Church and State in American History

Church and State in American History

Key Documents, Decisions, and Commentary from the Past Three Centuries

THIRD EDITION
Expanded and Updated

John F. Wilson
and
Donald L. Drakeman,
Editors

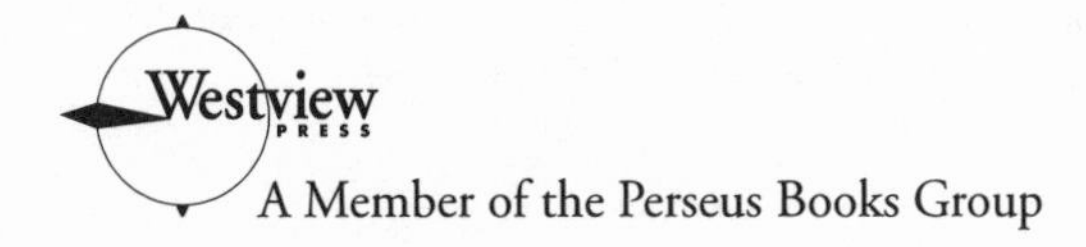

A Member of the Perseus Books Group

Westview Press books are available at special discounts for bulk purchases in the United States by corporations, institutions, and other organizations. For more information, please contact the Special Markets Department at The Perseus Books Group, 11 Cambridge Center, Cambridge, MA 02142, or call (617) 252-5298, (800)255-1514 or e-mail j.mccrary@perseusbooks.com

First edition published in 1965 by D. C. Heath and Company.
Revised and expanded edition published in 1987 by Beacon Press.
Third Edition: Published in 2003 in the United States of America by Westview Press, 5500 Central Avenue, Boulder, Colorado 80301–2877, and in the United Kingdom by Westview Press, 12 Hid's Copse Road, Cumnor Hill, Oxford 0X2 9JJ.

Find us on the World Wide Web at www.westviewpress.com

Cataloging-in-Publication Data is available from the Library of Congress.
ISBN: 0-8133-6558-9 (pb); 0-8133-6582-1 (hc)

The paper used in this publication meets the requirements of the American National Standard for Permanence of Paper for Printed Library Materials Z39.48–1984.

10 9 8 7 6 5 4 3 2 1

Contents

PREFACE

"It was the last struggle of the separation of Church and State," Lyman Beecher opined in 1820, when commenting on the end of state support for religion in Connecticut. To be sure, firm belief in the separation of church and state has become a hallmark of the American consciousness. When asked what he thought about as a young pilot shot down in shark-infested waters during World War II, President George H.W. Bush spoke of meditating on "God and faith, and the separation of church and state." But the meaning of the phrase "separation of church and state," as applied to specific issues such as prayer in the public schools, state aid for religious organizations and the like, is not as widely shared by the American public as is belief in the general principle. Put differently, had Beecher accurately envisioned a future America where church-state questions were merely the subject of historical reflection, there would be little need for a revised and expanded edition of this volume. In the nearly two centuries since Beecher's optimistic, if somewhat premature, pronouncement that church and state had been separated once and for all, however, the proper relationship of religious institutions and civil governments has not only remained unresolved but has become even more complex. The classic church-state question has ramified into a multitude of issues involving churches, synagogues, mosques and many other religious institutions interacting with every species of federal, state, and local governments. Pluralism—of both religions and governments—has been a critical force in the continual reshaping of church-state issues, from the founding period to the present day.

For much of American history, issues of pluralism frequently led to literally multiple results, that is, church-state questions were often local issues resolved by the communities that were most affected, and often decided differently from place to place depending on who held political power. More recently, the nature of decisionmaking about church-state issues has been dramatically reshaped. For the first several hundred years after the settling of the American colonies, such matters were debated and determined primarily by the legislative branches of local governments—and frequently decided quite differently in various state houses. But for the past fifty years or so they have quite literally become federal cases. And those cases have almost invariably fallen within the jurisdiction of the United States Supreme Court, a judicial body that decided a mere handful of church-state cases in the 175 years between the adoption of the First Amendment's "religion clauses" and the publication of the first edition of this book in 1965. By the second edition, just twenty years later, the Supreme Court had increased that number of cases by several fold, and the growth has been nearly exponential since then, making church-state jurisprudence one of the most active and complex areas of modern constitutional decisionmaking. In sum, the Supreme Court established itself as the arbiter of national, rather than local, standards for the interaction of religion and government.

Throughout the several editions of this volume, the critical issues have remained essentially the same. "Church and state" refers to the institutional interplay between two sets of powerful forces at work in societies, religion and politics. Although the issues arising on American soil have typically been formulated on the basis of experiences in social orders strongly shaped by Western Christianity, other societies manifest parallel or comparable phenomena. This book was initially designed to provide primarily documents and interpretive materials that would introduce readers to the complexity of these issues in the American experience, beginning with settlement of the English colonies. Subsequent revisions have tried to bring coverage of these questions down to the present—now into a new century—while remaining dedicated to the same objective.

Certain basic questions have been constant across the centuries. For example, does religion rightfully make special claims against governments or the state? Is religion privileged among the forces that form modern societies? Should political regime defer to religious authority? Can governments control or make use of religious institutions? But if questions like these remain relatively unchanged, particular expressions given to them have evolved markedly since the 1960s.

The first edition made much of the recognition in post–World War II America that our society has become religiously pluralistic. It would have been difficult at that point, however, to imagine the many and diverse expressions of tension between religion and politics that have become commonplace in our new century. We hope that this edition will prove to be a challenging and useful guide for new generations, at once opening up problem topics and equipping readers to understand them more effectively.

John F. Wilson
Donald L. Drakeman

ACKNOWLEDGMENTS

Church and State in American History was first published in 1965 with strong encouragement by Gerald E. Stearn. More than two decades later we reissued it in a much augmented and jointly edited version. This third edition continues the collaboration, adding excerpts from numerous recent court cases and recasting the earlier sections. Through these several versions, the authors have benefited greatly from students' comments, colleagues' suggestions, and assistance from coworkers. We hope that the volume will continue to prove useful as introduction to a perennial issue, namely, how the line should be drawn between, on the one hand, religious belief and behavior and, on the other, political authorities and the rights of citizens. It is evident that this problem continues to challenge this nation, and increasingly other nations face it as well.

John F. Wilson
Donald L. Drakeman

Introduction

The phrase "church and state" designates a certain tension in our pluralistic society. Aid to parochial schools, public-school prayer, tax exemption for religious institutions, religious beliefs of political candidates, abortion, and the nuclear arms race—all of these issues (and many others as well) have been thought to involve questions of church and state.

Some of these social issues were first widely recognized in post–World War II America. Others have a long history in American society. Even when applied to the most contemporary problem, however, the term "church and state" suggests that the issue in question expresses an ancient differentiation between two kinds of institutions that have organized the life of men and women in Western societies. One structure of authority has been primarily concerned with temporal life as an end in itself; the other has been concerned with temporal life as a means to "spiritual" ends. To identify certain points of tension in our common life as entailing questions of church and state is to say that the spheres of temporal and spiritual authorities may diverge or that conflicting claims arise in the exercise of temporal and spiritual powers.

In one respect the phrase "church and state" is unfortunate because its connotations are excessively formalistic. It suggests that one spiritual authority structure confronts a single temporal authority structure as was essentially the case in some periods in Western history. In fact the colonial period of U.S. history exhibits some attempts to realize classical kinds of relationship between a single spiritual authority structure—the Church—and a single temporal authority structure—the colonial State. But the colonial period also illustrates how different sorts of ingredients in American society—for example, the diversity of ethnic groups and the separatist impulses of evangelical activism—worked to make classical church-state patterns outmoded. On the religious side of the equation, one church could not embody the manifold spiritual life of the American people. Consequently, the federal government was constructed on the assumption that there could—and should—be no national establishment of religion. Although largely nominal state establishments did continue, in one case until 1833, it became increasingly evident that, even of this level, a single spiritual authority structure was not a realistic option. This pattern, which has subsequently characterized American society, has often been described as "the separation of church and state."

Some interpreters argue that the formal disengagement of these authority structures of church and state dissolved the ancient problems of their relationship. If there is no one church recognized by the state, the argument runs, how can there be any church-state problems? If difficulties exist, the argument continues, it is only because the separation of the two has been insufficiently rigorous. The confusion embodied in this position is produced, obviously, by the misleadingly formal character of the church-state formula. There is no single authority structure—or combination of them—that could presume to embody the religious or spiritual life of America. In shorthand fashion this situation is usually designated as "religious pluralism," that is, many different religious movements exist in America and they pursue relatively autonomous courses without prejudice. Therefore the classical term "church"—in denotation as well as connotation—might appear alien to the American scene.

It ought to be equally obvious that no single authority structure embodies the temporal life of Americans—that is, a single state is no more an empirical reality than a single church. Like religious pluralism, governmental pluralism involves multiple authorities that exercise overlapping jurisdictions within our society. Thus citizens experience rule by federal, state, county, and local governments, and all contribute to the structuring of the common life. Sometimes they are mutually reinforcing; on other occasions they counterbalance each other. Although the federal government has precedence (and it certainly has a preemptive power among governmental institutions without parallel among religious institutions), in practice its agencies display considerable deference toward local authorities. The federal constitution was framed with the intent that there should not be an American "state" in the classical sense. Powers were divided at the national level, and manifold governments were fostered at other levels as well. In addition, the development of semiautonomous bureaucratic structures and quasi-judicial commissions (not continuously subordinated to explicit political review) further pluralized the process of governing American society. Also, large corporate entities exercise powers in our society that any formal state would reserve to itself. Thus there simply is no classical state in American experience that corresponds either to the medieval or modern European uses of this term. Accordingly, the term "church and state"breaks down completely if the attempt is made to use it in a traditional fashion.

Is "church and state" at all useful, then, in comprehending American society? Clearly, a variety of spiritual authority structures interact with each other and with a complex set of temporal authority structures. We have in America not "church" and "state" but religions and governments—all interacting within society. Some argue it would be desirable to give up this designation altogether and seek one more in accord with American experience. To do so, however, would be to accept only the most formalistic definition of the term. For it is as wrong to suggest that the tensions between temporal and spiritual life in America are wholly unprecedented as it is to argue that church-state problems disappeared with the adoption of the First Amendment, especially as applied to the states through the due process clause of the Fourteenth. The substance of the church-state tradition is still with us, but it is with us in new forms. The historical terms apply inexactly, but the tradition designated by the terms is very much to the point in comprehending America's past and present. Through analyzing the historical development of the concept of "church and state" it may be possible, on the one hand, to modify its formalistic connotations and, on the other, to denote more precisely what it has meant in the past and may legitimately signify now.

Consequently, this introduction addresses the following topics: first, the origin, development, and content of the traditional church-state distinction in Western history; second, the range of patterns that have existed in the historical relationships between religious and political authorities; third, the relatively distinctive pattern of church-state relations in America, together with the sources and significance of those relations.

I

The distinction between church and state in Western history inevitably refers back to classic texts of early Christianity recurrently cited in discussions of the issue. Perhaps the chief one is Jesus's response (as reported in the synoptic gospels: Matthew 22:15–22, Mark 12:13–17, Luke 20:20–26) to a question about rendering tribute to Caesar: "Is it lawful to pay taxes to Caesar, or not?" (Mark 12:14). Jesus's injunction was to "Render to Caesar the things that are Caesar's, and to God the things that are God's" (Mark 12:17). Another text, scarcely less significant, is located in Paul's Letter to the Romans. As a whole the section runs to seven verses (Romans 13:1–7), but its principle is summed up in the first verse alone: "Let every person be subject to the governing authorities. For there is no authority except from God, and those that exist have been instituted by God." Other biblical texts are less significant than these two, and none refers directly to "church and state." Rather, they presuppose that faithfulness to God requires also appropriate obedience to worldly authorities since such are instituted by God. In early Christianity this might even have demanded "obedience unto death." Early Christian canonical writings did not explore the church-state relationship in a fashion relevant to later needs because, among other reasons, the "State" did not acknowledge the legitimacy of the "Church" as a competing authority structure. To recognize the Church as such would be to say that in principle the State should be limited to activities relating to temporal ends. Thus the possibility of a formal church-state pattern emerged only after Constantine as emperor was converted to Christianity in the early part of the fourth century. This resulted in the Constantinian settlement in which the Christian movement was at first accepted and then favored over alternate (and generally more syncretistic) religious movements with which it had been competing. Through its persistent obedience to God (and thus to Caesar), the Church gained recognition from Caesar allowing it to possess an authority structure in some measure independent from, while also paralleling, the State. In the eastern half of the empire, the Church remained closely associated with the State—even wholly subordinated to it. It was in Western Christendom, therefore, that the distinction between church and state developed its particular significance.

At the end of the fifth century Pope Gelasius I articulated the fundamental premise concerning Church and State that has characterized Western history. The premise was, simply, there are two. "Two swords" or "two authority structures" meant a single society under two jurisdictions—one temporal and the other spiritual. From a theological point of view, the coming of Christ and the establishment of the Church had made it unlawful for both authorities to be administered by one figure. So there were two. Priest and prince, or church and state, each needed the other, but both were separate aspects of one society. This separated double authority structure is what marked off

Western Christendom from Eastern Christianity, and it properly locates the significance of "church and state." A universal Christian society was presupposed that had a twofold government or rule. While the Church embodied the spiritual order of that society, the Empire organized the same society in temporal terms. The perduring problem was the interaction between the ecclesiastical and civil authority structures. What should be the relationship of these two jurisdictions?

From the ninth until roughly the middle of the eleventh century a pattern emerged that derived from the Emperor Charlemagne. Generally the pope was subordinated to the emperor, and thus the Church to the Empire. Subsequently Pope Gregory VII challenged the emperor (Henry IV), however, and on the immediate question at issue—lay investiture of bishops—the papal interests won a partial victory in the Concordat of Worms (1122). The further Gregorian ambition was to assert at once the spiritual autonomy of the Church and the monarchical rule of the Church by the pope: "If kings are to be judged by priests for their sins, by whom should they be judged with better right than by the Roman pontiff?" By the end of the twelfth century, Innocent III made even further claims, likening the papal church to the sun and the imperial dominion to the moon, which derived its light from the former. The maximum claim for papal authority in the Church and ecclesiastical authority over the Empire, however, was made by Boniface VIII in his *Unam Sanctam* (1302). It called for the subordination of the temporal to the spiritual, reversing completely the earlier Carolingian pattern. "Both are in the power of the Church, the spiritual sword and the material sword. But the latter is to be used for the Church, the former by her; the former by the priest, the latter by kings and captains but at the will and by the sufferance of the priest. The one sword, then, should be under the other, and the temporal authority subject to the spiritual." Even as Boniface advanced such unqualified claims, however, the papacy was humiliated through being held captive at Avignon. Concurrently, England and France began to develop as new nation-states that would sustain their own national churches in place of universal Latin Christendom ordered in a twofold pattern. Concurrently Aristotelian naturalists, for example, Marsilius of Padua, argued for the restriction of spiritual authority in the name of an autonomous secular realm. By the late Middle Ages, church and state as two swords or authorities no longer meant pope and emperor as jointly quarreling trustees of a universal Christian society. No longer was the church the spiritual structure of a universal society. Instead, it was either the religious expression of a national entity or an association of like-minded individuals more often than not in conflict with a repressive state. The ground was present in which both the religious sectarianism and the secular states of modern Europe would grow.

From this perspective, the Protestant Reformation was an ambiguous event. At once it was allied with the centrifugal national forces that were destroying what remained of universal society while concurrently attempting to reexpress the two-authority doctrine that had been so characteristic of Western Christendom. Thus it was neither wholly modern nor wholly reactionary but a curious combination of both. The Lutheran branch of the Reformation identified the two authorities as two realms each dependent directly on God so that both faithless prince and faithful believer had a vocation in the divine economy. The Calvinist branch, by contrast, usually sought to locate temporal authority in the hands of those saints who were responsive to the spiritual authority of the Church. In either case it was impossible to recover universalism, as Protestants (and Catholics also) discovered in the bloody religious wars.

This cursory review of the developing church-state pattern ought to make clear that through the sixteenth century a static relationship between religious and political authorities never existed in Western history. Nor was its essence embodied, for instance, in the relationship of emperor and pope in the thirteenth century. On the contrary, the common substance of church-state relationships was recognition of two authority structures in the corporate life of humanity—one essentially temporal and the other primarily spiritual. In shorthand form these were respectively designated as "state" and "church," but there were manifold expressions of this relationship long before the terms and the rubric were introduced into American history. Therefore, to explore "church and state in American history," our inquiry turns to consider the relationships between temporal and spiritual authority structures—or religious institutions and civil governments. It is self-evident that these relationships neither began nor ended with the adoption of the First (or the Fourteenth) Amendment.

II

Another approach to analysis of "church and state" may help suggest the range of patterns properly designated under this heading. In another way this should establish why the church-state designation must not be identified with one particular example of that relationship, such as papal church and imperial magistracy within a single and inclusive Christian society. To this end, the question is asked, What are the formal patterns in the relationships between the temporal and spiritual authority structures? It is useful to arrange responses to this question schematically. One sort of pattern curiously brackets bitter antagonists. Both would deny that there should be two authority structures, that is, that human life is to be comprehended under the dual aspect of temporal and spiritual concerns. The parties to this strange consensus disagree, of course, as to which of the two authority structures should absorb the other. On the one hand a hierocratic regime authorizes the priests to hold all power—spiritual and temporal—in their hands. By contrast a statist or consistent totalitarian position refuses to recognize an independent spiritual authority structure and may not only create a subservient temporal religion but also prosecute and proscribe dissenting religious faiths. While the latter position has been a common one in the modern West, hierocracies have been uncommon since the destruction of ancient Israel. Both priest-king and commissar deny the traditional Western assumption about church and state—that independence of the two authority structures is fundamental.

Another kind of pattern allows a certain independence of the two institutions, but it ultimately subordinates one to the other. Like the previous position it may also be resolved into clearly opposed alternatives. One option decrees the subordination of spiritual authority to temporal authority—at the extreme the utilization and manipulation of the church by the state. Usually this alternative is designated as Erastianism after a sixteenth-century Swiss theologian, Thomas Erastus, who argued that where there is uniformity of religion, ecclesiastical jurisdiction should be exercised under the review of the civil authorities. Although the label is usually applied only to the situation of nation-states from the sixteenth century on, the principle involved (subordination of spiritual to temporal authority) expresses the pretensions of many emperors beginning with Charlemagne. The other form of subordination argues that spiritual ends take precedence over temporal ones. Such, of course, were the classical papal claims. This position also characterized Calvinists as they pursued the ideal of the holy community. It is appropriate to label such an alternative theocratic as long as that term is distinguished from the hierocratic pattern, which denies all autonomy to the temporal authority. This broader theocratic tradition, whether in Rome, Geneva, or Massachusetts Bay, was not essentially the rule of priests (or preachers for that matter) over temporal matters. Rather it presupposed that the consciences of the lay civil authorities—autonomous in temporal matters—should be formed by, and their outward practice conformed to, proper religious faith. The whole society—in its dual aspect—was created by God, and both authorities were to be appropriately conformed to supposed divine intentions for it. The medievalism of early Protestant ideals is apparent once again.

A third type of pattern presumes that there are separate authority structures and proposes that they should be disengaged from each other. Again, however, there are different ways in which this independence can be construed. One alternative is the segregation of the spiritual authority structure from the temporal authority structure. This is close to the Protestant Anabaptist ideal. In another way this would seem to be implied in the Jeffersonian metaphor concerning a "wall of separation" as well as a great deal of contemporary rhetoric about the "separation of church and state." Another kind of independence between church and state is a recognition of mutually supportive roles. While the spiritual authority structure or structures ought to lend their power to the civil order, the temporal authorities should recognize and assist religious institutions.

Such an exercise in arranging patterns of institutional authority is surely artificial, although it is sufficiently flexible to comprehend reasonably well most concrete instances of church-state relationships. Its chief significance, however, ought to be the weight it lends to the argument of this essay that if "church and state" is to be a useful phrase, it must be broad and flexible enough to cover a wide variety of historical relationships between spiritual and temporal authority structures. The term is relatively useless if it is primarily identified with one particular pattern that is considered normative.

III

This study will identify seven different periods of church and state in American history. Each one is relatively distinctive because it represents a new phase in the relationship between religious institutions and civil governments in light of the changing history of religious pluralism in America. In these stages ideological resources have joined with social circumstances to create a series of experimental resolutions of the tensions between spiritual and temporal authority structures. Before briefly surveying these periods, it is important to recognize that the American experiments in church-state relations have almost universally assumed the dual-authority pattern of Western societies that was discussed above. America has not provided congenial soil, for example, for the anticlerical sentiment that was so widespread in Europe during the nineteenth century and that understandably resulted in a defensive posture on the part of religious institutions. Some might argue that the more militant forms of modern secularism effectively deny this presumption of two realms. But American secularism characteristically has been little more than indifferent toward the claim that the spiritual dimension of life has an authority of its own. Again—contrary to many interpretations of New England Puritanism—there have been few attempts at a hierocratic melding of spiritual and temporal authorities in American history. Perhaps the most interesting, and certainly the only significant, experiment with this kind of order was the early Mormon venture. Followers thought that in the person of Joseph Smith, Jr., the offices of prophet, priest, and king were once again united. Brigham Young and his associates received this mantle and structured the Salt Lake Valley community accordingly. The mainstream of American experience, however, has taken for granted that there should be two authority structures—although significantly varying interpretations have been offered.

Chapter 1

The seventeenth-century Atlantic colonies represent a useful first period in this study. There we find traditional church-state terms very much present. We are introduced to the language of establishment that was simply taken for granted—for even someone like Roger Williams, although he denied the propriety of established religion, could make his case only in those same terms. It is important to grasp that—aside from the lively experiment of Rhode Island—all of the colonies erected establishments of some sort. No one would deny the vastly different degrees of rigor (both in conceiving and realizing their establishments) that characterized, for example, Massachusetts Bay and Pennsylvania. But it is entirely wrong to so emphasize Pennsylvania's relative latitude that the common language used by both is hidden from view. The New England Puritans did not set up the hierocratic regimes so often attributed to them. John Cotton was neither a latter-day Sadducee nor a Joseph Smith, Jr., born before his time. The New England Puritan assumptions were far more akin to the ideals of Innocent III. Theirs was to be a commonwealth, ruled in temporal affairs by Christian laymen whose consciences were formed by the preaching of the Word (if not nourished by the administration of the Eucharist). Not all of the colonies aspired to such a formally theocratic constitution of the relationship between church and state. By virtue of economic necessity, if not ideological programs, some represented more nearly the Erastian position that the religious institution should be subordinated to (though not absorbed in) the temporal regime and its needs. Nevertheless in this first period the language of establishment was essentially universal.

Chapter 2

During the first six decades of the eighteenth century the establishment language that had been taken for granted was challenged by the diversification of religious life in the colonies. The overwhelming number of colonists were Protestant in sympathy—even if they were not allowed or willing to become active church members. But different kinds of Protestant families and groups relentlessly immigrated; even the relatively homogeneous New England settlements yielded, first on the fringes and then at the center as well, Scotch-Irish Presbyterians in Anglican Virginia, "German" Mennonites in Quaker Pennsylvania, Anglicans in Congregational Connecticut and Massachusetts. In addition, the upheavals of the Great Awakening split asunder the Presbyterians and Congregationalists and served to expand the slim Baptist ranks. Given the circumstances of colonial development, this proliferation of Protestant groups made necessary the practice of toleration. Toleration of dissent is perfectly compatible with a pattern of establishment. It does not, however, make credible the theocratic subordination of state to religion, nor on the other hand does it render society religiously uniform—which is the great attraction of a subordination of church to state. Therefore the first six decades of the eighteenth century represent a transitional period during which the language of establishment became outdated. In no sense was the fundamental assumption of dualism denied—there were two realms, each with its appropriate institutional expression. But radical competition among the religious groups made it inevitable (though the illusion died hard) that a single spiritual authority structure could not be realized.

Chapter 3

During the third period, which runs between 1760 and approximately 1820, the problem of religious establishment was directly confronted. Simply to indicate some of the factors that were present makes evident how a basic reevaluation of the traditional pattern had become necessary. As the colonies were drawn into a closer network, the multiplicity of Protestant groups was all the more evident. Continuing feeble efforts to regularize if not prefer the Church of England in the colonies dramatized for proto-Americans that the scope or latitude present in their religious lives was precious. Religious liberty as a positive ideal was openly discussed. The Enlightenment estimate of religion exerted an effect. The net result of these and other elements can be seen with particular clarity in the public newspaper debate during the 1760s over the scheme to appoint Church of England bishops in America. The colonial critics of this proposal did everything in their power to marshal public resistance toward it through belittling and ridiculing it. In the course of this argument they articulated notions about religion that would have been unthinkable a century earlier, for example, that plural religious institutions were desirable, or that clergymen should be meagerly paid so that their pretension and power would not corrupt the exercise of their spiritual ministry. Such sentiments indicate how tenuous the traditional language of establishment had become. In the Virginia struggle for religious freedom and disestablishment, however, we find the first consistent political arguments supporting the independence of church and state.

Jefferson's passion for religious freedom is well known, and he later bequeathed that attractive if confusing metaphor of a "wall of separation" between church and state, which continues to echo throughout the common life. But James Madison is probably the more significant figure, both in the Virginia struggle and in the adoption of the First Amendment, which undergirds religious freedom and prohibits congressional legislation "respecting an establishment of religion." With the debate over the bishops and with Madison's contribution, the American future in church-state relations seemed clearly to have been pointed in the direction of an independence between spiritual and temporal authority structures.

Chapter 4

This revolution in the position of the churches gives significance to the next period—roughly extending to the Civil War. To be sure, numerous relevant developments were under way that would in their own time influence church-state relationships in America, for example, the influx of large contingents of Catholic immigrants as well as significant numbers of "German Jews." While these and other events quietly set the stage for the post–Civil War period, however, the evangelical forces in America took aggressive action to recover in an informal way what had been their legal position before disestablishment. During this "era of republican Protestantism" a great "united front" of interdenominational agencies developed that aspired to make America a Protestant Christian republic in substance if not in form. The reader will have to judge how profoundly this collaborative enterprise shaped and formed the common life so that even more than a century and a half after its maximum activity, American political, social, and economic—as well as religious—idioms testify to its vital impact. This effort had its contemporary critics, and many of its coveted projects failed. But the concept of an indirect relationship between religious and political authority structures tried to turn to advantage the condition that there was no direct mutually supporting relationship between religious institutions and civil governments. Madison's theory had not allowed for cooperation among evangelical denominations any more than he had anticipated the development of political parties (not altogether dissimilar entities). One broader question concerns the degree to which this strategy was an indigenous American movement and how much it was part of the conservative Anglo-American response to the French Revolution.

Chapter 5

After the Civil War the ethnic multiplication and religious diversification that had proceeded relentlessly throughout the previous era could no longer remain unrecognized and unacknowledged. Even before the Civil War, the public schools became the focus of the conflicting claims made by temporal and spiritual authority structures. It is interesting that where the fact (and burden) of religious pluralism was explicitly recognized, a position favoring a neutral relationship between church and state emerged. This position clearly repudiated the assumption that a religious uniformity underlying republican Protestantism was desirable. This anticipated, of course, more modern discussions. For Roman Catholics this situation required dissent from European interpretations of the normative relationships between the two authority structures and led to the advocacy of an "Americanism" that appeared almost heretical to

Europeans. For Protestants it set an even harder task. Beneath and behind that sense of national mission and anti-Roman animus nourished by the evangelical tradition, the Protestants had to locate more ancient resources that would equip them to comprehend church-state alternatives other than the ideal so dear to them. As the eighteenth century had been a transitional period during which formal disestablishment became necessary, so this period (1860–1920) was also transitional, a period of disestablishment—in this case not of state-recognized churches but of a Protestant religious privilege.

Chapter 6

In the period between the First World War and the election of a president in 1960 who was Roman Catholic, that ancient problem of the relationship of temporal and spiritual authority structures became widely discussed in at least three different perspectives, all in the context of an American religious pluralism encompassing the three major religions: Protestantism, Judaism, and Roman Catholicism. The church-state issue was viewed under the aspect of a theological-religious problem, in the guise of political struggles within a pluralist society, and finally as a constitutional and legal issue. A responsible consensus seemed to ensure that the United States, as a matter of necessity if not choice, must develop its particular pattern on the basis of independence between church and state. The existence of two authority structures seemed to be recognized in principle if not always honored in practice, and the historical alternatives of subordinating one to the other were not widely viewed as plausible formal options. There was, however, no consensus as to whether the independence of church and state should be one of segregation, neutrality, or mutual support. Most important, the issues had become constitutionalized through construing the two clauses of the First Amendment as providing a national template for all questions relating to church and state. Thus the religious liberty and establishment clauses were incorporated by means of the Fourteenth Amendment to frame interactions among religions and governments for the remaining decades of the twentieth century and into the twenty-first.

Chapter 7

Commencing in the early 1960s, the meaning of the term "pluralism" has been expanded to include additional and very diverse religious groups. This era has been marked by a willingness within American institutions to give unprecedented recognition to claims for equal treatment made by a variety of ethnic, racial, religious, and other minority bodies. Not all Americans have welcomed the new religious and cultural pluralism that extends well beyond the Protestant-Catholic-Jewish mainstream. Readings from salient cases decided by the Supreme Court in these decades reflect various specific issues that also disclose deeper social tensions. Thus in recent decades a struggle has been taking place about religion in society. The essential question is, Should the government disregard or take formal account of those Western values (often called Judeo-Christian) thought by many to be at the foundation of our national culture? More broadly speaking, the church-state divide in the contemporary era separates those who think that government should accommodate and encourage the sort of religion that they see as a foundation of our culture from those who think that in the name of religious liberty the government should not extend aid or support to religion in any way. In short, this is a struggle between those who endorse what the Supreme Court has called "benevolent neutrality" and proponents of a more inclusive construction of religious liberty. While this battle over the legitimacy of governmental aid to religion continues to rage, the issue of religiously based activity in the political realm has returned in recent years as a diverse array of groups has lobbied in God's name for various political programs. These continuing struggles suggest that many Americans have not abandoned the concept that at some fundamental level there remains a spiritual authority that should instruct the state and receive support from it in spite of governmental, religious, and cultural pluralism.

IV

Within the framework so sketched, this book presents texts and documents that exemplify the church-state question as it has developed in American history. These readings delineate the range of tensions between the temporal and spiritual forces of our society. Critical interpretive selections propose some points for discussion. Introductions and suggested further readings amplify the text. Taken as a whole, this book should position its readers to understand the importance in American history of the church-state issue and its continuing influence within modern culture.

Accordingly, this book offers readings about the relationships between those authority structures shaped primarily for temporal purposes and those dedicated by spiritual ends throughout American history. Understood in these terms American experience has derived from continental European civilization, although its church-state patterns have not been identical with either historic or contemporary developments across the Atlantic. As a historical collection, the book places major emphasis on the interrelationships of political, legal, and religious phenomena in any given period and, as important, the necessity of interpreting these phenomena. This means other options have been excluded. For instance, it would be possible to construe the church-state issue in purely legal terms, assembling the relevant legal texts from charters, constitutions, legislation, and judicial decisions. In such a study the legal relationships between churches and governments would be the unifying theme. For another example, it would be possible to develop a study of the relationships between religion and politics in American history that would be a very different book, focused by another theme. Yet again, a collection of readings in ecclesiastical polities and public affairs would meet another sort of need in the present day. No one of these options, however, would be consistently directed to church-state issues in the way this book is designed to be.

A great deal of literature allegedly about church and state really concerns the achievement of religious toleration as a reality and the development of religious liberty as an ideal. Toleration and religious liberty have certainly influenced the question of church and state. But it is entirely mistaken to assume that the church-state relationship is either resolved or dissolved by the religious latitude so highly valued by modern American society. Those who are concerned with toleration and religious liberty really disclose the persistence of individualistic categories in American intellectual life. Analysis of social dynamics and appreciation for collective languages are not widely present in American thought. Consequently, corporate issues—for example, the relationships of religious and governmental authority structures—have often been discussed as if they were to be understood as the sum of individual religious and political relationships within society. From this point of view religious liberty for the individual has seemed to be the substantial goal that "separation of church and state" guaranteed. Attractive as such a formula is, it does not accord with the empirical reality of religious and governmental authority structures nor with the persistently collective behavior of Americans past and present. The significance of "church and state" as an intellectual framework is that it requires the analysis of our social history against the background of Western European history with its richer experience and traditions, and its more exact and comprehensive language. This is an illuminating point of view for readers weaned on the individualistic social discourse of American life, which is reinforced by the canned rhetoric of contemporary mass media.

The phrase "church and state" has echoed throughout American history. In this sense it has been a constant from the colonial settlements to the latest term of the Supreme Court. By no means, however, has it always carried the same meaning or referred to comparable social realities. Like all terms that function in political life, the church-and-state language has undergone a metamorphosis in the past three hundred years as radical as the transformation experienced by society on the North American continent during that period. Like all terms that function in religious life, the church-and-state language has retained traditional connotations even when inappropriate and clearly misleading for purposes of description. Like all terms that function in legal contexts, the church-and-state vocabulary has a formalistic character insufficiently empirical for analytic usage. Thus a volume of readings titled *Church and State in American History* necessarily has a twofold character—it must exhibit these several languages as they are used and concurrently analyze those special patterns to which the languages have responded. Accordingly, this is a historical study of the interrelationships between the legal, political, and religious structures of American society as they have embodied the temporal and spiritual dimensions of Western life. For this reason this volume is selective in representing events and documents that are related to the theme. Most fundamentally, *Church and State in American History* is directed toward introducing the assumptions in terms of which the events were shaped and the documents were framed.

1

The Language of Colonial Establishments (–1700)

At one time it was fashionable to weigh the alleged "motives" that contributed to the colonization of America. Accordingly, arguments erupted about the relative significance of commercial and religious impulses, partisans of each position supporting their cases with polemic as well as evidence. Unfortunately such an approach inhibits any study of seventeenth-century America. During that century, especially in the English-speaking world, theology was still a primary language. It was a fundamental mode of thought in which public endeavors were comprehended and advocated. As a matter of course, people of the early seventeenth century—especially Puritan English folk, the prime movers in the Virginia and New England ventures—assumed that religious authority should contribute to the structuring of their experiments. The society they intended to plant was to be a cutting from that English Protestant society they knew under Elizabeth and James. An example may clarify this point. Historians have often indicated the discrepancy between the settlers' expressed intentions of converting the Indians to Christianity and their achievements in this regard. To conclude that, because of their miserable failure in these programs, the colonists were hypocritical in their religious professions is to miss the crucial point. They failed because the Indians—apart from the likes of Pocahontas—would not be refashioned after the English pattern, they would not abandon their own society for that offered to them in the name of God and King. In the contemporary idiom, "civilitie of life" and "vertue" were necessarily linked with the "true worship of God." Thus failure to convert the Indians is less indicative of religious hypocrisy than it is of how alien the English Protestant mind was in the new environment—and how stubbornly the colonists clung to their convictions and preconceptions. One of these preconceptions was that church and state should have a correlative relationship.

Accordingly this section on the language of colonial establishments has two purposes. The first is to display the theological mode of thought in the terms in which trade and politics, no less than religious activities, were carried on. It will be most appropriate to illustrate this mentality as it sought to articulate the relationship of church and state as it was implied in that view of the world. The second purpose is to indicate the different patterns of religious establishment, which were developed in the several colonies. It is important to recognize that although these patterns embody significant diversities, the fundamental theological assumptions about society were not disrupted.

There is little doubt that theological literature and discourse is more prominent in the remains of Massachusetts Bay, for instance, than in the legacies from other colonial endeavors. This is largely to be explained, however, in the circumstances of the various settlements. For instance, the Virginia Company and its primary officers resided in London, and delegated officials managed the plantation, while the Massachusetts Bay Company transported itself and its charter across the Atlantic. Again, after achieving successful settlement the Virginia enterprise was involved in a decade-long struggle for subsistence as a garrison state while the attention of the London investors was given to their Bermuda project. By contrast, Massachusetts Bay rapidly developed during a decade of intensive immigration once the plan for a significant colony had been decided on. It is evident that a fully developed religious establishment could not have been introduced into Virginia under these circumstances. Yet that colony relied on the mutual reinforcement of spiritual and temporal authorities as much as the New England experiments did. On the principle of intelligibility, then, special attention will be given to the literature from New England.

Thomas Hooker, clerical leader of the exodus from Newton (now Cambridge) in Massachusetts Bay to the Connecticut River settlements around Hartford, expressed the conventional presuppositions about "Church and State" in a sentence: "Men sustain a double relation."[1] They were, first, "members of the commonwealth," which was a civil relationship touching the outer man—or men's bodies. Secondly, they were "members of a Church," which was a spiritual relationship involving the souls and consciences of men. Both of these "relations" were among men and between men and God. Thus the civil life, or the life of the commonwealth, had its relationship to God that was not exclusively mediated through the institution of the Church. Hooker's was a particular version of a Calvinistic scheme, which itself was a variant of a traditional Christian position. For him state and church were coordinated and mutually dependent since both were ordained by God to support each other. Temporal life required spiritual orientation no less than spiritual life presupposed temporal order.

The point to be emphasized is that civil and religious life remained distinguished in the assumptions undergirding the various seventeenth-century efforts to colonize America. There were variations within the pattern, but the dual ends of human life were never denied. Certainly a hierocracy was not established; civil polity was not subordinated to ecclesiastical direction. "Church and State" were explicitly coordinated with the exception of Rhode Island, and that exception—as will be evident in the readings—was articulated in the language of the day. Otherwise the means and degrees of correlation between civil and religious life varied among the colonies. The variety was certainly a major factor in the eventual disestablishment of the colonial churches. But that development cannot be comprehended without appreciating the terms in which differentiation occurred. The language of establishment was the language of the day.

JOHN COTTON

A Discourse About Civil Government

The leaders of Massachusetts Bay lavishly expounded their theory of society and their understanding of the relationship between church and state. Enough of this literature is still available to discredit facile pronouncements that the colony was a potential democracy corrupted by clerical tyranny. One of the classic texts about the relationship between civil and religious life has not been readily available, perhaps because of a longstanding confusion over its authorship. A New Haven Colony was early projected as an improvement upon the Massachusetts experiment, and its founders hoped to clarify some of the "problems" that were becoming apparent here. Apparently the Rev. John Davenport sought out the advice of his friend and mentor, the Rev. John Cotton of Boston. At issue was whether the franchise for civil government ought to be restricted to church members. In answering this question John Cotton, a dominant figure in the Bay, displayed the chief marks of Puritan scholasticism and effectively rehearsed the major assumptions about "Church and State." The "double relation" men sustained to church and commonwealth will be evident in Cotton's exposition. On the confused question of authorship of this tract refer to "The Authorship of 'A Discourse,'" by I. M. Calder in the *American Historical Review* (Volume XXXVII, pp 267 ff.).

Reverend Sir,

I have reviewed [your writing] and find, as I formerly expressed to yourself, that the question is mis-stated by you.[2] The arguments which you produce to prove that which is not denied are (in reference to this question) spent in vain, as arrows are when they fall wide of the marks they should hit though they strike in a white which the archer is not called to shoot at.

The terms wherein you state the question are these: "Whether the right and power of choosing civil magistrates belongs to the Church of Christ?"

To omit all critical inquiries, in your stating [of] the question I utterly dislike two things.

1. You speak of the civil magistrates indefinitely and without limitation—under which notion all magistrates . . . are included, Turks and Indians and idolaters as well as Christian. Now no man, I think, holdeth or imagineth that the Church of Christ hath power and right to choose all civil magistrates throughout the world. For:

A. In some countries there is no Church of Christ, all the inhabitants being heathen men and idolaters, and among those who are called Christian, the number of Churches of Christ will be found to be so small, and the members of them so few and mean, that it is impossible that the right and power of choosing civil magistrates in all places should belong to the Churches of Christ.

B. Nor have the churches countenance of state in all countries, but [they] are under restraint and persecution in some. . . .

C. In some countries the churches are indeed under the protection of magistrates, as foreigners, permitted quietly to sit down under their wings. But neither are the members capable of magistracy there, nor have they the power of voting in the choice of magistrates. . . .

D. In some countries sundry nations are so mingled that they have severally an equal right unto several parts of the country. . . .

Now he that should affirm that the Churches of Christ as such have right and power of choosing civil magistrates in such places seemeth to me more to need physick than arguments to recover him from his error.

2. The second thing that I dislike in your stating [of] the question is that you make the Churches of Christ to be the subject of this right and power of choosing civil magistrates. For:

A. The church so considered is a spiritual political body consisting of diverse members male and female, bond and free—sundry of which are not capable of magistracy, nor of voting in the choice of magistrates inasmuch as none have that right and power but free burgesses, among whom women and servants are not reckoned although they may be and are church members.

B. The members of the Churches of Christ are [to be considered] under a twofold respect answerable to the twofold man which is in all the members of the Church while they are in this world: the inward and the outward man (II Corinthians 4:16). Whereunto the only wise God hath fitted and appointed two sorts of administrators, ecclesiastical and civil. Hence they are capable of a twofold relation, and of action and power suitable to them both, viz., civil and spiritual, and accordingly [they] must be exercised about both in their seasons without confounding those two different states or destroying either of them. What they transact in civil affairs is done by virtue of their civil relation, their church-state only fitting them to do it according to God.

Now that the state of the question may appear I think it seasonable and necessary to premise a few distinctions to prevent all mistakes if it may be.

First let us distinguish between the two administrations or polities, ecclesiastical and civil, which men commonly call the church and commonwealth. I incline rather to those who speak of a Christian communion, [and] make the communion to be the genus and the states ecclesiastical and civil to be species of it. For in a Christian Communion there are . . . different administrations or polities or states, ecclesiastical and civil: ecclesiastical administrators are a divine order appointed to believers for holy communing of holy things, civil administrators are a human order appointed by God to men for civil fellowship of human things. . . .

1. Though both agree in this—that there is order in their administrations—yet with this difference: the guides in the Church have not a despotical but economical power only [since they are] not lords over Christ's heritage but stewards and ministers of Christ and of the Church, the dominion and law-giving power being reserved to Christ alone as the only Head of the Church. But in the other state he hath given lordly power, authority, and dominion unto men.
2. Though both agree in this—that man is the common subject of both—yet with this difference: Man by nature being a reasonable and social creature, capable of

civil order, is or may be the subject of civil power and state. But man by Grace called out of the world to fellowship with Jesus Christ and with His people is the only subject of church power. Yet [even] so the outward man of church members is subject to the civil power in common with other men while their inward man is the subject of spiritual order and administrations.

3. Though they both agree in this—that God is the efficient [cause] and author of both, and that by Christ—yet not [identically]. For God as the creator and governor of the world is the author of civil order and administrations, but God as in covenant with his people in Christ is the author of church-administrations. So likewise Christ, as the efficient Word and Wisdom of God creating and governing the world, is the efficient [cause] and fountain of civil order and administrations. But as mediator of the new covenant and Head of the Church he establishes ecclesiastical order.
4. Though they both agree in this—that they have the same last end, viz., the glory of God—yet they differ in their next ends. For the next end of civil order and administration is the preservation of human societies in outward honor, justice, and peace. But the next ends of church order and administrations are the conversions, edification, and salvation of souls, pardon of sin, power against sin, peace with God, &c.
5. Hence arises another difference about the objects of these different states. For though they both agree in this—that they have the common welfare for their aim and scope—yet the things about which the civil power is primarily conversant are bodies . . . I Corinthians 6:4, or . . . the things of this life [such] as goods, lands, honor, the liberties and peace of the outward man. The things whereabout the church power is exercised are . . . the things of God [such] as the souls and consciences of men, the doctrine and worship of God, the communion of saints. Hence also they have: (a) different laws, (b) different officers, (c) different power whereby to reduce men to order according to their different objects and ends.

Now [in order] that a just harmony may be kept between these two different orders and administrations two extremes must be avoided:

1. That they be not confounded either by giving the spiritual power—which is proper to the church—into the hand of the civil magistrate (as Erastus would have done in the matter of excommunication) . . . or [in the other case] by giving civil power to church-officers who are called to attend only to spiritual matters and the things of God, and therefore may not be distracted from them by secular entanglements. (I say church-officers, not church-members, for they—not being limited as the officers are by God—are capable of two different employments [according to the] two different men in them in different respects, as has been said. As they may be lawfully employed about things of this life so they are of all men fittest, being sanctified and dedicated to God to carry on all worldly and civil business to God's ends, as we shall declare in due time.) . . .
2. The second extreme to be avoided is that these two different orders and states—ecclesiastical and civil—be not set in opposition as contraries [so] that one

> should destroy the other, but as coordinate states in the same place reaching forth help mutually each to [the] other for the welfare of both according to God. Both officers and members of Churches [should] be subject, in respect of the outward man, to the civil power of those who bear rule in the civil state according to God. . . . Civil magistrates and officers in regard to the outward man [ought to] subject themselves spiritually to the power of Christ in church-ordinances, and by their civil power preserve the same in outward peace and purity. This will best be attained when the pastor may say to the magistrate. . . , "Thou rulest with Christ and administerest to Christ. Thou hast the sword for him. Let this gift which thou hast received from him be kept pure for him." The civil magistrate in his church-state [should fit] Ambrose ['s] description of a good emperor: "A good magistrate is within the church, not above it." . . . So much shall serve to have been spoken concerning the first distinction.

The second distinction to be premised for clearing the true state of the question is . . . between a commonwealth already settled and a commonwealth yet to be settled wherein men are free to choose what form they shall judge best. . . . Men that profess the fear of God, if they be free to make choice of their civil judges (as in this new plantation we are), . . . should rather choose such as are members of the Church for that purpose than others who are not in that state.

The third distinction premised for clearing the truth in this point is between free burgesses and free inhabitants in a civil state. Concerning which there must be had a different consideration. This difference of people living under the same civil jurisdiction is held and observed in all countries (as well heathen as others)—as may be proven, if it were needful, out of the histories of all nations and times. And the experience of our times as well in our own native country as in other places confirms it. In all [of] which many are inhabitants that are not citizens, that are never likely to be numbered among *archontes,* or rulers. [So it is] in the case now in question. When we urge that magistrates be chosen out of such as are members of these churches we do not thereby go about to exclude those that are not in church-order from any civil right or liberty that is due unto them as inhabitants and planters, as if none should have lots in due proportion with other men, nor the benefit of justice under the government where they live [except] church-members—for this were indeed to have the commonwealth swallowed up [by] the church. But [since] there ever will be differences between the world and the church in the same place, and [since] men of the world are allowed [by] God [to have] the use and enjoyment . . . of civil government for their quiet and comfortable subsistance in the world, and [since] church members (though called out of the world unto fellowship with Christ) [will ever be] living in the world and having many worldly necessities and business in common with men of the world who live among them, [both] stand in need of the civil power to right them against civil injuries and to protect them in their right and outward orderly use of their spirituals against those who are apt to be injurious to them in the one or in the other respect. [Those who are outside the church] are not under the church's power and yet, living within the verge of the same civil jurisdiction, [both] are under the civil power of the magistrates. Hence it is that we plead for this order to be set in civil affairs that such a course may be taken as will best secure to ourselves and our posterities the fruitful managing of civil government for the common welfare of all, as well [those] in the church as without. [This will] most certainly be effected when the public trust and power of these matters is committed to such men as are most approved according to God. These are church-members—as shall afterward, God assisting, be proved.

The fourth distinction to be premised for clearing the truth and to prevent mistakes in this question shall be between the actions of church-members. For some actions are done by them all jointly as a spiritual body in reference to spiritual ends, and some actions are done only by some of the body in reference to civil ends. . . . Members fitly chosen out of the church and made free burgesses are fitter to judge and determine according to God than other men [are]. . . .

The fifth distinction to be premised . . . is between places where all, or the most considerable part, of the first and free planters profess their desire and purpose of entering into church-fellowship according to Christ and of enjoying in that state all the ordinances in purity and peace and of securing the same unto their posterity so far as men are able, and those places where all or the most considerable part of the first and free planters are other-wise minded and profess the contrary. Our question is of the first sort, not of the second.

So much shall seem to have been spoken to the distinctions (which having been premised) we now proceed to declare the true state of the question which is as followeth:

> Whether a new plantation where all or the most considerable part of free planters profess their purpose and desire of securing to themselves and to their posterity the pure and peaceable enjoyment of Christ's ordinances, whether, I say, such planters are bound in laying the foundations of church and civil state to take order that all the free burgesses be such as are in the fellowship of the church or churches which are or may be gathered according to Christ? And [further] that those free burgesses have the only power of choosing from among themselves civil magistrates and men to be entrusted with transacting all public affairs of importance according to the rules and directions of Scripture?

I hold the affirmative part of this question upon this ground, that this course will [be] most conduc[ive] to the good of both states and by consequence to the common welfare of all—[to which] all men are bound principally to attend in laying the foundation of a common-wealth lest posterity rue the first miscarriages when it will be too late to redress them.

Argument 1: Theocracy, or to make the Lord God our governor, is the best form of government in a Christian commonwealth, and . . . men who are free to choose (as in a new plantation they are) ought to establish [it]. . . . That form of government where, (a) the people who have the power of choosing their governors are in covenant with God, (b) wherein the men chosen by them are godly men and fitted with a spirit of government, (c) in which the laws they rule by are the laws of God, (d) wherein laws are executed, inheritances alloted, and civil differences are composed according to God's appointment, [and] (e) in which men of God are consulted [about] all hard cases and in matters of religion, [this] is the form which was received and established among the people of Israel while the Lord God was their governor.

Argument 2: The form of government which gives unto Christ his due preeminence is the best form of government in a Christian commonwealth. . . .

Argument 3: That form of government [in which] the best provision is made for the good both of the church and of the civil state is the best form of government in a Christian communion. . . . Junius, [who speaks] of the consent and harmony of the Church and civil state in the concurrence of their several administrations to the welfare of a Christian Commonwealth, . . . expresses it by the conjunction of the soul and body in a man. . . .

Argument 4: That form of government [in which] the power of civil administration is denied unto unbelievers and [is] committed to the saints is the best form of government in a Christian Commonwealth. . . .

Argument 5: That form of government [in which] the power of choosing from among themselves men to be entrusted with managing all public affairs of importance is committed to those who are furnished with the best helps for securing to a Christian state the full discharge of such a trust is the best form of government in a Christian Commonwealth. . . .

Argument 6: [There is a danger of devolving power upon those not members of the church.]

It seems to be a principle imprinted in the minds and hearts of all men in the equity of it that such a form of government as best serves to establish their religion should, by the consent of all, be established in the civil state.

ROGER WILLIAMS

Queries of Highest Consideration (1644)

Against the rest of New England the settlements around Narragansett Bay provide vivid contrast on the issue of church and state. To its orthodox contemporaries this minute and quarrelsome colony was a cesspool. Moderns have wished to locate vital stirrings of "democracy" in its troubled waters. Either judgment fails to distill the dual significance of Rhode Island. Modernists fail to appreciate the continuing medievalism in Roger Williams's tortuous argument with his former colleagues. The colleagues themselves recognized no more than Williams himself did the practical success which would eventually attend the segregation of religious authority from civil jurisdiction. Williams's checkered career need not be recounted here. His *Queries of Highest Consideration* appeared in London during 1644 when he was there seeking support in the Long Parliament for the struggling settlement. The pamphlet was not addressed to Cotton—that exchange was published separately. But if not to Cotton the *Queries* was addressed to men of his stripe on the English scene. Some of the Dissenting Brethren, indeed, counted Cotton as a spiritual father. Arguing against an established church for England (under discussion in the Westminster Assembly during the first civil war), Williams did not deny that "double-relation," which was fundamental to seventeenth-century thought about church and state. But he did deny that a coordination of spiritual and temporal authorities logically followed from that premise. For Williams such "coordination" inevitably meant subordination of the spiritual to the temporal. For the sake of the "spiritual relation" or the "inward man" he advocated that church sustenance be denied to the state. He argued that civil society had to be secularized in order that religious life might be authentically spiritual. The *Queries* was directed to participants in the Westminster Assembly, but his personal quarrel was with the established church of Massachusetts Bay in which Cotton was the great ornament.

Addressed to the Dissenting Brethren and the Scottish Commissioners at the Westminster Assembly in London

Worthy sirs,

In serious examination of your late apologies we shall in all due respect and tenderness humbly query:[3]

First, what precept or pattern hath the Lord Jesus left you in his last will and testament for your Synod or Assembly of Divines by virtue of which you may expect his preference and assistance?

If you say (as all Popish synods and councils do), the pattern is plain, Acts 15, we ask if two or three particular congregations at Antioch sent to that first mother church at Jerusalem where the Apostles were . . . [who] had power to make decrees for all churches, Acts 16, we ask whether this be a pattern for a nation or kingdom . . . to reform or form a religion, &c.?

We pray you to consider [rather] if the golden image [of Daniel 3] be not a type and figure of the several national and state religions which all nations set up and ours hath done, for which the wrath of God is now upon us?

Query II. Whereas you both agree (though with some differences) that the civil magistrate must reform the church, establish religion, and so consequently must first judge and judicially determine which is true [and] which is false, . . . we now query—since the Parliament (being the representative commonwealth) hath no other power but what the common weale derive [unto] and betrust it with—whether it will not evidently follow that the commonweal, the nation, the kingdom, and (if it were in Augustus' time) the whole world must rule and govern the Church and [also] Christ himself as the Church is called, I Corinthians 12:12.

Furthermore if the Honourable Houses (the representative commonweal) shall erect a spiritual court for the judging of spiritual men and spiritual causes (although a new name be put upon it) [we query] whether or not such a court is not in the true nature and kind of it an High Commission? And is not this a reviving of Moses and the sanctifying of a new land of Canaan of which we hear nothing in the Testament of Jesus Christ, nor of any other holy nation but the particular Church of Christ? (I Peter 2:9)

Is not this to subject this holy nation, this heavenly Jerusalem, the wife and spouse of Jesus, the pillar and ground of truth to the uncertain and changeable mutations of this present evil world?

Query III. Whether, since you prefer to be builders, you have not cause to fear and tremble lest you be found to reject the cornerstone [i.e., Jesus Christ] in not fitting to him only living stones [i.e., true believers]. . . ?

Query IV. Whether in your consciences before God you be not persuaded—notwithstanding your promiscuous joining with all—that few of the people of England and Scotland (and fewer of the nobles and gentry) are such spiritual matter, living stones, truly regenerate and converted? And therefore whether it be not the greatest courtesy in the world which you may possibly perform unto them to aquaint them impartially with their condition and how impossible it is for a dead stone to have fellowship with the living God, and for any man to enter the kingdom of God without a second birth? John 3.

Query VII. We query where you now find one footstep, print, or pattern in this doctrine of the Son of God for a national holy covenant and so, consequently, . . . a national church? Where find you evidence of a whole nation, country or kingdom converted to the faith, and of Christ's appointing of a whole nation or kingdom to walk in one way of religion?

Again we ask whether . . . the constitution of a national church . . . can possibly be framed without a racking and tormenting of souls as well as of the bodies of persons, for it seems not possible to fit it to every conscience?

Query VIII. We readily grant [that] the civil magistrate [is] armed by God with a civil sword (Romans 13) to execute vengeance against robbers, murderers, tyrants, &c. Yet where it concerns Christ we find [that] when his disciples desire vengeance upon offenders (Luke 9) he meekly answers, "You know not what spirit you are of. I came not to destroy men's lives but to save them." If ever there were cause for the servants of Christ Jesus to fight, it was when—not his truth, or servants, or ordinances, but—his own most holy person was in danger, Matthew 26. Yet then that Lamb of God checks Peter [who was] beginning to fight for him, telling him that all who take the sword shall perish by the sword. . . . Unto which may also be added John 18:35: "My kingdom is not of this world. If my kingdom were of this world then would my servants fight that I should not be delivered, &c."

We query—if security be taken by the wisdom of the state for civil subjection—why even the Papists themselves and their consciences may not be permitted in the world? For otherwise if England's government were the government of the whole world not only they but a world of idolaters of all sorts—yea, the whole world—must be driven out of the world?

Query X. Since you report your opposing and suppressing of heresies and [your] glorious success, &c, we query whether that be a demonstrative argument from the scriptures for a truth of a church or government of it since even the Church of Rome may boast of the same against many schisms and heresies, and doth triumph with wonderful success even against the truth and the witness to it according to Daniel's and John's prophecies? Daniel 11, Revelation 13.

Query XII. Since you both profess to want more light and that a greater light is to be expected . . . we query how you can profess and swear to persecute all others as schismatics, heretics, &c, who believe they see a further light and dare not join with either of your churches? [We query] whether the Lamb's wife has received any such commission or disposition from the Lamb (her husband) so to practice? [We query] whether (as King James once wrote upon Revelation 20) it be not a true mark and character of a false church to persecute? It being the nature only of a wolf to hurt the lambs and sheep, but impossible for a lamb or sheep—or a thousand flocks of sheep—to persecute one wolf (we speak of spiritual sheep and spiritual wolves). For other wolves against the civil state we profess it to be the duty of the civil state to persecute and suppress them.

And lastly, whether the States of Holland which tolerate (though not own, as you say) the several sects among them which differ from them and are of another conscience and worship, [we query] whether or not they come not nearer to the holy pattern and command of the Lord Jesus to permit the tares to have a civil being in the field of the world until the harvest, the end of it? (Matthew 13)

We know the allegations against this counsel [of mine]: the [archetype of such practice] is from Moses (no Christ), his pattern is the typical land of Canaan, the kings of Israel and Judah, &c. We believe [that this] will be found [to be] but one of Moses' shadows which vanished at the coming of the Lord Jesus—yet such a shadow as is directly opposite to the very testament and coming of the Lord Jesus. [It is] opposite to the very nature of a Christian Church, the only holy nation and Israel of God. [It is] opposite to the very tender bowels of humanity (and how much more Christianity?), [which] abhors to pour out the blood of men merely for their souls' belief and worship. [It is] opposite to the very essentials and fundamentals of the nature of a civil magistracy, a civil common weal or combination of men which can only respect civil things. [It is] opposite to the Jews conversion to Christ by not permitting them a civil life or being. [It is] opposite to the civil peace and the lives of millions slaughtered upon this ground in mutual persecuting of each other's consciences, especially the Protestant and the Papist. [It is] opposite to the souls of all men who by persecutions are ravished into a dissembled worship which their hearts embrace not. [It is] opposite to the best of God's servants who, in all Popish and Protestant states, have been commonly esteemed and persecuted as the only schismatics, heretics, &c. [It is] opposite to that light of scripture which is expected yet to shine [but] which must, by that doctrine, be suppressed as a new or old heresy or novelty. All this in all ages experience testifies [to], [ages] which never saw any long lived fruit of peace or righteousness grow upon that fatal tree.

ANNE HUTCHINSON

The Examination of Anne Hutchinson (1637)

As the colonial establishment sought to clarify the relationships between church and state, they faced occasional protest or opposition from religious dissenters. Roger Williams's separatist views caused him to be exiled from the Massachusetts Bay Colony in 1635, which led to a legacy of broader religious toleration in Rhode Island than in the Bay Colony. Not long after Williams' exile, the Puritan colony was again challenged, this time by Anne Hutchinson, a midwife and theologian who held religious services in her home and spoke of receiving "immediate revelation" from God "by the voice of his own spirit to my soul."

The Examination of Anne Hutchinson

John Winthrop, Governor (JW): Mrs. Hutchinson, you are called here as one of those that have troubled the peace of the commonwealth and the churches here; you are known to be a woman that hath had a great share in the promoting and divulging of those opinions that are causes of this trouble, and to be nearly joined not only in affinity and affection with some of those the court had taken notice of and passed censure upon, but you have spoken diverse things (as we have been informed) very prejudicial to the honour of the churches and ministers thereof[.][4] [A]nd you have maintained a meeting and an assembly in your house that hath been condemned by the general assembly as a thing not tolerable nor comely in the sight of God nor fitting for your sex. . . .

Anne Hutchinson (AH): I am called here to answer before you, but I hear no things laid to my charge.

JW: I have told you some already and more I can tell you.

AH: Name one, Sir.

JW: Have I not named some already?

AH: What have I said or done?

JW: Why for your doings, this you did harbour and countenance those that are parties in this faction that you have heard of.

AH: That's matter of conscience, Sir.

JW: Your conscience you must keep, or it must be kept for you. . . .

AH: If you please to give me leave, I shall give you the ground of what I know to be true. Being much troubled to see the falseness of the constitution of the church of England, I had like to have turned separatist[.] [W]hereupon I kept a day of solemn humiliation and pondering, this scripture was brought unto me—he that denies Jesus Christ is the antichrist[.] This I considered of and in considering found that the papists did not deny him to be come in the flesh, nor we did not deny him: who then was antichrist? Was the Turk antichrist only? The Lord knows that I could not open scripture; he must by his prophetical office open it unto me. So after that being unsatisfied in the thing, the Lord was pleased to bring this scripture out of the Hebrews. He that denies the testament denies the testator, and in this did open unto me and give me to see that those which did not teach the new covenant had the spirit of antichrist, and upon this he did discover the ministry unto me; and, ever since, I bless the Lord, he hath let me see which was the clear ministry and which the wrong. Since that time I confess I have been more choice and he hath left me to distinguish between the voice of my beloved and the voice of Moses, the voice of John Baptist and the voice of antichrist, for all those voices are spoken of in scripture. Now if you do condemn me for speaking what in my conscience I know to be truth, I must commit myself unto the Lord.

Second Officer of the Court: How do you know that that was the spirit?

AH: How did Abraham know that it was God that bid him offer his son, being a breach of the sixth commandment?

Third Officer: By an immediate voice.

AH: So to me by an immediate revelation.

Third Officer: How! an immediate revelation.

AH: By the voice of his own spirit to my soul. I will give you another scripture, Jer. 46: 27, 28—out of which the Lord showed me what he would do for me and the rest of his servants. But after he was pleased to reveal himself to me I did presently like Abraham run to Hagar. And after that he did let me see the atheism of my own heart, for which I begged of the Lord that it might not remain in my heart, and being thus, he did show me this (a twelvemonth after) which I told you of before. . . . Therefore, I desire you to look to it, for you see this scripture fulfilled this day and therefore I desire you that as you tender the Lord and the church and commonwealth to consider and look what you do. You have power over my body but the Lord Jesus hath power over my body and soul; and assure yourselves thus much, you do as much as in you lies to put the Lord Jesus Christ from you, and if you go on in this course you begin, you will bring a curse upon you and your posterity, and the mouth of the Lord hath spoken it.

Articles, Lawes, and Orders, Divine, Politic, and Martiall for the Colony in Virginia (1610–1611)

From its "planting" in 1607 until 1624 when it was taken over as a royal colony, the Virginia settlement was controlled by a company that held "power and authority of government" according to several charters from James I. While the Virginia Company resided in London, delegated officials actually managed the affairs of the plantation. Without exception the charters and related documents were phrased in that language used by Cotton and Williams, and they illustrate the close association of divine and mundane authorities that reinforced each other's administrations. A full establishment was out of the question in the early garrison state where the ministers were really chaplains. "Dale's Laws" embody the regimen introduced by Sir Thomas Gates, Lord Delaware, and Sir Thomas Dale, which helped to rescue the faltering plantation from extinction. The complete set of thirty-seven laws was to be read to the assemblies every Sunday by the clergymen. More significantly, perhaps, a long and orthodox prayer was appointed to be read twice daily on the Court of the Guard by the captain or other officer. If the laws and the prayer seemed "ancient and common," it was only because "these grounds are the same constant Asterismes [constellations] and starres which must guide all that travell in these perplexed wayes and paths of publique affairs." By the middle of the seventeenth century Virginia society had developed its own pattern for the relationship between Anglican parish churches and the colonial government, which gave unique authority to the local vestry in the absence of both a hereditary patron and an accessible bishop.

Whereas his Majesty like himself a most zealous prince hath in his own realms a principal care of true Religion and reverence to God, and hath always strictly commanded his generals and governors with all his forces wheresoever to let their ways be like his ends for the glory of God, . . . I have . . . adhered unto the laws divine, and orders politic and martial of his Lordship . . . an addition of such others as I have found either the necessity of the present state of the Colony to require, or the infancy and weakness of the body thereof . . . able to digest. . . .[5]

1. First, since we owe our highest and supreme duty, our greatest and all our allegiance, to him from whom all power and authority is derived and flows as from the first and only fountain, and being special soldiers empressed in this sacred cause, we must alone expect our success from him who is only the blesser of all good attempts, the King of Kings, the commander of commanders, and Lord of Hosts, I do strictly command and charge all captains and officers, of what quality or nature soever . . . , to have a care that the Almighty God be duly and daily served, and that they call upon their people to hear sermons, as that also they diligently frequent Morning and Evening Prayer themselves by their own example and daily life and duty herein encourage others thereunto, and that such who shall often and willfully absent themselves be duly punished according to the martial law in that case provided.
2. That no man speak impiously or maliciously against the holy and blessed Trinity or any of the three persons, that is to say, against God the Father, God the Son, and God the holy Ghost, or against the known articles of the Christian faith, upon pain of death.
3. That no man blaspheme God's holy name upon pain of death, or use unlawful oaths, taking the name of God in vain, curse or ban, upon pain of severe punishment for the first offence so committed, and for the second to have a bodkin thrust through his tongue, and if he continue the blaspheming of God's holy name, for the third time so offending, he shall be brought to a martial court and there receive censure of death for his offence.
4. No man shall use any traiterous words against his Majesty's Person, or royal authority, upon pain of death.
5. No man shall speak any word or do any act which may tend to the derision or despight of God's holy word upon pain of death. Nor shall any man unworthily demean himself unto any preacher or minister of the same but generally hold them in reverent regard. . . .
6. Every man and woman duly twice a day upon the first tolling of the bell shall upon the working days repair unto the Church to hear divine service upon pain of losing his or her days allowance for the first omission, for the second to be whipped, and for the third to be condemned to the Gallies for six months. Likewise no man or woman shall dare to violate or break the sabbath by any gaming, public, or private abroad, or at home, but duly sanctify and observe the same, both himself and his family, by preparing themselves at home with private prayer, that they may be the better fitted for the public according to the commandments of God and the orders of our Church, as also every man and woman shall repair in the morning to the divine service and sermons preached upon the sabbath day, and in the afternoon to divine service and catechizing, upon pain for the first fault to lose their provision and allowance for the whole week following, for the second to lose the said allowance and also to be whipped, and for the third to suffer death.

7. All preachers or ministers within this our colony or colonies shall . . . choose unto him four of the most religious and better disposed as well to inform of the abuses and neglects of the people in their duties and service to God as also to the due reparation and keeping of the church handsome and fitted with all reverent observances thereunto belonging. Likewise every minister shall keep a faithful and true record or church book of all christenings, marriages, and deaths of such [of] our people as shall happen. . . .
10. No man shall be found guilty of sacrilege which is a trespass as well committed in violating and abusing any sacred ministry, duty or office of the church irreverently or profanely as by being a church robber to filch, steal or carry away anything out of the church appertaining thereunto or unto any holy and consecrated place to the divine service of God which no man should do upon pain of death. . . .
13. No manner of person whatsoever, contrary to the word of God (which ties every particular and private man, for conscience sake, to obedience and duty [to] the magistrate and such as shall be placed in authority over them) shall detract, slander, calumnate, murmur, mutiny, resist, disobey, or neglect the commandments either of the Lord Governor . . . or any authorized . . . public officer. . . .
33. There is not one man or woman in this colony now present, or hereafter to arrive, but shall give up an account of his and their faith and religion, and repair unto the minister that by his conference with them he may understand and gather whether heretofore they have been sufficiently instructed and catechised in the principles and grounds of religion. . . .
37. . . . Every minister or preacher shall every sabbath day before catechising read all these laws and ordinances publicly in the assembly of the congregation upon pain of his entertainment check for that week.

Preface to the Fundamental Orders of Connecticut (1638–1639)

In the case of Massachusetts Bay, sufferage had been explicitly restricted to church members as early as 1631. It is likely that this act should be understood as an expediential means, adopted by the General Court, to secure and assure its control over the separated settlements within the patent as immigration rapidly increased. The Hartford settlements did not adopt a similar restriction, a fact that is erroneously interpreted as indicating the presence of an incipient democracy in the Connecticut Valley. Actually its territory was small, its location isolated, and its population comparatively homogeneous. Thomas Hooker, a dominant figure in the settlement, casually offered the following postulates, which would have warranted such a restriction if it had been needed: 1. "A right opinion and worship of God should be openly professed within the territories and jurisdiction of a state . . . as that which comes within the . . . object of the state and policy to attend" and 2. "Hence the supreme magistrate hath liberty and power both to inquire and judge of professions and religions, which is true and ought to be maintained, which is false and ought to be rejected."[6] The Preface to the Fundamental Orders indicates how intimately church and state were coordinated in that venture. In the Bay

Colony, church attendance was required of all inhabitants, and all were required to support the organization. The correlation of spiritual and temporal authorities was simply an expression of the medieval principle that the unity of society was guaranteed by the uniformity of religion. The principle that heresy is treason logically followed, and by 1644 Massachusetts Bay required banishment for Baptists.

Forasmuch as it hath pleased the Almighty God by the wise disposition of his divine providence so to order and dispose of things that we the inhabitants and residents of Windsor, Hartford, and Wethersfield are now cohabiting and dwelling in and upon the River of Connecticut and the lands thereunto adjoining; And well knowing that where a people are gathered together the Word of God requires that to maintain the peace and union of such a people there should be an orderly and decent government established according to God to order and dispose of the affairs of the people at all seasons as occasion shall require: [we] do therefore associate and conjoin ourselves to be as one public state or commonwealth; and do, for ourselves and our successors and such as shall be adjoined to us at any time hereafter, enter into combination and confederation together to maintain and preserve the liberty and purity of the gospel of our Lord Jesus Christ which we now profess, as also the discipline of the churches which according to the truth of the said gospel is now practised among us; As also in our civil affairs to be guided and governed according to such Laws, Rules, Orders and Decrees as shall be made, ordered & decreed, as followeth:[7]

An Act Concerning Religion in the Maryland Colony (1649)

The Maryland Colony represents a peculiar chapter in the records of church-state relationships in colonial America. Although sponsored by Lord Baltimore in the 1630s as a refuge for English Catholics, from the beginning a significant number of Protestants joined in the venture. During the 1640s—against the background of the civil war in England—hostility between Protestants and Catholics became bitter, especially since it was encouraged by outside agitators from Virginia. In this situation Baltimore attempted to undergird his tolerant policy through "An Act Concerning Religion." Within five years it had been repealed and the Catholics outlawed by the ascendant and militant Puritan party. After a series of complex developments Maryland finally became a royal colony after the Glorious Revolution. Whether Baltimore's policy of toleration was primarily idealistic or a political calculation, times were not ready for it. It is curious that this act has become known as the Act of Toleration. To be sure it does authorize some latitude in religious belief and observance. Read in its entirety, however, it is yet another exercise in that "language of establishment," which was so nearly universal to the seventeenth century. An analysis and assessment of the act may be found in M. P. Andrews, *The Founding of Maryland* (New York, 1933), pp. 143 ff.

Forasmuch as in a well governed and Christian commonwealth matters concerning religion and the honor of God ought in the first place to be taken into serious consideration and endeavoured to be settled, be it therefore ordered and enacted by the Right Honorable Cecilius Lord Baron of Baltimore absolute Lord and Proprietary of this province with the advice and consent of this General Assembly:[8]

That whatsoever person or persons within this province . . . shall from henceforth blaspheme God, that is curse him, or deny our Saviour Jesus Christ to be the Son of God, or shall deny the holy Trinity . . . , or the Godhead of any of the said three persons of the Trinity or the Unity of the Godhead, or shall use or utter any reproachful speeches, words or language concerning the said holy Trinity, or any of the said three persons thereof, shall be punished with death and confiscation or forfeiture of all his or her lands and goods to the Lord Proprietary and his heirs.

And be it also enacted by the authority and with the advice and assent aforesaid, That whatsoever person or persons shall from henceforth use or utter any reproachful words or speeches concerning the blessed Virgin Mary the Mother of our Saviour or the holy Apostles or Evangelists or any of them shall in such case for the first offence forfeit to the said Lord Proprietary . . . the sum of five pound sterling or the value thereof. . . . And that every such offender or offenders for every second offence shall forfeit ten pound sterling or the value thereof. . . . And that every person or persons before mentioned offending herein the third time shall for such third offence forfeit all his lands and goods and be forever banished and expelled out of this province.

And be it also further enacted by the same authority, advice and assent that whatsoever person or persons shall from henceforth upon any occasion of offence or otherwise in a reproachful manner or way declare, call or denominate any person or persons whatsoever . . . within this province . . . an heretic, schismatic, idolator, puritan, Independent, Presbyterian, popish priest, Jesuit, Jesuited papist, Lutheran, Calvinist, Anabaptist, Brownist, Antinomian, Barrowist, Roundhead, Separatist, or any other name or term in a reproachful manner relating to matter of religion shall for every such offence forfeit and lose the sum of ten shillings sterling or the value thereof. . . , the one half thereof to be forfeited and paid unto the person and persons of whom such reproachful words are or shall be spoken or uttered, and the other half thereof to the Lord Proprietary. . . .

And be it further likewise enacted by the authority and consent aforesaid that every person and persons within this province that shall at any time hereafter profane the Sabbath or Lord's Day called Sunday by frequent swearing, drunkenness or by any uncivil or disorderly recreation, or by working on that day when absolute necessity doth not require it, shall for every first offence forfeit two shillings six pence sterling or the value thereof, and for the second offence five shillings sterling or the value thereof, and for the third offence and so for every time he shall offend in like manner afterwards ten shillings sterling or the value thereof. . . .

And whereas the enforcing of the conscience in matters of religion hath frequently fallen out to be of dangerous consequences in those commonwealths where it hath been practised, and for the more quiet and peaceable government of this province, and the better to preserve mutual love and amity among the inhabitants thereof; be it therefore also by the Lord Proprietary with the advice and consent of this Assembly ordained and enacted (except as in this present Act is before declared and set forth) that no person or persons whatsoever within this province . . . professing to believe in

Jesus Christ shall from henceforth be in any ways troubled, molested or discountenanced for or in respect of his or her religion, nor in the free exercise thereof within this province of the islands thereunto belonging, nor in any way compelled to the belief or exercise of any other religion against his or her consent, so [long] as they be not unfaithful to the Lord Proprietary, or molest or conspire against the civil government established or to be established in this province under him or his heirs. . . . The freemen have assented. Tho: Hatton Enacted by the Governor. Willm Stone

The Charter of Rhode Island and Providence Plantations (1663)

To actualize Williams's segregation of spiritual authority and temporal jurisdiction was also to make practically possible the social being of Providence Plantations and Rhode Island, which were populated by a mixed lot according to any classification of the day. Rabid religionists of several stripes shared the meagre and marginal land with traders, adventurers, individualists, and Indians. Thus when Dr. John Clarke finally did obtain a charter from Charles II in 1663 that granted religious liberty, it did mark a "lively experiment" as to whether social cohesion could be achieved apart from a common religious allegiance. Neither Williams, the "theological windmill," nor the reluctant experiment of the charter make any sense, however, apart from the idiom of the seventeenth century.

Whereas his Majesty has been informed by the petition of John Clarke, on behalf of . . . the purchasers and free inhabitants of the island called Rhode Island the rest of the colony of Providence Plantations in Narragansett Bay in New England, that they, pursuing with loyal minds their serious intentions of godly edifying themselves in the holy Christian faith as they were persuaded, together with the conversion of the Indian natives, did not only with the encouragement of his Majesty's progenitors transport themselves unto America but, not being able to bear in those parts their different apprehensions in religious concernments, again left their desirable habitations and transplanted themselves into the midst of the most potent Indian people of that country where (by the good Providence of God, from whom the plantations have taken their name) they have not only been preserved to admiration, but have prospered and become possessed by purchase from the natives of lands, rivers, harbors, &c, very convenient for plantations, ship building, supply of pipe-staves, and commerce with his Majesty's southern plantations, and by their friendly society with the great body of Narragansett Indians have given them encouragement to subject themselves to his Majesty.[9] And whereas they have declared that it is much on their hearts to hold forth a lively experiment that a flourishing civil state may best be maintained among his Majesty's subjects with full religious liberty, and that true piety will give the greatest security for sovereignty and true loyalty, His Majesty, willing to preserve to them that liberty in the worship of God which they have sought with so much travail and loyal subjection, and because some of them cannot conform to the liturgy, ceremonies, and articles of the Church of England, and hoping that the same—by reason of distance—may be no breach of the uniformity established in this nation, hereby grants and declares that no person within the said colony shall hereafter be any wise molested or called in question for any difference in opinion in matters of religion that does not disturb the civil peace of the colony, and that they shall enjoy the benefit of his Majesty's late Act of Indemnity and free pardon.

WILLIAM PENN

Preface to the Frame of Government of Pennsylvania (1682)

The seventeenth-century language of establishment is often overlooked by those who are concerned to locate instances of official toleration or allowance of religious liberty in colonial affairs. The Articles of Capitulation on the Reduction of New Netherland, for instance, are cited because Clause 8 allowed the Dutch the "liberty of their consciences in Divine Worship and Church Discipline." The significant implication, of course, is that a single establishment of religion seemed right and proper and that this departure from that practice was an expediential arrangement. In a similar way, while William Penn is justly celebrated for granting civil liberties to all who confessed "God as the Lord of conscience," this should not obscure the fact that such was a Quaker version of the conventional "language of establishment." Because man's "spiritual relation" was "free and mental" the church could not be "corporeal and compulsive." Yet government was said to be divinely authored—"sacred in its institution and end"—not only to restrain sin but to regulate "many other affairs," and Penn required confession of God on the part of the inhabitants and profession of Jesus Christ as Saviour on the part of the rulers. This might be contrasted with Williams's proposal that spiritual and temporal affairs be radically segregated. It is natural that we should be sympathetic toward Penn's charity in comparing him with many of his contemporaries. This does not mean, however, that the Pennsylvania experiment was more than another change rung on the medieval theme that man's double relation required coordination of his religious and civil lives.

When the great and wise God had made the world, of all his creatures it pleased him to choose man his deputy to rule it. And to fit him for so great a charge and trust he did not only qualify him with skill and power, but with integrity to use them justly.[10] This native goodness was equally his honour and his happiness. And while he stood here all went well. There was no need of coercive or compulsive means; the precept of divine love and truth in his bosom was the guide and keeper of his innocency. But lust prevailing against duty made a lamentable breach upon it. And the law that before had no power over him took place upon him and his disobedient posterity that such as would not live conformable to the holy law within should fall under the reproof and correction of the just law without in a judicial administration.

[Saint Paul] settles the divine right of government beyond exception, and that for two ends: first, to terrify evil doers; secondly, to cherish those that do well—which gives government a life beyond corruption and makes it as durable in the world as good men shall be. So that government seems to me a part of religion itself, a thing sacred in its institution and end. For if it does not directly remove the cause it crushes the effects of evil and is as such (though a lower, yet) an emanation of the same divine power that is both author and object of pure religion. The difference [between them lies] here: the one is more free and mental, the other more corporeal and compulsive in its operations. But that is only to evil doers, government itself being otherwise as capable of kindness, goodness, and charity as a more private society. They weakly err that think there is no other use of government than correction which is the coarsest part of it. Daily experience tells us that the care and regulation of many other affairs, more soft and daily necessary, make up much of the greatest part of government and [this] must have followed the peopling of the world had Adam never fell, and will continue among men, on earth, under the highest attainments they may arrive at by the coming of the blessed Second Adam, the Lord from Heaven. Thus much of government in general, as to its rise and end.

The Fundamental Constitutions of Carolina (1669–1698)

The Fundamental Constitutions have been of antiquarian interest because John Locke is thought to have had a hand in drafting the original (1669) version. Actually it is unlikely that he was deeply involved in the project. Of far more significance is the fact that the Lords Proprietors of Carolina attempted to provide an essentially feudal civil government for their colony, which they intended to be perpetual. The document—never fully in effect, apparently—passed through at least five versions. The original one contained several paragraphs that represent once again a statement of those traditional assumptions regarding church-state relations. This selection is from the final version (1698). Although very important changes took place in the other provisions during the revisions, the clauses relating to religion and religious institutions are substantially identical to those of the earliest draft.

25. No man shall be permitted to be a Freeman of Carolina or to have any estate or habitation within it who does not acknowledge a God, & that God is publically & solemnly to be worshipped.[11]
26. As the country comes to be sufficiently planted & distributed into fit divisions it shall belong to the Parliament to take care for the building of churches and the public maintenance of divines to be employed in the exercise of religion according to the Church of England, which being the only true & orthodox & national religion of the King's dominions is so also of Carolina, and therefore it alone shall be allowed to receive public maintenance by grant of Parliament.
27. Any seven or more persons agreeing in any religion shall constitute a church or a profession to which they shall give some name to distinguish it from others.
28. The terms of admittance & communion with any church or profession shall be written in a book and therein be subscribed by all the members of the said church or profession which shall be kept by the public Register of the Precinct wherein they reside.

29. The time of every ones subscription and admittance shall be dated in the said book of religious records.
30. In the terms of communion of every church or profession these following shall be there without which no agreement or assembly of men upon pretence of religion shall be accounted a church or profession within these rules:

    1st That there is a God.

    2nd That God is publicly to be worshipped.

    3rd That it is lawful and the duty of every man being thereunto called by those that govern to bear witness to truth, and that every church or profession shall in their terms of communion set down the external way whereby they witness a truth, as in the presence of God whether it be by laying hands on or kissing the Bible as in the Church of England or by holding up the hand or any sensible way.
31. No person above seventeen years of age shall have any benefit or protection of the law, or be capable of any place of profit or honor, who is not a member of some church or profession (having his name recorded in some one and but one religious record at once).
32. No person of any church or profession shall disturb or molest any religious assembly.
33. No person whatsoever shall speak anything in their religious assembly irreverently or seditiously of the government or governor or of state matters.
34. Any person subscribing the terms of communion in the record of the said church or profession before the precinct register and any five members of the said church or profession shall be thereby made a member of the said church or profession.
35. Any person striking out his own name out of any religious record, or his name being struck out by any officer there-unto authorized by each church or profession respectively, shall cease to be a member of that church or profession.
36. No man shall use any reproachful, reviling or abusive language against the religion of any church or profession, that being the certain way of disturbing the peace & hindering the conversion of any to the truth by engaging them in quarrels & animosities to the hatred of the professors and that profession which otherwise they may be brought to assent to.
37. Since charity obliges us to wish well to the souls of all men, and religion ought to alter nothing in any man's civil estate or right, it shall be lawful for slaves as well as others to enter themselves and be of what church or profession any of them shall think best & thereof be as fully members as any freeman. But yet no slave shall hereby be exempted from that civil dominion his master has over him, but in all other things in the same state & condition he was in before.
38. Assemblies upon what pretence soever of religion not observing & performing the abovesaid rule shall not be esteemed as churches but [as] unlawful meetings, and be punished as other riots.
39. No person whatsoever shall disturb, molest or persecute another for his speculative opinions in religion or his way of worship.
40. Every freeman of Carolina shall have absolute power & authority over his negro slaves of what opinion or religion soever.

A. LEON HIGGINBOTHAM, JR.

Race and the American Legal Process: The Colonial Period

Christian slaveholders in the South did not consider slavery inconsistent with their religious faith. But they were concerned about what their faith and laws might require if the slaves were to adopt the Christianity. Writing in 1978, A. Leon Higginbotham, Jr., judge of the Federal Third Circuit Court of Appeals, describes Virginia's legislative solution to this quandary.

Christianity: Meaningful for Whites but Irrelevant for Blacks

Virginians had to clarify how seriously they accepted the concept of true human brotherhood for those blacks who had adopted the white man's Christian faith.[12] Did conversion to Christianity entitle the slave to freedom? That was the crucial question, and it was answered in 1667 when the colonial assembly passed an act providing that baptism would not affect the bondage of blacks or Indians.

> 1667. Act III. Whereas some doubts have arisen whether children that are slaves by birth, and by the charity and pity of their owners made partakers of the blessed sacrament of baptism, should by virtue of their baptism be made free, it is enacted that *baptism does not alter the condition of the person as to his bondage of freedom; masters freed from this doubt may more carefully propagate Christianity by permitting slaves to be admitted to that sacrament.*

Once masters were reassured that it was the skin color and not the heathenism of their black and Indian slaves that "justified" their subjugation, they were not as hesitant to have their slaves baptized. In fact, a slave's baptism was often seen as a sign of his docility. Eventually some ministers began to use even Christianity as a means of extorting obedience from their slaves. In his sermon to a Maryland slave congregation, Reverend Thomas Bacon stressed that slaves who desired to be good Christians could become so only by being "good slaves":

> And pray, do not think that I want to deceive you, when I tell you, that your *masters* and *mistresses* are God's *overseers,*—and that if you are faulty towards them, God himself will punish you severely for it in the next world, unless you repend it and strive to make amends, by your *faithfulness and Diligence.*

In 1670, three years after the assembly had made clear that baptism would not alter a black man's bondage, it passed an act further clarifying the black servants' status in the colony by dividing non-Christian servants into two classes: those imported into this colony by shipping, who "shall be slaves for their lives"; and those who "shall come by land," who "shall serve, if boys or girles; untill thirty yeares of age: if men or women twelve yeares and no longer." This act favored the Indian, who usually came by land, and fixed the status of the non-Christian African as that of slave for life. It also anticipated later judicial and legislative pronouncements that all Africans were presumed to be slaves. The distinctions established by the 1670 statute were eliminated in 1682 when all imported non-Christians were made slaves.

If one juxtaposes the 1670 statute (and the 1682 modification), which fixed the status of blacks and Indians upon entry into the colony, with the earlier 1667 statute, which declared that baptism did not alter slave status, one realizes that by 1682 slavery was placed squarely on a racial foundation. Yet even these legislative enactments did not prevent masters who wanted to from creating their own arrangements. For instance, in 1678, a "Spanish Mullato, by name Antonio," sold by John Indicott of Boston to Richard Madlicott, to serve "But for Tenn yeares from the day he shall Disembarke in Virginia, and at the expiration of the said Tenn yeares the s'd Mullato, Antony, to be a free man to goe wherever he pleaseth."

Notes

1. Thomas Hooker, *A Survey of the Summe of Church Discipline* (London, 1648), part I, pp. 4f.

2. Abridged and edited to conform more nearly to current usage [Ed.].

3. Abridged and edited to conform more nearly to current usage. A full text may be consulted in *Publications of the Narragansett Club,* vol. II (Providence, R.I.: Narragansett Club, 1867), pp. 11 ff. (second so numbered) or in *The Complete Writings of Roger Williams* (New York: Russell & Russell, 1963), same volume and pages (facsimile of the former).

4. Reprinted by permission of the publisher from "The Examination of Mrs. Ann Hutchinson at the Court at Newtown," Appendix II, pp. 366–391 in *The History of the Colony and Province of Massachusetts-Bay*: Volume II by Thomas Hutchinson, edited by Lawrence Shaw Mayo, pp. 366, 383–384, Cambridge, Mass.: Harvard University Press, copyright © 1936 by the President and Fellows of Harvard College.

5. Abridged and edited to conform more nearly to current usage. A full text may be consulted in Peter Force, ed., *Tracts and Other Papers,* vol. III (Washington, 1844).

6. Thomas Hooker, *A Survey of the Summe of Church Discipline* (London, 1648), part IV, p. 75 (57).

7. Edited to conform more nearly to current usage. Text may be consulted in J. H. Trumbull, ed., *The Public Records of Connecticut* (Hartford, 1850), pp. 20 f.

8. Abridged and edited to conform more nearly to current usage. The text may be located in *The Proceedings and Acts of the General Assembly of Maryland,* January 1637/8–September 1664 (Baltimore, 1883), pp. 244 ff.

9. Edited to conform more nearly to current usage. The text may be consulted in *The Calendar of State Papers,* "Colonial America and West Indies, 1661–68," no. 512 (July 8, 1663), p. 148 .

10. Abridged and edited to conform more nearly to current usage. The text is available in ed. F. N. Thorpe, ed., *The Federal and State Constitutions* (Washington, 1909), vol. V, pp. 3052 f.

11. Abridged and edited to conform more nearly to current usage. The text is available in W. L. Saunders, ed., *The Colonial Records of North Carolina* vol. II (Raleigh, 1886), pp. 852 ff. The five versions of The Fundamental Constitutions may be compared in M. E. E. Parker, ed., *North Carolina Charters and Constitutions, 1578–1698* (Raleigh, 1963), pp. 128 ff.

12. From *In the Matter of Color: Race and the American Legal Process 1: The Colonial Period* by A. Leon Higginbotham, Jr., copyright © 1978 by Oxford University Press, Inc. Used by permission of Oxford University Press, Inc.

2

Ethnic Diversity and Evangelical Differentiation (1700–1760)

The language of establishment took for granted that there was a uniformity of religious life within society. Even as this idiom continued to be used in the eighteenth-century colonies, however, developments were taking place that would render it wholly obsolete. The religious life of the colonies—never completely uniform separately, let alone collectively—was becoming so pluralized that an establishment of religion could mean little more than public financial support and preference for one "denomination" of Christians. This was a far cry from that coordination and interpenetration of spiritual and temporal concerns that had been the earlier virtually universal ideal and had been substantially realized particularly in several of the early New England settlements. The critical issue in this development was not so much a latitude in creed or liberalism of spirit. Nor was it a worldliness stimulated by commercial endeavors. Such attitudes were perfectly compatible with personal indifference toward establishments and support of them for the public good. What rendered the older language anachronistic was the differentiation of religious life itself. Thus numerous religious groups, all of which considered themselves autonomous spiritually, were placed beside each other and together—rather than independently—they constituted the common life. This differentiation resulted in conviction confronting belief and zeal challenging prejudice. As a consequence, the colonies were set on a road to disestablishment although that destination was not at all clear in the beginning. Broadly speaking a distinction must be drawn between two sources that gave rise to this pluralization of religious life. One source was rooted in the ethnic diversity that soon became a reality in the colonies. The second source was in the evangelical energies that sought to transform the existing churches but that more often led to the formation of new ones. Frequently these causes acted in the same situation and contributed to the same results, but for purposes of analysis it is necessary to distinguish them.

It is no part of this study to offer a systematic consideration of how immigration has influenced American religious ideas and practices. It is appropriate to observe, however, that early in the eighteenth century the colonies, most of which had been fundamentally English in composition, began to receive an increasingly diverse population. Thus the Scots started to immigrate after the Act of Union in 1708. The Ulstermen began to arrive about 1717. German, or "Dutch," groups of Germans and Swiss came between 1720 and 1740. From the point of view of the religious life of the colonies this immigration introduced no form of Protestantism radically different from those already on the scene. But while the earlier pattern had been one—especially in the northern and southern colonies—of relative religious homogeneity, the new settlers juxtaposed their ethnically defined religious patterns beside the existing ones. Thus the Scottish Presbyterian in Carolina was "foreign" no less than the Irish Presbyterian was in New England. And Pennsylvania took into itself not only the Calvinistic Ulstermen but also such exotic continental groups as the Moravians and the Mennonites. This pattern of ethnic-religious diversification of American life became even more significant in the nineteenth century, and its effects continue to be important in twenty-first century American life. Nevertheless the early role of this factor in creating conditions making necessary disestablishment requires attention in the present context.

If the colonies were receiving a population that diversified their religious life, Protestant evangelicalism within the colonies was also working upon the population in such a way as to lead to that same end. The Great Awakening is the name usually given to the religious turmoil that troubled the East Coast settlements during the second quarter of the eighteenth century. Arising out of a desire to intensify the authentic religious life of the faithful, it broke out in New Jersey, went through a New England phase, and disturbed the southern colonies also. George Whitefield, the English evangelist, preached to great throngs up and down the coast while lesser figures itinerated on local circuits. Where old churches could not or would not be renewed, new ones were formed. These new churches frequently represented classes of the population that had been effectively excluded from the original churches. No less than the ethnic-based churches "imported" from Europe, this domestic development made the ideal of religious homogeneity wholly irrelevant to the American scene. Accordingly "religious establishment" could only be an empty phrase signifying little more than financial support and civic preference for a particular institution. The language of establishment might still be used, but its meaning had shifted.

The Connecticut Establishment and Provision for Dissent (1708)

Connecticut, along with Massachusetts Bay, took for granted the desirability of a rigorous and exclusive church establishment.[1] Connecticut was able to realize this pattern more successfully, however, due chiefly to a greater insularity. The Connecticut system was incorporated in the Saybrook Platform, which was adopted in 1708.[2] Contemporaneously with this legislation of an establishment, nevertheless, external circumstances made it necessary to recognize the presence of "dissenters" and to grant them the appearance if not a measure of toleration. Quakers and members of the Church of England, it was correctly feared, might influence the Crown to proceed with the intended consolidation of the New England Colonies under a governor of his appointment. England itself had recognized dissenters with its Toleration Act of 1689. Thus the dissenters' act and the related provision that qualified the Saybrook Platform were loopholes for the Baptist or Anglican who would submit to double taxation. The Quaker—who would not submit to the oath of allegiance—was not really helped at all.

And it is further enacted, for the ease of such as soberly dissent from the way of worship and ministry established by the ancient laws of this government (and still continuing), That if any such persons shall at the county court of that county they belong to qualify themselves according to an act made in the first year of the late King William and Queen Mary, granting liberty of worshipping God in a way separate from that which is by law established, they shall enjoy the same liberty and priviledge in any place within this Colony, without any let, hindrance, and molestation whatsoever. Provided always that nothing herein shall be construed to the prejudice of the rights and priviledges of the churches as by law established in this government, or to the excusing [of] any person from paying any such minister or town dues as are now or shall hereafter be due from them.

The Confession of Faith of the Christians Called Mennonites

The Mennonites took their name from Menno Simons (d. 1561), who was an Anabaptist leader of the continental Reformation. His followers were incorrectly grouped with the revolutionaries and spiritualists by both Protestants and Catholics, and all were severely persecuted. The Mennonites actually sought to recover primitive Christianity, taking the historical Jesus as the norm for their life. Accordingly they asked only to be left undisturbed, a radical request since it made religious uniformity impossible. Although chiefly from the Netherlands (which had granted a measure of toleration to them) the Mennonites who came to America in the eighteenth century were known as Germans. In Pennsylvania they found a welcome respite from their harrassed life. In order to introduce themselves they published an English translation of their Confession of Faith along with an Appendix that includes the following passages about their view of government and magistrates. The selection discloses the spirit in which they sought to recover early Christianity while also indicating the diversity of population that outmoded religious establishments. A modern discussion of this group in its early years may be found in *The Anabaptist View of the Church* by Franklin H. Littell (Boston, 1952, 1958).

And now if some will conclude out of our doctrine and wrongfully judge us as if we cast off, dispised or set at nought the Office of the Magistrates, they may be pleased to know that we utterly deny such reproaches for we acknowledge it freely that [the office] is ordained by God, and therefore the Powers are called "The Ministers of God, and are ordained to punish the evil doers, and defend the just," according to the doctrine and testimony of Saint Paul. (Romans, Chapter 13)[3]

And though we can find no exact rule or example in the New Testament, like as it is in the Old, after which that office should be served, or how the high and heavy worldly business should be ruled, [and though we] also cannot see that they are ruled according to the Godly commands of the Old Testament but in most places are ruled according to the Constitution or appointment of the Emperors, Kings, Lords and higher powers, their commands, laws and customs (which are diverse from one another), and yet it behoves and becomes a right and true Christian that he should be little and low in this World, and shun the greatness of the same, and keep himself like the lowly ones. And therefore we (as also because of the manifold encumberances which befall this office) think ourselves too low and find ourselves too weak to undertake the same or to rule the same. But yet we will declare herewith, and also at all times endeavor to show, that we hold it in great worth and honor as an ordinance of God, as it is written: "his work is worthy of praise and honor," or, as others translate it, "what He orders is honorable and glorious, &c." (Psalm 111) And [we] judge or account no body cursed in our hearts by reason of his office if he do walk upright in the true Christian religion and according to his duty.

Which may be taken . . . that we hold and acknowledge ourselves for conscience sake and duty towards God to honor them and [we] also herewith (as at other times we commonly do) very friendly and not less earnestly exhort all our fellow members . . . that they not only behave themselves with due respect to the powers, and give them all honor, but also as it becomes loyal and obedient subjects to assist them with all uprightness, truth and obedience according to the holy Gospel, and to follow their Christian calling and duty according to the doctrine of Paul as above mentioned, and to pay all required taxes, tolls, excises, and convoy charges truly and willingly without any deficiency.

This is that which our Lord and Teacher commands, "Render unto Caesar the things which are Caesar's," Matthew 22. And above that, that everyone, not only in all meetings or places of worship but also by all other opportunities both day and night, make mention of them in their ejaculations or hearty prayers to God. . . .

Thus we have thought it good to publish the here before-going Confession and also this appendix in the English Language and no longer to withhold [from] our English friends in their hearty desires. And if we find that this is welcome to them—that we Dutch learn to speak English. . . .—then we will hope that our powers (which are set by God over countries and nations) may take it in a Christian like consideration if it is not better for their countries and cities, and also if it were not worthy of praise for their own persons, that they ruled and dealt with patience, meekness, and peaceableness with their subjects and inhabitants that are of another religion, and that they did not let themselves be moved by anybody to forcing of conscience nor hinder their subjects of their inward worship. . . .

When all this is seriously considered and weighed in the balance of God's holy Word, then we will hope and steadfastly believe that nobody will rule and deal otherwise with his subjects than he willingly would that he or his, living under the powers of another religion, should be dealt with and ruled, and to live according to that kingly command which teaches, "To do to another as we willingly would that [it] should be done to us."

And, Ah! if it might please all—who aforetime have been so zealous in these things—in time to come to deal lovingly with and patiently suffer their subjects which are of another religion, like as our eminent powers in this province do who protect and defend us, and therefore serve as an excellent example to all others to follow the same. And those that will be like them in the same shall also have the like praise and honor. They will give occasion to their subjects to bring their earnest prayers [for them] to the Lord. . . .

Soli Deo Gloria

Grievances Against the Connecticut Establishment (1751)

The following memorial addressed to the Connecticut Legislature by a separate Congregational Church at Preston petitions for relief from the requirement that they support the stated ministry (the established Congregational Church) and that they accept the Saybrook Platform (the ideological establishment). In this regard the Connecticut pattern was probably the extreme case of an establishment seeking to preserve its prerogatives—it certainly should not be considered typical. But the plea for toleration was characteristic because such a development represented the only practicable solution to the colonial religious situation in the mid-eighteenth century. Toleration within the patterns of establishment was not sufficiently radical, however, to serve as the religious condition for a federal government—or, for that matter, for the constitutive states.

To the Honourable General Assembly of the Colony of Connecticut to be convened at New Haven In said Colony on the Second thirsday of October A. D. 1751 the Memorial of John Avery and others the Subscribers hereunto Humbly Shueth that your Memorialists live Some of us within the first, and some of us within the Second Eccleciastical Societys In the Town of Preston Some few within the Second Society In Groton and Some few within the South Society in Norwich and Some In the Second Society of Stonington, that we are that one of the Very Many Sects of Professors of Christianity that are Commonly Called Separates that we Have truly and Contientiously Desented and Separated from all the Churches and Religious Societyes within whose limits we live That we are Settled according to the Present Establishment of this Government, that our Habitations are Generally Compact none of us living more than 7 or 8 miles from the Place of our Public worship most of us within Two Miles, that the Number of families Is About forty and the Number of Souls about 300, of which there are more than fifty Church Members all belonging to our Communion and of our Profession that we Have at our own Cost Settled a Minister & built a Meeting House for Divine worship & have long since been Imbodied Into Church Estate that Nevertheless we are Compelled to pay towards the Support of the Ministry & for the building of Meeting Houses In these Societies from which we have Respectively Sepperated and Desented as aforsesaid and for our Neglect to Make Payment of Such Rates we have Many of us been Imprisoned others have had their Estates Torn

& sold to the almost ruining of some familyes wherefore we Intreat the attention of this Honnourable Assembly and Pray Your Honnours to Suffer us to Say that we always have & for the future most Chearfully Shall Contribute our Proportion towards the Support of Civil Government & we not only Prise & value but Humbly Claim and Challenge our Right In the Immunities of the Present Constitution.[4]

Our Religion or Principles are no ways Subversive of Government and we are not only Inclining but Engaging to Support It—and there Is no Difference between us and other Members of the Community but what is Merely Ecclesiastical In which Respect also they Differ one from another & the whole Christian World no less.

Our Religious Sentiments and way of worship No ways affect the State.

We are as Industrious In our business and as Punctual in our Contracts as If we were Anabaptists or Quakers and we Challenge to hold enjoy and Improve what Is our own by the Same Rules and Laws as all other Denominations of Christians Do.

And we Suppose there is (In the nature of things) no Reason we Should maintain & Support any Religion or way of worship but what we our Selves Embrace and Propose to receive the advantage of and that No body has right to Impede or Hinder us In that way of worship which in our Consciense we think to be Right for us. In all matters Civil we are accountable to the State So in all Matters of worship we are accountable to him who Is the object of It. to whom alone we must stand or fall and on these Principles are founded all acts of Toleration. Your Memorialists therefore humbly Intreat the Interposition and Protection of this honnourable Assembly that your honnours would order and Grant that your Memorialists and all such as adhere to or shall be Joined & attend the Publick worship with them may for the future be Released and Exempted from Paying Taxes for the Building of Meetinghouses or for the Support of the ministry in any of the Societies from which we have Sepperated (within the compass of eight miles from the place of Publick worship or Such other Limmits as your honnours Shall See fit) or that your honnours would grant us the Same Ease and Liberty as by law is Provided for the Ease of Anabaptists and Quakers or otherwise Grant Such Relief as in your wisdom you Shall Judge Just and your Memorialists are Ready to Qualify themselves according to the act of Toleration.

And as In Duty Bound Ever Pray.

Dated the 10th Day of September A. D. 1751.

Samuel Davies on Behalf of Dissenters in Virginia (1752)

Samuel Davies, who became fourth president of the College of New Jersey (Princeton) in 1759, was instrumental in organizing Presbyterianism in Virginia. His most significant contribution was to secure the right of dissent from the established Anglican Church under the English Act of Toleration. Through correspondence with Philip Doddridge—an English dissenting minister—Davies learned that the Bishop of London was concerned about dissenters in Virginia. He grasped the opportunity to address a long apology to the Bishop on behalf of his fellow colonists. The following excerpts are from that letter, which was written from Hanover, Virginia, during January 1752. Although the Bishop for whom it was intended never saw it, the letter in this way failing to fulfill its intention, it does represent the theme of this chapter in a striking fashion. The ethnically based religious complexity of the colonies was reinforced and compounded by the effects of evangelical faith, which Davies equally embodied.

I hope, my lord, you will not suspect I have so much arrogance as to encounter your lordship as a disputant, if I presume to make some free and candid remarks. . . .[5] My only design is to do justice to a misrepresented cause, which is the inalienable right of the meanest innocent; and as an impartial historical representation will be sufficient for this purpose, 'tis needless to tire your lordship with tedious argumentation.

The frontier counties of this colony, about an hundred miles west and southwest from Hanover, have been lately settled by people that chiefly came from Ireland originally, and immediately from the Northern colonies, who were educated Presbyterians, and had been under the care of the ministers belonging to the Synod of New York (of which I am a member) during their residence there. Their settling in Virginia has been many ways beneficial to it, which I am sure most of them would not have done, had they expected any restraint in the inoffensive exercise of their religion, according to their consciences. After their removal, they continued to petition the Synod of New York, and particularly the Presbytery of Newcastle, which was nearest to them, for ministers to be sent among them. But as the ministers of said Synod and Presbytery were few, and vastly disproportioned to the many congregations under their care, they could not provide these vacancies with settled pastors. . . . The only expedient in their power (was) to appoint some of their members to travel, alternately, into these destitute congregations, and officiate among them as long as would comport with their circumstances. It was this, my lord, that was the first occasion, as far as I can learn, of our being stigmatized *itinerant preachers.*

The dissenters here, my lord, are but sufficiently numerous to form two distinct organized congregations, or particular churches, and did they live contiguous, two meeting-houses would be sufficient for them, and neither they nor myself, would desire more. But they are so dispersed that they cannot convene for public worship, unless they have a considerable number of places licensed; and so few that they cannot form a particular organized church at each place. There are seven meeting-houses licensed in five different counties. . . . But the extremes of my congregation lie eighty or ninety miles apart; and the dissenters under my care are scattered through six or seven different counties. . . . The counties here are large, generally forty or fifty miles in length, and about twenty or thirty miles in breadth; so that though they lived in one county, it might be impossible for them all to convene at one place; and much more when they are dispersed through so many. Though there are now seven places licensed, yet the nearest are twelve or fifteen miles apart; and many of the people have ten, fifteen, or twenty miles to the nearest, and thirty, forty, or sixty miles to the rest; nay, some of them have thirty or forty miles to the nearest. That this is an impartial representation of our circumstances, I dare appeal to all that know anything about them.

All the dissenters here depend entirely on me to officiate among them, as there is no other minister of their own denomination within two hundred miles, except when one of my brethren from the northern colonies is appointed to pay them a transient visit, for two or three Sabbaths, once in a year or two: and as I observed they cannot attend on my ministry at one or two places by reason of their distance; nor constitute a complete particular church at each place of meeting, by reason of the smallness of their number.

These things, my lord, being impartially considered, I dare submit it to your lordship,

Whether my itinerating in this manner in such circumstances be illegal? And whether, though I cannot live in five different counties at once, as your lordship observes, I may not lawfully officiate in them, or in as many as the peculiar circumstances of my congregation, . . . render necessary?

Whether contiguity of residence is necessary to entitle dissenters to the liberties granted by the Act of Toleration? Whether when they cannot convene at one place, they may not, according to the true intent and meaning of that Act, obtain as many houses licensed as will render public worship accessible to them all? And whether if this liberty be denied them, they can be said to be tolerated at all? i.e. Whether *dissenters are permitted to worship in their own way,* (which your lordship observes was the intent of the Act) who are prohibited from worshipping in their own way, unless they travel thirty, forty or fifty miles every Sunday?

Whether, when there are a few dissenting families in one county and a few in another, and they are not able to form a distinct congregation or particular church at each place, and yet all of them conjunctly are able to form one, though they cannot meet statedly at one place; whether, I say, they may not legally obtain sundry meeting-houses licensed, in these different counties, where their minister may divide his time according to the proportion of the people, and yet be looked upon as one organized church? And whether the minister of such a dispersed church, who alternately officiates at these sundry meeting-houses should on this account be branded as an itinerant?

Whether, when a number of dissenters, sufficient to constitute two distinct congregations, each of them able to maintain a minister, can obtain but one by reason of the scarcity of ministers, they may not legally share in the labours of that one, and have as many houses licensed for him to officiate in, as their distance renders necessary? And whether the minister of such an united congregation, though he divides his labours at seven different places, or more, if their conveniency requires it, be not as properly a *settled* minister as though he preached but at one place, to but one congregation?

I beg leave, my lord, farther to illustrate the case by a relation of a matter of fact, and a very possible supposition.

It very often happens in Virginia, that the parishes are twenty, thirty, forty, and sometimes fifty or sixty miles long, and proportionably broad; which is chiefly owing to this, that people are not so thick settled, as that the inhabitants in a small compass should be sufficient for a parish. The Legislature here has wisely made provision to remedy this inconveniency, by ordering sundry churches or chapels of ease to be erected in one parish, that one of them at least may be tolerably convenient to all the parishioners; and all these are under the care of one minister, who shares his labours at each place in proportion to the number of people there.

Now, I submit it to your lordship, whether there be not at least equal reason that a plurality of meeting-houses should be licensed for the use of the dissenters here, since they are more dispersed and fewer in numbers? . . . I submit it also to your lordship, whether there be not as little reason for representing me as an itinerant preacher, on account of my preaching at so many places for the conveniency of one congregation, as that the minister of a large parish, where there are sundry churches or chapels of ease, should be so called for preaching at these sundry places, for the convenience of one parish?

But I find I have been represented to your lordship as an uninvited intruder into these parts:

To justify me from this charge, my lord, it might be sufficient to observe, that the meeting-houses here were legally licensed before I preached in them, and that the licenses were petitioned for by the people,

But to give your lordship a just view of this matter, I shall present you with a brief narrative of the rise and increase of the dissenters in and about this county, and an account of the circumstances of my settling among them.

About the year 1743, upon the petition of the Presbyterians in the frontier counties of this colony, the Rev. Mr. Robinson, who now rests from his labours, was sent by order of Presbytery to officiate for some time among them. A little before this about four or five persons, heads of families, in Hanover, had dissented from the established church, not from any scruples about her ceremonial peculiarities, much less about her excellent Articles of Faith, but from a dislike of the doctrines generally delivered from the pulpit, as not savouring of experimental piety, nor suitably intermingled with the glorious peculiarities of the religion of Jesus. It does not concern me at present, my lord, to inquire or determine whether they had sufficient reason for their dislike. They concluded them sufficient; and they had a legal as well as natural right to follow their own judgment. These families were wont to meet in a private house on Sundays to hear some good books read, particularly Luther's; whose writings I can assure your lordship were the principal cause of their leaving the Church; which I hope is a presumption in their favour. After some time sundry others came to their society, and upon hearing these books, grew indifferent about going to church, and chose rather to frequent these societies for reading. At length the number became too great for a private house to contain them, and they agreed to build a meeting-house, which they accordingly did.

Thus far, my lord, they had proceeded before they had heard a dissenting minister at all. (Here again I appeal to all that know any thing of the matter to attest this account.) They had not the least thought at this time of assuming the denomination of Presbyterians, as they were wholly ignorant of that Church: but when they were called upon by the court to assign the reasons of their absenting themselves from church, and asked what denomination they professed themselves of, they declared themselves Lutherans, not in the usual sense of that denomination in Europe, but merely to intimate that they were of Luther's sentiments, particularly in the article of Justification.

Hence, my lord, it appears that neither I nor my brethren were the first instruments of their separation from the Church of England. And this leads me back to my narrative again.

While Mr. Robinson was preaching in the frontier counties, about an hundred miles from Hanover, the people here having received some information of his character and doctrines, sent him an invitation by one or two of their number to come and preach among them; which he complied with and preached four days successively to a mixed multitude; many being prompted to attend from curiosity. Tis true many after this joined with those that had formerly dissented; but their sole reason at first was, the prospect of being entertained with more profitable doctrines among the dissenters than they were wont to hear in the parish churches, and not because Mr. Robinson had poisoned them with bigoted prejudices against the established church. And permit me, my lord, to declare, . . . that I have been . . . the joyful witness of the happy effect of these four sermons. Sundry thoughtless impenitents, and sundry abandoned profligates have ever since given good evidence of a thorough conversion, not from party to party, but from sin to holiness, by an universal devotedness to God, and the conscientious practice of all the social and personal virtues.

It is true, my lord, there have been some additions made to the dissenters here since my settlement, and some of them by occasion of my preaching. They had but five meeting-houses then, in three different counties, and now they have seven in five counties, and stand in need of one or two more. But here I must again submit it to your lordship, whether the laws of England forbid men to change their opinions, and act according to them when changed? And whether the Act of Toleration was intended to tolerate such only as were dissenters by birth and education? Whether professed dissenters are prohibited to have meeting-houses licensed convenient to them, where there are conformists adjacent, whose curiosity may at first prompt them to hear, and whose judgments may afterwards direct them to join with the dissenters? Or whether, to avoid the danger of gaining proselytes, the dissenters, in such circumstances, must be wholly deprived of the ministration of the gospel?

—And here, my lord, that I may unbosom myself with all the candid simplicity of a gospel minister, I must frankly own, that abstracting the consideration of the disputed peculiarities of the established church, which have little or no influence in the present case, I am verily persuaded . . . those of the Church of England in Virginia do not generally enjoy as suitable means for their conversion and edification as they might among the dissenters. I cannot help thinking that they who generally entertain their hearers with languid harangues on morality or insipid speculations, omitting or but slightly touching upon the glorious doctrines of the gospel, which will be everlastingly found the most effectual means to reform a degenerate world; such as the corruption of human nature in its present lapsed state; the nature and necessity of regeneration, and of divine influences to effect it; the nature of saving faith, evangelical repentance, &c.

I am surprised, my lord, to find any intimations in the letter from Virginia about the validity and legality of the licenses for seven meeting-houses granted by the General Court, especially if that letter came from the Commissary. These were granted by the supreme authority of this colony; and cannot be called in question by the Council without questioning the validity of their own authority, at least the legal exercise of it in this instance.

EDWIN S. GAUSTAD

Institutional Effects of the Great Awakening

The Great Awakening in New England by Edwin S. Gaustad is a classic study of that event. This selection includes excerpts from chapter 7 of the book.

The revival had set off explosive effects: that much was clear. But were the effects for good or ill?[6] It was within Congregationalism that the aftermath was first and most keenly felt. The most immediate result of the revival was the making of new converts: this awakening power was sufficiently evident to win for the movement the name by which it is known. Nevertheless, an attempt to estimate the number of "new births" in the period is fraught with difficulty. Later writers are content to state simply and vaguely that "thousands" were added to the churches at this time, while earlier writers took refuge in that biblical generality, "multitudes." In the *Christian History,* statistics of the number of persons becoming full church members are seldom given. Where they are given, however, they reveal that the Great Awakening was not a mass movement of repentant sinners clamoring for acceptance by the churches. During 1741 and for some years after, the *Boston Gazette* noted the number of additions to the Boston churches during the preceding week. Since the total weekly number for all the churches hovered around ten or twelve during the height of the revival, it is evident that the crowded "sawdust trails" of later revivalism were absent. Joseph Seccombe, who in 1744 acclaimed the "good Fruits and Effects" of the revival in his parish at Harvard, Massachusetts, noted that since 1739 there had been nearly one hundred additions to his church, a yearly average of about twenty. At the height of the excitement Seccombe wrote, "scarce a Sacrament pass'd (which is with us once in eight Weeks) without some Additions to the Church . . . tho' twelve is the greatest Number that has been received at once." In East Lyme, which parish "consists of betwixt 60 and 70 Families, leaving out the Churchmen and Baptists," one hundred white persons and thirteen Indians were admitted to the church between April, 1741, and January, 1744. In the most successful month, July, 1741, there were thirty-two additions. Successes of similar proportion were attained in Groton, North Stonington, and Franklin, Connecticut.

Much more numerous and more frequently mentioned than the conversions were the signs of repentance and concern. William Cooper of Brattle Street Church remarked that in one week, at the height of the revival, more persons came to him in anxiety and concern than in the preceding twenty-four years of his ministry. Meanwhile, John Webb of New North Church declared "that he had five Hundred and Fifty Persons noted down in his Book (besides some Strangers) that have been with him in their Soul Troubles within a Quarter of a Year." This concern might fully awaken the sinner and it might also revive the saint. Prince noted that many of those coming to confer with their ministers about the state of their souls "had been in full communion and going on in a course of religion many years." The recurrent phrase "especially among young people," in connection with this visible concern for religion, suggests that many converts were formerly in the Half-Way Covenant. Depending upon the practice of each church, such a convert might or might not be reckoned a new church member. Visiting preachers or itinerant evangelists, as a rule, ventured only to indicate the numbers "under great Concern for their Souls," recognizing that longer observation was needed to determine the true conversions—if indeed such a determination was possible at all. It was at least apparent to most of the standing as well as to the traveling ministry that the anxiety was extensive and that many were asking, "What must I do to be saved?"

This concern, manifesting itself in more conspicuous ways than pastoral consultations and anxious queries, provoked a deeper loyalty to the externals of religion. Church attendance increased, while many agitated for more church services. If the meetinghouses did not open their doors with a frequency sufficient to satisfy the zealous and earnestly desirous, then religious exercises would be held in private homes. Cooper noted that

> Religion is now much more the Subject of Conversation at Friends Houses, than ever I knew it. The Doctrines of Grace are espoused and relished. Private religious Meetings are greatly multiplied. . . . There is indeed an extraordinary Appetite after the sincere Milk of the Word.

An enterprising pastor would move from one private society to another, offering here a prayer or there a few words of exhortation. Young people formed their own groups for "Prayer and reading Books of Piety." "If at any Time Neighbours met, the great Affairs of Salvation were the Subject of Discourse." Weekly lectures, i.e., sermons on a weekday, were added to the schedule of many churches, Chauncy reporting in 1742 that "Evening-lectures were set up in one Place and another; no less than six in this Town, four weekly, and two monthly ones. . . ." The Massachusetts General Court responded to public interest by enforcing a more strict observance of the "Lords-Day." The concern of many young converts did not end with the reading of good and proper literature, but expressed itself in an earnest, if often unguided, evangelism. Itineracy and lay preaching with all their patent defects did much to destroy "puritan tribalism." When a church or minister refused to become evangelistic, a schism or secession would often result, this leading to the formation of a new and fervent group or to an alliance with some already existing ecclesiastical body whose missionary concern was obvious. Thus cells of self-commissioned ambassadors for Christ increased. The long-neglected Indian now received more attention both on the frontier and in the settled areas, two of the outstanding missionaries to the Indians being earnest friends of the revival. These were David Brainerd who labored effectively though briefly among the Indians of New Jersey, and Eleazar Wheelock whose Indian School at Lebanon was later moved to New Hampshire where it became Dartmouth College. In the days that followed the Awakening, people were not simply inquiring about salvation: they were striving to become both recipients of and agents for that gift of grace.

Had the Great Awakening never occurred, it is doubtful that Edwards would have written *An Humble Inquiry into the Rules of the Word of God, concerning The Qualifications Requisite to a Complete Standing and Full Communion in the Visible Christian*

Church. This treatise was Edwards' public confession of a conviction he had long harbored: that none but the converted should be permitted to share in the privileges of full church membership and to receive communion. Reflection upon regeneration and conversion during the years of the Northampton and the New England revivals forced upon Edwards the revolt against Stoddardeanism, whatever the effects of such a revolt might be on "my own reputation, future usefulness, and my very subsistence." As he "became more studied in divinity" and "improved in experience," he grew convinced that only a negative answer was proper to the question: "Whether any adult persons but such as are in profession and appearance endued with Christian grace or piety, ought to be admitted to the Christian Sacraments; particularly whether they ought to be admitted to the Lord's Supper." Thereafter, those who presented themselves for church membership at Northampton were to be required to sign a confession of faith and to acknowledge their personal experience of divine grace.

The major result of this important step taken by Edwards is that it represented a return to the "sect ideal." To primitive Congregationalism, the church was a group of believers separated from the world, regularly purified through a careful discipline, emphasizing personal achievement in religion and in ethics. It was a "holy community," which should not lower its standards or erase its requirements in order to include the whole of society. The Cambridge Platform had without equivocation declared that "the matter of a visible church are Saints by calling." With reference to the admission of members, it decreed that "the things which are requisite to be found in all church members, are, Repentance from sin, & faith in Jesus Christ. And therefore these are the things whereof men are to be examined. . . ." Churches should exclude from their fellowship those who do not continue to live as saints. And the sacrament of communion was the keystone in the structure of a pure church, for its observance was an occasion when strict examination of the communicants was possible and excommunication, if necessary, forthcoming. To achieve a visible church that conformed as nearly as possible to the invisible one was, beneath all the bitterness, self-righteousness and censoriousness of the New Lights, a major purpose of their separations. To purify the parish church and to alter its status from an established church for all society to a holy community for saints alone was the aim of the *Humble Inquiry.*

Where indifference to religion is widespread, tolerance is no problem; but when religion becomes intensely vital, bigotry becomes more pervasive. In Connecticut the immediate effect of the Great Awakening on religious liberty was detrimental. Elsewhere democracy and individualism in religion sprang ahead, and ultimately even in the land of steady habits, religion was made free. In the 1720's Connecticut had granted a measure of toleration to Anglicans, Quakers, and Baptists, allowing them freedom of worship and, upon proper registration, exemption from the support of any other form of worship. When in the divisive days of 1741 and after, Presbyterians and Congregationalists withdrew from the established churches to form new ones, they expected like other dissenters to be permitted to support their own ministry and to be released from the public taxation for support of the standing ministry. But the General Assembly, now acting in such a way as to make the Saybrook Platform obligatory, ruled "that those commonly called Presbyterians or Congregationalists should not take the benefit of that Toleration Act." When New

Lights started changing the names of their churches to "Baptist" in order to come under the terms of the Toleration Act, that act was repealed. Other laws, already noted, provided for the arrest and punishment of New Light itinerants, and restricted ordination of ministers to graduates of approved schools, while New Light civil officials were deprived of their offices.

To Solomon Paine, the radical preacher of Canterbury, this alliance of church and state was all wrong.

> The cause of a just separation of the saints from their fellow men in their worship, is not that there are hypocrites in the visible church of Christ, *nor* that some fall into scandalous sins in the Church, *nor* because the minister is flat, formal, or ever saith he is a minister of Christ, and is not, and doth lie; but it is their being yoked together, or incorporated into a corrupt constitution, under the government of another supreme head than Christ, and governed by the precepts of men, put into the hands of unbelievers, which will not purge out any of the corrupt fruit, but naturally bears it and nourishes it, and decries the power of godliness, both in the government and gracious effects of it.

The Separate church gathered at Preston March 17, 1747, characterized the church from which it withdrew as one

> which caled it Self Partly Congregational & Partly Presbyterial; who submitted to the Laws of the Government to Settle articles of faith; to govern the Gathering of the Church & Settlement & Support of its ministers building of meeting houses, Preaching, Exhorting &c . . .

The Opposers, or Old Lights, were not everywhere, if anywhere, the leading exponents of a free and catholic spirit. The standing ministry was for peace, to be sure, wrote Reuben Fletcher, "an Independant," but

> upon the same terms that the Pope is for peace, for he wants to rule over all Christians throughout the whole world, and they want to rule from one town to another, throughout the whole country. If they could have their wills, separates and Baptists would have no more liberties here than the protestants have in France or Rome. What tyrant would not desire peace on the same terms that they do?

A generation after the revival Ezra Stiles was still justifying the despotism of Congregationalism in Connecticut.

Presbyterianizing died hard in Connecticut, but it died. In 1784 the Saybrook Platform was repealed, and though complete disestablishment was not achieved until 1818, long before that time both the government and the consociation had ceased to be ruling powers in local church affairs.

The problem of ecclesiastical freedom was not so complicated in Massachusetts where a more liberal charter and a more vocal Anglican minority precluded—even before the Awakening—an effective partnership of church and state. Though church schisms were not so plentiful in Massachusetts, theological division in the Bay colony was sharper than elsewhere. This diversity here as in Connecticut prevented rigid control by consociations. Finally there was in Massachusetts a strong voice for congregational polity. Nathanael Emmons, of Edwards' theological school and of the tradition of John Wise as well, strenuously opposed any step which seemed to compromise the autonomy of the local congregation. He resisted even the establishment of an association of the Massachusetts churches, concerning which he is reported to have said: "Associationism leads to Consociationism; Consociationism leads to Presbyterianism; Presbyterianism leads to Episcopacy; Episcopacy leads to Roman Catholicism; and Roman Catholicism is an ultimate fact." Over a century later, the Congregational historian Leonard Bacon rejoiced that in this period the churches learned to content themselves "with the simple and Scripture policy which rejects all ecumenical, national, provincial, and classical judicatures ruling the churches of Christ, and recognizes no church on earth save the local or parochial assembly and fellowship of believers. . . ."

With reference to freedom within the local church, the change is more difficult to trace. Several factors suggest, however, that even as greater liberties were enjoyed by the churches, so were the parishioners under less restraint. The emphasis upon a personal religious experience had then, as always, the effect of making converts less dependent on external authority—scriptural or ecclesiastical. Those to whom religion in the 1740's had suddenly become meaningful knew that the kingdom of God was within them; their private divine vocation, be it called new light, inner light, or sense of the heart, was their ultimate and occasionally their only appeal. To them only one covenant was of pressing significance: the covenant of grace. The church covenant was important, but secondary. Mediation was unnecessary, priesthood was universal. The civil covenant was obsolete, and society was shattered, but into members not classes.

Religious democratization of this sort found fullest expression, of course, in New Light churches. But in Old Light communions too the "power of the keyes" rested ultimately in the pew instead of in the pulpit, or even in an aggregate of pulpits. The breaking up of the prevailing parish system further weakened intrachurch discipline as well as interchurch control. After the Awakening it was possible, even fashionable, to leave the established church to join a separate society, a Baptist or Anglican church, or perhaps to hold religious services in a private home. Church minorities were now more outspoken than ever before, and could generally muster a council or committee that shared its ecclesiastical or more often its theological position. And, as Ezra Stiles ingenuously remarked, ". . . such are the circumstances of our churches, so intermixt with sects of various communion, that it is impolitic to use extreme and coercive measures—since universal liberty permits the oppressed to form into voluntary coalitions for religious worship." The "circumstance of our churches" together with the abundance of immediate personal religion in some of the churches promoted greater individual freedom from ecclesiastical control.

Notes

1. Edited to conform more nearly to current usage. The text is located in *The Public Records of the Colony of Connecticut*, vol. V (Hartford, 1870), p. 50. Enacted May 13, 1708. See also the legislative acceptance of the Saybrook proposals on September 9, 1708, Ibid., p. 87.

2. Cf. Williston Walker, *The Creeds and Platforms of Congregationalism* (New York: Scribners, 1893; Boston: Pilgrim, 1960).

3. "Published . . . in the Low-Dutch, and translated . . . into the English Language, 1725. (Philadelphia: . . . 1727)," pp. 26–29, 35–39 Abridged and edited to conform more nearly to current usage.

4. From Leroy S. Blake, *The Separates* (Boston: Pilgrim, 1902), pp. 118–121.

5. The above are selected excerpts. The full text may be consulted in William Foote, *Sketches of Virginia,* vol. I (Philadelphia, 1850), pp. 178 ff.

6. From Edwin S. Gaustad, *The Great Awakening in New England* (New York: Harper & Row, 1957), pp. 103–113. Reprinted by permission of the author.

3

The Struggle for Independence and the Terms of Settlement (1760–1820)

If ethnic diversity and evangelical differentiation had set the conditions that ultimately would lead to the pattern of religious disestablishment, that consequence was by no means self-evident to the American colonists during the first half of the eighteenth century. As a result of the Church of England seeking entrance into all of the colonies, however, it became clear how jealous the colonists were in their ecclesiastical liberties. The threat of an established Church of England equipped with a resident bishop provided a rallying point for colonial solidarity. Although the campaign for an American bishop had proceeded fitfully since the late seventeenth century, by the 1760s it became an issue in the public press as a response to *An Appeal to the Public in Behalf of the Church of England in America* by Thomas Bradbury Chandler. A pamphleteering conflict ensued that was initiated by William Livingston with help from New York associates and Philadelphia friends; Chandler's colleagues answered immediately and in kind. In this exchange the colonial critics of Anglican designs introduced many of the arguments and much of the rhetoric that would become so much more significant in the next decades when a different though related sort of independence was at stake. The debate between these parties also dramatizes for us the extent to which the conditions requiring disestablishment were already in existence, at least in some of the colonies, and how far a rationalistic temper toward religion had come to operate in the public realm.

The actual struggle for disestablishment was pressed in Virginia with large roles being taken by Jefferson and Madison. Their classic texts have been reproduced here simply because they disclose that kind of understanding of religion and religious institutions that had become possible in the colonies among a number of sophisticated men at the close of the eighteenth century. Religion—in a typically enlightenment point of view—had shown itself to be a *private* affair. Its public consequences were all that might concern the government. This was not to equate traditional religions with superstition and to seek to suppress them through secular cults, as happened on the continent. That sort of development presupposed a formalistic conception of the state that was deeply alien to American colonial experience. But it did suggest—as "The American Whig" and "The Centinel" had implied in the "Bishops War"—that religion was only one among several "interests" of man. Madison went so far in *Federalist* #10 as to bracket religion as a source of faction along with a "rage for paper money" and other "improper or wicked project[s]." Religion did not provide a pattern or design for the good life or a good beyond life. Rather the "good life" proceeded from the interchange and exchange between these interests. Thus by the end of the eighteenth century the traditional language of the "two relations" was beginning to give way in substance as well as form. Whereas for John Cotton and the seventeenth century the two relations had been those of the inward spiritual man and the outward temporal man—both of concern within the common life—within a century and a half the two relations came to be distinguished in the terms of private versus public matters. Connecticut might retain an establishment (meaning tax support for the Congregational Church) until 1818 and Massachusetts until 1833, but already signs of a new ordering of the relationship of church and state began to appear: The Danbury Connecticut Baptists had been fortified with Jefferson's "wall of separation," and a Treaty of Peace and Friendship with the Bey and Subjects of Tripoli had formally stated that the Federal Union was not "founded on the Christian religion."[1]

Although the Jeffersonian and Madisonian ideas on the subject might be counted as advanced, such an "independence of Church and State" as they worked for was ultimately adopted by all of the states as they followed Virginia's lead in disestablishing churches and guaranteeing religious liberty. That process took half a century, however, and in the meantime, the new federal government was constituted. When several states complained that individual liberties were insufficiently addressed in the new Constitution, the First Congress took up the subject of a "bill of rights." In doing so, this group of "founding fathers" was given an opportunity to consider how the newly formed national government should deal with the subject of church and state in a context in which Virginia had visibly disestablished the Anglican church while New England states like Massachusetts, New Hampshire, and Connecticut maintained strong "standing orders" of state-supported churches. In reviewing the debates surrounding the adoption of the religion clauses of the First Amendment—"Congress shall make no law respecting the establishment of religion, or prohibiting the free exercise thereof"—it is sometimes difficult to decide whether the First Congress intended to sever any remaining bonds between church and state, to allow the government to employ its secular resources to accommodate the religiosity of its people, or simply to exempt itself from legislating on church-state matters, leaving the entire subject in the hands of the individual states. Although the First Amendment was adopted with relatively little fanfare in the eighteenth century, these issues of the founding fathers' original intentions have often become central to the modern Supreme Court's church-state jurisprudence two centuries later.

The Threat of an Anglican Establishment

THOMAS BRADBURY CHANDLER

Chandler's Appeal on Behalf of Anglicans in America (1767)

Thomas Bradbury Chandler was prominent in the second generation of indigenous Anglicans who looked back to the defection of Timothy Cutler of Yale from the Connecticut establishment early in the eighteenth century for the origins of their party. In his *Appeal* Chandler was, at least on the surface, merely recalling a topic that very much concerned all members of the Church of England in America. Without a resident bishop the Anglican churches were crippled in their administration. Chandler's opponents, as the subsequent readings will make evident, saw other issues at stake in this matter.

The favourable Opportunity which has so long been waited for, in the Opinion of many wise and judicious Persons in America, now presents itself—and such, in several Respects, as the Circumstances of the Nation have never, until now, afforded.[2] As the Tumults of War have ceased, and the public Tranquillity is restored, without any reasonable Suspicions of a speedy Interruption—so, the greatest Harmony subsists between our Mother-Country and most of the Colonies, the late Disputes having been brought, by the Wisdom and good Temper of the former, to a happy Termination—the Plan of an American Episcopate has been previously settled, and adjusted in such a Manner, that the religious Privileges of none can be violated or endangered—and, which we should ever acknowledge with all Thankfulness, we are, at this Time, so happy as to have a Prince on the Throne, from whose most unquestionable Disposition to promote the general Interest of Virtue and Religion, from whose sincere Affection for the Church, and from whose most gracious Declarations on the Subject before us, we cannot possibly doubt of the Royal Approbation and Concurrence—while a wise and virtuous Ministry cannot fail of being ready, to afford to so good a Cause, all needful Assistance. These are the Advantages, which now happily concur to favour the American Church, and which peculiarly mark the present Period.

It ought to be farther considered, that the Arguments for sending Bishops to America, were never so urgent and forcible as they are at present. When such Progress was made towards obtaining for this Country an Episcopate, in the former Part of this Century, the Number of American Clergy and Professors of the Church, . . . was small and inconsiderable, in Comparison with the Amount of their present Number. The amazing natural Increase of the Colonists, and the vast Accession of Europeans to the British America, have, in the Compass of Fifty or Sixty Years, enlarged the Number of its Inhabitants, and proportionably of the Members of the Church.

Should it be said, that the Church of England in America contains now near *a Million* of Members, the Assertion might be justified. It is not easy to ascertain the Number exactly, in a Country so widely extended and unequally peopled; but from general Calculations it has been frequently said of late Years, that the proper Subjects of the British Crown in America amount to *Three Millions.*

An actual Survey of the Number of Inhabitants in 1762, with a Distribution of them into Classes, according to their religious Professions, is said to have been carefully made: and it was then found, that, not including the new Colonies ceded by the last general Treaty of Peace, they amounted to between Two and Three Millions, in the Colonies and Islands. Of the *Whites,* the Professors of the Church were about a third Part—the Presbyterians, Independents and Anabaptists were not so many—the Germans, Papists and other Denominations, amounted to more.

Let this Representation be carefully considered, and it will appear in a very evident and striking Light, that the Wants of the American Church, as it has been destitute of Bishops, must have naturally increased, and can amount now to little less than an absolute Necessity. In these Circumstances, could such a Number of Christians, even under a Pagan Government, unless in a State of open Persecution, provided they had always proved themselves loyal and faithful Subjects, apply in vain for a Favour, so needful for themselves, and so harmless to others? How much less Reason then can the Church in America have to fear a Refusal in the present Case, not only from a Christian Nation, famed for its prudent Indulgence to all religious Denominations in general—but from a Nation, which is moreover disposed to befriend it, from peculiar Reasons both of Affection and Policy?

This Argument taken from the *Number* of those who belong to the Church of England in America, will receive great additional Force, from a Consideration of the State of the *Blacks* in our Islands and Colonies; who were found, in the above-mentioned Survey, to be about Eight Hundred and Forty-four Thousand. Although many of these, it is to be feared, through the Neglect of their Masters, are not Christians at all; yet, as they are connected with, and under the immediate Government of, Persons who profess Christianity, they may be said, in an imperfect Sense, to belong to the respective religious Classes of their Owners. However, their Situation is undoubtedly such, that in Proportion as a Sense of Religion prevails in their Masters, they will receive Benefit. Now as these are known chiefly to belong to the Professors of the Church, if an Episcopate will naturally tend to improve the State of Religion in the Church of England, it must consequently, . . . have a general good Effect upon more than half a Million of poor Creatures, Sharers with us of the same common Nature—sent into the World as Probationers and Candidates for the same glorious Immortality—whom Christ equally purchased by his precious blood-shedding—who notwithstanding, as they are bred up in Ignorance and Darkness, are suffered, to the eternal Disgrace of their Owners, to walk on "in the Shadow of Death," without a Ray of rational religious Hope to chear them.

Another Argument for granting an American Episcopate, arises from the Obligations of Gratitude; a national Sense of which, it is humbly conceived, ought, at this Time, to have a peculiar Efficacy in Favour of Religion in the American Plantations. By a signal Interposition of Divine Providence, the British Arms in America have triumphed over all that opposed them, our Colonies have been prodigiously extended, and our new Acquisitions, together with our old Settlements, have been secured, not only by Treaty, but by a total Annihilation of that Power on this Continent, whereby our former Safety was chiefly endangered.

Every *wise* Nation sees and acknowledges the Hand of God in the Production of such Events; and every *religious* Nation will endeavour to make some suitable Returns to him for such extraordinary Favours. And what Returns are proper to be made in such Cases, one Moment's serious Reflection will clearly discover. The Circumstances of Things evidently point out two Duties to our Governors, on this Occasion, both of them important in themselves, and of indispensible Obligation: *One* is, the farther Security and Support of the true Religion in America, in those Places where it already is; and the *other,* the Propagation of it in those Places, to which it has not hitherto been extended.

As America is the Region, wherein the Divine Goodness has been more remarkably displayed, in Favour of the British Nation; so, America is evidently the very Ground, on which some suitable Monument of religious Gratitude ought to be erected. This should be of such a Nature as to be visible to the World, and, that the Honour of the Supreme Ruler of Events may be thereby immediately promoted. Now as the Honour of God is most directly promoted by public Worship—as that Worship must be most acceptable to him, wherein the Praises and Adorations of his Creatures are regularly offered him, in the solemn Offices of the purest and best Religion—and as the national Religion must be supposed best to answer these Characters, in the national Opinion; it necessarily follows, that the State of the national Religion here has a Right, on this Occasion, to the peculiar Attention and Consideration of those, who are intrusted with the Direction of our public Affairs.

What then does the present State of this Religion in America require to be done? What is *possible* to be done for its Benefit and Advantage? These are the Questions that must naturally arise. And every one that professes it, every Witness of its suffering Condition, is able to answer:—The Church of England in America, is perishing for Want of common Necessaries. She has long been imploring Relief, under such Diseases as must prove fatal to her, if much longer neglected. She therefore earnestly requests, and she *only* requests, that proper Remedies may be provided for her present Sufferings. And she leaves it, with all due Submission to the Wisdom of her Superiors, whether any Thing farther is proper to be done, to strengthen and improve her Interests. She wishes for nothing, which shall be thought inconsistent with the Rights and Safety of others. She asks nothing, but what has been granted to others, without any ill Consequences; and she relies on the common Affection and Justice of the Nation, to raise her to this Equality. And, whether there is any Thing presumptuous or unreasonable in these Expectations, let Heaven and Earth judge!

Colonial Criticism of the Appeal (1768)

William Livingston (d. 1791) graduated from Yale in 1740 and subsequently read law, becoming a whig and staunchly anti-Anglican in his religious sentiment. He later became first governor of the state of New Jersey. Livingston is credited with chief responsibility for "The American Whig," a series published in the *New York Gazette* beginning on March 14, 1768. "The Centinel" was apparently written by a circle of Philadelphia friends including Francis Alison, John Dickinson, and others. It was published in the *Pennsylvania Journal* beginning on March 24, 1768. They exhibit both an explicit attitude toward religion and an implicit temper of mind that were wholly alien to that language of establishment that had been current at the time of colonial settlement.

"The Centinel," No. I

Dr. Chandler's *Appeal to the Public* . . . , which from his own Account, seems rather to be the united Effort of all the CLERGY in New-York and New-Jersey, perfected by the kind assistance of the CLERGY from the neighbouring Provinces, may by this time be supposed to have circulated pretty generally.[3] And as the season advances, when we presume these clergy are again to meet in voluntary convention, this may be the proper time to propose a few Questions for their, or if the Dr. pleases, for his consideration. The performance seems replete with bold extravagant assertions of Facts, many of which have no foundation in Truth; it is pretty deficient in Christian Charity, tho' not deficient in low craft, and seems dangerous to the Civil and Religious Liberties of the Colonies in America. . . .

He begins with informing us "that application has been made to our Superiors, by the clergy of the several colonies, requesting one or more Bishops to be sent to America"; he complains of "unprecedented hardships" and "intolerable grievances," suffered by the "Church," the "American Church," the "Church of England in America" for want of "an American Episcopate," and upon this founds his Appeal to the Public.

We should be obliged to the Doctor, if he would inform us in plain terms, who are these Superiors to whom the clergy have applied; by whom these Bishops are to be sent; by what authority this American Episcopate is to be established; or who are the authors of their *intolerable Grievances* and *unprecedented Hardships,* that we may better judge whether the apprehensions on account of our civil liberties, which this avowed application has raised in the minds of many people, be well or ill founded. . . .

The claims of the Doctor, without an establishment, notwithstanding all his seeming modesty and candor, are too great not to awaken jealousies in the minds of free born Americans, if none had been conceived there before.

The "Church," the "American Church," "the Church of England in America," are the names by which he affects to distinguish that denomination of Christians to which he belongs. I wish the Doctor would please to define his terms, and tell us what he means by Church, and why that name should be applied to English Episcopalians only. Are not the Lutheran & Calvinist Churches, are not the Congregational, Consociated and Presbyterian Churches; are not the Baptist, the Quaker and all other Churches in America, of what denomination soever they be, Members of Christ's Catholic Church, if they profess faith in Christ and hold the great essentials of Christianity? Or does he mean to lay such a stress on the unbroken Succession, and on Episcopacy as established by law in England, as to make these essential to the being of a Church?. . .

We apprehend this is not a meer impropriety of speech adopted by a man who seems not to be one of the most correct writers, but a phrase artfully introduced with a sinister design.

The Doctor cannot have read so little either of Civil or Ecclesiastical History, or be so very little acquainted with mankind, as not to know the magic of words and the blind devotion paid to Names and Sounds. . . .

The "National Religion" is another phrase of the Doctors wherewith he graces the peculiar tenets of his Church. . . . We would ask him, why might not Christianity have been allowed the honor of being called the National Religion? Or why is Episcopacy alone honored with that name? Is it because it is established by law in England? Is not Presbyterianism also established by law, and was it not established in 1707—a more enlightened age surely than that in which Episcopacy was established at the Reformation?. . .

It is not doubted but every man who wishes to be free will by all lawful ways in his power oppose the establishment of any one denomination in America, the preventing of which is the only means of securing their natural rights to all those at least who may differ from that denomination. . . .

One thing more I would beg to know from the Doctor; what assurances (besides his own, which are too weak to be relied on in so momentous an affair) are we to have that Bishops will be sent over with such limited powers? Attempts are made upon American liberty from a quarter where it ought not to be expected. A temper is shown by some leading Prelates even now in England that will not suffer us to place a confidence in them. . . .

We hope the Doctor will explain himself fully, and resolve the doubts and queries we have here propounded.

"The Centinel," No. III

Having opened the general tendency of Dr. Chandler's APPEAL, &c., I shall now proceed to make some remarks on the inconveniences and mischiefs of religious establishments.[4]

Whoever peruses ecclesiastical history, ever since the time of Constantine, will find it contains little else than the follies, absurdities, frauds, rapine, pride, domination, rage, and cruelty of spiritual tyrants; who practised every artifice to persuade or cajole the temporal rulers to support their measures. . . .

I would not be understood to assert that the principles of the episcopal Churches tend more particularly to these abuses than those of others; but it is the fault of human nature [that it] cannot bear great power with equanimity, and perhaps is most apt to abuse it in religious matters. The high rank and large revenues of the Bishops in England must tempt them, however, into this error more easily than the leaders in Churches whose influence depends on personal qualifications only.

Religious establishments are very hardly kept from great corruption. But if the provision made for the clergy be large, and the leaders are enabled to live in grandeur, it is not likely they should long continue pure. Ambitious worldly-minded men, who seek the fleece and not the well being of the flock, will insinuate themselves into the chief offices; their example or influence will mislead or discourage others who in better company might have been usefully employed; the industry and vigilance of the spiritual guides in the proper business of their function will be relaxed; and that skill in their profession which practice, study, and attention alone can give will not be attained. . . . And should the evil proceed yet further, and the clergy, instead of being examples to their flock, set before them patterns of irregular living, open immorality, and daring wickedness, will it not be readily granted that there can be no religion at all among the zealots for an establishment so enormously corrupted?

But still worse than this: there is no probability of religion's being reformed under these ecclesiastical polities. Nothing less than a state convulsion effected the reformation in most of the countries where it took place. . . . But above all the most dreadful evil is the danger of persecution which worldly minded men, to gratify their own pride and lust for power, are forward on proper occasions to practice and which weak men with better intentions are too apt to be lead into. We too readily think ourselves secure from error if we have the wise, the powerful, and the many [with us] in our opinions. Those who differ from us we conclude must be obstinate and perverse and [we are] without much difficulty brought to look on it as an act of charity as well as duty to administer some wholesome restraints and severities to such manifest heretics. Thus is the pride of supposed right opinion nourished under establishments. . . .

Such are some of the mischiefs which spring from the civil powers meddling with religion. Beware! O beware then my countrymen, of countenancing this mistake!

"The Centinel," No. IX

The abuse of power has, in all ages, furnished the most copious fund of materials to the moralist and to the historian and has ever given the greatest perplexity to the legislator.[5] Private persons doubtless affect the public weal by their vices and their crimes; but standing singly and alone their transgressions are easily corrected. Whereas those who by the advantages of birth, fortune, office, or superior abilities are enabled to influence others and to direct the public views and councils, are not without difficulty and address kept within the bounds of law and justice. The passions and prejudices of men are constantly leading them into one mistake or another; and the remonstrances of reason and duty alone are but feeble restraints. In order therefore to curb the licentiousness of leading men, it has been found expedient to distribute the powers of government among the different orders of which the community is composed, as to excite and employ those of one rank and interest to correct the irregularities of another.

Although this may seem to lay a foundation for constant debate and faction, yet even this is a small inconvenience compared to the galling and oppressive yoke of absolute monarchy, or even the jealous severity of an aristocratic senate. But the common disadvantages of the mixed forms of government will be found neither very considerable nor lasting in case the distribution of power is made with judgment. . . .

The circumstances of the British colonies, just rising out of the difficulties of an infant state, do not admit of such a regular distribution of power [as the British Constitution admirably supplies.] . . .

In this state of things it behooves the People of North-America to consider fully what political consequences and effects the introduction of diocesan Bishops among them may produce. By Dr. Chandler's account of them . . . we find they are not to be merely voluntary Bishops . . . but prelates commissioned by his Majesty as Head of the Church and authorized by the nation as branching from the ecclesiastical establishment in England. . . .

In their zeal for their hierarchy these gentlemen, possibly, have not considered what they are about in this [regard]. Or if any of them have glanced so much beside their own concernments as to have perceived the obvious effects of their proposal on political affairs, they may have reconciled to themselves the pursuit of so dangerous a measure by the prospect of the spiritual advantage they expect will flow from it.

For my part I have often esteemed it a great advantage to the northern Colonies that their clergy have very little weight in government. This is owing to the moderate salaries paid them, to their debates and divisions about the modes and circumstantials of religion, and to the want of general connection among themselves and with the churches established in Britain. By their dissensions we are secured from the usurpations and encroachments they might otherwise make as a body; for one denomination carefully watches another and sounds the alarm on occasion of any schemes that may be devised to the prejudice of the public. This also keeps up a spirit of free-enquiry and prevents the ill effects of a . . . superstitious credulity.

But here is a measure proposed that directly tends to form and combine this order of men into a regular and powerful band, and to put them under the direction of superior officers invested with great powers over the rest. It is also calculated to connect them by uniformity, establishment and interest with the Church established in England.

While for civil government the British dominions on the continent are already divided into seventeen provinces, the Episcopal clergy . . . will be collected and disciplined under twenty or more Bishops, and a Primate appointed from home. What restraint or check will there be on the views and schemes of a body so well compacted, so weighty, so well established by statute, and so well allied to powerful hierarchies in Europe. Without an order of nobility to stand on equal footing with the prelates, without courts of common law (of jurisdiction extensive enough to issue prohibitions and correct the proceedings of the Archbishop and his suffragans when they exceed their proper limits . . .), without a General Assembly of the Colonies or other association for civil purposes, in what circumstances must the laity be to guard themselves against the ambitious designs of the spiritual power? In short they must lie entirely at the mercy and moderation of the clergy: And what these are let Spain, let Italy, let the history of England in the papal times (and even since the Reformation under the government of the House of Stuart) picture out to the reader. Men in all ages and of every character are much the same in regard to the abuse of power, and their conduct when they get above control loudly proclaims the necessity of attending to the proper distribution of it in every free government that would preserve its constitution.

"The American Whig," XV

If there be any force or conclusion in his argument, it plainly consists in this position: that episcopacy and not Christianity is the national religion.[6] This is evidently implied in that bright chain of reasoning which, to do it full justice, my readers shall have in his own words. After having excited our gratitude and called for public testimonials in honour to the deity, he argues thus: "as this honour is most directly promoted by public worship; as that worship must be most acceptable to him wherein the praises and adorations of his creatures are regularly offered him, in the solemn offices of the purest and best religion; and as the national religion must be supposed best to answer these characters, in the national opinion;" it necessarily follows—mark the conclusion—

that the state of the "national religion here has a right on this occasion to the peculiar attention and consideration of those who are entrusted with the direction of our public affairs." The same argument would doubtless be as conclusive in the mouth of a Musselman and in an address to the Grand Signor. It is not a plea for Christianity. It is a claim for distinction in favor of the national religion. For it cannot be denied that all other religious denominations among us, except Judaism, are at least as zealous possessors of the religion of Jesus as those of the Doctor's persuasion which he is pleased to call the national religion. . . . Hence also it is clear that the reason for establishing episcopacy in America is not that its doctrines are more pure, the practice of its professors more regular and uninterrupted than those of other denominations, or—in other words—that the Church of England is properly and exclusively the Church of Christ, in which alone all true Christians must allow the honour of God can be duly promoted but because it is, as the Doctor asserts, the national religion. . . .

But at all events the Doctor is involved in this dilemma: he must either be understood as asserting that the honour of God cannot be duly promoted in America for want of that Christian purity and perfection to which we are now strangers and which cannot be introduced among us [except] by the means of an episcopacy, or that the honour of God is not so much promoted by the purity and perfection of a Christian Church as by a national establishment of religion however corrupt it may appear to be if tested by the sacred oracles, the divine canon of Scripture. . . . Now to consider his reasoning in a just light it evidently amounts to this: it is the duty of the legislature of a country to promote the national religion whatever it may be. In Turkey, therefore, the lawgivers should advance Mohametanism, in France, Spain, and Portugal, Popery, in the British Empire, Protestant Episcopacy, in China Idolatry—all which in their several places are calculated to promote the honour of God because, in the national opinion, they must respectively be supposed best adapted to that purpose. This is certainly most excellent doctrine from the pen of a Church of England divine, and a Doctor too.

In truth every establishment of religion, if such establishments are in themselves justifiable, ought to be maintained (as well as those which are merely of a civil nature) by the infliction of temporal punishments on transgressors of the law. Nor, indeed, can its efficiency as an establishment consist in anything else. Hence therefore it is evident, in the Doctor's judgment . . . , that we cannot make suitable returns to the great author of all our benefits [except] by establishing English episcopacy in America, and enforcing it—for it otherwise cannot be an establishment—by pains and penalties. . . . It requires a very slender capacity to discern that the principles upon which the Doctor builds his claim to the peculiar attention of those who are entrusted with the direction of our public affairs "in favour of the national religion" lead directly and necessarily to the full and complete establishment of episcopacy.

But before I conclude it may not be amiss to enquire into the propriety of that expression upon which so much is built and by the major force of which we are taught that whoever is opposed to the establishment of episcopacy in the colonies is unmindful of those signal deliverances which have lately been wrought for us by the finger of God. To talk of a national religion of France, in Spain, or in Turkey would be to speak with propriety; but to apply this character to any Church in the British Empire is absurd. In England prelacy is established, in Scotland Presbyterianism, in New-England colonies Congregationalism, and in almost all the other colonies they have no religious establishment at all. How then—when by religion is meant not Christianity itself, but a particular denomination of Christians—how, I say, can any religion in the King's realm or dominions be called national? Truly I cannot conceive how unless by a well known figure in rhetoric which puts the part for the whole. But upon a subject of so much importance, and in an APPEAL TO THE PUBLIC, it is inexcusable to deal in figures. I am therefore rather of the opinion that the Doctor supposes that England, though a part only of the great whole, has exclusively considered a right in the plain and common sense of the words, as they are used and understood by British Protestants, to extend her ecclesiastical establishment throughout the colonies of the British Empire and to load Americans with burdens which neither they nor their forefathers could bear. And whether the sound of this doctrine is more agreeable to an American ear than the unmusical periods of the stamp-act I leave to my American readers to determine.

The Founding Fathers on the Issue of Establishment

JAMES MADISON

Madison's Memorial and Remonstrance (1785)

In a letter to George Mason written in 1826 Madison described the origin of this document and its relationship to the enactment of Jefferson's Bill for Establishing Religious Freedom.

During the session of the General Assembly, 1784–'5, a Bill was introduced into the House of Delegates, providing for the legal support of Teachers of the Christian Religion; and being patronized by the most popular talents in the House, seemed likely to obtain a majority of votes.[7] In order to arrest its progress, it was insisted, with success, that the Bill should be postponed till the ensuing session; and, in the meantime, be printed for public consideration. That the sense of the people might be better called forth, your highly distinguished ancestor, Col. George Mason, Col. George Nicholas, also possessing much public weight, and some others, thought it advisable that a remonstrance against the Bill should be prepared for general circulation and signature; and imposed on me the task of drawing up such a paper. The draught having received their sanction, a large number of printed copies were distributed, and so extensively signed by the people of every religious denomination, that at the ensuing session, the projected measure was entirely frustrated, and under the influence of the public sentiment thus manifested, the celebrated Bill "Establishing Religious Freedom" enacted into a permanent barrier against future attempts on the rights of conscience, as declared in the great charter prefixed to the Constitution of the State.

A Memorial and Remonstrance To the Honourable the General Assembly of the Commonwealth of Virginia.

We, the subscribers, citizens of the said Commonwealth, having taken into serious consideration a Bill printed by order of the last session of the General Assembly, entitled "A Bill establishing a provision for Teachers of the Christian Religion," and conceiving that the same, if finally armed with the sanctions of a law, will be a dangerous abuse of power, are bound, as faithful members of a free State, to remonstrate against it; and to declare the reasons by which we are determined. We remonstrate against the said Bill—

Because, We hold it for a fundamental and undeniable truth, "that Religion, or the duty which we owe to our Creator, and the manner of discharging it, can be directed only by reason and conviction, not by force or violence." The Religion, then, of every man must be left to the conviction and conscience of every man; and it is the right of every man to exercise it as these may dictate. This right is in its nature an unalienable right. It is unalienable, because the opinions of men, depending only on the evidence contemplated in their own minds, cannot follow the dictates of other men: It is unalienable also, because what is here a right towards men is a duty towards the Creator. It is the duty of every man to render to the Creator such homage, and such only, as he believes to be acceptable to him; this duty is precedent, both in order of time and in degree of obligation, to the claims of civil society. Before any man can be considered a member of civil society, he must be considered as a subject of the Governor of the Universe: And if a member of civil society, who enters into any subordinate association, must always do it with a reservation of his duty to the general authority, much more must every man who becomes a member of any particular civil society do it with a saving of his allegiance to the Universal Sovereign. We maintain, therefore, that in matters of religion, no man's right is abridged by the institution of civil society; and that religion is wholly exempt from its cognizance. True it is, that no other rule exists by which any question which may divide a society can be ultimately determined but the will of the majority; but it is also true that the majority may trespass on the rights of the minority.

Because, If religion be exempt from the authority of the society at large, still less can it be subject to that of the legislative body. The latter are but the creatures and vicegerents of the former. Their jurisdiction is both derivative and limited. It is limited with regard to the co-ordinate departments: more necessarily is it limited with regard to the constituents. The preservation of a free government requires not merely that the metes and bounds which separate each department of power be invariably maintained; but more especially, that neither of them be suffered to overleap the great barrier which defends the rights of the people. The rulers who are guilty of such an encroachment exceed the commission from which they derive their authority, and are tyrants. The people who submit to it are governed by laws made neither by themselves nor by any authority derived from them, and are slaves.

Because, It is proper to take alarm at the first experiment on our liberties. We hold this prudent jealousy to be the first duty of citizens, and one of the noblest characteristics of the late Revolution. The freemen of America did not wait till usurped power had strengthened itself by exercise, and entangled the question in precedents. They saw all the consequences in the principle, and they avoided the consequences by denying the principle. We revere this lesson too much, soon to forget it. Who does not see that the same authority which can establish Christianity, in exclusion of all other religions, may establish with the same ease any particular sect of Christians, in exclusion of all other sects? That the same authority which can force a citizen to contribute three pence only of his property for the support of any one establishment, may force him to conform to any other establishment in all cases whatsoever.

Because, The Bill violates that equality which ought to be the basis of every law, and which is more indispensable in proportion as the validity or expediency of any law is more liable to be impeached. If "all men are by nature equally free and independent," all men are to be considered as entering into society on equal conditions, as relinquishing no more, and therefore retaining no less, one than another of their rights. Above all, are they to be considered as retaining an "*equal* title to the free exercise of religion according to the dictates of conscience," Whilst we assert for ourselves a freedom to embrace, to profess, and to observe, the religion which we believe to be of divine origin, we cannot deny an equal freedom to those whose minds have not yet yielded to the evidence which has convinced us. If this freedom be abused, it is an offence against God, not against man: To God, therefore, not to men, must an account of it be rendered. As the Bill violates equality by subjecting some to peculiar burdens, so it violates the same principle, by granting to others peculiar exemptions. Are the Quakers and Menonists the only sects who think a compulsive support of their religions unnecessary and unwarrantable? Can their piety alone be entrusted with the care of public worship? Ought their religions to be endowed, above all others, with extraordinary privileges, by which proselytes may be enticed from all others? We think too favorably of the justice and good sense of these denominations, to believe that they either covet pre-eminences over their fellow citizens, or that they will be seduced by them from the common opposition to the measure.

Because, The Bill implies, either that the Civil Magistrate is a competent judge of religious truth, or that he may employ religion as an engine of civil policy. The first is an arrogant pretension, falsified by the contradictory opinions of rulers in all ages, and throughout the world: The second, an unhallowed perversion of the means of salvation.

Because, The establishment proposed by the Bill is not requisite for the support of the Christian Religion. To say that it is, is a contradiction to the Christian Religion itself; for every page of it disavows a dependence on the powers of this world: It is a contradiction to fact; for it is known that this Religion both existed and flourished, not only without the support of human laws, but in spite of every opposition from them; and not only during the period of miraculous aid, but long after it had been left to its own evidence, and the ordinary care of Providence: Nay, it is a contradiction in terms: for, a Religion not invented by human policy must have pre-existed and been supported before it was established by human policy. It is moreover to weaken in those who profess this Religion, a pious confidence in its innate excellence, and the patronage of its author; and to foster in those who still reject it, a suspicion that its friends are too conscious of its fallacies to trust it to its own merits.

Because, Experience witnesseth that eclesiastical establishments, instead of maintaining the purity and efficacy of religion, have had a contrary operation. During almost fifteen centuries, has the legal establishment of Christianity been on trial. What have been its fruits? More or less, in all places, pride and indolence in the Clergy; ignorance and servility in the laity; in both, superstition, bigotry and persecution. Inquire of the teachers of Christianity for the ages in which it appeared in its greatest lustre; those of every sect point to the ages prior to its incorporation with civil policy. Propose a restoration of this primitive state, in which its teachers depended on the voluntary rewards of their flocks; many of them predict its downfall. On which side ought their testimony to have greatest weight, when for or when against their interest?

Because, The establishment in question is not necessary for the support of civil government. If it be urged as necessary for the support of civil government only as it is a means of supporting religion, and if it be not necessary for the latter purpose, it cannot be necessary for the former. If religion be not within the cognizance of civil government, how can its legal establishment be said to be necessary to civil government? What influence, in fact, have eclesiastical establishments had on civil society? In some instances they have been seen to erect a spiritual tyranny on the ruins of the civil authority; in many instances they have civil authority; in many instances they have been seen upholding the thrones of political tyranny; in no instance have they been seen the guardians of the liberties of the people. Rulers who wished to subvert the public liberty, may have found an established clergy convenient auxiliaries. A just government, instituted to secure and perpetuate it, needs them not. Such a government will be best supported by protecting every citizen in the enjoyment of his Religion, with the same equal hand which protects his person and his property; by neither invading the equal rights of any sect, nor suffering any sect to invade those of another.

Because, The proposed establishment is a departure from that generous policy which, offering an asylum to the persecuted and oppressed of every nation and religion, promised a lustre to our country, and an accession to the number of its citizens. What a melancholy mark is the bill of sudden degeneracy? Instead of holding forth an asylum to the persecuted, it is itself a signal of persecution. It degrades from the equal rank of citizens all those whose opinions in religion do not bend to those of the legislative authority. Distant as it may be, in its present form, from the Inquisition, it differs from it only in degree. The one is the first step, the other the last, in the career of intolerance. The magnanimous sufferer under this cruel scourge in foreign regions, must view the bill as a beacon on our coast, warning him to seek some other haven, where liberty and philanthropy, in their due extent, may offer a more certain repose from his troubles.

Because, It will have a like tendency to banish our citizens. The allurements presented by other situations are every day thinning their number. To superadd a fresh motive to emigration, by revoking the liberty which they now enjoy, would be the same species of folly which has dishonored and depopulated flourishing kingdoms.

Because, It will destroy that moderation and harmony which the forbearance of our laws to intermeddle with Religion has produced amongst its several sects. Torrents of blood have been spilt in the old world, by vain attempts of the secular arm to extinguish religious discord, by proscribing all difference in religious opinions. Time has at length revealed the true remedy. Every relaxation of narrow and rigorous policy, wherever it has been tried it has been found to assuage the disease. The American theatre has exhibited proofs that equal and complete liberty, if it does not wholly eradicate it, sufficiently destroys its malignant influence on the health and prosperity of the State. If with the salutary effects of this system under our own eyes, we begin to contract the bonds of religious freedom, we know no name that will too severely reproach our folly. At least let warning be taken at the first fruits of the threatened innovation. The very appearance of the bill has transformed "that Christian forbearance, love and charity," which of late mutually prevailed, into animosities and jealousies, which may not soon be appeased. What mischiefs may not be dreaded, should this enemy to the public quiet be armed with the force of a law?

Because, The policy of the bill is adverse to the diffusion of the light of Christianity. The first wish of those who enjoy this precious gift, ought to be, that it may be imparted to the whole race of mankind. Compare the number of those who have as yet received it, with the number still remaining under the dominion of false religions; and how small is the former? Does the policy of the bill tend to lessen the disproportion? No: it at once discourages those who are strangers to the light of revelation from coming into the region of it; and countenances, by example, the nations who continue in darkness, in shutting out those who might convey it to them. Instead of levelling as far as possible every obstacle to the victorious progress of truth, the bill, with an ignoble and unchristian timidity, would circumscribe it, with a wall of defence, against the encroachments of error.

Because, Attempts to enforce by legal sanctions acts obnoxious to so great a proportion of citizens, tend to enervate the laws in general, and to slacken the bands of society. If it be difficult to execute any law which is not generally deemed necessary or salutary, what must be the case where it is deemed invalid and dangerous? And what may be the effect of so striking an example of impotency in the government, on its general authority?

Because, A measure of such singular magnitude and delicacy ought not to be imposed without the clearest evidence that it is called for by the majority of citizens: And no satisfactory method is yet proposed by which the voice of the majority in this case may be determined, or its influence secured. "The people of the respective counties are indeed requested to signify their opinion respecting the adoption of the Bill to the next session of Assembly." But the representation must be made equal, before the voice either of the representatives, or of the counties, will be that of the people. Our hope is, that neither of the former will, after due consideration, espouse the dangerous principle of the bill. Should the event disappoint us, it will still leave us in full confidence that a fair appeal to the latter will reverse the sentence against our liberties.

Because, Finally, "The equal right of every citizen to the free exercise of his religion, according to the dictates of conscience," is held by the same tenure with all our other rights. If we recur to its origin, it is equally the gift of nature; if we weigh its importance, it cannot be less dear to us; if we consult the "declaration of those rights which pertain to the good people of Virginia, as the basis and foundation of government," it is enumerated with equal solemnity, or rather studied emphasis. Either, then, we must say, that the will of the Legislature is the only measure of their authority, and that in the plenitude of this authority they may sweep away all our fundamental rights; or that they are bound to leave this particular right untouched and sacred. Either we must say, that they may control the freedom of the press; may abolish the trial by jury; may swallow up the executive and judiciary powers of the State; nay, that they may despoil us of our very right of suffrage, and erect themselves into an independent and hereditary Assembly; or we must say, that they have no authority to enact into law the Bill under consideration. We, the subscribers, say, that the General Assembly of this Commonwealth have no such authority. And that no effort may be omitted on our part against so dangerous an usurpation, we oppose to it this remonstrance; earnestly praying, as we are in duty bound, that the Supreme Law-giver of the Universe, by illuminating those to whom it is addressed, may, on the one hand, turn their councils from every act which would affront his holy prerogative, or violate the trust committed to them: And on the other, guide them into every measure which may be worthy of his blessing, may redound to their own praise, and may establish more firmly the liberties, the prosperity, and the happiness of the Commonwealth.

Jefferson's Act for Establishing Religious Freedom (1786)

Although the General Assembly received this bill in 1779, it was not enacted until 1786 in reaction against proposed assessments for the establishment which had been in part stimulated and focused by Madison's Memorial. As passed by the assembly a clause of the Virginia Declaration of Rights was substituted in the text as here reproduced. It is widely noted that Jefferson ranked this act as one of his most significant achievements.

SECTION I. Well aware that the opinions and belief of men depend not on their own will, but follow involuntarily the evidence proposed to their minds; that Almighty God hath created the mind free, and manifested his supreme will that free it shall remain by making it altogether insusceptible of restraint; that all attempts to influence it by temporal punishments, or burthens, or by civil incapacitations, tend only to beget habits of hypocrisy and meanness, and are a departure from the plan of the holy author of our religion, who being lord both of body and mind, yet choose not to propagate it by coercions on either, as was in his Almighty power to do, but to exalt it by its influence on reason alone; that the impious presumption of legislature and ruler, civil as well as ecclesiastical, who, being themselves but fallible and uninspired men, have assumed dominion over the faith of others, setting up their own opinions and modes of thinking as the only true and infallible, and as such endeavoring to impose them on others, hath established and maintained false religions over the greatest part of the world and through all time: That to compel a man to furnish contributions of money for the propagation of opinions which he disbelieves and abhors, is sinful and tyrannical; that even the forcing him to support this or that teacher of his own religious persuasion, is depriving him of the comfortable liberty of giving his contributions to the particular pastor whose morals he would make his pattern, and whose powers he feels most persuasive to righteousness; and is withdrawing from the ministry those temporary rewards, which proceeding from an approbation of their personal conduct, are an additional incitement to earnest and unremitting labours for the instruction of mankind; that our civil rights have no dependance on our religious opinions, any more than our opinions in physics or geometry; and therefore the proscribing any citizen as unworthy the public confidence by laying upon him an incapacity of being called to offices of trust or emolument, unless he profess or renounce this or that religious opinion, is depriving him injudiciously of those privileges and advantages to which, in common with his fellow-citizens, he has a natural right; that it tends also to corrupt the principles of that very religion it is meant to encourage, by bribing with a monopoly of worldly honours and emoluments, those who will externally profess and conform to it; that though indeed these are criminals who do not withstand such temptation, yet neither are those innocent who lay the bait in their way; that the opinions of men are not the object of civil government, nor under its jurisdiction; that to suffer the civil magistrate to intrude his powers into the field of opinion and to restrain the profession or propagation of principles on supposition of their ill tendency is a dangerous falacy, which at once destroys all religious liberty, because he being of course judge of that tendency will make his opinions the rule of judgment, and approve or condemn the sentiments of others only as they shall square with or differ from his own; that it is time enough for the rightful purposes of civil government for its officers to interfere when principles break out into overt acts against peace and good order; and finally, that truth is great and will prevail if left to herself; that she is the proper and sufficient antagonist to error, and has nothing to fear from the conflict unless by human interposition disarmed of her natural weapons, free argument and debate; errors ceasing to be dangerous when it is permitted freely to contradict them.[8]

SECTION II. We the General Assembly of Virginia do enact that no man shall be compelled to frequent or support any religious worship, place, or ministry whatsoever, nor shall be enforced, restrained, molested, or burthened in his body or goods, or shall otherwise suffer, on account of his religious opinions or belief; but that all men shall be free to profess, and by argument to maintain, their opinions in matters of religion, and that the same shall in no wise diminish, enlarge, or affect their civil capacities.

SECTION III. And though we well know that this assembly, elected by the people for their ordinary purposes of legislation only, have no power to restrain the acts of succeeding Assemblies, constituted with powers equal to our own, and that therefore to declare this act to be irrevocable would be of no effect in law; yet we are free to declare, and do declare, that the rights hereby asserted are of the natural rights of mankind, and that if any act shall be hereafter passed to repeal the present or to narrow its operations, such act will be an infringement of natural right.

A Petition Relating to Church Establishment (1786)

This petition is in Madison's handwriting, and it is probable that he was instrumental in drafting it. A Bill for the Incorporation of the Protestant Episcopal Church was passed by the General Assembly in 1785, which gave considerable autonomy to the Church. Yet by the next session of the assembly the statute was under attack, and it was repealed early in 1787.

To the honourable the Speaker & Gentlemen The General Assembly of Virginia:

We the subscribers members of the protestant episcopal Church claim the attention of your honourable Body to our objections to the law passed at the last Session of Assembly for incorporating the protestant Episcopal church; and we remonstrate against the said law—

Because the law admits the power of the Legislative Body to interfere in matters of Religion which we think is not included in their jurisdiction.[9]

Because the law was passed on the petition of some of the Clergy of the Protestant Episcopal Church without any application from the other members of that Church on whom the law is to operate, and we conceive it to be highly improper that the Legislature should regard as the sense of the whole Church the opinion of a few interested members who were in most instances originally imposed on the people without their consent & who were not authorized by even the smallest part of this community to make such a proposition.

Because the law constitutes the Clergy members of a convention who are to legislate for the laity contrary to their fundamental right of chusing their own Legislators.

Because by that law the most obnoxious & unworthy Clergyman cannot be removed from a parish except by the determination of a body, one half of whom the people have no confidence in & who will always have the same interest with the minister whose conduct they are to judge of.

Because—by that law power is given to the convention to regulate matters of faith & the obsequious vestries are to engage to change their opinions as often as the convention shall alter theirs.

Because a system so absurd and servile will drive the members of the Episcopal Church over to the Sects where there will be more consistency & liberty.

We therefore hope that the wisdom & impartiality of the present assembly will incline them to repeal a law so pregnant with mischief & injustice.

House and Senate Debates (1789)

Adoption of the United States Constitution was very controversial. In response to concerns that the Constitution did not adequately protect individual liberties, James Madison introduced a number of amendments that he called a "bill of rights." The following excerpts from the House and Senate debates show the progress of the proposals that ultimately became the religion clauses of the First Amendment.

Debates in Congress
June 8, 1789

Mr. MADISON . . . The amendments which have occurred to me, proper to be recommended by Congress to the State Legislatures, are these:[10]

. . . That in article 1st, section 9, between clauses 3 and 4, be inserted these clauses, to wit: The civil rights of none shall be abridged on account of religious belief or worship, nor shall any national religion be established, nor shall the full and equal rights of conscience be in any manner, or on any pretext, infringed. . . .

That in article 1st, section 10, between clauses 1 and 2, be inserted this clause, to wit:

No State shall violate the equal rights of conscience, or the freedom of the press, or the trial by jury in criminal cases.

Saturday, August 15 [1789]

The House again went into a Committee of the whole on the proposed amendments to the constitution, Mr. BOUDINOT in the chair.

The fourth proposition being under consideration, as follows:

Article 1. Section 9. Between paragraphs two and three insert "no religion shall be established by law, nor shall the equal rights of conscience be infringed."

Mr. SYLVESTER had some doubts of the propriety of the mode of expression used in this paragraph. . . . He feared it might be thought to have a tendency to abolish religion altogether.

Mr. VINING suggested the propriety of transposing the two members of the sentence.

Mr. GERRY said it would read better if it was, that no religious doctrine shall be established by law.

Mr. SHERMAN thought the amendment altogether unnecessary, inasmuch as Congress had no authority whatever delegated to them by the constitution to make religious establishments; he would, therefore, move to have it struck out.

Mr. CARROLL.—As the rights of conscience are, in their nature, of peculiar delicacy, and will little bear the gentlest touch of governmental hand; and as many sects have concurred in opinion that they are not well secured under the present constitution, he said he was much in favor of adopting the words. . . . He would not contend with gentlemen about the phraseology. . . .

Mr. MADISON said, he apprehended the meaning of the words to be, that Congress should not establish a religion, and enforce the legal observation of it by law, nor compel men to worship God in any manner contrary to their conscience. Whether the words are necessary or not, he did not mean to say, but they had been required by some of the State Conventions, who seemed to entertain an opinion that under the clause of the constitution, which gave power to Congress to make all laws necessary and proper to carry into execution the constitution, and the laws made under it, enabled them to make laws of such a nature as might infringe the rights of conscience, and establish a national religion; to prevent these effects he presumed the amendment was intended, and he thought it as well expressed as the nature of the language would admit.

Mr. HUNTINGTON said that he feared, with the gentleman first up on this subject, that the words might be taken in such latitude as to be extremely hurtful to the cause of religion. He understood the amendment to mean what had been expressed by the gentleman from Virginia; but others might find it convenient to put another construction upon it. . . .

By the charter of Rhode Island, no religion could be established by law; he could give a history of the effects of such a regulation; indeed the people were now enjoying the blessed fruits of it. He hoped, therefore, the amendment would be made in such a way as to secure the rights of conscience, and a free exercise of the rights of religion, but not to patronize those who professed no religion at all.

Mr. MADISON thought, if the word national was inserted before religion, it would satisfy the minds of honorable gentlemen. He believed that the people feared one sect might obtain a pre-eminence, or two combine together, and establish a religion to which they would compel others to conform. He thought if the word national was introduced, it would point the amendment directly to the object it was intended to prevent.

Mr. LIVERMORE was not satisfied with that amendment; but he did not wish them to dwell long on the subject. He thought it would be better if it was altered, and made to read in this manner, that Congress shall make no laws touching religion, or infringing the rights of conscience.

Mr. GERRY did not like the term national, proposed by the gentleman from Virginia, and he hoped it would not be adopted by the House. . . .

Mr. MADISON withdrew his motion, but observed that the words "no national religion shall be established by law," did not imply that the Government was a national one; the question was then taken on Mr. LIVERMORE'S motion, and passed in the affirmative, thirty-one for, and twenty against it. . . .

Monday, August 17 [1789]

The committee then proceeded to the fifth proposition:

Article 1. section 10. between the first and second paragraph, insert "no State shall infringe the equal rights of conscience, nor the freedom of speech or of the press, nor of the right of trial by jury in criminal cases."

Mr. TUCKER.—This is offered, I presume, as an amendment to the constitution of the United States, but it goes only to the alteration of the constitutions of particular States. It will be much better, I apprehend, to leave the State Governments to themselves, and not to interfere with them more than we already do; and that is thought by many to be rather too much. I therefore move, sir, to strike out these words.

Mr. MADISON conceived this to be the most valuable amendment to the whole list. If there was any reason to restrain the Government of the United States from infringing upon these essential rights, it was equally necessary that they should be secured against the State Governments. He thought that if they provided against the one, it was as necessary to provide against the other, and was satisfied that it would be equally grateful to the people.

Mr. LIVERMORE had no great objection to the sentiment, but he thought it not well expressed. He wished to make it an affirmative proposition; "the equal rights of conscience, the freedom of speech or of the press, and the right of trial by jury in criminal cases, shall not be infringed by any State."

This transposition being agreed to, and Mr. TUCKER's motion being rejected, the clause was adopted. . . .

Thursday, August 20 [1789]

The House resumed the consideration of the report of the Committee of the whole on the subject of amendment to the constitution. . . .

On motion of Mr. AMES, the fourth amendment was altered so as to read "Congress shall make no law establishing religion, or to prevent the free exercise thereof, or to infringe the rights of conscience." This being adopted,

The first proposition was agreed to. . . .

Senate Journal September 3, 1789

On Motion, To amend Article third, and to strike out these words, "Religion or prohibiting the free Exercise thereof," and insert, "One Religious Sect or Society in preference to others," It passed in the Negative.

On Motion, For reconsideration, It passed in the affirmative.

On Motion, That Article the third be stricken out, It passed, in the Negative.

On Motion, To adopt the following, in lieu of the third Article, "Congress shall not make any law infringing the rights of conscience, or establishing any Religious Sect or Society," It passed in the Negative.

On Motion, To amend the third Article, to read thus—"Congress shall make no law establishing any particular denomination of religion in preference to another, or prohibiting the free exercise thereof, nor shall the rights of conscience be infringed"—It passed in the Negative.

On Motion, To adopt the third Article proposed in the Resolve of the House of Representatives, amended by striking out these words—"Nor shall the rights of conscience be infringed"—It passed in the Affirmative.

* * *

[On September 7, 1789, the Senate rejected (without any record of the debates) the amendment passed by the House of Representatives that would prohibit the states from infringing the rights of conscience.]

September 9, 1789

. . . [The Senate agreed] To amend Article the third, to read as follows "Congress shall make no law establishing articles of faith or a mode of worship, or prohibiting the free exercise of religion. . . ."

Debates in Congress
September 24, 1789

The House proceeded to consider the report of a Committee of Conference, on the subject matter of the amendments depending between the two Houses to the several articles of amendment to the Constitution of the United States, as proposed by this House: whereupon, it was resolved, that they recede from their disagreement to all the amendments; provided that the two articles, which, by the amendments of the Senate, are now proposed to be inserted as the third and eighth articles, shall be amended to read as follows:

> ART. 3. Congress shall make no law respecting an establishment of religion, or prohibiting a free exercise thereof, or abridging the freedom of speech, or of the press, or the right of the people peaceably to assemble, and to petition the Government for a redress of grievances. . . .

Occasional Letters Regarding Religion and Government

To some extent informal letters written during the later years of Jefferson's and Madison's lives are at least as important in understanding their attitudes toward the question of church and state as the formal documents they drafted or the constitutional arrangements they contrived. The following represent rather than exhaust this kind of source.

Jefferson's Letter to the Danbury Baptists

Readers will note how the letter is a wholly conventional response, and might question whether it provides a likely foundation for the "wall of separation" it allegedly supports.

Messrs. Nehemiah Dodge, Ephraim Robbins, and Stephen S. Nelson,
a Committee of the Danbury Baptist Association, in the State of Connecticut.

January 1, 1802.

Gentlemen—The affectionate sentiments of esteem and approbation which you are so good as to express towards me, on behalf of the Danbury Baptist Association, give me the highest satisfaction.[11] My duties dictate a faithful and zealous pursuit of the interests of my constituents, and in proportion as they are persuaded of my fidelity to those duties, the discharge of them becomes more and more pleasing.

Believing with you that religion is a matter which lies solely between man and his God, that he owes account to none other for his faith or his worship, that the legislative powers of government reach actions only, and not opinions, I contemplate with sovereign reverence that act of the whole American people which declared that their legislature should "make no law respecting an establishment of religion, or prohibiting the free exercise thereof," thus building a wall of separation between church and State. Adhering to this expression of the supreme will of the nation in behalf of the rights of conscience, I shall see with sincere satisfaction the progress of those sentiments which tend to restore to man all his natural rights, convinced he has no natural right in opposition to his social duties.

I reciprocate your kind prayers for the protection and blessing of the common Father and Creator of man, and tender you for yourselves and your religious association, assurances of my high respect and esteem.

Jefferson on the Question of Fast Days

To the Rev. Mr. Millar

Washington, January 23, 1808.

Sir,—I have duly received your favor of the 18th, and am thankful to you for having written it, because it is more agreeable to prevent than to refuse what I do not think myself authorized to comply with.[12] I consider the government of the United States as interdicted by the Constitution from intermeddling with religious institutions, their doctrines, discipline, or exercises. This results not only from the provision that no law shall be made respecting the establishment or free exercise of religion, but from that also which reserves to the States the powers not delegated to the United States. Certainly, no power to prescribe any religious exercise, or to assume authority in religious discipline, has been delegated to the General Government. It must then rest with the States, as far as it can be in any human authority. But it is only proposed that I should *recommend,* not prescribe a day of fasting and prayer. That is, that I should *indirectly* assume to the United States an authority over religious exercises, which the Constitution has directly precluded them from. It must be meant, too, that this recommendation is to carry some authority, and to be sanctioned by some penalty on those who disregard it; not indeed of fine and imprisonment, but of some degree of proscription, perhaps in public opinion. And does the change in the nature of the penalty make the recommendation less a *law* of conduct for those to whom it is directed? I do not believe it is for the interest of religion to invite the civil magistrate to direct its exercises, its discipline, or its doctrines; nor of the religious societies; that the General Government should be invested with the power of effecting any uniformity of time or matter among them. Fasting and prayer are religious exercises; the enjoining them an act of discipline. Every religious society has a right to determine for itself the times for these exercises, and the objects proper for them, according to their own particular tenets; and this right can never be safer than in their own hands, where the Constitution has deposited it.

I am aware that the practice of my predecessors may be quoted. But I have ever believed, that the example of State executives led to the assumption of that authority by the General Government, without due examination, which would have discovered that what might be a right in a State government, was a violation of that right when assumed by another. Be this as it may, every one must act according to the dictates of his own reason, and mine tells me that civil powers alone have been given to the President of the United States, and no authority to direct the religious exercises of his constituents.

I again express my satisfaction that you have been so good as to give me an opportunity of explaining myself in a private letter, in which I could give my reasons more in detail than might have been done in a public answer; and I pray you to accept the assurances of my high esteem and respect.

Madison on the Relation of Christianity to Civil Government

In 1832, only several years before his death, Madison took the time to comment upon a sermon that had been sent to him by an Episcopal clergyman. The Rev. Jasper Adams (d. 1841) was President of Charleston College in South Carolina.

private
To Rev. [Jasper] Adams

Charleston, S. C.

I received in due time the printed copy of your Convention sermon on the relation of Xnity to Civil Government with a manuscript request of my opinion on the subject.[13]

There appears to be in the nature of man what insures his belief in an invisible cause of his present existence, and anticipation of his future existence. Hence the propensities & susceptibilities in that case of religion which with a few doubtful or individual exceptions have prevailed throughout the world.

Waiving the rights of Conscience, not included in the surrender implied by the social State, and more or less invaded by all religious Establishments, the simple question to be decided is whether a support of the best & purest religion, the Xn religion itself ought not so far at least as pecuniary means are involved, to be provided for by the Government rather than be left to the voluntary provisions of those who profess it. And on this question experience will be an admitted Umpire, the more adequate as the connection between Governments & Religion have existed in such various degrees & forms, and now can be compared with examples where connection has been entirely dissolved.

In the Papal System, Government and Religion are in a manner consolidated, & that is found to be the worst of Governments.

In most of the Governments of the old world, the legal establishment of a particular religion and without or with very little toleration of others makes a part of the Political and Civil organization and there are few of the most enlightened judges who will maintain that the system has been favorable either to Religion or to Government.

Until Holland ventured on the experiment of combining a liberal toleration with the establishment of a particular creed, it was taken for granted, that an exclusive & intolerant establishment was essential, and notwithstanding the light thrown on the subject by that experiment, the prevailing opinion in Europe, England not excepted, has been that Religion could not be preserved without the support of Government nor Government be supported without an established religion that there must be at least an alliance of some sort between them.

It remained for North America to bring the great & interesting subject to a fair, and finally to a decisive test.

In the Colonial State of the Country, there were four examples, R. I., N. J., Pennsylvania, and Delaware, & the greater part of N. Y. where there were no religious Establishments; the support of Religion being left to the voluntary associations & contributions of individuals; and certainly the religious condition of those Colonies, will well bear a comparison with that where establishments existed.

As it may be suggested that experiments made in Colonies more or less under the Controul of a foreign Government, had not the full scope necessary to display their tendency, it is fortunate that the appeal can now be made to their effects under a compleat exemption from any such controul.

It is true that the New England States have not discontinued establishments of Religion formed under very peculiar circumstances; but they have by successive relaxations advanced towards the prevailing example; and without any evidence of disadvantage either to Religion or good Government.

And if we turn to the Southern States where there was, previous to the Declaration of independence, a legal provision for the support of Religion; and since that event a surrender of it to a spontaneous support by the people, it may be said that the difference amounts nearly to a contrast in the greater purity & industry of the Pastors and in the greater devotion of their flocks, in the latter period than in the former. In Virginia the contrast is particularly striking, to those whose memories can make the comparison. It will not be denied that causes other than the abolition of the legal establishment of Religion are to be taken into view in accounting for the change in the Religious character of the community. But the existing character, distinguished as it is by its religious features, and the lapse of time now more than 50 years since the legal support of Religion was withdrawn sufficiently prove that it does not need the support of Government and it will scarcely be contended that Government has suffered by the exemption of Religion from its cognizance, or its pecuniary aid.

The apprehension of some seems to be that Religion left entirely to itself may run into extravagances injurious both to Religion and to social order; but besides the question whether the interference of Government *in any form* would not be more likely to increase than controul the tendency, it is a safe calculation that in this as in other cases of excessive excitement, Reason will gradually regain its ascendancey. Great excitements are less apt to be permanent than to vibrate to the opposite extreme.

Under another aspect of the subject there may be less danger that Religion, if left to itself, will suffer from a failure of the pecuniary support applicable to it than that an omission of the public authorities to limit the duration of their Charters to Religious Corporations, and the amount of property acquirable by them, may lead to an injurious accumulation of wealth from the lavish donations and bequests prompted by a pious zeal or by an atoning remorse. Some monitory examples have already appeared.

Whilst I thus frankly express my view of the subject presented in your sermon, I must do you the justice to observe that you very ably maintained yours. I must admit moreover that it may not be easy, in every possible case, to trace the line of separation between the rights of religion and the Civil authority with such distinctness as to avoid collisions & doubts on unessential points. The tendency to a usurpation on one side or the other, or to a corrupting coalition or alliance between them, will be best guarded against by an entire abstinance of the Government from interference in any way whatever, beyond the necessity of preserving public order, & protecting each sect against trespasses on its legal rights by others.

I owe you Sir an apology for the delay in complying with the request of my opinion on the subject discussed in your sermon; if not also for the brevity & it may be thought crudeness of the opinion itself. I must rest the apology on my great age now in its 83rd year, with more than the ordinary infirmities, and especially on the effect of a chronic Rheumatism, combined with both, which makes my hand & fingers as averse to the pen as they are awkward in the use of it.

Be pleased to accept Sir a tender of my cordial & respectful salutations.

ROBERT T. HANDY

The Magna Charta of Religious Freedom in America

Robert T. Handy was Professor of Church History at Union Theological Seminary, New York, for many decades. The following essay, which deals primarily with the constitutional guarantee of religious freedom, suggests the variety of forces that joined together to enact the establishment and free exercise clauses of the First Amendment.

The spell cast over human affairs by the idea of Christendom has been a long one; many who rejected its outward forms were still drawn to its central vision.[14] When we remember that in 1750 there were church establishments of one kind or another in nine of the 13 colonies, and recall how deeply embedded in the western tradition the idea of establishment was, the constitutional events that set the new nation on the path of religious freedom show their revolutionary significance. Most of the young nation's chosen representatives were at least nominally committed to Christianity while some of them were adherents of churches still established in a few of the states; how could such persons approve the First Amendment, and how could the state legislatures ratify it?

At least three general perspectives informed various individuals and groups as they worked for religious freedom. Some were dominated by one of these approaches, and yet were also influenced to some degree by the others. . . . The representatives of the three perspectives which guided those who shaped and passed the First Amendment can for the sake of convenience be called the enlightened, the dissenters, and the accommodationists.

The Enlightened

So much has been written about the impact of the Enlightenment on the revolutionary generation in general and on those in particular who shaped the Constitution and the Bill of Rights that the point need not be extensively elaborated here. Deeply impressed by the remarkable discoveries of science, which seemed to be sweeping mystery from the world, and repelled by the inhumanity and barbarity of the series of religious wars of the sixteenth and seventeenth centuries, the thinkers of the Enlightenment proposed to discover the truth about God and the universe by a rational examination of nature. . . .

Thomas Jefferson's great contributions to religious freedom were significantly shaped by the perspectives of Enlightenment. At various times he called himself a "Deist," a "Theist," a "Unitarian," and a "rational Christian." He distilled the Enlightenment's characteristic emphasis on natural religion in his "Bill for Establishing Religious Freedom," framed by him in 1777, and finally enacted with some minor changes early in 1786 by the Virginian House of Delegates and Senate as "An act for establishing religious freedom." In this statute, which he rated as second in importance among all his writings only to the Declaration of Independence, Jefferson insisted "that our civil rights have no dependence on our religious opinions, any more than our opinions in physics or geometry; that therefore the proscribing of any citizen as unworthy [of] the public confidence by laying upon him an incapacity of being called to offices of trust and emolument, unless he profess or renounce this or that religious opinion, is depriving him injuriously of those privileges and advantages to which in common with his fellow citizens he has a natural right.". . .

Some of those who articulated the view of the Enlightenment on religion, such as Tom Paine and Ethan Allen, were sharper in their criticisms of organized religion than Jefferson, and they had their own spheres of influence. But probably of greater significance for the passage of the First Amendment was the way the thought of the Enlightenment pervaded the general intellectual and cultural atmosphere of the times and left its mark on those who remained otherwise devoted to the perspectives of revealed religion. . . . Hence those who cannot themselves be classed directly among the leaders of the Enlightenment were shaped, sometimes decisively, by its perspectives.

How to classify James Madison religiously is not easy, for he was reluctant to speak about such matters. His family had close connections with the Episcopal Church; he was a regular attendant, and he is usually listed as an Episcopalian. He was also strongly influenced by the Presbyterian president of the College of New Jersey at Princeton, John Witherspoon, who brought the Scottish Enlightenment to Princeton, and who was an ardent believer in religious freedom. Madison's own commitment to religious freedom had several taproots, one of which was unquestionably the social and religious thought of the Enlightenment. This was brilliantly displayed in his "Memorial and Remonstrance Against Religious Assessments," written in response to a bill "establishing a provision for teachers of the Christian religion" before the Virginia House of Delegates in 1784–1785. Insisting on the right of every person to the free exercise of religion, Madison argued that "this right is in its nature an unalienable right. . . . because the opinions of men, depending only in the evidence contemplated by their own minds, cannot follow the dictates of other men." He saw that freedom for one meant freedom for all: "Whilst we assert for ourselves a freedom to embrace, to profess and to observe the Religion which we believe to be of divine origin, we cannot deny an equal freedom to those whose minds have not yet yielded to the evidence which has convinced us." He summed up the case against the legal establishment of religion in phrases that echo the work of the philosophes: "What have been its fruits? More or less in all places, pride and indolence in the Clergy; ignorance and servility in the laity; in both, superstition, bigotry and persecution." It was Madison who presented the first draft of what became the Bill of Rights, and who participated actively in the Congressional debates that led to the final form of the First Amendment, which he also wrote. As the process of the ratification of the amendments proceeded until the Virginia approval of December 17, 1791 put them into effect, the way had been prepared by the perspectives on Enlightenment. . . .

The Dissenters

No one term can serve adequately to cover those Americans of various religious viewpoints who were positively oriented to freedom of religion largely for religious reasons. The term "dissenter" is used here to refer to those who were in disagreement with views held by the majority of Americans in the colonial period that religion should be established in some form or other. Often the dissenters believed in, worked for, and sometimes suffered for the separation of church and state. Individuals and groups whose origins can be traced back to the left wing of the Reformation (chiefly Mennonites) and to the left wing of Puritanism (primarily Baptists, Separate Congregationalists, and Quakers) were from the early decades of colonial history devoted to religious freedom.

Anabaptists in Europe refused to be part of any church-state system, often suffering intense persecution as a result. Their descendants in America continued to work and witness for religious freedom. Contributing significantly to the ferment of freedom in colonial America were such figures as John Clarke, Roger Williams, and William Penn, all of whom emerged from the left wing of Puritanism. They were involved in creating states without establishment of religion—a novel and revolutionary step in the history of European civilization. They proved it could be done. . . . The examples thus provided were frequently cited in later years, especially when the struggles to separate churches from states were going on in the late eighteenth century. So, in 1791, the colorful John Leland, that outspoken Jeffersonian Baptist, could say,

> The state of Rhode Island has stood above one hundred and sixty years without any religious establishment. . . . New Jersey claims the same. Pennsylvania has also stood from its first settlement until now upon a liberal foundation; and if agriculture, the mechanical arts and commerce, have not flourished in these states, equal to any of the others, I judge wrong.

Leland was but one of the more prominent figures among the growing hosts of Baptists who struggled for religious freedom in the revolutionary era. . . . Their growth in the colonial period had been stimulated by the Great Awakening, that remarkable movement of religious revival that swept through the colonies in the half-century before the Revolution. Its force was indeed still operative in the South during the war years. The unestablished evangelical bodies profited greatly from this intercolonial movement, increasing in size and number. As Baptists participated in the Revolution, they sought every opportunity also to press for religious freedom. In 1774, they sent a memorial to the Continental Congress which read in part, "The free exercises of private judgment, and the unalienable rights of conscience, are of too high a rank and dignity to be submitted to the decrees of councils, or the imperfect laws of fallible legislatures. The merciful Father of mankind is the alone Lord of conscience." The story of the way the Baptists cooperated with Jefferson and Madison in the disestablishment drive in Virginia has been told many times.

[T]here were thousands of Baptists, and hundreds of representatives of other of the left-wing traditions of the Reformation and of Puritanism who played some part in the struggle for religious freedom and the separation of church and state. . . . [Especially in local] arenas the dissenters played major roles in the rise of religious freedom.

The Accommodationists

There were many Americans who had supported the Revolution and believed in religious liberty as they defined it but who also still were convinced that the United States was and should continue to be a Christian nation. Some of them were willing to give up establishments of religion, others to accommodate existing state or town establishments to the general trend towards freedom by letting other denominations share in them in some form of "multiple establishment." Such persons generally did not feel threatened by the First Amendment; they had been represented in the Congressional debate by those who shared their views. The Bill of Rights was ratified by the necessary number of states in the relatively short period of 26 months with a notable lack of protest or negative comment. The history of religion in America in the nineteenth century cannot be well understood without an awareness of the importance of the accommodative perspective which was clearly evident in the last quarter of the eighteenth. Mark DeWolfe Howe has asserted that "among the most important purposes of the First Amendment was the advancement of the interests of religion." Many church leaders came to believe that the Christian state for which they worked could be better realized under the First Amendment, as they interpreted it, than under the older, coercive mechanisms of confessional states. . . .

[As one example, the] Maryland Constitution of 1776 ended the establishment of the Church of England so that "for the first time since the beginning of the century all Christian denominations were now equal before the law in Maryland." The old confessional state with its establishment was swept aside, but what emerged was a specifically Christian state. Article XXXIII of the constitution provided that "All persons professing the Christian religion are equally entitled to protection in their religious liberty." Persons did not have to declare their belief in Christianity to vote, but they did to hold office. It was not the Jews who were regarded as a threat to this Christian state, but the Deists, whom many in the Maryland constitutional convention regarded as infidels. . . . In this and in similar episodes what I have elsewhere called "the long spell of Christendom" exerted its power in modified or accommodated form in the late eighteenth and early nineteenth centuries. Three New England states clung to their form of the religious establishment of Congregationalism until the early nineteenth century, but their church leaders insisted on their devotion to freedom, especially in the way they avoided infringing on the rights of others. . . . [W]hen Massachusetts adopted a new Constitution of 1780, it accommodated the desire for religious freedom within the framework of a Christian state by allowing a form of multiple establishment. Key clauses that show the tension and its resolution are these selected from Articles II and III. Article II said in part that "no subject shall be hurt, molested, or restrained, in his person, liberty, or estate for worshipping GOD in the manner and season most agreeable to the dictates of his own conscience"; but III went on to state that

> As the happiness of a people, and the good order and preservation of civil government, essentially depend upon piety, religion, and morality: Therefore, to promote their happiness, and to secure the good order and preservation of their government, the people of this commonwealth have a right to invest their legislature with power to authorize and require, the several towns, parishes, precincts, and other bodies politic, or religious societies, to make suitable provision, at their own expense, for the institution of the public worship of GOD: and for the support and maintenance of public Protestant teachers of piety, religion, and morality, in all cases where such provision shall not be made voluntarily.

It was more than a half-century before this pattern of establishment was ended.

Though Massachusetts did not finally ratify the Bill of Rights, the joint committee of the Senate and House endorsed it without any mention of religion, for the state's form of establishment appeared secure. Thus there were a considerable number of people in the late eighteenth and early nineteenth centuries who accommodated a belief in religious freedom to a form of a Christian state, which in some cases was to be maintained by establishments of religion at state or local levels.

Overlappings

There was considerable overlapping among the three main groups described here—overlapping that may seem quite inconsistent to the twentieth-century mind. It may be a bit surprising to find James Madison presenting to the Virginia legislature in

1785 "A Bill for Punishing Disturbers of Religious Worship and Sabbath Breakers"; it is even more surprising to find that the bill had been drafted by Thomas Jefferson. The measure provided that a ten-shilling fine would be levied "If any person on Sunday shall himself be found labouring at his own or any other trade or calling." The authors of *Freedom From Federal Establishment* conclude that "apparently such governmental accommodation to the interests of the Christian religion was deemed both good social policy and also constitutional under the state charter by James Madison and his fellow Virginians." The act was passed in the following year. This illustrates overlapping between enlightened and accommodationist viewpoints, overlapping which blended concerns for religious freedom with some aspects of a Christian state.

Dissenters often showed that they too sought a Christian state. . . . Even [Baptist Issac] Backus showed that he believed in a Christian state when he spoke in praise of a Massachusetts provision that stated, "No man can take a seat in our legislature till he solemnly declares, 'I believe the Christian religion and have a firm persuasion of its truth.'" Although the three general view-points outlined here can be distinctly discerned, they are not to be seen as mutually exclusive ideal types; they were held by persons who lived in a particular historical period, and they do overlap in certain ways. We are dealing with eighteenth-century and not twentieth-century minds.

Notes

1. 8 *U.S. Statutes at Large,* 155 (November 4, 1796), article XI.
2. From T. B. Chandler, *An Appeal to the Public* (New York, 1767), pp. 54–60.
3. Abridged and edited from the *Pennsylvania Journal,* March 24, 1768.
4. Abridged and edited from the *Pennsylvania Journal,* April 7, 1768.
5. Abridged and edited from the *Pennsylvania Journal,* May 19, 1768.
6. Abridged and edited from the *New York Gazette,* June 20, 1768.
7. Reprinted from "Principles of Religious Equality," printed by Rothwell and Ustick (n.p., n.d.). The *Memorial* may also be located in Volume I of the "Congress" edition of Madison's *Writings* (Philadelphia, 1865).
8. From Thomas Jefferson, *The Works of Thomas Jefferson,* ed. Paul L. Ford (New York, 1904), vol. II, pp. 438 ff.
9. From James Madison, *The Writings of James Madison,* ed. G. Hunt, vol. II, 1783–1787 (New York, 1901), pp. 212–214.
10. The text of the House debate can be found in *Annals of the Congress of the United States: The Debates and Proceedings in the Congress of the United States,* vol. I, compiled from Authentic Materials by Joseph Gales, Sr. (Washington, D.C., 1834). The Senate debates can be found in Linda Grant Depauw, ed., *Documentary History of the First Federal Congress of the United States of America* (Baltimore: Johns Hopkins University Press, 1977).
11. From Thomas Jefferson, *The Writings of Thomas Jefferson,* vol. VIII, ed. Paul L. Ford and H. A. Washington (New York, 1854), pp. 113 f.
12. From Thomas Jefferson, *The Writings of Thomas Jefferson,* vol. V, ed. H. A. Washington (Washington, 1853), pp. 236–238.
13. From James Madison, *The Writings of James Madison,* vol. IX (1819–1836), ed. G. Hunt (New York: G. P. Putnam's Sons, 1910), pp. 484–488. Reprinted by permission. *The Relation of Christianity to Civil Government in the United States* passed through several editions.
14. From R. T. Handy, "The Magna Charta of Religious Freedom in America," *Union Seminary Quarterly Review* XXXVIII, nos. 3 and 4 (1984). Reprinted by permission of the publisher.

4

The Era of Republican Protestantism (1820–1860)

That same religious ardor that had been raised up to support ecclesiastical independence from the Church of England was also called forth as sentiment for political independence. It has long been recognized that the preachers did yeoman service in the cause for independence, publicizing it, recruiting men, sustaining morale. More recently it has been observed that at the same time, ironically, they were undermining whatever remained of that traditional structure of life—the formal "double relation" in which the churches embodied the one side while civil governments represented the other. So wholly did the colonial Calvinists commit themselves to the cause of independence that the achievement of their political aspiration fulfilled a religious vision. Having supported independence as a quasi-religious goal, an "establishment" on the part of the federal union (and perhaps even the constituent states) became illogical as well as impossible on practical grounds. American Protestantism had effectively done itself out of that established position in the common life that had been largely taken for granted during earlier periods, until the pattern was effectively challenged in Virginia. From this perspective the significant church-and-state development of the national period was the Protestant attempt to recover that position it had lost—albeit expressed in an informal mode.[1]

This new republican Protestantism embodied a two-fold thrust. On the one side it emphasized that evangelical concern with the individual and his salvation, which had proved to be so dynamic in the Great Awakening a century earlier. Under nineteenth-century conditions this led to the perfection of revivalism as the nearly universal pattern of Protestant religious life in America. Available energies were directed toward the conversion of souls, and at the hands of a Charles G. Finney the impulse was shaped into a system that virtually excluded any other conception of religious life. On the other side, republican Protestantism utilized that principle of voluntary association that so intrigued an observer of America like de Tocqueville.[2] Technically speaking, the churches were no more than a species of association within the broader community that included many other kinds of association as well. This position constituted, in contrast to earlier periods, a great reduction in prestige and position. No longer did churches represent the formal expression of the spiritual end of the whole society—this had been the traditional meaning of establishment as we have seen. But from another point of view, this new conception meant that the churches were liberated to work within the society in new ways. One of these ways was through vast cooperating interdenominational agencies that undertook to reform the life of the new nation. The United States might not be Protestant Christian in form, but republican Protestantism sought to make it so in substance. Such a development was directly counter to the intention, shared by Jefferson and Madison, to disengage political and religious life. On the theoretical level it required that the evangelical groups work together for common ends rather than follow the Madisonian expectation that their mutual jealousies would hold each other's ambitions in check.

The concern of this section is not with the agencies and the goals of republican Protestantism per se. Rather the point to be emphasized is the conception that underlay this vast Protestant effort. It was no less than a vision of the United States as a Protestant Christian nation conformed to the divine will, not through a formal—even a "theocratic"—establishment of religion, but through a common life renewed by evangelical religion and thus spontaneously God-oriented. Churches and governments might be independent of each other, but the common subject of both was that individual whose conversion the revivalistic system was designed to effect. The readings in the section include contemporary criticisms of this republican Protestantism from a number of significantly different points of view.

JOSEPH STORY

Joesph Story on the Religion Clauses of the Bill of Rights (1833)

Joseph Story (d. 1845), associate justice of the Supreme Court, was a colleague of John Marshall's, and together they were conservative pillars of a conservative institution. His *Commentaries on the Constitution* indicates how—in spite of the influence Jefferson and Madison exerted in shaping the religious "settlement"—the Christian religion might be presumed necessary to social stability. In this perspective an informal Protestant establishment such as the evangelicals set out to create could seem to fulfil the true intention of the Constitution—and the Bill of Rights in particular.

Commentaries on the Bill of Rights

1863. Let us now enter upon the consideration of the amendments, which, it will be found, principally regard subjects properly belonging to a bill of rights.[3]

1864. The first is, "Congress shall make no law respecting an establishment of religion, or prohibiting the free exercise thereof; or abridging the freedom of speech, or of the press; or the right of the people peaceably to assemble, and to petition government for a redress of grievances."

1865. And first, the prohibition of any establishment of religion, and the freedom of religious opinion and worship.

How far any government has a right to interfere in matters touching religion, has been a subject much discussed by writers upon public and political law. The right and the duty of the interference of government, in matters of religion, have been maintained by many distinguished authors, as well those, who were the warmest advocates of free governments, as those, who were attached to governments of a more arbitrary character. Indeed, the right of a society or government to interfere in matters of religion will hardly be contested by any persons, who believe that piety, religion, and morality are intimately connected with the well being of the state, and indispensable to the administration of civil justice. The promulgation of the great doctrines of religion, the being, and attributes, and providence of one Almighty God; the responsibility to him for all our actions, founded upon moral freedom and accountability; a future state of rewards and punishments; the cultivation of all the personal, social, and benevolent virtues;—these never can be a matter of indifference in any well ordered community. It is, indeed, difficult to conceive, how any civilized society can well exist without them. And at all events, it is impossible for those, who believe in the truth of Christianity, as a divine revelation, to doubt, that it is the especial duty of government to foster, and encourage it among all the citizens and subjects. This is a point wholly distinct from that of the right of private judgment in matters of religion, and of the freedom of public worship according to the dictates of one's conscience.

1866. The real difficulty lies in ascertaining the limits, to which government may rightfully go in fostering and encouraging religion. Three cases may easily be supposed. One, where a government affords aid to a particular religion, leaving all persons free to adopt any other; another, where it creates an ecclesiastical establishment for the propagation of the doctrines of a particular sect of that religion, leaving a like freedom to all others; and a third, where it creates such an establishment, and excludes all persons, not belonging to it, either wholly, or in part, from any participation in the public honours, trusts, emoluments, privileges, and immunities of the state. For instance, a government may simply declare, that the Christian religion shall be the religion of the state, and shall be aided, and encouraged in all the varieties of sects belonging to it; or it may declare, that the Catholic or Protestant religion shall be the religion of the state, leaving every man to the free enjoyment of his own religious opinions; or it may establish the doctrines of a particular sect, as of Episcopalians, as the religion of the state, with a like freedom; or it may establish the doctrines of a particular sect, as exclusively the religion of the state, tolerating others to a limited extent, or excluding all, not belonging to it, from all public honours, trusts, emoluments, privileges, and immunities.

1867. Now, there will probably be found few persons in this, or any other Christian country, who would deliberately contend, that it was unreasonable, or unjust to foster and encourage the Christian religion generally, as a matter of sound policy, as well as of revealed truth. In fact, every American colony, from its foundation down to the revolution, with the exception of Rhode Island, (if, indeed, that state be an exception,) did openly, by the whole course of its laws and institutions, support and sustain, in some form, the Christian religion; and almost invariably gave a peculiar sanction to some of its fundamental doctrines. And this has continued to be the case in some of the states down to the present period, without the slightest suspicion, that it was against the principles of public law, or republican liberty. Indeed, in a republic, there would seem to be a peculiar propriety in viewing the Christian religion, as the great basis, on which it must rest for its support and permanence, if it be, what it has ever been deemed by its truest friends to be, the religion of liberty.

1868. Probably at the time of the adoption of the constitution, and of the amendment to it, now under consideration, the general, if not the universal, sentiment in America was, that Christianity ought to receive encouragement from the state, so far as was not incompatible with the private rights of conscience, and the freedom of religious worship. An attempt to level all religions, and to make it a matter of state policy to hold all in utter indifference, would have created universal disapprobation, if not universal indignation.

1869. It yet remains a problem to be solved in human affairs, whether any free government can be permanent, where the public worship of God, and the support of religion, constitute no part of the policy or duty of the state in any assignable shape. The future experience of Christendom, and chiefly of the American states, must settle this problem, as yet new in the history of the world, abundant, as it has been, in experiments in the theory of government.

1871. The real object of the amendment was, not to countenance, much less to advance Mahometanism, or Judaism, or infidelity, by prostrating Christianity; but to exclude all rivalry among Christian sects, and to prevent any national ecclesiastical establishment, which should give to an hierarchy the exclusive patronage of the national government. It thus cut off the means of religious persecution, (the vice and pest of former ages,) and of the subversion of the rights of conscience in matters of religion, which had been trampled upon almost from the days of the Apostles to the present age.

LYMAN BEECHER

Lyman Beecher on Disestablishment in Connecticut (1820)

Lyman Beecher (d. 1863) studied at Yale under Timothy Dwight and became the latter's right-hand man in the defense of the Congregational establishment—or "standing order"—in Connecticut. These reflections about the "fall of the standing order" in 1820 are from his autobiography.

The habit of legislation from the beginning had been to favor the Congregational order and provide for it.[4] Congregationalism was the established religion. All others were dissenters, and complained of favoritism. The ambitious minority early began to make use of the minor sects on the ground of invidious distinctions, thus making them restive. So the democracy, as it rose, included nearly all the minor sects, besides the Sabbath-breakers, rum-selling tippling folk, infidels, and ruff-scuff generally, and made a dead set at us of the standing order.

It was a long time, however, before they could accomplish any thing, so small were the sects and so united the Federal phalanx. After defeat upon defeat, and while other state delegations in Congress divided, ours, for twenty years a unit, Pierrepont Edwards, a leader of the Democrats, exclaimed, "As well attempt to revolutionize the kingdom of heaven as the State of Connecticut!"

But throwing Treadwell over in 1811 broke the charm and divided the party; persons of third-rate ability, on our side, who wanted to be somebody, deserted; all the infidels in the state had long been leading on that side; the minor sects had swollen, and complained of having to get a certificate to pay their tax where they liked; our efforts to enforce reformation of morals by law made us unpopular; they attacked the clergy unceasingly, and myself in particular, in season and out of season, with all sorts of misrepresentation, ridicule, and abuse; and, finally, the Episcopalians, who had always been stanch Federalists, were disappointed of an appropriation for the Bishop's Fund, which they asked for, and went over to the Democrats.

That overset us. They slung us out like a stone from a sling.

C. E. B. "I remember seeing father, the day after the election, sitting on one of the old-fashioned, rush-bottomed kitchen chairs, his head dropping on his breast, and his arms hanging down. 'Father,' said I, 'what are you thinking of?' He answered, solemnly, 'THE CHURCH OF GOD.'"

It was a time of great depression and suffering. It was the worst attack I ever met in my life, except that which Wilson made. I worked as hard as mortal man could, and at the same time preached for revivals with all my might, and with success, till at last, what with domestic afflictions and all, my health and spirits began to fail. It was as dark a day as ever I saw. The odium thrown upon the ministry was inconceivable. The injury done to the cause of Christ, as we then supposed, was irreparable. For several days I suffered what no tongue can tell *for the best thing that ever happened to the State of Connecticut.* It cut the churches loose from dependence on state support. It threw them wholly on their own resources and on God.

They say ministers have lost their influence; the fact is, they have gained. By voluntary efforts, societies, missions, and revivals, they exert a deeper influence than ever they could by queues, and shoebuckles, and cocked hats, and gold-headed canes.

* * *

Revivals now began to pervade the state. The ministers were united, and had been consulting and praying. Political revolution had cut them off from former sources of support, and caused them to look to God. Then there came such a time of revival as never before in the state.

I remember how we all used to feel before the revolution happened. Our people thought they should be destroyed if the law should be taken away from under them. They did not think any thing about God—did not seem to. And the fact is, we all felt that our children would scatter like partridges if the tax law was lost. We saw it coming. In Goshen they raised a fund. In Litchfield the people bid off the pews, and so it has been ever since.

But the effect, when it did come, was just the reverse of the expectation. When the storm burst upon us, indeed, we thought we were dead for a while. But we found we were not dead. Our fears had magnified the danger. We were thrown on God and on ourselves, and this created that moral coercion which makes men work. Before we had been standing on what our fathers had done, but now we were obliged to develop all our energy.

"On the other hand, the other denominations lost all the advantage they had had before, so that the very thing in which the enemy said, "Raze it—raze it to the foundations," laid the corner-stone of our prosperity to all generations. The law compelling every man to pay somewhere was repealed. The consequence unexpectedly was, first, that the occasion of animosity between us and the minor sects was removed, and infidels could no more make capital with them against us, and they then began themselves to feel the dangers of infidelity, and to react against it, and this laid the basis of cooperation and union of spirit.

And, besides, that tax law had for more than twenty years really worked to weaken us and strengthen them. All the stones that shelled off and rolled down from our eminence lodged in their swamp. Whenever a man grew disaffected, he went off and paid his rates with the minor sects; but on the repeal of the law there was no such temptation.

Take this revolution through, it was one of the most desperate battles ever fought in the United States. It was the last struggle of the separation of Church and State.

ABNER KNEELAND

Blasphemy on Trial (1838)

The classic story of the Puritans fleeing persecution in England and seeking religious freedom in the New World is balanced, to some extent, by the strong tendencies of those same Puritans and their descendants to be intolerant of the unorthodox practices or beliefs of their fellow Americans. This case, which took place in Massachusetts in the 1830s, and as described by Leonard W. Levy, appears to have involved the last criminal penalty for blasphemy in the United States.

Abner Kneeland was a heretic—a cantankerous, inflexible heretic.[5] Worse still, he was regarded as an immoral being who had crawled forth from the darkness of the Stygian caves to menace Massachusetts in the 1830's. Believe Kneeland, though, and one would think he was a mere harbinger of free thought and a noble exponent of liberty of conscience. His name might now be shrouded in oblivion but for the fact that an outraged community, upon which he inflicted his opinions, retaliated by inflicting martyrdom upon him. He was the last man to be jailed by Massachusetts for the crime of blasphemy.

In the *Bible of Reason* which Kneeland preached to his audiences, Samuel Gridley Howe, the humanitarian, had read with alarm "that infidelity is spreading like wildfire, and that in fifty years Christianity will be professed only by a miserable minority of male bigots and female fools." With the reformer's urgency, Dr. Howe had reached for his pen "to make the public aware of the leprosy that is creeping over the body politic." He demonstrated that Kneeland, "the hoary-headed apostle of Satan," had characterized the rich as tyrants; judges and lawyers as knaves; the clergy as hypocrites; and the *Holy Bible* as a string of lies. Kneeland also incited class hatreds, counseled a union of farmers and workingmen, railed against property, complained of high prices, derided the sacredness of marriage, and taught sex-education.

What made Kneeland a danger was not alone his damnable views, but the fact that his lectures at Boston's Federal Street Theatre attracted throngs of two thousand, and a like number subscribed to his . . . *Investigator.* This periodical, according to a political enemy, was "a lava stream of blasphemy and obscenity which blasts the vision and gangrenes the very soul of the uncorrupted reader." . . .

It was the *Investigator* that got Kneeland into the legal controversy which agitated Massachusetts for four years. Orthodox descendants of the Puritans, in erecting their government during the Revolution, had apparently thought it necessary to appease the vanity of God by implementing a constitutional recognition of his existence with an act against blasphemy, passed in 1782. Under this statute, an indictment was brought against the editor of the *Investigator* for having "unlawfully and wickedly" published, on December 20, 1833, a "scandalous, impious, obscene, blasphemous and profane libel" of and concerning God.

If the indictment for the Commonwealth recalled to Kneeland the memory of witchhunting days, some of the penalties admissible under the anti-blasphemy act gave him justification. Any person wilfully blaspheming the name of God by denying him, or by cursing or contumeliously reproaching him, or any part of the Trinity, or the Bible, would be punished "by Imprisonment not exceeding Twelve Months, by sitting in the Pillory, by Whipping, or sitting on the Gallows with a Rope about the Neck, or binding to the good Behaviour, at the discretion of the Supreme Judicial Court."

The indictment contained three counts based on articles published in the *Investigator.* The first count alleged a gutter obscenity relating to the Immaculate Conception; the second, an irreverent ridicule of prayer, and the third was based on part of a published letter to the editor of the Universalist *Trumpet*—the only article written by Kneeland himself—in which the variations of blasphemy had been contemptuously exhausted. He had written:

> 1. Universalists believe in a god which I do not; but believe that their god . . . is nothing more than a chimera of their own imagination. 2. Universalists believe in Christ, which I do not; but believe that the whole story concerning him is as much a fable and fiction as that of the god Prometheus. . . . 3. Universalists believe in miracles, which I do not; but believe that every pretension to them is to be attributed to mere trick and imposture. 4. Universalists believe in the resurrection of the dead, immortality and eternal life, which I do not; but believe that all life is material, that death is an eternal extinction of life. . . .

The case against the incarnate Robespierre was loaded with explosive political implications. In 1835, John Barton Derby, who had once been "a nut of old Hickory," brought a hard fist cracking down on the yet loyal heads; when the kernels were separated from the shells, one Abner Kneeland emerged as a leader of the Democratic radicals:

> I assert, as a fact beyond contradiction, that nineteen-twentieths of the followers of Abner Kneeland were and are now Jacksonmen, . . . I venture to declare that if any person will procure the Boston AntiBank Memorial, he shall find among its subscribers nearly every man who attends the Infidel orgies at the Federal-street Theatre. I have no doubt that the Infidel party constitutes at least one-third of the Jackson party of the City at this moment. . . .

Appropriately enough, Kneeland was represented by Andrew Dunlap, a high-ranking member of the Massachusetts Democratic party and formerly state attorney-general.

Whiggery had small occasion for regret at the conviction of the *Investigator's* editor by the dozen God-fearing men who sat as a jury . . . But only the first of five trials had been completed. Kneeland appealed his cause, and in the spring of 1834, the second trial began before Judge Samuel Putnam of the Supreme Judicial Court. . . .

The case of *Commonwealth v. Kneeland* was heard in March of 1836. Only one man could act as Kneeland's counsel: himself. He was a scriptural scholar, a carpenter, a minister, a phonetics expert, a legislator, a philosopher, author of common-school spellers, and something of an obstetrician. Why not advocate of his own cause?. . .

Kneeland appeared before the court, he said, "like a lofty oak that has braved the storms of more than sixty winters, and yet remains . . . pure as the mountain snow. . . ." He repeated all of [the prosecution's] arguments and more, arguing, first, that the charges as recorded in the indictment constituted no offense. [One of the judges] had admitted that even an atheist might propagate his opinions, and [another] had admitted that the truth of the Scriptures might be denied, although both annexed the condition of speaking decently. Were his crimes, then, merely an offense against delicacy? Yet he had by no means transcended the usual ferocity and extremism of theological controversy—a fact for which he offered proof.

There was no blasphemy in that article on the Miraculous Conception. The Virgin wasn't even named in the statute. And where after all was the obscenity charged that had made strong men blench? There was merely a quotation from Voltaire's *Philosophical Dictionary* which circulated in the respectable Athenaeum and in the Harvard library.[6] If an indelicate word (testicle), derived from a classical language and found in any school dictionary, was regarded by some as obscene—well, shrugged Kneeland, "Evil to him who evil thinks."

There was no blasphemy in that article on prayers. Certain modes of prayers had been satirized, yes, but the Puritans had disparaged prayers, too, and Chauncey, second President of Harvard, had attacked them as a "hell bred superstition," an ebullition of bitterness not poured forth in the *Investigator.* Christians who took offense at the *Investigator's* satire admitted its truth: "Birds do not generally flutter till they are hit."

Nor was there blasphemy in the public letter he had addressed to the Universalist editor, the count in the indictment mainly relied upon by [the prosecution]. That letter had been written in the mildest of language, without cursing or contumelious reproach. A disbelief in the doctrines of Christianity was not prohibited by the statute. Anyway, Kneeland continued, he had simply expressed a disbelief in the creed of the Universalists,—a fact which he sought to prove by an elaborate grammatical analysis of his words, "Universalists believe in a god which I do not; but believe that their god," etc. Yet, even if his words be construed to express a general disbelief in the existence of God, it would not be a *denial* of God within meaning of the statute. A disbelief is an expression of doubt; a denial is a positive assertion without any doubt; and the statute referred only to wilful denial. "I do say," Kneeland declared, "and shall until my dying breath, I never intended to express even a disbelief in, much less a denial of, God."

Was this Boston's Robespierre speaking, Satan's apostle? What was Kneeland's creed? In that same letter to the Universalist editor he had written, "I am not an Atheist but a Pantheist." He did believe in God; God was everything, Nature and the Universe. "I believe," he had written, "that it is in God we live, move, and have our being; and that the whole duty of man consists . . . in promoting as much happiness as he can while he lives." Here was a creed as spiritual and benevolent as that of the Transcendentalists!

Having argued that he had not blasphemed even under that law "as cruel as the laws against witchcraft," Kneeland proceeded to argue its unconstitutionality. He proposed that it violated Article II of the Massachusetts Declaration of Rights which declared that no subject would be restrained "for worshipping God in the manner and season most agreeable to the dictates of his own conscience; or for his religious professions and sentiments." [The judge's] instructions in the former trial had stripped Kneeland of this protection by holding that his atheistic denial of God's existence was an *irreligious* profession; Kneeland had moved in arrest of judgment because of this charge.

He thought Article II should be interpreted broadly, under the maxim of Jefferson, that "error of opinion may be safely tolerated, when reason is left free to combat it." To Kneeland, the words of Article II proclaimed the principle of "universal toleration." His own sentiments, he urged, were religious, not irreligious, but the article protected *all* sentiments respecting religion. If the court could brand his sentiments as irreligious, this

> discreditable quibble would destroy the whole object of the provision in the Bill of Rights, leaving it in the power of the Legislature and Courts to harass by penal prosecutions all who might maintain a profession or sentiment in or respecting religion which the Legislature and Courts might choose to consider irreligious.

Conformists, he declared, were in no danger of being persecuted; Article II was intended for those who needed protection, those who professed unpopular sentiments respecting religion. Concluding, Kneeland said:

> I stand on a ground as broad as space, and as firm as the rock of ages; to wit, on the right of conscience, together with the privilege of the freedom of speech and the liberty of the press.

More than two years passed before the court gave its opinion. But the case was not forgotten. There were men in Massachusetts who valued "the right of conscience." William Lloyd Garrison could recall that when every Christian church in Boston turned him down, Kneeland had offered him the use of his meetinghouse. Emerson, working on his Divinity School Address, might have remembered that George Ripley had been censured by the Orthodox for teaching transcendentalism. Theodore Parker knew that George Noyes, the biblical scholar, had once been threatened by Attorney-General Austin with prosecution for heresy. Almost all who were given to heterodox ideas—utopians, abolitionists, and transcendentalists—balked at using the strong arm of the state to silence Kneeland. In March of 1839, Dr. Channing wrote to Ellis Gray Loring, the abolitionist lawyer: "My intention is to see and converse with Judge Shaw on the subject. That a man should be punished for his opinion would be shocking,—an offense at once to the principles and feelings of the community."

All was in vain. In April, Chief Justice Shaw delivered the opinion of the court, sustaining Kneeland's conviction. No American jurist outside the Supreme Court of the United States, and few who have been members of the body, exercised a more profound influence on American law than Shaw. His opinion in the Kneeland case, however, does not so much reveal his greatness as it confirms the observation of Richard Henry Dana that Shaw, a conservative Unitarian and Whig, was "a man of intense and doting biases." It was no coincidence that the one judge who dissented from Shaw's opinion was Marcus Morton, the only Jacksonian on the bench.

Shaw explained that the delay in handing down the decision was occasioned by the "intrinsic difficulty attending some of the questions raised in the case, and a difference of opinion among the judges." He thought the first question for decision was whether the language of the defendant as set forth in the indictment constituted blasphemy within the meaning of the statute. Blasphemy, wrote Shaw, may be described as

> speaking evil of the Deity with an impious purpose to derogate from the divine majesty, and to alienate the minds of others from the love and reverence of God. It is purposely using words concerning God, calculated and designed to impair and destroy the reverence, respect, and confidence due to him. . . . It is a wilful and malicious attempt to lessen men's reverence of God.

The offense to be prohibited by the statute was the "wilful denial of God . . . with an intent and purpose to impair and destroy the reverence due to him."

The Chief Justice had "no doubt" that Kneeland's public letter amounted to the offense. Although Kneeland had couched his language in the form of a disbelief, "if" he had intended a wilful denial of God's existence, his disbelief constituted a denial. Whether his language was, in fact, used with unlawful intent

> was a question upon the whole indictment and all the circumstances, and after verdict, if no evidence was erroneously admitted or rejected, and no incorrect directions in matter of law were given, *it is to be taken as proved,* that the language was used in the sense, and under the circumstances, and with the intent and purpose, laid in the indictment, so as to bring the act within the statute.

For more than two years this decision had been in the making, and in the end, the fundamental question—had Kneeland blasphemed?—was settled without considered judgment; it was "taken as proved" simply by accepting the verdict of guilty. Furthermore, Shaw neglected to determine whether Kneeland was liable for the articles which he had not written. What then had been the purpose of hearing the cause on the "whole indictment and all the circumstances" as the court itself had ordered at the very beginning? All that Shaw had offered was a definition of blasphemy which could meet disagreement from no quarter; Kneeland himself had proposed the same definition to prove that he had committed no offense. Thus far, Shaw's opinion was—and remained—a neatly orchestrated abstraction at no point contaminated by the realities of the case.

The Chief Justice next addressed himself to the argument that the statute was repugnant to the constitution. He cited with approval a decision by Kent that blasphemy was a *common law* crime not to be abrogated by a constitution which carried the doctrine of unlimited tolerance.[7] Here was an intolerable implication that in spite of the constitution, and whether or not the statute was valid, Kneeland was guilty at common law because Christianity was incorporated therein. Shaw proceeded, however, to examine the provisions of the Declaration of Rights which were supposed to have been violated by the statute.

Article XVI provided that "the liberty of the press is essential to the security of freedom in a state; it ought not therefore to be restrained in the Commonwealth." Shaw construed these words to mean only that individuals would be at liberty to print, although responsible for the matter printed, without previous permission of any officer of the government. Kneeland's argument relative to the liberty of the press, said Shaw, was best refuted by reformulating it: "every act, however injurious or criminal, which may be committed by the use of language, may be committed with impunity if such language is printed."

> Not only would the article in question become a general license for scandal, calumny, and falsehood against individuals, institutions and governments . . . but all incitation to treason, assassination, and all other crimes however atrocious, if conveyed in printed language, would be dispunishable.

There was not the least basis for this characterization of Kneeland's argument. On the contrary, he is officially reported to have said: "I do not contend, however, that a man who slanders his neighbor in print, shall not be answerable for the injury he inflicts"; he had only contended that Article XVI guaranteed him the right to propagate his sentiments on religion or any other subject. Nevertheless Shaw ruled that Article XVI was no ground for excusing publication of the articles specified in the indictment or for invalidating the statute. Shaw's construction of the article as a mere prohibition of prior restraints upon publication emasculated its guarantee of liberty of the press, by reading into it the very common law definition of a free press which its framers sought to supplant.

Shaw found no violation either of Article II which guaranteed religious liberty. The statute merely made it penal wilfully to blaspheme the name of God. "Wilfully," said Shaw, meant "with a bad purpose," in this statute, an intent "to calumniate and disparage the Supreme Being." But, Shaw added, the statute did not prohibit the fullest inquiry and freest discussion for "honest" purposes; it did not even prohibit a "simple and sincere avowal of a disbelief in the existence and attributes of God." So construed, declared Shaw, the statute did not restrain the profession of any religious sentiments; it was intended merely to punish acts which have "a tendency to disturb the public peace."

This section of the opinion possessed the dubious distinction of ignoring the case at bar of a man who had, at worst, quoted Voltaire, satirized prayer, and denied God. If the statute had not prohibited free discussion, Kneeland should have been tending his presses instead of anticipating jail. If his purposes had not been honest, and if he had disturbed the peace in a manner not protected by the guarantees of civil liberties, then Shaw evaded reasoned judgment on the particulars.

The majority opinion grieved Judge Morton, a champion of the laboring classes and civil liberties. He regretted that he was driven to lengthy dissent, but he had strong convictions on the matter. He considered as illiberal the view that Article II embraced only religious, as contrasted to irreligious, professions. To Morton the article was a "general proposition" enacted "for the protection of the rights of the people."

> Being interwoven in the frame of the government, it was intended to continue in force as long as that should endure. It should . . . receive a liberal construction, unrestrained by the prevailing tenets of any particular time or place.

Thus, all beliefs and *disbeliefs* concerning religion were protected to the extent that no individual was responsible to any human tribunal for his opinions on the existence of God; "operations of the human mind especially in the adoption of its religious faith" are "entirely above all civil authority," added Morton. Religious truths did not need the "dangerous aid" of legislation.

The act against blasphemy Morton considered constitutional only when construed not to penalize a mere denial of God. "No one may advocate an opinion which another may not controvert." Criminality depended upon motive, a fact which provided a broad boundary between liberty and license. The denial "must be *blasphemously* done": there must be a denial inspired by corruption and malice for the purpose of injuring others. A wilful denial imparted no crime because "wilful," at worst, meant *obstinately:*

> Every person has a constitutional right to discuss the subject of a God, to affirm or deny his existence. I cannot agree that a man may be punished for *wilfully* doing what he has a legal right to do.

"This conviction," concluded Morton, "rests very heavily upon my mind." . . .

On June 1, 1838, Kneeland wrote a letter to Shaw cruelly attributing the death of his infant son to the severe shock of the mother, as a "consequence of my being again summoned to Court after more than two years silence, to hear the decision and probable sentence which would have left her unprotected in the critical and most trying hour." In spite of his grief, Kneeland informed Shaw, he was as prepared as he ever would be "to undergo the penalty of that barbarous, cruel, absurd law, of witchcraft memory." He wanted it known that he refused to say anything which might mitigate his punishment, since his son's death had made him "totally indifferent as to the amount of punishment." He was fortified in the knowledge that

> the current of public opinion is turned so much against this odious persecution, that every iota of suffering which I shall have to endure . . . will help the cause in which I am engaged; for which cause, if need be, I am willing to suffer; yea, more willing, if I can un-

> derstand the account, than was the pattern of christian [sic] patience; for even should my agony cause me to sweat blood . . . I shall never offer up the fruitless prayer, "if it be possible let this cup pass from me;" much less would I *blasphemously* say, "My God, my God, why hast thou forsaken me?"

The arrogant letter closed with the information that Kneeland would submit proudly and endure the penalty indignantly, but he requested that his sentence begin early: "'whatever thou dost, do quickly.'"

Shaw had delayed entering judgment on the verdict. It was within his power to suspend sentence and bind Kneeland to good behavior, but the latter's letter scarcely stimulated magnanimity. On August 8, Theodore Parker wrote to George Ellis:

> . . . Abner was jugged for sixty days; but he will come out as beer from a bottle, all foaming, and will make others foam. . . . The charm of all is that Abner got Emerson's address to the students, and read it to his followers, as better infidelity than he could write himself. . . .

Abner Kneeland served his time. Upon his release from prison, he emigrated, with members of his First Society of Free Inquirers, to the free air of frontier Iowa. There he established an unsuccessful utopian community, "Salubria," and became active in Democratic politics. He died unreconstructed at seventy-one, in 1844. . . .

EZRA STILES ELY

A Christian Party in Politic (1827)[8]

> The Rev. Ezra Stiles Ely delivered this sermon in Philadelphia on the fourth of July 1827. Having gone so far as to declare, "that other things being equal, I would prefer for my chief magistrate, and judge, and ruler, a sound Presbyterian," Ely's proposal provided a convenient target for contemporary anticlericalism, which was convinced that a conspiracy existed to unite church and state.

We have assembled, fellow citizens, on the anniversary of our Nation's birth day, in a rational and religious manner, to celebrate our independence of all foreign domination, and the goodness of God in making us a free and happy people. On what subject can I, on the present occasion, insist with more propriety, than on the duty of all the rulers and citizens of these United States in the exercise and enjoyment of all their political rights, to honour the Lord Jesus Christ.

Let it then be distinctly stated and fearlessly maintained IN THE FIRST PLACE, that every member of this christian nation, from the highest to the lowest, ought to serve the Lord with fear, and yield his sincere homage to the Son of God. Every ruler *should be* an avowed and a sincere friend of Christianity. He should know and believe the doctrines of our holy religion, and act in conformity with its precepts. This *he ought* to do; because as a man he is required to serve the Lord; as a public ruler he is called upon by divine authority to "kiss the Son." The commandment contained in Proverbs iii. 6. *"in all thy ways acknowledge him,"* includes public as well as private ways, and political no less than domestic ways. It is addressed equally to the man who rules, and to the person who is subject to authority. If we may not disown our God and Saviour in *any* situation, it will follow that we are to own him in *every* situation. Infinite wisdom has taught us, that *he who ruleth over men must be just, ruling in the fear of God.* No *Christian* can gainsay this decision. Let all then admit, that our civil rulers ought to act a religious part in all the relations which they sustain. Indeed, they ought preeminently to commit their way unto the Lord that he may direct their steps; delight themselves in him, and wait patiently for him; because by their example, if good, they can do more good than private, less known citizens; and if evil, more harm. Their official station is a talent entrusted to them for usefulness, for which they must give account to their Maker. They are like a city set on a hill, which cannot be hid; and it is a fact indisputable, that wickedness in high places does more harm than in obscurity.

I would guard, however, against misunderstanding and misrepresentation, when I state, that all our rulers ought in their official stations to serve the Lord Jesus Christ. I do not wish any religious test to be prescribed by constitution, and proposed to a man on his acceptance of any public trust. Neither can any intelligent friend of his country and of true religion desire the establishment of any one religious sect by civil law. Let the religion of the Bible rest on that everlasting rock, and on those spiritual laws, on which Jehovah has founded his kingdom: let Christianity by the spirit of Christ in her members support herself: let Church and State be for ever distinct: but, still, let the doctrines and precepts of Christ govern all men, in all their relations and employments. If a ruler is not a Christian he ought to be one, in this land of evangelical light, without delay; and he ought, being a follower of Jesus, to honour him even as he honours the FATHER. In this land of religious freedom, what should hinder a civil magistrate from believing the gospel, and professing faith in Christ, any more than any other man? If the Chief Magistrate of a nation may be an irreligious man, with impunity, who may not? It seems to be generally granted, that our political leaders in the national and state governments ought not to be notoriously profane, drunken, abandoned men in their moral conduct; but if they may not be injurious to themselves and their fellow men, who shall give them permission to contemn God? If they ought to be just towards men, ought they not also to abstain from robbing God, and to render unto him that honour which is HIS due?

Our rulers, like any other members of the community, who are under law to God as rational beings, and under law to Christ, since they have the light of divine revelation, ought to search the scriptures, assent to the truth, profess faith in Christ, keep the Sabbath holy to God, pray in private and in the domestic circle, attend on the public ministry of the word, be baptized, and celebrate the Lord's supper. None of our rulers have the consent of their Maker, that they should be Pagans, Socinians, Mussulmen, Deists, the opponents of Christianity; and a religious people should never think of giving them permission, as public officers, to be and do, what they might not lawfully be and do, as private individuals. If a man may not be a gambler and drink to intoxication in the western wilds, he may not at the seat of government; if he may not with the approbation of his fellow citizens, in a little village of the north, deny "the true God and eternal life," he may not countenance, abet, and support those who deny the Deity of our Lord Jesus Christ at Washington. In other words, our Presidents, Secretaries of the Government, Senators and other Representatives in Congress, Governors of States, Judges, State Legislators, Justices of the Peace, and City Magistrates, are just as much bound as any other persons in the United States, to be orthodox in their faith, and virtuous and religious in their whole deportment. They may no more lawfully be bad husbands, wicked parents, men of heretical opinions, or men of dissolute lives, than the obscure individual who would be sent to Bridewell for his blasphemy or debauchery.

God, my hearers, requires a Christian faith, a Christian profession, and a Christian practice of all our public men; and we as Christian citizens ought, by the publication of our opinions to require the same.

SECONDLY, Since it is the duty of all our rulers to serve the Lord and kiss the Son of God, it must be most manifestly the duty of all our Christian fellow-citizens to honour the Lord Jesus Christ and promote christianity by electing and supporting as public officers the friends of our blessed Saviour. Let it only be granted, that Christians have the same rights and privileges in exercising the elective franchise, which are here accorded to Jews and Infidels, and we ask no other evidence to show, that those who prefer a Christian ruler, may unite in supporting him, in preference to any one of a different character. It shall cheerfully be granted, that every citizen is eligible to every office, whatever may be his religious opinions and moral character; and that every one may constitutionally support any person whom he may *choose;* but it will not hence follow, that he is without accountability to his Divine Master for his choice; or that he may lay aside all his Christian principles and feelings when he selects his ticket and presents it at the polls. "*In all* thy ways acknowledge him," is a maxim which should dwell in a Christian's mind on the day of a public election as much as on the Sabbath; and which should govern him when conspiring with others to honour Christ, either at the Lord's table, or in the election of a Chief Magistrate. In elucidating the duty of private Christians in relation to the choice of their civil rulers, it seems to me necessary to remark,

1. That every Christian who has the right and the opportunity of exercising the elective franchise ought to do it. Many pious people feel so much disgust at the manner in which elections are conducted, from the first nomination to the closing of the polls, that they relinquish their right of voting for years together. But if all *pious* people were to conduct thus, then our rulers would be wholly elected by the *impious.* If all *good men* are to absent themselves from elections, then the *bad* will have the entire transaction of our public business.

If the wise, the prudent, the temperate, the friends of God and of their country do not endeavour to control our elections, they will be controlled by others: and if *one* good man may, without any reasonable excuse, absent himself, then *all* may. Fellow Christians, the love of Christ and of our fellow-men should forbid us to yield the choice of our civil rulers into the hands of selfish office hunters, and the miserable tools of their party politics. If all the truly religious men of our nation would be punctual and persevering in their endeavours to have good men chosen to fill all our national and state offices of honour, power and trust, THEIR WEIGHT would soon be felt by politicians; and those who care little for the religion of the Bible, would, for their own interest, consult the reasonable wishes of the great mass of Christians throughout our land.

I propose, fellow-citizens, a new sort of union, or, if you please, *a Christian party in politics,* which I am exceedingly desirous all good men in our country should join: not by *subscribing a constitution* and the formation of a new society, to be added to the scores which now exist; but by adopting, avowing, and determining to act upon, truly religious principles in all civil matters. I am aware that the true Christians of our country are divided into many different denominations; who have, alas! too many points of jealousy and collision; still, a union to a very great extent, and for the most valuable purposes is not impracticable. For,

2. All Christians, of all denominations, may, and ought to, agree in determining, that they will never wittingly support for any public office, any person whom they know or believe to sustain, at the time of his proposed election, a bad moral character. In this, thousands of moralists, who profess no experimental acquaintance with Christianity, might unite and co-operate with *our Christian party.* And surely, it is not impossible, nor unreasonable for all classes of Christians to say within themselves, no man that we have reason to think is a liar, thief, gambler, murderer, debauchee, spendthrift, or openly immoral person in any way, shall have our support at any election. REFORMATION should not only be allowed, but encouraged; for it would be requiring too much to insist upon it, that a candidate for office *shall always have sustained an unblemished moral character,* and it would be unchristian not to forgive and support one who has proved his repentance by recantation and a considerable course of new obedience.

Some of the best of men were once vile; but they have been washed from their sins. Present good moral character should be considered as essential to every candidate for the post of honour. In this affair I know we are very much dependent on testimony, and that we may be deceived; especially in those controverted elections in which all manner of falsehoods are invented and vended, wholesale and retail, against some of the most distinguished men of our country: but after all, we must exercise our candour and best discretion, as we do in other matters of belief. We must weigh evidence, and depend most on those who appear the most competent and credible witnesses. It will be natural for us to believe a man's neighbours and acquaintances in preference to strangers. When we have employed the lights afforded us for the illumination of our minds, we shall feel peace of conscience, if we withhold our vote from every one whom we believe to be an immoral man.

Come then, fellow Christians, and friends of good morals in society, let us determine thus far to unite; for thus far we may, and ought to, and shall unite, if we duly weigh the importance of a good moral character in a ruler. Let no love of *the integrity of a party* prevent you from striking out the name of every dishonest and base man from your ticket. You have a right to choose, and you glory in your freedom: make then your own election: and when all good men act on this principle it will not be a vain thing. Candidates then, must be moral men, or seem to be, or they will not secure an election.

3. All who profess to be Christians of any denomination ought to agree that they will support no man as a candidate for any office, who is not professedly friendly to Christianity, and a believer in divine Revelation. We do not say that true or even pretended Christianity shall be made a constitutional test of admission to office; but we do affirm that Christians may in their elections lawfully prefer the avowed friends of the Christian religion to Turks, Jews, and Infidels. Turks, indeed, might naturally prefer Turks, if they could elect them; and Infidels might prefer Infidels; and I should not wonder if a conscientious Jew should prefer a ruler of his own religious faith; but it would be passing strange if a Christian should not desire the election of one friendly to his own system of religion. While every religious system is tolerated in our country, and no one is established by law, it is still possible for me to think, that the friend of Christianity will make a much better governor of this commonwealth or President of the United States, than the advocate of Theism or Polytheism. We will not pretend to search the heart; but surely all sects of Christians may agree in opinion, that it is more desirable to have a Christian than a Jew, Mohammedan, or Pagan, in any civil office; and they may accordingly settle it in their minds, that they will never vote for any one to fill any office in the nation or state, who does not profess to receive the Bible as the rule of his faith. If three or four of the most numerous denominations of Christians in the United States, the Presbyterians, the Baptists, the Methodists and Congregationalists for instance, should act upon this principle, our country would never be dishonoured with an *avowed infidel* in her national cabinet or capitol. The Presbyterians alone could bring *half a million of electors* into the field, in opposition to any known advocate of Deism, Socinianism, or any species of avowed hostility to the truth of Christianity. If to the denominations above named we add the members of the Protestant Episcopal church in our country, the electors of these five classes of true Christians, united in the sole requisition of apparent friendship to Christianity in every candidate for office whom they will support, could govern every public election in our country, without infringing in the least upon the charter of our civil liberties. To these might be added, in this State and in Ohio, the numerous German Christians, and in New York and New Jersey the members of the Reformed Dutch Church, who are all zealous for the fundamental truths of Christianity. What should prevent us from cooperating in such a union as this? Let a man be of good moral character, and let him profess to believe in and advocate the Christian religion, and we can all support him. At one time he will be a Baptist, at another an Episcopalian, at another a Methodist, at another a Presbyterian of the American, Scotch, Irish, Dutch, or German stamp, and always a friend to our common Christianity. Why then should we ever suffer an enemy, an open and known enemy of the true religion of Christ, to enact our laws or fill the executive chair? Our Christian rulers will not oppress Jews or Infidels; they will *kiss the Son and serve the Lord;* while we have the best security for their fidelity to our republican, and I may say scriptural forms of government.

It deprives no man of his right for me to prefer a Christian to an Infidel. If Infidels were the most numerous electors, they would doubtless elect men of their own sentiments; and unhappily such men not unfrequently get into power in this country, in which ninety-nine hundredths of the people are believers in the divine origin and authority of the Christian religion. If hundreds of thousands of our fellow citizens should agree with us in an effort to elect men to public office who read the Bible, profess to believe it, reverence the Sabbath, attend public worship, and sustain a good moral character, who could complain? Have we not as much liberty to be the supporters of the Christian cause by our votes, as others have to support anti-christian men and measures?

Let us awake, then, fellow Christians, to our sacred duty to our Divine Master; and let us have no rulers, with our consent and co-operation, who are not known to be avowedly Christians.

LYMAN BEECHER

Beecher's Strategy for the West (1835)

After his conversion to the "voluntary principle" Lyman Beecher moved to a parish in Boston and subsequently agreed to head up the Lane Theological Seminary in Cincinnati—a strategically placed institution in the campaign to win the West for Protestantism. *A Plea for the West* is the published version of fundraising lectures Beecher delivered to East Coast audiences to gain support for Lane Seminary. In these brief excerpts it is clear that republican Protestantism embodied a great deal of anti–Roman Catholic sentiment and fear of despotic government—often failing to distinguish the two issues.

The great experiment is now making . . . in the West, whether the perpetuity of our republican institutions can be reconciled with universal suffrage.[9] Without the education of the head and heart of the nation, they cannot be; and the question to be decided is, can the nation, or the vast balance power of it be so imbued with intelligence and virtue, as to bring out, in laws and their administration, a perpetual self-preserving energy? We know that the work is a vast one, and of great difficulty; and yet we believe it can be done.

We know that we have reached an appalling crisis; that the work is vast and difficult, and is accumulating upon us beyond our sense of danger and deliberate efforts to meet it. It is a work that no legislation alone can reach, and nothing but an undivided, earnest, decided public sentiment can achieve; and that, too, not by anniversary resolutions and fourth of July orations, but by well systematized voluntary associations; counting the worth of our institutions, the perils that surround them, and the means and the cost of their preservation, and making up our minds to meet the exigency.

It is a union of church and state, which we fear, and to prevent which we lift up our voice: a union which never existed without corrupting the church and enslaving the people, by making the ministry independent of them and dependent on the state, and to a great extent a sinecure aristocracy of indolence and secular ambition, auxiliary to the throne and inimical to liberty. No treason against our free institutions would be more fatal than a union of church and state; none, when perceived would bring on itself a more overwhelming public indignation, and which all Protestant denominations would resist with more loathing and abhorrence.

And is there, therefore, no danger of a church and state union, because all denominations cannot unite, and no one can elude the vigilant resistance of the rest? Is there no other door at which the innovation can come in? How has the union been constituted in times past? Not as coveted by the church, and secured by her artifice or power; but as coveted by the state, and sought for purposes of secular ambition to strengthen the arm of despotic power.

But in republics the temptation and the facilities of courting an alliance with church power may be as great as in governments of less fluctuation. Amid the competitions of party and the struggles of ambition, it is scarcely possible that the clergy of a large denomination should be able to give a direction to the suffrage of their whole people, and not become for the time being the most favored denomination, and in balanced elections the dominant sect, whose influence in times of discontent may perpetuate power against the unbiased verdict of public opinion. The free circulation of the blood is not more essential to bodily health, than the easy, unobstructed movement of public sentiment in a republic. All combinations to forestall and baffle its movements tend to the destruction of liberty. Its fluctuations are indeed an evil; but the power to arrest its fluctuations and chain it down is despotism; and when it is accomplished by the bribed alliance of ecclesiastical influence in the control of suffrage, it appears in its most hateful and alarming form.

We say, then, . . . only keep the church and state apart, and there will be no danger. But while you watch the door at which the alliance never did come, do not forget to watch the door at which it always has entered—the door of the state, inviting the alliance of church power to sustain its own weakness, and nerve its arm for despotic dominion.

> But why so much excitement about the Catholic religion? Is not one religion just as good as another?

It is an anti-republican charity . . . which would shield the Catholics, or any other religious denomination, from the animadversion of impartial criticism. Denominations, as really as books, are public property, and demand and are benefited by criticism. And if ever the Catholic religion is liberalized and assimilated to our institutions, it must be done, not by a sickly sentimentalism screening it from animadversion, but by subjecting it to the tug of controversy, and turning upon it the searching inspection of the public eye, and compelling it, like all other religions among us, to pass the ordeal of an enlightened public sentiment.

RICHARD M. JOHNSON

A Jacksonian Criticism of the Protestant Phalanx (1829)

Richard M. Johnson (d. 1850) served in the House and the Senate as well as in the vice presidency under Martin van Buren. His nomination to this latter position was according to the wishes of President Jackson, with whom he had been close. His report to the Senate "on the subject of mails on the Sabbath" is significant in indicating one kind of resistance to the evangelicals' pressure within the common life. It is all the more significant when compared with the report presented to the House on the same issue, which recommended that mails be neither transported nor delivered on Sunday: "It is believed that the history of legislation in this country affords no

> instance in which a stronger expression has been made, if regard be had to the numbers, the wealth or the intelligence of the petitioners."[10]

That some respite is required from the ordinary vocations of life, is an established principle, sanctioned by the usages of all nations, whether Christian or Pagan.[11] One day in seven has also been determined upon as the proportion of time; and in conformity with the wishes of the great majority of citizens of this country, the first day of the week, commonly called Sunday, has been set apart to that object. The principle has received the sanction of the national legislature, so far as to admit a suspension of all public business on that day, except in cases of absolute necessity, or of great public utility. This principle, the committee would not wish to disturb. If kept within its legitimate sphere of action, no injury can result from its observance. It should, however, be kept in mind, that the proper object of government is, to protect all persons in the enjoyment of their religious, as well as civil rights; and not to determine for any, whether they shall esteem one day above another, or esteem all days alike holy.

We are aware, that a variety of sentiment exists among the good citizens of this nation, on the subject of the Sabbath day; and our government is designed for the protection of one, as much as for another. The Jews, who, in this country are as free as Christians, and entitled to the same protection from the laws, derive their obligation to keep the Sabbath day from the fourth commandment of their decalogue, and in conformity with that injunction, pay religious homage to the seventh day of the week, which we call Saturday. One denomination of Christians among us, justly celebrated for their piety, and certainly as good citizens as any other class, agree with the Jews in the moral obligation of the Sabbath, and observe the same day. There are also many Christians among us, who derive not their obligation to observe the Sabbath from the decalogue, but regard the Jewish Sabbath as abrogated. From the example of the Apostles of Christ, they have chosen the first day of the week, instead of that day set apart in the decalogue, for their religious devotions. These have generally regarded the observance of the day as a devotional exercise, and would not more readily enforce it upon others, than they would enforce secret prayer or devout meditations. Urging the fact, that neither their Lord nor his disciples, though often censured by their accusers for a violation of the Sabbath, ever enjoined its observance, they regard it as a subject on which every person should be fully persuaded in his own mind, and not coerce others to act upon his persuasion. Many Christians again differ from these, professing to derive their obligation to observe the Sabbath from the fourth commandment of the Jewish decalogue, and bring the example of the Apostles, who appear to have held their public meetings for worship on the first day of the week, as authority for so far changing the decalogue, as to substitute that day for the seventh. The Jewish government was a theocracy, which enforced religious observances; and though the committee would hope that no portion of the citizens of our country could willingly introduce a system of religious coercion in our civil institutions, the example of other nations should admonish us to watch carefully against its earliest indication.

With these different religious views, the committee are of opinion that Congress cannot interfere. It is not the legitimate province of the legislature to determine what religion is true, or what false. Our government is a civil, and not a religious institution. Our Constitution recognises in every person, the right to choose his own religion, and to enjoy it freely, without molestation. Whatever may be the religious sentiments of citizens, and however variant, they are alike entitled to protection from the government, so long as they do not invade the rights of others.

The transportation of the mail on the first day of the week, it is believed, does not interfere with the rights of conscience. The petitioners for its discontinuance appear to be actuated from a religious zeal, which may be commendable if confined to its proper sphere; but they assume a position better suited to an ecclesiastical than to a civil institution. They appear, in many instances, to lay it down as an axiom, that the practice is a violation of the law of God. Should Congress, in their legislative capacity, adopt the sentiment, it would establish the principle, that the Legislature is a proper tribunal to determine what are the laws of God. It would involve a legislative decision in a religious controversy; and on a point in which good citizens may honestly differ in opinion, without disturbing the peace of society, or endangering its liberties. If this principle is once introduced, it will be impossible to define its bounds. Among all the religious persecutions with which almost every page of modern history is stained, no victim ever suffered, but for the violation of what government denominated the law of God. To prevent a similar train of evils in this country, the Constitution has wisely withheld from our government the power of defining the Divine Law. It is a right reserved to each citizen; and while he respects the equal rights of others, he cannot be held amenable to any human tribunal for his conclusions.

Extensive religious combinations, to effect a political object, are, in the opinion of the committee, always dangerous. This first effort of the kind, calls for the establishment of a principle, which, in the opinion of the committee, would lay the foundation for dangerous innovations upon the spirit of the Constitution, and upon the religious rights of the citizens. If admitted, it may be justly apprehended, that the future measures of government will be strongly marked, if not eventually controlled, by the same influence. All religious despotism commences by combination and influence; and when that influence begins to operate upon the political institutions of a country, the civil power soon bends under it; and the catastrophe of other nations furnishes an awful warning of the consequence.

Under the present regulations of the Post Office Department, the rights of conscience are not invaded. Every agent enters voluntarily, and it is presumed conscientiously, into the discharge of his duties, without intermeddling with the conscience of another. Post offices are so regulated, as that but a small proportion of the first day of the week is required to be occupied in official business. In the transportation of the mail on that day, no one agent is employed many hours. Religious persons enter into the business without violating their own consciences, or imposing any restraints upon others. Passengers in the mail stages are free to rest during the first day of the week, or to pursue their journeys at their own pleasure. While the mail is transported on Saturday, the Jew and the Sabbatarian may abstain from any agency in carrying it, from conscientious scruples. While it is transported on the first day of the week, another class may abstain, from the same religious scruples. The obligation of government is the same to both of these classes; and the committee can discover no principle on which the claims of one should be more respected than those of the other, unless it should be admitted that the consciences of the minority are less sacred than those of the majority.

It is the opinion of the committee, that the subject should be regarded simply as a question of expediency, irrespective of its religious bearing. In this light, it has hitherto been considered. Congress have never legislated upon the subject. It rests, as it ever has done, in the legal discretion of the Postmaster General, under the repeated refusals of Congress to discontinue the Sabbath mails. His knowledge and judgment in all the concerns of that department, will not be questioned. His intense labors and assiduity have resulted in the highest improvement of every branch of his department. It is practised only on the great leading mail routes, and such others as are necessary to maintain their connexions. To prevent this, would, in the opinion of the committee, be productive of immense injury, both in its commercial, political, and in its moral bearings.

Nor can the committee discover where the system could consistently end. If the observance of a holyday becomes incorporated in our institutions, shall we not forbid the movement of an army; prohibit an assault in time of war; and lay an injunction upon our naval officers to lie in the wind while upon the ocean on that day? Consistency would seem to require it. Nor is it certain that we should stop here. If the principle is once established, that religion, or religious observances, shall be interwoven with our legislative acts, we must pursue it to its ultimatum. We shall, if consistent, provide for the erection of edifices for the worship of the Creator, and for the support of Christian ministers, if we believe such measures will promote the interests of Christianity. It is the settled conviction of the committee, that the only method of avoiding these consequences, with their attendant train of evils, is to adhere strictly to the spirit of the Constitution, which regards the general government in no other light than that of a civil institution, wholly destitute of religious authority.

What other nations call religious toleration, we call religious rights. They are not exercised in virtue of governmental indulgence, but as rights, of which government cannot deprive any portion of citizens, however small. Despotic power may invade those rights, but justice still confirms them. Let the national legislature once perform an act which involves the decision of a religious controversy, and it will have passed its legitimate bounds. The precedent will then be established, and the foundation laid for that usurpation of the Divine prerogative in this country, which has been the desolating scourge to the fairest portions of the old world. Our Constitution recognises no other power than that of persuasion, for enforcing religious observances. Let the professors of Christianity recommend their religion by deeds of benevolence—by Christian meekness—by lives of temperance and holiness. Let them combine their efforts to instruct the ignorant—to relieve the widow and the orphan—to promulgate to the world the gospel of their Saviour, recommending its precepts by their habitual example: government will find its legitimate object in protecting them. It cannot oppose them, and they will not need its aid. Their moral influence will then do infinitely more to advance the true interests of religion, than any measures which they may call on Congress to enact.

The petitioners do not complain of any infringement upon their own rights. They enjoy all that Christians ought to ask at the hand of any government—protection from all molestation in the exercise of their religious sentiments.

Resolved, That the Committee be discharged from the further consideration of the subject.

WILLIAM ELLERY CHANNING

A Religious Liberal's Criticism of the Protestant Strategy (1829)

William Ellery Channing (d. 1842) was a broad churchman within Boston Congregationalism who was instrumental in the emergence of American Unitarianism during the 1820s. It is wrong to see Channing as a philosophic radical—rather he was a liberal Christian with a social conscience. His moral concern for the social life is evident in this criticism of the evangelical program.

In truth, one of the most remarkable circumstances or features of our age is the energy with which the principle of combination, or of action by joint forces, by associated numbers, is manifesting itself.[12] It may be said, without much exaggeration, that every thing is done now by societies. Men have learned what wonders can be accomplished in certain cases by union, and seem to think that union is competent to every thing. You can scarcely name an object for which some institution has not been formed. Would men spread one set of opinions or crush another? They make a society. Would they improve the penal code, or relieve poor debtors? They make societies. Would they encourage agriculture, or manufactures or science? They make societies. Would one class encourage horse-racing, and another discourage travelling on Sunday? They form societies. We have immense institutions spreading over the country, combining hosts for particular objects. We have minute ramifications of these societies, penetrating everywhere except through the poor-house, and conveying resources from the domestic, the laborer, and even the child, to the central treasury. This principle of association is worthy the attention of the philosopher, who simply aims to understand society and its most powerful springs. To the philanthropist and the Christian it is exceedingly interesting, for it is a mighty engine, and must act either for good or for evil, to an extent which no man can foresee or comprehend.

That this mode of action has advantages and recommendations is very obvious. The principal arguments in its favor may be stated in a few words. Men, it is justly said, can do jointly what they cannot do singly. The union of minds and hands works wonders. Men grow efficient by concentrating their powers. Joint effort conquers nature, hews through mountains, rears pyramids, dikes out the ocean. Man, left to himself, living without a fellow,—if he could indeed so live,—would be one of the weakest of creatures. Associated with his kind, he gains dominion over the strongest animals, over the earth and the sea, and, by his growing knowledge, may be said to obtain a kind of property in the universe.

The great principle from which we start in this preliminary discussion, and in which all our views of the topics above proposed are involved, may be briefly expressed. It is this:—Society is chiefly important as it ministers to, and calls forth, intellectual and moral energy and freedom. Its action on the individual is beneficial in proportion as it awakens in him a power to act on himself, and to control or withstand the social influences to which he is at first subjected. Society serves us by furnishing objects, occasions, materials, excitements, through which the whole soul may be brought into vigorous exercise, may acquire a consciousness of its free and responsible nature, may become a law to itself, and may rise to the happiness and dignity of framing and improving itself without limit or end. Inward, creative energy is the highest good which accrues to us from our social principles and connections. The mind is enriched, not by what it passively receives from others, but by its own action on what it receives. We would especially affirm of virtue that it does not consist in what we inherit, or what comes to us from abroad. It is of inward growth, and it grows by nothing so much as by resistance of foreign influences, by acting from our deliberate convictions, in opposition to the principles of sympathy and imitation. According to these views, our social nature and connections are means. Inward power is the end,—a power which is to triumph over and control the influence of society.

The truth is, and we need to feel it most deeply, that our connection with society, as it is our greatest aid, so it is our greatest peril. We are in constant danger of being spoiled of our moral judgment, and of our power over ourselves; and in losing these, we lose the chief prerogatives of spiritual beings. We sink, as far as mind can sink, into the world of matter, the chief distinction of which is, that it wants self-motion, or moves only from foreign impulse. The propensity in our fellow-creatures which we have most to dread is that which, though most severely condemned by Jesus, is yet the most frequent infirmity of his followers,—we mean the propensity to rule, to tyrannize, to war with the freedom of their equals, to make themselves standards for other minds, to be lawgivers, instead of brethren and friends, to their race. Our great and most difficult duty, as social beings, is, to derive constant aid from society without taking its yoke; to open our minds to the thoughts, reasonings, and persuasions of others, and yet to hold fast the sacred right of private judgment; to receive impulses from our fellow-beings, and yet to act from our own souls; to sympathize with others, and yet to determine our own feelings; to act with others, and yet to follow our own consciences; to unite social deference and self-dominion; to join moral self-subsistence with social dependence; to respect others without losing self-respect; to love our friends and to reverence our superiors, whilst our supreme homage is given to that moral perfection which no friend and no superior has realized, and which, if faithfully pursued, will often demand separation from all around us. Such is our great work as social beings, and to perform it, we should look habitually to Jesus Christ, who was distinguished by nothing more than by moral independence,—than by resisting and overcoming the world.

It is interesting and encouraging to observe, that the enslaving power of society over the mind is decreasing, through what would seem at first to threaten its enlargement;—we mean, through the extension of social intercourse. . . .

We regret that religion has not done more to promote this enlarged intercourse of minds,—the great means, as we have seen, of reconciling social aids with personal independence. As yet, religion has generally assumed a sectarian form, and its disciples, making narrowness a matter of conscience, have too often shunned connection with men of different views as a pestilence, and yielded their minds to the exclusive influences of the leaders and teachers of their separate factions. Indeed, we fear that in no department of life has the social principle been perverted more into an instrument of intellectual thraldom than in religion. We could multiply proofs without end, but will content ourselves with a single illustration drawn from what are called "revivals of religion." We have many objections to these as commonly conducted; but nothing offends us more than their direct and striking tendency to overwhelm the mind with foreign influences, and to strip it of all self-direction. In these feverish seasons, religion, or what bears the name, is spread, as by contagion, and to escape it is almost as difficult as to avoid a raging epidemic. Whoever knows any thing of human nature, knows the effect of excitement in a crowd. When systematically prolonged and urged onward, it subverts deliberation and self-control. The individual is lost in the mass, and borne away as in a whirlwind. The prevalent emotion, be it love or hatred, terror or enthusiasm, masters every mind which is not fortified by a rare energy, or secured by a rare insensibility. In revivals, a multitude are subjected at once to strong emotions, which are swelled and perpetuated by the most skilful management. The individual is never suffered to escape the grasp of the leading or subordinate agents in the work. A machinery of social influences, of "inquiry meetings," of "anxious meetings," of conferences, of prayer meetings, of perpetual private or public impulses, is brought to bear on the diseased subject, until, exhausted in body and mind, he becomes the passive, powerless recipient of whatever form or impressions it may be thought fit to give him.

Our first remark is, that we should beware of confounding together, as of equal importance, those associations which are formed by our Creator, which spring from our very constitution, and are inseparable from our being, and those of which we are now treating, which man invents for particular times and exigencies. Let us never place our weak, short-sighted contrivances on a level with the arrangements of God. We have acknowledged the infinite importance of society to the development of human powers and affections. But when we speak thus of society, we mean chiefly the relations in which God has placed us; we mean the connections of family, of neighborhood, of country, and the great bond of humanity, uniting us with our whole kind, and not missionary societies, peace societies, or charitable societies, which men have contrived. These last have their uses, and some do great good; but they are no more to be compared with the societies in which nature places us, than the torches which we kindle on earth in the darkness of night are to be paralleled with the all-pervading and all-glorifying light of the sun. We make these remarks, because nothing is more common than for men to forget the value of what is familiar, natural, and universal, and to ascribe undue importance to what is extraordinary, forced, and rare, and therefore striking. Artificial associations have their use, but are not to be named with those of nature; and to these last, therefore, we are to give our chief regard.

We now proceed to our second remark, in which we proposed to suggest a principle by which the claims of different associations may be estimated. It is this: The value of associations is to be measured by the energy, the freedom, the activity, the moral power, which they encourage and diffuse. In truth, the great object of all benevolence is to give power, activity, and freedom to others. We cannot, in the strict sense of the word, *make* any being happy. We can give others the *means* of happiness, together with motives to the faithful use of them; but on this faithfulness, on the free and full exercise of their own powers, their happiness depends. There is thus a fixed, impassable limit to human benevolence. It can only make men happy through themselves, through their own freedom and energy. We go further. We believe that God has set the same limit to his own benevolence. He makes no being happy in any other sense than in that of giving him means, powers, motives, and a field for exertion. We have here, we think, the great consideration to guide us in judging of associations.

. . . We beg our readers to carry with them the principle now laid down in judging of associations; to inquire how far they are fitted to call forth energy, active talent, religious inquiry, a free and manly virtue. We insist on these remarks, because not a few associations seem to us exceedingly exceptionable, on account of their tendency to fetter men, to repress energy, to injure the free action of individuals and society, and because this tendency lurks, and is to be guarded against, even in good institutions. On this point we cannot but enlarge, for we deem it of the highest importance.

Associations often injure free action by a very plain and obvious operation. They accumulate power in a few hands, and this takes place just in proportion to the surface over which they spread. In a large institution, a few men rule, a few do every thing; and, if the institution happens to be directed to objects about which conflict and controversy exist, a few are able to excite in the mass strong and bitter passions, and by these to obtain an immense ascendency. Through such an association, widely spread, yet closely connected by party feeling, a few leaders can send their voices and spirit far and wide, and, where great funds are accumulated, can league a host of instruments, and by menace and appeals to interest can silence opposition. Accordingly, we fear that in this country an influence is growing up, through widely spread societies, altogether at war with the spirit of our institutions, and which, unless jealously watched, will gradually but surely encroach on freedom of thought, of speech, and of the press. It is very striking to observe how, by such combinations, the very means of encouraging a free action of men's minds may be turned against it. We all esteem the press as the safeguard of our liberties, as the power which is to quicken intellect by giving to all minds an opportunity to act on all. Now, by means of tract societies spread over a whole community, and acting under a central body, a few individuals, perhaps not more than twenty, may determine the chief reading for a great part of the children of the community, and for a majority of the adults, and may deluge our country with worthless sectarian writings, fitted only to pervert its taste, degrade its intellect, and madden it with intolerance. Let associations devoted to any objects which excite the passions be everywhere spread and leagued together for mutual support, and nothing is easier than to establish a control over newspapers. We are persuaded that, by an artful multiplication of societies, devoted apparently to different objects, but all swayed by the same leaders, and all intended to bear against a hated party, as cruel a persecution may be carried on in a free country as in a despotism. Public opinion may be so combined, and inflamed, and brought to bear on odious individuals or opinions, that it will be as perilous to think and speak with manly freedom as if an inquisition were open before us. It is now discovered that the way to rule in this country is by an array of numbers which a prudent man will not like to face. Of consequence, all associations aiming or tending to establish sway by numbers ought to be opposed. They create tyrants as effectually as standing armies. Let them be withstood from the beginning. No matter whether the opinions which they intend to put down be true or false. Let no opinion be put down by such means. Let no error be suppressed by an instrument which will be equally powerful against truth, and which must subvert that freedom of thought on which all truth depends. Let the best end fail if it cannot be accomplished by right and just means. For example, we would have criminals punished, but punished in the proper way, and by a proper authority. It were better that they should escape than be imprisoned or executed by any man who may think fit to assume the office; for sure we are that, by this summary justice, the innocent would soon suffer more than the guilty; and, on the same principle, we cannot consent that what we deem error should be crushed by the joint cries and denunciations of vast societies directed by the tyranny of a few; for truth has more to dread from such weapons than falsehood, and we know no truth against which they may not be successfully turned. In this country, few things are more to be dreaded than organizations or institutions by which public opinion may be brought to bear tyrannically against individuals or sects. From the nature of things, public opinion is often unjust; but, when it is not embodied and fixed by pledged societies, it easily relents, it may receive new impulses, it is opened to influences from the injured. On the contrary, when shackled and stimulated by vast associations, it is in danger of becoming a steady, unrelenting tyrant, brow-beating the timid, proscribing the resolute, silencing free speech, and virtually denying the dearest religious and civil rights. We say not that all great associations *must* be thus abused. We know that some are useful. We know, too, that there are cases in which it is important that public opinion should be condensed, or act in a mass. We feel, however, that the danger of great associations is increased by the very fact that they are sometimes useful. They are perilous instruments. They ought to be suspected. They are a kind of irregular government created within our constitutional government. Let them be watched closely. As soon as we find them resolved or disposed to bear down a respectable man or set of men, or to force on the community measures about which wise and good men differ, let us feel that a dangerous engine is at work among us, and oppose to it our steady and stern disapprobation.

CALVIN COLTON

Colton on the True Character of the Evangelical Enterprise (1836)

Calvin Colton went from Yale to Andover Seminary and thereafter into a Presbyterian Church until his voice failed him. Later he became an Episcopalian clergyman for a short period although already journalistic ambition had become evident. At one point he attacked the separation of church and state in America. The book from which this selection is taken is a criticism initially directed at the Temperance Movement. His comments apply, however, to the whole Protestant enterprise which sought to refashion the common life through the voluntary societies. After writing significant political and biographical pieces he held a chair of political economy at Trinity College, Hartford, Connecticut, until his death.

It is a remarkable fact, that in less than the period that belongs to a single generation, the economy of society in this country, in all that pertains to moral reform and religious enterprise, has been formed on a model entirely new to ourselves, but not without type in history.[13]

It is the assumption of a controlling influence by a few, who stand at the head of moral and religious organizations of various names. The public generally are simple, honest, confiding; and do not note operations of this kind. That is, they do not understand when and how the whole frame of society is getting into a new structure, leaving the great mass in subjection to the will and control of select, and often self-elected, combinations of individuals. They do not even suspect, that societies, formed for such good purposes, could have in them the leaven of ambition; and they allow themselves to be formed into minor and subsidiary organizations, comprehending the whole mass of the community, to uphold these supervisory establishments by contributions drawn from every source and from every hand. Most extraordinary measures are devised to obtain funds; itinerating mendicants are flying in all directions, traversing the country from east to west, and from north to south; every part of the complicated machinery is well contrived to answer the end; the system is thorough and perfect; and at the head of all sit a few eminent individuals, looking down upon and managing this work of their own hands, themselves independent and secure in their places by provisions which cannot fail while their influence lasts.

The process of corruption—for such we think proper to call it, without pretending to measure its degrees—in these high officers, and in the societies under their control, is always gradual. The men come into these places ordinarily under the influence of very pure designs; it was, perhaps, an unexpected elevation; certainly there was neither experience nor custom in it; they are transplanted from a circumscribed to a wide sphere of action and influence; their views are expanded; their duties require them to travel, and to form extensive acquaintances with the public; they see the world in constantly new and shifting forms; are ever concerting and scheming for the attainment of their objects; the economy of social organization for these purposes becomes a study, and themselves adepts; practice makes perfect; they enlarge their plans, and attempt to improve them; they attain, finally, not only a high and commanding position in society, but an almost unlimited influence; and "who," think they, at last, "can govern the world better than we? We have discovered how it can be done; we are competent; and we think it will be safest in our hands." And they set themselves about it, on the principle that all men have a right to that influence which they can command. They have no scruples; they have found out that the world must be governed by a few; that it is all effected by scheming; that perfect honesty and openness are inconsistent with such an art, and impolitic; that the secrets of government must be in the keeping of governors; that the wide public are to be informed only on points which concern them to know, and as they may be convenient instruments of power; that, in view of rival institutions, sects, or parties, all plans are to be formed and executed on principles of policy; and policy becomes, at last, the reigning principle. In spite of themselves, they and their work are transformed; they are not the things they were when they first set out. It is the unavoidable, the irresistible tendency of such organizations in such relations. It can no more be prevented than the course of nature, because it is identical with that course. These men will as necessarily become ambitious and aspiring, grasping at power and loving to wield it, and will as certainly scheme for themselves, as the infant will come to be a man; and observing the scope, and feeling the motives, of the wide field before him, will make the most of it. And never was a community more effectually brought under this dominion than we are at this moment. It is a new form indeed; but it is the operation of the same principle. A few irresponsible societies, with a few men at their head, govern this land in all that relates to our moral and religious interests; and they govern it for themselves. At least, they govern it in a way that is agreeable to themselves; and such is the ascendency of their influence, that their will is irresistible. It is a revival of the reign of Jesuitism, adapted to our time and circumstances.

We think it fair to say, that the clergy generally, and the religious public, who have been drawn into these schemes, are most remote from any participation in unworthy motives. It is the perfection of such policies, that a few lead the many, and ride upon their shoulders—while the many are persuaded that their leaders are as uncorrupt as themselves. Nor would we intimate that, for the most part, these societies have not espoused interests of importance, and most worthy of support. Our diffidence relates entirely to the character of the organizations, and their inherent tendencies to corruption and abuse. The change we desire to see is not the abandonment of these interests, but that they should be restored to the control of that public that is called upon to support them.

If the clergy of this land and the Christian public will open their eyes, they will see that the interests of moral and religious reform in the country are, almost entirely, in the hands and under the control of a few combinations of individuals, who are themselves not only above any suitable control, and irresponsible, but who have devised and put in operation a system of measures, which, by their own supervision and that of their sub-agents, force the wide community, socially and individually, into their schemes, while the public have no voice in concerting them. The measures are not submitted, but imposed. In the present posture of these affairs, there is no chance for that general control which is the only safety of a community of rights and privileges. And the ascendency of these combinations is perpetually rising; this control is becoming more uncontrollable; by a consciousness of power they are growing more confident; and no man can openly oppose them without the risk of being crushed by their influence. Their eyes are everywhere; they see and understand all movements; and not a whisper of discontent can be breathed, but that the bold remonstrant will feel the weight of their displeasure. The whole community, on whom they rely, are marshalled and disciplined to their will.

However important, therefore, those interests may be which have thus accidentally fallen into such hands, and for the very reason that they are important, it becomes the solemn duty of the public to see that they do not receive detriment on that account. Some of them have already been grossly mismanaged, and threatened with a complete wreck—such, for example, as the Temperance reformation. We do not desire to expose the faults we have noticed in the management of other enterprises, because we indulge the hope that they may yet be corrected; nor are we willing to diminish public confidence in them so long as that hope remains. Our principal aim has been to point out the defects and dangerous tendencies of organizations of a specific character, in the hands of which these interests are extensively vested, believing that they are radically and essentially Jesuitical.

VINCENT HARDING

The Black Struggle for Freedom in America

Although white Christians often hoped that conversion to Christianity would encourage slaves to submit to the authority of their masters, the slaves also heard a message of freedom in the gospel. Professor Vincent Harding, who has combined an academic career with work in the civil rights movement, describes the power of the spoken word in the black community and how it contributed to the freedom movement. He then goes on to describe the kinds of laws enacted by some southern states to control the spread of that word following the violent slave insurrection in 1831 led by the black preacher Nat Turner.

In the slave castles and by the riversides of Africa, where our ancestors had gathered for the long journey into American captivity, the spoken word had many functions.[14] It provided a bridge between and among them, to draw them together for the unity those first efforts demanded. On the ships the word was used to strengthen men and women and urge them toward the dangers of participation. It was often on the ships that the word, for the first sustained length of time, was directed toward the white captors. Early, in such a setting, the word was used in protest, in statements of black rights and white wrongs, of black people's determination to be men and women in spite of European attempts to dehumanize them. There, too, the word publicly spoken to white men often served as a rallying point for the Africans. For in many cases the word was openly uttered in spite of the rules and laws of the whites, spoken in the face of threats and punishment and even death. Such courageous speakers of the word understandably evoked strength and courage and hope in other captives.

Similar situations often prevailed when the black-white struggle moved from the prison ships into the fields and forests of the New World prison state. In the South, the word was used as an organizing tool for the flight into the outlyers' camps or toward the North. In many such situations it spoke the truth about white oppression, black suffering, and the potential power of organized black will. Such a word strengthened and encouraged friends to continue the struggle to survive, to bide their time toward the struggle to overcome. And on many occasions, the prison states exacted the same cruel penalties as the prison ships for the honest, defiant, encouraging black word. For such words were radical acts.

No less dangerous to white power in the South were the words spoken honestly from the Bible, the Word, telling men and women of a humanity no one could deny them, reminding a people that God opposed injustice and the oppression of the weak, encouraging believers to seek for messianic signs in the heavens, for blood on the leaves. On the tongues of black people—and in their hands—the Word might indeed become a sword. . . .

One major white reaction to slave uprisings was to attempt to intercept and oppose all black messengers from God, who brought the Word to the captive African people of America. Shortly after the Turner insurrection, the Richmond *Enquirer* raised the alarm: "The case of Nat Turner warns us. No black man ought to be permitted to turn a preacher through the country. The law must be enforced—or the tragedy of Southhampton appeals to us in vain." From Washington, D.C., an unidentified, but not atypical, correspondent wrote to express a widespread white fear of the power of such independent black religion: "It is much to be regretted that many insurrectionary plots are instigated by fierce, ignorant fanatics, assuming to be preachers. . . . I foresee that this land must one day or another, become a field of blood."

Out of such fear, a congeries of new laws swept across the South. There were laws prohibiting the captives from being taught how to read and write, and forbidding them to preach; laws insisting on increased white vigilance; laws interfering with black meetings—all of them testifying to the fact that similar earlier laws simply had not worked. Yet the strenuous legal effort went on. Just as on the slave ships it was necessary for white men to pour out great expenditures of time, energy, and money to keep the hidden black forces from springing into sight, so the white South remained constantly on its guard lest the rebellious black presence break out like fire, like flood, onto the decks of the society. So in Mississippi shortly after Turner's insurrection, this statute was enacted: "It is unlawful for any slave, free Negro, or mulatto to preach the gospel upon pain of receiving thirty-nine lashes upon the naked back of the . . . preacher."

But since when had lashes, even to the death, impeded the movement of the river? Before long, black people responded to the laws inspired by Nat Turner with an answer whites could hear without really understanding. Like so many black answers, it was disguised in a song:

> You might be Carroll from Carrollton
> Arrive here night afo' Lawd make creation
> But you can't keep the World from movering round
> And not turn her back from the gaining ground.

Only when that last ambiguous line was repeated again and again might it become clear that "not turn her" was old Prophet Nat in disguise, alive on the lips of his people, still on the gaining ground.

JAMES F. MACLEAR

"The True American Union" of Church and State

Professor James Fulton Maclear, in the article from which this selection is taken, views Protestant efforts as a "reconstruction of the theocratic tradition," which was the legacy of the American Puritans.

By the end of the 1780's . . . the ecclesiastical crisis of New England had become acute.[15] And in the next decade the appearance of the Republican party brought the church question to sharpest focus. Here the fusion of political radicals with dissenters was completed, the antitheocratic traditions made politically relevant, and disestablishment transformed from a visionary ideal into an imminent possibility. Jeffersonian

Baptists like John Leland expressed the new militancy: "The very idea of toleration is despicable. . . . All should be equally free, Jews, Turks, Pagans and Christians. . . . A general assessment (forcing all to pay some preacher) amounts to an establishment." Thus the stage was set for a final assault on the ancient New England ideal of a Christian republic. Could the Puritans' heirs so restate this ideal that it might again become relevant to the vision of an altered New England and to the wider American destiny to which New England had become committed?

* * *

"For several days I suffered what no tongue can tell *for the best thing that ever happened to the State of Connecticut.*" This often-quoted statement of Lyman Beecher suggests both the painfulness and the thoroughness of conservative readjustment, but not the eventual acceptance of the liberal philosophy of church-state separation, as has sometimes been said. Instead, the year after Connecticut disestablishment Beecher was lecturing civil magistrates on their duties to the church as if nothing had happened. This constancy to the old loyalties was general, even though the necessity of accepting legal separation was gradually being recognized. The sermon preached before the Connecticut legislature in 1823 by Nathaniel W. Taylor, Beecher's closest friend and late pastor of the Center Church, New Haven, was typical. "There were dangers and evils without the change, it is believed, greater than exist with it," was Taylor's unenthusiastic judgment. But he then went on to repeat most of the essentials of Dwight's argument:

> Why should not legislators, judges, magistrates of every description, with every friend of his country, uphold those institutions which are its strength and its glory? . . . Shall clamors about the rights of conscience induce us to throw away Heaven's richest legacy to earth? . . . But you will make men Christians. And what if we do? . . . But you will make sectarians. God forbid. We plead for no such influence. We only ask for those provisions of law, and that patronage from every member of the community in behalf of a common Christianity, which are its due as a nation's strength and a nation's glory.

The continuity displayed here was consciously promoted through later decades. Nowhere was there apology for New England's past. Seventeenth-century religious persecution was dismissed as a subordinate theme and the historic religious qualification for office justified as "a necessary measure, to prevent the ascendency of new adventurers, having different principles, who might, had they been allowed to vote, have destroyed the foundations on which all our invaluable institutions now rest." . . .

Yet disestablishment gravely affected the Puritan tradition. And as Beecher suggested, its effect was ultimately beneficial. . . . Specifically, what were the services of disestablishment to this revival of the theocratic tradition?

First, constitutional separation stimulated the completion of a radical reformulation of principles. The encumbrance of political alliances, emphasizing an older and now untenable theory of church-state relations and vitiating Congregational pretensions to denominational equalitarianism, was cast off. Accordingly, by 1823 Beecher had come to oppose any direct entanglement in the political process, though one of his reasons—that no party can "in a popular government, be sufficiently secure from change to render it safe"—indicated that his thinking on this issue was only partially reformed. Indeed, it was now not only possible but essential to explore new theoretical alternatives, for in the altered circumstances a convincing justification of theocracy depended on exploiting new departures.

Moreover, disestablishment now made it possible to disarm opposition by adopting the semblance of antitheocratic principles without actually embracing their meaning. For one thing, sectarian opposition was quieted by the apparent acceptance of voluntaryism. Congregationalism no longer made exclusive claims to christianize the entire community. Indeed, the Second Awakening, promoted by Dwight and his party at least partly to strengthen the Standing Order, had already restored the insistence on the "gathered church." With disestablishment, Congregationalism's last tie with the more churchly conception of its mission seemingly was gone. Similarly, the opposition from the American liberal tradition was undermined. For New England clergy now uniformly spoke the language of religious freedom and discoursed on the "deadly embrace" of state churches. . . . And yet, despite this apparent conversion, the essentials of underlying Puritan assumptions were maintained intact.

Lastly and perhaps most significantly for future American history, church-state separation emancipated the Puritan tradition from its purely local reference. At last the New England ecclesiastical situation was constitutionally identical with that in the remainder of the Union. Consequently, any reconstruction undertaken for New England would also apply to the rest of the United States. Leading Congregational writers were soon aware of this too. By the 1820's provincialism had been shed, and references were ordinarily being made to the general American scene. Hence the theocratic tradition was no longer on the defensive. Just as New England's political conservatism was changing from a moribund Federalism to the vigorous Whiggery of the 1840's so also the Puritan heritage was preparing to awaken as the gospel of the "true American union" of church and people—a gospel which was to flourish in the Puritan homeland and successfully invade other denominations and sections.

This further reformulation preserved every essential element of the Puritan concept of a Christian commonwealth. State support to a national religious faith which in turn would keep the United States a Christian nation, a government informed by the light of Christianity, the organic union and interdependence of church and state—all were maintained. Only such adjustments were made as were required by the new constitutional situation. What were these adjustments?

Public support for a national church was still considered essential, but both the national church and the character of support were differently conceived. Enlarging on the concept of comprehension developed earlier, writers now demanded state support to a church coextensive with the national community of Christians. In effect, the idea of a denominational grand alliance, so alarming to many Americans, was here being replaced by the more politically prudent concept of the church invisible in America. . . . In addition, the nature of the support which rulers were to bestow was different. This became clear in the 1830's when Channing ascribed political ambitions to the orthodox and Moses Stuart replied, admitting, "We do fully believe that no good government on earth can be long maintained" without piety, "but this is an influence of religion on government and a connection with it which are *indirect.*" Emphasis on indirection was now conventional in discussions of the subject. The day might be gone when governors could call synods, recommend creeds, and force attendance at public worship, but they were not thereby emancipated from duties to the gospel. "Our civil rulers owe to God and their country now, the same illustrious piety, the same estimation of the doctrines of God's Word, the same attendance upon the ordinances of the Gospel and co-operation for their support, and the same strict and pure morality, which rendered the civil Fathers of our land so illustrious."

As this has already suggested, the religious character of the state was also retained. Though not so closely identified with confessionalism as formerly, rulers were still to be visibly sympathetic with the Christian cause. "There are certain guarantees of integrity, and of security to the general interests of religion, which as Christians, we are bound to require," said Beecher. . . . Of magistracy, as distinct from particular magistrates, even more was required. Government was still founded on divine institution, not civil compact. It was still obliged to heed revelation. . . . The state's religious commitment even limited the freedom which it could legitimately offer. Moses Stuart thought that Jews, Mohammedans, pagans, and Deists might enjoy liberty in America, but not to the extent of showing contempt for Christians or blaspheming the Christian religion. Daniel Webster argued at law against the right of a Philadelphia philanthropist to establish a secular orphanage: "Christianity—general, tolerant Christianity—Christianity independent of sects and parties—that Christianity to which the sword and the fagot are unknown—general, tolerant Christianity is the law of the land!" Because of this adjustment to an indirect connection of church and state New England leaders felt that they had digested disestablishment without injury. . . .

But the work of reconstruction was not yet completed. It was necessary also to deal with that organic inter-relationship of church and state which Puritans had assumed and Dwight had made explicit as the state's dependence on morality and religion. Now a further dimension of relevance appeared. Specific emphasis was placed on the services of religion to republics and particularly to the American republic. Conceivably, Old World monarchies and despotisms might rule by force and terror, but a free republic depended solely upon mass moral restraint. Thus "there is no form of government better than our own for a virtuous community; and none worse for a vicious community." The problem was especially great since immigration and electoral reforms had placed government "within the reach of a perverted and profligate suffrage." Beecher in 1829 could not be optimistic, but he knew that in Christianity rested the only hope of saving the American experiment: "It is hard to elevate the mass, and harder to sustain it; and none but by the help of God and his institutions have been able to do it."

Throughout the decades leading to the Civil War this argument was repeated with variations for each of the perils confronting America. Was the United States becoming huger in territory and population with every passing year? Heman Humphrey's solution was "an immense moral power to control twenty, thirty, *fifty* millions of daring and enterprising republicans, spread over a vast territory." Did sectional passions raise the specter of coming storms and bloody conflict? Beecher's recourse was to "God's government and the institutions of Christianity" inculcating the intelligence and moral principle capable of maintaining national unity. Were increasingly bitter partisan battles destroying the fraternal bonds of republican unity? Bushnell cited Christianity as an integrating center, for "if we go to the same churches and tables of communion, receiving there the common principles and lessons of God's truth, and thence go forth to bless our country, as citizens . . . we may differ warmly and earnestly as to the mode, but we cannot be sundered into state factions." Lastly, were the American people moving apart in class and wealth? Was the republic threatened with bitter social division? Beecher admitted the situation: "There is pervading the entire class of relative poverty a strong feeling of dissatisfaction, as if they were injured, and as if the rich were the aggressors, and were revelling on the spoils which had been wrested from them." But he also knew where salvation lay. "Explosion and revolution" would never erupt, despite political radicals and universal suffrage, so long as Christianity fortified the mind and conscience. Thus the Christian gospel and its institutions were the real sustaining powers of American democracy. "On this influence depends our rise or fall—our glorious immortality or our hasty dissolution." It is not surprising that the result should have been that fusion of patriotism, republicanism, and religion which was noted by foreign visitors. Here, in this complex, the triumph of the theocratic element over its alienation from the American liberal faith was revealed. At the death of Jefferson Heman Humphrey complained of the tendency to call every American statesman a Christian, but he had himself contributed not a little to the blurring of the distinction.

To safeguard this invisible union of church and state, Beecher, it will be recalled, had experimented with techniques for re-establishing the church influence in politics, even before the collapse of the Standing Order in Connecticut. These techniques were now further developed. In a democracy, Taylor warned, public opinion is "absolutely paramount." According to Beecher, the contest for its control was already raging, "and by this generation, in the city and in country, it is to be decided whether an evangelical or a worldly influence shall prevail." Hence it was necessary for Christians to close ranks and face the task together. "Religious principle must be applied throughout the nation, and no *one* denomination *can* do it." Revivals must be encouraged and the suffrage exploited. Every freeman must "inquire concerning the candidate for whom he is solicited to vote—is he an enemy of the Bible, or the doctrines and institutions of the Gospel;—is he a duellist, or an intemperate man, or a sabbath-breaker or dissolute, or dishonest?" The ultimate goal was a "public opinion which shall accord with the morality of the Gospel."

To implement this purpose organization was needed. Therefore, coincident with the fall of the New England Establishments, an expansion of interdenominational voluntary societies was undertaken. The Connecticut Moral Society of 1812 was the beginning of many such foundations, spreading from New England to New York and the Middle West. These moral societies were seconded by organizations for allied purposes—tract societies, Bible societies, temperance societies, missionary societies, Sabbath School societies—all striving to extend "that influence which the law could no longer apply." Concerning the motivation behind such foundations, Beecher was candid: "These are the providential substitutes for those legal provisions of our fathers, which are now inapplicable by change of circumstances." By the 1830's the seriousness of such professions was being illustrated in effective political action. The General Union for Promoting the Observance of the Christian Sabbath had already launched a national campaign, deluging Congressmen with petitions against the carrying of the mails on Sundays, and in the next decade temperance societies were to begin winning public opinion to a program of legal action which secured its first striking victory in the Maine Prohibition Law. The re-establishment of the Christian interest in the politics of American democracy was taking place.

* * *

The idea of a Christian commonwealth was once again a force in American intellectual history. Toward the end of his life a melancholy John Leland looked back to note that the menace of religious oppression "in the old way" had been vanquished only to have it return with the increased strength of a "Christian Phalanx." "If my painful fears on this head are ever realized, the glory of America will depart—the blood and treasure expended in the revolution will all be lost." Though his understanding of the "new way" was confused, Leland did have a correct intuition of the restored vitality of the theocratic challenge. For these ideas now flourished outside the region and denomination where this rejuvenation had taken place.

Notes

1. Perry Miller suggests this broad interpretation in his chapter "From Covenant to Revival," in James W. Smith and Leland Jamison, eds., *The Shaping of Religion in America* (Princeton: Princeton University Press, 1961). He is particularly concerned in this chapter with the metamorphosis of the covenant concept that loomed so large in his interpretation of the "New England mind."

2. Cf. *Democracy in America,* vol. I (New York: Vintage, 1954), pp. 198 ff.

3. From Joseph Story, *Commentaries on the Constitution of the United States,* vol. III (Boston, 1833), pp. 722 ff.

4. From Lyman Beecher, *Autobiography, Correspondence, etc., of Lyman Beecher, D.D.*, ed. Charles Beecher, 2 vols. (New York, 1864). Selections are from vol. I, pp. 342–344 and pp. 452–453. (A new edition edited by Barbara M. Cross was published in 1961 by the Harvard University Press, Cambridge, Mass.)

5. Levy, Leonard W. "Satan's Last Apostle in Massachusetts." *American Quarterly* 5:1 (1953), 16–30. © The American Studies Association. Reprinted with permission of the Johns Hopkins University Press.

6. Voltaire had derided the idea of the Virgin Birth by suggesting the improbability of conception without the intervention of the male genitals [footnote by the editor, Leonard W. Levy].

7. *People v. Ruggles, Johnson's Reports* VIII NY 290 ff. (1811). The facts of this case differed from Kneeland's in that Ruggles had blasphemed beyond doubt, by calling Jesus Christ a "bastard" and Mary a "whore. . . " [footnote by the editor, Leonard W. Levy].

8. From Ezra Stiles Ely, *The Duty of Christian Freemen to Elect Christian Rulers* (Philadelphia, 1828), pp. 4–12.

9. From Lyman Beecher, *A Plea for the West,* 2nd ed. (Cincinnati, New York, 1835), pp. 42–87 (excerpts).

10. Report from the House Committee on the Post Office and Post Roads, 20th Congr., 2nd sess., 1828–1829, H. Report No. 65 (Feb. 3, 1829).

11. From *Public Documents,* printed by order of the Senate of the U.S., 20th Cong., 2nd sess., 1828–1829, no. 46, January 19, 1829, abridged.

12. From William E. Channing, *The Works of William E. Channing, D. D.* (Boston, 1878), pp. 138–149.

13. From A Protestant, *Protestant Jesuitism* (New York, 1836), pp. 107–112.

14. Excerpts from *There Is a River: The Black Struggle for Freedom In America,* copyright © 1981 by Vincent Harding, reprinted by permission of Harcourt, Inc.

15. From James Fulton Maclear, "The True American Union of Church and State: The Reconstruction of the Theocratic Tradition," *Church History* 28 (1959): 41–62. Reprinted with permission from the American Society of Church History.

5

The Recognition of American Pluralism (1860–1920)

While the evangelical forces had labored to realize their "true American Union of Church and State," vast changes had been taking place within American society. Large contingents of hitherto unrepresented ethnic groups—frequently locating their identities through their Roman Catholic or Jewish religious practices—were arriving year after year. The frontier was relentlessly conquered, and urban areas were developing concurrently. Inventions and investments transformed the American economy and with it American society. Also a fratricidal conflict disclosed deep conflicts within the United States. Thus, although the Protestant revivalistic endeavors continued and the united front activities proceeded, the premise on which they had originated did not have continuing validity. The United States was no longer overwhelmingly Protestant. It was ceasing to be in large part rural. It would never again have the potential to be a Christian Republic—the vision that had inspired the evangelical efforts. Thus the years between the Civil War and World War I represent a period of transition in some ways analogous to the first half of the eighteenth century—at least when viewed in the perspective of church and state. The responses of Protestantism during these years to the changes in American society were manifold, and no such nearly universal consensus as republican Protestantism began to develop. In this section our concern is primarily with the kinds of tension between the religiously plural society coming into existence and the older paradigms of church-state relations—especially republican Protestantism but also continental Roman Catholicism—which did not readily comprehend either the situation of post–Civil War America or the legacy of the Constitutional epoch.

Understandably an early and continuing issue was built into the development of the public school systems. Usually, in the East at least, the common schools were direct outgrowths of schools that had originated under religious auspices, and their conventions as well as their curriculum—both Protestant in character—were bitterly resented by "foreigners" and especially "Catholic foreigners." Although, for instance, the Massachusetts public schools were allegedly purged of sectarian practices well before the Civil War, and these reforms influenced other systems, the issue continued to trouble the common life—even as it does today. One of the better-known conflicts—representing many more—occurred in Cincinnati, Ohio, during the early 1870s. The local school board had been responsive to pressures for making the schools less overtly Protestant in the experience of Roman Catholic children. Specifically at issue was the reading of a Protestant version of the Bible as an opening exercise. Although the lower court upheld the traditional practice that the school board had modified, the State Supreme Court reversed that decision and reaffirmed the board's action. This incident—or ones substantially identical—occurred frequently as the burden of religious pluralism became a reality in the common life. That it took such issues to recall the Jeffersonian and Madisonian ideal indicates how successful the evangelical Protestants had been in establishing their own conception of the relationship between religious and civil authority structures.

Generally the Roman Catholic Church found it quite possible to be reconciled to an independence of church and state as it grew in numbers and power. Some American Roman Catholics became such partisans of the American circumstances that their orthodoxy was suspect in Europe. The Vatican actually went so far as to warn the faithful about the errors of "Americanism." European Roman Catholics, for whom separation of church and state meant facing a hostile state and perhaps even civil penalties, were understandably uneasy about the enthusiasm of their coreligionists across the Atlantic for the pattern in which the two authority structures were disengaged—also known as a "separation." By contrast to the actual—if not ideological—acceptance of the American pattern on the part of Roman Catholics, the Protestant response often took the form of a strident reaffirmation of the evangelical dream of a Protestant America. Whether expressed in the scurrilous literature surveyed by Washington Gladden or embodied in the more sophisticated tract of Josiah Strong, Protestant Americanism could not easily accept that substantive independence of church and state as the prerequisite to the life of a religiously plural community. In this perspective the prohibition era of the 1920s was a last major victory for that anachronistic Protestant mentality.

Despite the tensions in the common life during this period church and state were not directly linked, as the estimates of Lord Bryce, Thomas Cooley, and Philip Schaff all indicate. Along with the growing perception of the burden went recognition of that formal framework for a religiously plural community that was becoming a reality. In the years since World War I this framework has been articulated, or, to change the figure, the rules of the game have been under discussion.

The Public Schools as Divisive

JUDGE STORER

The Bible in the Common Schools

From their organization in 1829 the common schools of Cincinnati had opening exercises in which teachers or "scholars" read parts of the "Holy Scriptures." In 1842 it was provided that a pupil might be excused from reading the "Protestant

Testament and Bible" if his parents or guardians wished it. By 1852 it was decided that, at the desire of their parents, pupils might read from the version of their preference. Finally in 1869 a majority of the Board of Education resolved to exclude religious instruction and the reading of religious books and to terminate Bible reading at the opening exercises. The minority of the Board protested the decision, and the issue went to the Superior Court of Cincinnati where Judge Storer rendered the decision of a two-to-one court—an injunction against the majority's resolutions.

Separated . . . from the mass of irrelevant matter in which the question before us has been involved by the learning and the industry of the counsel who have addressed us, if we regard the different standpoints from which they have argued, the propositions to be solved are simply these: Had the defendants, in the exercise of the discretion given them to direct the course of study and decide upon the text books to be used, the legal right to declare the Bible should no longer be read in the schools, where for nearly half a century it had been used as the daily exercise, and, coupled with its exclusion, the denial of all religious instruction and the reading of religious books shall be prohibited.[1]

If no such power existed, may we not adjudge the board has acted *"ultra vires,"* and their resolutions are void. What, then, does our present Constitution prescribe. By sec. 7, art. 1, it is ordained that "Religion, morality and knowledge being essential to good government, it shall be the duty of the General Assembly to pass suitable laws to protect all religious denominations in the peaceable enjoyment of their own mode of public worship, and to encourage schools and the means of instruction." The section commences with the assertion that "all men have a natural and indefeasible right to worship Almighty God according to the dictates of their own conscience. No persons shall be compelled to, erect or support any place of worship, or maintain any form of worship, and no preference shall be given by law to any religious society, nor shall any interference with the rights of conscience be permitted." This may be said to be a literal transcript of sec. 3, art. 8, of the Constitution of 1802, and that in substance is borrowed from art. 3 of the Ordinance of 1787. These are the affirmations of a great truth, and to vindicate which we believe they were inserted in our organic law.

They recognize the existence of a Supreme Being, and the fact is judicially admitted that religion, as well as morality and knowledge, are essential to good government, and consequently, make it imperative that schools and the means of education shall be regulated by the Legislature.

Now it will be admitted that no preference can be given to religious sects, as such, as difference of opinion upon religious subjects is not only tolerated, but the right to enjoy it is given to its fullest extent. There is a manifest distinction, however, between religion and religious denominations, as they present all shades of theoretic as well as practical belief. Hence it is we may recur to the clause so prominently presented in the section of our Bill of Rights that secures to all the worship of Almighty God, as the exponent of what we may rationally conclude the founders of the Constitution intended by the general term religion. . . .

The whole argument that seems to us reaches the real question before us is predicated upon the supposition that the Bible is a volume whose teachings lead to sectarianism, and which ought not, therefore, to remain in the schools.

We do not admit the assertion, either in whole or in part. What we understand by sectarianism is the work of man, not of the Almighty. We are taught in the Scriptures that we are all the children of a common Parent, who is our Father and our Friend, that we are all of the same blood, a common unity pervading the race. Such, however, is not the human lesson. Learned men are not satisfied with the plain statement of revelation. They have divided the human family into distinct parts, giving to each a separate origin. We learn from the Bible to forgive injuries, to deal justly, to elevate our conceptions above the objects that surround us, and feel we were born to be immortal. Not so are we thoroughly taught by the profoundest system of human philosophy.

A volume that unfolds the origin of men, the beginning of time, and the assurance of an eternity when the present dispensation shall end, can not, upon any rational principle, be said to indicate religious exclusiveness. It has, we admit, seen its dark days, and has contended with bitter foes, yet it has suffered as much, if it could suffer at all, from the mistaken zeal, or the dogmatism and intolerance, of its professed friends. . . .

We marvel not that the mixtures and devices of men have obscured revelation when scarcely a week passes by without the annunciation of some new annotation or analysis, or the defence of some peculiar dogma.

All these, we admit, tend to the same result, which is necessarily a devotion to a sect. But we can not admit that the Bible necessarily induces any such consequences.

If it is candidly examined, studied without preconceived prejudice, its truths admitted to the test of enlightened conscience, we doubt not the answer always will be as it ever has been, the acknowledgement of its sacred character, and a veneration for its truthfulness.

It is urged, however, that the conscience of the Catholic parent can not permit the ordinary version to be read as an exercise, as no religious teaching is permitted by his church, unless it is directed by the clergy or authorized by the church itself, and it is, therefore, offensive to the moral sense of those who are compelled to listen when any portion of the Bible is read; but the rule has long since been abolished requiring children to be present, or to read from the version now in use, if it should be the expressed wish of the parents first communicated to the teachers.

The reason of the objection, then, would seem to have ceased. More than this, it is in evidence before us that our Catholic friends have their own separate schools, and very few of their children attend the common schools, while in one of these schools the Douay translation of the Bible is read as a daily exercise.

But is it consistent with this claim of counsel that, even if the Bible should be prohibited, Catholic children would not attend the common schools, unless subject to the teachings of their spiritual guides? The schools have been denominated godless, while the Scriptures are yet read as a daily exercise. What must they become, and what will they be termed, when the Scriptures are forbidden?

What appears to us to underlie this view of the case, is the alleged injustice that Catholic parents, in common with other property-holders, should be taxed for the support of schools that are independent of the control of the Church, and consequently, opposed to its whole economy.

This has been pressed in argument, though no one of the counsel for the plaintiffs or defendants have intimated there should be a division of the school fund. With the justice or injustice, therefore, of the mode of taxation, we have nothing to do in deciding the questions submitted to us. If the point should ever arise, we trust we shall attentively consider all the objections that may be raised to the present organization of the schools; but it furnishes no ground of argument against the reading of the Bible that the taxes for the support of the schools are not equally assessed or properly distributed. We can not believe that any portion of the community, either from prejudice or the belief of wrong done, when the judicial tribunals are open, and their complaints may be heard, would imitate the strong man of old by laying their hands upon the pillars which support the temple, when the inevitable result would be a common ruin.

We therefore conclude upon this branch of the case, that the premises upon which the whole argument of the defendants depends as to the rights of conscience being violated, have been assumed, and not proved to exist. On the other hand, we may well suppose the consciences of the many thousands who protest against the resolutions of the Board of Education, if any wrong may have been done, have equal cause to complain.

Nor do we think that the mere reading of the Scriptures without note or comment, and in detached sentences, can be deemed an act of worship, in its commonly received definition. The lessons selected are, in all probability, those which elevate the mind and soften the heart—an exercise not only proper, but desirable to calm the temper of children, while it impresses the truth of personal responsibility for good or evil conduct. It furnishes a perfect standard of moral rectitude not to be found elsewhere, which is immutable as it is authoritative. No prayer is required of the teacher or the scholar, though the simple and beautiful *pater noster* would not, we believe, be out of place.

If, then, "no religious test," to use the language of the Bill of Rights, is required of teacher or scholar, if no act of worship, in a sectarian sense, is performed, if no sectarian or denominational teaching is introduced, and even the possibility of either is prevented by the resolution long since promulgated, that those who desire it may be exempted from the general rule, we can not see how the defendants can justify the exclusion from the schools of what has been permitted there for nearly half a century without rebuke. It can not be that a new revelation has been received by the Board of Education of what is their responsibility to the public, or that they, as a body, have become wiser, better informed, or have a clearer perception of moral duty than their predecessors, for these suppositions were not made, much less suggested, and we are consequently led to believe that there has been hasty, unnecessary and unauthorized legislation, neither demanded by the state of fact upon which that legislation is said to be based, nor yet the wish of those whose sons and daughters have heretofore been or are now being educated in the public schools.

On the whole case we are satisfied that we have complete jurisdiction of the subject before us, and of the parties; that the matters alleged by the plaintiffs and admitted by the defendants present just and equitable grounds for our interference. We so decide, because we are satisfied that the powers conferred on the defendants have been transcended; that the resolutions prohibiting the Bible and all religious instruction are *ultra vires,* and therefore void.

We have not referred to any adjudicated case, as those quoted by one of our colleagues fully justify us. We stand upon the admitted principle, as true in law as in equity, that the unauthorized acts of a corporate body or trustees, whose powers are prescribed by law, may be restrained. While we hold that every form of religious worship is to be alike protected by law, and the conscience of every man can not be questioned; while the broad shield of the Constitution is over all our citizens, without distinction of race or sect, we can not ignore the right of the petitioners to the relief they have sought, nor can we, with our views of legal duty, sustain the action of the defendants.

A majority of the Court are of this opinion, and a perpetual injunction will be therefore decreed, as prayed for in the petition.

JUDGE WELCH

The Bible in the Public Schools

The judgment of the Superior Court was appealed, and the Supreme Court of Ohio reversed the decision: The original petition was dismissed, and the majority of the Board was upheld.

The arguments in this case have taken a wide range, and counsel have elaborately discussed questions of state policy, morality, and religion, which, in our judgment, do not belong to the case.[2] We are not called upon as a court, nor are we authorized to say whether the Christian religion is the best and only true religion. There is no question before us of the wisdom or unwisdom of having "the Bible in the schools," or of withdrawing it therefrom. Nor can we, without usurping legislative functions, undertake to decide what religious doctrines, if any, ought to be taught, or where, when, by whom, or to whom it would be best they should be taught. These are questions which belong to the people and to other departments of the government.

The case, as we view it, presents merely or mainly a question of the courts' rightful authority to interfere in the management and control of the public schools of the state. In other words, the real question is, has the court jurisdiction to interfere in the management and control of such schools, to the extent of enforcing religious instructions, or the reading of religious books therein?

There is a total absence . . . of any legislation looking to the enforcement of religious instruction, or the reading of religious books in the public schools; and we are brought back to the question, what is the true meaning and effect of these constitutional provisions on this subject? Do they enjoin religious instructions in the schools? and does this injunction bind the courts, in the absence of legislation? We are unanimous in the opinion that both these questions must be answered in the negative.

The truth is that these are matters left to legislative discretion, subject to the limitations on legislative power, regarding religious freedom, contained in the bill of rights; and subject also to the injunction that laws shall be passed, such as in the judgment of the legislature are "suitable" to encourage general means of instruction, including, among other means, a system of common schools.

Equally plain is it to us, that if the supposed injunction to provide for religious instructions is to be found in the clauses of the constitution in question, it is one that rests exclusively upon the legislature. In both sections the duty is expressly imposed upon the "general assembly." The injunction is, to "pass suitable laws." Until these "laws" are passed, it is quite clear to us that the courts have no power to interpose. The courts can only execute the laws when passed. They can not compel the general assembly to pass them.

This opinion might well end here. Were the subject of controversy any other branch of instructions in the schools than religion, I have no doubt it might safely end here, and the unanimous opinion of the court thus rendered be satisfactory to all. The case is of peculiar importance, however, in the fact that it touches our religious convictions and prejudices, and threatens to disturb the harmonious working of the state government, and particularly of the public schools of the state. I deem it not improper, therefore, to consider briefly some of the points and matters so ably and elaborately argued by counsel, although really lying outside of the case proper, or only bearing on it remotely.

The real claim here is, that by "religion," in this clause of the constitution, is meant "Christian religion," and that by "religious denomination" in the same clause is meant "Christian denomination." If this claim is well founded, I do not see how we can consistently avoid giving a like meaning to the same words and their cognates, "worship," "religious society," "sect," "conscience," "religious belief," throughout the entire section. To do so, it will readily be seen, would be to withdraw from every person not of Christian belief the guaranties therein vouchsafed, and to withdraw many of them from Christians themselves. . . .

If, by this generic word "religion," was really meant "the Christian religion," or "Bible religion," why was it not plainly so written? Surely the subject was of importance enough to justify the pains, and surely it was of interest enough to exclude the supposition that it was written in haste, or thoughtlessly slurred over. At the time of adopting our present constitution, this word "religion" had had a place in our old constitution for half a century, which was surely ample time for studying its meaning and effect, in order to make the necessary correction or alteration, so as to render its true meaning definite and certain. The same word "religion," and in much the same connection, is found in the constitution of the United States. The latter constitution, at least, if not our own also, in a sense, speaks to *mankind,* and speaks of the rights of *man.* Neither the word "Christianity," "Christian," nor "Bible," is to be found in either. When they speak of "religion," they must mean the religion of man, and not the religion of any *class* of men. When they speak of "all men" having certain rights, they can not mean merely "all Christian men." Some of the very men who helped to frame these constitutions were themselves not Christian men.

We are told that this word "religion" must mean "Christian religion," because "Christianity is a part of the common law of this country," lying behind and above its constitutions. Those who make this assertion can hardly be serious, and intend the real import of their language. If Christianity is a *law* of the state, like every other law, it must have a *sanction.* Adequate penalties must be provided to enforce obedience to all its requirements and precepts. No one seriously contends for any such doctrine in this country, or, I might almost say, in this age of the world. The only foundation—

rather, the only excuse—for the proposition, that Christianity is part of the law of this country, is the fact that it is a Christian country, and that its constitutions and laws are made by a Christian people. And is not the very fact that those laws do *not* attempt to *enforce* Christianity, or to place it upon exceptional or vantage ground, itself a strong evidence that they *are* the laws of a Christian people, and that their religion is the best and purest of religions? It is strong evidence that their religion is indeed a religion "without partiality," and *therefore* a religion "without hypocrisy." True Christianity asks no aid from the sword of civil authority. It began without the sword, and wherever it has taken the sword it has perished by the sword. . . .

But it will be asked, how can religion, in this general sense, be essential to good government? Is atheism, is the religion of Buddha, of Zoroaster, of Lao-tse, conducive to good government? Does not the best government require the best religion? Certainly the best government requires the best religion. It is the child of true religion, or of truth on the subject of religion, as well as on all other subjects. But the real question here is, not what is the best religion, but how shall this best religion be secured? I answer, it can best be secured by adopting the doctrine of this 7th section in our own bill of rights, and which I summarize in two words, by calling it the doctrine of "hands off." Let the state not only keep its own hands off, but let it also see to it that religious sects keep their hands off each other. Let religious doctrines have a fair field, and a free, intellectual, moral, and spiritual conflict. The weakest—that is, the intellectually, morally, and spiritually weakest—will go to the wall, and the best will triumph in the end. This is the golden truth which it has taken the world eighteen centuries to learn, and which has at last solved the terrible enigma of "church and state." Among the many forms of stating this truth, as a principle of government, to my mind it is nowhere more fairly and beautifully set forth than in our own constitution. Were it in my power, I would not alter a syllable of the form in which it is there put down. It is the true republican doctrine. It is simple and easily understood. It means a free conflict of opinions as to things divine; and it means masterly inactivity on the part of the state, except for the purpose of keeping the conflict free, and preventing the violation of private rights or of the public peace. Meantime, the state will impartially aid all parties in their struggles after religious truth, by providing means for the increase of general knowledge, which is the handmaid of good government, as well as of true religion and morality. It means that a man's right to his own religious convictions, and to impart them to his own children, and his and their right to engage, in conformity thereto, in harmless acts of worship toward the Almighty, are as sacred in the eye of the law as his rights of person or property, and that although in the minority, he shall be protected in the full and unrestricted enjoyment thereof. The "protection" guaranteed by the section in question, means protection to the minority. The majority can protect itself. Constitutions are enacted for the very purpose of protecting the weak against the strong; the few against the many.

* * *

It follows that the judgment of the Superior Court will be reversed, and the original petition dismissed.

Judgment accordingly.

SAMUEL T. SPEAR

Religion and the State

Samuel T. Spear was an Episcopalian clergyman in Brooklyn, N.Y. His book *Religion and the State* (1876) was first published as a series of articles in the *Independent.* They arose out of what he called "the much debated school question" and were intended to contribute "some help to the public mind in arriving at [its] true solution."

The direct and immediate issue before the American people is not the general question of Church and State, but the specific question of Bible reading and religious instruction and worship in our public schools.[3] This question is merely a branch of the larger one that relates to the attitude which civil government should assume and maintain with reference to religion. All the general principles that are applicable to the latter are equally so to the former.

The conclusion reached from the survey of the more extended field is that civil government, as such, should have nothing to do with the work of administering, sustaining, or teaching religion, and that on this subject its only legitimate function consists in affording an impartial protection to all the people in the exercise of their religious liberty, while so limiting this exercise as to make it compatible with the peace and good order of civil society. It has taken the world a long time to discover and embody this elementary truth; and even now the discovery and embodiment are limited to a small portion of the race. It is practically an unknown truth to the greater part of mankind.

The acceptance of this general doctrine in regard to the province of civil government settles the School question and all other questions that come within the range of its application. The public school, as an institution of the State, exists and is regulated by its authority, and is, moreover, supported by compulsory taxation. To prescribe for it a religious system to be taught therein, or forms of worship to be there observed, is to determine by the authority of the State what the system or forms of worship shall be, and then to compel the people to pay the expenses thereof. Such a coerced support of religion is equivalent to a State religion in the public school, and that, too, whether the religion and the worship accord with the views and wishes of the majority or not.

All this and much more would be very proper, provided the administration or teaching of religion comes within the rightful province of civil government. But, if this province be simply that of impartial protection, and not at all that of administration or teaching, then besides being highly improper, it is a trespass upon the rights and religious liberty of the people. It is such because it compels them by law to do what should be left to their own discretion. It is especially such in a country where there is great diversity in the religious faith of the people. A school system in which a specific form of religion shall be taught or practiced at the public expense, is among such a people unjust to all who dissent from that religion, but are, nevertheless, compelled to contribute to its support. It puts civil government in a false attitude. It invests it with a function that does not belong to it. On this generic ground we believe it both impolitic and wrong to employ our public school system as the means of propagating any form of religion.

We have in this country a system of *secular* governments, established by the authority of the people for secular and not for religious purposes, which, when coming in contact with religion, are planned to afford protection to the people in the peaceable exercise and enjoyment of their religion, but not to regulate, support, or teach that religion, or to make any discriminations on religious grounds. The Constitution of the United States, so far as applicable to the subject at all, is constructed on this general principle; and the same is for the most part true of the constitutions of the several States.

Any divergence from this great principle, as is the fact in some of the State constitutions, is merely exceptional to the general spirit and purpose of our governmental system. A religious test as a qualification to hold office, or to perform any political or civil duty, or to enjoy any political or civil right, is such an exception. In two of the States the power of taxation for the support of religion is granted by their constitutions; yet this, too, is an exception. So, also, in most of the States religious corporations are exempted from taxation; yet this, while an inconsistency surviving by the force of habit and usage after the theory which gave it birth is dead, is not based on religious grounds. Notwithstanding the exceptions that mar the absolute unity and harmony of the system, considered in relation to religion, it is, nevertheless, true that the system, taken as a whole, disclaims all jurisdiction over religion, all right to discriminate among the people for religious reasons, and all right to impose any tax burdens for the support or propagation of religion. We express this general fact by the oft-repeated declaration that in this country we have no union between Church and State. One need but to study its fundamental laws to see this truth.

The proper solution of the School question. That solution is clearly the one which grows out of and accords with the fundamental principles of our national and State organization. We can accept no other, and put no other into practice, without contradicting these principles. The Puritan public school, with the religious catechism and the Bible in it—which was once the public school of New England as New England then was—does not conform to the standard furnished by the American doctrine of civil government. It gave preference to a religious sect, and at the public expense inculcated the special ideas of that sect; and this is plainly contrary to the doctrine.

The same objection applies with equal force to the Protestant public school, in which King James's version of the Sacred Scriptures and religious exercises, Protestant in their type and tendency, are incorporated into its educational system. The Catholic, the Jew, the Infidel, and, indeed, all who dissent from Protestantism, being citizens in common with Protestants and having precisely the same rights, complain of the injustice done to them in taxing them for the support of such a school. Their complaint is a valid one. We do not see how it is possible to answer it without ignoring the cardinal principles upon which our national and State life is founded. The same method of reasoning is equally applicable to a Catholic public school, a Jewish public school, or any public school which is made the organ of religious instruction or worship in any form.

The fatal difficulty with all such schools consists in the fact that, while they assign to civil government functions that do not belong to it, they come into direct collision with the American doctrine as to the nature and scope of its functions. They make the

State a religious teacher at the public expense, and this is just what it cannot be in consistency with its own doctrine. Shall, then, the doctrine, when applied to popular education, be abandoned as false, or shall our public school system be adjusted to it? Shall all religious and all anti-religious sects be placed on a common ground in the full and impartial enjoyment of their citizen-rights, with no discrimination against or in favor of any class? Shall the public school be the *common* school of the people, of *all* the people, and *for* all the people, and in this respect be like the government that authorizes it, and taxes the people for its support? Shall it, by a wise and just omission, remit the subject of religion in all the forms of the idea, and in all the processes of its propagation, to other agencies, neither controlled nor supported by the State, but left entirely free at their own charges to consult their own pleasure?

. . . The true answer to these questions is this:—THE PUBLIC SCHOOL, LIKE THE STATE, UNDER WHOSE AUTHORITY IT EXISTS, AND BY WHOSE TAXING POWER IT IS SUPPORTED, SHOULD BE SIMPLY A CIVIL INSTITUTION, ABSOLUTELY SECULAR AND NOT AT ALL RELIGIOUS IN ITS PURPOSES, AND ALL PRACTICAL QUESTIONS INVOLVING THIS PRINCIPLE SHOULD BE SETTLED IN ACCORDANCE THEREWITH.

Protestants who, as Protestants, fight Catholics and seek to resist their demands in respect to the public school, are handling very dangerous weapons, though many of them do not seem to know it. They conduct the war upon a principle which may at any time be turned against themselves.

The true ground, whether for attack or defense, is the one that places the Protestant and the Catholic on an equal footing; and the moment the former takes this position, the whole power of our system of government at once comes to his support. The position is impregnable; and taking it, the Protestant is sure of a victory, not as a Protestant, but as a citizen. He concedes to the Catholic all his rights and simply claims his own. He demands for himself no more than he is willing to grant to others. This position is a strong one, because it is just and because it exactly accords with the letter and spirit of our civil constitutions.

"Americanism," Protestant and Catholic

WASHINGTON GLADDEN

The Anti-Catholic Crusade

Washington Gladden was a Congregational clergyman in Columbus, Ohio, from 1882 until his death in 1918. He is best known for his social Christianity, or his concern to make Christianity relevant to the common life. This assessment of anti–Roman Catholic agitation in the American Protective Association (APA) indicates the author's liberal sympathies no less than it reports on the bias against Rome, which was so deep-seated in American Protestantism. This sort of agitation, among other things, was one expression of Protestant frustration in an America that was becoming so religiously plural.

The year of the Parliament of Religions witnessed a most discouraging outbreak of religious rancor in the United States.[4] It is the ancient feud of Protestant and Romanist, and the new form which it has taken is worse than the old Know-nothingism. The animus of that party was ostensibly its opposition to foreigners; the present movement is directed solely against Roman Catholics.

The time seems inopportune for such an outbreak. The occupant of the papal throne is perhaps the most enlightened and the most progressive pontiff who has ever occupied that throne: the whole policy of the Church under his administration has been tending toward a reconciliation with modern civilization, thus in effect reversing the tendencies of the preceding reign; the right of the people to govern themselves under republican forms has been distinctly affirmed by Pope Leo XIII.; his deliverances upon the social question have manifested a large intelligence and quick human sympathy; and we are told by those who ought to know that the Pope is not alone in this liberalism—that he is heartily supported by the whole Curia, and by public sentiment at Rome. This is the administration which the anti-Catholic zealots have chosen to attack; it is in the presence of these hopeful movements of the Roman ecclesiasticism that they are seeking to uncover the smoldering embers of religious animosity.

Several secret orders are taking part in this crusade. Just now they are very strong in Ohio and in Michigan, and in all the States farther West. I learn that many of the local governments in eastern Michigan are in their possession; in some portions of Ohio they have been able to control municipal elections. In my own county, at the last election, every man but one upon the county ticket of one of the parties was reputed to be a member of one of these orders. It was also said, during the campaign, that a large proportion of the legislative candidates of one of the parties belonged to this order.

The methods employed by these orders in gathering their adherents seem to be tolerably uniform. The campaign opens with the furtive circulation of certain documents. . . .

When the ground has been well prepared by the dissemination of such dreadful documents and such harrowing tales, the work of organization proceeds. The meeting-places of these orders are intended to be secret; all their operations are carried on in the most stealthy manner. It will be readily seen, however, that a class of persons who could accept as genuine the documents which I have described would not be likely to preserve such secrets, and the existence and the main purpose of these orders speedily transpire.

Chief among these anti-Catholic secret orders is the American Protective Association, better known by its initials. The platform of principles which this order publishes in the newspapers sounds well; most platforms do. It is not, however, always easy to find in its platform the animus of a political party; much less safe is it to accept those statements of its designs which a secret political society publishes in the newspapers. If its real purposes could be published in the newspapers, there would appear to be no reason for secrecy.

The platform of the A. P. A. makes these declarations:

> We attack no man's religion so long as he does not attempt to make his religion an element of politicial power.
>
> We are in favor of preserving constitutional liberty and maintaining the government of the United States.
>
> We regard all religio-political organizations as the enemies of civil and religious liberty.

This is the exoteric doctrine. The esoteric differs widely, as may be seen by comparing these statements with the oath taken at their initiation by all members of the order. This oath has been published in several places, having been derived, apparently, from independent sources. Some verbal differences appear in these versions, but their substantial identity is conclusive evidence of their essential genuineness. The cardinal obligations of this oath are two: (1) A promise never to favor or aid the nomination, election, or appointment of a Roman Catholic to any political office. (2) A promise never to employ a Roman Catholic in any capacity if the services of a Protestant can be obtained. The evidence that the oath of the order contains these two obligations is abundant and conclusive. Sane and reputable men, members of the order, in controversy with me upon the subject, have acknowledged this; and the challenge to men of known veracity to come forward and deny it has not been accepted. If the oath is not substantially as published, such a denial would violate no obligation.

In the light of this oath, which every member of the A. P. A. takes with his hand upon his heart, we must interpret those outgivings printed in the newspapers. When he says that he attacks no man's religion so long as he does not intrude it into politics, we explain his saying as well as we can, in view of his oath that he will not employ a Roman Catholic in any capacity if he can obtain the services of a Protestant, and that he will never countenance or aid the nomination, election, or appointment to public office by any Roman Catholic. Not a word is said in this oath about any distinction between Roman Catholics who attempt to make their religion an element of political power and Roman Catholics who do not; Roman Catholics, as such, are sweepingly proscribed. And when the champion of this order tells us in the newspapers that he is "in favor of preserving constitutional liberty," we must bear in mind that he has sworn to violate the first principle of American constitutional liberty, which forbids discrimination against men on account of their religious belief. The Constitution of the United States declares that "no religious test shall ever be required as a qualification to any office or public trust under the United States." All the State constitutions embody the same principle. The oath of the A. P. A. binds its members to apply a religious test to every candidate for office—to give political office to none but Protestants. This is what they mean when they say that they are "in favor of preserving constitutional liberty."

What may be done by secret conclaves of men, bound together by such an oath as this, meeting at night in concealed places, and carefully hiding all their operations from the public eye, any man is at liberty to conjecture. It is evident that these assemblies will be hotbeds of malicious rumor. The men who have accepted as genuine the "Instructions to Catholics" and the pseudo-encyclical are prepared to believe anything. The most preposterous lies can be started in these conclaves, for there is no one there to challenge them; and thence they can pass from mouth to mouth until they have filled the whole community with their malarious influence. A system of espionage falls in with this scheme, and spies are detailed to attend Catholic churches to watch the priests and the bishops, and to dog the footsteps of those who are supposed to be friendly to the Roman Catholics. Suspicions and fears are thus plentifully engendered, and many communities have been filled with terror. . . .

The people of . . . rural neighborhoods are told the most lurid tales of what is going on in the cities. My correspondent had heard that a year ago all the public-school teachers in Columbus were Roman Catholics; the fact was that out of 349 teachers not more than 12 were Roman Catholics. The most blood-curdling reports had also reached that hamlet of the preparations for war which the Catholics in Columbus were making. Thus the secret propaganda is able to work very effectively in the rural districts. A large proportion of these councils are found in country places.

But credulity is not confined to the country. A minister of the gospel in Columbus told me that *all* our county officers were Roman Catholics, and that 95 per cent. of the police of our city were Catholics. The fact was that at that time 5 out of 20 county officials were of that faith, and 45 out of 112 policemen.

That in this year of grace a secret political society, built on such foundations of forgery, and bound together with such an oath, should be sweeping over the land like the Russian epidemic, is certainly a fact for patriots and Christians to ponder. The depth and density of that popular ignorance which permits the use of such documents as I have cited is certainly appalling.

The silence of the pulpit in many instances is explained by the fact that members of the church are members of the order, and the pastor is unwilling to alienate any of his supporters. There are few churches, I suppose, in the Western cities in which members of this order are not found. But a more influential reason for this silence is a feeling which is shared by the great majority of Protestant ministers, that Roman Catholics, as such, are a very dangerous class of persons, and that any kind of opposition to them is therefore to be welcomed. The extermination or repression of the Roman Catholic Church seems to these pious men a desirable end, and they are therefore inclined to argue that any means to that end are justifiable.

The political proscription of Roman Catholics which the oath requires is justified on the plea that Roman Catholics are not and cannot be loyal Americans; that their doctrine of the papal supremacy puts them completely under the power of a foreign potentate. Roman Catholic scholars dispute this interpretation of their allegiance, and insist that they owe no obedience to the Pope which can interfere with their duty to their country. I will not argue this question. Let us admit for the sake of the argument that the logic of the papal theory would require the Roman Catholic to disobey, at the Pope's command, the laws of his country. But is it true that we all follow our theories to their logical results? The logic of his doctrine requires every Presbyterian to believe in infant damnation; do Presbyterians generally believe in infant damnation? The logic of his theory requires the Baptist to unchurch all other Christians. Does the Baptist follow his logic? "That good dose of inconsistency which," as Cousin says, "common sense often prescribes for philosophy" is all that saves a good many of us from being fanatics or fools. That good dose of inconsistency has been well shaken and taken by millions of Roman Catholics. They are not really any more consistent than the rest of us, and the attempt to include them in the condemnation of alienism and treason is not a sane procedure. Roman Catholics have proved their loyalty to this nation on many a bloody battle-field; and those who imagine that the Pope's orders always find them tame, spiritless subjects of his will should read of his attempted interference with the recent "Plan of Campaign" in Ireland.

The relation of the oath of this order to the oath of office taken by all high officials under our Government demands consideration. It is evident that the contradiction between the two is absolute. The oath of office promises obedience to the constitution of the State and of the nation, and these constitutions forbid any distinction or preference among men on account of their religious belief. The oath of the order binds a man to make precisely these distinctions. . . .

That the prevalence of this insanity will be brief is certain; but it may spread widely enough and last long enough to do incalculable mischief. May I not venture to call upon all intelligent Protestants, and especially upon Protestant clergymen, to consider well their responsibilities in relation to this epidemic? Can we afford, as Protestants, to approve, by our silence, such methods of warfare against Roman Catholics as this society is employing? For the honor of Protestantism, is it not high time to separate ourselves from this class of "patriots?" In any large town, if the leading Protestant clergymen will speak out clearly, the plague will be stayed or abated.

JOSIAH STRONG

America the Embodiment of Christian Anglo-Saxon Civilization

Josiah Strong (d. 1916) was a Congregational minister and agent throughout the middle West until, with the publication of *Our Country* (1885), he became an author with a national following. In one sense he should be seen as trying to rally a new Protestant evangelical alliance that would do for the last years of the nineteenth and the first years of the twentieth centuries what the "evangelical united front" had done in the National period. But it was a program in the mode of its own time reflecting social Darwinism and suggestive of John Fiske. This vision indicates no less than the APA how deep Protestant frustrations ran, and how incapable the broad movement had become of comprehending the church-state, or dual–authority structure, problem in American society. Republican Protestantism so dominated the Protestant past that the denominations were alienated from their own more classical past, that is, Puritanism and the continental reformation, which could have provided theological resources for coming to terms with an ever more religiously plural society.

It is not necessary to argue to those for whom I write that the two great needs of mankind, that all men may be lifted up into the light of the highest Christian civilization, are, first, a pure, spiritual Christianity, and, second, civil liberty.[5] Without controversy, these are the forces which, in the past, have contributed most to the elevation of the human race, and they must continue to be, in the future, the most efficient ministers to its progress. It follows, then, that the Anglo-Saxon, as the great representative of these two ideas, the depository of these two greatest blessings, sustains peculiar relations to the world's future, is divinely commissioned to be, in a peculiar sense, his brother's keeper. Add to this the fact of his rapidly increasing strength in modern times, and we have well nigh a demonstration of his destiny. In 1700 this race numbered less than 6,000,000 souls. In 1800, Anglo-Saxons (I use the term somewhat broadly to include all English-speaking peoples) had increased to about 20–500,000, and in 1880 they numbered nearly 100,000,000, having multiplied almost five-fold in eighty years.

At the end of the reign of Charles II. the English colonists in America numbered 200,000. During these two hundred years, our population has increased two hundred and fifty-fold. And the expansion of this race has been no less remarkable than its multiplication. In one century the United States has increased its territory ten-fold, while the enormous acquisition of foreign territory by Great Britain—and chiefly within the last hundred years—is wholly unparalleled in history. . . . It is not unlikely that, before the close of the next century, this race will outnumber all the other civilized races of the world. Does it not look as if God were not only preparing in our Anglo-Saxon civilization the die with which to stamp the peoples of the earth, but as if he were also massing behind that die the mighty power with which to press it? My confidence that this race is eventually to give its civilization to mankind is not based on mere numbers—China forbid! I look forward to what the world has never yet seen united in the same race; viz., the greatest numbers, *and* the highest civilization.

There can be no reasonable doubt that North America is to be the great home of the Anglo-Saxon, the principal seat of his power, the center of his life and influence. Not only does it constitute seven-elevenths of his possessions, but his empire is unsevered, while the remaining four-elevenths are fragmentary and scattered over the earth. Australia will have a great population; but its disadvantages, as compared with North America, are too manifest to need mention. Our continent has room and resources and climate, it lies in the pathway of the nations, it belongs to the zone of power, and already, among Anglo-Saxons, do we lead in population and wealth. . . .

It may be easily shown, and is of no small significance, that the two great ideas of which the Anglo-Saxon is the exponent are having a fuller development in the United States than in Great Britain. There the union of Church and State tends strongly to paralyze some of the members of the body of Christ. Here there is no such influence to destroy spiritual life and power. Here, also, has been evolved the form of government consistent with the largest possible civil liberty. Furthermore, it is significant that the marked characteristics of this race are being here emphasized most. Among the most striking features of the Anglo-Saxon is his money-making power—a power of increasing importance in the widening commerce of the world's future. . . .

Again, another marked characteristic of the Anglo-Saxon is what may be called an instinct or genius for colonizing. His unequaled energy, his indomitable perseverance, and his personal independence, made him a pioneer. He excels all others in pushing his way into new countries. . . .

Again, nothing more manifestly distinguishes the Anglo-Saxon than his intense and persistent energy; and he is developing in the United States an energy which, in eager activity and effectiveness, is peculiarly American. This is due partly to the fact that Americans are much better fed than Europeans, and partly to the undeveloped resources of a new country, but more largely to our climate, which acts as a constant stimulus. . . . Moreover, our social institutions are stimulating. In Europe the various ranks of society are, like the strata of the earth, fixed and fossilized. There can be no great change without a terrible upheaval, a social earthquake. . . . Thus many causes co-operate to produce here the most forceful and tremendous energy in the world.

What is the significance of such facts? These tendencies infold the future; they are the mighty alphabet with which God writes his prophecies. May we not, by a careful laying together of the letters, spell out something of his meaning? *It seems to me that God, with infinite wisdom and skill, is training the Anglo-Saxon race for an hour sure to come in the world's future.* Heretofore there has always been in the history of the world a comparatively unoccupied land westward, into which the crowded countries of the East have poured their surplus populations. But the widening waves of migration, which millenniums ago rolled east and west from the valley of the Euphrates meet today on our Pacific coast. There are no more new worlds. The unoccupied arable lands of the earth are limited, and will soon be taken. The time is coming when the pressure of population on the means of subsistence will be felt here as it is now felt in Europe and Asia. Then will the world enter upon a new stage of its history—*the final competition of races, for which the Anglo-Saxon is being schooled.* Long before the thousand millions are here, the mighty *centrifugal* tendency, inherent in this stock and strengthened in the United States, will assert itself. Then this race of unequaled energy, with all the majesty of numbers and the might of wealth behind it—the representative, let us hope, of the largest liberty, the purest Christianity, the highest civilization—having developed peculiarly aggressive traits calculated to impress its institutions upon mankind, will spread itself over the earth. If I read not amiss, this powerful race will move down upon Mexico, down upon Central and South America, out upon the islands of the sea, over upon Africa and beyond. And can any one doubt that the result of this competition of races will be the "survival of the fittest"?. . . "In every corner of the world," says Mr. Froude, "there is the same phenomenon of the decay of established religions. . . . Among Mohammedans, Jews, Buddhists, Brahmins, traditionary creeds are losing their hold. An intellectual revolution is sweeping over the world, breaking down established opinions, dissolving foundations on which historical faiths have been built up." The contact of Christian with heathen nations is awaking the latter to new life. Old superstitions are loosening their grasp. The dead crust of fossil faiths is being shattered by the movements of life underneath. In Catholic countries, Catholicism is losing its influence over educated minds, and in some cases the masses have already lost all faith in it. Thus, while on this continent God is training the Anglo-Saxon race for its mission, a complemental work has been in progress in the great world beyond. God has two hands. Not only is he preparing in our civilization the die with which to stamp the nations, but, by what Southey called the "timing of Providence," he is preparing mankind to receive our impress.

Is there room for reasonable doubt that this race, unless devitalized by alcohol and tobacco, is destined to dispossess many weaker races, assimilate others, and mold the remainder, until, in a very true and important sense, it has Anglo-Saxonized mankind? Already "the English language, saturated with Christian ideas, gathering up into itself the best thought of all the ages, is the great agent of Christian civilization throughout the world; at this moment affecting the destinies and molding the character of half the human race." . . .

In my own mind, there is no doubt that the Anglo-Saxon is to exercise the commanding influence in the world's future; but the exact nature of that influence is, as yet, undetermined. How far his civilization will be materialistic and atheistic, and how long it will take thoroughly to Christianize and sweeten it, how rapidly he will hasten the coming of the kingdom wherein dwelleth righteousness, or how many ages he may retard it, is still uncertain; but *it is now being swiftly determined.* Let us weld together in a chain the various links of our logic which we have endeavored to forge. Is it manifest that the Anglo-Saxon holds in his hands the destinies of mankind for ages to come? Is it evident that the United States is to be the home of this race, the principal seat of his power, the great center of his influence? Is it true that the great West is to dominate the nation's future? Has it been shown that this generation is to determine the character, and hence the destiny, of the West? Then may God open the eyes of this generation! . . .

E. B. BRADY

An American Catholic on Church and State

Protestant responses to loss of place in the national life included the actions of the APA and the fantasies of a Josiah Strong (as well as more moderate and relevant activities). By contrast Roman Catholic acclimation to post–Civil War America was not so stormy. For one thing Catholics were concentrated in urban settlements and had contrived mutually satisfactory relationships between the religious and political institutions within their communities. But at the same time a tradition within American Roman Catholicism—from the Revolutionary period on—had fully appreciated the independence of church and state and the substantial congruence of this pattern with the classical Catholic position. Edward Brady, a Paulist Father, was among the American Roman Catholic liberals of the later nineteenth century.

The church . . . does claim due recognition in the Christian state, and she holds that the best interests of Christian society are secured by an *entente cordiale* between the civil power and the ecclesiastical authority.[6] And Pius IX., in his famous *Syllabus,* condemns as false the proposition which asserts that there should be absolutely no union between church and state. But the most earnest and the most enlightened defenders of the church and her rights in the world to-day disclaim all idea of such political union as sometimes existed in the past, and which had bequeathed a legacy of weakness to the church the evil effects of which are felt in some countries even to this day. The march of mankind, though halting and circuitous, is ever onward, and we must not turn backwards. Not to restore the past, but to try to improve the present and save the future, should be the aim of all enlightened zeal. The political ideas and methods of the mediæval age would be as much out of place in the nineteenth century as its dungeons and its cumberous coats of mail, and the church would no more think of restoring the politicial conditions of that bygone time than of resuscitating the dust of its dead kings and warriors from their long-forgotten graves. The most intense churchman has no yearning to see the past restored in this particular; such a reactionary spirit would be the height of folly. The church, like everything else in the world, must accommodate herself to her changed surroundings, and she has always done so. Her power of adaptation to the circumstances of all times and places and races is not the least evidence of her divine organization. While her doctrines are unchangeable her discipline is ever changing. But the Catholic Church has her rights in the nineteenth century as well as in the twelfth, and she never hesitates to assert them, though the ages of faith and chivalry have passed away.

From the very beginning the church claimed the right to determine the "things of God"; she made this claim when hid away in the catacombs as well as when she stood uncovered in the palace of the Cæsars. Her very existence is founded upon this right, for her mission in the world is to point out the divine law and secure its observance, and without at least the negative co-operation of the state she cannot fulfil her mission. The legislation of the civil power must be in harmony with the divine law, or at all events not opposed to it; otherwise there must necessarily be conflict between the church and the state.

The church never has questioned and never can question the absolute authority of the state in its own proper sphere, and she deprecates all idea of interference in the functions of the state. The words of Pope Leo XIII., in his encyclical on the "Christian Character of States," ought to be sufficient evidence of the church's teaching on this subject. "God," he says, "has divided the care of the human race between two powers, the ecclesiastical and the civil; the one placed over divine things, the other over human. Each is without *superior* in its own sphere; each has fixed bounds in which it is contained, and these defined by the nature and proximate cause of each one, so that a kind of circle is drawn within which the acts proper to each, each does of its own right." But while the church thus maintains the absolute authority of the state within its own sphere, she holds, with St. Paul, that "there is no power except from God," and hence "in every kind of government those who rule should keep their eyes fixed on God, the Sovereign Ruler of the world, and have him before them in executing their civil duties as their example and law." Rulers and law-makers as well as private individuals must recognize the principles of divine right and justice, and be guided by them in their official conduct and in the enactment of laws. This much the church insists upon. As the exponent of the higher law of God to Christian legislators, she demands that the laws of Cæsar shall not interfere with "the things of God," but shall render due homage to them; and, on the other hand, she commands full obedience to the laws of the state, and a strict rendering to Cæsar "the things that are Cæsar's."

This is the absolute claim of the church in her relation to the state and its laws, and a careful examination of her past history will show that this has been her real attitude all along. No doubt there have been ambitious churchmen who in their relations with the civil power contended for much more than this, as there have been ambitious statesmen who wanted to rule over spiritual as well as temporal affairs; but individuals, however high their office, are not the church, and their aims must not be confounded with those of the church, which are *essentially spiritual;* and just as grasping, unscrupulous statesmen have brought and still bring odium upon their government or their party by their abuse of power, so misguided churchmen have brought odium upon the church by trying to make her the instrument of their own personal schemes and ignoble ambitions.

But if this be the actual state of the case, if the church admits that she has no right or title to interfere in the remotest manner with the affairs of the state except where the things of God are clearly concerned, why the constant friction between church and state all adown the ages? Simply because the state has all along tried to ignore the rights of God where they actually exist, and the church has tried to enforce them. Let us take a few examples. Is not marriage a sacrament, a divine institution, in the eyes of the church, and do not the laws relating to civil marriage and divorce concern the things of God? Does not the observance of Sunday concern them? Does not Christian education concern them? Does not the maintenance of public decency and morality concern them? If the church have no right to a hearing on such matters as these, her mission is a mere mockery, and her power and her authority in the world at large is null and void. She is only a dumb dog that cannot bark.

Those and those only who hold to the purely pagan idea of a state supreme in all things and over all things can deny the rights of religion here. No one with a particle of Christian faith or feeling can question them. If Christianity is true, the claims of the church in this particular are also true. Every Catholic, I had almost said every Christian, must needs unite with Leo XIII. in saying that "to exclude the church from influence on life, from law, from the education of youth, from the family, is a great and pernicious error. A state cannot be moral if you take away religion." The experiment of a purely secular state has never yet succeeded, and certainly the results of recent attempts in this direction do not give any sufficient evidence to show that it ever will succeed. There can be no stability in human affairs without some recognition of the divine order of things. When the civil and religious elements are in full accord and move harmoniously together the best interests of society are secured.

There may be abuses, there have been abuses on both sides; but is there anything in this world that is not subject to abuse, and has there ever been any arrangement of human society that worked perfectly? Conservative governments are liable to curtail the just rights of the people, liberal governments are liable to fail in the enforcement of law; so there is some danger in every form of government. A very common, but none the less a very erroneous idea is that the Catholic Church is in favor of extreme conservatism, or even absolutism, in government, and is the uncompromising foe of all liberal constitutions. The truth is the church is not wedded to any particular form of government; all forms that fulfil the functions of government and promote the public welfare and the common good are alike to her, and she loyally supports all just constitutions, whether monarchical or republican. . . .

The rabid, unreasoning opponents of Catholicity sometimes amuse us by prophesying what the church would do should she ever gain the ascendency in this country. Their prophetic fears are not only groundless, but to us they seem supremely absurd. We know very well what the church would do under the circumstances. She would do away with divorce; she would establish a system of Christian education for her own children (she would not impose it upon others); she would try to root out public as well as private corruption; she would endeavor to secure an honest ballot and anathematize any party or individual that should by bribery or other methods pollute the sources of our political life; but she would not touch a single stone in the noble fabric of our constitution—nay, she would safeguard to the utmost of her power our free institutions, and teach her children to be willing at any moment to die in their defence.

It were a grievous injustice to the church to suppose that the few Catholic politicians who from time to time become prominent in public life represent Catholic principles in their political action. Most of them represent nothing but themselves; some there are who carry their Catholic consciences into their official conduct, and they are an honor to us and a blessing to the state; but unhappily the majority go with the tide and recognize no principle but expediency, and the church must not be held responsible for them. As for the low and venal crew of pot-house politicians who batten on bribery and the perjured spoils of office, they are a libel on humanity as well as on Christianity. The true, consistent Christian, the man who brings his Christian principles everywhere with him and acts upon them, is always the best citizen, and the words of St. Augustine on this subject are as true to-day as when they were first written, nearly fourteen centuries ago. "Let those who say the teaching of Christ is opposed to the republic," exclaims the great doctor, "give it soldiers such as the teaching of Christ bids them to be; let them give such governors of provinces, such husbands, such wives, such parents, such children, such masters, such servants, such kings, such judges—finally, such payers and exactors of the debts due the revenue itself, the very agent of the government; all these such as Christian principles commend them to be, and let them dare to say the church is hostile to the republic; nay, let them acknowledge that she is, if obeyed, the great source of safety to the state."

JOHN IRELAND, D.D.

Catholicism and Americanism

The Rev. John Ireland (d. 1918), archbishop of Saint Paul, Minnesota, was a very colorful figure in the ranks of those American Catholic clergy who were at the same time loyal Catholics and loyal Americans. The following short excerpt from a relatively late address indicates the terms in which separation or independence of church and state was congenial to many Americans who were also members of the Roman Catholic Church.

My religious faith is that of the Catholic Church—Catholicism, integral and unalloyed—Catholicism, unswerving and soul swaying—the Catholicism, if I am to put it into more positive and concrete form, taught by the supreme chieftain of the Catholic Church, the Bishop, the Pope of Rome.[7]

My civil and political faith is that of the Republic of the United States of America—Americanism, purest and brightest; yielding in strength and loyalty to the Americanism of none other American; surpassed in spirit of obedience and sacrifice by that of none other citizen, none other soldier; sworn to uphold in peace and in war America's Star Spangled Banner.

Between my religious faith and my civil and political faith, between my creed and my country, it has been said, there is discord and contradiction, so that I must smother something of the one when I bid the other burst forth into ardent burning, that I must subtract something from my allegiance to the one when I bend my full energy to service to the other. Those who so speak misunderstand either my creed or my country; they belie either the one or the other. The accord of one with the other is the theme of the address I am privileged this evening to make.

No room is there for discord or contradiction. Church and State cover separate and distinct zones of thought and action: The Church busies itself with the spiritual, the State with the temporal. The Church and the State are built for different purposes, the Church for Heaven, the State for earth. The line of demarcation between the two jurisdictions was traced by the unerring finger of Him who is the master of both. The law of God is—"Render to Cæsar the things that are Cæsar's; and to God the things that are God's."

The partition of jurisdiction into the spiritual and the temporal is a principle of Catholicism; no less is it a principle of Americanism. Catholicism and Americanism are in complete agreement.

The Constitution of the United States reads: "Congress shall make no law respecting an establishment of religion, or prohibiting the free exercise thereof." It was a great forward leap on the part of the new nation towards personal liberty and the consecration of the rights of conscience. Not so had it heretofore been on the soil of America. Save in Maryland while reigned there the spirit of the Catholic Lord Baltimore, and in Pennsylvania under the sweet-tempered rule of William Penn, religious freedom was barred by law in the Colonies,—Protestant creeds warring one with the other, all warring with the Catholic. But it was decreed that the new flag must be unsullied by religious persecution, the new nation must be, on every score, the daughter of freedom, the guardian angel of personal rights in each and every American.

ROBERT D. CROSS

Catholicism and a Non-Catholic State

This selection is from a highly regarded study, *The Emergence of Liberal Catholicism in America,* by Professor Cross.

In theory, the appearance of the modern state required no alteration in the traditional Catholic argument that all authority flowed from God, was subject to His laws, and therefore required the superintendence or instruction of the Church.[8] It had always been necessary for the Church to decide what authority could be delegated to the secular power, what methods of control to employ, and what role the individual Catholic should play in supporting and perfecting the state. But as the state changed from being a bare preponderance of force, remote from the lives of most people, and became a monopoly of force which daily affected the lives of everyone, and as it assumed forms and adopted techniques unknown to theologians of the past, Catholics found that questions of "Church and State" constituted some of the most perplexing problems in the relationship of Christianity and culture.

Traditionalists, looking longingly back to the states of the past whose kings considered themselves the particular defenders of Catholicism, found it hard to believe that the newly declared sovereign people would respect the Church's teachings as conscientiously as would a prince religiously trained and especially consecrated. Conservative suspicions deepened as nineteenth-century radicals, identifying republicanism with the drastic curtailment of the Church's influence, found an ideal of statesmanship in Cavour's attempt to construct a free state wholly separate from the Church. Like Cavour, they were willing to despoil the Church of much of its property and privilege. In bitter condemnation, Father Thébaud admitted that the modern state was not yet completely the "incarnation of Antichrist," but it was in such "a great degree ruled over by really anti-Christian ideas" that the Church and the state "are evidently now arrayed against each other and engaged in a deadly conflict." The Syllabus vigorously denounced all attempts to limit the Church's control over the state.

America, as one of the first republics of the age, had always been an object of admiration for European radicals; and non-Catholic Americans proclaimed to all who would listen that the states, both federal and local, were completely separated from the control of any church. To many Catholics, the states seemed to behave that way. Immigrant groups did not need theological demonstrations to conclude that the state was no helpmate, at least to the True Church. Through favoritism to Protestant clergymen, by the enforcement of Protestant ideals of public morals, by legal restrictions on the Church's property-holding powers, by the support of "godless" public schools, it seemed as much the enemy of the Church as the governments of Francesco Crispi and Jules Ferry. "The truth is," the conservative Church Progress of St. Louis complained, "that in the whole world there is not a Catholic country with a non-Catholic population of any importance which does not show more respect for the conscience of the non-Catholic minority than the United States manifests for the conscience of Catholics there." To American Catholics of these convictions, the censures of the Syllabus were badly needed condemnations of the political system under which they lived.

The liberal Catholics resented the innuendo that the American polity was as deeply undesirable as the laicizing states of Europe. Usually taking care not to contradict explicitly the traditional Catholic teaching, they proudly declared, nevertheless, their deepfelt satisfaction with the relations between the Church and the American "state." In their testimonials they seldom bothered to distinguish between the federal government—prohibited by the Bill of Rights from directly supporting any church—and the state governments, still theoretically free to create a full-fledged Establishment. It was in this genial spirit that Cardinal Gibbons declared "'America, with all thy faults I love thee still.'" Like the other liberals he never doubted that the "state" in all its divisions was every year growing more responsive to Catholic rights and interests.

The state's unwillingness to provide direct financial aid was, the liberals devoutly believed, a blessing. The laity had responded with a generous enthusiasm that contrasted strikingly with the sullenness and outright disinterest that characterized lay activities in many "Catholic" countries. "Liberty has, indeed, its inconveniences, its dangers even," Bishop Spalding said, "but the atmosphere it creates is the native air of generous, fair, and noble souls; and where it is not, man's proper good and honor are not found." All the liberals asked was a fair field and no favor. "We are content," Father Hewit wrote, "with the total separation of Church and state . . . leaving us at liberty to propagate our religion. . . . We are content that all Christian sects, Jews, and in general all associations which do not conspire against the laws, should enjoy equal liberty." "None love more ardently" than do Catholics, Bishop Stephen Ryan insisted, "the freedom they enjoy; none have profited more by the liberty of conscience and equality of rights guaranteed to all."

Conversely, the liberals were sure that a closer connection between church and state than existed in America inevitably harmed religion by committing its interests to the whim of political officials. The filiations with the state during the Middle Ages were only "accident," Spalding wrote, not the Catholic ideal; and they had cost the Church the liberty to appoint whom it wished, at the same time that they allowed the clergy and laity to grow lax and indifferent. "The outward honor shown to the Church has generally been at the expense of her inward force," the bishop concluded. Dependence on the state made the Middle Ages "a nightmare" for the Church, Father Joseph Tracy of Boston maintained; dependence today would surely have the same sad result. Father McGlynn announced that he was "willing to go in for perfect, absolute union of Church and State in the Kingdom of Heaven beyond the grave, or in the communities of angelic men," but nowhere else. And Professor Thomas O'Gorman, in his history of the American Church, noted that "if the close union of church and state in the early Christianity of California was of some advantage to the church . . . it was also productive of some disadvantages. *It cannot be* otherwise . . . so long as human nature is what it is." The liberals rejoiced that the American Church was "free and unshackled by concordats," which necessarily limited her "action," and cramped her "energy."

In a dominantly Protestant America, it was relatively easy for the liberal Catholics to accept the "separation of church and state." It was a bolder step to assert, as unambiguously as they did, that closer relations had always been harmful. Yet some of the liberals went even further and happily forecast that when Catholics predominated in America, the separation would be maintained. Such avowals were highly reassuring to the many Protestants who suspected that the Church was libertarian only when Catholics were in a minority. Bishop Keane promised that, however much of America was converted, so long as real disagreement on questions of social and political morality existed, the Church was too tolerant to impose its beliefs by coercive laws. Keane cited the Church's approval of the charter of liberties granted in the Catholic France of Louis XVIII, and in Catholic Belgium. And he repeated Cardinal Manning's assurances to Gladstone that, should Catholics gain controlling political power, there would be no laws of constraint or privation enacted against dissenters. The Paulist Father Edward Brady amplified Keane's reply. Should virtually all Americans become Catholic, divorce would be abolished, and the Church would insist on a Christian education for Catholic children,—"(she would not impose it upon others)." She would try to provide an honest ballot and an upright administration of justice. But "she would not touch a single stone in the noble fabric of our constitution—nay, she would safeguard to the utmost of her power our free institutions, and teach her children to be willing at any moment to die in their defense."

The liberals claimed that American Catholics had demonstrated fine tolerance even when local conditions made it possible for them to have acted otherwise. Richard Clarke testified that the several Protestant boys cared for in the Catholic Protectory he managed were respectfully escorted to a Protestant church every Sunday. Cardinal Gibbons used his personal influence to prevent the city of Baltimore from suppressing an atheistical "Sunday School." And the cardinal liked to praise Lord Baltimore for voluntarily establishing religious freedom in his personal colony. His "noble stature" would "reflect unfading glory" on himself, on his state, and on his Church.

The liberals regularly asserted that the Spanish Inquisition had been primarily a political institution, and that American Catholics wished one no more than did American politicians. One Catholic writer maintained that an inquisition would never reappear, because "all history is a record of progress from ignorance to knowledge, from weakness to strength, from bondage to freedom." Cardinal Gibbons, claiming the backing of "every Catholic Priest and layman in the land," emphatically renounced "every species of violence" in religious affairs, and asserted that in the future, doctrinal orthodoxy would be preserved, not by physically coercive means, but by the sword of the spirit, and the fire of the love of Christ.

Even such traditional methods of control as the *imprimatur* and the Index might well, the liberals suggested, be dispensed with. The *Catholic World* cited with approval an English Jesuit's opinion that, in the ideal state of the future, censorship of opinion might well be less necessary and less desirable. "The *imprimatur* might be either . . . obligatory or merely a matter of counsel to obtain it. We are not to adopt promiscuously all the praiseworthy customs of our forefathers." When conservatives in Europe and America demanded that Henry George's *Progress and Poverty* be placed on the Index, the liberals were able to block the move, and their protests implied grave doubts whether such censorship was any longer a useful practice. Canon William Barry, an English ally, stated flatly that the Index was an anachronism.

The liberals made their professions of perpetual loyalty to the American system, serene in the conviction that America had long enjoyed far better relations between churches and the state than either Catholic ultramontanes or American secularists would acknowledge. To the saturnine John Gilmary Shea, many of the founding fathers seemed no better than "base drivelling slaves of the old anti-Catholic bigotry and fanaticism, shutting their eyes to the light and full of fiendish hatred." Even Hecker was, on occasion, less than flattering in his estimate of the religious instincts of the founding fathers. But McGlynn declared firmly that it was a "calumny" to assert that the founders were "irreligious men," and Richard Clarke concluded that Washington's "relations with Catholics were friendly and intimate. . . , always just and sympathetic, characterized by . . . a particular leaning towards them." Bishop Stephen Ryan wrote his clergy on the hundredth anniversary of Washington's inauguration that "when we contrast a Washington, and the illustrious founders of our great Republic—men of deep religious convictions, men of broad, liberal minds, of genuine Christian instincts . . . with the pigmy statesmen, pretended liberals, and radical revolutionaries of other lands," it became obvious why the revolution they led and the government they established were more acceptable to Catholics than anything in Europe. In fact, one layman insisted, the Revolution did not seek to destroy religion, but only to eliminate religious bigotry. The revolt was so certainly "providential," that Gibbons rejoiced in the mistaken notion that no Catholics served with the Tories.

The "governmental spirit of the United States" from the first was not, of course, Christian in the traditional mode, and so the French Canadian Jules Tardivel intransigently concluded that it had always been "by every necessity" dominated by an "anti-Christian spirit." This kind of logic disgusted the *Catholic World.* Relations between church and state were established in America by righteous men dealing wisely with existing conditions, "not by a frantic advocacy of antique methods, or of a state of things which ought to be in the abstract, or of what emotional or traditional temperaments might desire—all legitimate enough, but barred out of here by the sovereign rule" of what the *World* was frank to call "providential conditions." A great deal of "unmistakably Christian sentiment" was "infused into our institutions," the journal continued, as would be obvious to anyone who dispassionately considered the actual operations of the state today.

In salient contrast to conditions in France and Italy, the Church in America could hold all the property it wished. Conservatives remained indignant that civil law regulated the transfer of property titles, as if the Church could be rightfully treated as the creature or subject of the state. But liberals like John Ireland concentrated on the fact that most states had dropped requirements common in mid-century that laymen of the vicinity share in Church property holding. Most bishops were now permitted to designate themselves corporations sole, and where this privilege was not available, Ireland blamed Catholics for not having made clear to the state their desire for it.

Though states did not directly finance the work of the Church, some granted aid to Catholic hospitals and asylums, ostensibly on the grounds of material interest, but often in the desire to help churches in any way constitutional. It was true that some Americans noisily denounced such subsidies, but a proposed amendment to the Federal Constitution "to perfect the cleavage between church and state" never mustered much popular support. Protests made against tax exemption of church property were similarly ineffectual.

The state deferred to the church by recognizing her clergy as civil officials for such functions as marriage. It appointed and paid chaplains to the armed services; during the Civil War, enough Catholic chaplains had been selected to weaken the old tradition that the faith was discriminated against. The custom of asking clergymen, including Catholics on occasion, to offer prayers at important public meetings had virtually acquired the sanction of law. Most officials took a solemn oath upon the Bible before assuming office. And the proclamation of a day of thanksgiving to God impressed both Americans and foreigners; "what difference is there," a visiting French cleric asked, after reading Cleveland's declaration of Thanksgiving Day, "between this beautiful proclamation of a state leader and the decree of a Catholic bishop?"

Despite these quasi-religious activities, none of the states could be deemed "Catholic," since none explicitly acknowledged the authority of the Church or carried out all its recommendations. One conservative protested that even the Christianity implicit in the common law had been eroded away by the courts; in its place, the legislatures, oblivious of their obligations to enforce the natural law, were "attempting to fabricate a crude religious and moral code, without the guidance of inspiration and influenced solely by temporary prejudice or a mistaken view of public policy." Hecker, on the other hand, was sure that the courts would continue to punish not only violations of the natural law, but also clear transgressions of revealed religious duty as crimes "against good government." Cardinal Gibbons declared that statute laws were almost invariably so "intimately interwoven with the Christian religion," that the faith had nothing to fear from their application. He was confident that the common law still virtually guaranteed the Christianity of the states.

By appealing to practices rather than to principles, the American liberals tried hard to mediate between the demands of a traditionalist Catholicism and those of contemporary culture. When a popular movement developed to put "God in the Constitution," Gibbons pleased ardent defenders of the separation of church and state by declaring his opposition; at the same time, he placated Catholics by stating that he was not agitated over constitutional phrases so long as the government continued to be guided in so much of its work by a manifestly Christian spirit. A Paulist advised fellow Catholics to work not for union, but rather a more perfect *"entente cordiale"* between church and state.

American Governments and Religious Institutions

PHILIP SCHAFF

The American Theory and System

Philip Schaff (d. 1893), originally Swiss, came to Mercersburg Seminary (Pennsylvania) in 1843 having been trained as a church historian in Germany. Schaff's contribution to the American scene was many-sided—including attempts to "explain" America and American ways to Europe. This selection is from an essay titled "Church and State in the United States," which Schaff prepared for publication in the studies of the recently founded American Historical Association.

The relationship of church and state in the United States secures full liberty of religious thought, speech, and action, within the limits of the public peace and order. It makes persecution impossible.[9]

Religion and liberty are inseparable. Religion is voluntary, and cannot, and ought not to be forced.

This is a fundamental article of the American creed, without distinction of sect or party. Liberty, both civil and religious, is an American instinct. All natives suck it in with the mother's milk; all immigrants accept it as a happy boon, especially those who flee from oppression and persecution abroad. Even those who reject the modern theory of liberty enjoy the practice, and would defend it in their own interest against any attempt to overthrow it.

Such liberty is impossible on the basis of a union of church and state, where the one of necessity restricts or controls the other. It requires a friendly separation, where each power is entirely independent in its own sphere. The church, as such, has nothing to do with the state except to obey its laws and to strengthen its moral foundations; the state has nothing to do with the church except to protect her in her property and liberty; and the state must be equally just to all forms of belief and unbelief which do not endanger the public safety.

* * *

The American relationship of church and state differs from all previous relationships in Europe and in the colonial period of our history; and yet it rests upon them and reaps the benefit of them all. For history is an organic unit, and American history has its roots in Europe.

1: The American system differs from the ante-Nicene or pre-Constantinian separation of church and state, when the church was indeed, as with us, self-supporting and self-governing, and so far free within, but under persecution from without, being treated as a forbidden religion by the then heathen state. In America the government protects the church in her property and rights without interfering with her internal affairs. By the power of truth and the moral heroism of martyrdom the church converted the Roman Empire and became the mother of Christian states.

2: The American system differs from the hierarchical control of the church over the state, or from priest government, which prevailed in the Middle Ages down to the Reformation, and reached its culmination in the Papacy. It confines the church to her proper spiritual vocation, and leaves the state independent in all the temporal affairs of the nation. The hierarchical theory was suited to the times after the fall of the Roman Empire and the ancient civilization, when the state was a rude military despotism, when the church was the refuge of the people, when the Christian priesthood was in sole possession of learning and had to civilize as well as to evangelize the barbarians of northern and western Europe. By her influence over legislation the church abolished bad laws and customs, introduced benevolent institutions, and created a Christian state controlled by the spirit of justice and humanity, and fit for self-government.

3: The American system differs from the Erastian or Cæsaro-Papal control of the state over the church, which obtained in the old Byzantine Empire, and prevails in modern Russia, and in the Protestant states of Europe, where the civil government protects and supports the church, but at the expense of her dignity and independence, and deprives her of the power of self-government. The Erastian system was based on the assumption that all citizens are also Christians of one creed, but is abnormal in the mixed character of government and people in the modern state. In America, the state has no right whatever to interfere with the affairs of the church, her doctrine, discipline, and worship, and the appointment of ministers. It would be a great calamity if religion were to become subject to our ever-changing politics.

4: The American system differs from the system of toleration, which began in Germany with the Westphalia Treaty, 1648; in England with the Act of Toleration, 1689, and which now prevails over nearly all Europe; of late years, nominally at least, even in Roman Catholic countries, to the very gates of the Vatican, in spite of the protest of the Pope. Toleration exists where the government supports one or more churches, and permits other religious communities under the name of sects (as on the continent), or dissenters and nonconformists (as in England), under certain conditions. In America, there are no such distinctions, but only churches or denominations on a footing of perfect equality before the law. To talk about any particular denomination as *the* church, or *the American* church, has no meaning, and betrays ignorance or conceit. Such exclusiveness is natural and logical in Romanism, but unnatural, illogical, and contemptible in any other church. The American laws know no such institution as "the church," but only separate and independent organizations.

Toleration is an important step from state-churchism to free-churchism. But it is only a step. There is a very great difference between toleration and liberty. Toleration is a concession, which may be withdrawn; it implies a preference for the ruling form of faith and worship, and a practical disapproval of all other forms. It may be coupled with many restrictions and disabilities. We tolerate what we dislike, but cannot alter; we tolerate even a nuisance if we must. Acts of toleration are wrung from a government by the force of circumstances and the power of a minority too influential to be disregarded. In this way even the most despotic governments, as those of Turkey and of Russia, are tolerant; the one toward Christians and Jews, the other toward Mohammedans and dissenters from the orthodox Greek Church; but both deny the right of self-extension and missionary operations except in favor of the state religion, and both forbid and punish apostasy from it. . . .

In our country we ask no toleration for religion and its free exercise, but we claim it as an inalienable right. "It is not toleration," says Judge Cooley, "which is established in our system, but religious equality." Freedom of religion is one of the greatest gifts of God to man, without distinction of race and color. He is the author and lord of conscience, and no power on earth has a right to stand between God and the conscience. A violation of this divine law written in the heart is an assault upon the majesty of God and the image of God in man. Granting the freedom of conscience, we must, by logical necessity, also grant the freedom of its manifestation and exercise in public worship. To concede the first and to deny the second, after the manner of despotic governments, is to imprison the conscience. To be just, the state must either support all or none of the religions of its citizens. Our government supports none, but protects all.

5: Finally—and this we would emphasize as especially important in our time,—the American system differs radically and fundamentally from the infidel and red-republican theory of religious freedom. The word freedom is one of the most abused words in the vocabulary. True liberty is a positive force, regulated by law; false liberty is a negative force, a release from restraint. True liberty is the moral power of self-government; the liberty of infidels and anarchists is carnal licentiousness. The American separation of church and state rests on respect for the church; the infidel separation, on indifference and hatred of the church, and of religion itself.

The infidel theory was tried and failed in the first Revolution of France. It began with toleration, and ended with the abolition of Christianity, and with the reign of terror, which in turn prepared the way for military despotism as the only means of saving society from anarchy and ruin. Our infidels and anarchists would re-enact this tragedy if they should ever get the power. They openly profess their hatred and contempt of our Sunday-laws, our Sabbaths, our churches, and all our religious institutions and societies. Let us beware of them! The American system grants freedom also to irreligion and infidelity, but only within the limits of the order and safety of society. The destruction of religion would be the destruction of morality and the ruin of the state. Civil liberty requires for its support religious liberty, and cannot prosper without it. Religious liberty is not an empty sound, but an orderly exercise of religious duties and enjoyment of all its privileges. It is freedom *in* religion, not freedom *from* religion; as true civil liberty is freedom *in* law, and not freedom *from* law. . . .

Republican institutions in the hands of a virtuous and God-fearing nation are the very best in the world, but in the hands of a corrupt and irreligious people they are the very worst, and the most effective weapons of destruction. An indignant people may rise in rebellion against a cruel tyrant; but who will rise against the tyranny of the people in possession of the ballotbox and the whole machinery of government? Here lies our great danger, and it is increasing every year.

Destroy our churches, close our Sunday-schools, abolish the Lord's Day, and our republic would become an empty shell, and our people would tend to heathenism and barbarism. Christianity is the most powerful factor in our society and the pillar of our institutions. It regulates the family; it enjoins private and public virtue; it builds up moral character; it teaches us to love God supremely, and our neighbor as ourselves; it makes good men and useful citizens; it denounces every vice; it encourages every virtue; it promotes and serves the public welfare; it upholds peace and order. Christianity is the only possible religion for the American people, and with Christianity are bound up all our hopes for the future.

JAMES BRYCE

The Churches and the Clergy

Lord Bryce (d. 1922) published *The American Commonwealth* on the basis of three visits to the United States. It was widely accepted as a valuable analysis of American society. In this selection it is evident that his assessment of the relationships between governments and religious institutions is close to those of Schaff and Cooley, which were roughly contemporaneous.

It is accepted as an axiom by all Americans that the civil power ought to be not only neutral and impartial as between different forms of faith, but ought to leave these matters entirely on one side, regarding them no more than it regards the artistic or literary pursuits of the citizens.[10] There seem to be no two opinions on this subject in the United States. Even the Protestant Episcopalian clergy, who are in many ways disposed to admire and envy their brethren in England; even the Roman Catholic bishops, whose creed justifies the enforcement of the true faith by the secular arm, assure the European visitor that if State establishment were offered them they would decline it, preferring the freedom they enjoy to any advantages the State could confer. Every religious community can now organize itself in whatever way it pleases, lay down its own rules of faith and discipline, create and administer its own system of judicature, raise and apply its funds at its uncontrolled discretion. A church established by the State would not be able to do all these things, because it would also be controlled by the State, and it would be exposed to the envy and jealousy of other sects.

The only controversies that have arisen regarding State action in religious matters have turned upon the appropriation of public funds to charitable institutions managed by some particular denomination. Such appropriations are expressly prohibited in the constitutions of some States. But it may happen that the readiest way of promoting some benevolent public purpose is to make a grant of money to an institution already at work, and successfully serving that purpose. As this reason may sometimes be truly given, so it is also sometimes advanced where the real motive is to purchase the political support of the denomination to which the institution belongs, or at least of its clergy. In some States, and particularly in New York, State or city legislatures are often charged with giving money to Roman Catholic institutions for the sake of securing the Catholic vote. In these cases, however, the money always purports to be voted not for a religious but for a philanthropic or educational purpose. No ecclesiastical body would be strong enough to obtain any grant to its general funds, or any special immunity for its ministers. The passion for equality in religious as well as secular matters is everywhere in America far too strong to be braved, and nothing excites more general disapprobation than any attempt by an ecclesiastical organization to interfere in politics. The suspicion that the Roman Catholic church uses its power over its members to guide their votes for its purposes has more than once given rise to strong anti-Catholic or (as they would be called in Canada) Orange movements, such as that which has recently figured so largely in Ohio, Indiana, Michigan, and Illinois under the name of the American Protective Association. So the hostility to Mormonism was due not merely to the practice of polygamy, but also to the notion that the hierarchy of the Latter Day Saints constitutes a secret and tyrannical *imperium in imperio* opposed to the genius of democratic institutions.

The refusal of the civil power to protect or endow any form of religion is commonly represented in Europe as equivalent to a declaration of contemptuous indifference on the part of the State to the spiritual interests of its people. A State recognizing no church is called a godless State; the disestablishment of a church is described as an act of national impiety. Nothing can be farther from the American view, to an explanation of which it may be well to devote a few lines.

The abstention of the State from interference in matters of faith and worship may be advocated on two principles, which may be called the political and the religious. The former sets out from the principles of liberty and equality. It holds any attempt at compulsion by the civil power to be an infringement on liberty of thought, as well as on liberty of action, which could be justified only when a practice claiming to be religious is so obviously anti-social or immoral as to threaten the well-being of the community. Religious persecution, even in its milder forms, such as disqualifying the members of a particular sect for public office, is, it conceives, inconsistent with the conception of individual freedom and the respect due to the primordial rights of the citizen which modern thought has embraced. Even if State action stops short of the imposition of disabilities, and confines itself to favouring a particular church, whether by grants of money or by giving special immunities to its clergy, this is an infringement on equality, putting one man at a disadvantage compared with others in respect of matters which are (according to the view I am stating) not fit subjects for State cognizance.

The second principle, embodying the more purely religious view of the question, starts from the conception of the church as a spiritual body existing for spiritual purposes, and moving along spiritual paths. It is an assemblage of men who are united by their devotion to an unseen Being, their memory of a past divine life, their belief in the possibility of imitating that life, so far as human frailty allows, their hopes for an illimitable future. Compulsion of any kind is contrary to the nature of such a body, which lives by love and reverence, not by law. It desires no State help, feeling that its strength comes from above, and that its kingdom is not of this world. It does not seek for exclusive privileges, conceiving that these would not only create bitterness between itself and other religious bodies, but might attract persons who did not really share its sentiments, while corrupting the simplicity of those who are already its members. Least of all can it submit to be controlled by the State, for the State, in such a world as the present, means persons many or most of whom are alien to its beliefs and cold to its emotions. The conclusion follows that the church as a spiritual entity will be happiest and strongest when it is left absolutely to itself, not patronized by the civil power, not restrained by law except when and in so far as it may attempt to quit its proper sphere and intermeddle in secular affairs.

Of these two views it is the former much more than the latter that has moved the American mind. The latter would doubtless be now generally accepted by religious people. But when the question arose in a practical shape in the earlier days of the Republic, arguments of the former or political order were found amply sufficient to settle it, and no practical purpose has since then compelled men either to examine the spiritual basis of the church, or to inquire by the light of history how far State action has during fifteen centuries helped or marred her usefulness. There has, however, been another cause at work, I mean the comparatively limited conception of the State itself which Americans have formed. The State is not to them, as to Germans or Frenchmen, and even to some English thinkers, an ideal moral power, charged with the duty of forming the characters and guiding the lives of its subjects. It is more like a commercial company, or perhaps a huge municipality created for the management of certain business in which all who reside within its bounds are interested, levying contributions and expending them on this business of common interest, but for the most part leaving the shareholders or burgesses to themselves. That an organization of this kind should trouble itself, otherwise than as matter of policy, with the opinions or conduct of its members, would be as unnatural as for a railway company to inquire how many of the shareholders were total abstainers. Accordingly it never occurs to the average American that there is any reason why State churches should exist, and he stands amazed at the warmth of European feeling on the matter.

Just because these questions have been long since disposed of, and excite no present passion, and perhaps also because the Americans are more practically easy-going than pedantically exact, the National government and the State governments do give to Christianity a species of recognition inconsistent with the view that civil government should be absolutely neutral in religious matters. Each House of Congress has a chaplain, and opens its proceedings each day with prayers. The President annually after the end of harvest issues a proclamation ordering a general thanksgiving, and occasionally appoints a day of fasting and humiliation. So prayers are offered in the State legislatures, and State governors issue proclamations for days of religious observance. Congress in the crisis of the Civil War (July, 1863) requested the President to appoint a day for humiliation and prayer. In the army and navy provision is made for religious services, conducted by chaplains of various denominations, and no difficulty seems to have been found in reconciling their claims. In most States there exist laws punishing blasphemy or profane swearing by the name of God (laws which, however, are in some places openly transgressed and in few or none enforced), laws restricting or forbidding trade or labour on the Sabbath, as well as laws protecting assemblages for religious purposes, such as camp-meetings or religious processions, from being disturbed. The Bible is (in most States) read in the public State-supported schools, and though controversies have arisen on this head, the practice is evidently in accord with the general sentiment of the people.

The matter may be summed up by saying that Christianity is in fact understood to be, though not the legally established religion, yet the national religion. So far from thinking their commonwealth godless, the Americans conceive that the religious character of a government consists in nothing but the religious belief of the individual citizens, and the conformity of their conduct to that belief. They deem the general acceptance of Christianity to be one of the main sources of their national prosperity, and their nation a special object of the Divine favour.

The legal position of a Christian church is in the United States simply that of a voluntary association, or group of associations, corporate or unincorporate, under the ordinary law. There is no such thing as a special ecclesiastical law; all questions, not only of property but of church discipline and jurisdiction, are, if brought before the courts of the land, dealt with as questions of contract; and the court, where it is obliged to examine a question of theology, as for instance whether a clergyman has advanced opinions inconsistent with any creed or formula to which he has bound himself—for it will prefer, if possible, to leave such matters to the proper ecclesiastical authority—will treat the point as one of pure legal interpretation, neither assuming to itself theological knowledge, nor suffering considerations of policy to intervene.

As a rule, every religious body can organize itself in any way it pleases. The State does not require its leave to be asked, but permits any form of church government, any ecclesiastical order, to be created and endowed, any method to be adopted of vesting church property, either simply in trustees or in corporate bodies formed either under the general law of the State or under some special statute. Sometimes a limit is imposed on the amount of property, or of real estate, which an ecclesiastical corporation can hold; but, on the whole, it may be said that the civil power manifests no jealousy of the spiritual, but allows the latter a perfectly free field for expansion. Of course if any ecclesiastical authority were to become formidable either by its wealth or by its control over the members of its body, this easy tolerance would disappear; all I observe is that the difficulties often experienced, and still more often feared, in Europe, from the growth of organizations exercising tremendous spiritual powers, have in the United States never proved serious. No church has anywhere a power approaching that of the Roman Catholic Church in Lower Canada. Religious bodies are in so far the objects of special favour that their property is in most States exempt from taxation; and this is reconciled to theory by the argument that they are serviceable as moral agencies, and diminish the expenses incurred in respect of police administration. Two or three States impose restrictions on the creation of religious corporations, and one, Maryland, requires the sanction of the legislature to dispositions of property to religious uses. But, speaking generally, religious bodies are the objects of legislative favour.

T. M. COOLEY

Constitutional Limitations Regarding Religious Liberty

Thomas McIntyre Cooley (d. 1898) served on the Michigan State Supreme Court for twenty years while also teaching law at the University of Michigan. *A Treatise on the Constitutional Limitations Which Rest upon the Legislative Power of the States of the American Union* was his most important work and continued to be issued in revised editions even after his death. This selection summarizes the pattern of "Church-State relationships" existing in the legal provisions of the states.

A careful examination of the American constitutions will disclose the fact that nothing is more fully set forth or more plainly expressed than the determination of their authors to preserve and perpetuate religious liberty, and to guard against the slightest approach towards the establishment of an inequality in the civil and political rights of citizens, which shall have for its basis only their differences of religious belief.[11] The American people came to the work of framing their fundamental laws, after centuries of religious oppression and persecution, sometimes by one party or sect and sometimes by another, had taught them the utter futility of all attempts to propagate religious opinions by the rewards, penalties, or terrors of human laws. They could not fail to perceive, also, that a union of Church and State, like that which existed in England, if not wholly impracticable in America, was certainly opposed to the spirit of our institutions, and that any domineering of one sect over another was repressing to the energies of the people, and must necessarily tend to discontent and disorder. Whatever, therefore, may have been their individual sentiments upon religious questions, or upon the propriety of the State assuming supervision and control of religious affairs under other circumstances, the general voice has been, that persons of every religious persuasion should be made equal before the law, and that questions of religious belief and religious worship should be questions between each individual man and his Maker. Of these questions human tribunals, so long as the public order is not disturbed, are not to take cognizance, except as the individual, by his voluntary action in associating himself with a religious organization, may have conferred upon such organization a jurisdiction over him in ecclesiastical matters. These constitutions, therefore, have not established religious toleration merely, but religious equality; in that particular being far in advance not only of the mother country, but also of much of the colonial legislation, which, though more liberal than that of other civilized countries, nevertheless exhibited features of discrimination based upon religious beliefs or professions.

Considerable differences will appear in the provisions in the State constitutions on the general subject of the present chapter; some of them being confined to declarations and prohibitions whose purpose is to secure the most perfect equality before the law of all shades of religious belief, while some exhibit a jealousy of ecclesiastical authority by making persons who exercise the functions of clergyman, priest, or teacher of any religious persuasion, society, or sect, ineligible to civil office; and still others show some traces of the old notion, that truth and a sense of duty do not consort with skepticism in religion. There are exceptional clauses, however, though not many in number; and it is believed that, where they exist, they are not often made use of to deprive any person of the civil or political rights or privileges which are placed by law within the reach of his fellows.

Those things which are not lawful under any of the American constitutions may be stated thus:

1: Any law respecting an establishment of religion. The legislatures have not been left at liberty to effect a union of Church and State, or to establish preferences by law in favor of any one religious persuasion or mode of worship. There is not complete religious liberty where any one sect is favored by the State and given an advantage by law over other sects. . . .
2: Compulsory support, by taxation or otherwise, of religious instruction. Not only is no one denomination to be favored at the expense of the rest, but all support of religious instruction must be entirely voluntary. It is not within the sphere of government to coerce it.
3: Compulsory attendance upon religious worship. Whoever is not led by choice or a sense of duty to attend upon the ordinances of religion is not to be compelled to do so by the State. . . .
4: Restraints upon the free exercise of religion according to the dictates of the conscience. No external authority is to place itself between the finite being and the Infinite when the former is seeking to render the homage that is due, and in a mode which commends itself to his conscience and judgment as being suitable for him to render, and acceptable to its object.
5: Restraints upon the expression of religious belief. An earnest believer usually regards it as his duty to propagate his opinions, and to bring others to his views. To deprive him of this right is to take from him the power to perform what he considers a most sacred obligation.

These are the prohibitions which in some form of words are to be found in the American constitutions, and which secure freedom of conscience and of religious worship. No man in religious matters is to be subjected to the censorship of the State or of any public authority; and the State is not to inquire into or take notice of religious belief, when the citizen performs his duty to the State and to his fellows, and is guilty of no breach of public morals or public decorum.

But while thus careful to establish, protect, and defend religious freedom and equality, the American constitutions contain no provisions which prohibit the authorities from such solemn recognition of a superintending Providence in public transactions and exercises as the general religious sentiment of mankind inspires, and as seems meet and proper in finite and dependent beings. Whatever may be the shades of religious belief, all must acknowledge the fitness of recognizing in important human affairs the superintending care and control of the great Governor of the Universe, and of acknowledging with thanksgiving His boundless favors, of bowing in contrition when visited with the penalties of His broken laws. No principle of constitutional law is violated when thanksgiving or fast days are appointed; when chaplains are designated for the army and navy; when legislative sessions are opened with prayer or the reading of the Scriptures, or when religious teaching is encouraged by a general exemption of the houses of religious worship from taxation for the support of State government. Undoubtedly the spirit of the constitution will require, in all these cases, that care be taken to avoid discrimination in favor of or against any one religious denomination or sect; but the power to do any of these things does not become unconstitutional simply because of its susceptibility to abuse. . . .

Nor, while recognizing a superintending Providence, are we always precluded from recognizing also, in the rules prescribed for the conduct of the citizen, the notorious fact that the prevailing religion in the States is Christian. . . . The moral sense is largely regulated and controlled by the religious belief; and therefore it is that those things which, estimated by a Christian standard, are profane and blasphemous, are properly punished as crimes against society, since they are offensive in the highest degree to the general public sense, and have a direct tendency to undermine the moral support of the laws, and to corrupt the community.

It is frequently said that Christianity is a part of the law of the land. In a certain sense and for certain purposes this is true. The best features of the common law, and especially those which regard the family and social relations; which compel the parent to support the child, the husband to support the wife; which make the marriage tie permanent and forbid polygamy,—if not derived from, have at least been improved and strengthened by the prevailing religion and the teachings of its sacred Book. But the law does not attempt to enforce the precepts of Christianity on the ground of their sacred character or divine origin. . . .

Whatever deference the constitution or the laws may require to be paid in some cases to the conscientious scruples or religious convictions of the majority, the general policy always is, to avoid with care any compulsion which infringes on the religious scruples of any, however little reason may seem to others to underlie them. Even in the important matter of bearing arms for the public defense, those who cannot in conscience take part are excused, and their proportion of this great and sometimes imperative burden is borne by the rest of the community.

Some Limitations on Religious Freedom

Reynolds v. United States (1879)

The federal government set out in the nineteenth century to eliminate the practice of polygamy. The prosecution of George Reynolds, private secretary to Mormon leader Brigham Young, under a federal statute criminalizing bigamy, provided the Supreme Court with its first significant opportunity to consider the reach of the First Amendment's protections.

Mr. Chief Justice Waite delivered the opinion of the court:

This is an indictment for bigamy under Section 5352, Revised Statutes, which, omitting its exceptions, is as follows:[12]

"Every person having a husband or wife living, who marries another, whether married or single, in a Territory, or other place over which the United States have exclusive jurisdiction, is guilty of bigamy; and shall be punished by a fine of not more than $500, and by imprisonment for a term of not more than five years." . . .

On the trial, the plaintiff in error, the accused, proved that at the time of his alleged second marriage he was, and for many years before had been, a member of the Church of Jesus Christ of Latter-Day Saints, commonly called the Mormon Church, and a believer in its doctrines; that it was an accepted doctrine of that Church "That it was the duty of male members of said Church, circumstances permitting, to practice polygamy; * * * that this duty was enjoined by different books which the members of said Church believed to be of divine origin, and among others the Holy Bible, and also that the members of the Church believed that the practice of polygamy was directly enjoined upon the male members thereof by the Almighty God, in a revelation to Joseph Smith, the founder and prophet of said Church; that the failing or refusing to practice polygamy by such male members of said Church, when circumstances would admit, would be punished, and that the penalty for such failure and refusal would be damnation in the life to come." He also proved "That he had received permission from the recognized authorities in said Church to enter into polygamous marriage; * * * that Daniel H. Wells, one having authority in said Church to perform the marriage ceremony, married the said defendant on or about the time the crime is alleged to have been committed, to some woman by the name of Schofield, and that such marriage ceremony was performed under and pursuant to the doctrines of said Church."

Upon this proof he asked the court to instruct the jury that if they found from the evidence that he "was married as charged (if he was married) in pursuance of and in conformity with what he believed at the time to be a religious duty, that the verdict must be 'not guilty.'" This request was refused, and the court did charge "That there must have been a criminal intent, but that if the defendant, under the influence of a religious belief that it was right—under an inspiration, if you please, that it was right—deliberately married a second time, having a first wife living, the want of consciousness of evil intent, the want of understanding on his part that he was committing a crime, did not excuse him; but the law inexorably in such case implies the criminal intent."

Upon this charge and refusal to charge the question is raised, whether religious belief can be accepted as a justification of an overt act made criminal by the law of the land. The inquiry is not as to the power of Congress to prescribe criminal laws for the Territories, but as to the guilt of one who knowingly violates a law which has been properly enacted, if he entertains a religious belief that the law is wrong.

Congress cannot pass a law for the government of the Territories which shall prohibit the free exercise of religion. The first amendment to the Constitution expressly forbids such legislation. Religious freedom is guarantied everywhere throughout the United States, so far as congressional interference is concerned. The question to be determined is, whether the law now under consideration comes within this prohibition.

The word "religion" is not defined in the Constitution. We must go elsewhere, therefore, to ascertain its meaning, and nowhere more appropriately, we think, than to the history of the times in the midst of which the provision was adopted. The precise point of the inquiry is, what is the religious freedom which has been guarantied?

Before the adoption of the Constitution, attempts were made in some of the Colonies and States to legislate not only in respect to the establishment of religion, but in respect to its doctrines and precepts as well. The people were taxed, against their will, for the support of religion, and sometimes for the support of particular sects to whose tenets they could not and did not subscribe. Punishments were prescribed for a failure to attend upon public worship, and sometimes for entertaining heretical opinions. The controversy upon this general subject was animated in many of the States, but seemed at last to culminate in Virginia. In 1784, the House of Delegates of that State having under consideration "A bill establishing provision for teachers of the Christian religion," postponed it until the next session, and directed that the bill should-be published and distributed, and that the People be requested "to signify their opinion respecting the adoption of such a bill at the next session of Assembly."

This brought out a determined opposition. Amongst others, Mr. Madison prepared a "Memorial and Remonstrance," which was widely circulated and signed, and in which he demonstrated "that religion, or the duty we owe the Creator," was not within the cognizance of civil government. Semple's Virginia Baptists, Appendix. At the next session the proposed bill was not only defeated, but another, "for establishing religious freedom," drafted by Mr. Jefferson, . . . was passed. In the preamble of this Act, . . . religious freedom is defined; and after a recital "That to suffer the civil magistrate to intrude his powers into the field of opinion, and to restrain the profession or propagation of principles on supposition of their ill tendency, is a dangerous fallacy which at once destroys all religious liberty," it is declared "that it is time enough for the rightful purposes of civil government for its officers to interfere when principles break out into overt acts against peace and good order." In these two sentences is found the true distinction between what properly belongs to the Church and what to the State.

In a little more than a year after the passage of this statute the convention met which prepared the Constitution of the United States. Of this convention Mr. Jefferson was not a member, he being then absent as minister to France. As soon as he saw the draft of the Constitution proposed for adoption, he, in a letter to a friend, expressed his disappointment at the absence of an express declaration insuring the freedom of religion, . . . but was willing to accept it as it was, trusting that the good sense and honest intentions of the people would bring about the necessary alterations. . . . Five of the States, while adopting the Constitution, proposed amendments. Three, New Hampshire, New York and Virginia, included in one form or another a declaration of religious freedom in the changes they desired to have made, as did also North Carolina, where the convention at first declined to ratify the Constitution until the proposed amendments were acted upon. Accordingly, at the first session of the first Congress the amendment now under consideration was proposed with others by Mr. Madison. It met the views of the advocates of religious freedom, and was adopted. Mr. Jefferson afterwards, in reply to an address to him by a committee of the Danbury Baptist Association, . . . took occasion to say: "Believing with you that religion is a matter which lies solely between man and his God; that he owes account to none other for his faith or his worship; that the legislative powers of the Government reach actions only, and not opinions, I contemplate with sovereign reverence that act of the whole American people which declared that their Legislature should 'make no law respecting an establishment of religion or prohibiting the free exercise thereof,' thus building a wall of separation between Church and State. Adhering to this expression of the supreme will of the Nation in behalf of the rights of conscience. I shall see, with sincere satisfaction, the progress of those sentiments which tend to restore man to all his natural rights, convinced he has no natural right in opposition to his social duties." Coming as this does from an acknowledged leader of the advocates of the measure, it may be accepted almost as an authoritative declaration of the scope and effect of the amendment thus secured. Congress was deprived of all legislative power over mere opinion, but was left free to reach actions which were in violation of social duties or subversive of good order.

Polygamy has always been odious among the Northern and Western Nations of Europe and, until the establishment of the Mormon Church, was almost exclusively a feature of the life of Asiatic and African people. At common law, the second marriage was always void, . . . and from the earliest history of England polygamy has been treated as an offense against society. After the establishment of the ecclesiastical courts, and until the time of James I., it was punished through the instrumentality of those tribunals, not merely because ecclesiastical rights had been violated, but because upon the separation of the ecclesiastical courts from the civil, the ecclesiastical were supposed to be the most appropriate for the trial of matrimonial causes and offenses against the rights of marriage; just as they were for testamentary causes and the settlement of the estates of deceased persons.

By the Statute of 1 James I., ch. 11, the offense, if committed in England or Wales, was made punishable in the civil courts, and the penalty was death. As this statute was limited in its operation to England and Wales, it was at a very early period re-enacted, generally with some modifications, in all the Colonies. In connection with the case we are now considering, it is a significant fact that on the 8th of December, 1788, after the passage of the Act establishing religious freedom, and after the convention of Virginia had recommended as an amendment to the Constitution of the United States the declaration in a Bill of Rights that "All men have an equal, natural and unalienable right to the free exercise of religion, according to the dictates of conscience," the Legislature of that State substantially enacted the Statute of James I., death penalty included, because as recited in the preamble, "It hath been doubted whether bigamy or polygamy be punishable by the laws of this Commonwealth." . . . From that day to this we think it may safely be said there never has been a time in any State of the Union when polygamy has not been an offense against society, cognizable by the civil courts and punishable with more or less severity. In the face of all this evidence, it is impossible to believe that the constitutional guaranty of religious freedom was intended to prohibit legislation in respect to this most important feature of social life. Marriage, while from its very nature a sacred obligation, is, nevertheless, in most civilized nations, a civil contract, and usually regulated by law. Upon it society may be said to be built, and out of its fruits spring social relations and social obligations and duties, with which government is necessarily required to deal. In fact, according as monogamous or polygamous marriages are allowed, do we find the principles on which the Government of the People, to a greater or less extent, rests. Professor Lieber says: polygamy leads to the patriarchal principle, and which, when applied to large communities, fetters the people in stationary despotism, while that principle cannot long exist in connection with monogamy. . . . An exceptional colony of polygamists under an exceptional leadership may sometimes exist for a time without appearing to disturb the social condition of the people who surround it; but there cannot be a doubt that, unless restricted by some form of constitution, it is within the legitimate scope of the power of every civil government to determine whether polygamy or monogamy shall be the law of social life under its dominion.

In our opinion the statute immediately under consideration is within the legislative power of Congress. It is constitutional and valid as prescribing a rule of action for all those residing in the Territories, and in places over which the United States have exclusive control. This being so, the only question which remains is, whether those who make polygamy a part of their religion are excepted from the operation of the statute. If they are, then those who do not make polygamy a part of their religious belief may be found guilty and punished, while those who do must be acquitted and go free. This would be introducing a new element into criminal law. Laws are made for the government of actions, and while they cannot interfere with mere religious belief and opinions, they may with practices. Suppose one believed that human sacrifices were a necessary part of religious worship, would it be seriously contended that the civil government under which he lived could not interfere to prevent a sacrifice? Or if a wife religiously believed it was her duty to burn herself upon the funeral pile of her dead husband, would it be beyond the power of the civil government to prevent her carrying her belief into practice?

So here, as a law of the organization of society under the exclusive dominion of the United States, it is provided that plural marriages shall not be allowed. Can a man excuse his practices to the contrary because of his religious belief? To permit this would be to make the professed doctrines of religious belief superior to the law of the land, and in effect to permit every citizen to become a law unto himself. Government could exist only in name under such circumstances. . . .

Davis v. Beason (1890)

Following the *Reynolds* case, the United States continued its efforts to wipe out polygamy among the Mormons in the Western territories, in this case, by requiring voters to swear that they were not members of an organization encouraging polygamy. The Supreme Court subsequently upheld a federal law revoking the charter of the Mormon church and confiscating much of its property (in the 1890 case of *Church of Jesus Christ of Latter-Day Saints v. United States*). Faced with public antipathy, the potential of widespread criminal prosecutions, and the forfeiture of the church's property, the president of the Mormon church issued a proclamation saying that polygamous marriages were no longer sanctioned. Ultimately, there was a grant of amnesty and presidential pardon for all who abstained from polygamy after the proclamation.

Statement by *Mr. Justice* Field:

In April, 1889, the appellant, Samuel D. Davis, was indicted in . . . the Territory of Idaho, in the County of Oneida, in connection with divers persons named, and divers other persons whose names were unknown to the grand jury, for a conspiracy to unlawfully pervert and obstruct the due administration of the laws of the Territory in this, that they would unlawfully procure themselves to be admitted to registration as electors of said County of Oneida for the general election then next to occur in that county, when they were not entitled to be admitted to such registration, by appearing before the respective registrars of the election precincts in which they resided, and taking the oath prescribed by the Statute of the State, in substance as follows:[13] "I do swear (or affirm) that I am a male citizen of the United States of the age of twenty-one years (or will be on the 6th day of November, 1888); and that I have (or will have) actually resided in this Territory four months and in this county for thirty days next preceding the day of the next ensuing election; that I have never been convicted of treason, felony or bribery; and that I am not registered or entitled to vote at any other place in this Territory; and I do further swear that I am not a bigamist or polygamist; that I am not a member of any order, organization or association which teaches, advises, counsels or encourages its members, devoices or any other person to commit the crime of bigamy or polygamy, or any other crime defined by law as a duty arising or resulting from membership in such order, organization or association, or which practices bigamy, polygamy or plural or celestial marriage as a doctrinal right of such organization; that I do not and will not, publicly or privately, or in any manner whatever, teach, advise, counsel or encourage any person to commit the crime of bigamy or polygamy, or any other crime defined by law, either as a religious duty or otherwise; that I do regard the Constitution of the United States and the laws thereof and the laws of this Territory, as interpreted by the courts, as the supreme laws of the land, the teachings of any order, organization or association to the contrary notwithstanding, so help me God," when, in truth, each of the defendants was a member of an order, organization and association, namely, the Church of Jesus Christ of Latter-Day Saints, commonly known as the Mormon Church, which they knew taught, advised, counseled and encouraged its members and devotees to commit the crimes of bigamy and polygamy as duties arising and resulting from membership in said order, organization and association, and which order, organization and association, as they all knew, practiced bigamy and polygamy and plural and celestial marriage as doctrinal rights of said organization; and that in pursuance of said conspiracy the said defendants went before the registrars of different precincts of the county (which are designated) and took and had administered to them respectively the oath aforesaid. . . .

On the trial which followed on the 12th of September, 1889, the jury found the defendant Samuel D. Davis guilty as charged in the indictment. The defendant was thereupon sentenced to pay a fine of $500, and in default of its payment to be confined in the county jail of Oneida County for a term not exceeding 250 days, and was remanded to the custody of the sheriff until the judgment should be satisfied.

Mr. Justice Field delivered the opinion of the court:

On this appeal our only inquiry is whether the District Court of the Territory had jurisdiction of the offense charged in the indictment of which the defendant was found guilty. . . . We cannot look into any alleged errors in its rulings on the trial of the defendant. . . . Nor can we inquire whether the evidence established the fact alleged, that the defendant was a member of an order or organization known as the Mormon Church, called the Church of Jesus Christ of Latter Day Saints, or the fact that the order or organization taught and counseled its members and devotees to commit the crimes of bigamy and polygamy as duties arising from membership therein. On this hearing we can only consider whether, these allegations being taken as true, an offense was committed of which the territorial court had jurisdiction to try the defendant. And on this point there can be no serious discussion or difference of opinion, Bigamy and polygamy are crimes by the laws of all civilized and Christian countries. They are crimes by the laws of the United States, and they are crimes by the laws of Idaho. They tend to destroy the purity of the marriage relation, to disturb the peace of families, to degrade woman and to debase man. Few crimes are more pernicious to the best interests of society and receive more general or more deserved punishment. To extend exemption from punishment for such crimes would be to shock the moral judgment of the community. To call their advocacy a tenet of religion is to offend the common sense of mankind. If they are crimes, then to teach, advise and counsel their practice is to aid in their commission, and such leaching and counseling are themselves criminal and proper subjects of punishment, as aiding and abetting crime are in all other cases.

The term "religion" has reference to one's views of his relations to his Creator, and to the obligations they impose of reverence for his being and character, and of obedience to his will. It is often confounded with the *cultus* or form of worship of a particular sect, but is distinguishable from the latter. The First Amendment to the Constitution, in declaring that Congress shall make no law respecting the establishment of religion, or forbidding the free exercise thereof, was intended to allow everyone under the jurisdiction of the United States to entertain in such notions respecting his relations to his Maker and the duties they impose as may be approved by his judgment and conscience, and to exhibit his sentiments in such form of worship as be may think proper, not injurious to the equal rights of others, and to prohibit legislation for the support of any religious tenets, or the modes of worship of any sect. The oppressive measures adopted, and the cruelties and punishments inflicted by the governments of Europe for many ages, to compel parties to conform in their religious beliefs and modes of worship to the views of the most numerous sect, and the folly of attempting in that way to control the mental operations of persons and enforce an outward conformity to a prescribed standard, led to the adoption of the Amendment in question. It was never intended or supposed that the Amendment could be invoked as a protection against legislation for the punishment of acts inimical to the peace, good order and morals of society. With man's relations to his Maker and the obligations he may think they impose, and the manner in which an expression shall be made by him of his belief on those subjects, no interference can be permitted, provided always the laws of society, designed to secure its peace and prosperity, and the morals of its people; are not interfered with. However free the exercise of religion may be, it must be subordinate to the criminal laws of the country, passed with reference to actions regarded by general consent as properly the subjects of punitive legislation. There have been sects which denied as a part of their religious tenets that there should be any marriage tie, and advocated promiscuous intercourse of the sexes as prompted by the passions of their members. And history discloses the fact that the necessity of human sacrifices, on special occasions, has been a tenet of many sects. Should a sect of either of these kinds ever find its way into this country, swift punishment would follow the carrying into effect of its doctrines, and no heed would be given to the pretense that, as religious beliefs, their supporters could be protected in their exercise by the Constitution of the United States. Probably never before in the history of this country has it been seriously contended that the whole punitive power of the government, for acts recognized by the general consent of the Christian world in modern times as proper matters for prohibitory legislation, must be suspended in order that the tenets of a religious sect encouraging crime may be carried out without hindrance. . . .

It is assumed by counsel of the petitioner that, because no mode of worship can be established or religious tenets enforced in this country, therefore any form of worship may be followed and any tenets, however destructive of society, may be held and advocated, if asserted to be a part of the religious doctrines of those advocating and practicing them. But nothing is further from the truth. Whilst legislation for the establishment of a religion is forbidden, and its free exercise permitted, it does not follow that everything which may be so called can be tolerated. Crime is not the less odious because sanctioned by what any particular sect may designate as religion.

Notes

1. Published as *The Bible in the Common Schools* (Cincinnati, 1870). The case was *John D. Minor, et al. v. Board of Education of Cincinnati, et al.* It was decided in the General Term, February 1870, of the Superior Court of Cincinnati. Excerpts are from pp. 373–389.

2. Published as *The Bible in the Public Schools* (Cincinnati, 1873). This was extracted from vol. 23 of the Ohio State Reports, pp. 238–254.

3. From *Religion and the State, or, the Bible and the Public Schools* (New York, 1876), pp. 377–387.

4. From *The Century,* XLVII, no. 5 (March 1894), pp. 789–795.

5. From Josiah Strong, *Our Country: Its Possible Future and Its Present Crises* (New York, 1885), Chap. XIII, pp. 161 ff.

6. From E. B. Brady, C.S.P., "Church and State," in *The Catholic World,* LIV, no. 321 (December 1891): 391–396 (New York, 1892).

7. From John A. Ryan and M. F. X. Millar, eds., *The State and the Church* (New York: Macmillan Company, 1924), pp. 282–283, 285. Reprinted by permission.

8. Reprinted by permission of the publisher from "Catholicism and A Non-Catholic State" in *The Emergence of Liberal Catholicism in America* by Robert D. Cross, pp. 71–78, Cambridge, Mass.: Harvard University Press, copyright © 1958 by the President and Fellows of Harvard College.

9. From Philip Schaff, "Church and State in the United States," *Papers of the American Historical Association* II, no. 4 (1888): 9–10 and 12–16.

10. From James Bryce, *The American Commonwealth,* 3rd ed., vol. 2 (New York: Macmillan, 1894), pp. 698–704.

11. From T. M. Cooley, "Of Religious Liberty," *A Treatise on the Constitutional Limitations Which Rest upon the Legislative Power of the States of the American Union,* 7th ed. (Boston: Little, Brown, 1903), which followed the last text revised by Cooley dated in 1896. This section—regarding text—was substantially unchanged from at least the 4th ed. (Boston: Little, Brown, 1878).

12. *Reynolds v. United States* 98 U.S. 145 (1879).

13. *Davis v. Beason* 133 U.S. 333 (1890).

6

Mainstream Pluralism (1920–1960)

Between 1920 and 1960 there were continuing attempts to define what "independence of Church and State" might mean in a society self-conscious of its religious pluralism—at least to the extent of its three major faiths. Each of these religious communities rethought its traditions in light of its American experiences. The spirit that led to the nineteenth-century liberal American Catholic "heresy" of Americanism (even if the heresy per se never existed) found new expression in liberating Catholic self-understanding from dated European categories. Many Protestants also rethought their positions on the church-state issue, conscious that their pre–Civil War aspirations should not (or could not) necessarily prevail in a more pluralistic era. The Jewish community—vocal out of proportion to its numbers—frequently contributed to this discussion. Sharing with the Roman Catholics a sense of tradition and a sense of outrage at the second-class status they both experienced for so long, the Jews were exceptionally articulate in defending their substantial religious freedom in America. In particular, they championed the separation of church and state with fervor akin to that earlier associated with the Baptists. Thus the Jewish community nicely mediated between the far larger Protestant and Catholic communities.

As the religious communities sought to delineate institutional aspects of church and state, another facet of the ancient problem received considerable public attention—the relationship between religion and politics. Some have argued that religion is an entirely private affair, and thus it should have no significant relationship to the realm of politics, yet others assert with equal vehemence that religious and political views are inseparable. The relationship includes such issues as ecclesiastical pressure on political processes, the "religious vote," and selection of candidates according to the religious vote they may be expected to pull (if not a de facto religious test for office). Understandably, primary interest in these questions has been focused at the level of national politics, but religious authority structures and political behavior interact at all levels of community life. Twice during this period the question arose of whether a Roman Catholic could be elected president. It is probably wrong to attribute the defeat of Al Smith in the 1928 campaign to his Roman Catholic faith. It is possible, however, that religion significantly affected the outcome of the 1960 election, in which John F. Kennedy safely won the electoral college while failing to receive a majority of the popular vote.

During this period, the United States Supreme Court became an important force in church-state matters. Guided both by the historical roots of the religion clauses of the First Amendment and by the need to address contemporary questions, the court has had an increasingly influential role in defining the American church-state question. Starting at least with the *Everson* case in 1947, almost every issue involving religion and government became a potential source of litigation under either the free exercise clause or the establishment clause.

It can be argued that the rubric of church and state has application only where a religious institution and a political institution express the twofold life of a single community. If that is the case the phrase would seem to have little relevance for much of intervening American history. But if it designates the manifold interactions among religious and political aspects of a complex modern society—where each is presumed to have a certain autonomy—then the term continues to be appropriate to an America self-conscious of its religious pluralism and eager to preserve its heritage of voluntary associations and limited civil governments.

Church and State in Religious Perspectives

JOHN A. RYAN

Comments on the "Christian Constitution of States"

John A. Ryan, professor of moral theology at Catholic University of America, was at once traditionalistic in his interpretation of Roman Catholic church-state thought and a liberal in social issues. His exegesis of Pope Leo XIII's encyclical *Immortale Dei* (November 1, 1885) was an important statement of the conservative Roman Catholic position.

Public Profession of Religion by the State

To the present generation this is undoubtedly "a hard saying."[1] The separation of Church and State, which obtains substantially in the majority of countries, is generally understood as forbidding the State to make "a public profession of religion." Nevertheless, the logic of Pope Leo's argument is unassailable. Men are obliged to worship God, not only as individuals, but also as organized groups. Societies have existence and functions over and above the existence and functions of their individual members. Therefore, they are dependent upon God for their corporate existence and functions, and as moral persons owe corporate obedience to His laws, formal recognition of His authority, and appropriate acts of worship. To deny these propositions is to maintain the illogical position that man owes God religious worship under only one aspect of his life, in only one department of his life.

Since the State is by far the most important of the secular societies to which man belongs, its obligation to recognize and profess religion is considerably greater and stricter than is the case with the lesser societies. And the failure of the State to discharge this obligation produces evil results of corresponding gravity. It exhibits in most extensive proportions the destructive power of bad example.

Attitude of the State Toward the Church

But Pope Leo goes further. He declares that the State must not only "have care for religion," but recognize the *true* religion. This means the form of religion professed by the Catholic Church. It is a thoroughly logical position. If the State is under moral compulsion to profess and promote religion, it is obviously obliged to profess and promote only the religion that is true; for no individual, no group of individuals, no society, no State is justified in supporting error or in according to error the same recognition as to truth.

Those who deny this principle may practically all be included within three classes: First, those who hold that truth will by its own power speedily overcome error, and that the State should consequently assume an attitude of impartiality toward both; second, those who assume that all forms of religion are equally good and true; third, those who hold that it is impossible to know which is the true one. The first theory is contradicted and refuted by the persistence of a hundred errors side by side with truth for centuries. In the long run and with sufficient enlightenment, truth will be sufficiently mighty to prevail by its own force and momentum, but its victory can be greatly hastened by judicious assistance from the State and, indeed, from every other kind of organized social power. The successful opposition of the Church to the Protestant Reformation in those countries where the Church had the sympathy and assistance of the State, is but one of a vast number of historical illustrations. Against the theory that all forms of religion are equally sound, it is sufficient to cite the principle of contradiction; two contradictory propositions cannot be true, any more than yes can be identified with no. Finally, it is not impossible to know which religion is the right one, inasmuch as the Church of Christ comes before men with credentials sufficient to convince all those who will deliberately examine the evidence with a will to believe. The argument and the proofs are summarized by Pope Leo in the paragraphs immediately following the one now under consideration. Such is the objective logic of the situation. In a particular case the public authorities can reject and frequently have rejected the evidence for the divinity of the Catholic Church.

It is not of such rulers or such States that Pope Leo is speaking in this part of the encyclical. The principle that he is here defending has complete and unconditional application only to Catholic States. Between these and the Catholic Church the normal relation is that of formal agreement and mutual support; in other words, what is generally known as the union of Church and State. In his encyclical on "Catholicity in the United States," the same Pope gave generous praise to the attitude of our government and laws toward religion, but immediately added:

"Yet, though all this is true, it would be very erroneous to draw the conclusion that in America is to be sought the type of the most desirable status of the Church, or that it would be universally lawful or expedient for State and Church, to be, as in America, dissevered and divorced. The fact that Catholicity with you is in good condition, nay, is even enjoying a prosperous growth, is by all means to be attributed to the fecundity with which God has endowed His Church, in virtue of which unless men or circumstances interfere, she spontaneously expands and propagates herself; but she would bring forth more abundant fruits if, in addition to liberty, she enjoyed the favor of the laws and the patronage of public authority."

Occasionally some Catholics are found who reject this doctrine on the ground that alliances between Church and State have done more harm than good. Space is wanting here for an adequate discussion and refutation of this contention. Nor is a formal criticism necessary. Men who take this position are indulging in what the logicians call "the fallacy of the particular instance." Because they find some forms of union between Church and State working badly in some countries for certain periods of time, they rush to the conclusion that all forms are bad, at all times, in all countries. An adequate evaluation of the arrangement, a judicious weighing of the good effects against the bad effects, supposes a knowledge of history far more comprehensive than is possessed by any of these critics. Men who lack this knowledge ought to show a becoming modesty and hesitancy in making any general pronouncement on the complex effects of this policy.

One observation may be made which is calculated to prevent much misconception and false reasoning on this subject. It is that the *principle* of union between Church and State is not necessarily dependent upon *any particular form of union that has actually been in operation.* When men condemn the principle because they see that State support of the clergy, or State nomination of bishops, has in certain cases been harmful to the Church, they are laboring under a false assumption. Neither of these particular arrangements is required by the principle. Other critics identify the principle with the particular application of it that obtained in the Middle Ages. This assumption is likewise illogical and incorrect. The distinguished German theologian, Father Pohle, writes thus: "The intimate connection of both powers during the Middle Ages was only a passing and temporary phenomenon, arising neither from the essential nature of the State nor from that of the Church." In the same article, he points out three grave evil results of this intimate connection; namely, excessive meddling by ecclesiastical authorities in political affairs, conflicts between the two powers which produced diminished popular respect for both, and "the danger that the clergy, trusting blindly to the interference of the secular arm in their behalf, may easily sink into dull resignation and spiritual torpor, while the laity, owing to the religious surveillance of the State, may develop rather into a race of religious hypocrites and pietists than into inwardly convinced Christians."

All that is essentially comprised in the union of Church and State can be thus formulated: The State should officially recognize the Catholic religion as the religion of the commonwealth; accordingly it should invite the blessing and the ceremonial participation of the Church for certain important public functions, as the opening of legislative sessions, the erection of public buildings, etc., and delegate its officials to attend certain of the more important festival celebrations of the Church; it should recognize and sanction the laws of the Church; and it should protect the rights of the Church, and the religious as well as the other rights of the Church's members.

Does State recognition of the Catholic religion necessarily imply that no other religion should be tolerated? Much depends upon circumstances and much depends upon what is meant by toleration. Neither unbaptized persons nor those born into a non-Catholic sect, should ever be coerced into the Catholic Church. This would be fundamentally irrational, for belief depends upon the will and the will is not subject to physical compulsion. Should such persons be permitted to practice their own form of worship? If these are carried on within the family, or in such an inconspicuous manner as to be an occasion neither of scandal nor of perversion to the faithful, they may properly be tolerated by the State. At least, this is the approved Catholic doctrine concerning the religious rites of the non-baptized. Only those religious practices of unbelievers which are contrary to the natural law, such as idolatry, human sacrifice and debauchery, should be repressed. The best indication of the Church's attitude on this question is the toleration and protection accorded all through the Middle Ages to Judaism and Jewish worship by the Popes in their capacity of civil rulers of the Papal States. The same principle regarding freedom of worship seems fairly applicable to baptized persons who were born into a non-Catholic sect. For their participation in false worship does not necessarily imply a wilful affront to the true Church nor a menace to public order or social welfare. In a Catholic State which protects and favors the Catholic religion and whose citizens are in great majority adherents of the true faith, the religious performances of an insignificant and ostracized sect will constitute neither a scandal nor an occasion of perversion to Catholics. Hence there exists no sufficient reason to justify the State in restricting the liberty of individuals.

Quite distinct from the performance of false religious worship and preaching to the members of the erring sect, is the propagation of the false doctrine among Catholics. This could become a source of injury, a positive menace, to the religious welfare of true believers. Against such an evil they have a right of protection by the Catholic State. On the one hand, this propaganda is harmful to the citizens and contrary to public welfare; on the other hand, it is not among the natural rights of the propagandists. Rights are merely means to rational ends. Since no rational end is promoted by the dissemination of false doctrine, there exists no right to indulge in this practice. The fact that the individual may in good faith think that his false religion is true gives no more right to propagate it than the sincerity of the alien anarchist entitles him to advocate his abominable political theories in the United States, or than the perverted ethical notions of the dealer in obscene literature confer upon him a right to corrupt the morals of the community. No State could endure on the basis of the theory that the citizen must always be accorded the prerogative of doing whatever he thinks right. Now the actions of preaching and writing are at once capable of becoming quite as injurious to the community as any other actions and quite as subject to rational restraint.

Superficial champions of religious liberty will promptly and indignantly denounce the foregoing propositions as the essence of intolerance. They are intolerant, but not therefore unreasonable. Error has not the same rights as truth. Since the profession and practice of error are contrary to human welfare, how can error have rights? How can the voluntary toleration of error be justified? As we have already pointed out, the men who defend the principle of toleration for all varieties of religious opinion, assume either that all religions are equally true or that the true cannot be distinguished from the false. On no other ground is it logically possible to accept the theory of indiscriminate and universal toleration.

To the objection that the foregoing argument can be turned against Catholics by a non-Catholic State, there are two replies. First, if such a State should prohibit Catholic worship or preaching on the plea that it was wrong and injurious to the community, the assumption would be false; therefore, the two cases are not parallel. Second, a Protestant State could not logically take such an attitude (although many of them did so in former centuries) because no Protestant sect claims to be infallible. Besides, the Protestant principle of private judgment logically implies that Catholics may be right in their religious convictions, and that they have a right to hold and preach them without molestation.

Such in its ultimate rigor and complete implications is the Catholic position concerning the alliance that should exist between the Church and a Catholic State. While its doctrinal premises will be rejected by convinced non-Catholics, its logic cannot be denied by anyone who accepts the unity of religious truth. If there is only one true religion, and if its possession is the most important good in life for States as well as individuals, then the public profession, protection, and promotion of this religion and the legal prohibition of all direct assaults upon it, becomes one of the most obvious and fundamental duties of the State. For it is the business of the State to safeguard and promote human welfare in all departments of life. In the words of Pope Leo, "civil society, established for the common welfare, should not only safeguard the well-being of the community, but have also at heart the interests of its individual members, in such mode as not in any way to hinder, but in every manner to render as easy as may be, the possession of that highest and unchangeable good for which all should seek."

In practice, however, the foregoing propositions have full application only to the completely Catholic State. This means a political community that is either exclusively, or almost exclusively, made up of Catholics. In the opinion of Father Pohle, "there is good reason to doubt if there still exists a purely Catholic State in the world." The propositions of Pope Pius IX condemning the toleration of non-Catholic sects do not now, says Father Pohle, "apply even to Spain or the South American republics, to say nothing of countries possessing a greatly mixed population." He lays down the following general rule: "When several religions have firmly established themselves and taken root in the same territory, nothing else remains for the State than either to exercise tolerance towards them all, or, as conditions exist today, to make complete religious liberty for individuals and religious bodies a principle of government." Father Moulart makes substantially the same statement: "In a word, it is necessary to extend political toleration to dissenting sects which exist in virtue of a fact historically accomplished."

The reasons which justify this complete religious liberty fall under two heads: First, rational expediency, inasmuch as the attempt to proscribe or hamper the peaceful activities of established religious groups would be productive of more harm than good; second, the positive provisions of religious liberty found in the constitutions of most modern States. To quote Father Pohle once more: "If religious freedom has been accepted and sworn to as a fundamental law in a constitution, the obligation to show this tolerance is binding in conscience." The principle of tolerance, he continues, cannot be disregarded even by Catholic States "without violation of oaths and loyalty, and without violent internal convulsions."

But constitutions can be changed, and non-Catholic sects may decline to such a point that the political proscription of them may become feasible and expedient. What protection would they then have against a Catholic State? The latter could logically tolerate only such religious activities as were confined to the members of the dissenting group. It could not permit them to carry on general propaganda nor accord their organization certain privileges that had formerly been extended to all religious corporations, for example, exemption from taxation. While all this is very true in logic and in theory, the event of its practical realization in any State or country is so remote in time and in probability that no practical man will let it disturb his equanimity or affect his attitude toward those who differ from him in religious faith. It is true, indeed, that some zealots and bigots will continue to attack the Church because they fear that some five thousand years hence the United States may become overwhelmingly Catholic and may then restrict the freedom of non-Catholic denominations. Nevertheless, we cannot yield up the principles of eternal and unchangeable truth in order to avoid the enmity of such unreasonable persons. Moreover, it would be a futile policy; for they would not think us sincere.

Therefore, we shall continue to profess the true principles of the relations between Church and State, confident that the great majority of our fellow citizens will be sufficiently honorable to respect our devotion to truth, and sufficiently realistic to see that the danger of religious intolerance toward non-Catholics in the United States is so improbable and so far in the future that it should not occupy their time or attention.

JOHN COURTNEY MURRAY, S.J.

Civil Unity and Religious Integrity

Father John Courtney Murray, S.J., was professor of theology at Woodstock College. He is best known for his re-expression of the Roman Catholic position on church and state in terms that take account of the American political traditions and practices. Many of his articles were brought together in *We Hold These Truths,* from which the following selection is taken.

The Distinction of Church and State

If the demands of social necessity account for the emergence in America of religious freedom as a fact, they hardly account for certain peculiarities of the first of our prejudices and for the depth of feeling that it evokes.[2] Another powerful historical force must be considered, namely, the dominant impulse toward self-government, government by the people in the most earnest sense of the word. Above all else the early Americans wanted political freedom. And the force of this impulse necessarily acted as a corrosive upon the illegitimate "unions" of church and state which the post-Reformation era had brought forth. The establishments of the time were, by and large, either theocratic, wherein the state was absorbed in the church, or Erastian, wherein the church was absorbed in the state. In both cases the result was some limitation upon freedom, either in the form of civil disabilities imposed in the name of the established religion, or in the form of religious disabilities imposed in the name of the civil law of the covenanted community. The drive toward popular freedom would with a certain inevitability sweep away such establishments. Men might share the fear of Roger Williams, that the state would corrupt the church, or the fear of Thomas Jefferson, that the church would corrupt the state. In either case their thought converged to the one important conclusion, that an end had to be put to the current confusions of the religious and political orders. The ancient distinction between church and state had to be newly reaffirmed in a manner adapted to the American scene. Calvinist theocracy, Anglican Erastianism, Gallican absolutism—all were vitiated by the same taint: they violated in one way or another this traditional distinction.

The dualism of mankind's two hierarchically ordered forms of social life had been Christianity's cardinal contribution to the Western political tradition, as everyone knows who has looked into the monumental work of the two Carlyles, *Medieval Political Thought in the West.* Perhaps equally with the very idea of law itself it had been the most fecund force for freedom in society. The distinction had always been difficult to maintain in practice, even when it was affirmed in theory. But when it was formally denied the result was an infringement of man's freedom of religious faith or of his freedom as a citizen—an infringement of either or both. Hence the generalized American impulse toward freedom inevitably led to a new and specially emphatic affirmation of the traditional distinction.

The distinction lay readily within the reach of the early American lawyers and statesmen; for it was part of the English legal heritage, part of the patrimony of the common law. One can see it appearing, for instance, in Madison's famous *Memorial and Remonstrance,* where it is interpreted in a manner conformable to the anti-ecclesiasticism which he had in common with Jefferson. But the interesting figure here is again Roger Williams. Reading him, the Catholic theorist is inclined to agree with those "juditious persons" whose verdict was reluctantly and belatedly recorded by Cotton Mather. They "judged him," said Mather, "to have the root of the matter in him."

In the present question the root of the matter is this distinction of the spiritual and temporal orders and their respective jurisdictions. One is tempted to think that he got hold of this root at least partly because of his early acquaintance with English law. He was for a time secretary to the great Sir Edward Coke and it is at least not unlikely that he continued his legal interests at Cambridge. In any event, this distinction was a key principle with Williams. He had his own special understanding of it, but at least he understood it. What is more, in 1636 he felt in his own flesh, so to speak, the effects of its violations in the Massachusetts colony. Of his banishment from Massachusetts in that year he later wrote: "Secondly, if he (John Cotton) means this civil act of banishing, why should he call a civil sentence from a civil state, within a few weeks execution in so sharp a time of New England's cold, why should he call this a banishment from the churches except he silently confess that the frame or constitution of their churches is implicitly national (which yet they profess against)? For otherwise, why was I not yet permitted to live in the world or commonweal except for this reason, that the commonweal and church is yet but one, and he that is banished from the one must necessarily be banished from the other also?" This was his constant accusation against the New England Way. He says on another occasion: "First, it will appear that in spiritual things they make the garden and the wilderness (as I often have intimated), I say, the garden and the wilderness, the church and the world are all one." The same charge is lodged against "holy men, emperors and bishops" throughout history, that "they made the garden of the church and the field of the world to be all one. . . ."

However erroneously Williams may have understood the "garden," the church, as having no relation whatsoever to the "wilderness," at least he knew that church and civil society are not one but two. To make them "all one" is to violate the nature of the church and also the nature of civil society, as this latter had been understood in the liberal Christian political tradition.

As has been said, Roger Williams was not a Father of the Federal Constitution. He is adduced here only as a witness, in his own way, to the genuine Western tradition of politics. The point is that the distinction of church and state, one of the central assertions of this tradition, found its way into the Constitution. There it received a special embodiment, adapted to the peculiar genius of American government and to the concrete conditions of American society.

How this happened need not concern us here. Certainly it was in part because the artisans of the Constitution had a clear grasp of the distinction between state and society, which had been the historical product of the distinction between church and state, inasmuch as the latter distinction asserted the existence of a whole wide area of human concerns which were remote from the competence of government. Calhoun's "force of circumstances" also had a great deal of influence; here again it was a matter of the Fathers building better than they knew. Their major concern was sharply to circumscribe the powers of government. The area of state—that is, legal—concern was limited to the pursuit of certain enumerated secular purposes (to say that the purposes are secular is not to deny that many of them are also moral; so for instance the establishment of justice and peace, the promotion of the general welfare, etc). Thus made autonomous in its own sphere, government was denied all competence in the field of religion. In this field freedom was to be the rule and method; government was powerless to legislate respecting an establishment of religion and likewise powerless to prohibit the free exercise of religion. Its single office was to take legal or judicial steps necessary on given occasions to make effective the general guarantee of freedom.

The concrete applications of this, in itself quite simple, solution have presented great historical and legal difficulties. This has been inevitable, given the intimacy with which religion is woven into the whole social fabric, and given, too, the evolution of government from John Adams' "plain, simple, intelligible thing, quite comprehensible by common sense," to the enormously complicated and sprawling thing which now organizes a great part of our lives, handles almost all education, and much social welfare. In particular, we have not yet found an answer to the question whether government can make effective the primary intention of the First Amendment, the guarantee of freedom of religion, simply by attempting to make more and more "impregnable" what is called, in Rogers Williams' fateful metaphor, the "wall of separation" between church and state. However, what concerns us here is the root of the matter, the fact that the American Constitution embodies in a special way the traditional principle of the distinction between church and state.

For Catholics this fact is of great and providential importance for one major reason. It serves sharply to set off our constitutional system from the system against which the Church waged its long-drawn-out fight in the nineteenth century, namely, Jacobinism, or (in Carlton Hayes's term) sectarian Liberalism, or (in the more definitive term used today) totalitarian democracy.

It is now coming to be recognized that the Church opposed the "separation of church and state" of the sectarian Liberals because in theory and in fact it did not mean separation at all but perhaps the most drastic unification of church and state which history had known. The Jacobin "free state" was as regalist as the *ancien régime,* and even more so. Writing as a historian, de Tocqueville long ago made this plain. And the detailed descriptions which Leo XIII, writing as a theologian and political moralist, gave of the Church's "enemy" make the fact even more plain. Within this "free state" the so-called "free church" was subject to a political control more complete than the Tudor or Stuart or Bourbon monarchies dreamed of. The evidence stretches all the way from the Civil Constitution of the Clergy in 1790 to the Law of Separation in 1905.

In the system sponsored by the sectarian Liberals, as has been well said, "The state pretends to ignore the Church; in reality it never took more cognizance of her." In the law of 1905, the climactic development, the Church was arrogantly assigned a juridical statute articulated in forty-four articles, whereby almost every aspect of her organization and action was minutely regulated. Moreover, this was done on principle—the principle of the primacy of the political, the principle of "everything within the state, nothing above the state." This was the cardinal thesis of sectarian Liberalism, whose full historical development is now being witnessed in the totalitarian "people's democracies" behind the Iron Curtain. As the Syllabus and its explicatory documents—as well as the multitudinous writings of Leo XIII—make entirely clear, it was this thesis of the juridical omnipotence and omnicompetence of the state which was the central object of the Church's condemnation of the Jacobin development. It was because freedom of religion and separation of church and state were predicated on this thesis that the Church refused to accept them as a thesis.

This thesis was utterly rejected by the founders of the American Republic. The rejection was as warranted as it was providential, because this thesis is not only theologically heterodox, as denying the reality of the Church; it is also politically revolutionary, as denying the substance of the liberal tradition. The American thesis is that government is not juridically omnipotent. Its powers are limited, and one of the principles of limitation is the distinction between state and church, in their purposes, methods, and manner of organization. The Jacobin thesis was basically philosophical; it derived from a sectarian concept of the autonomy of reason. It was also theological, as implying a sectarian concept of religion and of the church. In contrast, the American thesis is simply political. It asserts the theory of a free people under a limited government, a theory that is recognizably part of the Christian political tradition, and altogether defensible in the manner of its realization under American circumstances.

It may indeed be said that the American constitutional system exaggerates the distinction between church and state by its self-denying ordinances. However, it must also be said that government rarely appears to better advantage than when passing self-denying ordinances. In any event, it is one thing to exaggerate a traditional distinction along the lines of its inherent tendency; it is quite another thing to abolish the distinction. In the latter case the result is a vicious monistic society; in the former, a faultily dualistic one. The vice in the Jacobin system could only be condemned by the Church, not in any way condoned. The fault in the American system can be recognized as such, without condemnation. There are times and circumstances, Chesterton jocosely said, when it is necessary to exaggerate in order to tell the truth. There are also times and circumstances, one may more seriously say, when some exaggeration of the restrictions placed on government is necessary in order to insure freedom. These circumstances of social necessity were and are present in America.

The Freedom of the Church

Here then is the second leading reason why the American solution to the problem of religious pluralism commends itself to the Catholic conscience. In the discourse already cited Pius XII states, as the two cardinal purposes of a Concordat, first, "to assure to the Church a stable condition of right and of fact within society," and second, "to guarantee to her a full independence in the fulfillment of her divine mission." It may be maintained that both of these objectives are sufficiently achieved by the religious provisions of the First Amendment. It is obvious that the Church in America enjoys a stable condition in fact. That her status at law is not less stable ought to be hardly less obvious, if only one has clearly in mind the peculiarity of the American affirmation of the distinction between church and state. This affirmation is made through the imposition of limits on government, which is confined to its own proper ends, those of temporal society. In contrast to the Jacobin system in all its forms, the American Constitution does not presume to define the Church or in any way to supervise her exercise of authority in pursuit of her own distinct ends. The Church is entirely free to define herself and to exercise to the full her spiritual jurisdiction. It is legally recognized that there is an area which lies outside the competence of government. This area coincides with the area of the divine mission of the Church, and within this area the Church is fully independent, immune from interference by political authority.

The juridical result of the American limitation of governmental powers is the guarantee to the Church of a stable condition of freedom as a matter of law and right. It should be added that this guarantee is made not only to the individual Catholic but to the Church as an organized society with its own law and jurisdiction. The reason is that the American state is not erected on the principle of the unity and indivisibility of sovereignty which was the post-Renaissance European development. Nowhere in the American structure is there accumulated the plenitude of legal sovereignty possessed in England by the Queen in Parliament. In fact, the term "legal sovereignty" makes no sense in America, where sovereignty (if the alien term must be used) is purely political. The United States has a government, or better, a structure of governments operating on different levels. The American state has no sovereignty in the classic Continental sense. Within society, as distinct from the state, there is room for the independent exercise of an authority which is not that of the state. This principle has more than once been affirmed by American courts, most recently by the Supreme Court in the *Kedroff* case. The validity of this principle strengthens the stability of the Church's condition at law.

Perhaps the root of the matter, as hitherto described, might be seen summed up in an incident of early American and Church history. This is Leo Pfeffer's account of it in his book, *Church, State and Freedom:*

> In 1783 the papal nuncio at Paris addressed a note to Benjamin Franklin suggesting that, since it was no longer possible to maintain the previous status whereunder American Catholics were subject to the Vicar Apostolic at London, the Holy See proposed to Congress that a Catholic bishopric be established in one of the American cities, Franklin transmitted the note to the [Continental] Congress, which directed Franklin to notify the nuncio that "the subject of his application to Doctor Franklin being purely spiritual, it is without the jurisdiction and powers of Congress, who have no authority to permit or refuse it, these powers being reserved to the several states individually." (Not many years later the several states would likewise declare themselves to "have no authority to permit or refuse" such a purely spiritual exercise of ecclesiastical jurisdiction.)

The good nuncio must have been mightily surprised on receiving this communication. Not for centuries had the Holy See been free to erect a bishopric and appoint a bishop without the prior consent of government, without prior exercise of the governmental right of presentation, without all the legal formalities with which Catholic states had fettered the freedom of the Church. In the United States the freedom of the Church was completely unfettered; she could organize herself with the full independence which is her native right. This, it may be confidently said, was a turning point in the long and complicated history of church-state relations.

JOHN COLEMAN BENNETT

Patterns of Church-State Relations—Grounds for Separation

The Rev. John C. Bennett was president of Union Theological Seminary in New York City. He had been a close associate of Reinhold Niebuhr both as a colleague and in editing a lively journal called *Christianity and Crisis.* Mr. Bennett wrote widely on social, political, and religious problems from the point of view of a Christian ethicist.

There is no Protestant doctrine concerning Church-State relations.[3] There is a Baptist doctrine that is very clear and that has always had great influence in this country. There is an American doctrine which has been developing since the beginning of the Republic and some aspects of it are still being clarified by the courts.

When the Federal Government was formed, it was possible to begin with a clean slate so far as its relation to Churches was concerned. Today the idea of separation of Church and state is so much taken for granted in this country that it is difficult to realize what an adventurous step it was. The Constitution itself prohibits all religious tests for federal office holders and this was an important start in separating the

Church from the state though of itself this is not inconsistent with some forms of religious establishment. Religious tests were abandoned in Britain over a century ago. The very general words of the First Amendment to the Constitution laid down the lines along which our institutions were to develop: "Congress shall make no law respecting an establishment of religion, or prohibiting the free exercise thereof." This amendment did not apply to the states but only to the actions of Congress, and it was not until 1923 that in matters of religious liberty the guarantee of liberty by the Fourteenth Amendment ("Nor shall any State deprive any person of life, liberty, or property, without due process of law") was extended to actions by the states.

It should be noted that the word "separation" is not in the Constitution. It was Jefferson's word and it came to be the popular American word for this constitutional provision; later the Supreme Court was to use Jefferson's metaphor, "wall of separation," as a fitting description of the American Church-State pattern. I agree with those who believe that this is an unfortunate metaphor because there can be no such wall between institutions which have to so large an extent the same constituency and which share many of the same concerns for the same national community. I also believe that it would have been better if the popular word for the American system were "independence" rather than "separation." But, I am not quibbling over that and in what follows I shall speak of the separation of Church and state. . . . There are three reasons why I believe that this general pattern of "separation" is best for both Church and state and that changes in other countries which have established Churches should be (and, in fact, are) in this direction.

(1) The first reason for emphasizing the separation of Church and state is that it is the only way of assuring the complete freedom of the Church: Established Churches in Europe are all attempting to gain the substance of freedom but this still remains a difficult struggle. Anglican leaders now declare that if the British Parliament ever again uses its acknowledged legal right to interfere with the doctrine or worship of the Church, the Church must insist on its freedom even at the cost of disestablishment.

In this country the freedom of the Church from state control is not a real problem. Freedom of the Church from control by the community or by movements of public opinion is a problem, but I am not discussing that here. The Church-State problems that call for solution in this country are basically in a different area, but they usually raise the question as to whether the Church should relate any of its efforts or its institutions to the state in such a way that the state might come to exercise control over them. But no one suspects any agency of the state in this country of trying to dictate to the Churches. I remember how great a furor there was when Mayor La Guardia of New York, who was in charge of civil defense during the Second World War, sent around to the clergy some very innocent suggestions concerning a sermon that might be preached. This was a blunder on his part, as he soon learned, but he obviously had no intention of trying to dictate to the clergy. The American Churches are extremely sensitive on matters of this sort. For example, it took a long time for enough of them to agree to have the Federal Social Security made *optional* for ministers on the basis of self-employment to enable this to become law, though it is difficult to see how this can threaten the freedom of the Church. If any Churches become lax on matters affecting their freedom they get a strong reminder from the Baptists who are in a special way watch-dogs concerning the freedom of the Church, and it is good to have them perform this function.

In this country the Churches live independently with a friendly state and the American form of separation is in the first instance as good a guarantee of the freedom of the Church as Churches have ever had in their long history.

(2) The second reason for believing in the separation of Church and State is the preservation of the state from control by the Church. This freedom from control by the Church takes two forms. One is freedom from ecclesiastical pressure on the state itself on matters of public policy. In a later chapter I shall discuss what forms of influence or even pressure by the Churches upon the state are not open to objection. Much of this influence or pressure is a part of the democratic process itself. When the constituencies of Churches express their views on public questions, this is a part of the process of the formation of public opinion. There is nothing about the role of the Church here that need be regarded as unfair pressure or ecclesiastical manipulation. . . .

There is another aspect of this freedom of the state from Church control which is related to the ecclesiastical pressure upon government but it is in itself so central in the concern of Americans that I shall lift it up for special emphasis: the freedom of all religious minorities, and of those who reject all forms of religious faith, from pressure from any Church or group of Churches of the kind that comes through the use of the power of the state.

Today when Church-State problems are discussed in this country the one concern that ranks above all others is the fear that one Church or a group of Churches may finally be able to use the state to bring about discrimination against citizens on grounds of religion or to limit the freedom of any religious bodies. The people who belong to no religious body are afraid that all religious bodies may combine against them. The Jewish community usually takes their part because it fears that if there is any such combining of religious bodies, the Christians will control the combination. So, Jews take their position with the Baptists as watch-dogs in all matters that affect religious liberty. Both in practice often make common cause with the various forms of secularists. . . .

The religious liberty which we have in this country and which we should seek to preserve here and to encourage in every country is, of course, not only liberty within the walls of the church. Religious liberty should include in addition to this the liberty of public witness, of evangelism. It should be the liberty not only to convert, but also to be converted in the sense of changing one's religious affiliation. It should be the liberty of public teaching not only about religious matters in the narrow sense, but also about all social, economic and political questions concerning which there is a religious judgment. It should include the liberty of Churches and other religious institutions to do all that is necessary to preserve their freedom as organizations, to hold property, to choose their own leaders. It is significant that the First Amendment in the very sentence that speaks of religious liberty also mentions freedom of speech, of the press, of "the right of people peaceably to assemble, and to petition the government for redress of grievances." It is fitting that religious liberty should be related so closely to these other liberties for there can be no religious liberty unless there is religious freedom to speak, unless there is freedom for religious books and periodicals, unless there is freedom for congregations and many other religious groups to assemble, and unless there is freedom to petition on all matters that affect the rights of Churches or of the individual conscience. Whenever any state clamps down on these rights of citizens on political grounds, religious liberty even in the narrowest sense is in danger for there is always the possibility of claiming that religious teaching is politically subversive. And when governments clamp down on religious liberty, any group of citizens who express political ideas that are regarded as subversive may be accused of religious heresy. So interdependent are all these freedoms of the mind and spirit.

(3) The third reason for emphasizing the separation of Church and state is that it is best for the Church to be on its own. Here we can distinguish between two considerations.

The first is that in contrast to the experience of the national Church, it is important to have a Christian body that is distinguishable from the national community. Where the national Church does include almost the whole nation it is difficult to find any such body at all except the clergy. They in their training and function are set apart; they are the visible churchmen. I have referred to the fact that there is in some national Churches no synod representing clergy and laymen and the reason for this is that the national parliament is supposed to act in that capacity for most of its members are baptized churchmen. Once there was reality behind this arrangement, but now it is fictional and very bad for the Church. I should emphasize the fact that most national Churches are fully aware of the problems to which I refer and changes are rapidly taking place.

The second consideration which is involved in the proposition that it is best for the Church to be on its own is that a free Church must support itself. It cannot rely on funds from the state or on the remarkable system of church-taxes which are compulsory for all who acknowledge membership in the Church even though such membership is not compulsory. It is our experience in the United States that the activity of the laymen in their financial support of the Church has created an extraordinary momentum of lay interest in the Church. It is significant that the Churches that have to support themselves have the greatest resources available for missions and other benevolences. At the present time, the vitality of the American Churches amaze all who observe it and this vitality is in considerable measure the result of the very active and often sacrificial interest of the laymen. The Church's use of laymen increases their sense of responsibility and their loyalty to the Church. I realize that there is much debate as to how much depth or how much understanding of the Gospel or how much distinctively Christian commitment there is in all of this lay activity. Certainly it is all very mixed. The popularity of the Church does tend to lead to the secularizing of the Church and it is ironical that Churches that are not national Churches in this country actually seem more organic to the community as a whole than do national Churches. But after all of the criticisms of this vitality in the American Churches, one can hardly deny that it provides a tremendous opportunity for the Churches to mediate the truth and the grace of the Gospel to people.

In this chapter I have set forth the main reasons for believing in the separation of Church and state. I have always kept in mind the fact that these reasons have a special application to the United States but, while they do not necessarily suggest that the

American form of separation is good for all countries, they do suggest that older forms of the national Church should everywhere give way to new patterns which do justice to the freedom of the Church, to the religious liberty of all citizens and to the need of developing distinctively Christian communities characterized by lay initiative.

RICHARD L. RUBENSTEIN

Church and State: The Jewish Posture

When he wrote this article, Richard L. Rubenstein was director of the B'nai B'rith Hillel Foundations and chaplain to Jewish students at the University of Pittsburgh, Carnegie Institute of Technology, Chatham College, and Duquesne University. His discussion of this subject nicely represents the challenge faced by the Jewish community in American society.

In modern times, Jewish equality of status within the political order has been possible only when and where official Christianity has ceased to be privileged.[4] Where the special pre-eminence of the Christian church remained a relevant political fact, Jews have never been able to attain genuine equality of condition within that community. Jews have also fared best in multi-national and multi-ethnic political communities such as the old Austro-Hungarian Empire or contemporary America.

The fact that Jewish emancipation was largely the result of the temporary triumph of secular humanism in France does not necessarily mean that Jews have uniformly favored the underlying secular humanist ideology which produced the disestablishment of the church. Because Jews were among those who gained most visibly from the destruction of the old order, those who continued to oppose the French Revolution and its entailments tended to identify the Revolution in some sense with Jewish ends and purposes. This was strategically useful, in any event, because of the utility of the unpopular Jews as opponents. A similar identification of ends and ideology took place after the Russian Revolution. In neither upheaval was there a real coincidence of aim or interest between the Jewish community and its emancipators. Religious Jews of whatever bent could not and do not favor many of the tenets of the secular humanist ideology which led to Jewish emancipation. Those Jews who participated most wholeheartedly in the revolutionary movements were precisely those least concerned with the preservation of their identity as Jews.

The problem of theological anthropology, the religious doctrine of man [is] relevant to the problem of the separation of church and state. It is no accident that the American doctrine of separation was the product of a culture deeply Protestant in its ethos and influenced by Lockean deism and rationalism. Although it is difficult to make generalized statements about any of the major religious communities, it would seem that Protestantism has felt more decisively the tension and opposition between God and the world, the spirit and the flesh, and the religious and political orders than have either Judaism or Catholicism. Ernest Troeltsch's distinction between the church-type and the sect-type religious communities is very much to the point. Both Judaism and Catholicism are essentially church-type structures in that religious status is obligatory and hence proves nothing with regard to the member's virtue. The sect, defined by Max Weber as "a voluntary association of only those who are . . . religiously and morally qualified" is a more typically Protestant structure. Sects are founded by people who feel strongly the opposition between the political and the religious orders. They have despaired of the world and seek to maintain the community of the elect, undisturbed by the world's corruption. For members of sectarian religious communities, separation of the religious and political orders is absolutely necessary because of the incurable corruption of the political and social order.

Non-Christians who cannot accept the doctrine of the Incarnation are nevertheless frequently at one with its fundamental insight that there is an existential and an axiological continuum between the spirit and the flesh, between God and man. Those who affirm this continuum cannot really accept the separation of the religious and the political orders as their theological ideal. Nevertheless, it would be consistent with this position to suggest that the union of the two orders will only truly be achieved at the End of Time, the Time of the Messiah for Jews and the Parousia for Christians. In our imperfect and alienated world, the preponderant weight of social necessity favors separation.

I have attempted to stress a number of elements that arose out of religious and cultural perspectives most religious Jews do not and cannot entirely accept, but which were present in the culture which created Jewish emancipation in Europe and the First Amendment in America. In modern times there have been many attempts to identify Judaism largely or entirely with the culture of its neighbors. The identity of Judaism and "the German spirit" has understandably not stood the test of time. It has been supplanted by an assertion of the identity of Judaism and the roots of American democracy. There is undoubtedly far more reason to assert the latter identity than the former. Nevertheless, as we have seen, there are important areas in which the Enlightenment and sect-type Protestantism part company with fundamental Jewish convictions. There is nothing inherently sacred about the current American way of handling church-state problems. Under other circumstances other modes of dealing with the problem would be equally appropriate and suitable to Jewish needs.

There are, however, urgent *practical* reasons why there is near unanimity of opinion among Jews favoring the strongest possible guarantees of the separation of the religious and the political orders. As I have already suggested, the basic strategy of the Jewish community in modern times has been, wherever possible, withdrawal from Christian influence. Only in a society neutral to the practice of religion could Jews hope to attain that normalcy of life-situation which has eluded them for almost two thousand years. The ways in which Christian influence, perhaps unconsciously, excludes Jews from full participation in the national culture of even relatively secularized, contemporary France has been depicted by the French-Jewish-Tunisian novelist Albert Memmi in his *Portrait of a Jew.* As Memmi points out, Jews are alienated from the national culture at precisely those moments when the rest of the population is most strongly united in a shared community of aspiration and remembrance. Even the relatively formal and symbolic act of including prayers by rabbis as well as priests and ministers on public occasions is token of a legal equality in America which is unthinkable in Europe to this day.

Jews basically want nothing more than the opportunity to participate in American life under conditions of maximum equality with their fellow citizens. This is the simple practical basis for Jewish sentiment favoring separation of church and state in the United States. The Jewish community has had the experience of living as a minority for a very long time. Out of this experience, it has come to understand the incompatibility of any position other than absolute political neutrality in religious matters with the demands of equality. As has been indicated, nothing within Jewish tradition favors the separation of the religious and political orders. Nevertheless, everything within Jewish experience does. Were there none but Jews in America and were there a unanimity of Jewish assent on religious matters, there would probably be no such separation. Theologically speaking, one might describe the current situation as a concomitant of the confusion of tongues. I believe most responsible Jewish leaders would agree with Martin Marty's comment that "pluralism is a ground rule and not an altar." It is called for, not by our ideologies, but by the facticity of our concrete, limited situations. As long as America remains a multi-ethnic and multi-religious community, there can be no equitable alternative to political neutrality in religious affairs.

Even in an America agreed upon religious affirmation and affiliation, there would always be the question of the right of the atheist or the agnostic not to be forced to suffer the intrusion of an unwelcome religiosity in the public domain toward which he contributes his fair share. Although most Jewish leaders part company with secular humanist ideology, they most emphatically do *not* agree with those who assert that the American posture of religious neutrality excludes the irreligious. This position seems to occur more frequently among Catholic commentators on church-state affairs than among either their Protestant or their Jewish counterparts. If Jewish participants in the dialogue can not accept the Lockean conception of religion as a purely voluntary association, they do assert the practical necessity of acting *as if* the Lockean conception were true. Jewish law includes Jewish atheists in the Jewish religious community. Nevertheless, Jewish leaders would hardly insist, even had they the power so to do, upon a religious commitment from those who find such a commitment meaningless.

What I am suggesting is that Jewish concern for the individual goes beyond securing for him the opportunity to follow his own beliefs. It insists, particularly in a pluralistic society, that as far as possible his right to participate fully in the life of the community be recognized. Neutrality of the state toward religion is the only way to avoid excluding from full participation in community life the many secular humanists who share with the most devoted followers of any Western religion respect for human dignity and the worth of the individual. Recognition of this helps explain the position taken by Jews on many church-state issues.

America represents a new experiment for Jews. It offers the promise of an equality of condition which Jews have never known, even in the most advanced European nations. Like every human ideal, this promise cannot be extricated from the human context in which it is offered. The ideals implicit in law can never entirely be fulfilled. At best, they can be reasonably approximated. Jews do not really expect that the separation of the religious and political orders will ever be completely achieved. This would be possible only if the human beings who constitute the raw material of both orders were capable of an almost schizophrenic act of self-division. The absolute application of logic to human affairs leads not to justice but to murder, as the terror of the French Revolution and the rational terror of communism and nazism demonstrate. Nevertheless, historical Jewish experience has taught us that the ideal of a government neutral in religious matters offers the only hope for equality of condition for all men in a multi-ethnic and multi-religious community. Historical experience has also taught us that nothing is gained by the failure of the Jew to seek his rights under law when and where it is possible so to do. Finally, Jews are absolutely convinced that the decisions of our courts must be obeyed and respected. No insight is as deeply or as persistently present in Judaism as the conviction that society is radically imperiled when men assert a priority of personal inclination over the majesty of the law, for in Judaism God Himself is the Bestower and Teacher of the Law.

Church and State as a Political Issue

Catholic and Patriot: Governor Smith Replies

Al Smith was Democratic nominee for president in 1928. Having come up from lower Manhattan through Tammany Hall he became a distinguished and long-term governor of New York State. Although his religion was certainly a factor, it seems that his overwhelming defeat at the hands of Herbert Hoover probably reflected other issues more directly, among them his stand against prohibition and his very progressive record at Albany. In April 1927 the *Atlantic Monthly* published "An Open Letter to The Honourable Alfred E. Smith," by Charles C. Marshall. Smith replied in the May issue with the help of Father Francis P. Duffy. This might be compared to John F. Kennedy's Houston speech.

Charles C. Marshall, Esq.

Dear Sir:

In your open letter to me in the April *Atlantic Monthly* you "impute" to American Catholics views which, if held by them, would leave open to question the loyalty and devotion to this country and its Constitution of more than twenty million American Catholic citizens.[5] I am grateful to you for defining this issue in the open and for your courteous expression of the satisfaction it will bring to my fellow citizens for me to give "a disclaimer of the convictions" thus imputed. Without mental reservation I can and do make that disclaimer. These convictions are held neither by me nor by any other American Catholic, as far as I know. . . .

Taking your letter as a whole and reducing it to commonplace English, you imply that there is conflict between religious loyalty to the Catholic faith and patriotic loyalty to the United States. Everything that has actually happened to me during my long public career leads me to know that no such thing as that is true. I have taken an oath of office in this State nineteen times. Each time I swore to defend and maintain the Constitution of the United States. All of this represents a period of public service in elective office almost continuous since 1903. I have never known any conflict between my official duties and my religious belief. No such conflict could exist. Certainly the people of this State recognize no such conflict. They have testified to my devotion to public duty by electing me to the highest office within their gift four times. You yourself do me the honor, in addressing me, to refer to "your fidelity to the morality you have advocated in public and private life and to the religion you have revered; your great record of public trusts successfully and honestly discharged." During the years I have discharged these trusts I have been a communicant of the Roman Catholic Church. If there were conflict, I, of all men, could not have escaped it, because I have not been a silent man, but a battler for social and political reform. These battles would in their very nature disclose this conflict if there were any.

But, wishing to meet you on your own ground, I address myself to your definite questions, against which I have thus far made only general statements. I must first call attention to the fact that you often divorce sentences from their context in such a way as to give them something other than their real meaning. I will specify. . . . You quote from the *Catholic Encyclopedia* that my Church "regards dogmatic intolerance, not alone as her incontestable right, but as her sacred duty." And you say that these words show that Catholics are taught to be politically, socially, and intellectually intolerant of all other people. If you had read the whole of that article in the *Catholic Encyclopedia,* you would know that the real meaning of these words is that for Catholics alone the Church recognizes no deviation from complete acceptance of its dogma. These words are used in a chapter dealing with that subject only. The very same article in another chapter dealing with toleration toward non-Catholics contains these words: "The intolerant man is avoided as much as possible by every high-minded person. . . . The man who is tolerant in every emergency is alone lovable." The phrase "dogmatic intolerance" does not mean that Catholics are to be dogmatically intolerant of other people, but merely that inside the Catholic Church they are to be intolerant of any variance from the dogma of the Church.

Similar criticism can be made of many of your quotations. But, beyond this, by what right do you ask me to assume responsibility for every statement that may be made in any encyclical letter? As you will find in the *Catholic Encyclopedia* (Vol. V p. 414), these encyclicals are not articles of our faith. The Syllabus of Pope Pius IX, which you quote on the possible conflict between Church and State, is declared by Cardinal Newman to have "no dogmatic force." You seem to think that Catholics must be all alike in mind and in heart, as though they had been poured into and taken out of the same mould. You have no more right to ask me to defend as part of my faith every statement coming from a prelate than I should have to ask you to accept as an article of your religious faith every statement of an Episcopal bishop, or of your political faith every statement of a President of the United States. So little are these matters of the essence of my faith that I, a devout Catholic since childhood, never heard of them until I read your letter. Nor can you quote from the canons of our faith a syllable that would make us less good citizens than non-Catholics. . . .

Under our system of government the electorate entrusts to its officers of every faith the solemn duty of action according to the dictates of conscience. I may fairly refer once more to my own record to support these truths. No man, cleric or lay, has ever directly or indirectly attempted to exercise Church influence on my administration of any office I have ever held, nor asked me to show special favor to Catholics or exercise discrimination against non-Catholics.

It is a well-known fact that I have made all of my appointments to public office on the basis of merit and have never asked any man about his religious belief. In the first month of this year there gathered in the Capitol at Albany the first Governor's cabinet that ever sat in this State. It was composed, under my appointment, of two Catholics, thirteen Protestants, and one Jew. The man closest to me in the administration of the government of the State of New York is he who bears the title of Assistant to the Governor. He had been connected with the Governor's office for thirty years, in subordinate capacities, until I promoted him to the position which makes him the sharer with me of my every thought and hope and ambition in the administration of the State. He is a Protestant, a Republican, and a thirty-second-degree Mason. In my public life I have exemplified that complete separation of Church from State which is the faith of American Catholics to-day.

I summarize my creed as an American Catholic. I believe in the worship of God according to the faith and practice of the Roman Catholic Church. I recognize no power in the institutions of my Church to interfere with the operations of the Constitution of the United States or the enforcement of the law of the land. I believe in absolute freedom of conscience for all men and in equality of all churches, all sects, and all beliefs before the law as a matter of right and not as a matter of favor. I believe in the absolute separation of Church and State and in the strict enforcement of the provisions of the Constitution that Congress shall make no law respecting an establishment of religion or prohibiting the free exercise thereof. I believe that no tribunal of any church has any power to make any decree of any force in the law of the land, other than to establish the status of its own communicants within its own church. I believe in the support of the public school as one of the corner stones of American liberty. I believe in the right of every parent to choose whether his child shall be educated in the public school or in a religious school supported by those of his own faith. I believe in the principle of noninterference by this country in the internal affairs of other nations and that we should stand steadfastly against any such interference by whomsoever it may be urged. And I believe in the common brotherhood of man under the common fatherhood of God.

In this spirit I join with fellow Americans of all creeds in a fervent prayer that never again in this land will any public servant be challenged because of the faith in which he has tried to walk humbly with his God.

Very truly yours,
Alfred E. Smith

PAUL BLANSHARD

The Catholic Plan for America

With his *American Freedom and Catholic Power* (1949) Paul Blanshard struck a responsive chord in many Americans who—consciously or not—had reservations about the political implications of growing Roman Catholic influence in American life. Mr. Blanshard was an important figure in Protestants and Other

Americans United—a lobbying group that staunchly supported a rigorous separation of church and state. A counter statement to Mr. Blanshard's may be found in *Catholicism and American Freedom* by James M. O'Neill (New York, 1952).

Back in the days of the most virulent anti-Catholic bigotry, when "The Menace" was a national institution and candidates for public office openly reviled the Pope, one dramatic question was frequently asked at anti-Catholic mass meetings: "What will become of American democracy if the United States is captured by the Papists?"[6] That last word was usually hissed or whispered in a way to make shivers run up and down the spine.

The question was more reasonable than its source. In fact, the bigoted character of the source has tended to divert attention from a valid and important question. Many American liberals have been deterred from an honest analysis of the implications of Catholic rule by fear of being associated with anti-Catholic fanatics. They have allowed the Catholic hierarchy, unchallenged, to use American freedom as a cloak for the systematic cultivation of separatism and intolerance among the American Catholic people.

Recent developments in Europe and Latin America suggest that the future role of the Roman Catholic Church in American politics should be re-examined with some care. What would happen to American democracy if our alleged twenty-six million Catholics grew to be a majority in the population and followed the direction of their priests? Suppose that, on some magic carpet of time, we could pass over the next two centuries and find ourselves in a predominantly Catholic America. What would American democracy look like?

The democratic *form* of our leading institutions might not be altered very much. Probably the most striking effect of Catholic control would be apparent in the *spirit* of those institutions and the *use* to which they would be put. The Catholic hierarchy is perfectly willing to compromise with democratic forms of government so long as its own special areas of power are respected. In a Catholic America the principal institutions of American democracy might be permitted to continue if they were operated for Catholic objectives.

The most striking and immediate result of Catholic ascendancy in our democracy would be the transfer of control of education, religion and family relationships to the Catholic hierarchy. After Catholics had attained a majority in three-fourths of our states, this transfer could be accomplished by three comprehensive amendments to the United States Constitution. Let us draft them in outline.

The first Catholic amendment to the Constitution might be called, for educational purposes, the "Christian Common-wealth Amendment." In all likelihood, it would include all of the following statements:

1: The United States is a Catholic Republic, and the Catholic Apostolic and Roman religion is the sole religion of the nation.

2: The authority of the Roman Catholic Church is the most exalted of all authorities; nor can it be looked upon as inferior to the power of the United States government, or in any manner dependent upon it, since the Catholic Church as such is a sovereign power.

3: Priests and members of religious orders of the Roman Catholic Church who violate the law are to be tried by an ecclesiastical court of the Roman Catholic

Church, and may, only with the consent of the competent Catholic authority, be tried by the courts of the United States or the states.

4: Apostate priests or those incurring the censure of the Roman Catholic Church cannot be employed in any teaching post or any office or employment in which they have immediate contact with the public.

5: Non-Catholic faiths are tolerated, but public ceremonies and manifestations other than those of the Roman Catholic religion will not be permitted.

6: The First Amendment to the Constitution of the United States is hereby repealed.

The second Catholic amendment to the Constitution of the United States might well be described for propaganda purposes as the "Christian Education Amendment." It could be expected with confidence to be phrased in forms like these:

1: American religious education belongs pre-eminently to the Roman Catholic Church, by reason of a double title in the supernatural order, conferred exclusively upon her by God Himself.

2: The Roman Catholic Church has the inalienable right to supervise the entire education of her children in all educational institutions in the United States, public or private, not merely in regard to the religious instruction given in such institutions, but in regard to every other branch of learning and every regulation in so far as religion and morality is concerned.

3: Compulsory education in public schools exclusively shall be unlawful in any state in the Union.

4: It shall be unlawful for any neutral or non-Catholic school to enroll any Catholic child without permission of the Church.

5: Since neutral schools are contrary to the fundamental principles of education, public schools in the United States are lawful only when both religious instruction and every other subject taught are permeated with Catholic piety.

6: The governments of the United States and of the states are permitted to operate their own schools for military and civic training without supervision by the Roman Catholic Church, provided they do not injure the rights of the said Church, and provided that only the Roman Catholic Church shall have power to impart any religious instructions in such schools.

7: With due regard to special circumstances, co-education shall be unlawful in any educational institution in the United States whose students have attained the age of adolescence.

8: The governments of the United States and the states shall encourage and assist the Roman Catholic Church by appropriate measures in the exercise of the Church's supreme mission as educator.

The third Catholic amendment to the Constitution of the United States might be called the "Christian Family Amendment," although, in the campaign for its adoption, the sanctity of womanhood and the defeat of communism would, doubtless, play a major part. The amendment probably would read:

1: The government of the United States, desirous of restoring to the institution of matrimony, which is the basis of the family, that dignity conformable to the traditions of its people, assigns as civil effects of the sacrament of matrimony all that is attributed to it in the Canon Law of the Roman Catholic Church.

2: No matrimonial contract in the United States that involves a Catholic can be valid unless it is in accordance with the Canon Law of the Roman Catholic Church.

3: Marriages of non-Catholics are subject to the civil authority of the state, but all civil laws that contradict the Canon Law of the Roman Catholic Church on marriage are hereby declared null and void.

4: All marriages are indissoluble, and the divorce of all persons is prohibited throughout the territory of the United States: provided that nothing herein shall affect the right of annulment and remarriage in accordance with the Canon Law of the Roman Catholic Church.

5: Attempted mixed marriages or unions between members of the Roman Catholic Church and non-Catholics are null and void, and the children of such unions are illegitimate, unless a special dispensation is obtained from the ecclesiastical authority of the Catholic Church.

6: Birth control, or any act that deliberately frustrates the natural power to generate life, is a crime.

7: Direct abortion is murder of the innocent even when performed through motives of misguided pity when the life of a mother is gravely imperiled.

8: Sterilization of any human being is forbidden except as an infliction of grave punishment under the authority of the government for a crime committed.

I remember a verse from Job which is appropriate at this moment: "If I justify myself, mine own mouth shall condemn me." That is meant for Catholic liberals whose temperature has been rising while they have been reading these three amendments. As most of my readers have doubtless guessed, there is not an original thought and scarcely an original word in my entire three Catholic amendments. They are mosaics of official Catholic doctrine. *Every concept, almost every word and phrase, has been plagiarized line by line from Catholic documents.* The most important phrases are derived from the highest documents of Catholicism, the encyclicals of the Popes. The provisions on education come from Pius XI's *Christian Education of Youth,* and those on family life from his *Casti Connubii,* both of them accepted universally in the Catholic Church as the Bibles of present-day educational and family policy. A few provisions are taken directly from Canon Law, the recent laws of Catholic countries like Spain, and the 1929 Concordat between Mussolini and the Vatican, all of which have been publicly approved by Catholic authorities. Only place-names and enabling clauses have been added to give the Papal principles local application.

JOHN F. KENNEDY

Remarks on Church and State

John F. Kennedy, unlike Al Smith, who was reluctant to discuss it, confronted the "religious issue" both directly and often.[7] This was so much the case that in the

West Virginia primary, in which he ran against Hubert Humphrey, a vote for Humphrey became a vote for bigotry. He subsequently spoke directly to his clerical critics in Texas. From that encounter he gained their respect if not their votes. In spite of these efforts the issue remained hotly contested in the 1960 campaign until the end.

I am grateful for your generous invitation to state my views.

While the so-called religious issue is necessarily and properly the chief topic here tonight, I want to emphasize from the outset that I believe that we have far more critical issues in the 1960 election: the spread of Communist influence, until it now festers only ninety miles off the coast of Florida—the humiliating treatment of our President and Vice-President by those who no longer respect our power—the hungry children I saw in West Virginia, the old people who cannot pay their doctor's bills, the families forced to give up their farms—an America with too many slums, with too few schools, and too late to the moon and outer space.

These are the real issues which should decide this campaign. And they are not religious issues—for war and hunger and ignorance and despair know no religious barrier.

But because I am a Catholic, and no Catholic has ever been elected President, the real issues in this campaign have been obscured—perhaps deliberately in some quarters less responsible than this. So it is apparently necessary for me to state once again—not what kind of church I believe in, for that should be important only to me, but what kind of America I believe in.

I believe in an America where the separation of church and state is absolute—where no Catholic prelate would tell the President (should he be a Catholic) how to act and no Protestant minister would tell his parishioners for whom to vote—where no church or church school is granted any public funds or political preference—and where no man is denied public office merely because his religion differs from the President who might appoint him or the people who might elect him.

I believe in an America that is officially neither Catholic, Protestant nor Jewish—where no public official either requests or accepts instructions on public policy from the Pope, the National Council of Churches or any other ecclesiastical source—where no religious body seeks to impose its will directly or indirectly upon the general populace or the public acts of its officials—and where religious liberty is so indivisible that an act against one church is treated as an act against all.

For while this year it may be a Catholic against whom the finger of suspicion is pointed, in other years it has been, and may someday be again, a Jew—or a Quaker—or a Unitarian—or a Baptist. It was Virginia's harassment of Baptist preachers, for example, that led to Jefferson's statute of religious freedom. Today, I may be the victim—but tomorrow it may be you—until the whole fabric of our harmonious society is ripped apart at a time of great national peril.

Finally, I believe in an America where religious intolerance will someday end—where all men and all churches are treated as equal—where every man has the same right to attend or not attend the church of his choice—where there is no Catholic vote, no anti-Catholic vote, no bloc voting of any kind—and where Catholics, Protestants and Jews, both the lay and the pastoral level, will refrain from those attitudes of disdain and division which have so often marred their works in the past, and promote instead the American ideal of brotherhood.

That is the kind of America in which I believe. And it represents the kind of Presidency in which I believe—a great office that must be neither humbled by making it the instrument of any religious group, nor tarnished by arbitrarily withholding it, its occupancy, from the members of any religious group. I believe in a President whose views on religion are his own private affair, neither imposed upon him by the nation or imposed by the nation upon him as a condition to holding that office.

I would not look with favor upon a President working to subvert the First Amendment's guarantees of religious liberty (nor would our system of checks and balances permit him to do so). And neither do I look with favor upon those who would work to subvert Article VI of the Constitution by requiring a religious test—even by indirection—for if they disagree with that safeguard, they should be openly working to repeal it.

I want a Chief Executive whose public acts are responsible to all and obligated to none—who can attend any ceremony, service or dinner his office may appropriately require him to fulfill—and whose fulfillment of his Presidential office is not limited or conditioned by any religious oath, ritual or obligation.

This is the kind of America I believe in—and this is the kind of America I fought for in the South Pacific and the kind my brother died for in Europe. No one suggested then that we might have a "divided loyalty," that we did "not believe in liberty" or that we belonged to a disloyal group that threatened "the freedoms for which our forefathers died."

And in fact this is the kind of America for which our forefathers did die when they fled here to escape religious test oaths, that denied office to members of less favored churches, when they fought for the Constitution, the Bill of Rights, the Virginia Statute of Religious Freedom—and when they fought at the shrine I visited today—the Alamo. For side by side with Bowie and Crockett died Fuentes and McCafferty and Bailey and Bedillio and Carey—but no one knows whether they were Catholics or not. For there was no religious test there.

I ask you tonight to follow in that tradition, to judge me on the basis of fourteen years in the Congress—on my declared stands against an ambassador to the Vatican, against unconstitutional aid to parochial schools, and against any boycott of the public schools (which I attended myself)—instead of judging me on the basis of these pamphlets and publications we have all seen that carefully select quotations out of context from the statements of Catholic Church leaders, usually in other countries, frequently in other centuries, and rarely relevant to any situation here—and always omitting, of course, that statement of the American bishops in 1948 which strongly endorsed church-state separation.

I do not consider these other quotations binding upon my public acts—why should you? But let me say, with respect to other countries, that I am wholly opposed to the state being used by any religious group, Catholic or Protestant, to compel, prohibit or persecute the free exercise of any other religion. And that goes for any persecution at any time, by anyone, in any country.

And I hope that you and I condemn with equal fervor those nations which deny their Presidency to Protestants and those which deny it to Catholics. And rather than cite the misdeeds of those who differ, I would also cite the record of the Catholic Church in such nations as France and Ireland—and the independence of such statesmen as de Gaulle and Adenauer.

But let me stress again that these are my views—for, contrary to common newspaper usage, I am not the Catholic candidate for President. I am the Democratic Party's candidate for President, who happens also to be a Catholic.

I do not speak for my church on public matters—and the church does not speak for me.

Whatever issue may come before me as President, if I should be elected—on birth control, divorce, censorship, gambling, or any other subject—I will make my decision in accordance with these views, in accordance with what my conscience tells me to be in the national interest, and without regard to outside religious pressure or dictate. And no power or threat of punishment could cause me to decide otherwise.

But if the time should ever come—and I do not concede any conflict to be remotely possible—when my office would require me to either violate my conscience, or violate the national interest, then I would resign the office, and I hope any other conscientious public servant would do likewise.

But I do not intend to apologize for these views to my critics of either Catholic or Protestant faith, nor do I intend to disavow either my views or my church in order to win this election. If I should lose on the real issues, I shall return to my seat in the Senate, satisfied that I tried my best and was fairly judged.

But if this election is decided on the basis that 40,000,000 Americans lost their chance of being President on the day they were baptized, then it is the whole nation that will be the loser in the eyes of Catholics and non-Catholics around the world, in the eyes of history, and in the eyes of our own people.

But if, on the other hand, I should win this election, I shall devote every effort of mind and spirit to fulfilling the oath of the Presidency—practically identical, I might add, with the oath I have taken for fourteen years in the Congress. For, without reservation, I can, and I quote, "solemnly swear that I will faithfully execute the office of President of the United States and will to the best of my ability preserve, protect and defend the Constitution, so help me God."

Church and State as a Juridical Problem

Cantwell v. Connecticut (1940)

This first of the "Jehovah's Witness cases" concerned the conviction of Newton Cantwell and two of his sons under Connecticut statutes for proselytizing in a heavily Roman Catholic section of New Haven, Connecticut "*Cantwell*" explicitly applies the religion clauses of the First Amendment to the states through the "due process clause" of the Fourteenth. Brief excerpts follow.

Mr. Justice Roberts Delivered the Opinion of the Court.

* * *

First. We hold that the statute, as construed and applied to the appellants, deprives them of their liberty without due process of law in contravention of the Fourteenth Amendment.[8] The fundamental concept of liberty embodied in that Amendment embraces the liberties guaranteed by the First Amendment. The First Amendment declares that Congress shall make no law respecting an establishment of religion or prohibiting the free exercise thereof. The Fourteenth Amendment has rendered the legislatures of the states as incompetent as Congress to enact such laws. The constitutional inhibition of legislation on the subject of religion has a double aspect. On the one hand, it forestalls compulsion by law of the acceptance of any creed or the practice of any form of worship. Freedom of conscience and freedom to adhere to such religious organization or form of worship as the individual may choose cannot be restricted by law. On the other hand, it safeguards the free exercise of the chosen form of religion. Thus the Amendment embraces two concepts,—freedom to believe and freedom to act. The first is absolute but, in the nature of things, the second cannot be. Conduct remains subject to regulation for the protection of society. The freedom to act must have appropriate definition to preserve the enforcement of that protection. In every case the power to regulate must be so exercised as not, in attaining a permissible end, unduly to infringe the protected freedom. . . .

Nothing we have said is intended even remotely to imply that, under the cloak of religion, persons may, with impunity, commit frauds upon the public. Certainly penal laws are available to punish such conduct. Even the exercise of religion may be at some slight inconvenience in order that the state may protect its citizens from injury. . . .

Second. We hold that, in the circumstances disclosed, the conviction of Jesse Cantwell on the fifth count must be set aside. . . .

The offense known as breach of the peace embraces a great variety of conduct destroying or menacing public order and tranquility. It includes not only violent acts but acts and words likely to produce violence in others. No one would have the hardihood to suggest that the principle of freedom of speech sanctions incitement to riot or that religious liberty connotes the privilege to exhort others to physical attack upon those belonging to another sect. When clear and present danger of riot, disorder, interference with traffic upon the public streets, or other immediate threat to public safety, peace, or order, appears, the power of the State to prevent or punish is obvious. Equally obvious is it that a State may not unduly suppress free communication of views, religious or other, under the guise of conserving desirable conditions. . . .

In the realm of religious faith, and in that of political belief, sharp differences arise. In both fields the tenets of one man may seem the rankest error to his neighbor. To persuade others to his own point of view, the pleader, as we know, at times, resorts to exaggeration, to vilification of men who have been, or are, prominent in church or state, and even to false statement. But the people of this nation have ordained in the light of history, that, in spite of the probability of excesses and abuses, these liberties are, in the long view, essential to enlightened opinion and right conduct on the part of the citizens of a democracy.

The essential characteristic of these liberties is, that under their shield many types of life, character, opinion and belief can develop unmolested and unobstructed. Nowhere is this shield more necessary than in our own country for a people composed of many races and of many creeds. There are limits to the exercise of these liberties. The danger in these times from the coercive activities of those who in the delusion of racial or religious conceit would incite violence and breaches of the peace in order to deprive others of their equal right to the exercise of their liberties, is emphasized by events familiar to all. These and other transgressions of those limits the States appropriately may punish.

Minersville School District v. Gobitis (1940)

The simple school ritual of saluting the flag became a constitutional issue when two Pennsylvania schoolchildren were expelled for refusing to do so on the grounds that it was forbidden by their Jehovah's Witness faith. The case arose during the Second World War, a time when many felt the need for national unity, and the court upheld the expulsions. This case and its virtual twin (which follows), in which the *Gobitis* decision is repudiated, showcase two critical issues: first, the extent to which the free exercise clause may serve as the basis for an exemption to otherwise generally applicable laws and, second, the proper roles of the legislative and judicial branches in authoritatively interpreting the Constitution and the individual liberties it guarantees.

Mr. Justice Frankfurter delivered the opinion of the Court:

A grave responsibility confronts this Court whenever in course of litigation it must reconcile the conflicting claims of liberty and authority.[9] But when the liberty invoked is liberty of conscience, and the authority is authority to safeguard the nation's fellowship, judicial conscience is put to its severest test. Of such a nature is the present controversy.

Lillian Gobitis, aged twelve, and her brother William, aged ten, were expelled from the public schools of Minersville, Pennsylvania, for refusing to salute the national flag as part of a daily school exercise. The local Board of Education required both teachers and pupils to participate in this ceremony. . . . The Gobitis family are affiliated with "Jehovah's Witnesses," for whom the Bible as the Word of God is the supreme authority. The children had been brought up conscientiously to believe that such a gesture of respect for the flag was forbidden by command of scripture.

The Gobitis children were of an age for which Pennsylvania makes school attendance compulsory. Thus they were denied a free education, and their parents had to put them into private schools. To be relieved of the financial burden thereby entailed, their father, on behalf of the children and in his own behalf, brought this suit. He sought to enjoin the authorities from continuing to exact participation in the flag-salute ceremony as a condition of his children's attendance at the Minersville school. . . .

We must decide whether the requirement of participation in such a ceremony, exacted from a child who refuses upon sincere religious grounds, infringes without due process of law the liberty guaranteed by the Fourteenth Amendment.

Centuries of strife over the erection of particular dogmas as exclusive or all-comprehending faiths led to the inclusion of a guarantee for religious freedom in the Bill of Rights. The First Amendment, and the Fourteenth through its absorption of the First, sought to guard against repetition of those bitter religious struggles by prohibiting the establishment of a state religion and by securing to every sect the free exercise of its faith. So pervasive is the acceptance of this precious right that its scope is brought into question, as here, only when the conscience of individuals collides with the felt necessities of society.

Certainly the affirmative pursuit of one's convictions about the ultimate mystery of the universe and man's relation to it is placed beyond the reach of law. Government may not interfere with organized or individual expression of belief or disbelief. Propagation of belief—or even of disbelief in the supernatural—is protected, whether in church or chapel, mosque or synagogue, tabernacle or meeting-house. Likewise the Constitution assures generous immunity to the individual from imposition of penalties for offending, in the course of his own religious activities, the religious views of others, be they a minority or those who are dominant in government. . . .

But the manifold character of man's relations may bring his conception of religious duty into conflict with the secular interests of his fellow-men. When does the constitutional guarantee compel exemption from doing what society thinks necessary for the promotion of some great common end, or from a penalty for conduct which appears dangerous to the general good? To state the problem is to recall the truth that no single principle can answer all of life's complexities. The right to freedom of religious belief, however dissident and however obnoxious to the cherished beliefs of others—even of a majority—is itself the denial of an absolute. But to affirm that the freedom to follow conscience has itself no limits in the life of a society would deny that very plurality of principles which, as a matter of history, underlies protection of religious toleration. . . . Our present task then, as so often the case with courts, is to reconcile two rights in order to prevent either from destroying the other. But, because in safeguarding conscience we are dealing with interests so subtle and so dear, every possible leeway should be given to the claims of religious faith.

In the judicial enforcement of religious freedom we are concerned with a historic concept. The religious liberty which the Constitution protects has never excluded legislation of general scope not directed against doctrinal loyalties of particular sects. Judicial nullification of legislation cannot be justified by attributing to the framers of the Bill of Rights views for which there is no historic warrant. Conscientious scruples have not, in the course of the long struggle for religious toleration, relieved the individual from obedience to a general law not aimed at the promotion or restriction of religious beliefs. The mere possession of religious convictions which contradict the relevant concerns of a political society does not relieve the citizen from the discharge of political responsibilities. The necessity for this adjustment has again and again been recognized. In a number of situations the exertion of political authority has been sustained, while basic considerations of religious freedom have been left inviolate. . . . In all these cases the general laws in question, upheld in their application to those who refused obedience from religious conviction, were manifestations of specific powers of government deemed by the legislature essential to secure and maintain that orderly, tranquil, and free society without which religious toleration itself is unattainable. Nor does the freedom of speech assured by Due Process move in a more absolute circle of immunity than that enjoyed by religious freedom. Even if it were assumed that freedom of speech goes beyond the historic concept of full opportunity to utter and to disseminate views, however heretical or offensive to dominant opinion, and includes freedom from conveying what may be deemed an implied but rejected affirmation, the question remains whether school children, like the Gobitis children, must be excused from conduct required of all the other children in the promotion of national cohesion. We are dealing with an interest inferior to none in the hierarchy of legal values. National unity is the basis of national security. To deny the legislature the right to select appropriate means for its attainment presents a totally different order of problem from that of the propriety of subordinating the possible ugliness of littered streets to the free expression of opinion through distribution of handbills. . . .

Situations like the present are phases of the profoundest problem confronting a democracy—the problem which Lincoln cast in memorable dilemma: "Must a government of necessity be too *strong* for the liberties of its people, or too *weak* to maintain its own existence?" No mere textual reading or logical talisman can solve the dilemma. And when the issue demands judicial determination, it is not the personal notion of judges of what wise adjustment requires which must prevail.

Unlike the instances we have cited, the case before us is not concerned with an exertion of legislative power for the promotion of some specific need or interest of secular society—the protection of the family, the promotion of health, the common defense, the raising of public revenues to defray the cost of government. But all these specific activities of government presuppose the existence of an organized political society. The ultimate foundation of a free society is the binding tie of cohesive sentiment. Such a sentiment is fostered by all those agencies of the mind and spirit which may serve to gather up the traditions of a people, transmit them from generation to generation, and thereby create that continuity of a treasured common life which constitutes a civilization. "We live by symbols." The flag is the symbol of our national unity, transcending all internal differences, however large, within the framework of the Constitution. This Court has had occasion to say that ". . . the flag is the symbol of the Nation's power, the emblem of freedom in its truest, best sense . . . it signifies government resting on the consent of the governed; liberty regulated by law; the protection of the weak against the strong; security against the exercise of arbitrary power; and absolute safety for free institutions against foreign aggression.". . .

The case before us must be viewed as though the legislature of Pennsylvania had itself formally directed the flag-salute for the children of Minersville; had made no exemption for children whose parents were possessed of conscientious scruples like those of the Gobitis family; and had indicated its belief in the desirable ends to be secured by having its public school children share a common experience at those periods of development when their minds are supposedly receptive to its assimilation, by an exercise appropriate in time and place and setting, and one designed to evoke in them appreciation of the nation's hopes and dreams, its sufferings and sacrifices. The precise issue, then, for us to decide is whether the legislatures of the various states and the authorities in a thousand counties and school districts of this country are barred from determining the appropriateness of various means to evoke that unifying sentiment without which there can ultimately be no liberties, civil or religious. To stigmatize legislative judgment in providing for this universal gesture of respect for the symbol of our national life in the setting of the common school as a lawless inroad on that freedom of conscience which the Constitution protects, would amount to no less than the pronouncement of pedagogical and psychological dogma in a field where courts possess no marked and certainly no controlling competence. The influences which help toward a common feeling for the common country are manifold. Some may seem harsh and others no doubt are foolish. Surely, however, the end is legitimate. And the effective means for its attainment are still so uncertain and so unauthenticated by science as to preclude us from putting the widely prevalent belief in flag-saluting beyond the pale of legislative power. It mocks reason and denies our whole history to find in the allowance of a requirement to salute our flag on fitting occasions the seeds of sanction for obeisance to a leader.

The wisdom of training children in patriotic impulses by those compulsions which necessarily pervade so much of the educational process is not for our independent judgment. Even were we convinced of the folly of such a measure, such belief would be no proof of its unconstitutionality. For ourselves; we might be tempted to say that the deepest patriotism is best engendered by giving unfettered scope to the most crochety beliefs. Perhaps it is best, even from the standpoint of those interests which ordinances like the one under review seek to promote, to give to the least popular sect leave from conformities like those here in issue. But the courtroom is not the arena for debating issues of educational policy. It is not our province to choose among competing considerations in the subtle process of securing effective loyalty to the traditional ideals of democracy, while respecting at the same time individual idiosyncracies among a people so diversified in racial origins and religious allegiances. So to hold would in effect make us the school board for the country. That authority has not been given to this Court, nor should we assume it.

We are dealing here with the formative period in the development of citizenship. Great diversity of psychological and ethical opinion exists among us concerning the best way to train children for their place in society. Because of these differences and because of reluctance to permit a single, iron-cast system of education to be imposed upon a nation compounded of so many strains, we have held that, even though public education is one of our most cherished democratic institutions, the Bill of Rights bars a state from compelling all children to attend the public schools. . . . But it is a very different thing for this Court to exercise censorship over the conviction of legislatures that a particular program or exercise will best promote in the minds of children who attend the common schools an attachment to the institutions of their country.

What the school authorities are really asserting is the right to awaken in the child's mind considerations as to the significance of the flag contrary to those implanted by the parent. In such an attempt the state is normally at a disadvantage in competing with the parent's authority, so long—and this is the vital aspect of religious toleration—as parents are unmolested in their right to counteract by their own persuasiveness the wisdom and rightness of those loyalties which the state's educational system is seeking to promote. Except where the transgression of constitutional liberty is too plain for argument, personal freedom is best maintained—so long as the remedial channels of the democratic process remain open and unobstructed—when it is ingrained in a people's habits and not enforced against popular policy by the coercion of adjudicated law. That the flag-salute is an allowable portion of a school program for those who do not invoke conscientious scruples is surely not debatable. But for us to insist that, though the ceremony may be required, exceptional immunity must be given to dissidents, is to maintain that there is no basis for a legislative judgment that such an exemption might introduce elements of difficulty into the school discipline, might cast doubts in the minds of the other children which would themselves weaken the effect of the exercise.

The preciousness of the family relation, the authority and independence which give dignity to parenthood, indeed the enjoyment of all freedom, presuppose the kind of ordered society which is summarized by our flag. A society which is dedicated to the preservation of these ultimate values of civilization may in self-protection utilize the educational process for inculcating those almost unconscious feelings which bind men together in a comprehending loyalty, whatever may be their lesser differences and difficulties. That is to say, the process may be utilized so long as men's right to believe as they please, to win others to their way of belief, and their right to assemble in their chosen places of worship for the devotional ceremonies of their faith, are all fully respected.

Judicial review, itself a limitation on popular government, is a fundamental part of our constitutional scheme. But to the legislature no less than to courts is committed the guardianship of deeply-cherished liberties. . . . Where all the effective means of inducing political changes are left free from interference, education in the abandonment of foolish legislation is itself a training in liberty. To fight out the wise use of legislative authority in the forum of public opinion and before legislative assemblies rather than to transfer such a contest to the judicial arena, serves to vindicate the self-confidence of a free people. . . .

West Virginia State Board of Education v. Barnette (1943)

The following are excerpts from a "Flag Salute Case." After the Gobitis decision (1940), on the basis of state legislation, the West Virginia State Board of Education required the flag salute in public schools.[10] The following decision, as the text makes clear, explicitly overturned the earlier ruling.

Mr. Justice Jackson Delivered the Opinion of the Court.

* * *

The Gobitis decision . . . assumed, as did the argument in that case and in this, that power exists in the State to impose the flag salute discipline upon school children in general. The Court only examined and rejected a claim based on religious beliefs of immunity from an unquestioned general rule. The question which underlies the flag salute controversy is whether such a ceremony so touching matters of opinion and political attitude may be imposed upon the individual by official authority under powers committed to any political organization under our Constitution. We examine rather than assume existence of this power and, against this broader definition of issues in this case, re-examine specific grounds assigned for the Gobitis decision.

1. It was said that the flag-salute controversy confronted the Court with "the problem which Lincoln cast in memorable dilemma: 'Must a government of necessity be too strong for the liberties of its people, or too weak to maintain its own existence?'" and that the answer must be in favor of strength.

We think these issues may be examined free of pressure or restraint growing out of such considerations.

It may be doubted whether Mr. Lincoln would have thought that the strength of government to maintain itself would be impressively vindicated by our confirming power of the state to expel a handful of children from school. Such oversimplification, so handy in political debate, often lacks the precision necessary to postulates of judicial reasoning. If validly applied to this problem, the utterance cited would resolve every issue of power in favor of those in authority and would require us to override every liberty thought to weaken or delay execution of their policies.

Government of limited power need not be anemic government. Assurance that rights are secure tends to diminish fear and jealousy of strong government, and by making us feel safe to live under it makes for its better support. Without promise of a limiting Bill of Rights it is doubtful if our Constitution could have mustered enough strength to enable its ratification. To enforce those rights today is not to choose weak government over strong government. It is only to adhere as a means of strength to individual freedom of mind in preference to officially disciplined uniformity for which history indicates a disappointing and disastrous end.

The subject now before us exemplifies this principle. Free public education, if faithful to the ideal of secular instruction and political neutrality, will not be partisan or enemy of any class, creed, party, or faction. If it is to impose any ideological discipline, however, each party or denomination must seek to control, or failing that, to weaken the influence of the educational system. Observance of the limitations of the Constitution will not weaken government in the field appropriate for its exercise.

2. It was also considered in the Gobitis case that functions of educational officers in states, counties and school districts were such that to interfere with their authority "would in effect make us the school board for the country."

The Fourteenth Amendment, as now applied to the States, protects the citizen against the State itself and all of its creatures—Boards of Education not excepted. These have, of course, important, delicate, and highly discretionary functions, but none that they may not perform within the limits of the Bill of Rights. That they are educating the young for citizenship is reason for scrupulous protection of Constitutional Freedoms of the individual, if we are not to strangle the free mind at its source and teach youth to discount important principles of our government as mere platitudes.

3. The Gobitis opinion reasoned that this is a field "where courts possess no marked and certainly no controlling competence," that it is committed to the legislatures as well as the courts to guard cherished liberties and that it is constitutionally appropriate to "fight out the wise use of legislative authority in the form of public opinion and before legislative assemblies rather than to transfer such a contest to the judicial arena," since all the "effective means of inducing political changes are left free."

The very purpose of a Bill of Rights was to withdraw certain subjects from the vicissitudes of political controversy, to place them beyond the reach of majorities and officials and to establish them as legal principles to be applied by the courts. One's right to life, liberty, and property, to free speech, a free press, freedom of worship and assembly, and other fundamental rights may not be submitted to vote; they depend on the outcome of no elections.

4. Lastly, and this is the very heart of the Gobitis opinion, it reasons that "National unity is the basis of national security," that the authorities have "the right to select appropriate means for its attainment," and hence reaches the conclusion that such compulsory measures toward "national unity" are constitutional. Upon the verity of this assumption depends our answer in this case.

National unity as an end which officials may foster by persuasion and example is not in question. The problem is whether under our Constitution compulsion as here employed is a permissible means for its achievement.

Struggle to coerce uniformity of sentiment in support of some end thought essential to their time and country have been waged by many good as well as by evil men. Nationalism is a relatively recent phenomenon but at other times and places the ends have been racial or territorial security, support of a dynasty or regime, and particular plans for saving souls. As first and moderate methods to attain unity have failed, those bent on its accomplishment must resort to an ever increasing severity. . . .

It seems trite but necessary to say that the First Amendment to our Constitution was designed to avoid these ends by avoiding these beginnings. There is no mysticism in the American concept of the State or of the nature or origin of its authority. We set up government by consent of the governed, and the Bill of Rights denies those in power any legal opportunity to coerce that consent. Authority here is to be controlled by public opinion, not public opinion by authority.

The case is made difficult not because the principles of its decision are obscure but because the flag involved is our own. Nevertheless, we apply the limitations of the Constitution with no fear that freedom to be intellectually and spiritually diverse or even contrary will disintegrate the social organization. To believe that patriotism will not flourish if patriotic ceremonies are voluntary and spontaneous instead of a compulsory routine is to make an unflattering estimate of the appeal of our institutions to free minds. We can have intellectual individualism and the rich cultural diversities that we owe to exceptional minds only at the price of occasional eccentricity and abnormal attitudes. When they are so harmless to others or to the State as those we deal with here, the price is not too great. But freedom to differ is not limited to things that do not matter much. That would be a mere shadow of freedom. The test of its substance is the right to differ as to things that touch the heart of the existing order.

If there is any fixed star in our constitutional constellation, it is that no official, high or petty, can prescribe what shall be orthodox in politics, nationalism, religion, or other matters of opinion or force citizens to confess by word or act their faith therein. If there are any circumstances which permit an exception, they do not now occur to us.

We think the action of the local authorities in compelling the flag salute and pledge transcends constitutional limitations on their power and invades the sphere of intellect and spirit which it is the purpose of the First Amendment to our Constitution to reserve from all official control.

The decision of this Court in Minersville School District v. Gobitis and the holdings of those few per curiam decisions which preceded and foreshadowed it are overruled, and the judgment enjoining enforcement of the West Virginia Regulation is affirmed.

Mr. Justice Roberts and Mr. Justice Reed adhere to the views expressed by the Court in Minersville School District v. Gobitis and are of the opinion that the judgment below should be reversed.

Mr. Justice Frankfurter, Dissenting.

The essence of the religious freedom guaranteed by our Constitution is . . . this: no religion shall either receive the state's support or incur its hostility. Religion is outside the sphere of political government. This does not mean that all matters on which religious organizations or beliefs may pronounce are outside the sphere of government. Were this so, instead of the separation of church and state, there would be the subordination of the state on any matter deemed within the sovereignty of the religious conscience. Much that is the concern of temporal authority affects the spiritual interests of men. But it is not enough to strike down a non-discriminatory law that it may hurt or offend some dissident view. It would be too easy to cite numerous prohibitions and injunctions to which laws run counter if the variant interpretations of the Bible were made the tests of the obedience to law. The validity of secular laws cannot be measured by their conformity to religious doctrines. It is only in a theocratic state that ecclesiastical doctrines measure legal right or wrong.

An act compelling profession of allegiance to a religion, no matter how subtly or tenuously promoted, is bad. But an act promoting good citizenship and national allegiance is within the domain of governmental authority and is therefore to be judged by the same considerations of power and of constitutionality as those involved in the many claims of immunity from civil obedience because of religious scruples.

That claims are pressed on behalf of sincere religious convictions does not of itself establish their constitutional validity. Nor does waving the banner of religious freedom relieve us from examining the power we are asked to deny the states. Otherwise the doctrine of separation of church and state, so cardinal in the history of this nation and for the liberty of our people, would mean not the disestablishment of a state church but the establishment of all churches and of all religious groups.

The subjection of dissidents to the general requirement of saluting the flag, as a measure conducive to the training of children in good citizenship, is very far from being the first instance of exacting obedience to general laws that have offended deep religious scruples. Compulsory vaccination, compulsory medical treatment, these are but illustrations of conduct that has often been compelled in the enforcement of legislation of general applicability even though the religious consciences of particular individuals rebelled at the exaction.

Law is concerned with external behavior and not with the inner life of man. It rests in large measure upon compulsion. Socrates lives in history partly because he gave his life for the conviction that duty of obedience to secular law does not pre-suppose consent to its enactment or belief in its virtue. The consent upon which free government rests is the consent that comes from sharing in the process of making and unmaking laws. The state is not shut out from a domain because the individual conscience may deny the state's claim. The individual conscience may profess what faith it chooses. It may affirm and promote that faith—in the language of the Constitution, it may "exercise" it freely—but it cannot thereby restrict community action through political organs in matters of community concern, so long as the action is not asserted in a discriminatory way either openly or by stealth. One may have the right to practice one's religion and at the same time owe the duty of formal obedience to laws that run counter to one's beliefs.

Everson v. Board of Education (1947)

This case concerned the practice of reimbursing parents of parochial school children (as well as those whose children attended public schools) for fares spent to reach their schools on regular buses of the public transportation system. Here the applicability of the establishment clause was openly confronted in a very close (five to four) decision.

Mr. Justice Black Delivered the Opinion of the Court.

Since there has been no attack on the statute on the ground that a part of its language excludes children attending private schools operated for profit from enjoying state payment for their transportation, we need not consider this exclusionary language; it has no relevancy to any constitutional question here presented. . . .[11]

The only contention here is that the State statute and the resolution, in so far as they authorized reimbursement to parents of children attending parochial schools, violate the Federal Constitution in these two respects, which to some extent, overlap. First. They authorize the State to take by taxation the private property of some and bestow it upon others, to be used for their own private purposes. This, it is alleged, violates the due process clause of the Fourteenth Amendment. Second. The statute and the resolution forced inhabitants to pay taxes to help support and maintain schools which are dedicated to, and which regularly teach, the Catholic Faith. This is alleged to be a use of State Power to support church schools contrary to the prohibition of the First Amendment which the Fourteenth Amendment made applicable to the states.

First. The due process argument that the State law taxes some people to help others carry out their private purposes is framed in two phases. The first phase is that a state cannot tax A to reimburse B for the cost of transporting his children to church schools. This is said to violate the due process clause because the children are sent to these church schools to satisfy the personal desires of their parents, rather than the public's interest in the general education of all children. This argument, if valid, would apply equally to prohibit state payment for the transportation of children to any non-public school, whether operated by a church, or any other non-government individual or group. But, the New Jersey legislature has decided that a public purpose will be served by using tax-raised funds to pay the bus fares of all school children, including those who attend parochial schools. The New Jersey Court of Errors and Appeals has reached the same conclusion. The fact that a state law, passed to satisfy a public need, coincides with the personal desires of the individuals most directly affected is certainly an inadequate reason for us to say that a legislature has erroneously appraised the public need.

Insofar as the second phase of the due process argument may differ from the first, it is by suggesting that taxation for transportation of children to church schools constitutes support of a religion by the State. But if the law is invalid for this reason, it is because it violates the First Amendment's prohibition against the establishment of religion by law. This is the exact question raised by appellant's second contention, to consideration of which we now turn.

Second. The New Jersey statute is challenged as a "law respecting an establishment of religion." The First Amendment, as made applicable to the states by the Fourteenth, commands that a state "shall make no law respecting an establishment of religion, or prohibiting the free exercise thereof." . . .

The meaning and scope of the First Amendment, preventing establishment of religion or prohibiting the free exercise thereof, in the light of its history and the evils it was designed forever to suppress, have been several times elaborated by the decisions of this Court prior to the application of the First Amendment to the states by the Fourteenth. The broad meaning given the Amendment by these earlier cases has been accepted by this Court in its decisions concerning an individual's religious freedom rendered since the Fourteenth Amendment was interpreted to make the prohibitions of the First applicable to state action abridging religious freedom. There is every reason to give the same application and broad interpretation to the "establishment of religion" clause. The interrelation of these complementary clauses was well summarized in a statement of the Court of Appeals of South Carolina, quoted with approval by this Court, in Watson v. Jones, "The structure of our government has, for the preservation of civil liberty, rescued the temporal institutions from religious interference. On the other hand, it has secured religious liberty from the invasions of the civil authority."

The "establishment of religion" clause of the First Amendment means at least this: Neither a state nor the Federal Government can set up a church. Neither can pass laws which aid one religion, aid all religions, or prefer one religion over another. Neither can force nor influence a person to go to or to remain away from church against his will or force him to profess a belief or disbelief in any religion. No person can be punished for entertaining or professing religious beliefs or disbeliefs, for church attendance or non-attendance. No tax in any amount, large or small, can be levied to support any religious activities or institutions, whatever they may be called, or whatever form they may adopt to teach or practice religion. Neither a state nor the Federal Government can, openly or secretly, participate in the affairs of any religious organizations or groups and vice versa. In the words of Jefferson, the clause against establishment of religion by law was intended to erect "a wall of separation between Church and State."

We must consider the New Jersey statute in accordance with the foregoing limitations imposed by the First Amendment. But we must not strike that state statute down if it is within the state's constitutional power even though it approaches the verge of that power. New Jersey cannot consistently with the "establishment of religion" clause of the First Amendment contribute tax-raised funds to the support of an institution which teaches the tenets and faith of any church. On the other hand, other language of the amendment commands that New Jersey cannot exclude individual Catholics, Lutherans, Mohammedans, Baptists, Jews, Methodists, Non-believers, Presbyterians, or the members of any other faith, because of their faith, or lack of it, from receiving the benefits of public welfare legislation. While we do not mean to intimate that a state could not provide transportation only to children attending public schools, we must be careful, in protecting the citizens of New Jersey against state-established churches, to be sure that we do not inadvertently prohibit New Jersey from extending its general State law benefits to all its citizens without regard to their religious belief.

Measured by these standards, we cannot say that the First Amendment prohibits New Jersey from spending tax-raised funds to pay the bus fares of parochial school pupils as a part of a general program under which it pays the fares of pupils attending public and other schools. It is undoubtedly true that children are helped to get to church schools. There is even a possibility that some of the children might not be sent to the church schools if the parents were compelled to pay their children's bus fares out of their own pockets when transportation to a public school would have been paid for by the State. The same possibility exists where the state requires a local transit company to provide reduced fares to school children including those attending parochial schools, or where a municipally owned transportation system undertakes to carry all school children free of charge. Moreover, state-paid policemen, detailed to protect children going to and from church schools from the very real hazards of traffic, would serve much the same purpose and accomplish much the same result as state provisions intended to guarantee free transportation of a kind which the state deems to be best for the school children's welfare. And parents might refuse to risk their children to the serious danger of traffic accidents going to and from parochial schools, the approaches to which were not protected by policemen. Similarly, parents might be reluctant to permit their children to attend schools which the state had cut off from such general government services as ordinary police and fire protection, connections for sewage disposal, public high-ways and sidewalks. Of course, cutting off church schools from these services, so separate and so indisputably marked off from the religious function, would make it far more difficult for the schools to operate. But such is obviously not the purpose of the First Amendment. That Amendment requires the state to be a neutral in its relations with groups of religious believers and non-believers; it does not require the state to be their adversary. State power is no more to be used so as to handicap religions, than it is to favor them.

This Court has said that parents may, in the discharge of their duty under state compulsory education laws, send their children to a religious rather than a public school if the school meets the secular educational requirements which the state has power to impose. It appears that these parochial schools meet New Jersey's requirements. The State contributes no money to the schools. It does not support them. Its legislation, as applied, does no more than provide a general program to help parents get their children, regardless of their religion, safely and expeditiously to and from accredited schools.

The First Amendment has erected a wall between church and state. That wall must be kept high and impregnable. We could not approve the slightest breach. New Jersey has not breached it here.

Affirmed.

Mr. Justice Jackson, Dissenting.

I find myself, contrary to first impressions, unable to join in this decision. I have a sympathy, though it is not ideological, with Catholic citizens who are compelled by law to pay taxes for public schools, and also feel constrained by conscience and discipline to support other schools for their own children. Such relief to them as this case involves is not in itself a serious burden to taxpayers and I had assumed it to be as little serious in principle. Study of this case convinces me otherwise. The Court's opinion marshals every argument in favor of state aid and puts the case in its most favorable light, but much of its reasoning confirms my conclusions that there are no good grounds upon which to support the present legislation. In fact the undertones of the opinion, advocating complete and uncompromising separation of Church from State, seem utterly discordant with its conclusion yielding support to their commingling in educational matters. The case which irresistibly comes to mind as the most fitting precedent is that of Julia who according to Byron's reports, "whispering 'I will ne'er consent,'—consented."

It seems to me that the basic fallacy in the Court's reasoning, which accounts for its failure to apply the principles it avows, is in ignoring the essentially religious test by which beneficiaries of this expenditure are selected. A policeman protects a Catholic, of course—but not because he is a Catholic, it is because he is a man and a member of our society. The fireman protects the Church school—but not because it is a Church school; it is because it is property, part of the assets of our society. Neither the fireman nor the policeman has to ask before he renders aid "Is this man or building identified with the Catholic Church?" But before these school authorities draw a check to reimburse for a student's fare they must ask just that question, and if the school is a Catholic one they may render aid because it is such, while if it is of any other faith or is run for profit, the help must be withheld. To consider the converse of the Court's reasoning will best disclose its fallacy. That there is no parallel between police and fire protection and this plan of reimbursement is apparent from the incongruity of the limitation of this Act if applied to police and fire service. Could we sustain an Act that said police shall protect pupils on the way to or from public schools and Catholic schools but not while going to and coming from other schools, and firemen shall extinguish a blaze in public or Catholic school buildings but shall not put out a blaze in Protestant Church schools or private schools operated for profit? That is the true analogy to the case we have before us and I should think it pretty plain that such a scheme would not be valid.

This policy of our Federal Constitution has never been wholly pleasing to most religious groups. They all are quick to invoke its protections; they all are irked when they feel its restraints. This Court has gone a long way, if not an unreasonable way, to hold that public business of such paramount importance as maintenance of public order, protection of the privacy of the home, and taxation may not be pursued by a state in a way that even indirectly will interfere with religious proselyting.

But we cannot have it both ways. Religious teaching cannot be a private affair when the state seeks to impose regulations which infringe on it indirectly, and a public affair when it comes to taxing citizens of one faith to aid another, or those of no faith to aid all. If these principles seem harsh in prohibiting aid to Catholic education, it must not be forgotten that it is the same Constitution that alone assures Catholics the right to maintain these schools at all when predominant local sentiments would forbid them. Nor should I think that those who have done so well without this aid would want to see this separation between Church and State broken down. If the state may aid these religious schools, it may therefore regulate them. Many groups have sought aid from tax funds only to find that it carried political controls with it. Indeed this Court has declared that "It is hardly lack of due process for the Government to regulate that which it subsidizes."

But in any event, the great purposes of the Constitution do not depend on the approval or convenience of those they restrain. I cannot read the history of the struggle to separate political from ecclesiastical affairs, well summarized in the opinion of Mr. Justice Rutledge in which I generally concur, without a conviction that the Court today is unconsciously giving the clock's hands a backward turn.

Mr. Justice Frankfurter joins in this opinion.

Mr. Justice Rutledge, with Whom Mr. Justice Frankfurter, Mr. Justice Burton Agree, Dissenting.

Our constitutional policy . . . does not deny the value or the necessity for religious training, teaching or observance. Rather it secures their free exercise. But to that end it does deny that the state can undertake or sustain them in any form or degree. For this reason the sphere of religious activity, as distinguished from the secular intellectual liberties, has been given the twofold protection and, as the state cannot forbid, neither can it perform or aid in performing the religious function. The dual prohibition makes that function altogether private. It cannot be made a public one by legislative act. This was the very heart of Madison's Remonstrance, as it is of the Amendment itself.

It is not because religious teaching does not promote the public or the individual's welfare, but because neither is furthered when the state promotes religious education, that the Constitution forbids it to do so. Both legislatures and courts are bound by that distinction. In failure to observe it lies the fallacy of the "public function"-"social legislation" argument, a fallacy facilitated by easy transference of the argument's basing from due process unrelated to any religious aspect to the First Amendment.

By no declaration that a gift of public money to religious uses will promote the general or individual welfare, or the cause of education generally, can legislative bodies overcome the Amendment's bar. Nor may the courts sustain their attempts to do so by finding such consequences for appropriations which in fact give aid to or promote religious uses. Legislatures are free to make, and courts to sustain, appropriations only when it can be found that in fact they do not aid, promote, encourage or sustain religious teaching or observances, be the amount large or small. No such finding has been or could be made in this case. The Amendment has removed this form of promoting the public welfare from legislative and judicial competence to make a public function. It is exclusively a private affair.

The reasons underlying the Amendment's policy have not vanished with time or diminished in force. Now as when it was adopted the price of religious freedom is double. It is that the church and religion shall live both within and upon that freedom. There cannot be freedom of religion, safeguarded by the state, and intervention by the church or its agencies in the state's domain or dependency on its largesse. The great condition of religious liberty is that it be free from sustenance, as also from other interferences, by the state. For when it comes to rest upon that secular foundation it vanishes with the resting. Public money devoted to payment of religious costs, educational or other, brings the quest for more. It brings too the struggle of sect against sect for the larger share or for any. Here one by numbers alone will benefit most, there another. That is precisely the history of societies which have had an established religion and dissident groups. It is the very thing Jefferson and Madison experienced and sought to guard against, whether in its blunt or in its more screened forms. The end of such strife cannot be other than to destroy the cherished liberty. The dominating group will achieve the dominant benefit; or all will embroil the state in their dissensions.

Illinois ex rel. McCollum v. Board of Education (1948)

The McCollum Case dealt with a Champaign, Illinois, "released time" plan.

Mr. Justice Black Delivered the Opinion of the Court.

This case relates to the power of a state to utilize its tax-supported public school system in aid of religious instruction insofar as that power may be restricted by the First and Fourteenth Amendments to the Federal Constitution.[12]

Although there are disputes between the parties as to various inferences that may or may not properly be drawn from the evidence concerning the religious program, the following facts are shown by the record without dispute. In 1940 interested members of the Jewish, Roman Catholic, and a few of the Protestant faiths formed a voluntary association called the Champaign Council on Religious Education. They obtained permission from the Board of Education to offer classes in religious instruction to public school pupils in grades four to nine inclusive. Classes were made up of pupils whose parents signed printed cards requesting that their children be permitted to attend; they were held weekly, thirty minutes for the lower grades, forty-five minutes for the higher. The council employed the religious teachers at no expense to the school authorities, but the instructors were subject to the approval and supervision of the superintendent of schools. The classes were taught in three separate religious groups by Protestant teachers, Catholic priests, and a Jewish rabbi, although for the past several years there have apparently been no classes instructed in the Jewish religion. Classes were conducted in the regular classrooms of the school building for pursuit of their secular studies. On the other hand, students who were released from secular study for the religious instructions were required to be present at the religious classes. Reports of their presence or absence were to be made to their secular teachers.

The foregoing facts, without reference to others that appear in the record, show the use of tax-supported property for religious instruction and the close cooperation between the school authorities and the religious council in promoting religious education. The operation of the state's compulsory education system thus assists and is integrated with the program of religious instruction carried on by separate religious sects. Pupils compelled by law to go to school for secular education are released in part from their legal duty upon the condition that they attend the religious classes. This is beyond all question a utilization of the tax-established and tax-supported public school system to aid religious groups to spread their faith. And it falls squarely under the ban of the First Amendment (made applicable to the States by the Fourteenth) as we interpreted it in Everson v. Board of Education.

The majority in the Everson case, and the minority . . . agreed that the First Amendment's language, properly interpreted, had erected a wall of separation between Church and State. They disagreed as to the facts shown by the record and as to the proper application of the First Amendment's language to those facts.

Recognizing that the Illinois program is barred by the First and Fourteenth Amendments if we adhere to the views expressed both by the majority and the minority in the Everson case, counsel for the respondents challenge those views as dicta and urge that we reconsider and repudiate them. They argue that historically the First Amendment was intended to forbid only government preference of one religion over another, not an impartial governmental assistance of all religions. In addition they ask that we distinguish or overrule our holding in the Everson case that the Fourteenth Amendment made the "establishment of religion" clause of the First Amendment applicable as a prohibition against the states. After giving full consideration to the arguments presented we are unable to accept either of these contentions.

To hold that a state cannot consistently with the First and Fourteenth Amendments utilize its public school system to aid any or all religious faiths or sects in the dissemination of their doctrines and ideals does not, as counsel urge, manifest a governmental hostility to religion or religious teachings. A manifestation of such hostility would be at war with our national tradition as embodied in the First Amendment's guaranty of the free exercise of religion. For the First Amendment rests upon the premise that both religion and government can best work to achieve their lofty aims if each is left free from the other within its respective sphere. Or, as we said in the Everson case, the

First Amendment has erected a wall between Church and State which must be kept high and impregnable.

Here not only are the state's tax-supported public school buildings used for the dissemination of religious doctrines. The State also affords sectarian groups an invaluable aid in that it helps to provide pupils for their religious classes through use of the state's compulsory public school machinery. This is not separation of Church and State.

The cause is reversed and remanded to the State Supreme Court for proceedings not inconsistent with this opinion.

Mr. Justice Frankfurter Delivered The Following Opinion, In Which Mr. Justice Jackson, Mr. Justice Rutledge And Mr. Justice Burton Join.

We dissented in Everson v. Board of Education, because in our view the Constitutional principle requiring separation of Church and State compelled invalidation of the ordinance sustained by the majority. Illinois has here authorized the commingling of sectarian with secular instruction in the public schools. The Constitution of the United States forbids this.

Separation means separation, not something less. Jefferson's metaphor in describing the relation between Church and State speaks of a "wall of separation," not of a fine line easily overstepped. The public school is at once the symbol of our democracy and the most pervasive means for promoting our common destiny. In no activity of the State is it more vital to keep out divisive forces than in its schools. To avoid confusing, not to say fusing, what the Constitution sought to keep strictly apart. "The great American principle of eternal separation"—Elihu Root's phrase bears repetition—is one of the vital reliances of our Constitutional system for assuring unities among our people stronger than our diversities. It is the Court's duty to enforce this principle in its full integrity.

We renew our conviction that "we have staked the very existence of our country on the faith that complete separation between the state and religion is best for the state and best for religion." If nowhere else, in the relation between Church and State, "good fences make good neighbors."

Mr. Justice Reed, Dissenting.

This Court summarized the amendment's accepted reach into the religious field, as I understand its scope, in Everson v. Board of Education. The Court's opinion quotes the gist of the Court's reasoning in Everson. I agree as there stated that none of our governmental entities can "set up a church." I agree that they cannot "aid" all or any religions or prefer one "over another." But "aid" must be understood as a purposeful assistance directly to the church itself or to some religious group or organization doing religious work of such a character that it may fairly be said to be performing ecclesiastical functions. "Prefer" must give an advantage to one "over another." I agree that pupils cannot "be released in part from their legal duty" of school attendance upon condition that they attend religious classes. But as Illinois has held that it is within the discretion of the School Board to permit absence from school for religious instruction no legal duty of school attendance is violated. . . . Of course, no tax can be levied to support organizations intended "to teach or practice religion." I agree too that the state cannot influence one toward religion against his will or punish him for his beliefs. Champaign's religious education course does none of these things.

With the general statements in the opinions concerning the constitutional requirement that the nation and states, by virtue of the First and Fourteenth Amendments, may "make no law respecting an establishment of religion," I am in agreement. But, in the light of the meaning given to those words by the precedents, customs, and practices which I have detailed above, I cannot agree with the Court's conclusion that when pupils compelled by law to go to school for secular education are released from school so as to attend the religious classes, churches are unconstitutionally aided. Whatever may be the wisdom of the arrangement as to the use of the school buildings made with The Champaign Council of Religious Education, it is clear to me that past practice shows such cooperation between the schools and a nonecclesiastical body is not forbidden by the First Amendment. When actual church services have always been permitted on government property, the mere use of the school buildings by a non-sectarian group for religious education ought not to be condemned as an establishment of religion. For a non-sectarian organization to give the type of instruction here offered cannot be said to violate our rule as to the establishment of religion by the state. The prohibition of enactments respecting the establishment of religion do not bar every friendly gesture between church and state. It is not an absolute prohibition against every conceivable situation where the two may work together any more than the other provisions of the First Amendment—free speech, free press—are absolutes. If abuses occur such as the use of the instruction hour for sectarian purposes, I have no doubt . . . that Illinois will promptly correct them. If they are of a kind that tend to the establishment of a church or interfere with the free exercise of religion, this Court is open for a review of any erroneous decision. This Court cannot be too cautious in upsetting practices embedded in our society by many years of experience. A state is entitled to have great leeway in its legislation when dealing with the important social problems of its population. A definite violation of legislative limits must be established. The Constitution should not be stretched to forbid national customs in the way courts act to reach arrangements to avoid federal taxation. Devotion to the great principle of religious liberty should not lead us into a rigid interpretation of the constitutional guarantee that conflicts with accepted habits of our people. This is an instance where, for me, the history of past practices is determinative of the meaning of a constitutional clause not a decorous introduction to the study of its text. The judgment should be affirmed.

Zorach v. Clauson (1952)

Within four years a similar case had reached the Supreme Court. The chief difference was that the pupils (who desired to be) were not released to receive religious instruction in a specified classroom but were dismissed from school to attend the class in church buildings. Both the dissenters on the bench and commentators have questioned the significance given to this circumstance in the decision of the court.

Mr. Justice Douglas Delivered the Opinion of the Court.

New York City has a program which permits its public schools to release students during the school day so that they may leave the school buildings and school grounds and go to religious centers for religious instruction or devotional exercises.[13] A student is released on written request of his parents. Those not released stay in the class-rooms. The churches make weekly reports to the schools, sending a list of children who have been released from public school but who have not reported for religious instruction.

This "released time" program involves neither religious instruction in public school classrooms nor the expenditure of public funds. All costs, including the application blanks, are paid by the religious organizations. The case is therefore unlike McCollum v. Board of Education which involved a "released time" program from Illinois. In that case the classrooms were turned over to religious instructors. We accordingly held that the program violated the First Amendment which (by reason of the Fourteenth Amendment) prohibits the states from establishing religion or prohibiting its free exercise.

Appellants, who are taxpayers and residents of New York City and whose children attend its public schools, challenge the present law, contending it is in essence not different from the one involved in the McCollum case. Their argument, stated elaborately in various ways, reduces itself to this: the weight and influence of the school is put behind a program for religious instruction; public school teachers police it, keeping tab on students who are released; the classroom activities come to a halt while the students who are released for religious instruction are on leave; the school is a crutch on which the churches are leaning for support in their religious training; without the cooperation of the schools this "released time" program, like the one in the McCollum case, would be futile and ineffective. The New York Court of Appeals sustained the law against this claim of unconstitutionality. The case is here on appeal.

Our problem reduces itself to whether New York by this system has either prohibited the "free exercise" of religion or has made a law "respecting an establishment of religion" within the meaning of the First Amendment.

It takes obtuse reasoning to inject any issue of the "free exercise" of religion into the present case. No one is forced to go to the religious classroom and no religious exercise or instruction is brought to the classrooms of the public schools. A student need not take religious instruction. He is left to his own desires as to the manner or time of his religious devotions, if any.

Moreover, apart from that claim of coercion, we do not see how New York by this type of "released time" program has made a law respecting an establishment of religion within the meaning of the First Amendment. There is much talk of the separation of Church and State in the history of the Bill of Rights and in the decisions clustering around the First Amendment. See Everson v. Board of Education; McCollum v. Board of Education. There cannot be the slightest doubt that the First Amendment reflects the philosophy that Church and State should be separated. And so far as interference with the "free exercise" of religion and an "establishment" of religion are concerned, the separation must be complete and unequivocal. The First Amendment within the scope of its coverage permits no exception; the prohibition is absolute. The First Amendment, however, does not say that in every and all respects there shall be a separation of Church and State. Rather it studiously defines the manner, the specific ways, in which there shall be no concert or union or dependency one on the other. That is the common sense of the matter. Otherwise the state and religion would [be] aliens to each other—hostile, suspicious, and even unfriendly. Churches could not be required to pay even property taxes. Municipalities would not be permitted to render police or fire protection to religious groups. Policemen who helped parishioners into their places of worship would violate the Constitution. Prayers in our legislative halls; the appeals to the Almighty in the messages of the Chief Executive; the proclamations making Thanksgiving Day a holiday; "so help me God" in our courtroom oaths—these and all other references to the Almighty that run through our laws, our public rituals, our ceremonies would be flouting the First Amendment. A fastidious atheist or agnostic could even object to the supplication with which the Court opens each session: "God save the United States and this Honorable Court."

We would have to press the concept of separation of Church and State to these extremes to condemn the present law on constitutional grounds. The nullification of this law would have wide and profound effects. A Catholic student applies to his teacher for permission to leave the school during hours on a Holy Day of Obligation to attend a mass. A Jewish student asks his teacher for permission to be excused for Yom Kippur. A Protestant wants the afternoon off for a family baptismal ceremony. In each case the teacher requires parental consent in writing. In each case the teacher, in order to make sure the student is not a truant, goes further and requires a report from the priest, the rabbi, or the minister. The teacher in other words cooperates in a religious program to the extent of making it possible for her students to participate in it. Whether she does it occasionally for a few students, regularly for one, or pursuant to a systematized program designed to further the religious needs of all the students does not alter the character of the act.

We are a religious people whose institutions presuppose a Supreme Being. We guarantee the freedom to worship as one chooses. We make room for as wide a variety of beliefs and creeds as the spiritual needs of man deem necessary. We sponsor an attitude on the part of government that shows no partiality to any one group and that lets each flourish according to the zeal of its adherents and the appeal of its dogma. When the state encourages religious instruction or cooperates with religious authorities by adjusting the schedule of public events to sectarian needs, it follows the best of our traditions. For it then respects the religious nature of our people and accommodates the public service to their spiritual needs. To hold that it may not would be to find in the Constitution a requirement that the government show a callous indifference to religious groups. That would be preferring those who believe in no religion over those who do believe. Government may not finance religious groups nor undertake religious instruction nor blend secular and sectarian education nor use secular institutions to force one or some religion on any person. But we find no constitutional requirement which makes it necessary for government to be hostile to religion and to throw its weight against efforts to widen the effective scope of religious influence. The government must be neutral when it comes to competition between sects. It may not thrust any sect on any person. It may not make a religious observance compulsory. It may not coerce anyone to attend church, to observe a religious holiday, or to take religious instruction. But it can close its doors or suspend its operations as to those who want to repair to their religious sanctuary for worship or instruction. No more than that is undertaken here.

This program may be unwise and improvident from an educational or a community viewpoint. That appeal is made to us on a theory, previously advanced, that each case must be decided on the basis of "our own prepossessions." See McCollum v. Board of Education. Our individual preferences, however, are not the constitutional standard. The constitutional standard is the separation of Church and State. The problem, like many problems in constitutional law, is one of degree.

In the McCollum case the classrooms were used for religious instruction and the force of the public school was used to promote that instruction. Here, as we have said, the public schools do no more than accommodate their schedules to a program of outside religious instruction. We follow the McCollum case. But we cannot expand it to cover the present released time program unless separation of Church and State means that public institutions can make no adjustment of their schedules to accommodate the religious needs of the people. We cannot read into the Bill of Rights such a philosophy of hostility to religion.

Affirmed.

Mr. Justice Black, Dissenting.

I see no significant difference between the invalid Illinois system and that of New York here sustained. Except for the use of the school buildings in Illinois, there is no difference between the systems which I consider even worthy of mention. In the New York program, as in that of Illinois, the school authorities release some of the children on the condition that they attend the religious classes, get reports on whether they attend, and hold the other children in the school building until the religious hour is over. As we attempted to make categorically clear, the McCollum decision would have been the same if the religious classes had not been held in the school buildings. We said:

"Here not only are the State's tax-supported public school buildings used for the dissemination of religious doctrines. The State also affords sectarian groups an invaluable aid in that it helps to provide pupils for their religious classes through the use of the State's compulsory school machinery. This is not separation of Church and State." McCollum thus held that Illinois could not constitutionally manipulate the compelled classroom hours of its compulsory school machinery so as to channel children into sectarian classes. Yet that is exactly what the Court holds New York can do.

Mr. Justice Jackson, Dissenting.

This released time program is founded upon a use of the State's power of coercion, which, for me, determines its unconstitutionality. Stripped to its essentials, the plan has two stages, first, that the State compel each student to yield a large part of his time for public secular education and, second, that some of it be "released" to him on condition that he devote it to sectarian religious purposes.

No one suggests that the Constitution would permit the State directly to require this "released" time to be spent "under the control of a duly constituted religious body." This program accomplishes that forbidden result by indirection. If public education were taking so much of the pupils' time as to injure the public or the student's welfare by encroaching upon their religious opportunity, simply shortening everyone's school day would facilitate voluntary and optional attendance at Church classes. But that suggestion is rejected upon the ground that if they are made free many students will not go to the Church. Hence, they must be deprived of freedom for this period, with Church attendance put to them as one of the two permissible ways of using it.

A number of Justices just short of a majority of the majority that promulgates today's passionate dialectics joined in answering them in Illinois ex rel. McCollum v. Board of Education. The distinction attempted between that case and this is trivial, almost to the point of cynicism, magnifying its nonessential details and disparaging compulsion which was the underlying reason for invalidity. A reading of the Court's opinion in that case along with its opinion in this case will show such difference of overtones and undertones as to make clear that the McCollum case has passed like a storm in a teacup. The wall which the Court was professing to erect between Church and State has become even more warped and twisted than I expected. Today's judgment will be more interesting to students of psychology and of the judicial processes than to students of constitutional law.

MARK DE WOLFE HOWE

The Constitutional Question

Professor Howe was a highly respected authority on legal questions.

As the first step towards an analysis of law it seems important that the principal questions of history with which the Court has been concerned should be identified.[14]

The questions are two. The first concerns the interpretation of the religious clause of the First Amendment: "Congress shall make no law respecting an establishment of religion, or prohibiting the free exercise thereof . . ." The second—and in many ways more important—concerns the effect that adoption of the Fourteenth Amendment had on the power of the states. The relevant provisions of that Amendment are these: "No State shall make or enforce any law which shall abridge the privileges or immunities of citizens of the United States; nor shall any State deprive any person of life, liberty, or property, without due process of law; nor deny to any person within its jurisdiction the equal protection of the laws."

When Mr. Justice Rutledge [in his *Everson* dissent] sought to discover the intention of those who were responsible for the writing and enactment of the First Amendment, he chose, as others before him had chosen, to treat the opinions of Jefferson and Madison, as they had been formulated in Virginia's earlier struggle to safeguard religious liberty, as of predominant, if not controlling, importance. It is not my purpose either to contest this or to question the interpretation which Justice Rutledge gave to the views of Jefferson and Madison. I am willing to proceed on the assumption that the two Virginians sought in their own state not only to safeguard the individual's conscience but to oppose even those governmental aids to religion which did not appreciably infringe or endanger any individual's liberty. I shall also discuss the problems concerning the interpretation of the First Amendment on the more dubious assumption that Madison—and with him the American people—intended through that Amendment to impose upon the national government exactly those prohibitions which had successfully been imposed upon the Commonwealth of Virginia.

Having made these assumptions it will be well, I think, to emphasize their implications. The First Amendment thus interpreted would serve two purposes. In the first place, it would protect the individual's conscience from every form of Congressional violation, whether by means of legislation with respect to an establishment of religion or by more direct methods. In the second place, it would impose a disability upon the national government to adopt laws with respect to establishments whether or not their consequence would be to infringe individual rights of conscience.

To find this second purpose in the First Amendment involves, necessarily I think, the admission that the Amendment is something more than a charter of individual liberties. In making that admission one is emphasizing a fact which has too frequently been overlooked—that the Bill of Rights as a whole, and the First Amendment in particular, reflect not only a philosophy of freedom but a theory of federalism. We often forget that the framers were as much concerned with safeguarding the powers of the states as they were with protecting the immunities of the people. Some barriers to national power found their justification in theories of jurisdiction rather than in concepts of personal freedom. Yet it has been a tendency of judges and statesmen alike to read the Bill of Rights as if its provisions had no other purpose than to protect the citizen against the nation. The tendency may be usefully indicated by a reminder of the decision of the Supreme Court in *Cantwell* v. *Connecticut,* the first case of our time in which the Court indicated how the religious clauses of the First Amendment should be interpreted.

By this interpretation the sole purpose of the religious provisions in the First Amendment was to secure the liberty of individuals against national invasion. This interpretation contains no suggestion that national aid to religion or national recognition of religious interests is objectionable when the immunities of individuals are not significantly affected. There is not, in other words, any indication that the Court saw the non-establishment clause as a self-denying ordinance deriving some of its force from a theory of federalism rather than a philosophy of individual rights. To the extent that the Court in its *Cantwell* decision thus disregarded the possibility that the clause might outlaw legislation which does not concern the individual conscience it did not accept the Rutledge interpretation of Madisonian theory. By that rejection or neglect it would seem that Justice Roberts overlooked the aspects of a philosophy of federalism embodied in the First Amendment and the Bill of Rights.

In what I have said so far I have been willing to proceed on the assumption that the Rutledge court was substantially accurate when it described the views of Jefferson the Virginian and Madison the American. A similar assumption is less easily made when one turns to the other historical question which had critical importance to the disposition of the *McCollum* case.

When we remember that the Court which decided the *Cantwell* case, and for which Mr. Justice Roberts was speaking, had before it a case arising not under the First but under the Fourteenth Amendment, its failure to emphasize the principles of federalism is not surprising. . . . A few scholars and individual Justices of the Supreme Court have contended that the framers of the Fourteenth Amendment intended that its adoption should transform all the specific limitations on federal power found in the Bill of Rights into rigid limitations on state authority. If that interpretation were accepted it would mean, of course, that after 1868 no state could make a law "respecting an establishment of religion, or prohibiting the free exercise thereof." The prohibition would be enforced not because of the peculiar sanctity of the interests secured in the First Amendment but by virtue of the fact that the Amendment is a part of the Bill of Rights.

A majority of the Court has never been willing to accept such a mechanistic and revolutionary interpretation of the Fourteenth Amendment. Instead the Court has taken the view that though some of the specific prohibitions of the Bill of Rights have become applicable to the states, there are others which the states are not compelled to respect. The generalities which the Court has used for the classification of rights have served to separate those "immunities [that are] implicit in the concept of ordered liberty" (which the states must respect) from those which "are not so rooted in the traditions and conscience of our people as to be ranked as fundamental."

It is not surprising that the Supreme Court, after a period of some uncertainty, came to accept the view that the First Amendment's specific guarantee of freedom of speech and press had been made binding on the states by the Fourteenth Amendment. When that principle was settled it was clear that the free exercise of religion must enjoy similar protection—and it was given that protection with energetic vigor. When Mr. Justice Roberts in the *Cantwell* case found in the religious clauses of the First Amendment security for two religious freedoms, the one of belief, the other of action, he found it natural to assume that each had been rendered secure against state action by the adoption of the Fourteenth Amendment. It would, of course, have been absurd to say that though earlier decisions interpreting the Fourteenth Amendment had made good against the states the *relative* freedom of religious action the Court would not protect the *absolute* freedom of religious belief from state infringement. Surely if a freedom which the Court has classified as "relative" is considered essential to a scheme of ordered liberty the other freedom which it has described as "absolute" deserves no lower classification.

Had the Court in the *Everson* and *McCollum* cases done no more than apply the rule of incorporation enunciated by Mr. Justice Roberts seven years previously, its action might have been beyond criticism. It is the something more that happened which troubles many. By its re-examination of the purposes of the First Amendment the Court imposed, perhaps quite properly, special limitations on the powers of the national government which, as I have said, gain their strength from concepts of federalism rather than from principles of individual liberty. Yet it then proceeded, without discussion, to make those special, non-libertarian limitations on the national government effective against the states as if they were essential to the scheme of ordered liberty prescribed by the due process clause of the Fourteenth Amendment. The Court did not seem to be aware of the fact that some legislative enactments respecting an establishment of religion affect most remotely, if at all, the personal rights of religious liberty.

The Supreme Court of the United States has not yet re-examined its own interpretations of history either as they relate to the original meaning of the First Amendment or as they apply to the incorporation of the non-establishment clause of the Fourteenth. I find it hard to believe that a re-examination of the first matter is of critical importance. I would suggest, however, that public and judicial attention may well be directed to the second issue. If that effort should be made it seems to me that we might find ourselves generally satisfied with the resolution which a respect for history might compel us to adopt. We might find ourselves allowing the states to take such action in aid of religion as does not appreciably affect the religious or other constitutional rights of individuals while condemning all state action which unreasonably restricts the exercise and enjoyment of other constitutional rights. . . .

There is much evidence to support the belief that the framers of the First Amendment believed religious liberty was more important than other substantive rights to which they gave constitutional protection. To make that admission does not, however, involve a concession that all of the current demands which fly the colors of religious liberty are entitled to preferential respect. In particular, I think, it does not mean that government is under any affirmative responsibility to facilitate the fulfillment of a man's obligations to God. Yet this, I take it, has been the conclusion to which some of those who assert the priority of religious liberty would seek to carry us.

For two reasons I reject the conclusion. In the first place, it seems to me to violate a theory of government which was fundamental in the minds of the framers of the Constitution and which still plays an important and legitimate role in its administration. As I read the original document and its Bill of Rights it seems to me to expound a political theory which is grounded in the belief that liberty is the by-product of limitations on governmental power, not the objective of its existence.

One may fairly say that the conception that liberty becomes effective when the boundaries of governmental power are clearly defined reflects the naiveté of the eighteenth century. One must, however, acknowledge that the naiveté survived with such vigor that it not only defined in the nineteenth century the scope of the Fourteenth Amendment but in the twentieth has measured the significance of the Supreme Court's decision in the Segregation Cases. Just as the framers of the Bill of Rights thought that they had done enough when they protected certain rights from governmental infringement, so the draftsmen of the Fourteenth Amendment believed that they had secured the Negro's essential liberties when they restricted the powers of the states. In 1954 the Supreme Court went no further in its segregation decisions than to say that the states could not constitutionally compel segregation on racial grounds. The Court did not hold that the Fourteenth Amendment requires that Negro and white pupils be given an integrated education.

These distinctions are of profound importance. When they are forgotten we begin to use the word "rights" and the phrase "civil liberty" in misleading ways. Our rights, as the framers conceived them, were essentially certain specified immunities. They were not claims on, but assurances against, the government. In my judgment one of the greatest dangers in saying that some of our civil liberties are "natural rights" is that by the introduction of Nature or God into the discussion we seem to be asserting that an immunity against governmental interference has been transformed into an affirmative claim on government. When churchmen or others who believe that because religious liberty enjoys a preferential position the government is bound to take action that will make it effective, they ask us to abandon or overlook a central principle in the political theory of the Republic.

It may be urged that there is no reason why the twentieth century should feel itself compelled to respect an outmoded principle of eighteenth century political theory. We have learned from experience that rights considered as mere immunities are limp and inadequate. This realization has led our governments to act affirmatively in making racial equality, freedom of speech, and the dignity of man political realities. Why, therefore, it may be asked, should not the government give to persons who feel an obligation to fulfill their duties to God equivalent aids and supports?

The answer seems to me to lie in the stubborn fact that in so far as religion is concerned, the political theory of the eighteenth century is codified in the non-establishment clause of the First Amendment. Without a constitutional amendment we are not free to exclude its policies from our living tradition. When the framers of the First Amendment guaranteed religious liberty they accompanied that guarantee with specific prohibition against Congress' enacting any laws respecting an establishment of religion. At the very least that prohibition seems to me to have made the eighteenth century theory of liberty controlling in the area of religion. May it not fairly be argued that it was precisely because the framers granted a preferred status to religious liberty that they saw the need to minimize the consequences of that preference by making the central thesis of their political theory articulate in the non-establishment clause?. . .

The theses that I have offered for consideration are three.

First, I have urged that in so far as national power is concerned we are compelled by our respect for the intention of the framers to read the non-establishment clause of the First Amendment as a barrier not only to federal action which infringes religious and other liberties of individuals but as a prohibition of even those federal aids to religion which do not appreciably affect individual liberties.

Second, I have urged that when the limitations of the Fourteenth Amendment were imposed upon the states they lost not only the power directly to deny the free exercise of religion but to give any aid to religion which would significantly affect the secured liberties of individuals. In considering this problem I suggested that there is no justification for setting as high a barrier against state governments as must be recognized against the nation.

Third, I have suggested that the claim that religious liberty, either against the state or against the nation, has a more favorable status than other constitutional liberties is no longer justified. The denial of that preferential status seems to me to be required not only by the political theory on which our governments were founded but to be required by the policy of non-establishment, both as that policy has set limits to the power of the nation and as it has confined the authority of the states.

An added word of caution seems suitable in conclusion. There has been some tendency to assume that the dimensions of all interests relating to religion are dependent upon interpretations which the Supreme Court may give to the religious clauses of the First Amendment. This assumption is today mistaken, for as liberties and rights beyond the reach of that Amendment have secured recognition, the powers of government, as they relate to the interests and influence of religion, have necessarily been affected. Those persons who may be fearful of the possible consequences flowing from my suggestion that the states should be permitted to give more aid to religion than the nation is allowed to provide, may find real comfort, I suggest, in the fact that the equal protection clause of the Fourteenth Amendment sets limits to state power which did not exist when the First Amendment was adopted and which, perhaps, were not envisioned when the Fourteenth Amendment itself became binding on the states. A parallel expansion of constitutional rights against the federal government has significantly reduced the importance of the religious clauses of the First Amendment below the level they occupied in 1789. If those who demand for religious liberty today the same preferential status it enjoyed when the nation was founded will admit that their favorite liberty has been the beneficiary of an expanding constitutionalism, they might also be willing to surrender their outpost of intransigence. From the beginning of time men have found it difficult to live with each other. Reasonable men, however, have found it less difficult than have the impassioned.

Notes

1. From John A. Ryan and M. F. X. Millar, eds., *The State and the Church* (New York: Macmillan, 1924), pp. 29–39. Reprinted by permission.

2. From John Courtney Murray, S.J., *We Hold These Truths* (Kansas City, Miss:, Sheed and Ward, 1960), pp. 63–71. Used with permission.

3. Reprinted with the permission of Scribner, an imprint of Simon & Schuster Adult Publishing Group, from *Christians and the State* by John C. Bennett. Copyright © 1958 by John C. Bennett.

4. From *Religion and the Public Order*, ed. Donald A Giannella (Chicago, 1964), pp. 150–169. Reprinted by permission of the University of Chicago Press.

5. From Alfred E. Smith, "Governor Smith Replies," in *The Atlantic Monthly*, May 1927, 721–728. Reprinted by permission.

6. From Paul Blanshard, *American Freedom and Catholic Power* (Boston: Beacon Press, 1949; 1958), pp. 266–269. Reprinted by permission.

7. A transcript of Kennedy's statement along with the questions and answers that followed its delivery may be found in the *New York Times*, September 13, 1960, p. 22.

8. *Cantwell v. Connecticut* 310 U.S. 296 (1940).

9. *Minersville School District v. Gobitis* 310 U.S. 586 (1940).

10. *West Virginia State Board of Education v. Barnette* 319 US 624 (1943).

11. *Everson v. Board of Education* 330 U.S. 1 (1947).

12. *Illinois ex rel. McCollum v. Board of Education* 333 U.S. 203 (1948).

13. *Zorach v. Clauson* 343 U.S. 306 (1952).

14. Reprinted from Center for the Study of Democratic Institutions, *Religion in a Free Society* (Santa Barbara, Calif.: Center for the Study of Democratic Institutions, 1958).

7

Dimensions of Inclusive Pluralism (1960–)

In the 1960s any lingering sense of Protestant hegemony gave way to recognition of pluralism as the American cultural reality. This pluralism extended well beyond the Protestant-Catholic-Jewish mainstream, giving considerable support to the rights of both nonbelievers and adherents of new or uncommon faiths. Thus, as the nation approached its bicentennial celebration, it appeared for the first time to be manifestly plural in religion and genuinely secular in government. Yet, just as this process seemed complete, religious and political groups seeking to reunite God and country returned to the political arena with renewed vigor, challenging the movement toward religious pluralism and secular government as the creation of a godless nation.

These issues of cultural transformation have been shaped, in large part, by the resolution of church-state issues in a variety of forums. For example, during the second half of the twentieth century, there was a virtual explosion of judicial activity in the realm of church-state affairs. During this period, many Americans looked to the Supreme Court as the final arbiter of the American church-state question. And so, a series of lawsuits, typically concerned with whether a particular state program contravened the establishment clause of the First Amendment, began to wind their way through the federal courts. Thus, the establishment clause that lay virtually dormant for its first 150 years has become a regular source of litigation in recent decades.

The tremors created by the Supreme Court's establishment-clause decisions have been felt in the political arena. When the Court's opinions have challenged widespread beliefs, many people have turned to political action to restore the "American values" (or, perhaps, the republican Protestant values) they perceive as threatened or lost. For example, upon the Supreme Court's decision to strike down public school–sponsored prayer and Bible reading, the governors of all but one state called for a constitutional amendment to return prayer to the classroom. On the other hand, those opposed to official recognition of any consensus religiosity continue to fight to sever any remaining ties between church and state.

Thus, although the Supreme Court may be the final arbiter of the Constitution's meaning, it will not always have the last word on church-state questions. For over a century, legislators have periodically proposed a constitutional amendment acknowledging the sovereignty of Christ. During the 1980s, substantial political support was mustered behind a constitutional amendment sponsored by President Reagan to legalize school-sponsored prayers, although it did not become adopted. And, in 1993, the Congress tried to constrain the Supreme Court as it made decisions in cases under the free exercise clause with the enactment of the "Religious Freedom Restoration Act," the constitutionality of which was called into question in *Boerne v. Flores.*

Additionally, scholars of religion have begun to inquire more deeply into the role played by religion in American culture. These studies, many of which were stimulated by Robert Bellah's celebrated article "Civil Religion in America," show the manifold ways in which religion may be indelibly stamped on the American character, and hence its political structures, no matter how much church is formally and constitutionally separated from state. Whether there is a separate and distinct "civil religion" existing alongside the churches is debatable, and the debates over its existence may themselves be part of the effort to ensure that traditional values are not completely eradicated from American culture despite the upheavals of the recent decades. In any event, a vast number of Americans continue to see themselves as citizens of "one nation under God." So long as this religious underpinning remains a part of our culture, the church-state question will remain a challenge for scholars, judges, politicians, and, ultimately, the American people.

The following materials loosely represent three levels of interaction between religion and government—institutional, social, and cultural. The narrowest category is institutional interaction in which specific agencies of government, such as the Internal Revenue Service, deal with particular religious organizations. In other words, an organization representing the temporal authority structure is intersecting with an organization representing one branch of the spiritual authority structure. The second level of interaction, at the social level, involves the relationship of governmental institutions and religious activity. The best example of this is nondenominational prayers in public schools. Finally, the interaction is broadest at the cultural level. For many generations, the American dream has had religious connotations for a vast number of our citizens. This teleological link between America and the Kingdom of God can be heard in the rhetoric of virtually every president from George Washington to George W. Bush, and it shapes, in a fundamental way, the relationship of many Americans to their religion and their government.

Religion and Public Education

Engel v. Vitale (1962)[1]

The so-called Regents Prayer Case, when joined to the ruling that followed concerning Bible reading, meant that the neutrality required by the religion clauses of the First Amendment would no longer be satisfied by "nondenominational" Judeo-Christian exercises, at least in the public schools.

Mr. Justice Black delivered the opinion of the Court.

* * *

The respondent Board of Education of Union Free School District No. 9, New Hyde Park, New York, acting in its official capacity under state law, directed the School District's principal to cause the following prayer to be said aloud by each class in the presence of a teacher at the beginning of each school day:

> Almighty God, we acknowledge our dependence upon Thee, and we beg Thy blessings upon us, our parents, our teachers and our Country.

This daily procedure was adopted on the recommendation of the State Board of Regents, a governmental agency created by the State Constitution to which the New York Legislature has granted broad supervisory, executive, and legislative powers over the State's public school system. These state officials composed the prayer which they recommended and published as a part of their "Statement on Moral and Spiritual Training in the Schools," saying: "We believe that this Statement will be subscribed to by all men and women of good will, and we call upon all of them to aid in giving life to our program."

Shortly after the practice of reciting the Regents' prayer was adopted by the School District, the parents of ten pupils brought this action in a New York State Court insisting that use of this official prayer in the public schools was contrary to the beliefs, religions, or religious practices of both themselves and their children. Among other things, these parents challenged the constitutionality of both the state law authorizing the School District to direct the use of prayer in public schools and the School District's regulation ordering the recitation of this particular prayer on the ground that these actions of official governmental agencies violate that part of the First Amendment of the Federal Constitution which commands that "Congress shall make no law respecting an establishment of religion"—a command which was "made applicable to the State of New York by the Fourteenth Amendment of the said Constitution."...

We think that by using its public school system to encourage recitation of the Regents' prayer, the State of New York has adopted a practice wholly inconsistent with the Establishment Clause. There can, of course, be no doubt that New York's program of daily classroom invocation of God's blessings as prescribed in the Regents' prayer is a religious activity. It is a solemn avowal of divine faith and supplication for the blessings of the Almighty. The nature of such a prayer has always been religious, none of the respondents has denied this and the trial court expressly so found:

> The religious nature of prayer was recognized by Jefferson and has been concurred in

> by theological writers, the United States Supreme Court and State courts and administrative officials, including New York's Commissioner of Education. A committee of the New York Legislature has agreed.
>
> The Board of Regents as amicus curiae, the respondents and intervenors all concede the religious nature of prayer, but seek to distinguish this prayer because it is based on our spiritual heritage. . . .

The petitioners contend among other things that the state laws requiring or permitting use of the Regents' prayer must be struck down as a violation of the Establishment Clause because that prayer was composed by governmental officials as a part of a governmental program to further religious beliefs. For this reason, petitioners argue, the State's use of the Regents' prayer in its public school system breaches the constitutional wall of separation between Church and State. We agree with that contention since we think that the constitutional prohibition against laws respecting an establishment of religion must at least mean that in this country it is no part of the business of government to compose official prayers for any group of the American people to recite as a part of a religious program carried on by government.

It is a matter of history that this very practice of establishing governmentally composed prayers for religious services was one of the reasons which caused many of our early colonists to leave England and seek religious freedom in America. . . .

It is an unfortunate fact of history that when some of the very groups which had most strenuously opposed the established Church of England found themselves sufficiently in control of colonial governments in this country to write their own prayers into law, they passed laws making their own religion the official religion of their respective colonies. Indeed, as late as the time of the Revolutionary War, there were established churches in at least eight of the thirteen former colonies and established religions in at least four of the other five. But the successful Revolution against English political domination was shortly followed by intense opposition to the practice of establishing religion by law. This opposition crystallized rapidly into an effective political force in Virginia where the minority religious groups such as Presbyterians, Lutherans, Quakers and Baptists had gained such strength that the adherents to the established Episcopal Church were actually a minority themselves. In 1785–1786, those opposed to the established Church, led by James Madison and Thomas Jefferson, who, though themselves not members of any of those dissenting religious groups, opposed all religious establishments by law on grounds of principle, obtained the enactment of the famous "Virginia Bill for Religious Liberty" by which all religious groups were placed on an equal footing so far as the State was concerned. Similar though less far-reaching legislation was being considered and passed in other States.

By the time of the adoption of the Constitution, our history shows that there was a widespread awareness among many Americans of the dangers of a union of Church and State. These people knew, some of them from bitter personal experience, that one of the greatest dangers to the freedom of the individual to worship in his own way lay in the Government's placing its official stamp of approval upon one particular kind of prayer or one particular form of religious services. They knew the anguish, hardship and bitter strife that could come when zealous religious groups struggled with one another to obtain the Government's stamp of approval from each King, Queen, or Protector that came to temporary power. The Constitution was intended to avert a part of this danger by leaving the government of this country in the hands of the people rather than in the hands of any monarch. But this safeguard was not enough. Our Founders were no more willing to let the content of their prayers and their privilege of praying whenever they pleased be influenced by the ballot box than they were to let these vital matters of personal conscience depend upon the succession of monarchs. The First Amendment was added to the Constitution to stand as a guarantee that neither the power nor the prestige of the Federal Government would be used to control, support or influence the kinds of prayer the American people can say—that the people's religions must not be subjected to the pressures of government for change each time a new political administration is elected to office. Under that Amendment's prohibition against governmental establishment of religion, as reinforced by the provisions of the Fourteenth Amendment, government in this country, be it state or federal, is without power to prescribe by law any particular form of prayer which is to be used as an official prayer in carrying on any program of governmentally sponsored religious activity.

There can be no doubt that New York's state prayer program officially establishes the religious beliefs embodied in the Regents' prayer. The respondents' argument to the contrary, which is largely based upon the contention that the Regents' prayer is "non-denominational" and the fact that the program, as modified and approved by state courts, does not require all pupils to recite the prayer but permits those who wish to do so to remain silent or be excused from the room, ignores the essential nature of the program's constitutional defects. Neither the fact that the prayer may be denominationally neutral nor the fact that its observance on the part of the students is voluntary can serve to free it from the limitations of the Establishment Clause, as it might from the Free Exercise Clause, of the First Amendment, both of which are operative against the States by virtue of the Fourteenth Amendment. Although these two clauses may in certain instances overlap, they forbid two quite different kinds of governmental encroachment upon religious freedom. The Establishment Clause, unlike the Free Exercise Clause, does not depend upon any showing of direct governmental compulsion and is violated by the enactment of laws which establish an official religion whether those laws operate directly to coerce non-observing individuals or not. This is not to say, of course, that laws officially prescribing a particular form of religious worship do not involve coercion of such individuals. When the power, prestige and financial support of government is placed behind a particular religious belief, the indirect coercive pressure upon religious minorities to conform to the prevailing officially approved religion is plain. But the purposes underlying the Establishment Clause go much further than that. Its first and most immediate purpose rested on the belief that a union of government and religion tends to destroy government and to degrade religion. The history of governmentally established religion, both in England and in this country, showed that whenever government had allied itself with one particular form of religion, the inevitable result had been that it had incurred the hatred, disrespect and even contempt of those who held contrary beliefs. That same history showed that many people had lost their respect for any religion that had relied upon the support of government to spread its faith. The Establishment Clause thus stands as an expression of principle on the part of the Founders of our Constitution that religion is too personal, too sacred, too holy, to permit its "unhallowed perversion" by a civil magistrate. Another purpose of the Establishment Clause rested upon an awareness of the historical fact that governmentally established religions and religious persecutions go hand in hand. . . . It was in large part to get completely away from . . . systematic religious persecution that the Founders brought into being our Nation, our Constitution, and our Bill of Rights with its prohibition against any governmental establishment of religion. The New York laws officially prescribing the Regents' prayer are inconsistent both with the purposes of the Establishment Clause and with the Establishment Clause itself.

It has been argued that to apply the Constitution in such a way as to prohibit state laws respecting an establishment of religious services in public schools is to indicate a hostility toward religion or toward prayer. Nothing, of course, could be more wrong. The history of man is inseparable from the history of religion. And perhaps it is not too much to say that since the beginning of that history many people have devoutly believed that "More things are wrought by prayer than this world dreams of." It was doubtless largely due to men who believed this that there grew up a sentiment that caused men to leave the cross-currents of officially established state religions and religious persecution in Europe and come to this country filled with the hope that they could find a place in which they could pray when they pleased to the God of their faith in the language they chose. And there were men of this same faith in the power of prayer who led the fight for adoption of our Constitution and also for our Bill of Rights with the very guarantees of religious freedom that forbid the sort of governmental activity which New York has attempted here. These men knew that the First Amendment, which tried to put an end to governmental control of religion and of prayer, was not written to destroy either. They knew rather that it was written to quiet well-justified fears which nearly all of them felt arising out of an awareness that governments of the past had shackled men's tongues to make them speak only the religious thoughts that government wanted them to speak and to pray only to the God that government wanted them to pray to. It is neither sacrilegious nor antireligious to say that each separate government in this country should stay out of the business of writing or sanctioning official prayers and leave that purely religious function to the people themselves and to those the people choose to look to for religious guidance.

It is true that New York's establishment of its Regents' prayer as an officially approved religious doctrine of that State does not amount to a total establishment of one particular religious sect to the exclusion of all others—that, indeed, the governmental endorsement of that prayer seems relatively insignificant when compared to the governmental encroachments upon religion which were commonplace 200 years ago. To those who may subscribe to the view that because the Regents' official prayer is so brief and general there can be no danger to religious freedom in its governmental establishment, however, it may be appropriate to say in the words of James Madison, the author of the First Amendment:

> [I]t is proper to take alarm at the first experiment on our liberties. . . . Who does not see that the same authority which can establish Christianity, in exclusion of all other Religions, may establish with the same ease any particular sect of Christians, in exclusion of all other Sects? That the same authority which can force a citizen to contribute three pence only of his property for the support of any one establishment, may force him to conform to any other establishment in all cases whatsoever?

Mr. Justice Stewart, dissenting.

A local school board in New York has provided that those pupils who wish to do so may join in a brief prayer at the beginning of each school day, acknowledging their dependence upon God and asking His blessing upon them and upon their parents, their teachers, and their country. The court today decides that in permitting this brief nondenominational prayer the school board has violated the Constitution of the United States. I think this decision is wrong. . . .

With all respect, I think the Court has misapplied a great constitutional principle. I cannot see how an "official religion" is established by letting those who want to say a prayer say it. On the contrary, I think that to deny the wish of these school children to join in reciting this prayer is to deny them the opportunity of sharing in the spiritual heritage of our Nation. . . . We deal here not with the establishment of a state church, which would, of course, be constitutionally impermissible, but with whether school children who want to begin their day by joining in prayer must be prohibited from doing so. Moreover, I think that the Court's task, in this as in all areas of constitutional adjudication, is not responsibly aided by the uncritical invocation of metaphors like the "wall of separation," a phrase nowhere to be found in the Constitution. What is relevant to the issue here is . . . the history of the religious traditions of our people, reflected in countless practices of the institutions and officials of our government.

At the opening of each day's Session of this Court we stand, while one of our officials invokes the protection of God. Since the days of John Marshall our Crier has said, "God save the United States and this Honorable Court." Both the Senate and the House of Representatives open their daily Sessions with prayer. Each of our Presidents, from George Washington to John F. Kennedy, has upon assuming his office asked the protection and help of God.

The Court today says that the state and federal governments are without constitutional power to prescribe any particular form of words to be recited by any group of the American people on any subject touching religion. One of the stanzas of "The Star-Spangled Banner," made our National Anthem by Act of Congress in 1931, contains these verses:

> Blest with victory and peace, may the heav'n rescued land
> Praise the Pow'r that hath made and preserved us a nation!

Then conquer we must, when our cause it is just,
And this be our motto "In God is our Trust."

In 1954 Congress added a phrase to the Pledge of Allegiance to the Flag so that it now contains the words "one Nation *under God* indivisible, with liberty and justice for all." In 1952 Congress enacted legislation calling upon the President each year to proclaim a National Day of Prayer. Since 1865 the words "IN GOD WE TRUST" have been impressed on our coins.

Countless similar examples could be listed, but there is no need to belabor the obvious. It was all summed up by this Court just ten years ago in a single sentence: "We are a religious people whose institutions presuppose a Supreme Being."

I do not believe that this Court, or the Congress, or the President has by the actions and practices I have mentioned established an "official religion" in violation of the Constitution. And I do not believe the State of New York has done so in this case. What each has done has been to recognize and to follow the deeply entrenched and highly cherished spiritual traditions of our Nation—traditions which come down to us from those who almost two hundred years ago avowed their "firm Reliance on the Protection of divine Providence" when they proclaimed the freedom and independence of this brave new world.

I dissent.

School District of Abington Township v. Schempp (1963)[2]

The question of daily Bible readings as a part of opening school exercises finally reached the Supreme Court in a case which was argued during February of 1963 and decided on June 17. Excerpts follow.

Mr. Justice Clark Delivered the Opinion of the Court.

* * *

Once again we are called upon to consider the scope of the provision of the First Amendment to the United States Constitution which declares that "Congress shall make no law respecting an establishment of religion, or prohibiting the free exercise thereof. . . ." These companion cases present the issues in the context of state action requiring that schools begin each day with readings from the Bible. While raising the basic questions under slightly different factual situations, the cases permit of joint treatment. In light of the history of the First Amendment and of our cases interpreting and applying its requirements, we hold that the practices at issue and the laws requiring them are unconstitutional under the Establishment Clause, as applied to the States through the Fourteenth Amendment.

* * *

It is true that religion has been closely identified with our history and government. As we said in *Engel* v. *Vitale,* "The history of man is inseparable from the history of religion. And . . . since the beginning of that history many people have devoutly believed that 'More things are wrought by prayer than this world dreams of.'" In *Zorach* v. *Clauson* we gave specific recognition to the proposition that "[w]e are a religious people whose institutions pre-suppose a Supreme Being.". . .

This is not to say, however, that religion has been so identified with our history and government that religious freedom is not likewise as strongly imbedded in our public and private life. Nothing but the most telling of personal experiences in religious persecution suffered by our forebears . . . could have planted our belief in liberty of religious opinion any more deeply in our heritage. . . .

Almost a hundred years ago . . . Judge Alphonso Taft, father of the revered Chief Justice, . . . stated the ideal of our people as to religious freedom as one of

> absolute equality before the law, of all religious opinions and sects. . . .
>
> The government is neutral, and, while protecting all, it prefers none, and it *disparages* none.

Before examining this "neutral" position in which the Establishment and Free Exercise Clauses of the First Amendment place our Government it is well that we discuss the reach of the Amendment under the cases of this Court.

First, this Court has decisively settled that the First Amendment's mandate that "Congress shall make no law respecting an establishment of religion, or prohibiting the free exercise thereof" has been made wholly applicable to the States by the Fourteenth Amendment. . . . In a series of cases since *Cantwell* the Court has repeatedly reaffirmed that doctrine, and we do so now.

Second, this Court has rejected unequivocally the contention that the Establishment Clause forbids only governmental preference of one religion over another. Almost 20 years ago in *Everson* the Court said that "[n]either a state nor the Federal Government can set up a church. Neither can pass laws which aid one religion, aid all religions, or prefer one religion over another.". . .

While none of the parties to either of these cases has questioned these basic conclusions of the Court, both of which have been long established, recognized and consistently reaffirmed, others continue to question their history, logic and efficacy. Such contentions, in the light of the consistent interpretation in cases of this Court, seem entirely untenable and of value only as academic exercises.

The interrelationship of the Establishment and the Free Exercise Clauses was first touched upon by Mr. Justice Roberts for the Court in *Cantwell* v. *Connecticut* where it was said that their "inhibition of legislation" had

> a double aspect. On the one hand, it forestalls compulsion by law of the acceptance of any creed or the practice of any form of worship. Freedom of conscience and freedom to adhere to such religious organization or form of worship as the individual may choose can-

> not be restricted by law. On the other hand, it safeguards the free exercise of the chosen form of religion. Thus the Amendment embraces two concepts,—freedom to believe and freedom to act. The first is absolute but, in the nature of things, the second cannot be.

Finally, in *Engel* v. *Vitale,* only last year, these principles were so universally recognized that the Court, without the citation of a single case and over the sole dissent of Mr. Justice Stewart, reaffirmed them. The Court found the 22-word prayer used in "New York's program of daily classroom invocation of God's blessings as prescribed in the Regents' prayer . . . [to be] a religious activity." It held that "it is no part of the business of government to compose official prayers for any group of the American people to recite as a part of a religious program carried on by government." In discussing the reach of the Establishment and Free Exercise Clauses of the First Amendment the Court said:

> Although these two clauses may in certain instances overlap, they forbid two quite different kinds of governmental encroachment upon religious freedom. The Establishment Clause, unlike the Free Exercise Clause, does not depend upon any showing of direct governmental compulsion and is violated by the enactment of laws which establish an official religion whether those laws operate directly to coerce nonobserving individuals or not. This is not to say, of course, that laws officially prescribing a particular form of religious worship do not involve coercion of such individuals. When the power, prestige and financial support of government is placed behind a particular religious belief, the indirect coercive pressure upon religious minorities to conform to the prevailing officially approved religion is plain.

And in further elaboration the Court found that the "first and most immediate purpose [of the Establishment Clause] rested on the belief that a union of government and religion tends to destroy government and to degrade religion." When government, the Court said, allies itself with one particular form of religion, the inevitable result is that it incurs "the hatred, disrespect and even contempt of those who held contrary beliefs."

The wholesome "neutrality" of which this Court's cases speak thus stems from a recognition of the teachings of history that powerful sects or groups might bring about a fusion of governmental and religious functions or a concert or dependency of one upon the other to the end that official support of the State or Federal Government would be placed behind the tenets of one or of all orthodoxies. This the Establishment Clause prohibits. And a further reason for neutrality is found in the Free Exercise Clause, which recognizes the value of religious training, teaching and observance and, more particularly, the right of every person to freely choose his own course with reference thereto, free of any compulsion from the state. This the Free Exercise Clause guarantees. Thus, as we have seen, the two clauses may overlap. As we have indicated, the Establishment Clause has been directly considered by this Court eight times in the past score of years and, with only one Justice dissenting on the point, it has consistently held that the clause withdrew all legislative power respecting religious belief or the expression thereof. The test may be stated as follows: what are the purpose and the primary effect of the enactment? If either is the advancement or inhibition of religion then the enactment exceeds the scope of legislative power as circumscribed by the Constitution. That is to say that to withstand the strictures of the Establishment Clause there must be a secular legislative purpose and a primary effect that neither advances nor inhibits religion. The Free Exercise Clause, likewise considered many times here, withdraws from legislative power, state and federal, the exertion of any restraint on the free exercise of religion. Its purpose is to secure religious liberty in the individual by prohibiting any invasions thereof by civil authority. Hence it is necessary in a free exercise case for one to show the coercive effect of the enactment as it operates against him in the practice of his religion. The distinction between the two clauses is apparent—a violation of the Free Exercise Clause is predicated on coercion while the Establishment Clause violation need not be so attended.

Applying the Establishment Clause principles to the cases at bar we find that the States are requiring the selection and reading at the opening of the school day of verses from the Holy Bible and the recitation of the Lord's Prayer by the students in unison. These exercises are prescribed as part of the curricular activities of students who are required by law to attend school. They are held in the school buildings under the supervision and with the participation of teachers employed in those schools. None of these factors, other than compulsory school attendance, was present in the program upheld in *Zorach* v. *Clauson*. The trial court in No. 142 has found that such an opening exercise is a religious ceremony and was intended by the State to be so. We agree with the trial court's finding as to the religious character of the exercises. Given that finding, the exercises and the law requiring them are in violation of the Establishment Clause.

There is no such specific finding as to the religious character of the exercises in No. 119, and the State contends (as does the State in No. 142) that the program is an effort to extend its benefits to all public school children without regard to their religious belief. Included within its secular purposes, it says, are the promotion of moral values, the contradiction to the materialistic trends of our times, the perpetuation of our institutions and the teaching of literature. The case came up on demurrer, of course, to a petition which alleged that the uniform practice under the rule had been to read from the King James version of the Bible and that the exercise was sectarian. The short answer, therefore, is that the religious character of the exercise was admitted by the State. But even if its purpose is not strictly religious, it is sought to be accomplished through readings, without comment, from the Bible. Surely the place of the Bible as an instrument of religion cannot be gainsaid, and the State's recognition of the pervading religious character of the ceremony is evident from the rule's specific permission of the alternative use of the Catholic Douay version as well as the recent amendment permitting nonattendance at the exercises. None of these factors is consistent with the contention that the Bible is here used either as an instrument for nonreligious moral inspiration or as a reference for the teaching of secular subjects.

The conclusion follows that in both cases the laws require religious exercises and such exercises are being conducted in direct violation of the rights of the appellees and petitioners. Nor are these required exercises mitigated by the fact that individual students may absent themselves upon parental request, for that fact furnishes no defense to a claim of unconstitutionality under the Establishment Clause. . . . Further, it is no defense to urge that the religious practices here may be relatively minor encroachments on the First Amendment. . . .

It is insisted that unless these religious exercises are permitted a "religion of secularism" is established in the schools. We agree of course that the State may not establish a "religion of secularism" in the sense of affirmatively opposing or showing hostility to religion, thus "preferring those who believe in no religion over those who do believe.". . . We do not agree, however, that this decision in any sense has that effect. In addition, it might well be said that one's education is not complete without a study of comparative religion or the history of religion and its relationship to the advancement of civilization. It certainly may be said that the Bible is worthy of study for its literary and historic qualities. Nothing we have said here indicates that such study of the Bible or of religion, when presented objectively as part of a secular program of education, may not be effected consistently with the First Amendment. But the exercises here do not fall into those categories. They are religious exercises, required by the States in violation of the command of the First Amendment that the Government maintain strict neutrality, neither aiding nor opposing religion.

Finally, we cannot accept that the concept of neutrality, which does not permit a State to require a religious exercise even with the consent of the majority of those affected, collides with the majority's right to free exercise of religion. While the Free Exercise Clause clearly prohibits the use of state action to deny the rights of free exercise to *anyone,* it has never meant that a majority could use the machinery of the State to practice its beliefs. . . .

The place of religion in our society is an exalted one, achieved through a long tradition of reliance on the home, the church and the inviolable citadel of the individual heart and mind. We have come to recognize through bitter experience that it is not within the power of government to invade that citadel, whether its purpose or effect be to aid or oppose, to advance or retard. In the relationship between man and religion, the State is firmly committed to a position of neutrality. Though the application of that rule requires interpretation of a delicate sort, the rule itself is clearly and concisely stated in the words of the First Amendment. Applying that rule to the facts of these cases, we affirm the judgment in No. 142. In No. 119, the judgment is reversed and the cause remanded to the Maryland Court of Appeals for further proceedings consistent with this opinion.

It is so ordered.

Epperson v. Arkansas (1968)[3]

The courtroom clash over Tennessee's "monkey law"—which prohibited the schools from teaching Darwin's theory of evolution—pitted famed advocates Clarence Darrow and William Jennings Bryan against one another in the 1927 case of *Scopes* v. *State.* The issue came alive again forty years later when a similar Arkansas statute was challenged. Despite Darwin's triumph in this case, a debate continues to rage in some communities over whether the schools should teach "creation science" (generally based on the Genesis account) in addition to or instead of the theory of evolution.

Mr. Justice Fortas delivered the opinion of the Court.

* * *

This appeal challenges the constitutionality of the "anti-evolution" statute which the State of Arkansas adopted in 1928 to prohibit the teaching in its public schools and universities of the theory that man evolved from other species of life. The statute was a product of the upsurge of *"fundamentalist"* religious fervor of the twenties. The Arkansas statute was an adaptation of the famous Tennessee "monkey law" which that State adopted in 1925. The constitutionality of the Tennessee law was upheld by the Tennessee Supreme Court in the celebrated *Scopes* case in 1927.

The Arkansas law makes it unlawful for a teacher in any state-supported school or university "to teach the theory or doctrine that mankind ascended or descended from a lower order of animals," or "to adopt or use in any such institution a textbook that teaches" this theory. Violation is a misdemeanor and subjects the violator to dismissal from his position.

The present case concerns the teaching of biology in a high school in Little Rock. According to the testimony, until the events here in litigation, the official textbook furnished for the high school biology course did not have a section on the Darwinian Theory. Then, for the academic year 1965–1966, the school administration, on recommendation of the teachers of biology in the school system, adopted and prescribed a textbook which contained a chapter setting forth "the theory about the origin . . . of man from a lower form of animal." . . .

Susan Epperson, a young woman who graduated from Arkansas' school system and then obtained her master's degree in zoology at the University of Illinois, was employed by the Little Rock school system in the fall of 1964 to teach 10th grade biology at Central High School. At the start of the next academic year, 1965, she was confronted by the new textbook (which one surmises from the record was not unwelcome to her). She faced at least a literal dilemma because she was supposed to use the new textbook for classroom instruction and presumably to teach the statutorily condemned chapter; but to do so would be a criminal offense and subject her to dismissal.

She instituted the present action in the Chancery Court of the State, seeking a declaration that the Arkansas statute is void and enjoining the State and the defendant officials of the Little Rock school system from dismissing her for violation of the statute's provisions.

Only Arkansas and Mississippi have such "anti-evolution" or "monkey" laws on their books. There is no record of any prosecutions in Arkansas under its statute. It is possible that the statute is presently more of a curiosity than a vital fact of life in these States. Nevertheless, the present case was brought, the appeal is properly here, and it is our duty to decide the issues presented.

* * *

At the outset, it is urged upon us that the challenged statute is vague and uncertain and therefore within the condemnation of the Due Process Clause of the Fourteenth Amendment. . . .

[W]e do not rest our decision upon the asserted vagueness of the statute. On [any] interpretation of its language, Arkansas' statute cannot stand. It is of no moment whether the law is deemed to prohibit mention of Darwin's theory, or to forbid any or all of the infinite varieties of communication embraced within the term "teaching." Under either interpretation, the law must be stricken because of its conflict with the constitutional prohibition of state laws respecting an establishment of religion or prohibiting the free exercise thereof. The overriding fact is that Arkansas' law selects from the body of knowledge a particular segment which it proscribes for the sole reason that it is deemed to conflict with a particular religious doctrine; that is, with a particular interpretation of the Book of Genesis by a particular religious group.

* * *

The antecedents of today's decision are many and unmistakable. They are rooted in the foundation soil of our Nation. They are fundamental to freedom.

Government in our democracy, state and national, must be neutral in matters of religious theory, doctrine, and practice. It may not be hostile to any religion or to the advocacy of no-religion; and it may not aid, foster, or promote one religion or religious theory against another or even against the militant opposite. The First Amendment mandates governmental neutrality between religion and religion, and between religion and nonreligion. . . .

There is and can be no doubt that the First Amendment does not permit the State to require that teaching and learning must be tailored to the principles or prohibitions of any religious sect or dogma. . . .

While study of religions and of the Bible from a literary and historic viewpoint, presented objectively as part of a secular program of education, need not collide with the First Amendment's prohibition, the State may not adopt programs or practices in its public schools or colleges which "aid or oppose" any religion. This prohibition is absolute. It forbids alike the preference of a religious doctrine or the prohibition of theory which is deemed antagonistic to a particular dogma. . . .

The State's undoubted right to prescribe the curriculum for its public schools does not carry with it the right to prohibit, on pain of criminal penalty, the teaching of a scientific theory or doctrine where that prohibition is based upon reasons that violate the First Amendment. . . .

In the present case, there can be no doubt that Arkansas has sought to prevent its teachers from discussing the theory of evolution because it is contrary to the belief of some that the Book of Genesis must be the exclusive source of doctrine as to the origin of man. No suggestion has been made that Arkansas' law may be justified by considerations of state policy other than the religious views of some of its citizens. It is clear that fundamentalist sectarian conviction was and is the law's reason for existence. Its antecedent, Tennessee's "monkey law," candidly stated its purpose: to make it unlawful "to teach any theory that denies the story of the Divine Creation of man as taught in the Bible, and to teach instead that man has descended from a lower order of animals." Perhaps the sensational publicity attendant upon the *Scopes* trial induced Arkansas to adopt less explicit language. It eliminated Tennessee's reference to "the story of the Divine Creation of man" as taught in the Bible, but there is no doubt that the motivation for the law was the same: to suppress the teaching of a theory which, it was thought, "denied" the divine creation of man.

Arkansas' law cannot be defended as an act of religious neutrality. Arkansas did not seek to excise from the curricula of its schools and universities all discussion of the origin of man. The law's effort was confined to an attempt to blot out a particular theory because of its supposed conflict with the Biblical account, literally read. Plainly, the law is contrary to the mandate of the First, and in violation of the Fourteenth, Amendment to the Constitution.

Stone v. Graham (1980)[4]

Between *School District of Abington Township* v. *Schempp* in 1963 and *Stone* v. *Graham* in 1980, the Supreme Court developed a three-part test for establishment-clause cases. Often referred to as the *Lemon* test (because it was first crystalized in *Lemon* v. *Kurtzman* in 1971), this tripartite test was applied in *Stone* v. *Graham* to a Kentucky law requiring that the Ten Commandments be posted in every public school classroom.

Per Curiam Opinion.

* * *

A Kentucky statute requires the posting of a copy of the Ten Commandments, purchased with private contributions, on the wall of each public classroom in the State. Petitioners, claiming that this statute violates the Establishment and Free Exercise Clauses of the First Amendment, sought an injunction against its enforcement. . . .

This Court has announced a three-part test for determining whether a challenged state statute is permissible under the Establishment Clause of the United States Constitution:

> First, the statute must have a secular legislative purpose; second, its principal or primary effect must be one that neither advances nor inhibits religion. . . ; finally the statute must not foster "an excessive government entanglement with religion."

If a statute violates any of these three principles, it must be struck down under the Establishment Clause. We conclude that Kentucky's statute requiring the posting of the Ten Commandments in public schoolrooms had no secular legislative purpose, and is therefore unconstitutional.

The Commonwealth insists that the statute in question serves a secular legislative purpose, observing that the legislature required the following notation in small print at the bottom of each display of the Ten Commandments: "The secular application of the Ten Commandments is clearly seen in its adoption as the fundamental legal code of Western Civilization and the Common Law of the United States.". . .

The trial court found the "avowed" purpose of the statute to be secular, even as it labeled the statutory declaration "self-serving." Under this Court's rulings, however, such an "avowed" secular purpose is not sufficient to avoid conflict with the First Amendment. . . .

The pre-eminent purpose for posting the Ten Commandments on schoolroom walls is plainly religious in nature. The Ten Commandments is undeniably a sacred text in the Jewish and Christian faiths, and no legislative recitation of a supposed secular purpose can blind us to that fact. The Commandments do not confine themselves to arguably secular matters, such as honoring one's parents, killing or murder, adultery, stealing, false witness, and covetousness. See Exodus 20:12–17; Deuteronomy 5:16–21. Rather, the first part of the Commandments concerns the religious duties of believers: worshipping the Lord God alone, avoiding idolatry, not using the Lord's name in vain, and observing the sabbath day. See Exodus 20:1–11; Deuteronomy 5:6–15.

This is not a case in which the Ten Commandments are integrated into the school curriculum, where the Bible may constitutionally be used in an appropriate study of history, civilization, ethics, comparative religion, or the like. . . . Posting of religious texts on the wall serves no such educational function. If the posted copies of the Ten Commandments are to have any effect at all, it will be to induce the school children to read, meditate upon, perhaps to venerate and obey, the Commandments. However desirable this might be as a matter of private devotion, it is not a permissible state objective under the Establishment Clause.

It does not matter that the posted copies of the Ten Commandments are financed by voluntary private contributions, for the mere posting of the copies under the auspices of the legislature provides the "official support of the State . . . Government" that the Establishment Clause prohibits. Nor is it significant that the Bible verses involved in this case are merely posted on the wall, rather than read aloud as in *Schempp* and *Engel,* for "it is no defense to urge that the religious practices here may be relatively minor encroachments on the First Amendment.". . . We conclude that [the Kentucky statute] violates the first part of the [three-part] test, and thus the Establishment Clause of the Constitution.

Widmar v. Vincent (1981)[5]

Yet another approach to religion in the public schools is called "equal access." Under an equal-access approach, public schools having extracurricular activities must provide equal opportunity for both religious and secular organizations. In *Widmar* v. *Vincent* the Supreme Court upheld the constitutionality of the equal-access approach in the context of a public university. Following federal appellate court decisions suggesting that the equal-access approach in secondary schools is unconstitutional under the establishment clause, Congress enacted the Equal Access Act, which provided that public secondary schools receiving federal financial support must offer equal access to religious groups if they have a "limited open forum" for other types of student activities. The Supreme Court upheld the Equal Access Act in *Board of Education* v. *Mergens.* Although the Court's decision in *Widmar* v. *Vincent* is based on the free-speech clause of the First Amendment, some commentators have seen equal-access as an example of the inherent conflict within the religion clauses of the First Amendment. Students seeking equal access for religious groups rest their claims on free exercise (and free speech) grounds, while opponents argue that the establishment clause bars religious groups from meeting on school property.

Justice Powell Delivered the Opinion of the Court.

* * *

This case presents the question whether a state university, which makes its facilities generally available for the activities of registered student groups, may close its facilities to a registered student group desiring to use the facilities for religious worship and religious discussion.

* * *

It is the stated policy of the University of Missouri at Kansas City to encourage the activities of student organizations. The University officially recognizes over 100 student groups. It routinely provides University facilities for the meetings of registered organizations. Students pay an activity fee of $41 per semester (1978–1979) to help defray the costs to the University.

From 1973 until 1977 a registered religious group named Cornerstone regularly sought and received permission to conduct its meetings in University facilities. In 1977, however, the University informed the group that it could no longer meet in University buildings. The exclusion was based on a regulation, adopted by the Board of Curators in 1972, that prohibits the use of University buildings or grounds "for purposes of religious worship or religious teaching."

Eleven University students, all members of Cornerstone, brought suit to challenge the regulation in Federal District Court for the Western District of Missouri. They alleged that the University's discrimination against religious activity and discussion violated their rights to free exercise of religion, equal protection, and freedom of speech under the First and Fourteenth Amendments to the Constitution of the United States. . . .

* * *

Through its policy of accommodating their meetings, the University has created a forum generally open for use by student groups. Having done so, the University has assumed an obligation to justify its discriminations and exclusions under applicable constitutional norms. The Constitution forbids a State to enforce certain exclusions from a forum generally open to the public, even if it was not required to create the forum in the first place. . . .

The University's institutional mission, which it describes as providing a "*secular* education" to its students, does not exempt its actions from constitutional scrutiny. With respect to persons entitled to be there, our cases leave no doubt that the First Amendment rights of speech and association extend to the campuses of state universities. . . .

Here the University of Missouri has discriminated against student groups and speakers based on their desire to use a generally open forum to engage in religious worship and discussion. These are forms of speech and association protected by the First Amendment. . . .

In order to justify discriminatory exclusion from a public forum based on the religious content of a group's intended speech, the University must therefore satisfy the standard of review appropriate to content-based exclusions. It must show that its regulation is necessary to serve a compelling state interest and that it is narrowly drawn to achieve that end. . . .

In this case the University claims a compelling interest in maintaining strict separation of church and State. It derives this interest from the "Establishment Clauses" of both the Federal and Missouri Constitutions.

The University first argues that it cannot offer its facilities to religious groups and speakers on the terms available to other groups without violating the Establishment Clause of the Constitution of the United States. We agree that the interest of the University in complying with its constitutional obligations may be characterized as compelling. It does not follow, however, that an "equal access" policy would be incompatible with this Court's Establishment Clause cases. Those cases hold that a policy will not offend the Establishment Clause if it can pass a three-pronged test: "First, the [governmental policy] must have a secular legislative purpose; second, its principal or primary effect must be one that neither advances nor inhibits religion . . . ; finally, the [policy] must not foster 'an excessive government entanglement with religion.'" . . .

In this case two prongs of the test are clearly met. . . . [But] the University argues here, that allowing religious groups to share the limited public forum would have the "primary effect" of advancing religion.

The University's argument misconceives the nature of this case. The question is not whether the creation of a religious forum would violate the Establishment Clause. The University has opened its facilities for use by student groups, and the question is whether it can now exclude groups because of the content of their speech. In this context we are unpersuaded that the primary effect of the public forum, open to all forms of discourse, would be to advance religion.

We are not oblivious to the range of an open forum's likely effects. It is possible—perhaps even foreseeable—that religious groups will benefit from access to University facilities. But this Court has explained that a religious organization's enjoyment of merely "incidental" benefits does not violate the prohibition against the "primary advancement" of religion. . . .

We are satisfied that any religious benefits of an open forum at UMKC would be "incidental" within the meaning of our cases. Two factors are especially relevant.

First, an open forum in a public university does not confer any imprimatur of State approval on religious sects or practices. As the Court of Appeals quite aptly stated, such a policy "would no more commit the University . . . to religious goals," than it is "now committed to the goals of the Students for a Democratic Society, the Young Socialist Alliance," or any other group eligible to use its facilities.

Second, the forum is available to a broad class of non-religious as well as religious speakers; there are over 100 recognized student groups at UMKC. The provision of benefits to so broad a spectrum of groups is an important index of secular effect. . . . If the Establishment Clause barred the extension of general benefits to religious groups, "a church could not be protected by the police and fire departments, or have its public sidewalk kept in repair.". . . At least in the absence of empirical evidence that religious groups will dominate UMKC's open forum, we agree with the Court of Appeals that the advancement of religion would not be the forum's "primary effect."

* * *

Our holding in this case in no way undermines the capacity of the University to establish reasonable time, place, and manner regulations. Nor do we question the right of the University to make academic judgments as to how best to allocate scarce resources or "to determine for itself on academic grounds who may teach, what may be taught, how it shall be taught, and who may be admitted to study.". . . Finally, we affirm the continuing validity of cases . . . that recognize a University's right to exclude even First Amendment activities that violate reasonable campus rules or substantially interfere with the opportunity of other students to obtain an education.

The basis for our decision is narrow. Having created a forum generally open to student groups, the University seeks to enforce a content-based exclusion of religious speech. Its exclusionary policy violates the fundamental principle that a state regulation of speech should be content-neutral, and the University is unable to justify this violation under applicable constitutional standards. . . .

Wallace v. Jaffree (1985)[6]

The moment of silence has emerged as a potential way to return religion to the public school day. Defended as an entirely secular opportunity for students to start the day with a quiet moment, opponents (and some proponents) have seen it as a thinly disguised attempt to circumvent the prohibition of school-sponsored prayer in *Engel* v. *Vitale.* In this case, the Supreme Court held Alabama's moment of silence law (called here 316–1–20.1) unconstitutional, but a majority of the justices suggested that other moments of silence might pass muster. Also of note is Justice Rehnquist's call to the Court to abandon its entire approach to the establishment clause.

Justice Stevens delivered the opinion of the Court.. . .

Appellee Ishmael Jaffree is a resident of Mobile County, Alabama. On May 28, 1982, he filed a complaint on behalf of three of his minor children; two of them were second-grade students and the third was then in kindergarten. . . . The complaint . . . alleged that two of the children had been subjected to various acts of religious indoctrination "from the beginning of the school year in September, 1981"; that the defendant teachers had "on a daily basis" led their classes in saying certain prayers in unison; that the minor children were exposed to ostracism from their peer group class members if they did not participate; and that Ishmael Jaffree had repeatedly but unsuccessfully requested that the devotional services be stopped. . . .

[T]he District Court reviewed a number of opinions of this Court interpreting the Establishment Clause of the First Amendment, and then embarked on a fresh examination of the question whether the First Amendment imposes any barrier to the establishment of an official religion by the State of Alabama. After reviewing at length what it perceived to be newly discovered historical evidence, the District Court concluded that "the establishment clause of the first amendment to the United States Constitution does not prohibit the state from establishing a religion."

Our unanimous affirmance of the [reversal by the Court of Appeals of the District Court's decision] . . . makes it unnecessary to comment at length on the District Court's remarkable conclusion that the Federal Constitution imposes no obstacle to Alabama's establishment of a state religion. Before analyzing the precise issue that is presented to us, it is nevertheless appropriate to recall how firmly embedded in our constitutional jurisprudence is the proposition that the several States have no greater power to restrain the individual freedoms protected by the First Amendment than does the Congress of the United States.

As is plain from its text, the First Amendment was adopted to curtail the power of Congress to interfere with the individual's freedom to believe, to worship, and to express himself in accordance with the dictates of his own conscience. Until the Fourteenth Amendment was added to the Constitution, the First Amendment's restraints on the exercise of federal power simply did not apply to the States. But when the Constitution was amended to prohibit any State from depriving any person of liberty without due process of law, that Amendment imposed the same substantive limitations on the States' power to legislate that the First Amendment had always imposed on the Congress' power. This Court has confirmed and endorsed this elementary proposition of law time and time again.

Just as the right to speak and the right to refrain from speaking are complimentary [sic] components of a broader concept of individual freedom of mind, so also the individual's freedom to choose his own creed is the counterpart of his right to refrain from accepting the creed established by the majority. At one time it was thought that this right merely proscribed the preference of one Christian sect over another, but would not require equal respect for the conscience of the infidel, the atheist, or the adherent of a non-Christian faith such as Mohammedism or Judaism. But when the underlying principle has been examined in the crucible of litigation, the Court has unambiguously concluded that the individual freedom of conscience protected by the First Amendment embraces the right to select any religious faith or none at all. This conclusion derives support not only from the interest in respecting the individual's freedom of conscience, but also from the conviction that religious beliefs worthy of respect are the product of free and voluntary choice by the faithful, and from recognition of the fact that the political interest in forestalling intolerance extends beyond intolerance among Christian sects—or even intolerance among "religions"—to encompass intolerance of the disbeliever and the uncertain. . . . The State of Alabama, no less than the Congress of the United States, must respect that basic truth.

* * *

When the Court has been called upon to construe the breadth of the Establishment Clause, it has examined the criteria developed over a period of many years. Thus, in *Lemon* v. *Kurtzman* we wrote:

> Every analysis in this area must begin with consideration of the cumulative criteria developed by the Court over many years. Three such tests may be gleaned from our cases. First, the statute must have a secular legislative purpose; second, its principal or primary effect must be one that neither advances nor inhibits religion; finally, the statute must not foster "an excessive government entanglement with religion."

It is the first of these three criteria that is most plainly implicated by this case. . . . [E]ven though a statute that is motivated in part by a religious purpose may satisfy the first criterion, the First Amendment requires that a statute must be invalidated if it is entirely motivated by a purpose to advance religion.

In applying the purpose test, it is appropriate to ask "whether government's actual purpose is to endorse or disapprove of religion." In this case, the answer to that question is dispositive. For the record not only provides us with an unambiguous affirmative answer, but it also reveals that the enactment of § 16–1–20.1 was not motivated by any clearly secular purpose—indeed, the statute had *no* secular purpose.

The sponsor of the bill that became § 16–1–20.1, Senator Donald Holmes, inserted into the legislative record—apparently without dissent—a statement indicating that the legislation was an "effort to return voluntary prayer" to the public schools. Later Senator Holmes confirmed this purpose before the District Court. In response to the question whether he had any purpose for the legislation other than returning voluntary prayer to public schools, he stated, "No, I did not have no other purpose in mind." The State did not present evidence of *any* secular purpose. . . .

The Legislature enacted § . . . for the sole purpose of expressing the State's endorsement of prayer activities for one minute at the beginning of each school day. The addition of "or voluntary prayer" indicates that the State intended to characterize prayer as a favored practice. Such an endorsement is not consistent with the established principle that the Government must pursue a course of complete neutrality toward religion.

The importance of that principle does not permit us to treat this as an inconsequential case involving nothing more than a few words of symbolic speech on behalf of the political majority. For whenever the State itself speaks on a religious subject, one of the questions that we must ask is "whether the Government intends to convey a message of endorsement or disapproval of religion.". . . Keeping in mind, as we must, "both the fundamental place held by the Establishment Clause in our constitutional scheme and the myriad, subtle ways in which Establishment Clause values can be eroded," we conclude that § 16–1–20.1 violates the First Amendment.

* * *

Justice Rehnquist, dissenting.

* * *

Thirty-eight years ago this Court, in *Everson* v. *Board of Education,* summarized its exegesis of Establishment Clause doctrine thus:

> In the words of Jefferson, the clause against establishment of religion by law was intended to erect "a wall of separation between church and State."

It is impossible to build sound constitutional doctrine upon a mistaken understanding of constitutional history, but unfortunately the Establishment Clause has been expressly freighted with Jefferson's misleading metaphor for nearly forty years. Thomas Jefferson was of course in France at the time the constitutional amendments known as the Bill of Rights were passed by Congress and ratified by the states. His letter to the Danbury Baptist Association was a short note of courtesy, written fourteen years after the amendments were passed by Congress. He would seem to any detached observer as a less than ideal source of contemporary history as to the meaning of the Religion Clauses of the First Amendment.

Jefferson's fellow Virginian James Madison, with whom he was joined in the battle for the enactment of the Virginia Statute of Religious Liberty of 1786, did play as large a part as anyone in the drafting of the Bill of Rights. He had two advantages over Jefferson in this regard: he was present in the United States, and he was a leading member of the First Congress. But when we turn to the record of the proceedings in the First Congress leading up to the adoption of the Establishment Clause of the Constitution, including Madison's significant contributions thereto, we see a far different picture of its purpose than the highly simplified "wall of separation between church and State."

During the debates in the thirteen colonies over ratification of the Constitution, one of the arguments frequently used by opponents of ratification was that without a Bill of Rights guaranteeing individual liberty the new general government carried with it a potential for tyranny. The typical response to this argument on the part of those who favored ratification was that the general government established by the Constitution had only delegated powers, and that these delegated powers were so limited that the government would have no occasion to violate individual liberties. This response satisfied some, but not others, and of the eleven colonies which ratified the Constitution by early 1789, five proposed one or another amendments guaranteeing individual liberty. Three—New Hampshire, New York, and Virginia—included in one form or another a declaration of religious freedom. Rhode Island and North Carolina flatly refused to ratify the Constitution in the absence of amendments in the nature of a Bill of Rights. Virginia and North Carolina proposed identical guarantees of religious freedom.

On June 8, 1789, James Madison rose in the House of Representatives and "reminded the House that this was the day that he had heretofore named for bringing forward amendments to the Constitution.". . .

On the basis of the record of [the] proceedings in the House of Representatives, James Madison was undoubtedly the most important architect among the members of the House of the amendments which became the Bill of Rights, but it was James Madison speaking as an advocate of sensible legislative compromise, not as an advocate of incorporating the Virginia Statute of Religious Liberty into the United States Constitution. During the ratification debate in the Virginia Convention, Madison had actually opposed the idea of any Bill of Rights. His sponsorship of the amendments in the House was obviously not that of a zealous believer in the necessity of the Religion Clauses, but of one who felt it might do some good, could do no harm, and would satisfy those who had ratified the Constitution on the condition that Congress propose a Bill of Rights. His original language "nor shall any national religion be established" obviously does not conform to the "wall of separation" between church and State idea which latter day commentators have ascribed to him. His explanation on the floor of the meaning of his language—"that Congress should not establish a religion, and enforce the legal observation of it by law" is of the same ilk. When he replied to Huntington in the debate over the proposal which came from the Select Committee of the House, he urged that the language "no religion shall be established by law" should be amended by inserting the word "national" in front of the word "religion."

It seems indisputable from these glimpses of Madison's thinking, as reflected by actions on the floor of the House in 1789, that he saw the amendment as designed to prohibit the establishment of a national religion, and perhaps to prevent discrimination among sects. He did not see it as requiring neutrality on the part of government between religion and irreligion. Thus the Court's opinion in *Everson*—while correct in bracketing Madison and Jefferson together in their exertions in their home state leading to the enactment of the Virginia Statute of Religious Liberty—is totally incorrect in suggesting that Madison carried these views onto the floor of the United States House of Representatives when he proposed the language which would ultimately become the Bill of Rights.

The repetition of this error in the Court's opinion in [*Illinois* v. *McCollum* and *Engel* v. *Vitale*] does not make it any sounder historically. Finally, in *Abington School District* v. *Schempp,* the Court made the truly remarkable statement that "the views of Madison and Jefferson, preceded by Roger Williams came to be incorporated not only in the Federal Constitution but likewise in those of most of our States." On the basis of what evidence we have, this statement is demonstrably incorrect as a matter of history. And its repetition in varying forms in succeeding opinions of the Court can give it no more authority than it possesses as a matter of fact; *stare decisis* may bind courts as to matters of law, but it cannot bind them as to matters of history.

None of the other Members of Congress who spoke during the August 15th debate expressed the slightest indication that they thought the language before them from the Select Committee, or the evil to be aimed at, would require that the Government be absolutely neutral as between religion and irreligion. The evil to be aimed at, so far as those who spoke were concerned, appears to have been the establishment of a national church, and perhaps the preference of one religious sect over another; but it was definitely not concern about whether the Government might aid all religions evenhandedly. . . .

There is simply no historical foundation for the proposition that the Framers intended to build the "wall of separation" that was constitutionalized in *Everson.*

Notwithstanding the absence of an historical basis for this theory of rigid separation, the wall idea might well have served as a useful albeit misguided analytical concept, had it led this Court to unified and principled results in Establishment Clause cases. The opposite, unfortunately, has been true; in the 38 years since *Everson* our Establishment Clause cases have been neither principled nor unified. Our recent opinions, many of them hopelessly divided pluralities, have with embarrassing candor conceded that the "wall of separation" is merely a "blurred, indistinct, and variable barrier," which "is not wholly accurate" and can only be "dimly perceived.". . .

The "wall of separation between church and State" is a metaphor based on bad history, a metaphor which has proved useless as a guide to judging. It should be frankly and explicitly abandoned.

The Court has more recently attempted to add some mortar to *Everson*'s wall through the three-part test of *Lemon* v. *Kurtzman,* which served at first to offer a more useful test for purposes of the Establishment Clause than did the "wall" metaphor. Generally stated, the *Lemon* test proscribes state action that has a sectarian purpose or effect, or causes an impermissible governmental entanglement with religion.

[D]ifficulties arise because the *Lemon* test has no more grounding in the history of the First Amendment than does the wall theory upon which it rests. The three-part test represents a determined effort to craft a workable rule from an historically faulty doctrine; but the rule can only be as sound as the doctrine it attempts to service. The three-part test has simply not provided adequate standards for deciding Establishment Clause cases, as this Court has slowly come to realize. . . .

The true meaning of the Establishment Clause can only be seen in its history. . . . As drafters of our Bill of Rights, the Framers inscribed the principles that control today. Any deviation from their intentions frustrates the permanence of that Charter and will only lead to the type of unprincipled decisionmaking that has plagued our Establishment Clause cases since *Everson.*

The Framers intended the Establishment Clause to prohibit the designation of any church as a "national" one. The Clause was also designed to stop the Federal Government from asserting a preference for one religious denomination or sect over others. Given the "incorporation" of the Establishment Clause as against the States via the Fourteenth Amendment in *Everson,* States are prohibited as well from establishing a religion or discriminating between sects. As its history abundantly shows, however, nothing in the Establishment Clause requires government to be strictly neutral between religion and irreligion, nor does that Clause prohibit Congress or the States from pursuing legitimate secular ends through nondiscriminatory sectarian means. . . .

The State surely has a secular interest in regulating the manner in which public schools are conducted. Nothing in the Establishment Clause of the First Amendment, properly understood, prohibits any such generalized "endorsement" of prayer. I would therefore reverse the judgment of the Court of Appeals in *Wallace* v. *Jaffree.*

School Prayer Amendment

After the Supreme Court's decisions in *Engel* v. *Vitale* and *School District of Abington Township* v. *Schempp,* the governors of forty-nine states called for a constitutional amendment to overturn the Court's rulings. No amendment was adopted at that time, but the effort has been revitalized from time to time. The following school-prayer amendment, introduced with President Reagan's support, received serious attention from the Congress in 1984.

Nothing in this Constitution shall be construed to prohibit individual or group prayer in public schools or other public institutions. No person shall be required by the United States or by any State to participate in prayer.

Edwards v. Aguillard (1987)[7]

The debate over the teaching of evolution versus the Biblical version of creation in the public schools continues to the present day. In 1987, the Supreme Court heard another case on this topic. The case involved a Louisiana statute requiring the public schools of that state to teach "creation science" if they also taught evolution.

Justice Brennan delivered the opinion of the Court.

The question for decision is whether Louisiana's "Balanced Treatment for Creation-Science and Evolution-Science in Public School Instruction" Act (Creationism Act) . . . is facially invalid as violative of the Establishment Clause of the First Amendment.

The Creationism Act forbids the teaching of the theory of evolution in public schools unless accompanied by instruction in "creation science.". . . No school is required to teach evolution or creation science. If either is taught, however, the other must also be taught. . . .

The Establishment Clause forbids the enactment of any law "respecting an establishment of religion." The Court has applied a three-pronged test to determine whether legislation comports with the Establishment Clause. First, the legislature must have adopted the law with a secular purpose. Second, the statute's principal or primary effect must be one that neither advances nor inhibits religion. Third, the statute must not result in an excessive entanglement of government with religion. . . . State action violates the Establishment Clause if it fails to satisfy any of these prongs. . . .

The Court has been particularly vigilant in monitoring compliance with the Establishment Clause in elementary and secondary schools. Families entrust public schools with the education of their children, but condition their trust on the understanding that the classroom will not purposely be used to advance religious views that may conflict with the private beliefs of the student and his or her family. Students in such institutions are impressionable and their attendance is involuntary. . . . The State exerts great authority and coercive power through mandatory attendance requirements, and because of the students' emulation of teachers as role models and the children's susceptibility to peer pressure. . . . Furthermore, "[t]he public school is at once the symbol of our democracy and the most pervasive means for promoting our common destiny. In no activity of the State is it more vital to keep out divisive forces than in its schools. . . ."

* * *

Therefore, in employing the three-pronged Lemon test, we must do so mindful of the particular concerns that arise in the context of public elementary and secondary schools. We now turn to the evaluation of the Act under the Lemon test.

Lemon's first prong focuses on the purpose that animated adoption of the Act. . . . A governmental intention to promote religion is clear when the State enacts a law to serve a religious purpose. This intention may be evidenced by promotion of religion in general, . . . or by advancement of a particular religious belief. . . . If the law was enacted for the purpose of endorsing religion, "no consideration of the second or third criteria [of Lemon] is necessary.". . . In this case, appellants have identified no clear secular purpose for the Louisiana Act.

True, the Act's stated purpose is to protect academic freedom. . . . This phrase might, in common parlance, be understood as referring to enhancing the freedom of teachers to teach what they will. [But] the Act was not designed to further that goal. We find no merit in the State's argument that the "legislature may not [have] use[d] the terms 'academic freedom' in the correct legal sense. They might have [had] in mind, instead, a basic concept of fairness; teaching all of the evidence.". . . Even if "academic freedom" is read to mean "teaching all of the evidence" with respect to the origin of human beings, the Act does not further this purpose. The goal of providing a more comprehensive science curriculum is not furthered either by outlawing the teaching of evolution or by requiring the teaching of creation science.

* * *

. . .

It is clear from the legislative history that the purpose of the legislative sponsor, Senator Bill Keith, was to narrow the science curriculum. During the legislative hearings, Senator Keith stated: "My preference would be that neither [creationism nor evolution] be taught.". . . Such a ban on teaching does not promote—indeed, it undermines—the provision of a comprehensive scientific education.

It is equally clear that requiring schools to teach creation science with evolution does not advance academic freedom. The Act does not grant teachers a flexibility that they did not already possess to supplant the present science curriculum with the presentation of theories, besides evolution, about the origin of life. Indeed, . . . no law prohibited Louisiana public school teachers from teaching any scientific theory. . . .

If the Louisiana Legislature's purpose was solely to maximize the comprehensiveness and effectiveness of science instruction, it would have encouraged the teaching of all scientific theories about the origins of humankind. But under the Act's requirements, teachers who were once free to teach any and all facets of this subject are now unable to do so. Moreover, the Act fails even to ensure that creation science will be taught, but instead requires the teaching of this theory only when the theory of evolution is taught. . . .

[W]e need not be blind in this case to the legislature's preeminent religious purpose in enacting this statute. There is a historic and contemporaneous link between the teachings of certain religious denominations and the teaching of evolution. . . .

These same historic and contemporaneous antagonisms between the teachings of certain religious denominations and the teaching of evolution are present in this case. The preeminent purpose of the Louisiana Legislature was clearly to advance the religious viewpoint that a supernatural being created human-kind. The term "creation science" was defined as embracing this particular religious doctrine by those responsible for the passage of the Creationism Act. Senator Keith's leading expert on creation science, Edward Boudreaux, testified at the legislative hearings that the theory of creation science included belief in the existence of a supernatural creator. . . . The legislative history therefore reveals that the term "creation science," as contemplated by the legislature that adopted this Act, embodies the religious belief that a supernatural creator was responsible for the creation of humankind.

Furthermore, it is not happenstance that the legislature required the teaching of a theory that coincided with this religious view. The legislative history documents that the Act's primary purpose was to change the science curriculum of public schools in order to provide persuasive advantage to a particular religious doctrine that rejects the factual basis of evolution in its entirety. The sponsor of the Creationism Act, Senator Keith, explained during the legislative hearings that his disdain for the theory of evolution resulted from the support that evolution supplied to views contrary to his own religious beliefs. According to Senator Keith, the theory of evolution was consonant with the "cardinal principle[s] of religious humanism, secular humanism, theological liberalism, aetheistism [sic]." . . . The state senator repeatedly stated that scientific evidence supporting his religious views should be included in the public school curriculum to redress the fact that the theory of evolution incidentally coincided with what he characterized as religious beliefs antithetical to his own.

. . .

We do not imply that a legislature could never require that scientific critiques of prevailing scientific theories be taught. [T]eaching a variety of scientific theories about the origins of humankind to school-children might be validly done with the clear secular intent of enhancing the effectiveness of science instruction. But because the primary purpose of the Creationism Act is to endorse a particular religious doctrine, the Act furthers religion in violation of the Establishment Clause.

Lee v. Weisman (1992)[8]

Yet another example of prayer in the public schools is the relatively common phenomenon of invocations or benedictions at graduation ceremonies. Often these prayers are led by a local member of the clergy, sometimes on a rotating basis among Protestant, Roman Catholic, and Jewish religious leaders. In this case, the Supreme Court struggles to determine whether to permit such exercises. Note especially Justice Kennedy's discussion of whether there may be an American "civic religion," and Justice Scalia's sharply worded dissenting opinion.

Justice Kennedy delivered the opinion of the Court. . . .

Deborah Weisman graduated from Nathan Bishop Middle School, a public school in Providence, at a formal ceremony in June 1989. She was about 14 years old. For many years it has been the policy of the Providence School Committee and the Superintendent of Schools to permit principals to invite members of the clergy to give invocations and benedictions at middle school and high school graduations. Many, but not all, of the principals elected to include prayers as part of the graduation ceremonies. Acting for himself and his daughter, Deborah's father, Daniel Weisman, objected to any prayers at Deborah's middle school graduation, but to no avail. The school principal, petitioner Robert E. Lee, invited a rabbi to deliver prayers at the graduation exercises for Deborah's class. Rabbi Leslie Gutterman, of the Temple Beth El in Providence, accepted.

It has been the custom of Providence school officials to provide invited clergy with a pamphlet entitled "Guidelines for Civic Occasions," prepared by the National Conference of Christians and Jews. The Guidelines recommend that public prayers at nonsectarian civic ceremonies be composed with "inclusiveness and sensitivity," though they acknowledge that "[p]rayer of any kind may be inappropriate on some civic occasions.". . . The principal gave Rabbi Gutterman the pamphlet before the graduation and advised him the invocation and benediction should be nonsectarian.

[The rabbi delivered an invocation and a benediction at the graduation exercises that were addressed to "God" but otherwise appeared to be generally nonsectarian.]

The school board . . . argued that these short prayers and others like them at graduation exercises are of profound meaning to many students and parents throughout this country who consider that due respect and acknowledgement for divine guidance and for the deepest spiritual aspirations of our people ought to be expressed at an event as important in life as a graduation. We assume this to be so in addressing the difficult case now before us, for the significance of the prayers lies also at the heart of Daniel and Deborah Weisman's case.

These dominant facts mark and control the confines of our decision: State officials direct the performance of a formal religious exercise at promotional and graduation ceremonies for secondary schools. Even for those students who object to the religious exercise, their attendance and participation in the state-sponsored religious activity are in a fair and real sense obligatory, though the school district does not require attendance as a condition for receipt of the diploma.

This case does not require us to revisit the difficult questions dividing us in recent cases, questions of the definition and full scope of the principles governing the extent of permitted accommodation by the State for the religious beliefs and practices of many of its citizens. . . . The government involvement with religious activity in this case is pervasive, to the point of creating a state-sponsored and state-directed religious exercise in a public school. Conducting this formal religious observance conflicts with settled rules pertaining to prayer exercises for students, and that suffices to determine the question before us.

The principle that government may accommodate the free exercise of religion does not supersede the fundamental limitations imposed by the Establishment Clause. It is beyond dispute that, at a minimum, the Constitution guarantees that government may not coerce anyone to support or participate in religion or its exercise, or otherwise act in a way which "establishes a [state] religion or religious faith, or tends to do so."... The State's involvement in the school prayers challenged today violates these central principles.

That involvement is as troubling as it is undenied. A school official, the principal, decided that an invocation and a benediction should be given; this is a choice attributable to the State, and from a constitutional perspective it is as if a state statute decreed that the prayers must occur. The principal chose the religious participant, here a rabbi, and that choice is also attributable to the State. The reason for the choice of a rabbi is not disclosed by the record, but the potential for divisiveness over the choice of a particular member of the clergy to conduct the ceremony is apparent.

Divisiveness, of course, can attend any state decision respecting religions, and neither its existence nor its potential necessarily invalidates the State's attempts to accommodate religion in all cases. The potential for divisiveness is of particular relevance here though, because it centers around an overt religious exercise in a secondary school environment where... subtle coercive pressures exist and where the student had no real alternative which would have allowed her to avoid the fact or appearance of participation.

The State's role did not end with the decision to include a prayer and with the choice of clergyman. Principal Lee provided Rabbi Gutterman with a copy of the "Guidelines for Civic Occasions," and advised him that his prayers should be nonsectarian. Through these means the principal directed and controlled the content of the prayer. Even if the only sanction for ignoring the instructions were that the rabbi would not be invited back, we think no religious representative who valued his or her continued reputation and effectiveness in the community would incur the State's displeasure in this regard. It is a cornerstone principle of our Establishment Clause jurisprudence that "it is no part of the business of government to compose official prayers for any group of the American people to recite as a part of a religious program carried on by government," ... and that is what the school officials attempted to do.

Petitioners argue, and we find nothing in the case to refute it, that the directions for the content of the prayers were a good-faith attempt by the school to ensure that the sectarianism which is so often the flashpoint for religious animosity be removed from the graduation ceremony. The concern is understandable, as a prayer which uses ideas or images identified with a particular religion may foster a different sort of sectarian rivalry than an invocation or benediction in terms more neutral. The school's explanation, however, does not resolve the dilemma caused by its participation. The question is not the good faith of the school in attempting to make the prayer acceptable to most persons, but the legitimacy of its undertaking that enterprise at all when the object is to produce a prayer to be used in a formal religious exercise which students, for all practical purposes, are obliged to attend.

We are asked to recognize the existence of a practice of nonsectarian prayer, prayer within the embrace of what is known as the Judeo-Christian tradition, prayer which is more acceptable than one which, for example, makes explicit references to the God of Israel, or to Jesus Christ, or to a patron saint. There may be some support, as an empirical observation, to the statement of the Court of Appeals . . . that there has emerged in this country a civic religion, one which is tolerated when sectarian exercises are not. . . . If common ground can be defined which permits once conflicting faiths to express the shared conviction that there is an ethic and a morality which transcend human invention, the sense of community and purpose sought by all decent societies might be advanced. But though the First Amendment does not allow the government to stifle prayers which aspire to these ends, neither does it permit the government to undertake that task for itself.

The First Amendment's Religion Clauses mean that religious beliefs and religious expression are too precious to be either proscribed or prescribed by the State. The design of the Constitution is that preservation and transmission of religious beliefs and worship is a responsibility and a choice committed to the private sphere, which itself is promised freedom to pursue that mission. It must not be forgotten then, that while concern must be given to define the protection granted to an objector or a dissenting nonbeliever, these same Clauses exist to protect religion from government interference. . . .

These concerns have particular application in the case of school officials, whose effort to monitor prayer will be perceived by the students as inducing a participation they might otherwise reject. Though the efforts of the school officials in this case to find common ground appear to have been a good-faith attempt to recognize the common aspects of religions and not the divisive ones, our precedents do not permit school officials to assist in composing prayers as an incident to a formal exercise for their students. . . . And these same precedents caution us to measure the idea of a civic religion against the central meaning of the Religion Clauses of the First Amendment, which is that all creeds must be tolerated and none favored. The suggestion that government may establish an official or civic religion as a means of avoiding the establishment of a religion with more specific creeds strikes us as a contradiction that cannot be accepted.

The degree of school involvement here made it clear that the graduation prayers bore the imprint of the State and thus put school-age children who objected in an untenable position. We turn our attention now to consider the position of the students, both those who desired the prayer and she who did not.

To endure the speech of false ideas or offensive content and then to counter it is part of learning how to live in a pluralistic society, a society which insists upon open discourse towards the end of a tolerant citizenry. And tolerance presupposes some mutuality of obligation. It is argued that our constitutional vision of a free society requires confidence in our own ability to accept or reject ideas of which we do not approve, and that prayer at a high school graduation does nothing more than offer a choice. By the time they are seniors, high school students no doubt have been required to attend classes and assemblies and to complete assignments exposing them to ideas they find distasteful or immoral or absurd or all of these. Against this background, students may consider it an odd measure of justice to be subjected during the course of their educations to ideas deemed offensive and irreligious, but to be denied a brief, formal prayer ceremony that the school offers in return. This argument cannot prevail, however. It overlooks a fundamental dynamic of the Constitution.

The First Amendment protects speech and religion by quite different mechanisms. Speech is protected by insuring its full expression even when the government participates, for the very object of some of our most important speech is to persuade the government to adopt an idea as its own. . . . The method for protecting freedom of worship and freedom of conscience in religious matters is quite the reverse. In religious debate or expression the government is not a prime participant, for the Framers deemed religious establishment antithetical to the freedom of all. The Free Exercise Clause embraces a freedom of conscience and worship that has close parallels in the speech provisions of the First Amendment, but the Establishment Clause is a specific prohibition on forms of state intervention in religious affairs with no precise counterpart in the speech provisions. . . . The explanation lies in the lesson of history that was and is the inspiration for the Establishment Clause, the lesson that in the hands of government what might begin as a tolerant expression of religious views may end in a policy to indoctrinate and coerce. A state-created orthodoxy puts at grave risk that freedom of belief and conscience which are the sole assurance that religious faith is real, not imposed.

The lessons of the First Amendment are as urgent in the modern world as in the 18th Century when it was written. One timeless lesson is that if citizens are subjected to state-sponsored religious exercises, the State disavows its own duty to guard and respect that sphere of inviolable conscience and belief which is the mark of a free people. To compromise that principle today would be to deny our own tradition and forfeit our standing to urge others to secure the protections of that tradition for themselves.

As we have observed before, there are heightened concerns with protecting freedom of conscience from subtle coercive pressure in the elementary and secondary public schools. . . . Our decisions . . . recognize, among other things, that prayer exercises in public schools carry a particular risk of indirect coercion. The concern may not be limited to the context of schools, but it is most pronounced there. . . . What to most believers may seem nothing more than a reasonable request that the nonbeliever respect their religious practices, in a school context may appear to the nonbeliever or dissenter to be an attempt to employ the machinery of the State to enforce a religious orthodoxy.

We need not look beyond the circumstances of this case to see the phenomenon at work. The undeniable fact is that the school district's supervision and control of a high school graduation ceremony places public pressure, as well as peer pressure, on attending students to stand as a group or, at least, maintain respectful silence during the Invocation and Benediction. This pressure, though subtle and indirect, can be as real as any overt compulsion. Of course, in our culture standing or remaining silent can signify adherence to a view or simple respect for the views of others. And no doubt some persons who have no desire to join a prayer have little objection to standing as a sign of respect for those who do. But for the dissenter of high school age, who has a reasonable perception that she is being forced by the State to pray in a manner her conscience will not allow, the injury is no less real. There can be no doubt that for many, if not most, of the students at the graduation, the act of standing or remaining silent was an expression of participation in the Rabbi's prayer. That was the very point of the religious exercise. It is of little comfort to a dissenter, then, to be told that for her the act of standing or remaining in silence signifies mere respect, rather than participation. What matters is that, given our social conventions, a reasonable dissenter in this milieu could believe that the group exercise signified her own participation or approval of it.

Finding no violation under these circumstances would place objectors in the dilemma of participating, with all that implies, or protesting. We do not address whether that choice is acceptable if the affected citizens are mature adults, but we think the State may not, consistent with the Establishment Clause, place primary and secondary school children in this position. Research in psychology supports the common assumption that adolescents are often susceptible to pressure from their peers towards conformity, and that the influence is strongest in matters of social convention. . . . To recognize that the choice imposed by the State constitutes an unacceptable constraint only acknowledges that the government may no more use social pressure to enforce orthodoxy than it may use more direct means.

The injury caused by the government's action, and the reason why Daniel and Deborah Weisman object to it, is that the State, in a school setting, in effect required participation in a religious exercise. It is, we concede, a brief exercise during which the individual can concentrate on joining its message, meditate on her own religion, or let her mind wander. But the embarrassment and the intrusion of the religious exercise cannot be refuted by arguing that these prayers, and similar ones to be said in the future, are of a de minimis character. To do so would be an affront to the Rabbi who offered them and to all those for whom the prayers were an essential and profound recognition of divine authority. And for the same reason, we think that the intrusion is greater than the two minutes or so of time consumed for prayers like these. Assuming, as we must, that the prayers were offensive to the student and the parent who now object, the intrusion was both real and, in the context of a secondary school, a violation of the objectors' rights. That the intrusion was in the course of promulgating religion that sought to be civic or nonsectarian rather than pertaining to one sect does not lessen the offense or isolation to the objectors. At best it narrows their number, at worst increases their sense of isolation and affront. . . .

There was a stipulation in the [trial] that attendance at graduation and promotional ceremonies is voluntary. [But the law] reaches past formalism. And to say a teenage student has a real choice not to attend her high school graduation is formalistic in the extreme. True, Deborah could elect not to attend commencement without renouncing her diploma; but we shall not allow the case to turn on this point. Everyone knows that in our society and in our culture high school graduation is one of life's most significant occasions. A school rule which excuses attendance is beside the point. Attendance may not be required by official decree, yet it is apparent that a student is not free to absent herself from the graduation exercise in any real sense of the term "voluntary," for absence would require forfeiture of those intangible benefits which have motivated the student through youth and all her high school years. Graduation is a time for family and those closest to the student to celebrate success and express mutual wishes of gratitude and respect, all to the end of impressing upon the young person the role that it is his or her right and duty to assume in the community and all of its diverse parts.

The importance of the event is the point the school district and the United States rely upon to argue that a formal prayer ought to be permitted, but it becomes one of the principal reasons why their argument must fail. Their contention, one of considerable force were it not for the constitutional constraints applied to state action, is that the prayers are an essential part of these ceremonies because for many persons an occasion of this significance lacks meaning if there is no recognition, however brief, that human achievements cannot be understood apart from their spiritual essence. We think the Government's position that this interest suffices to force students to choose between compliance or forfeiture demonstrates fundamental inconsistency in its argumentation. It fails to acknowledge that what for many of Deborah's classmates and their parents was a spiritual imperative was for Daniel and Deborah Weisman religious conformance compelled by the State. While in some societies the wishes of the majority might prevail, the Establishment Clause of the First Amendment is addressed to this contingency and rejects the balance urged upon us. The Constitution forbids the State to exact religious conformity from a student as the price of attending her own high school graduation. This is the calculus the Constitution commands.

The Government's argument gives insufficient recognition to the real conflict of conscience faced by the young student. The essence of the Government's position is that with regard to a civic, social occasion of this importance it is the objector, not the majority, who must take unilateral and private action to avoid compromising religious scruples, here by electing to miss the graduation exercise. This turns conventional First Amendment analysis on its head. It is a tenet of the First Amendment that the State cannot require one of its citizens to forfeit his or her rights and benefits as the price of resisting conformance to state-sponsored religious practice. To say that a student must remain apart from the ceremony at the opening invocation and closing benediction is to risk compelling conformity in an environment analogous to the classroom setting, where we have said the risk of compulsion is especially high. . . .

Our society would be less than true to its heritage if it lacked abiding concern for the values of its young people, and we acknowledge the profound belief of adherents to many faiths that there must be a place in the student's life for precepts of a morality higher even than the law we today enforce. We express no hostility to those aspirations, nor would our oath permit us to do so. A relentless and all-pervasive attempt to exclude religion from every aspect of public life could itself become inconsistent with the Constitution. . . . We recognize that, at graduation time and throughout the course of the educational process, there will be instances when religious values, religious practices, and religious persons will have some interaction with the public schools and their students. . . . But these matters, often questions of accommodation of religion, are not before us. The sole question presented is whether a religious exercise may be conducted at a graduation ceremony in circumstances where, as we have found, young graduates who object are induced to conform. No holding by this Court suggests that a school can persuade or compel a student to participate in a religious exercise. That is being done here, and it is forbidden by the Establishment Clause of the First Amendment.

Justice Scalia, with whom The Chief Justice, Justice White, and Justice Thomas join, dissenting. . . .

In holding that the Establishment Clause prohibits invocations and benedictions at public-school graduation ceremonies, the Court—with nary a mention that it is doing so—lays waste a tradition that is as old as public-school graduation ceremonies themselves, and that is a component of an even more longstanding American tradition of nonsectarian prayer to God at public celebrations generally. As its instrument of destruction, the bulldozer of its social engineering, the Court invents a boundless, and boundlessly manipulable, test of psychological coercion. . . . Today's opinion shows more forcefully than volumes of argumentation why our Nation's protection, that fortress which is our Constitution, cannot possibly rest upon the changeable philosophical predilections of the Justices of this Court, but must have deep foundations in the historic practices of our people.

Justice Holmes' aphorism that "a page of history is worth a volume of logic," . . . applies with particular force to our Establishment Clause jurisprudence. As we have recognized, our interpretation of the Establishment Clause should "compor[t] with what history reveals was the contemporaneous understanding of its guarantees.". . .

The history and tradition of our Nation are replete with public ceremonies featuring prayers of thanks-giving and petition. . . .

From our Nation's origin, prayer has been a prominent part of governmental ceremonies and proclamations. The Declaration of Independence, the document marking our birth as a separate people, "appeal[ed] to the Supreme Judge of the world for the rectitude of our intentions" and avowed "a firm reliance on the protection of divine Providence." In his first inaugural address, after swearing his oath of office on a Bible, George Washington deliberately made a prayer a part of his first official act as President. . . .

Such supplications have been a characteristic feature of inaugural addresses ever since. . . .

The other two branches of the Federal Government also have a long-established practice of prayer at public events. . . . Congressional sessions have opened with a chaplain's prayer ever since the First Congress. . . . And this Court's own sessions have opened with the invocation "God save the United States and this Honorable Court" since the days of Chief Justice Marshall. . . .

In addition to this general tradition of prayer at public ceremonies, there exists a more specific tradition of invocations and benedictions at public-school graduation exercises. By one account, the first public-high-school graduation ceremony took place in Connecticut in July 1868—the very month, as it happens, that the Fourteenth Amendment (the vehicle by which the Establishment Clause has been applied against the States) was ratified—when "15 seniors from the Norwich Free Academy marched in their best Sunday suits and dresses into a church hall and waited through majestic music and long prayers."... As the Court obliquely acknowledges in describing the "customary features" of high school graduations, . . . the invocation and benediction have long been recognized to be "as traditional as any other parts of the [school] graduation program and are widely established."...

* * *

The Court presumably would separate graduation invocations and benedictions from other instances of public "preservation and transmission of religious beliefs" on the ground that they involve "psychological coercion." I find it a sufficient embarrassment that our Establishment Clause jurisprudence regarding holiday displays. . . has come to "requir[e] scrutiny more commonly associated with interior decorators than with the judiciary."... But interior decorating is a rockhard science compared to psychology practiced by amateurs. A few citations of "[r]esearch in psychology" that have no particular bearing upon the precise issue here . . . cannot disguise the fact that the Court has gone beyond the realm where judges know what they are doing. The Court's argument that state officials have "coerced" students to take part in the invocation and benediction at graduation ceremonies is, not to put too fine a point on it, incoherent. . . .

The Court declares that students' "attendance and participation in the [invocation and benediction] are in a fair and real sense obligatory."... But what exactly is this "fair and real sense"? According to the Court, students at graduation who want "to avoid the fact or appearance of participation" . . . in the invocation and benediction are *psychologically* obligated by "public pressure, as well as peer pressure, . . . to stand as a group or, at least, maintain respectful silence" during those prayers. . . . This assertion—*the very linchpin of the Court's opinion*—is almost as intriguing for what it does not say as for what it says. It does not say, for example, that students are psychologically coerced to bow their heads, place their hands in a Dürer-like prayer position, pay attention to the prayers, utter "Amen," or in fact pray. (Perhaps further intensive psychological research remains to be done on these matters.) It claims only that students are psychologically coerced "to stand . . . *or,* at least, maintain respectful silence."...

The Court's notion that a student who simply *sits* in "respectful silence" during the invocation and benediction (when all others are standing) has somehow joined—or would somehow be perceived as having joined—in the prayers is nothing short of ludicrous. We indeed live in a vulgar age. But surely "our social conventions" . . . have not coarsened to the point that anyone who does not stand on his chair and shout obscenities can reasonably be deemed to have assented to everything said in his presence. Since the Court does not dispute that students exposed to prayer at graduation ceremonies retain . . . the free will to sit, . . . there is absolutely no basis for the Court's decision. It is fanciful enough to say that: "a reasonable dissenter," standing head erect in a class of bowed heads, "could believe that the group exercise signified her own participation or approval of it" . . . It is beyond the absurd to say that she could entertain such a belief while pointedly declining to rise.

But let us assume the very worst, that the nonparticipating graduate is "subtly coerced" . . . to stand! Even that . . . does not remotely establish a "participation" (or an "appearance of participation") in a religious exercise. The Court acknowledges that "in our culture standing . . . can signify adherence to a view or simple respect for the views of others.". . . But if it is a permissible inference that one who is standing is doing so simply out of respect for the prayers of others that are in progress, then how can it possibly be said that a "reasonable dissenter . . . could believe that the group exercise signified her own participation or approval"? Quite obviously, it cannot. I may add, moreover, that maintaining respect for the religious observances of others is a fundamental civic virtue that government (including the public schools) can and should cultivate—so that even if it were the case that the displaying of such respect might be mistaken for taking part in the prayer, I would deny that the dissenter's interest in avoiding *even the false appearance of participation* constitutionally trumps the government's interest in fostering respect for religion generally.

The opinion manifests that the Court itself has not given careful consideration to its test of psychological coercion. For if it had, how could it observe, with no hint of concern or disapproval, that students stood for the Pledge of Allegiance, which immediately preceded Rabbi Gutterman's invocation? . . . The government can, of course, no more coerce political orthodoxy than religious orthodoxy. . . . Moreover, since the Pledge of Allegiance . . . include[s] the phrase "under God," recital of the Pledge would appear to raise the same Establishment Clause issue as the invocation and benediction. If students were psychologically coerced to remain standing during the invocation, they must also have been psychologically coerced, moments before, to stand for (and thereby, in the Court's view, take part in or appear to take part in) the Pledge. Must the Pledge therefore be barred from the public schools (both from graduation ceremonies and from the classroom)? . . .

I also find it odd that the Court concludes that high school graduates may not be subjected to this supposed psychological coercion, yet refrains from addressing whether "mature adults" may. . . . I had thought that the reason graduation from high school is regarded as so significant an event is that it is generally associated with transition from adolescence to young adulthood. Many graduating seniors, of course, are old enough to vote. Why, then, does the Court treat them as though they were first-graders? Will we soon have a jurisprudence that distinguishes between mature and immature adults?

* * *

The other "dominant fac[t]" identified by the Court is that "[s]tate officials direct the performance of a formal religious exercise" at school graduation ceremonies. . . . "Direct[ing] the performance of a formal religious exercise" has a sound of liturgy to it, summoning up images of the principal directing acolytes where to carry the cross, or showing the rabbi where to unroll the Torah. . . . All the record shows is that principals of the Providence public schools, acting within their delegated authority, have invited clergy to deliver invocations and benedictions at graduations; and that Principal Lee invited Rabbi Gutterman, provided him a two-page flyer, prepared by the National Conference of Christians and Jews, giving general advice on inclusive prayer for civic occasions, and advised him that his prayers at graduation should be nonsectarian. The Court identifies nothing in the record remotely suggesting that school officials have ever drafted, edited, screened or censored graduation prayers, or that Rabbi Gutterman was a mouthpiece of the school officials.

* * *

The deeper flaw in the Court's opinion does not lie in its wrong answer to the question whether there was state-induced "peer-pressure" coercion; it lies, rather, in the Court's making violation of the Establishment Clause hinge on such a precious question. The coercion that was a hallmark of historical establishments of religion was coercion of religious orthodoxy and of financial support *by force of law and threat of penalty.* Typically, attendance at the state church was required; only clergy of the official church could lawfully perform sacraments; and dissenters, if tolerated, faced an array of civil disabilities. . . . Thus, for example, in the colony of Virginia, where the Church of England had been established, ministers were required by law to conform to the doctrine and rites of the Church of England; and all persons were required to attend church and observe the Sabbath, were tithed for the public support of Anglican ministers, and were taxed for the costs of building and repairing churches. . . .

The Establishment Clause was adopted to prohibit such an establishment of religion at the federal level (and to protect state establishments of religion from federal interference). I will further acknowledge for the sake of argument that, as some scholars have argued, by 1790 the term "establishment" had acquired an additional meaning—"financial support of religion generally, by public taxation"—that reflected the development of "general or multiple" establishments, not limited to a single church. . . . But that would still be an establishment coerced *by force of law.* And I will further concede that our constitutional tradition, from the Declaration of Independence and the first inaugural address of Washington, quoted earlier, down to the present day, has, with a few aberrations, . . . ruled out of order government-sponsored endorsement of religion—even when no legal coercion is present, and indeed even when no ersatz, "peer-pressure" psycho-coercion is present—where the endorsement is sectarian, in the sense of specifying details upon which men and women who believe in a benevolent, omnipotent Creator and Ruler of the world, are known to differ (for example, the divinity of Christ). But there is simply no support for the proposition that the officially sponsored nondenominational invocation and benediction read by Rabbi Gutterman—with no one legally coerced to recite them—violated the Constitution of the United States. . . .

[A] happy aspect of the case is that it is only a jurisprudential disaster and not a practical one. Given the odd basis for the Court's decision, invocations and benedictions will be able to be given at public-school graduations next June, as they have for the past century and a half, so long as school authorities make clear that anyone who abstains from screaming in protest does not necessarily participate in the prayers. All that is seemingly needed is an announcement, or perhaps a written insertion at the beginning of the graduation program, to the effect that, while all are asked to rise for the invocation and benediction, none is compelled to join in them, nor will be assumed, by rising, to have done so. That obvious fact recited, the graduates and their parents may proceed to thank God, as Americans have always done, for the blessings He has generously bestowed on them and on their country. . . .

For the foregoing reasons, I dissent.

Rosenberger v. University of Virginia (1995)[9]

While the principal question before the Supreme Court in this case involved the funding of a student-run religious newspaper at a state university, the justices once again struggled to come to grips with an "Establishment Clause jurisprudence [that] is in hopeless disarray," according to Justice Thomas. In particular, note how claims under the free-speech and free-exercise clauses may potentially conflict with the establishment clause's prohibitions.

Justice Kennedy delivered the opinion of the Court.

The University of Virginia, an instrumentality of the Commonwealth for which it is named and thus bound by the First and Fourteenth Amendments, authorizes the payment of outside contractors for the printing costs of a variety of student publications. It withheld any authorization for payments on behalf of petitioners for the sole reason that their student paper "primarily promotes or manifests a particular belie[f] in or about a deity or an ultimate reality." That the paper did promote or manifest views within the defined exclusion seems plain enough. The challenge is to the University's regulation and its denial of authorization, the case raising issues under the Speech and Establishment Clauses of the First Amendment. . . .

Before a student group is eligible to submit bills from its outside contractors for payment by the fund described below, it must become a "Contracted Independent Organization" (CIO). CIO status is available to any group the majority of whose members are students, whose managing officers are fulltime students, and that complies with certain procedural requirements. . . . A CIO must file its constitution with the University; must pledge not to discriminate in its membership; and must include in dealings with third parties and in all written materials a disclaimer, stating that the CIO is independent of the University and that the University is not responsible for the CIO. . . . CIOs enjoy access to University facilities, including meeting rooms and computer terminals. . . . A standard agreement signed between each CIO and the University provides that the benefits and opportunities afforded to CIOs "should not be misinterpreted as meaning that those organizations are part of or controlled by the University, that the University is responsible for the organizations' contracts or other acts or omissions, or that the University approves of the organizations' goals or activities.". . .

Petitioners' organization, Wide Awake Productions (WAP), qualified as a CIO. Formed by petitioner Ronald Rosenberger and other undergraduates in 1990, WAP was established "[t]o publish a magazine of philosophical and religious expression," "[t]o facilitate discussion which fosters an atmosphere of sensitivity to and tolerance of Christian viewpoints," and "[t]o provide a unifying focus for Christians of multicultural backgrounds." WAP publishes Wide Awake: A Christian Perspective at the

University of Virginia. The paper's Christian viewpoint was evident from the first issue, in which its editors wrote that the journal "offers a Christian perspective on both personal and community issues, especially those relevant to college students at the University of Virginia." The editors committed the paper to a two-fold mission: "to challenge Christians to live, in word and deed, according to the faith they proclaim and to encourage students to consider what a personal relationship with Jesus Christ means." The first issue had articles about racism, crisis pregnancy, stress, prayer, C. S. Lewis' ideas about evil and free will, and reviews of religious music. In the next two issues, Wide Awake featured stories about homosexuality, Christian missionary work, and eating disorders, as well as music reviews and interviews with University professors. Each page of Wide Awake, and the end of each article or review, is marked by a cross. The advertisements carried in Wide Awake also reveal the Christian perspective of the journal. For the most part, the advertisers are churches, centers for Christian study, or Christian bookstores. By June 1992, WAP had distributed about 5,000 copies of Wide Awake to University students, free of charge.

WAP had acquired CIO status soon after it was organized. This is an important consideration in this case, for had it been a "religious organization," WAP would not have been accorded CIO status. As defined by the Guidelines, a "religious organization" is "an organization whose purpose is to practice a devotion to an acknowledged ultimate reality or deity."... At no stage in this controversy has the University contended that WAP is such an organization.

A few months after being given CIO status, WAP requested the SAF to pay its printer $5,862 for the costs of printing its newspaper. The Appropriations Committee of the Student Council denied WAP's request on the ground that Wide Awake was a "religious activity" within the meaning of the Guidelines, *i.e.,* that the newspaper "promote[d] or manifest[ed] a particular belie[f] in or about a deity or an ultimate reality." It made its determination after examining the first issue. WAP appealed the denial to the full Student Council, contending that WAP met all the applicable Guidelines and that denial of SAF support on the basis of the magazine's religious perspective violated the Constitution. The appeal was denied without further comment, and WAP appealed to the next level, the Student Activities Committee. In a letter signed by the Dean of Students, the committee sustained the denial of funding.

Having no further recourse within the University structure, WAP, Wide Awake, and three of its editors and members filed suit. . . . They alleged that refusal to authorize payment of the printing costs of the publication, solely on the basis of its religious editorial viewpoint, violated their rights to freedom of speech and press, to the free exercise of religion, and to equal protection of the law. . . .

It is axiomatic that the government may not regulate speech based on its substantive content or the message it conveys. . . . Other principles follow from this precept. In the realm of private speech or expression, government regulation may not favor one speaker over another. . . . Discrimination against speech because of its message is presumed to be unconstitutional. . . . These rules informed our determination that the government offends the First Amendment when it imposes financial burdens on certain speakers based on the content of their expression. . . . When the government targets not subject matter but particular views taken by speakers on a subject, the violation of the First Amendment is all the more blatant. . . . Viewpoint discrimination is thus an egregious form of content discrimination. The government must abstain from regulating speech when the specific motivating ideology or the opinion or perspective of the speaker is the rationale for the restriction. . . .

These principles provide the framework forbidding the State from exercising viewpoint discrimination, even when the limited public forum is one of its own creation. . . . The necessities of confining a forum to the limited and legitimate purposes for which it was created may justify the State in reserving it for certain groups or for the discussion of certain topics. . . . Once it has opened a limited forum, however, the State must respect the lawful boundaries it has itself set. The State may not exclude speech where its distinction is not "reasonable in light of the purpose served by the forum," . . . nor may it discriminate against speech on the basis of its viewpoint. . . . Thus, in determining whether the State is acting to preserve the limits of the forum it has created so that the exclusion of a class of speech is legitimate, we have observed a distinction, between, on the one hand, content discrimination, which may be permissible, if it preserves the purposes of that limited forum and, on the other hand, viewpoint discrimination, which is presumed impermissible when directed against speech otherwise within the forum's limitations. . . .

The SAF is a forum more in a metaphysical than in a spatial or geographic sense, but the same principles are applicable. . . .

The University does acknowledge (as it must in light of our precedents) that "ideologically driven attempts to suppress a particular point of view are presumptively unconstitutional in funding, as in other contexts," but insists that this case does not present that issue because the Guidelines draw lines based on content, not viewpoint. . . . As we have noted, discrimination against one set of views or ideas is but a subset or particular instance of the more general phenomenon of content discrimination. . . . And, it must be acknowledged, the distinction is not a precise one. It is, in a sense, something of an understatement to speak of religious thought and discussion as just a viewpoint, as distinct from a comprehensive body of thought. The nature of our origins and destiny and their dependence upon the existence of a divine being have been subjects of philosophic inquiry throughout human history. We conclude, nonetheless, that here . . . viewpoint discrimination is the proper way to interpret the University's objections to Wide Awake. By the very terms of the SAF prohibition, the University does not exclude religion as a subject matter but selects for disfavored treatment those student journalistic efforts with religious editorial viewpoints. Religion may be a vast area of inquiry, but it also provides, as it did here, a specific premise, a perspective, a standpoint from which a variety of subjects may be discussed and considered. The prohibited perspective, not the general subject matter, resulted in the refusal to make third-party payments, for the subjects discussed were otherwise within the approved category of publications.

The dissent's assertion that no viewpoint discrimination occurs because the Guidelines discriminate against an entire class of viewpoints reflects an insupportable assumption that all debate is bipolar and that anti-religious speech is the only response to religious speech. Our understanding of the complex and multifaceted nature of public discourse has not embraced such a contrived description of the marketplace of ideas. If the topic of debate is, for example, racism, then exclusion of several views on that problem is just as offensive to the First Amendment as exclusion of only one. It is as objectionable to exclude both a theistic and an atheistic perspective on the debate as it is to exclude one, the other, or yet another political, economic, or social viewpoint. The dissent's declaration that debate is not skewed so long as multiple voices are silenced is simply wrong; the debate is skewed in multiple ways. . . .

Vital First Amendment speech principles are at stake here. The first danger to liberty lies in granting the State the power to examine publications to determine whether or not they are based on some ultimate idea and if so for the State to classify them. The second, and corollary, danger is to speech from the chilling of individual thought and expression. That danger is especially real in the University setting, where the State acts against a background and tradition of thought and experiment that is at the center of our intellectual and philosophic tradition. . . . For the University, by regulation, to cast disapproval on particular viewpoints of its students risks the suppression of free speech and creative inquiry in one of the vital centers for the nation's intellectual life, its college and university campuses. . . .

Based on the principles we have discussed, we hold that the regulation invoked to deny SAF support, both in its terms and in its application to these petitioners, is a denial of their right of free speech guaranteed by the First Amendment. It remains to be considered whether the violation following from the University's action is excused by the necessity of complying with the Constitution's prohibition against state establishment of religion. . . .

A central lesson of our decisions is that a significant factor in upholding governmental programs in the face of Establishment Clause attack is their neutrality towards religion. . . . We have held that the guarantee of neutrality is respected, not offended, when the government, following neutral criteria and evenhanded policies, extends benefits to recipients whose ideologies and viewpoints, including religious ones, are broad and diverse. . . . More than once have we rejected the position that the Establishment Clause even justifies, much less requires, a refusal to extend free speech rights to religious speakers who participate in broad-reaching government programs neutral in design. . . .

The governmental program here is neutral toward religion. There is no suggestion that the University created it to advance religion or adopted some ingenious device with the purpose of aiding a religious cause. The object of the SAF is to open a forum for speech and to support various student enterprises, including the publication of newspapers, in recognition of the diversity and creativity of student life. The University's SAF Guidelines have a separate classification for, and do not make third-party payments on behalf of, "religious organizations," which are those "whose purpose is to practice a devotion to an acknowledged ultimate reality or deity." The category of support here is for "student news, information, opinion, entertainment, or academic communications media groups," of which Wide Awake was 1 of 15 in the 1990 school year. WAP did not seek a subsidy because of its Christian editorial viewpoint; it sought funding as a student journal, which it was. . . .

To obey the Establishment Clause, it was not necessary for the University to deny eligibility to student publications because of their viewpoint. The neutrality commanded of the State by the separate Clauses of the First Amendment was compromised by the University's course of action. The viewpoint discrimination inherent in the University's regulation required public officials to scan and interpret student publications to discern their underlying philosophic assumptions respecting religious theory and belief. That course of action was a denial of the right of free speech and would risk fostering a pervasive bias or hostility to religion, which could undermine the very neutrality the Establishment Clause requires. There is no Establishment Clause violation in the University's honoring its duties under the Free Speech Clause. . . .

Justice Thomas, concurring.

I write separately to express my disagreement with the historical analysis put forward by the dissent. Although the dissent starts down the right path in consulting the original meaning of the Establishment Clause, its misleading application of history yields a principle that is inconsistent with our Nation's long tradition of allowing religious adherents to participate on equal terms in neutral government programs.

Even assuming that the Virginia debate on the so-called "Assessment Controversy" was indicative of the principles embodied in the Establishment Clause, this incident hardly compels the dissent's conclusion that government must actively discriminate against religion. The dissent's historical discussion glosses over the fundamental characteristic of the Virginia assessment bill that sparked the controversy: The assessment was to be imposed for the support of clergy in the performance of their function of teaching religion. . . .

James Madison's Memorial and Remonstrance Against Religious Assessments (hereinafter Madison's Remonstrance) must be understood in this context. Contrary to the dissent's suggestion, Madison's objection to the assessment bill did not rest on the premise that religious entities may never participate on equal terms in neutral government programs. Nor did Madison embrace the argument that forms the linchpin of the dissent: that monetary subsidies are constitutionally different from other neutral benefits programs. Instead, Madison's comments are more consistent with the neutrality principle that the dissent inexplicably discards. . . .

Legal commentators have disagreed about the historical lesson to take from the Assessment Controversy. For some, the experience in Virginia is consistent with the view that the Framers saw the Establishment Clause simply as a prohibition on governmental preferences for some religious faiths over others. . . . Other commentators have rejected this view, concluding that the Establishment Clause forbids not only government preferences for some religious sects over others, but also government preferences for religion over irreligion. . . .

I find much to commend the former view. . . . The funding provided by the Virginia assessment was to be extended only to Christian sects, and the Remonstrance seized on this defect . . .

In addition . . . , "Madison's . . . arguments all speak, in some way, to the same intolerance, bigotry, unenlightenment, and persecution that had generally resulted from previous exclusive religious establishments.". . . The conclusion that Madison saw the principle of nonestablishment as barring governmental preferences for *particular* religious faiths seems especially clear in light of statements he made in the more-relevant context of the House debates on the First Amendment. . . . (Madison's views "as reflected by actions on the floor of the House in 1789, [indicate] that he saw the [First] Amendment as designed to prohibit the establishment of a national religion, and perhaps to prevent discrimination among sects," but not "as requiring neutrality on the part of government between religion and irreligion"). Moreover, even if more extreme notions of the separation of church and state can be attributed to Madison, many of them clearly stem from "arguments reflecting the concepts of natural law, natural rights, and the social contract between government and a civil society," . . . rather than the principle of nonestablishment in the Constitution. In any event, the views of one man do not establish the original understanding of the First Amendment.

But resolution of this debate is not necessary to decide this case. Under any understanding of the Assessment Controversy, the history cited by the dissent cannot support the conclusion that the Establishment Clause "categorically condemn[s] state programs directly aiding religious activity" when that aid is part of a neutral program available to a wide array of beneficiaries. . . . Even if Madison believed that the principle of nonestablishment of religion precluded government financial support for religion *per se* (in the sense of government benefits specifically targeting religion), there is no indication that at the time of the framing he took the dissent's extreme view that the government must discriminate against religious adherents by excluding them from more generally available financial subsidies.

In fact, Madison's own early legislative proposals cut against the dissent's suggestion. In 1776, when Virginia's Revolutionary Convention was drafting its Declaration of Rights, Madison prepared an amendment that would have disestablished the Anglican Church. This amendment (which went too far for the Convention and was not adopted) is not nearly as sweeping as the dissent's version of disestablishment; Madison merely wanted the Convention to declare that "no man or class of men ought, on account of religion[,] to be invested with *peculiar* emoluments or privileges. . . ." Likewise, Madison's Remonstrance stressed that "just government" is "best supported by protecting every citizen in the enjoyment of his Religion with the same equal hand which protects his person and his property; by neither invading the equal rights of any Sect, nor suffering any Sect to invade those of another.". . .

Stripped of its flawed historical premise, the dissent's argument is reduced to the claim that our Establishment Clause jurisprudence permits neutrality in the context of access to government *facilities* but requires discrimination in access to government *funds*. The dissent purports to locate the prohibition against "direct public funding" at the "heart" of the Establishment Clause, . . . but this conclusion fails to confront historical examples of funding that date back to the time of the founding. To take but one famous example, both Houses of the First Congress elected chaplains, . . . and that Congress enacted legislation providing for an annual salary of $500 to be paid out of the Treasury. . . . Madison himself was a member of the committee that recommended the chaplain system in the House. . . . This same system of "direct public funding" of congressional chaplains has "continued without interruption ever since that early session of Congress.". . .

The historical evidence of government support for religious entities through property tax exemptions is also overwhelming. As the dissent concedes, property tax exemptions for religious bodies "have been in place for over 200 years without disruption to the interests represented by the Establishment Clause" . . . In my view, the dissent's acceptance of this tradition puts to rest the notion that the Establishment Clause bars monetary aid to religious groups even when the aid is equally available to other groups. A tax exemption in many cases is economically and functionally indistinguishable from a direct monetary subsidy. In one instance, the government relieves religious entities (along with others) of a generally applicable tax; in the other, it relieves religious entities (along with others) of some or all of the burden of that tax by returning it in the form of a cash subsidy. Whether the benefit is provided at the front or back end of the taxation process, the financial aid to religious groups is undeniable. The analysis under the Establishment Clause must also be the same . . . .

Though our Establishment Clause jurisprudence is in hopeless disarray, this case provides an opportunity to reaffirm one basic principle that has enjoyed an uncharacteristic degree of consensus: The Clause does not compel the exclusion of religious groups from government benefits programs that are generally available to a broad class of participants. . . .

* * *

Justice Souter, with whom Justice Stevens, Justice Ginsburg, and Justice Breyer join, dissenting.

The Court today, for the first time, approves direct funding of core religious activities by an arm of the State. It does so, however, only after erroneous treatment of some familiar principles of law implementing the First Amendment's Establishment and Speech Clauses, and by viewing the very funds in question as beyond the reach of the Establishment Clause's funding restrictions as such. Because there is no warrant for distinguishing among public funding sources for purposes of applying the First Amendment's prohibition of religious establishment, I would hold that the University's refusal to support petitioners' religious activities is compelled by the Establishment Clause. . . .

* * *

The Court's difficulties will be all the more clear after a closer look at Wide Awake than the majority opinion affords. The character of the magazine is candidly disclosed on the opening page of the first issue, where the editor-in-chief announces Wide Awake's mission in a letter to the readership signed, "Love in Christ": it is "to challenge Christians to live, in word and deed, according to the faith they proclaim and to encourage students to consider what a personal relationship with Jesus Christ means.". . .

Using public funds for the direct subsidization of preaching the word is categorically forbidden under the Establishment Clause, and if the Clause was meant to accomplish nothing else, it was meant to bar this use of public money. Evidence on the subject antedates even the Bill of Rights itself, as may be seen in the writings of Madison, whose authority on questions about the meaning of the Establishment Clause is well settled. . . Four years before the First Congress proposed the First Amendment, Madison gave his opinion on the legitimacy of using public funds for religious purposes, in the Memorial and Remonstrance Against Religious Assessments, which played the central role in ensuring the defeat of the Virginia tax assessment bill in 1786 and framed the debate upon which the Religion Clauses stand:

> "Who does not see that . . . the same authority which can force a citizen to contribute three pence only of his property for the support of any one establishment, may force him to conform to any other establishment in all cases whatsoever?". . .

Madison wrote against a background in which nearly every Colony had exacted a tax for church support, . . . the practice having become "so commonplace as to shock the freedom-loving colonials into a feeling of abhorrence." . . . Madison's Remonstrance captured the colonists' "conviction that individual religious liberty could be achieved best under a government which was stripped of all power to tax, to support, or otherwise to assist any or all religions, or to interfere with the beliefs of any religious individual or group." Their sentiment as expressed by Madison in Virginia, led not only to the defeat of Virginia's tax assessment bill, but also directly to passage of the Virginia Bill for Establishing Religious Freedom, written by Thomas Jefferson. That bill's preamble declared that "to compel a man to furnish contributions of money for the propagation of opinions which he disbelieves, is sinful and tyrannical," Jefferson, A Bill for Establishing Religious Freedom, . . . and its text provided "[t]hat no man shall be compelled to frequent or support any religious worship, place, or ministry whatsoever. . . ." We have "previously recognized that the provisions of the First Amendment, in the drafting and adoption of which Madison and Jefferson played such leading roles, had the same objective and were intended to provide the same protection against governmental intrusion on religious liberty as the Virginia statute.". . .

The principle against direct funding with public money is patently violated by the contested use of today's student activity fee. Like today's taxes generally, the fee is Madison's threepence. The University exercises the power of the State to compel a student to pay it, . . . and the use of any part of it for the direct support of religious activity thus strikes at what we have repeatedly held to be the heart of the prohibition on establishment. . . .

The Court, accordingly, has never before upheld direct state funding of the sort of proselytizing published in Wide Awake and, in fact has categorically condemned state programs directly aiding religious activity. . . .

Even when the Court has upheld aid to an institution performing both secular and sectarian functions, it has always made a searching enquiry to ensure that the institution kept the secular activities separate from its sectarian ones, with any direct aid flowing only to the former and never the latter. . . .

Reasonable minds may differ over whether the Court reached the correct result in each of these cases, but their common principle has never been questioned or repudiated. "Although Establishment Clause jurisprudence is characterized by few absolutes, the Clause does absolutely prohibit government-financed . . . indoctrination into the beliefs of a particular religious faith.". . .

The Court is ordering an instrumentality of the State to support religious evangelism with direct funding. This is a flat violation of the Establishment Clause.

* * *

Given the dispositive effect of the Establishment Clause's bar to funding the magazine, there should be no need to decide whether in the absence of this bar the University would violate the Free Speech Clause by limiting funding as it has done. . . .

Santa Fe Independent School District v. Doe (2000)[10]

Prayer and the public schools continued to provide a litigious mix into the year 2000. Having previously considered official prayer and silent meditations, prayer during school, after school, and during graduation ceremonies, in *Santa Fe v. Doe* the Court was asked to rule on a Texas school practice in which students elected a chaplain to deliver a prayer before varsity football games.

Justice Stevens delivered the opinion of the Court.

* * *

Prior to 1995, the Santa Fe High School student who occupied the school's elective office of student council chaplain delivered a prayer over the public address system before each varsity football game for the entire season. This practice, along with others, was challenged in District Court as a violation of the Establishment Clause of the First Amendment. While these proceedings were pending in the District Court, the school district adopted a different policy that permits, but does not require, prayer initiated and led by a student at all home games. [The student council voted to have a prayer and subsequently elected a student to recite the prayer at each game.] The District Court entered an order modifying that policy to permit only nonsectarian, nonproselytizing prayer. . . .

In *Lee* v. *Weisman,* we held that a prayer delivered by a rabbi at a middle school graduation ceremony violated that Clause. Although this case involves student prayer at a different type of school function, our analysis is properly guided by the principles that we endorsed in *Lee.*

As we held in that case:

> The principle that government may accommodate the free exercise of religion does not supersede the fundamental limitations imposed by the Establishment Clause. It is beyond dispute that, at a minimum, the Constitution guarantees that government may not coerce anyone to support or participate in religion or its exercise, or otherwise act in a way which "establishes a [state] religion or religious faith, or tends to do so." . . .

In this case the District first argues that this principle is inapplicable to its October policy because the messages are private student speech, not public speech. It reminds us that "there is a crucial difference between *government* speech endorsing religion, which the Establishment Clause forbids, and *private* speech endorsing religion, which the Free Speech and Free Exercise Clauses protect.". . . We certainly agree with that distinction, but we are not persuaded that the pregame invocations should be regarded as "private speech."

These invocations are authorized by a government policy and take place on government property at government-sponsored school-related events. Of course, not every message delivered under such circumstances is the government's own. We have held, for example, that an individual's contribution to a government-created forum was not government speech. . . . Although the District relies heavily on *Rosenberger* and similar cases involving such forums, it is clear that the pregame ceremony is not the type of forum discussed in those cases. The Santa Fe school officials simply do not "evince either 'by policy or by practice,' any intent to open the [pregame ceremony] to 'indiscriminate use' . . . by the student body generally.". . . Rather, the school allows only one student, the same student for the entire season, to give the invocation. The statement or invocation, moreover, is subject to particular regulations that confine the content and topic of the student's message . . . "[S]elective access does not transform government property into a public forum."

Granting only one student access to the stage at a time does not, of course, necessarily preclude a finding that a school has created a limited public forum. Here, however, Santa Fe's student election system ensures that only those messages deemed "appropriate" under the District's policy may be delivered. That is, the majoritarian process implemented by the District guarantees, by definition, that minority candidates will never prevail and that their views will be effectively silenced. . . .

Once the student speaker is selected and the message composed, the invocation is then delivered to a large audience assembled as part of a regularly scheduled, school-sponsored function conducted on school property. The message is broadcast over the school's public address system, which remains subject to the control of school officials. It is fair to assume that the pregame ceremony is clothed in the traditional indicia of school sporting events, which generally include not just the team, but also cheerleaders and band members dressed in uniforms sporting the school name and mascot. The school's name is likely written in large print across the field and on banners and flags. The crowd will certainly include many who display the school colors and insignia on their school T-shirts, jackets, or hats and who may also be waving signs displaying the school name. It is in a setting such as this that "[t]he board has chosen to permit" the elected student to rise and give the "statement or invocation."

In this context the members of the listening audience must perceive the pregame message as a public expression of the views of the majority of the student body delivered with the approval of the school administration. In cases involving state participation in a religious activity, one of the relevant questions is "whether an objective observer, acquainted with the text, legislative history, and implementation of the statute, would perceive it as a state endorsement of prayer in public schools.". . . Regardless of the listener's support for, or objection to, the message, an objective Santa Fe High School student will unquestionably perceive the inevitable pregame prayer as stamped with her school's seal of approval.

The text and history of this policy, moreover, reinforce our objective student's perception that the prayer is, in actuality, encouraged by the school. When a governmental entity professes a secular purpose for an arguably religious policy, the government's characterization is, of course, entitled to some deference. But it is nonetheless the duty of the courts to "distinguis[h] a sham secular purpose from a sincere one."...

According to the District, the secular purposes of the policy are to "foste[r] free expression of private persons ... as well [as to] solemniz[e] sporting events, promot[e] good sportsmanship and student safety, and establis[h] an appropriate environment for competition." We note, however, that the District's approval of only one specific kind of message, an "invocation," is not necessary to further any of these purposes. Additionally, the fact that only one student is permitted to give a content-limited message suggests that this policy does little to "foste[r] free expression." Furthermore, regardless of whether one considers a sporting event an appropriate occasion for solemnity, the use of an invocation to foster such solemnity is impermissible when, in actuality, it constitutes prayer sponsored by the school. And it is unclear what type of message would be both appropriately "solemnizing" under the District's policy and yet non-religious.

Most striking to us is the evolution of the current policy from the long-sanctioned office of "Student Chaplain" to the candidly titled "Prayer at Football Games" regulation. This history indicates that the District intended to preserve the practice of prayer before football games. The conclusion that the District viewed the October policy simply as a continuation of the previous policies is dramatically illustrated by the fact that the school did not conduct a new election, pursuant to the current policy, to replace the results of the previous election, which occurred under the former policy. Given these observations, and in light of the school's history of regular delivery of a student-led prayer at athletic events, it is reasonable to infer that the specific purpose of the policy was to preserve a popular "state-sponsored religious practice."

School sponsorship of a religious message is impermissible because it sends the ancillary message to members of the audience who are nonadherants "that they are outsiders, not full members of the political community, and an accompanying message to adherants that they are insiders, favored members of the political community."... The delivery of such a message—over the school's public address system, by a speaker representing the student body, under the supervision of school faculty, and pursuant to a school policy that explicitly and implicitly encourages public prayer—is not properly characterized as "private" speech.

* * *

The District next argues that its football policy is distinguishable from the graduation prayer in *Lee* because it does not coerce students to participate in religious observances. Its argument has two parts: first, that there is no impermissible government coercion because the pregame messages are the product of student choices; and second, that there is really no coercion at all because attendance at an extracurricular event, unlike a graduation ceremony, is voluntary....

One of the purposes served by the Establishment Clause is to remove debate over this kind of issue from governmental supervision or control. We explained in *Lee* that the "preservation and transmission of religious beliefs and worship is a responsibility and a choice committed to the private sphere." . . . The election mechanism, when considered in light of the history in which the policy in question evolved, reflects a device the District put in place that determines whether religious messages will be delivered at home football games. The mechanism encourages divisiveness along religious lines in a public school setting, a result at odds with the Establishment Clause. . . .

The District further argues that attendance at the commencement ceremonies at issue in *Lee* "differs dramatically" from attendance at high school football games, which it contends "are of no more than passing interest to many students" and are "decidedly extracurricular," thus dissipating any coercion. . . . Attendance at a high school football game, unlike showing up for class, is certainly not required in order to receive a diploma. Moreover, we may assume that the District is correct in arguing that the informal pressure to attend an athletic event is not as strong as a senior's desire to attend her own graduation ceremony.

There are some students, however, such as cheerleaders, members of the band, and, of course, the team members themselves, for whom seasonal commitments mandate their attendance, sometimes for class credit. The District also minimizes the importance to many students of attending and participating in extracurricular activities as part of a complete educational experience. . . . High school home football games are traditional gatherings of a school community; they bring together students and faculty as well as friends and family from years present and past to root for a common cause. Undoubtedly, the games are not important to some students, and they voluntarily choose not to attend. For many others, however, the choice between whether to attend these games or to risk facing a personally offensive religious ritual is in no practical sense an easy one. The Constitution, moreover, demands that the school may not force this difficult choice upon these students for "[i]t is a tenet of the First Amendment that the State cannot require one of its citizens to forfeit his or her rights and benefits as the price of resisting conformance to state-sponsored religious practice." . . .

Religion and Politics

National Conference of Catholic Bishops on Religion and Politics[11]

In the 1980s, the American Roman Catholic bishops have become increasingly vocal on political issues. They issued a pastoral letter titled "Peace in the Modern World: Religious Perspectives and Principles" as well as a pastoral letter on the American economy. Additionally, individual bishops have made strong public statements on issues such as abortion. The following is a 1984 statement of Bishop James W. Mallone on behalf of the National Conference of Catholic Bishops.

The Administrative Board of the United States Catholic Conference . . . asked that I issue a statement reaffirming the Conference's position on the question of religion and politics. I am pleased to do so, since your pluralistic society should welcome discussion of the moral dimensions of public policy and thoughtful examination of the relationship of religious bodies to the political order.

As a nation we are constitutionally committed to the separation of church and state but not to the separation of religious and moral values from public life. The genius of the American political tradition lies in preserving religious freedom for all—but not at the price of excluding religious and moral content from discussions of domestic and foreign policy.

The question therefore is not whether we should discuss the relationship of religion, morality, and politics but how to discuss the relationship. While responsibility for the quality and character of this discussion rests with all citizens, it rests especially with religious leaders, political leaders, and the media.

[W]e do not take positions for or against particular parties or individual candidates.

Bishops are teachers in the Catholic Church entrusted with the responsibility of communicating the content of Catholic moral teaching and illustrating its relevance to social and political issues. We do not seek the formation of a voting bloc nor do we preempt the right and duty of individuals to decide conscientiously whom they will support for public office. Rather, having stated our positions, we encourage members of our own Church and all citizens to examine the positions of candidates on issues and decide who will best contribute to the common good of society.

The content of Catholic teaching leads us to take positions on many public issues; we are not a one-issue Church. . . .

[Our] concerns range from protecting human life from the attack of abortion, to safeguarding human life from the devastation of nuclear war; they extend to the enhancement of life through promoting human rights and satisfying human needs like nutrition, education, housing and health care, especially for the poor. We emphasize that the needs of the poor must be adequately addressed if we are to be considered a just and compassionate society. Attention to the least among us is the test of our moral vision, and it should be applied to candidates at every level of our government. . . .

[I]n speaking of human dignity and the sanctity of life, we give special emphasis to two issues today. They are the prevention of nuclear war and the protection of unborn human life.

These issues pertaining to the sanctity of human life itself are and cannot help but be matters of public morality. Evident in the case of war and peace, this is no less true in the case of abortion, where the human right to life of the unborn and society's interest in protecting it necessarily make this a matter of public, not merely private, morality.

On questions such as these, we realize that citizens and public officials may agree with our moral arguments while disagreeing with us and among themselves on the most effective legal and policy remedies. The search for political and public policy solutions to such problems as war and peace and abortion may well be long and difficult, but a prudential judgment that political solutions are not now feasible does not justify failure to undertake the effort.

Whether the issue be the control, reduction, and elimination of nuclear arms or the legal protection of the unborn, the task is to work for the feasibility of what may now be deemed unfeasible. The pursuit of complex objectives like these ought not to be set aside because the goals may not be immediately reachable. In debating such matters, there is much room for dialogue about what constitutes effective, workable responses; but the debate should not be about whether a response in the political order is needed.

None of these issues will be resolved quickly. All will extend far beyond the present political campaign. The discussion of religion and politics will also be pursued long after the campaign. Let us conduct our immediate dialogue with reason and civility, so that the resources of religious and moral vision and the method of rational political debate will be sustained and enhanced in our public life.

National Council of Churches on Religion and Politics[12]

In 1984 the National Council of the Churches of Christ in the United States issued the following guidelines, which it described as a drawing together of "long-standing positions" on the issue of religion and politics.

The continual controversy over religion and politics revolves around several points of confusion which could be clarified by reference to history.

1: *Religion, Morality and Law.* One of the purposes of law is to define and punish unacceptable behavior. Determining what behavior is unacceptable is the province of morality, which is essential to all civilized societies. Religion is one important source of moral insights, but it is not the only one. The legal tradition going back to the Codes of Hammurabi and Justinian is another source, as is the philosophical tradition going back to Socrates, Plato and Aristotle, and the medical tradition going back to Hippocrates and Galen. Every voice urging greater recognition and implementation of morality in this nation is entitled to respect and consideration, religion no less than any other. Not all voices will agree on the definition of morality, however, and not all forms of immorality need be, or can be, made punishable by law, so it is equally important that all voices urging the embodiment of morality in law be subject to debate and criticism, religion no less than any other. That is part of the essential public dialogue of a democracy.

2: *"Separation of Church and State."* It is not a violation of the separation of church and state for religious groups or their leaders to proclaim what they believe to be the right course for the nation, to try to persuade others to their point of view, to try to get laws passed which will advance what they believe is right, and to support candidates who will enact and enforce such laws. That is the right and duty of every citizen, and none are to be disqualified because of their religious commitments or convictions, but neither are they to be immune from criticism or opposition because of their religious commitments or convictions.

Preachers in their pulpits are entitled to exhort their followers and anyone else who will listen to work for the kind of public policy that will advance what they believe to be the right and moral course for the nation. That is what preachers are *supposed* to do, and so doing is not "imposing" their religious views on anyone because people can disregard their counsel—and often do—even if they declare that they are proclaiming the will of God or that those who disagree are sinful, pagan or bound for perdition. Preachers have done so throughout the history of the nation, and such activity is not only well within the bounds of freedom of speech and the free exercise of religion but is an important contribution to the shaping of the nation's public policy.

Preachers may even run for public office and serve if elected. The last state law banning clergy from civil office was struck down by a unanimous Supreme Court in 1978. . . . If clergy cannot be [banned] from candidacy for public office, how much less can they be [banned] from preaching on public issues or their followers be [banned] from acting on them politically.

However, a church which chooses to support or oppose specific candidates for public office runs the risk of losing its tax exemption, since Section 501(c)(3) of the Internal Revenue Code prohibits non-profit charitable organizations—including churches—from intervening in "any political campaign on behalf of any candidate for public office." That does not mean that it is illegal or unconstitutional to do so, but that there may be adverse tax consequences of so doing, which a church may in exceptional circumstances be willing to risk when it believes that its duty to God and humankind requires.

3: *Religion and the Candidate and Office Holder.* The Constitution forbids any religious test for public office. Therefore, a candidate's religious affiliation cannot disqualify him or her for election or appointment to public office in the United States. By the same token, a candidate's religion should not be show-cased as though it were a qualification or credential for public office. . . .

This view of the proper role of religion does not require the office-holder to be silent about his or her religious views when pertinent; far from it. The office-holder should seek in every way to advance what he or she believes the common good requires, and if that understanding of the common good derives in whole or in part from religious teaching or doctrine all the better! But others are not obliged to agree. Public policy proposals consonant with the office-holder's religious convictions should be neither accepted nor rejected for that reason, but should be debated on their secular merits and effects, like any others. If they do commend themselves to a majority as desirable public policy and are enacted into law, they are no more "imposed" on others than are any other laws duly enacted by the will of the majority.

What the office-holder should not do is to use the powers of office to advance the institutional interests of his or her faith-group at the expense of others or of religion at the expense of non-adherents of religion. Like-wise, the office-holder should not seek to implement in public policy the doctrinal teachings or tenets of her or his religion unless and to the extent they coincide with the secular common good. And candidates, though entitled to express their religious views while campaigning, should be wary of the temptation, if elected, to consider that they have somehow gained a "mandate" to advance those views as public policy without explicit authorization from the electorate. The office-holder (or candidate) should also avoid stigmatizing critics or opponents as irreligious or sinful just because they disagree.

By and large, the Presidents of the United States through more than two centuries of history have generally observed these principles in practice, and in this respect have set a good example for public servants at all levels.

National Jewish Community Relations Advisory Council on Religion and Politics

In 1985 the following statement on the role of religion and religious groups in the political process was adopted by the National Jewish Community Relations Advisory Council (NJCRAC). This council includes eleven national and over one hundred local organizations representing Orthodox, Conservative, and Reform Jewish groups.

We have long held that it is legitimate, indeed desirable, for religious groups and clergy to advocate policies that would shape society in ways that those faith communities view as fulfilling their ideal of the "good society." They have a Constitutional right not only to advocate their views on public-policy issues, but also to question candidates on their positions on those issues, to make their views known to their constituents and to the public at large, and to seek to build a community consensus in support of their positions. We would hope that religion, and religious groups, would speak to the ethics and morality of society in the public marketplace of ideas. We believe that all issues may be put on the table for discussion in the marketplace of ideas, but the manner of advocacy should respect our tradition of church-state separation, free of any hint of coercion or verbal violence. In the debate of public-policy issues, it is desirable that the focus be on the public good. These principles have guided Jewish organizations as we have spoken out on a wide array of public-policy issues.

Our concern grows out of what we perceive as growing dangerous tendencies in the political process which attempt to convert political parties into sectarian instruments and raise religious tests for public office. We witnessed in the 1984 election campaign such activities as a call by a candidate in a Congressional race against a Jewish member of Congress to "put a Christian in Congress"; questions addressed by a journalist in a nationally televised debate of the presidential candidates as to whether the presidential candidates were "born-again Christians," whether they attended church regularly, and whether they believed that abortion was a sin; a statement by the President that those who are against school prayer are "intolerant of religion"; clergy pressing members of their faith to subordinate to church beliefs their mandate as public officials to uphold the law and the Constitution; and, in Minnesota, some local political organizations demanding that school board candidates meet a religious test.

When church and synagogue officials command that their adherents who hold public office act in accordance with religious teaching inconsistent with responsibilities imposed by law, they threaten the very existence of a democracy whose citizens belong to a wide variety of faiths, or none. Such conduct goes well beyond the legitimate exercise of public advocacy. And while churches and synagogues have the right to judge whether their members' conduct meets the demands of the faith, the exercise of that right against public officials for actions taken in furtherance of their official duties is highly divisive.

The knowledge of the ravages of religious wars and religious persecution was what led the Founding Fathers, high-minded moralists, but also pragmatists, to erect, through the Bill of Rights, the wall of separation of church and state as part of the fundamental law of this land. It is important to recall that the Constitution specifically proscribes religious tests for public office. These guarantees not only have protected the rights of religious minorities, but also have fostered a society in which religious pluralism and freedom of religious expression have flourished and prospered.

Religious groups, as all groups in American society, have wide latitude in seeking to achieve their moral imperatives in the public arena. They can properly raise any issue for public debate; they can properly seek the redress of any government decision including, of course, decrees of the United States Supreme Court. The debate of public policy does not require the compromise of fundamental beliefs, including religious imperatives. It does require acting on the recognition that all the participants of the debate have that same right. It further requires respect for those whose views are bitterly opposed. The American democratic process benefits from public debate of differing views among people of good will, but is endangered when national debates degenerate into mortal combat between the forces of good and the forces of evil.

We recognize that religious groups in their hierarchies of social concern may feel a greater intensity about some issues than others, and they will act accordingly. While groups may legitimately coalesce around a single issue, the nation as a whole needs to respond wisely to the totality of needs of the American people.

While we believe that any issue may be debated in the marketplace of ideas under the rules of fair play, the Jewish community relations field will continue to assert vigorously our profound belief that there are issues that must be beyond the reach of government. We stand with Roger Williams, Jefferson, Madison, and those who followed, up to and including Justice William Brennan, in contending that the well-being of American society requires the inviolate protection of belief, and the sanctity of religious belief above all. They are beyond the jurisdiction of government. Even in areas like abortion, the Supreme Court has held that the Constitution requires limits on government intervention. We believe that in the uncertain area between private and public morality, the vindication of one religious tradition can come only at the expense of another. However, we do not deny the right of others to challenge these views in debates, but we urge that such advocacy be marked by civility and mutual respect.

The separation of religious dogma from politics is incumbent upon not only religious groups and their spokesmen, but also upon public officials, candidates for public office, and political parties. They, too, are called upon to avoid entangling the religious and political mainstreams of American life. They must stand guard against any who would identify American party politics with any brand of religious view. In conflicts over public policy, the determinant should be the public good rather than theological dogma. We look to them to reject categorically the pernicious notion that only one brand of politics or religion meets with God's approval and that others are necessarily evil. We look to them to recommit the major political parties of this nation to the spirit of religious tolerance and religious forbearance that is indispensable to a free society. Above all, we look to political and religious bodies to oppose any and all efforts, whether direct or subtle, to tamper with the First Amendment, the very foundation of American liberties.

DONALD L. DRAKEMAN

The Churches on Church and State[13]

During the latter half of the twentieth century, the mainline Protestant churches shifted their official policies from supporting school prayer and other links between government and religion to lobbying for a strict separation of church and state. In this article, Donald L. Drakeman explores this evolution in the churches' views and discusses how the churches' official positions on this public-policy issue diverge from the beliefs of the individual church members.

The Church-State Spectrum

From the earliest days of the Republic (and even further back to the Reformation), Protestant views on church and state have fallen at various points along a spectrum . . . The state-church model flourished during the colonial era when formally established churches were often the norm. In the nineteenth century, after the state-subsidized churches were finally disestablished, the government and the churches continued to share the belief that America is a "Christian nation." From Sunday closing laws to national days prayer and congressional chaplains, the government continued to put a Protestant stamp on the national character. For the most part, the practices were welcomed by the churches, which urged the government to "be mindful of its avowed faith in Almighty God as the fountainhead of our rights and on every public occasion to give due and proper recognition of this faith." . . .

During the last half century, however, Protestantism has been, in historian Leonard Sweet's words, "set upon by troublesome forces tart enough to sour honey." One of these pungent forces was the movement to eradicate from the public schools religious activities, such as prayers and Bible reading, that had a particularly Protestant flavor. . . . In 1962 the Supreme Court declared that the practice of reciting prayers in the public schools violated the Constitution's mandated separation of church and state; a year later, the Court followed suit and announced that school-sponsored Bible reading similarly contravened the establishment clause.

The Court's action left many with a sour taste in their mouths: fully 70 percent of the American public condemned the decisions; . . . and Episcopal bishop James Pike railed that the Court had "deconsecrated the nation." Whether reviled or acclaimed, the Court's pronouncements brought church-state issues into sharp focus throughout the land, and the Protestant churches were forced to decide whether to cling to traditional concepts of a "Christian nation" or to recognize that the force of pluralism required a new vision of the relationship of God and country.

Mainline Protestantism opted for pluralism; for example, the Presbyterian Church (U.S.A.) announced that "we have no right to claim that ours is and always has been a Christian nation." Despite these kinds of straightforward proclamations by denominational leaders, church-state issues remain contested even today. To get a sense of current Protestant approaches to the proper relationship of church and state, we need to [look] at the attitudes of [various "mainline"] churches through their official actions and statements as well as the beliefs of their clergy and their members.

Baptists

Many Baptists point proudly to a rich theological heritage calling for a high wall of separation between church and state. . . . In the 1930s, when many Protestant churches were still fully committed to the building of a "Christian nation," Southern and Northern Baptists jointly adopted the "American Baptist Bill of Rights," announcing that religious liberty is "indispensable to human welfare," and that Baptists "condemn every form of compulsion in religion."

In 1946, several Baptist conventions formed the Baptist Joint Committee on Public Affairs (BJC) in response to a number of perceived cracks in the wall of separation between church and state. . . . The BJC has consistently fought government involvement in religion on topics ranging from school prayer to parochial school aid. . . . Intra-Baptist disputes [exist], however, and the future of the BJC's role as church-state activist is unclear. Although some believe with Baptist minister Charles G. Adams that "Baptists pervert their own heritage by clamoring for a . . . 'Christian nation,'" many influential members of the Southern Baptist Convention, a body representing half the Baptists in America and providing 85 percent of the BJC's funding, have attacked the BJC's separationist posture. Among other things, the pastor of the largest Southern Baptist church has said on national television that "the separation of church and state is a figment of infidels' imagination.". . .

Presbyterians

In the early 1960s, the United Presbyterian Church adopted a policy statement promoting a stricter separation of church and state, particularly in the public schools, thus marking a sharp reversal from earlier statements extolling the benefits of a Christian nation. . . . In that same era, however, the Southern Presbyterian denomination, named the Presbyterian Church in the U.S., issued a report lamenting that the "absence of any sort of public acknowledgment of God [in public schools] could, in effect, be an unspoken suggestion that education is exclusively a secular pursuit without moral and spiritual considerations." These differences survived the union of the two major Presbyterian churches. . . .

Finally, in 1988, the Presbyterians officially resolved their differences as the General Assembly adopted a set of fairly separationist policy recommendations after a lengthy committee review. Among its many conclusions, the comprehensive report, *God Alone Is Lord of the Conscience,* strongly disapproved of a constitutional amendment to return prayer to the public schools, and called a Supreme Court decision permitting a municipal nativity scene "regrettable" because the "Court's emphasis on the secular nature of Christmas is offensive to Christians and transparently false to non-Christians.". . .

Lutherans

Shortly after the Supreme Court's school prayer decision, the president of the Lutheran Church in America issued a comment reflecting mixed emotions. Although the "elimination of the devotional practices did not entail much of a religious loss," it did signal that "the United States of America . . . is past the place where underlying Christian culture and beliefs are assumed in its life." By 1964, however, both the Lutheran Church in America and the American Lutheran Church had issued policy statements condemning efforts to overturn the Supreme Court's school prayer decisions as "unnecessary from a religious point of view and unwise from a public policy perspective." In particular, the statement of the Lutheran Church in America posited, "The more we . . . insist on common denominator religious exercise in public schools, the greater risk we run of diluting our faith and contributing to a vague religiosity which defines religion with patriotism and becomes a national folk religion.". . .

United Church of Christ

Since 1971, several national agencies of the United Church of Christ have released statements urging a separation of church and state in America and specifically supporting the Supreme Court's school prayer decision. . . .

Methodists

[In] 1968 the General Conference of the United Methodist Church . . . adopted a policy statement (reaffirmed in 1980) . . . declaring the church's opposition to "all establishment of religion by government." In particular, the statement proclaimed that the state should not use its authority to inculcate particular religious beliefs (including atheism) nor should it require prayer or worship in the public schools. . . .

Protestant Clergy and Laity

The polls make it clear that the American public shares the churches' dedication to the principle of strict separation. In a 1988 Gallup Poll, 77 percent of the public either "mostly" (29 percent) or "completely" (48 percent) agreed that "church and state should be separated.". . . [However,] virtually every time the public is surveyed approximately 70 percent favor prayer in the public schools. . . . These people were asked whether they would favor a constitutional amendment to "allow voluntary prayer in the public schools," and 84 percent of Protestants in 1983 said they would vote for the amendment. Greatest support came from the Baptists, and the smallest percent of school prayer advocates were the Methodists, 82 percent of whom favored the amendment.

Two years later, another Gallup Poll showed a drop in support for school prayer to 69 percent of all Americans, but 73 percent of Protestants continued to favor prayer. . . . [In fact,] a 1988 poll showed 59 percent of all Americans and *69 percent* of Protestant ministers in favor of prayer at public school athletic events. . . .

The results of a 1988 poll on church-state issues . . . demonstrated that 80 percent of the public would permit the government to display a crèche during the holiday season. . . . Once again, Protestant ministers supported this collaboration of church and state by a margin even greater than the public at large (85 percent). It is interesting, then, that in the year the survey was conducted, the [National Council of Churches] filed [a] brief in the Supreme Court arguing that publicly supported nativity scenes violate the Constitution's mandated separation of church and state. . . .

These . . . issues . . . point to sharp differences of opinion between the churches on the one hand and their members and clergy on the other. While the churches have shifted their positions on the church-state spectrum toward the strict separation side, their members—and perhaps most surprisingly, their ordained clergy—remain solidly within the "Christian nation" portion abandoned by the churches in the 1960s. . . .

ANNA GREENBERG

The Church and the Revitalization of Politics and Community[14]

Harvard professor Anna Greenberg has studied a variety of Protestant churches in Chicago to explore the role that churches play in connecting their members to political involvement, finding that churches can serve important roles in the political process while providing social services to their communities.

One typical Sunday morning, Father Jackson, the rector of a mainline African-American church, ended his sermon by making the weekly announcements. After reviewing the upcoming events, he asked his congregation for donations to fund scholarships for neighborhood children to participate in summer camp, noting simultaneously that the federal government had cut appropriations for poor teenagers. He then called attention to an announcement in the bulletin, asking members to "witness" for a living wage at a rally at City Hall. In this short interlude, Father Jackson simultaneously provided political information about the federal government's activities, engaged in institution building in a poor neighborhood, and provided his worshipers with an opportunity to make demands on local authorities. He demonstrated that the church can serve as an important political institution, generating ways to engage the political process and simultaneously providing social services through ministry in the face of declining government investment in poor neighborhoods. . . .

This article explores the role of religious institutions in generating civic engagement and their potential to connect people and political life through their networks of communal and political involvement. I argue that religious institutions have the potential to act as agents of political mobilization and as intermediaries between the individual and the state. Churches occupy this position because they are political institutions, serving as sources of political information, opportunities, resources, and incentives to engage the political process. At the same time, religious institutions are connected in important ways to the local community and the state, which makes them important locations of political empowerment. Churches create shared space for community groups and provide services for the disadvantaged, reaching beyond the immediate needs of the congregation. They bolster these services through partnerships with state agencies, which in turn both creates opportunities to influence public policy and to make demands upon the state. . . .

I use data collected during extensive field research in Protestant churches in Chicago, Illinois. These data are based on in-depth interviews and observation from participation in a variety of worship services and activities at eight churches across racial and theological traditions. The sample includes two white evangelical churches, three black evangelical churches, two white mainline churches, and one black mainline church. All respondents are Protestant women. . . .

Building Civic Engagement and Connection to Community

Ministerial Communication

The ministers in this study strongly believe in the importance of providing political information to their congregations, because in their view Christians have an important perspective to bring to political life. The ministers are disgusted with the state of political life, and for evangelicals in particular there is a strong belief in the embattled status of Christians in the public sphere. To rectify this situation, expressing a political voice is framed as part of the responsibilities of religious leaders and part of the requirements of living a Christian life. . . .

These ministers back up these beliefs by including political material in their sermons, giving political groups access to their congregations, and advertising political opportunities. Most frequently, leaders encourage members to perform their civic duty, for instance, by reminding them of impending elections. Political communication often stops here, however, as partisan and ideological politics are deemed inappropriate in the religious setting.

White evangelical leaders, however, circumvent opposition to excessively partisan politics by providing political information indirectly. Both white evangelical churches in the study allow conservative groups to distribute candidate score cards to their congregations during election season, though they stop short of telling people to vote for particular candidates. One evangelical church allowed an anti-abortion activist to conduct a teach-in at Sunday Morning Bible study and post relevant literature in the back of the chapel. The Illinois Citizens for Life organization leaves brochures in the back of the sanctuary that describe opportunities for political action, like letter writing, candidate information, and citizen lobbying trips to Springfield and Washington. Both evangelical churches in the study publicized additional anti-abortion activities, like the Evangelical Day of Life and fundraising walkathons for clinics.

In the black church, the partisan biases are more transparent, as the clergy frequently permit candidates to speak to congregations during services and strongly encourage political and community involvement. Support for political activity in the black church is widespread, usually uncontroversial, and important to Democratic party politics. Three of the four black churches in this sample have important ties to the Democratic party, either informally (candidate visits) or formally (overlapping organizational membership). At one large evangelical church, the co-pastors have strong connections to the Democratic party. . . . The imperative to engage politics in this church is explicit; the assistant pastor of this church admonishes every Sunday, "everyone in this congregation will give their tithe, will find a job, and will vote." The pastor of another evangelical church ran for alderman (though he lost to the machine) and rallied his congregation in support of a local African-American woman running for judge. Father Jackson, from the opening passage, makes sure all of his congregational members are registered to vote, and he served on the Board of Education.

White mainline churches are less politically engaged, though they certainly encourage performance of civic duty. One mainline church serves as a polling site, and members of both mainline churches in the study freely sign petitions at church to get candidates on the ballot. The Golden Fellowship at the more moderate mainline church hosts candidates during election season, though the pastor would never permit partisan discussion during worship services. But mainline white Protestantism has trouble grappling with political issues in church, in part because the leaders tend to be more ideologically committed and polarized than their members. As one mainline pastor explains: "I have a feeling that over the years, I've kind of watched, and I think there are probably some of the clergy who may be a little more liberal, more aware of some of the social issues than some of the parishioners are." This point is made graphically by some members of the more liberal mainline church, who complain about their pastor's extensive attention during worship services to issues like AIDS and prostitution.

Members' Voices

The attempts to make the linkage between religious and political goals are reflected in church members' orientation toward participation in politics. One white evangelical woman argues that Christian voices need to be heard in the public debate, at least in a "civil way." "We need to take an active part. Speak in that way. I'm not saying, like even the abortionists and the pro-lifers, some of the things they do is too strong, you know burning buildings, that's wrong too. You know, I don't think God intended, but there's things that we can do that need to be part of politics to voice our opinions, not by burning buildings, but do it in a civil way."

She also takes it upon herself to distribute mock letters or petitions against abortion that she finds in religious publications. One of her compatriots sees churches and religious individuals injecting certain sorts of values into political decision making: "I don't see how they cannot be involved in some ways, because it's the people making decisions. And if the church is not involved in those decisions, then I think they're not doing their part. I don't think they should get out and picket or, have riots and things when things are not going the way they want them to. But I think they should be involved in politics."

In the black church, community outreach efforts include both political and social action. A lay leader at a black evangelical church understands the ministry of Jesus Christ as fundamentally political and requires his followers to take on the same mission:

> I think that churches should be the light, wherever there is darkness in the community. And that means political, social, educational, I think the church should be there, being the light. . . . *Jesus was political.* And here at our church, we're so political, we expect that we will have politicians come, and we let them sit in our service, they get up and speak in the pulpit. They will sit on the pulpit and people say, OOHH! But we believe that that's what Jesus did. Jesus did it.

Another African-American evangelical woman argues that a religious commitment requires political involvement: "You can't grow [in] Him, if He's going to just say 'Well, I'm going to just concentrate on you. That's it.' And I don't think that's, if

Jesus's disciples did that, we wouldn't have Christianity today. And *I think they came into politics* and they came into all kind of areas." The political involvement of churches and religious people, as they understand it, would change the nature of politics. A member of the black mainline church thinks that the church should be an "example," arguing that if religious institutions were involved in politics, there would be fewer "problems." "You can't isolate yourself. You have to know what's going on. And if we had more involvement in the church, of the churches, we probably wouldn't have the problems we're having today. You know, in a positive role. Someone must get into office and get our hands dirty too. You're not an example then."

The disparity between the elite and the laity in mainline white Protestantism, however, is evident as members talk about the role of politics in church. They support community outreach through charity and ministry but object to partisan appeals in church. One member of the liberal mainline church thinks that religious values should influence political beliefs and priorities, but churches should eschew attempts to influence members' decisions:

> I don't like the idea. I'm in full agreement with the separation of church and state. I think they've gone a little bit far in some instances, but I do hold onto that as a tenet. I do believe that the church should have an impact on people's beliefs in political life and the way we are meant to go. That there's morals and ethics, and Lord knows, we all need help. And every political party. We should be striving for personal life, but also life in the community. But I don't believe, and more churches are doing it, they are telling people how to vote.

A member of the moderate mainline church is more emphatic: "[Should churches be involved in politics?] No. Not at all. Because I think everybody has their own ideas why they are voting for who and I don't . . . think that the church should get involved in that." On the other hand, these women do not shirk their civic duty; they vote at the same rates as other women in the sample, and they strongly believe in a compassionate orientation toward others through community outreach. The differences between mainline women and African-American women rest in a different conception of politics. Unlike African-American women, mainline women separate community outreach from political action, even if these activities have an implicit political component.

In sum, integration into religious institutions has a strong effect on an individual's propensity to get involved in politics. Leaders want their members to express their political voices, and congregational members believe that their voices can improve the political debate. To this end, leaders provide information and opportunities to engage the political process, even if this encouragement is limited to the fulfillment of civic duty. Empirically, this political exhortation is related to a variety of measures of political engagement and participation. The religiously involved vote at rates higher than the national average, regularly write letters to government officials, frequently belong to political organizations, and less frequently engage in collective action. It is fair to argue that religious participation creates an investment in the political process.

Church and Community in the Polity

These findings suggest that church involvement enhances individual engagement with the political process, as members acquire political information, resources, and opportunities to participate in politics. In isolation, however, the potential for building social capital and increasing political connectedness remains unrealized. Churches rarely sponsor political activity or direct action against the state. Rather, churches make the strongest connection to political life through the networks that religious institutions are embedded in and that they create through community outreach. Churches are important providers of social services and suppliers of space for community activity. In both of these capacities, religious institutions reach noncongregational members, empower community groups, and interact with state agencies. This activity is important for the political life of the congregation internally, but it also creates opportunities to influence policy making about important social problems.

There are approximately 300,000 congregations in the continental United States. Their most important function, of course, is religious ministry and education. But an overwhelming majority also provides some sort of community service, ranging from food pantries to arts education to health clinics. According to the Independent Sector's national survey of religious institutions, congregations engage in a broad range of activities—human services (87 percent, for example, meal services), international outreach (79 percent, refugee programs), public or societal benefit (70 percent, community development), health (68 percent, institutional care), arts (43 percent), culture and education (38 percent), and environmental improvement (27 percent).

These services and activities are made available beyond the church walls. A study of the activities of urban congregations recently released by the Partners for Sacred Places found widespread commitment to providing social services to the larger community. In its survey of 113 urban congregations in older buildings, Partners for Sacred Places found that 91 percent offer community services and that on average each congregation supports or houses at least four programs. A startling 81 percent of beneficiaries of these programs are not members of the congregations. Religious institutions open up space, moreover, to community and neighborhood groups. The Sacred Places study found that 45 percent of urban congregations share their space with other groups, frequently contributing funding and in-kind support (for example, heating). The Independent Sector survey found evidence of even greater support for the larger community, with 60 percent of their sample making space available for use by outside groups one day a week or more and 13 percent making their space available every day of the week.

Churches will play an even greater role in communities as the state institutionalizes its relationships with religious organizations in a number of areas, like housing and welfare. For instance, former Housing and Urban Development (HUD) Secretary Henry Cisneros created a program within HUD's Special Actions Office called the Religious Organizations Initiative to "provide extensive outreach to the faith community." In his report, *Higher Ground* (1996), Cisneros argues that not only are faith-based, community organizations central to developing affordable, decent housing, but that they should do so in partnership with government. This relationship, he argues, must be based on local assessment of needs and development of innovative solutions, which the government can then support. . . .

Similarly, the Charitable Choice provision embedded in the 1996 Personal Responsibility and Work Opportunity Reconciliation Act (or welfare reform), which allows religious organizations to provide welfare services with block grant money from state authorities, involves churches at the front end of policy making. For instance, in Sacramento, pastors and other clergy formed the Interfaith Service Bureau, which works with the Sacramento County Department of Human Assistance, to develop day care and job training programs. As the county's community development manager said, "Government can't do it on its own. There's no way."

This provision also allows churches and other congregations to compete for government contracts, generating incentives for religious initiative in this area. For instance, in Texas, one of the first states to take advantage of the Charitable Choice provisions, Governor George W. Bush has introduced legislation to allow religious organizations to participate in state-funded services. Governor Bush envisions aggressive competition among churches for welfare checks. As he puts it: "I envision a new welfare system, an energized, competitive program where a person who needs help would get a debit card, redeemable not just at a government agency, but at the Salvation Army or a church day-care facility.". . .

Churches in the study did take advantage of state resources to fund out-reach efforts, though these efforts are largely restricted to the black churches. One black evangelical church, for instance, built low-income transitional housing for women with children in partnership with HUD, as well as other state and local agencies. Another black church runs a large after-school program for area residents and church members, funded in part by the Board of Education. It is too early, however, to gauge if Charitable Choice will have an impact on the way churches deliver community services or how it will influence their relationships with the state. There is no question, however, that these provisions can change the relationship of churches to public policy making as they bring congregations into consultation with the state about important social and economic problems. . . .

Religion and Governmental Activity

McGowan v. Maryland (1961)[15]

In the nation's early history, state statutes often mandated various kinds of religious observances. James Madison, for example, introduced a bill in Virginia (originally drafted by Thomas Jefferson) that would punish "Sabbath-breakers." Similar laws have remained on the books of many states, and the Supreme Court in *McGowan* v. *Maryland* was faced with the issue of whether Sunday closing laws are an unconstitutional establishment of religion.

Mr. Chief Justice Warren Delivered the Opinion of the Court.

The issues in this case concern the constitutional validity of Maryland criminal statutes, commonly known as Sunday Closing Laws or Sunday Blue Laws. These statutes . . . generally proscribe all labor, business and other commercial activities on Sunday. . . .

Appellants are seven employees of a large discount department store located on a high-way in Anne Arundel County, Maryland. They were indicted for the Sunday sale of a three-ring loose-leaf binder, a can of floor wax, a stapler and staples, and a toy submarine in violation of Md. Ann. Code, Art. 27, § 521. Generally, this section prohibited, throughout the State, the Sunday sale of all merchandise except the retail sale of tobacco products, confectioneries, milk, bread, fruits, gasoline, oils, greases, drugs and medicines, and newspapers and periodicals. . . .

The essence of appellants' "establishment" argument is that Sunday is the Sabbath day of the predominant Christian sects; that the purpose of the enforced stoppage of labor on that day is to facilitate and encourage church attendance; that the purpose of setting Sunday as a day of universal rest is to induce people with no religion or people with marginal religious beliefs to join the predominant Christian sects; that the purpose of the atmosphere of tranquillity created by Sunday closing is to aid the conduct of church services and religious observance of the sacred day. In substantiating their "establishment" argument, appellants rely on the wording of the present Maryland statutes, on earlier versions of the current Sunday laws and on prior judicial characterizations of these laws by the Maryland Court of Appeals. Although only the constitutionality of § 521, the section under which appellants have been convicted, is immediately before us in this litigation, inquiry into the history of Sunday Closing Laws in our country, in addition to an examination of the Maryland Sunday closing statutes in their entirety and of their history, is relevant to the decision of whether the Maryland Sunday law in question is one respecting an establishment of religion. There is no dispute that the original laws which dealt with Sunday labor were motivated by religious forces. But what we must decide is whether present Sunday legislation, having undergone extensive changes from the earliest forms, still retains its religious character.

Sunday Closing Laws go far back into American history, having been brought to the colonies with a background of English legislation dating to the thirteenth century. In 1237, Henry III forbade the frequenting of markets on Sunday; the Sunday showing of wools at the staple was banned by Edward III in 1354; in 1409, Henry IV prohibited the playing of unlawful games on Sunday [etc.] . . . The law of the colonies to the time of the Revolution and the basis of the Sunday laws in the States was 29 Charles II, c. 7 (1677). It provided, in part:

> For the better observation and keeping holy the Lord's day, commonly called Sunday: be it enacted . . . that all the laws enacted and in force concerning the observation of the day, *and repairing to the church thereon,* be carefully put in execution; and that all and every person and persons whatsoever shall upon every Lord's day apply themselves to the observation of the same, by exercising themselves thereon in the duties of piety and true religion, publicly and privately; and that no tradesman, artificer, workman, laborer, or other person whatsoever, *shall do or exercise any worldly labor or business or work* of their ordinary callings upon the Lord's day, or any part thereof (works of necessity and charity only excepted). . . .

Observation of the above language, and of that of the prior mandates, reveals clearly that the English Sunday legislation was in aid of the established church.

The American colonial Sunday restrictions arose soon after settlement. Starting in 1650, the Plymouth Colony proscribed servile work, unnecessary travelling, sports, and the sale of alcoholic beverages on the Lord's day and enacted laws concerning church attendance. The Massachusetts Bay Colony and the Connecticut and New Haven Colonies enacted similar prohibitions, some even earlier in the seventeenth century. The religious orientation of the colonial statutes was equally apparent. For example, a 1629 Massachusetts Bay instruction began, "And to the end the Sabbath may be celebrated in a religious manner. . . ." These laws persevered after the Revolution and, at about the time of the First Amendment's adoption, each of the colonies had laws of some sort restricting Sunday labor. . . .

But, despite the strong religious origin of these laws, beginning before the eighteenth century, nonreligious arguments for Sunday closing began to be heard more distinctly and the statutes began to lose some of their totally religious flavor. In the middle 1700s, Blackstone wrote, "[T]he keeping one day in the seven holy, as a time of relaxation and refreshment as well as for public worship, is of admirable service to a state considered merely as a civil institution. It humanizes, by the help of conversation and society, the manners of the lower classes; which would otherwise degenerate into a sordid ferocity and savage selfishness of spirit; it enables the industrious workman to pursue his occupation in the ensuing week with health and cheerfulness.". . . The preamble to a 1679 Rhode Island enactment stated that the reason for the ban on Sunday employment was that "persons being evill minded, have presumed to employ in servile labor, more than necessity requireth, their servants. . . ." The New York law of 1788 omitted the term "Lord's day" and substituted "the first day of the week commonly called Sunday." Similar changes marked the Maryland statutes, discussed below. With the advent of the First Amendment, the colonial provisions requiring church attendance were soon repealed. . . .

More recently, further secular justifications have been advanced for making Sunday a day of rest, a day when people may recover from the labors of the week just passed and may physically and mentally prepare for the week's work to come. In England, during the First World War, a committee investigating the health conditions of munitions workers reported that "if the maximum output is to be secured and maintained for any length of time, a weekly period of rest must be allowed. . . . On economic and social grounds alike this weekly period of rest is best provided on Sunday."

. . .

Throughout the years, state legislatures have modified, deleted from and added to their Sunday statutes. Almost every State in our country presently has some type of Sunday regulation and over forty possess a relatively comprehensive system. Thus have Sunday laws evolved from the wholly religious sanctions that originally were enacted. . . .

In light of the evolution of our Sunday Closing Laws through the centuries, and of their more or less recent emphasis upon secular considerations, it is not difficult to discern that as presently written and administered, most of them, at least, are of a secular rather than of a religious character, and that presently they bear no relationship to establishment of religion as those words are used in the Constitution of the United States.

Throughout this century and longer, both the federal and state governments have oriented their activities very largely toward improvement of the health, safety, recreation and general well-being of our citizens. Numerous laws affecting public health, safety factors in industry, laws affecting hours and conditions of labor of women and children, week-end diversion at parks and beaches, and cultural activities of various kinds, now point the way toward the good life for all. Sunday Closing Laws, like those before us, have become part and parcel of this great governmental concern wholly apart from their original purposes or connotations. The present purpose and effect of most of them is to provide a uniform day of rest for all citizens; the fact that this day is Sunday, a day of particular significance for the dominant Christian sects, does not bar the State from achieving its secular goals. To say that the States cannot prescribe Sunday as a day of rest for these purposes solely because centuries ago such laws had their genesis in religion would give a constitutional interpretation of hostility to the public welfare rather than one of mere separation of church and State.

We now reach the Maryland statutes under review. The title of the major series of sections of the Maryland Code dealing with Sunday closing—Art. 27, §§ 492–534C—is "Sabbath Breaking"; § 492 proscribes work or bodily labor on the "Lord's day," and forbids persons to "profane the Lord's day" by gaming, fishing et cetera; § 522 refers to Sunday as the "Sabbath day." As has been mentioned above, many of the exempted Sunday activities in the various localities of the State may only be conducted during the afternoon and late evening; most Christian church services, of course, are held on Sunday morning and early Sunday evening. Finally, as previously noted, certain localities do not permit the allowed Sunday activities to be carried on within one hundred yards of any church where religious services are being held. This is the totality of the evidence of religious purpose which may be gleaned from the face of the present statute and from its operative effect.

The predecessors of the existing Maryland Sunday laws are undeniably religious in origin. . . .

Considering the language and operative effect of the current statutes, we no longer find the blanket prohibition against Sunday work or bodily labor. To the contrary, we find that § 521 of Art. 27, the section which appellants violated, permits the Sunday sale of tobaccos and sweets and a long list of sundry articles which we have enumerated above; we find that § 509 of Art. 27 permits the Sunday operation of bathing beaches, amusement parks and similar facilities; we find that Art. 2B, § 28, permits the Sunday sale of alcoholic beverages, products strictly forbidden by predecessor statutes; we are told that Anne Arundel County allows Sunday bingo and the Sunday playing of pin ball machines and slot machines, activities generally condemned by prior Maryland Sunday legislation. Certainly, these are not works of charity or necessity. Section 521's current stipulation that shops with only one employee may remain open on Sunday does not coincide with a religious purpose. These provisions, along with those which permit various sports and entertainments on Sunday, seem clearly to be fashioned for the purpose of providing a Sunday atmosphere of recreation, cheerfulness, repose and enjoyment. Coupled with the general proscription against other types of work, we believe that the air of the day is one of relaxation rather than one of religion. . . .

Marsh v. Chambers (1983)[16]

Colonial legislatures often commenced with a prayer, and the Continental Congress took up the practice in 1774. The tradition continues in the United States Congress and many state legislative halls. In *Marsh* v. *Chambers* the Supreme Court discussed the constitutionality of having a chaplain paid with tax dollars deliver an invocation prior to each session of the Nebraska legislature. This case also gave the Court the opportunity to elaborate further on its view of the concept of "neutrality" embodied in the First Amendment.

Chief Justice Burger delivered the opinion of the Court.

The Nebraska Legislature begins each of its sessions with a prayer offered by a chaplain who is chosen biennially by the Executive Board of the Legislative Council and paid out of public funds. Robert E. Palmer, a Presbyterian minister, has served as chaplain since 1965 at a salary of $319.75 per month for each month the legislature is in session. . . .

The opening of sessions of legislative and other deliberative public bodies with prayer is deeply embedded in the history and tradition of this country. From colonial times through the founding of the Republic and ever since, the practice of legislative prayer has coexisted with the principles of disestablishment and religious freedom. In the very courtrooms in which the United States District Judge and later three Circuit Judges heard and decided this case, the proceedings opened with an announcement that concluded, "God save the United States and this Honorable Court." The same invocation occurs at all sessions of this Court.

The tradition in many of the Colonies was, of course, linked to an established church, but the Continental Congress, beginning in 1774, adopted the traditional procedure of opening its sessions with a prayer offered by a paid chaplain. . . . Although prayers were not offered during the Constitutional Convention, the First Congress, as one of its early items of business, adopted the policy of selecting a chaplain to open each session with prayer. Thus, on April 7, 1789, the Senate appointed a committee "to take under consideration the manner of electing Chaplains." On April 9, 1789, a similar committee was appointed by the House of Representatives. On April 25, 1789, the Senate elected its first chaplain, [and] the House followed suit on May 1, 1789. A statute providing for the payment of these chaplains was enacted into law on September 22, 1789.

On September 25, 1789, three days after Congress authorized the appointment of paid chaplains, final agreement was reached on the language of the Bill of Rights. Clearly the men who wrote the First Amendment Religion Clause did not view paid legislative chaplains and opening prayers as a violation of that Amendment, for the practice of opening sessions with prayer has continued without interruption ever since that early session of Congress. It has also been followed consistently in most of the states, including Nebraska, where the institution of opening legislative sessions with prayer was adopted even before the State attained statehood. . . .

Standing alone, historical patterns cannot justify contemporary violations of constitutional guarantees, but there is far more here than simply historical patterns. . . .

No more is Nebraska's practice of over a century, consistent with two centuries of national practice, to be cast aside. It can hardly be thought that in the same week Members of the First Congress voted to appoint and to pay a chaplain for each House and also voted to approve the draft of the First Amendment for submission to the states, they intended the Establishment Clause of the Amendment to forbid what they had just declared acceptable. In applying the First Amendment to the states through the Fourteenth Amendment, it would be incongruous to interpret that Clause as imposing more stringent First Amendment limits on the states than the draftsmen imposed on the Federal Government.

This unique history leads us to accept the interpretation of the First Amendment draftsmen who saw no real threat to the Establishment Clause arising from a practice of prayer similar to that now challenged. We conclude that legislative prayer presents no more potential for establishment than the provision of school transportation . . . beneficial grants for higher education . . . or tax exemptions for religious organizations. . . .

Respondent . . . argues that we should not rely too heavily on "the advice of the Founding Fathers" because the messages of history often tend to be ambiguous and not relevant to a society far more heterogeneous than that of the Framers. . . . Respondent also points out that John Jay and John Rutledge opposed the motion to begin the first session of the Continental Congress with prayer. . . .

We do not agree that evidence of opposition to a measure weakens the force of the historical argument; indeed it infuses it with power by demonstrating that the subject was considered carefully and the action not taken thoughtlessly, by force of long tradition and without regard to the problems posed by a pluralistic society. Jay and Rutledge specifically grounded their objection on the fact that the delegates to the Congress "were so divided in religious sentiments . . . that [they] could not join in the same act of worship." Their objection was met by Samuel Adams, who stated that "he was no bigot, and could hear a prayer from a gentleman of piety and virtue, who was at the same time a friend to his country.". . .

This interchange emphasizes that the delegates did not consider opening prayers as a proselytizing activity or as symbolically placing the government's "official seal of approval on one religious view." Rather, the Founding Fathers looked at invocations as "conduct whose . . . effect . . . harmonize[d] with the tenets of some or all religions." The Establishment Clause does not always bar a state from regulating conduct simply because it "harmonizes with religious canons." Here, the individual claiming injury by the practice is an adult, presumably not readily susceptible to "religious indoctrination."

In light of the unambiguous and unbroken history of more than 200 years, there can be no doubt that the practice of opening legislative sessions with prayer has become part of the fabric of our society. To invoke Divine guidance on a public body entrusted with making the laws is not, in these circumstances, an "establishment" of religion or a step toward establishment; it is simply a tolerable acknowledgment of beliefs widely held among the people of this country. As Justice Douglas observed, "[w]e are a religious people whose institutions presuppose a Supreme Being." . . .

* * *

We turn then to the question of whether any features of the Nebraska practice violate the Establishment Clause. Beyond the bare fact that a prayer is offered, three points have been made: first, that a clergyman of only one denomination—Presbyterian—has been selected for 16 years; second, that the chaplain is paid at public expense; and third, that the prayers are in the Judeo-Christian tradition. Weighed against the historical background, these factors do not serve to invalidate Nebraska's practice.

The Court of Appeals was concerned that Palmer's long tenure has the effect of giving preference to his religious views. We cannot, any more than Members of the Congresses of this century, perceive any suggestion that choosing a clergyman of one denomination advances the beliefs of a particular church. To the contrary, the evidence indicates that Palmer was reappointed because his performance and personal qualities were acceptable to the body appointing him. Palmer was not the only clergyman heard by the legislature; guest chaplains have officiated at the request of various legislators and as substitutes during Palmer's absences. Absent proof that the chaplain's reappointment stemmed from an impermissible motive, we conclude that his long tenure does not in itself conflict with the Establishment Clause.

Nor is the compensation of the chaplain from public funds a reason to invalidate the Nebraska Legislature's chaplaincy; remuneration is grounded in historic practice initiated, as we noted earlier, by the same Congress that drafted the Establishment Clause of the First Amendment. . . . The content of the prayer is not of concern to judges where, as here, there is no indication that the prayer opportunity has been exploited to proselytize or advance any one, or to disparage any other, faith or belief. That being so, it is not for us to embark on a sensitive evaluation or to parse the content of a particular prayer. . . .

The unbroken practice for two centuries in the National Congress, for more than a century in Nebraska and in many other states, gives abundant assurance that there is no real threat "while this Court sits." . . .

Justice Brennan, with whom Justice Marshall joins, dissenting.

The Court today has written a narrow and, on the whole, careful opinion. In effect, the Court holds that officially sponsored legislative prayer, primarily on account of its "unique history," is generally exempted from the First Amendment's prohibition against "an establishment of religion." The Court's . . . limited rationale should pose little threat to the overall fate of the Establishment Clause. . . .

The Court makes no pretense of subjecting Nebraska's practice of legislative prayer to any of the formal "tests" that have traditionally structured our inquiry under the Establishment Clause. That it fails to do so is, in a sense, a good thing, for it simply confirms that the Court is carving out an exception to the Establishment Clause rather than reshaping Establishment Clause doctrine to accommodate legislative prayer. For my purposes, however, I must begin by demonstrating what should be obvious: that, if the Court were to judge legislative prayer through the unsentimental eye of our settled doctrine, it would have to strike it down as a clear violation of the Establishment Clause. . . .

That the "purpose" of legislative prayer is pre-eminently religious rather than secular seems to me to be self-evident. "To invoke Divine guidance on a public body entrusted with making the laws," is nothing but a religious act. Moreover, whatever secular functions legislative prayer might play—formally opening the legislative session, getting the members of the body to quiet down, and imbuing them with a sense of seriousness and high purpose—could so plainly be performed in a purely nonreligious fashion that to claim a secular purpose for the prayer is an insult to the perfectly honorable individuals who instituted and continue the practice.

The "primary effect" of legislative prayer is also clearly religious. As we said in the context of officially sponsored prayers in the public schools, "prescribing a particular form of religious worship," even if the individuals involved have the choice not to participate, places "indirect coercive pressure upon religious minorities to conform to the prevailing officially approved religion. . . ." More importantly, invocations in Nebraska's legislative halls explicitly link religious belief and observance to the power and prestige of the State. "[T]he mere appearance of a joint exercise of legislative authority by Church and State provides a significant symbolic benefit to religion in the minds of some by reason of the power conferred."

Finally, there can be no doubt that the practice of legislative prayer leads to excessive "entanglement" between the State and religion. . . . In the case of legislative prayer, the process of choosing a "suitable" chaplain, whether on a permanent or rotating basis, and insuring that the chaplain limits himself or herself to "suitable" prayers, involves precisely the sort of supervision that agencies of government should if at all possible avoid.

[E]xcessive "entanglement" might [also] arise out of "the divisive political potential" of a state statute or program.

> Ordinarily political debate and division, however vigorous or even partisan, are normal and healthy manifestations of our democratic system of government, but political division along religious lines was one of the principal evils against which the First Amendment was intended to protect. The potential divisiveness of such conflict is a threat to the normal political process. . . .

The principles of "separation" and "neutrality" implicit in the Establishment Clause serve many purposes. Four of these are particularly relevant here.

The first, which is most closely related to the more general conceptions of liberty found in the remainder of the First Amendment, is to guarantee the individual right to conscience. The right to conscience, in the religious sphere, is not only implicated when the government engages in direct or indirect coercion. It is also implicated when the government requires individuals to support the practices of a faith with which they do not agree.

The second purpose of separation and neutrality is to keep the state from interfering in the essential autonomy of religious life, either by taking upon itself the decision of religious issues, or by unduly involving itself in the supervision of religious institutions or officials.

The third purpose of separation and neutrality is to prevent the trivialization and degradation of religion by too close an attachment to the organs of government. The Establishment Clause "stands as an expression of principle on the part of the Founders of our Constitution that religion is too personal, too sacred, too holy, to permit its 'unhallowed perversion' by a civil magistrate."

Finally, the principles of separation and neutrality help assure that essentially religious issues, precisely because of their importance and sensitivity, not become the occasion for battle in the political arena. . . . With regard to most issues, the government may be influenced by partisan argument and may act as a partisan itself. In each case, there will be winners and losers in the political battle, and the losers' most common recourse is the right to dissent and the right to fight the battle again another day. With regard to matters that are essentially religious, however, the Establishment Clause seeks that there should be no political battles, and that no American should at any point feel alienated from his government because that government has declared or acted upon some "official" or "authorized" point of view on a matter of religion. . . .

Legislative prayer clearly violates the principles of neutrality and separation that are embedded within the Establishment Clause. . . . It intrudes on the right to conscience by forcing some legislators either to participate in a "prayer opportunity," with which they are in basic disagreement, or to make their disagreement a matter of public comment by declining to participate. It forces all residents of the State to support a religious exercise that may be contrary to their own beliefs. It requires the State to commit itself on fundamental theological issues. It has the potential for degrading religion by allowing a religious call to worship to be intermeshed with a secular call to order. And it injects religion into the political sphere by creating the potential that each and every selection of a chaplain, or consideration of a particular prayer, or even reconsideration of the practice itself, will provoke a political battle along religious lines and ultimately alienate some religiously identified group of citizens. . . .

Lynch v. Donnelly (1984)[17]

Christmas is a holiday laden with both sacred and secular meanings. In *Lynch* v. *Donnelly,* residents of Pawtucket, Rhode Island, challenged a traditional practice involving a "Seasons Greetings" display, sponsored by the city on private property, that included a nativity scene along with secular symbols of the holiday season.

Chief Justice Burger delivered the opinion of the Court.

* * *

Each year, in cooperation with the downtown retail merchants' association, the city of Pawtucket, R. I., erects a Christmas display as part of its observance of the Christmas holiday season. The display is situated in a park owned by a nonprofit organization and located in the heart of the shopping district. The display is essentially like those to be found in hundreds of towns or cities across the Nation—often on public grounds—during the Christmas season. The Pawtucket display comprises many of the figures and decorations traditionally associated with Christmas, including, among other things, a Santa Claus house, reindeer pulling Santa's sleigh, candy-striped poles, a Christmas tree, carolers, cutout figures representing such characters as a clown, an elephant, and a teddy bear, hundreds of colored lights, a large banner that reads "SEASONS GREETINGS," and the crèche at issue here. All components of this display are owned by the city.

The crèche, which has been included in the display for 40 or more years, consists of the traditional figures, including the Infant Jesus, Mary and Joseph, angels, shepherds, kings, and animals, all ranging in height from "5" to 5'". In 1973, when the present crèche was acquired, it cost the city $1,365; it now is valued at $200. The erection and dismantling of the crèche costs the city about $20 per year; nominal expenses are incurred in lighting the crèche. No money has been expended on its maintenance for the past 10 years. . . .

In every Establishment Clause case, we must reconcile the inescapable tension between the objective of preventing unnecessary intrusion of either the church or the state upon the other, and the reality that, as the Court has so often noted, total separation of the two is not possible.

The Court has sometimes described the Religion Clauses as erecting a "wall" between church and state. The concept of a "wall" of separation is a useful figure of speech probably deriving from views of Thomas Jefferson. The metaphor has served as a reminder that the Establishment Clause forbids an established church or anything approaching it. But the metaphor itself is not a wholly accurate description of the practical aspects of the relationship that in fact exists between church and state.

No significant segment of our society and no institution within it can exist in a vacuum or in total or absolute isolation from all the other parts, much less from government. "It has never been thought either possible or desirable to enforce a regime of total separation. . . ." Nor does the Constitution require complete separation of church and state; it affirmatively mandates accommodation, not merely tolerance, of all religions, and forbids hostility toward any. Anything less would require the "callous indifference" we have said was never intended by the Establishment Clause. Indeed, we have observed, such hostility would bring us into "war with our national tradition as embodied in the First Amendment's guaranty of the free exercise of religion."

The Court's interpretation of the Establishment Clause has comported with what history reveals was the contemporaneous understanding of its guarantees. A significant example of the contemporaneous understanding of that Clause is found in the events of the first week of the First Session of the First Congress in 1789. In the very week that Congress approved the Establishment Clause as part of the Bill of Rights for submission to the states, it enacted legislation providing for paid chaplains for the House and Senate. . . .

The interpretation of the Establishment Clause by Congress in 1789 takes on special significance in light of the Court's emphasis that the First Congress

> was a Congress whose constitutional decisions have always been regarded, as they should be regarded, as of the greatest weight in the interpretation of that fundamental instrument.

It is clear that neither the 17 draftsmen of the Constitution who were Members of the First Congress, nor the Congress of 1789, saw any establishment problem in the employment of congressional Chaplains to offer daily prayers in the Congress, a practice that has continued for nearly two centuries. It would be difficult to identify a more striking example of the accommodation of religious belief intended by the Framers.

There is an unbroken history of official acknowledgment by all three branches of government of the role of religion in American life from at least 1789. . . .

Our history is replete with official references to the value and invocation of Divine guidance in deliberations and pronouncements of the Founding Fathers and contemporary leaders. Beginning in the early colonial period long before Independence, a day of Thanksgiving was celebrated as a religious holiday to give thanks for the bounties of Nature as gifts from God. President Washington and his successors proclaimed Thanksgiving, with all its religious overtones, a day of national celebration and Congress made it a National Holiday more than a century ago. That holiday has not lost its theme of expressing thanks for Divine aid any more than has Christmas lost its religious significance.

Executive Orders and other official announcements of Presidents and of the Congress have proclaimed both Christmas and Thanksgiving National Holidays in religious terms. And, by Acts of Congress, it has long been the practice that federal employees are released from duties on these National Holidays, while being paid from the same public revenues that provide the compensation of the Chaplains of the Senate and the House and the military services. Thus, it is clear that Government has long recognized—indeed it has subsidized—holidays with religious significance.

Other examples of reference to our religious heritage are found in the statutorily prescribed national motto "In God We Trust," which Congress and the President mandated for our currency, and in the language "One nation under God," as part of the Pledge of Allegiance to the American flag. That pledge is recited by many thousands of public school children—and adults—every year.

Art galleries supported by public revenues display religious paintings of the 15th and 16th centuries, predominantly inspired by one religious faith. The National Gallery in Washington, maintained with Government support, for example, has long exhibited masterpieces with religious messages, notably the Last Supper, and paintings depicting the Birth of Christ, the Crucifixion, and the Resurrection, among many others with explicit Christian themes and messages. The very chamber in which oral arguments on this case were heard is decorated with a notable and permanent—not seasonal—symbol of religion: Moses with the Ten Commandments. Congress has long provided chapels in the Capitol for religious worship and meditation.

There are countless other illustrations of the Government's acknowledgment of our religious heritage and governmental sponsorship of graphic manifestations of that heritage. Congress has directed the President to proclaim a National Day of Prayer each year "on which [day] the people of the United States may turn to God in prayer and meditation at churches, in groups, and as individuals." Our Presidents have repeatedly issued such Proclamations. Presidential Proclamations and messages have also [been] issued to commemorate Jewish Heritage Week, and the Jewish High Holy Days. One cannot look at even this brief résumé without finding that our history is pervaded by expressions of religious beliefs. . . . Equally pervasive is the evidence of accommodation of all faiths and all forms of religious expression, and hostility toward none. . . .

* * *

This history may help explain why the Court consistently has declined to take a rigid, absolutist view of the Establishment Clause. We have refused "to construe the Religion Clauses with a literalness that would undermine the ultimate constitutional objective as *illuminated by history.*" In our modern, complex society, whose traditions and constitutional underpinnings rest on and encourage diversity and pluralism in all areas, an absolutist approach in applying the Establishment Clause is simplistic and has been uniformly rejected by the Court.

Rather than mechanically invalidating all governmental conduct or statutes that confer benefits or give special recognition to religion in general or to one faith—as an absolutist approach would dictate—the Court has scrutinized challenged legislation or official conduct to determine whether, in reality, it establishes a religion or religious faith, or tends to do so. . . .

In each case, the inquiry calls for line-drawing; no fixed, *per se* rule can be framed. The Establishment Clause . . . is not a precise, detailed provision in a legal code capable of ready application. The purpose of the Establishment Clause "was to state an objective, not to write a statute.". . .

In the line-drawing process we have often found it useful to inquire whether the challenged law or conduct has a secular purpose, whether its principal or primary effect is to advance or inhibit religion, and whether it creates an excessive entanglement of government with religion. But, we have repeatedly emphasized our unwillingness to be confined to any single test or criterion in this sensitive area. . . .

When viewed in the proper context of the Christmas Holiday season, it is apparent that, on this record, there is insufficient evidence to establish that the inclusion of the crèche is a purposeful or surreptitious effort to express some kind of subtle governmental advocacy of a particular religious message. In a pluralistic society a variety of motives and purposes are implicated. The city, like the Congresses and Presidents, however, has principally taken note of a significant historical religious event long celebrated in the Western World. The crèche in the display depicts the historical origins of this traditional event long recognized as a National Holiday. . . .

The narrow question is whether there is a secular purpose for Pawtucket's display of the crèche. The display is sponsored by the city to celebrate the Holiday and to depict the origins of that Holiday. These are legitimate secular purposes. . . .

Comparisons of the relative benefits to religion of different forms of governmental support are elusive and difficult to make. But to conclude that the primary effect of including the crèche is to advance religion in violation of the Establishment Clause would require that we view it as more beneficial to and more an endorsement of religion, for example, than expenditure of large sums of public money for textbooks supplied throughout the country to students attending church-sponsored schools; expenditure of public funds for transportation of students to church-sponsored schools; federal grants for college buildings of church-sponsored institutions of higher education combining secular and religious education; noncategorical grants to church-sponsored colleges and universities; and the tax exemptions for church properties. . . . It would also require that we view it as more of an endorsement of religion than . . . Sunday Closing Laws; the release program for religious training in *Zorach* . . . and the legislative prayers upheld in *Marsh*. . . .

We are unable to discern a greater aid to religion deriving from inclusion of the crèche than from these benefits and endorsements previously held not violative of the Establishment Clause. . . .

We are satisfied that the city has a secular purpose for including the crèche, that the city has not impermissibly advanced religion, and that including the crèche does not create excessive entanglement between religion and government. . . .

Of course the crèche is identified with one religious faith but no more so than the examples we have set out from prior cases in which we found no conflict with the Establishment Clause. . . . It would be ironic, however, if the inclusion of a single symbol of a particular historic religious event, as part of a celebration acknowledged in the Western World for 20 centuries, and in this country by the people, by the Executive Branch, by the Congress, and the courts for 2 centuries, would so "taint" the city's exhibit as to render it violative of the Establishment Clause. To forbid the use of this one passive symbol—the crèche—at the very time people are taking note of the season with Christmas hymns and carols in public schools and other public places, and while the Congress and legislatures open sessions with prayers by paid chaplains would be a stilted overreaction contrary to our history and to our holdings. If the presence of the crèche in this display violates the Establishment Clause, a host of other forms of taking official note of Christmas, and of our religious heritage, are equally offensive to the Constitution.

The Court has acknowledged that the "fears and political problems" that gave rise to the Religion Clauses in the 18th century are of far less concern today. We are unable to perceive the Archbishop of Canterbury, the Bishop of Rome, or other powerful religious leaders behind every public acknowledgment of the religious heritage long officially recognized by the three constitutional branches of government. Any notion that these symbols pose a real danger of establishment of a state church is far-fetched indeed. . . .

County of Allegheney v. American Civil Liberties Union (1989)[18]

The Supreme Court continued to deal with holiday displays in this 1989 case. The justices were sharply divided, and no one opinion was able to attract the votes of a majority of the justices. The role of religion in American history and culture is an important element of both Justice Blackmun's plurality opinion and the opinion of Justice Kennedy, who concurs with a part of the decision (allowing a menorah) but dissents from another portion (disallowing the display of a crèche).

Justice Blackmun announced the judgment of the Court. . . .

This litigation concerns the constitutionality of two recurring holiday displays located on public property in downtown Pittsburgh. The first is a crèche placed on the

Grand Staircase of the Allegheny County Courthouse. The second is a Chanukah menorah placed just outside the City-County Building, next to a Christmas tree and a sign saluting liberty. . . .

* * *

Since 1981, the county has permitted the Holy Name Society, a Roman Catholic group, to display a crèche in the county courthouse during the Christmas holiday season. . . . As observed in this Nation, Christmas has a secular, as well as a religious, dimension.

The crèche in the county court house, like other crèches, is a visual representation of the scene in the manger in Bethlehem shortly after the birth of Jesus, as described in the Gospels of Luke and Matthew. The crèche includes figures of the infant Jesus, Mary, Joseph, farm animals, shepherds, and wise men, all placed in or before a wooden representation of a manger, which has at its crest an angel bearing a banner that proclaims "Gloria in Excelsis Deo!"

During the 1986–1987 holiday season, the crèche was on display on the Grand Staircase from November 26 to January 9. . . . It had a wooden fence on three sides and bore a plaque stating: "This Display Donated by the Holy Name Society." Sometime during the week of December 2, the county placed red and white poinsettia plants around the fence. . . . The county also placed a small evergreen tree, decorated with a red bow, behind each of the two endposts of the fence. . . . These trees stood alongside the manger backdrop and were slightly shorter than it was. The angel thus was at the apex of the crèche display. Altogether, the crèche, the fence, the poinsettias, and the trees occupied a substantial amount of space on the Grand Staircase. No figures of Santa Claus or other decorations appeared on the Grand Staircase. . . .

* * *

The City-County Building is separate and a block removed from the county courthouse and, as the name implies, is jointly owned by the city of Pittsburgh and Allegheny County. . . .

For a number of years, the city has had a large Christmas tree under the middle arch outside the Grant Street entrance. Following this practice, city employees on November 17, 1986, erected a 45-foot tree under the middle arch and decorated it with lights and ornaments. . . . A few days later, the city placed at the foot of the tree a sign bearing the mayor's name and entitled "Salute to Liberty." Beneath the title, the sign stated:

> "During this holiday season, the city of Pittsburgh salutes liberty. Let these festive lights remind us that we are the keepers of the flame of liberty and our legacy of freedom.". . .

At least since 1982, the city has expanded its Grant Street holiday display to include a symbolic representation of Chanukah, an 8-day Jewish holiday that begins on the 25th day of the Jewish lunar month of Kislev. . . . The 25th of Kislev usually occurs in December, and thus Chanukah is the annual Jewish holiday that falls closest to Christmas Day each year. . . .

Chanukah, like Christmas, is a cultural event as well as a religious holiday. . . . Indeed, the Chanukah story always has had a political or national, as well as a religious, dimension: it tells of national heroism in addition to divine intervention. Also, Chanukah, like Christmas, is a winter holiday; according to some historians, it was associated in ancient times with the winter solstice. Just as some Americans celebrate Christmas without regard to its religious significance, some nonreligious American Jews celebrate Chanukah as an expression of ethnic identity, and "as a cultural or national event, rather than as a specifically religious event.". . .

On December 22 of the 1986 holiday season, the city placed at the Grant Street entrance to the City-County Building an 18-foot Chanukah menorah of an abstract tree-and-branch design. The menorah was placed next to the city's 45-foot Christmas tree, against one of the columns that supports the arch into which the tree was set. The menorah is owned by Chabad, a Jewish group, but is stored, erected, and removed each year by the city. . . .

* * *

. . .

In the course of adjudicating specific cases, this Court has come to understand the Establishment Clause to mean that government may not promote or affiliate itself with any religious doctrine or organization, may not discriminate among persons on the basis of their religious beliefs and practices, may not delegate a governmental power to a religious institution, and may not involve itself too deeply in such an institution's affairs. . . .

Our subsequent decisions further have refined the definition of governmental action that unconstitutionally advances religion. In recent years, we have paid particularly close attention to whether the challenged governmental practice either has the purpose or effect of "endorsing" religion, a concern that has long had a place in our Establishment Clause jurisprudence. . . .

Whether the key word is "endorsement," "favoritism," or "promotion," the essential principle remains the same. The Establishment Clause, at the very least, prohibits government from appearing to take a position on questions of religious belief or from "making adherence to a religion relevant in any way to a person's standing in the political community.". . .

* * *

We turn first to the county's crèche display. There is no doubt, of course, that the crèche itself is capable of communicating a religious message. . . . Indeed, the crèche in this lawsuit uses words, as well as the picture of the nativity scene, to make its religious meaning unmistakably clear. "Glory to God in the Highest!" says the angel in the crèche—Glory to God because of the birth of Jesus. This praise to God in Christian terms is indisputably religious—indeed sectarian—just as it is when said in the Gospel or in a church service.

Under the Court's holding in Lynch, the effect of a crèche display turns on its setting. Here, unlike in Lynch, nothing in the context of the display detracts from the crèche's religious message. The Lynch display composed a series of figures and objects, each group of which had its own focal point. Santa's house and his reindeer were objects of attention separate from the crèche, and had their specific visual story to tell. Similarly, whatever a "talking" wishing well may be, it obviously was a center of attention separate from the crèche. Here, in contrast, the crèche stands alone: it is the single element of the display on the Grand Staircase. . . .

Finally, the county argues that it is sufficient to validate the display of the crèche on the Grand Staircase that the display celebrates Christmas, and Christmas is a national holiday. This argument obviously proves too much. It would allow the celebration of the Eucharist inside a courthouse on Christmas Eve. While the county may have doubts about the constitutional status of celebrating the Eucharist inside the courthouse under the government's auspices, . . . this Court does not. The government may acknowledge Christmas as a cultural phenomenon, but under the First Amendment it may not observe it as a Christian holy day by suggesting that people praise God for the birth of Jesus. . . .

* * *

The display of the Chanukah menorah in front of the City-County Building may well present a closer constitutional question. The menorah, one must recognize, is a religious symbol: it serves to commemorate the miracle of the oil as described in the Talmud. But the menorah's message is not exclusively religious. The menorah is the primary visual symbol for a holiday that, like Christmas, has both religious and secular dimensions.

Moreover, the menorah here stands next to a Christmas tree and a sign saluting liberty. While no challenge has been made here to the display of the tree and the sign, their presence is obviously relevant in determining the effect of the menorah's display. The necessary result of placing a menorah next to a Christmas tree is to create an "overall holiday setting" that represents both Christmas and Chanukah—two holidays, not one. . . .

The mere fact that Pittsburgh displays symbols of both Christmas and Chanukah does not end the constitutional inquiry. If the city celebrates both Christmas and Chanukah as religious holidays, then it violates the Establishment Clause. . . .

Conversely, if the city celebrates both Christmas and Chanukah as secular holidays, then its conduct is beyond the reach of the Establishment Clause. Because government may celebrate Christmas as a secular holiday, it follows that government may also acknowledge Chanukah as a secular holiday. Simply put, it would be a form of discrimination against Jews to allow Pittsburgh to celebrate Christmas as a cultural tradition while simultaneously disallowing the city's acknowledgment of Chanukah as a contemporaneous cultural tradition.

Accordingly, the relevant question for Establishment Clause purposes is whether the combined display of the tree, the sign, and the menorah has the effect of endorsing both Christian and Jewish faiths, or rather simply recognizes that both Christmas and Chanukah are part of the same winter-holiday season, which has attained a secular status in our society. Of the two interpretations of this particular display, the latter seems far more plausible. . . .

The Christmas tree, unlike the menorah, is not itself a religious symbol. Although Christmas trees once carried religious connotations, today they typify the secular celebration of Christmas. . . . Numerous Americans place Christmas trees in their homes without subscribing to Christian religious beliefs, and when the city's tree stands alone in front of the City-County Building, it is not considered an endorsement of Christian faith. . . .

* * *

Lynch v Donnelly confirms, and in no way repudiates, the longstanding constitutional principle that government may not engage in a practice that has the effect of promoting or endorsing religious beliefs. The display of the crèche in the county courthouse has this unconstitutional effect. The display of the menorah in front of the City-County Building, however, does not have this effect, given its "particular physical setting." . . .

Justice Kennedy, with whom The Chief Justice, Justice White, and Justice Scalia join, concurring in the judgment in part and dissenting in part. . . .

The crèche display is constitutional, and, for the same reasons, the display of a menorah by the city of Pittsburgh is permissible as well. . . .

Government policies of accommodation, acknowledgment, and support for religion are an accepted part of our political and cultural heritage. . . .

The ability of the organized community to recognize and accommodate religion in a society with a pervasive public sector requires diligent observance of the border between accommodation and establishment. Our cases disclose two limiting principles: government may not coerce anyone to support or participate in any religion or its exercise; and it may not, in the guise of avoiding hostility or callous indifference, give direct benefits to religion in such a degree that it in fact "establishes a [state] religion or religious faith, or tends to do so." . . . These two principles, while distinct, are not unrelated, for it would be difficult indeed to establish a religion without some measure of more or less subtle coercion, be it in the form of taxation to supply the substantial benefits that would sustain a state-established faith, direct compulsion to observance, or governmental exhortation to religiosity that amounts in fact to proselytizing.

* * *

These principles are not difficult to apply to the facts of the cases before us. In permitting the displays on government property of the menorah and the creche, the city and county sought to do no more than "celebrate the season," . . . and to acknowledge, along with many of their citizens, the historical background and the religious, as well as secular, nature of the Chanukah and Christmas holidays. This interest falls well within the tradition of government accommodation and acknowledgment of religion that has marked our history from the beginning. It cannot be disputed that government, if it chooses, may participate in sharing with its citizens the joy of the holiday season, by declaring public holidays, installing or permitting festive displays, sponsoring celebrations and parades, and providing holiday vacations for its employees. All levels of our government do precisely that. . . .

The approach adopted by the majority contradicts important values embodied in the Clause. Obsessive, implacable resistance to all but the most carefully scripted and secularized forms of accommodation requires this Court to act as a censor, issuing national decrees as to what is orthodox and what is not. What is orthodox, in this context, means what is secular; the only Christmas the State can acknowledge is one in which references to religion have been held to a minimum. The Court thus lends its assistance to an Orwellian rewriting of history as many understand it. I can conceive of no judicial function more antithetical to the First Amendment. . . .

I might have voted against installation of these particular displays were I a local legislative official. But we have no jurisdiction over matters of taste within the realm of constitutionally permissible discretion. Our role is enforcement of a written Constitution. In my view, the principles of the Establishment Clause and our Nation's historic traditions of diversity and pluralism allow communities to make reasonable judgments respecting the accommodation or acknowledgment of holidays with both cultural and religious aspects. No constitutional violation occurs when they do so by displaying a symbol of the holiday's religious origins.

Capital Square v. Pinette (1995)[19]

The issue of whether religious displays on public land violate the establishment clause became further complicated in this 1995 case involving an application by the Ku Klux Klan to erect a cross in a public plaza in Columbus, Ohio. Note especially Justice Thomas's concurring opinion discussing the possibility that the Klan's use of the cross constituted a political message rather than religious speech.

Justice Scalia announced the judgment of the Court and delivered the opinion of the Court with respect to Parts I, II, and III, and an opinion with respect to Part IV, in which the Chief Justice, Justice Kennedy and Justice Thomas join. . . .

The question in this case is whether a State violates the Establishment Clause when, pursuant to a religiously neutral state policy, it permits a private party to display an unattended religious symbol in a traditional public forum located next to its seat of government.

I

Capital Square is a 10-acre, state-owned plaza surrounding the Statehouse in Columbus, Ohio. For over a century the square has been used for public speeches, gatherings, and festivals advocating and celebrating a variety of causes, both secular and religious. . . .

It has been the [City Advisory] Board's policy "to allow a broad range of speakers and other gatherings of people to conduct events on the Capital Square.". . . Such diverse groups as homosexual rights organizations, the Ku Klux Klan and the United Way have held rallies. The Board has also permitted a variety of unattended displays on Capital Square: a State-sponsored lighted tree during the Christmas season, a privately-sponsored menorah during Chanukah, a display showing the progress of a United Way fundraising campaign, and booths and exhibits during an arts festival. . . .

In November 1993, after reversing an initial decision to ban unattended holiday displays from the square during December 1993, the Board authorized the State to put up its annual Christmas tree. On November 29, 1993, the Board granted a rabbi's application to erect a menorah. That same day, the Board received an application from respondent Donnie Carr, an officer of the Ohio Ku Klux Klan, to place a cross on the square from December 8, 1993, to December 24, 1993. The Board denied that application on December 3. . . .

Two weeks later, having been unsuccessful in its effort to obtain administrative relief from the Board's decision, the Ohio Klan, through its leader, Vincent Pinette, filed the present suit. . . . The Board defended on the ground that the permit would violate the Establishment Clause. . . .

Respondents' religious display in Capital Square was private expression. Our precedent establishes that private religious speech, far from being a First Amendment orphan, is as fully protected under the Free Speech Clause as secular private expression. . . . Indeed, in Anglo-American history, at least, government suppression of speech has so commonly been directed *precisely* at religious speech that a free-speech clause without religion would be *Hamlet* without the prince. Accordingly, we have not excluded from free-speech protections religious proselytizing, . . . or even acts of worship, . . . Petitioners do not dispute that respondents, in displaying their cross, were engaging in constitutionally protected expression. They do contend that the constitutional protection does not extend to the length of permitting that expression to be made on Capital Square. . . .

There is no doubt that compliance with the Establishment Clause is a state interest sufficiently compelling to justify content-based restrictions on speech. . . . Whether that interest is implicated here, however, is a different question. . . .

Capital Square is a genuinely public forum, is known to be a public forum, and has been widely used as a public forum for many, many years. Private religious speech cannot be subject to veto by those who see favoritism where there is none.

The contrary view, most strongly espoused by Justice Stevens, *post*,. . . exiles private religious speech to a realm of less-protected expression heretofore inhabited only by sexually explicit displays and commercial speech. . . . It will be a sad day when this Court casts piety in with pornography, and finds the First Amendment more hospitable to private expletives . . . than to private prayers. This would be merely bizarre were religious speech simply *as* protected by the Constitution as other forms of private speech; but it is outright perverse when one considers that private religious expression receives *preferential* treatment under the Free Exercise Clause. It is no answer to say that the Establishment Clause tempers religious speech. By its terms that Clause applies only to the words and acts of *government:* It was never meant, and has never been read by this Court, to serve as an impediment to purely *private* religious speech connected to the State only through its occurrence in a public forum. . . .

If Ohio is concerned about misperceptions, nothing prevents it from requiring all private displays in the Square to be identified as such. That would be a content-neutral "manner" restriction which is assuredly constitutional. But the State may not, on the claim of misperception of official endorsement, ban all private religious speech from the public square, or discriminate against it by requiring religious speech alone to disclaim public sponsorship. . . .

*　*　*

Justice Thomas, concurring.

I join the Court's conclusion that petitioner's exclusion of the Ku Klux Klan's cross cannot be justified on Establishment Clause grounds. But the fact that the legal issue before us involves the Establishment Clause should not lead anyone to think that a cross erected by the Ku Klux Klan is a purely religious symbol. The erection of such a cross is a political act, not a Christian one.

There is little doubt that the Klan's main objective is to establish a racist white government in the United States. In Klan ceremony, the cross is a symbol of white supremacy and a tool for the intimidation and harassment of racial minorities, Catholics, Jews, Communists, and any other groups hated by the Klan. The cross is associated with the Klan not because of religious worship, but because of the Klan's practice of cross-burning. . . .

Although the Klan might have sought to convey a message with some religious component, I think that the Klan had a primarily nonreligious purpose in erecting the cross. The Klan simply has appropriated one of the most sacred of religious symbols as a symbol of hate. In my mind, this suggests that this case may not have truly involved the Establishment Clause, although I agree with the Court's disposition because of the manner in which the case has come before us. In the end, there may be much less here than meets the eye. . . .

Justice Stevens, dissenting.

The Establishment Clause should be construed to create a strong presumption against the installation of unattended religious symbols on public property. Although the State of Ohio has allowed Capital Square, the area around the seat of its government, to be used as a public forum and although it has occasionally allowed private groups to erect other sectarian displays there, neither fact provides a sufficient basis for rebutting that presumption. On the contrary, the sequence of sectarian displays disclosed by the record in this case illustrates the importance of rebuilding the "wall of separation between church and State" that Jefferson envisioned.

At issue in this case is an unadorned Latin cross, which the Ku Klux Klan placed, and left unattended, on the lawn in front of the Ohio State Capitol. The Court decides this case on the assumption that the cross was a religious symbol. I agree with that assumption notwithstanding the hybrid character of this particular object. The record indicates that the "Grand Titan of the Knights of the Ku Klux Klan for the Realm of Ohio" applied for a permit to place a cross in front of the State Capitol because "the Jews" were placing a "symbol for the Jewish belief" in the Square. Some observers, unaware of who had sponsored the cross, or unfamiliar with the history of the Klan and its reaction to the menorah, might interpret the Klan's cross as an inspirational symbol of the crucifixion and resurrection of Jesus Christ. More knowledgeable observers might regard it, given the context, as an antisemitic symbol of bigotry and disrespect for a particular religious sect. Under the first interpretation, the cross is plainly a religious symbol. Under the second, an icon of intolerance expressing an anti-clerical message should also be treated as a religious symbol because the Establishment Clause must prohibit official sponsorship of irreligious as well as religious messages. . . . This principle is no less binding if the anti-religious message is also a bigoted message. . . .

Thus, while this unattended, free-standing wooden cross was unquestionably a religious symbol, observers may well have received completely different messages from that symbol. Some might have perceived it as a message of love, others as a message of hate, still others as a message of exclusion—a Statehouse sign calling powerfully to mind their outsider status. In any event, it was a message that the State of Ohio may not communicate to its citizens without violating the Establishment Clause. . . .

Church and State: Institutional Issues

Walz v. Tax Commission (1970)[20]

Walz v. *Tax Commission* provided the Supreme Court with its first opportunity to consider whether tax exemptions for religious organizations run afoul of the Constitution's proscription of the establishment of religion. In upholding the tax exemption, the Court considered the effect of history on its interpretation of the First Amendment.

Mr. Chief Justice Burger delivered the opinion of the Court.

Appellant, owner of real estate in Richmond County, New York, sought an injunction in the New York courts to prevent the New York City Tax Commission from granting property tax exemptions to religious organizations for religious properties used solely for religious worship. The exemption from state taxes is authorized by Art. 16, § 1, of the New York Constitution, which provides in relevant part:

> Exemptions from taxation may be granted only by general laws. Exemptions may be altered or repealed except those exempting real or personal property used exclusively for religious, educational or charitable purposes as defined by law and owned by any corporation or association organized or conducted exclusively for one or more of such purposes and not operating for profit.

The essence of appellant's contention was that the New York City Tax Commission's grant of an exemption to church property indirectly requires the appellant to make a contribution to religious bodies and thereby violates provisions prohibiting establishment of religion under the First Amendment which under the Fourteenth Amendment is binding on the States. . . .

[F]or the men who wrote the Religion Clauses of the First Amendment the "establishment of a religion connoted sponsorship, financial support, and active involvement of the sovereign in religious activity. In England, and in some Colonies at the time of the separation in 1776, the Church of England was sponsored and supported by the Crown as a state, or established, church; in other countries "establishment" meant sponsorship by the sovereign of the Lutheran or Catholic Church. . . .

The Establishment and Free Exercise Clauses of the First Amendment are not the most precisely drawn portions of the Constitution. The sweep of the absolute prohibitions in the Religion Clauses may have been calculated; but the purpose was to state an objective not to write a statute. In attempting to articulate the scope of the two Religion Clauses, the Court's opinions reflect the limitations inherent in formulating general principles on a case-by-case basis. The considerable internal inconsistency in the opinions of the Court derives from what, in retrospect, may have been too sweeping utterances on aspects of these clauses that seemed clear in relation to the particular cases but have limited meaning as general principles.

The Court has struggled to find a neutral course between the two Religion Clauses, both of which are cast in absolute terms, and either of which, if expanded to a logical extreme, would tend to clash with the other. . . .

The course of constitutional neutrality in this area cannot be an absolutely straight line; rigidity could well defeat the basic purpose of these provisions, which is to insure that no religion be sponsored or favored, none commanded, and none inhibited. The general principle deducible from the First Amendment and all that has been said by the Court is this: that we will not tolerate either governmentally established religion or governmental interference with religion. Short of those expressly proscribed governmental acts there is room for play in the joints productive of a benevolent neutrality which will permit religious exercise to exist without sponsorship and without interference.

Each value judgment under the Religion Clauses must therefore turn on whether particular acts in question are intended to establish or interfere with religious beliefs and practices or have the effect of doing so. Adherence to the policy of neutrality that derives from an accommodation of the Establishment and Free Exercise Clauses has prevented the kind of involvement that would tip the balance toward government control of churches or governmental restraint on religious practice. . . .

In *Everson* the Court declined to construe the Religion Clauses with a literalness that would undermine the ultimate constitutional objective as illuminated by history. Surely, bus transportation and police protection to pupils who receive religious instruction "aid" that particular religion to maintain schools that plainly tend to assure future adherents to a particular faith by having control of their total education at an early age. No religious body that maintains schools would deny this as an affirmative if not dominant policy of church schools. But if as in *Everson* buses can be provided to carry and policemen to protect church school pupils, we fail to see how a broader range of police and fire protection given equally to all churches, along with nonprofit hospitals, art galleries, and libraries receiving the same tax exemption, is different for purposes of the Religion Clauses.

Similarly, making textbooks available to pupils in parochial schools in common with public schools was surely an "aid" to the sponsoring churches because it relieved those churches of an enormous aggregate cost for those books. Supplying of costly teaching materials was not seen either as manifesting a legislative purpose to aid or as having a primary effect of aid contravening the First Amendment. . . . In so holding the Court was heeding both its own prior decisions and our religious tradition.

With all the risks inherent in programs that bring about administrative relationships between public education bodies and church-sponsored schools, we have been able to chart a course that preserved the autonomy and freedom of religious bodies while avoiding any semblance of established religion. This is a "tight rope" and one we have successfully traversed.

* * *

The legislative purpose of a property tax exemption is neither the advancement nor the inhibition of religion; it is neither sponsorship nor hostility. New York, in common with the other States, has determined that certain entities that exist in a harmonious relationship to the community at large, and that foster its "moral or mental improvement," should not be inhibited in their activities by property taxation or the hazard of loss of those properties for nonpayment of taxes. It has not singled out one particular church or religious group or even churches as such; rather, it has granted exemption to all houses of religious worship within a broad class of property owned by non-profit, quasi-public corporations which include hospitals, libraries, playgrounds, scientific, professional, historical, and patriotic groups. The State has an affirmative policy that considers these groups as beneficial and stabilizing influences in community life and finds this classification useful, desirable, and in the public interest. Qualification for tax exemption is not perpetual or immutable; some tax-exempt groups lose that status when their activities take them outside the classification and new entities can come into being and qualify for exemption.

Governments have not always been tolerant of religious activity, and hostility toward religion has taken many shapes and forms—economic, political, and sometimes harshly oppressive. Grants of exemption historically reflect the concern of authors of constitutions and statutes as to the latent dangers inherent in the imposition of property taxes; exemption constitutes a reasonable and balanced attempt to guard against those dangers. The limits of permissible state accommodation to religion are by no means co-extensive with the noninterference mandated by the Free Exercise Clause. To equate the two would be to deny a national heritage with roots in the Revolution itself. . . . We cannot read New York's statute as attempting to establish religion; it is simply sparing the exercise of religion from the burden of property taxation levied on private profit institutions.

We find it unnecessary to justify the tax exemption on the social welfare services or "good works" that some churches perform for parishioners and others—family counselling, aid to the elderly and the infirm, and to children. Churches vary substantially in the scope of such services; programs expand or contract according to resources and need. As public-sponsored programs enlarge, private aid from the church sector may diminish. The extent of social services may vary, depending on whether the church serves an urban or rural, a rich or poor constituency. To give emphasis to so variable an aspect of the work of religious bodies would introduce an element of governmental evaluation and standards as to the worth of particular social welfare programs, thus producing a kind of continuing day-to-day relationship which the policy of neutrality seeks to minimize. Hence, the use of a social welfare yardstick as a significant element to qualify for tax exemption could conceivably give rise to confrontations that could escalate to constitutional dimensions.

Determining that the legislative purpose of tax exemption is not aimed at establishing, sponsoring, or supporting religion does not end the inquiry, however. We must also be sure that the end result—the effect—is not an excessive government entanglement with religion. The test is inescapably one of degree. Either course, taxation of churches or exemption, occasions some degree of involvement with religion. Elimination of exemption would tend to expand the involvement of government by giving rise to tax valuation of church property, tax liens, tax foreclosures, and the direct confrontations and conflicts that follow in the train of those legal processes.

Granting tax exemptions to churches necessarily operates to afford an indirect economic benefit and also gives rise to some, but yet a lesser, involvement than taxing them. In analyzing either alternative the questions are whether the involvement is excessive, and whether it is a continuing one calling for official and continuing surveillance leading to an impermissible degree of entanglement. Obviously a direct money subsidy would be a relationship pregnant with involvement and, as with most governmental grant programs, could encompass sustained and detailed administrative relationships for enforcement of statutory or administrative standards, but that is not this case. The hazards of churches supporting government are hardly less in their potential than the hazards of government supporting churches; each relationship carries some involvement rather than the desired insulation and separation. We cannot ignore the instances in history when church support of government led to the kind of involvement we seek to avoid.

The grant of a tax exemption is not sponsorship since the government does not transfer part of its revenue to churches but simply abstains from demanding that the church support the state. No one has ever suggested that tax exemption has converted libraries, art galleries, or hospitals into arms of the state or put employers "on the public payroll." There is no genuine nexus between tax exemption and establishment of religion. As Mr. Justice Holmes commented in a related context "a page of history is worth a volume of logic." The exemption creates only a minimal and remote involvement between church and state and far less than taxation of churches. It restricts the fiscal relationship between church and state, and tends to complement and reinforce the desired separation insulating each from the other.

Separation in this context cannot mean absence of all contact; the complexities of modern life inevitably produce some contact and the fire and police protection received by houses of religious worship are no more than incidental benefits accorded all persons or institutions within a State's boundaries, along with many other exempt organizations. . . .

All of the 50 States provide for tax exemption of places of worship, most of them doing so by constitutional guarantees. For so long as federal income taxes have had any potential impact on churches—over 75 years—religious organizations have been expressly exempt from the tax. Such treatment is an "aid" to churches no more and no less in principle than the real estate tax exemption granted by States. Few concepts are more deeply embedded in the fabric of our national life, beginning with pre-Revolutionary colonial times, than for the government to exercise at the very least this kind of benevolent neutrality toward churches and religious exercise generally so long as none was favored over others and none suffered interference.

It is significant that Congress, from its earliest days, has viewed the Religion Clauses of the Constitution as authorizing statutory real estate tax exemption to religious bodies. In 1802 the 7th Congress enacted a taxing statute for the County of Alexandria, adopting the 1800 Virginia statutory pattern which provided tax exemptions for churches. As early as 1813 the 12th Congress refunded import duties paid by religious societies on the importation of religious articles. During this period the City Council of Washington, D.C., acting under congressional authority, enacted a series of real and personal property assessments that uniformly exempted church property. In 1870 the Congress specifically exempted all churches in the District of Columbia and appurtenant grounds and property "from any and all taxes or assessments, national, municipal, or county."...

It is obviously correct that no one acquires a vested or protected right in violation of the Constitution by long use, even when that span of time covers our entire national existence and indeed predates it. Yet an unbroken practice of according the exemption to churches, openly and by affirmative state action, not covertly or by state inaction, is not something to be lightly cast aside....

Nothing in this national attitude toward religious tolerance and two centuries of uninterrupted freedom from taxation has given the remotest sign of leading to an established church or religion and on the contrary it has operated affirmatively to help guarantee the free exercise of all forms of religious belief. Thus, it is hardly useful to suggest that tax exemption is but the "foot in the door" or the "nose of the camel in the tent" leading to an established church. Any move that realistically "establishes" a church or tends to do so can be dealt with "while this Court sits."...

It is interesting to note that while the precise question we now decide has not been directly before the Court previously, the broad question was discussed by the Court in relation to real estate taxes assessed nearly a century ago on land owned by and adjacent to a church in Washington, D.C. At that time Congress granted real estate tax exemptions to buildings devoted to art, to institutions of public charity, libraries, cemeteries, and "church buildings, and grounds actually occupied by such buildings." In denying tax exemption as to land owned by but not used for the church, but rather to produce income, the Court concluded:

> In the exercise of this [taxing] power, Congress, like any state legislature unrestricted by constitutional provisions, may, at its discretion, wholly exempt certain classes of property from taxation, or may tax them at a lower rate than other property....

It appears that at least up to 1885 this Court, reflecting more than a century of our history and uninterrupted practice, accepted without discussion the proposition that federal or state grants of tax exemption to churches were not a violation of the Religion Clauses of the First Amendment. As to the New York statute, we now confirm that view.

State of Wisconsin v. Yoder (1972)[21]

In a 1925 case, *Pierce* v. *Society of Sisters,* the Supreme Court declared that parents have a constitutional right to send their children to private schools despite a state law mandating attendance at public schools. *Wisconsin* v. *Yoder* addresses whether the free-exercise clause permits the Old Order Amish to withdraw their children from any formal education after the eighth grade. It may be interesting to compare Chief Justice Burger's deference to the religious practices of the Amish to the Supreme Court's consideration of Native American religion in *Bowen* v. *Roy* and *Lyng* v. *Northwest Indian Cemetery Protection Association* and Hasidism in *Kiryas Joel Village School District* v. *Grumet.*

Mr. Chief Justice Burger delivered the opinion of the Court. . . .

* * *

Respondents Jonas Yoder and Wallace Miller are members of the Old Order Amish religion, and respondent Adin Yutzy is a member of the Conservative Amish Mennonite Church. They and their families are residents of Green County, Wisconsin. Wisconsin's compulsory school-attendance law required them to cause their children to attend public or private school until reaching age 16 but the respondents declined to send their children, ages 14 and 15, to public school after they completed the eighth grade. The children were not enrolled in any private school, or within any recognized exception to the compulsory-attendance law, and they are conceded to be subject to the Wisconsin statute.

On complaint of the school district administrator for the public schools, respondents were charged, tried, and convicted of violating the compulsory-attendance law in Green County Court and were fined the sum of $5 each. Respondents defended on the ground that the application of the compulsory-attendance law violated their rights under the First and Fourteenth Amendments. The trial testimony showed that respondents believed, in accordance with the tenets of Old Order Amish communities generally, that their children's attendance at high school, public or private, was contrary to the Amish religion and way of life. They believed that by sending their children to high school, they would not only expose themselves to the danger of the censure of the church community, but, as found by the county court, also endanger their own salvation and that of their children. The State stipulated that respondents' religious beliefs were sincere.

In support of their position, respondents presented as expert witnesses scholars on religion and education whose testimony is uncontradicted. They expressed their opinions on the relationship of the Amish belief concerning school attendance to the more general tenets of their religion, and described the impact that compulsory high school attendance could have on the continued survival of Amish communities as they exist in the United States today. The history of the Amish sect was given in some detail, beginning with the Swiss Anabaptists of the 16th century who rejected institutionalized churches and sought to return to the early, simple, Christian life de-emphasizing material success, rejecting the competitive spirit, and seeking to insulate themselves from the modern world. As a result of their common heritage, Old Order Amish communities today are characterized by a fundamental belief that salvation requires life in a church community separate and apart from the world and worldly influence. This concept of life aloof from the world and its values is central to their faith.

A related feature of Old Order Amish communities is their devotion to a life in harmony with nature and the soil, as exemplified by the simple life of the early Christian era that continued in America during much of our early national life. Amish beliefs require members of the community to make their living by farming or closely related activities. Broadly speaking, the Old Order Amish religion pervades and determines the entire mode of life of its adherents. Their conduct is regulated in great detail by the Ordnung, or rules, of the church community. Adult baptism, which occurs in late adolescence, is the time at which Amish young people voluntarily undertake heavy obligations, not unlike the Bar Mitzvah of the Jews, to abide by the rules of the church community.

Amish objection to formal education beyond the eighth grade is firmly grounded in these central religious concepts. They object to the high school, and higher education generally, because the values they teach are in marked variance with Amish values and the Amish way of life; they view secondary school education as an impermissible exposure of their children to a "worldly" influence in conflict with their beliefs. The high school tends to emphasize intellectual and scientific accomplishments, self-distinction, competitiveness, worldly success, and social life with other students. Amish society emphasizes informal learning-through-doing; a life of "goodness," rather than a life of intellect; wisdom, rather than technical knowledge; community welfare, rather than competition; and separation from, rather than integration with, contemporarly worldly society.

Formal high school education beyond the eighth grade is contrary to Amish beliefs, not only because it places Amish children in an environment hostile to Amish beliefs with increasing emphasis on competition in class work and sports and with pressure to conform to the styles, manners, and ways of the peer group, but also because it takes them away from their community, physically and emotionally, during the crucial and formative adolescent period of life. During this period, the children must acquire Amish attitudes favoring manual work and self-reliance and the specific skills needed to perform the adult role of an Amish farmer or housewife. They must learn to enjoy physical labor. Once a child has learned basic reading, writing, and elementary mathematics, these traits, skills, and attitudes admittedly fall within the category of those best learned through example and "doing" rather than in a classroom. And, at this time in life, the Amish child must also grow in his faith and his relationship to the Amish community if he is to be prepared to accept the heavy obligations imposed by adult baptism. In short, high school attendance with teachers who are not of the Amish faith—and may even be hostile to it—interposes a serious barrier to the integration of the Amish child into the Amish religious community. Dr. John Hostetler, one of the experts on Amish society, testified that the modern high school is not equipped, in curriculum or social environment, to impart the values promoted by Amish society.

The Amish do not object to elementary education through the first eight grades as a general proposition because they agree that their children must have basic skills in the "three R's" in order to read the Bible, to be good farmers and citizens, and to be able to deal with non-Amish people when necessary in the course of daily affairs. They view such a basic education as acceptable because it does not significantly expose their children to worldly values or interfere with their development in the Amish community during the crucial adolescent period. While Amish accept compulsory elementary education generally, wherever possible they have established their own elementary schools in many respects like the small local schools of the past. In the Amish belief higher learning tends to develop values they reject as influences that alienate man from God.

On the basis of such considerations, Dr. Hostetler testified that compulsory high school attendance could not only result in great psychological harm to Amish children, because of the conflicts it would produce, but would also, in his opinion, ultimately result in the destruction of the Old Order Amish church community as it exists in the United States today. The testimony of Dr. Donald A. Erickson, an expert witness on education, also showed that the Amish succeed in preparing their high school age children to be productive members of the Amish community. He described their system of learning through doing the skills directly relevant to their adult roles in the Amish community as "ideal" and perhaps superior to ordinary high school education. The evidence also showed that the Amish have an excellent record as law-abiding and generally self-sufficient members of society. . . .

* * *

There is no doubt as to the power of a State, having a high responsibility for education of its citizens, to impose reasonable regulations for the control and duration of basic education. . . . Providing public schools ranks at the very apex of the function of a State. Yet even this paramount responsibility was, in [a prior case] made to yield to the right of parents to provide an equivalent education in a privately operated system. There the Court held that Oregon's statute compelling attendance in a public school from age eight to age 16 unreasonably interfered with the interest of parents in directing the rearing of their offspring, including their education in church-operated schools. As that case suggests, the values of parental direction of the religious upbringing and education of their children in their early and formative years have a high place in our society. . . . Thus, a State's interest in universal education, however highly we rank it, is not totally free from a balancing process when it impinges on fundamental rights and interests, such as those specifically protected by the Free Exercise Clause of the First Amendment, and the traditional interest of parents with respect to the religious upbringing of their children so long as they . . . "prepare [them] for additional obligations.". . .

It follows that in order for Wisconsin to compel school attendance beyond the eighth grade against a claim that such attendance interferes with the practice of a legitimate religious belief, it must appear either that the State does not deny the free exercise of religious belief by its requirement, or that there is a state interest of sufficient magnitude to override the interest claiming protection under the Free Exercise Clause. Long before there was general acknowledgment of the need for universal formal education, the Religion Clauses had specifically and firmly fixed the right to free exercise of religious beliefs, and buttressing this fundamental right was an equally firm, even if less explicit, prohibition against the establishment of any religion by government. The values underlying these two provisions relating to religion have been zealously protected, sometimes even at the expense of other interests of admittedly high social importance. The invalidation of financial aid to parochial schools by government grants for a salary subsidy for teachers is but one example of the extent to which courts have gone in this regard, notwithstanding that such aid programs were legislatively determined to be in the public interest and the service of sound educational policy by States and by Congress. . . .

The essence of all that has been said and written on the subject is that only those interests of the highest order and those not otherwise served can overbalance legitimate claims to the free exercise of religion. We can accept it as settled, therefore, that, however strong the State's interest in universal compulsory education, it is by no means absolute to the exclusion or subordination of all other interests. . . .

We come then to the quality of the claims of the respondents concerning the alleged encroachment of Wisconsin's compulsory school-attendance statute on their rights and the rights of their children to the free exercise of the religious beliefs they and their forebears have adhered to for almost three centuries. In evaluating those claims we must be careful to determine whether the Amish religious faith and their mode of life are, as they claim, inseparable and interdependent. A way of life, however virtuous and admirable, may not be interposed as a barrier to reasonable state regulation of education if it is based on purely secular considerations; to have the protection of the Religion Clauses, the claims must be rooted in religious belief. Although a determination of what is a "religious" belief or practice entitled to constitutional protection may present a most delicate question, the very concept of ordered liberty precludes allowing every person to make his own standards on matters of conduct in which society as a whole has important interests. Thus, if the Amish asserted their claims because of their subjective evaluation and rejection of the contemporary secular values accepted by the majority, much as Thoreau rejected the social values of his time and isolated himself at Walden Pond, their claims would not rest on a religious basis. Thoreau's choice was philosophical and personal rather than religious, and such belief does not rise to the demands of the Religion Clauses.

Giving no weight to such secular considerations, however, we see that the record in this case abundantly supports the claim that the traditional way of life of the Amish is not merely a matter of personal preference, but one of deep religious conviction, shared by an organized group, and intimately related to daily living. That the Old Order Amish daily life and religious practice stem from their faith is shown by the fact that it is in response to their literal interpretation of the Biblical injunction from the Epistle of Paul to the Romans, "be not conformed to this world. . . ." This command is fundamental to the Amish faith. Moreover, for the Old Order Amish, religion is not simply a matter of theocratic belief. As the expert witnesses explained, the Old Order Amish religion pervades and determines virtually their entire way of life, regulating it with the detail of the Talmudic diet through the strictly enforced rules of the church community.

The record shows that the respondents' religious beliefs and attitude toward life, family, and home have remained constant—perhaps some would say static—in a period of unparalleled progress in human knowledge generally and great changes in education. The respondents freely concede, and indeed assert as an article of faith, that their religious beliefs and what we would today call "life style" have not altered in fundamentals for centuries. Their way of life in a church-oriented community, separated from the outside world and "worldly" influences, their attachment to nature and the soil, is a way inherently simple and uncomplicated, albeit difficult to preserve against the pressure to conform. Their rejection of telephones, automobiles, radios, and television, their mode of dress, of speech, their habits of manual work do indeed set them apart from much of contemporary society; these customs are both symbolic and practical.

As the society around the Amish has become more populous, urban, industrialized, and complex, particularly in this century, government regulation of human affairs has correspondingly become more detailed and pervasive. The Amish mode of life has thus come into conflict increasingly with requirements of contemporary society exerting a hydraulic insistence on conformity to majoritarian standards. So long as compulsory education laws were confined to eight grades of elementary basic education imparted in a nearby rural schoolhouse, with a large proportion of students of the Amish faith, the Old Order Amish had little basis to fear that school attendance would expose their children to the worldly influence they reject. But modern compulsory secondary education in rural areas is now largely carried on in a consolidated school, often remote from the student's home and alien to his daily home life. As the record so strongly shows, the values and programs of the modern secondary school are in sharp conflict with the fundamental mode of life mandated by the Amish religion; modern laws requiring compulsory secondary education have accordingly engendered great concern and conflict. The conclusion is inescapable that secondary schooling, by exposing Amish children to worldly influences in terms of attitudes, goals, and values contrary to beliefs, and by substantially interfering with the religious development of the Amish child and his integration into the way of life of the Amish faith community at the crucial adolescent stage of development, contravenes the basic religious tenets and practice of the Amish faith, both as to the parent and the child.

The impact of the compulsory-attendance law on respondents' practice of the Amish religion is not only severe, but inescapable, for the Wisconsin law affirmatively compels them, under threat of criminal sanction, to perform acts undeniably at odds with fundamental tenets of their religious beliefs. . . . Nor is the impact of the compulsory-attendance law confined to grave interference with important Amish religious tenets from a subjective point of view. It carries with it precisely the kind of objective danger to the free exercise of religion that the First Amendment was designed to prevent. As the record shows, compulsory school attendance to age 16 for Amish children carries with it a very real threat of undermining the Amish community and religious practice as they exist today; they must either abandon belief and be assimilated into society at large, or be forced to migrate to some other and more tolerant region.

In sum, the unchallenged testimony of acknowledged experts in education and religious history, almost 300 years of consistent practice, and strong evidence of a sustained faith pervading and regulating respondents' entire mode of life support the claim that enforcement of the State's requirement of compulsory formal education after the eighth grade would gravely endanger if not destroy the free exercise of respondents' religious beliefs.

* * *

Neither the findings of the trial court nor the Amish claims as to the nature of their faith are challenged in this Court by the State of Wisconsin. Its position is that the State's interest in universal compulsory formal secondary education to age 16 is so great that it is paramount to the undisputed claims of respondents that their mode of preparing their youth for Amish life, after the traditional elementary education, is an essential part of their religious belief and practice. Nor does the State undertake to meet the claim that the Amish mode of life and education is inseparable from and a part of the basic tenets of their religion—indeed, as much a part of their religious belief and practices as baptism, the confessional, or a sabbath may be for others.

Wisconsin concedes that under the Religion Clauses religious beliefs are absolutely free from the State's control, but it argues that "actions," even though religiously grounded, are outside the protection of the First Amendment. But our decisions have rejected the idea that religiously grounded conduct is always outside the protection of the Free Exercise Clause. It is true that activities of individuals, even when religiously based, are often subject to regulation by the States in the exercise of their undoubted power to promote the health, safety, and general welfare, or the Federal Government in the exercise of its delegated powers. . . . But to agree that religiously grounded conduct must often be subject to the broad police power of the State is not to deny that there are areas of conduct protected by the Free Exercise Clause of the First Amendment and thus beyond the power of the State to control, even under regulations of general applicability. . . . This case, therefore, does not become easier because respondents were convicted for their "actions" in refusing to send their children to the public high school; in this context belief and action cannot be neatly confined in logic-tight compartments. . . .

Nor can this case be disposed of on the grounds that Wisconsin's requirement for school attendance to age 16 applies uniformly to all citizens of the State and does not, on its face, discriminate against religions or a particular religion, or that it is motivated by legitimate secular concerns. A regulation neutral on its face may, in its application, nonetheless offend the constitutional requirement for governmental neutrality if it unduly burdens the free exercise of religion. . . . The Court must not ignore the danger that an exception from a general obligation of citizenship on religious grounds may run afoul of the Establishment Clause, but that danger cannot be allowed to prevent any exception no matter how vital it may be to the protection of values promoted by the right of free exercise. By preserving doctrinal flexibility and recognizing the need for a sensible and realistic application of the Religion Clauses "we have been able to chart a course that preserved the autonomy and freedom of religious bodies while avoiding any semblance of established religion. This is a 'tight rope' and one we have successfully traversed.". . .

We turn, then, to the State's broader contention that its interest in its system of compulsory education is so compelling that even the established religious practices of the Amish must give way. Where fundamental claims of religious freedom are at stake, however, we cannot accept such a sweeping claim; despite its admitted validity in the generality of cases, we must searchingly examine the interests that the State seeks to promote by its requirement for compulsory education to age 16, and the impediment to those objectives that would flow from recognizing the claimed Amish exemption. . . .

The State advances two primary arguments in support of its system of compulsory education. It notes, as Thomas Jefferson pointed out early in our history, that some degree of education is necessary to prepare citizens to participate effectively and intelligently in our open political system if we are to preserve freedom and independence. Further, education prepares individuals to be self-reliant and self-sufficient participants in society. We accept these propositions.

However, the evidence adduced by the Amish in this case is persuasively to the effect that an additional one or two years of formal high school for Amish children in place of their long-established program of informal vocational education would do little to serve those interests. Respondents' experts testified at trial, without challenge, that the value of all education must be assessed in terms of its capacity to prepare the child for life. It is one thing to say that compulsory education for a year or two beyond the eighth grade may be necessary when its goal is the preparation of the child for life in modern society as the majority live, but it is quite another if the goal of education be viewed as the preparation of the child for life in the separated agrarian community that is the keystone of the Amish faith. . . .

The State attacks respondents' position as one fostering "ignorance" from which the child must be protected by the State. No one can question the State's duty to protect children from ignorance but this argument does not square with the facts disclosed in the record. Whatever their idiosyncrasies as seen by the majority, this record strongly shows that the Amish community has been a highly successful social unit within our society, even if apart from the conventional "mainstream." Its members are productive and very law-abiding members of society; they reject public welfare in any of its usual modern forms. The Congress itself recognized their self-sufficiency by authorizing exemption of such groups as the Amish from the obligation to pay social security taxes.

It is neither fair nor correct to suggest that the Amish are opposed to education beyond the eighth grade level. What this record shows is that they are opposed to conventional formal education of the type provided by a certified high school because it comes at the child's crucial adolescent period of religious development. Dr. Donald Erickson, for example, testified that their system of learning-by-doing was an "ideal system" of education in terms of preparing Amish children for life as adults in the Amish community, and that "I would be inclined to say they do a better job in this than most of the rest of us do." As he put it, "These people aren't purporting to be learned people, and it seems to me the self-sufficiency of the community is the best evidence I can point to—whatever is being done seems to function well."

We must not forget that in the Middle Ages important values of the civilization of the Western World were preserved by members of religious orders who isolated themselves from all worldly influences against great obstacles. There can be no assumption that today's majority is "right" and the Amish and others like them are "wrong." A way of life that is odd or even erratic but interferes with no rights or interests of others is not to be condemned because it is different.

The State, however, supports its interest in providing an additional one or two years of compulsory high school education to Amish children because of the possibility that some such children will choose to leave the Amish community, and that if this occurs they will be ill-equipped for life. The State argues that if Amish children leave their church they should not be in the position of making their way in the world without the education available in the one or two additional years the State requires. However, on this record, that argument is highly speculative. There is no specific evidence of the loss of Amish adherents by attrition, nor is there any showing that upon leaving the Amish community Amish children, with their practical agricultural training and habits of industry and self-reliance, would become burdens on society because of educational shortcomings. Indeed, this argument of the State appears to rest primarily on the State's mistaken assumption, already noted, that the Amish do not provide any education for their children beyond the eighth grade, but allow them to grow in "ignorance." To the contrary, not only do the Amish accept the necessity for formal schooling through the eighth grade level, but continue to provide what has been characterized by the undisputed testimony of expert educators as an "ideal" vocational education for their children in the adolescent years.

There is nothing in this record to suggest that the Amish qualities of reliability, self-reliance, and dedication to work would fail to find ready markets in today's society. Absent some contrary evidence supporting the State's position, we are unwilling to assume that persons possessing such valuable vocational skills and habits are doomed to become burdens on society should they determine to leave the Amish faith, nor is there any basis in the record to warrant a finding that an additional one or two years of formal school education beyond the eighth grade would serve to eliminate any such problem that might exist.

Insofar as the State's claim rests on the view that a brief additional period of formal education is imperative to enable the Amish to participate effectively and intelligently in our democratic process, it must fall. The Amish alternative to formal secondary school education has enabled them to function effectively in their day-to-day life under self-imposed limitations on relations with the world, and to survive and prosper in contemporary society as a separate, sharply identifiable and highly self-sufficient community for more than 200 years in this country. In itself this is strong evidence that they are capable of fulfilling the social and political responsibilities of citizenship without compelled attendance beyond the eighth grade at the price of jeopardizing their free exercise of religious belief. When Thomas Jefferson emphasized the need for education as a bulwark of a free people against tyranny, there is nothing to indicate he had in mind compulsory education through any fixed age beyond a basic education. Indeed, the Amish communities singularly parallel and reflect many of the virtues of Jefferson's ideal of the "sturdy yeoman" who would form the basis of what he considered as the ideal of a democratic society. Even their idiosyncratic separateness exemplifies the diversity we profess to admire and encourage.

The requirement for compulsory education beyond the eighth grade is a relatively recent development in our history. Less than 60 years ago, the educational requirements of almost all of the States were satisfied by completion of the elementary grades, at least where the child was regularly and lawfully employed. The independence and successful social functioning of the Amish community for a period approaching almost three centuries and more than 200 years in this country are strong evidence that there is at best a speculative gain, in terms of meeting the duties of citizenship, from an additional one or two years of compulsory formal education. Against this background it would require a more particularized showing from the State on this point to justify the severe interference with religious freedom such additional compulsory attendance would entail. . . .

Aided by a history of three centuries as an identifiable religious sect and a long history as a successful and self-sufficient segment of American society, the Amish in this case have convincingly demonstrated the sincerity of their religious beliefs, the interrelationship of belief with their mode of life, the vital role that belief and daily conduct play in the continued survival of Old Order Amish communities and their religious organization, and the hazards presented by the State's enforcement of a statute generally valid as to others. Beyond this, they have carried the even more difficult burden of demonstrating the adequacy of their alternative mode of continuing informal vocational education in terms of precisely those overall interests that the State advances in support of its program of compulsory high school education. In light of this convincing showing, one that probably few other religious groups or sects could make, and weighing the minimal difference between what the State would require and what the Amish already accept, it was incumbent on the State to show with more particularity how its admittedly strong interest in compulsory education would be adversely affected by granting an exemption to the Amish. . . .

Nothing we hold is intended to undermine the general applicability of the State's compulsory school-attendance statutes or to limit the power of the State to promulgate reasonable standards that, while not impairing the free exercise of religion, provide for continuing agricultural vocational education under parental and church guidance by the Old Order Amish or others similarly situated. The States have had a long history of amicable and effective relationships with church-sponsored schools, and there is no basis for assuming that, in this related context, reasonable standards cannot be established concerning the content of the continuing vocational education of Amish children under parental guidance, provided always that state regulations are not inconsistent with what we have said in this opinion. . . .

Larson v. Valente (1982)[22]

Despite the First Amendment's establishment and free-exercise clauses, states periodically seek to regulate religious organizations that do not conform to the pattern set by mainstream religions. *Larson* v. *Valente* involves regulations and reporting requirements for religious organizations that receive most of their contributions from nonmembers.

Justice Brennan delivered the opinion of the Court.

The principal question presented by this appeal is whether a Minnesota statute, imposing certain registration and reporting requirements upon only those religious organizations that solicit more than fifty per cent of their funds from non-members, discriminates against such organizations in violation of the Establishment Clause of the First Amendment.

* * *

Appellants are John R. Larson, Commissioner of Securities, and Warren Spannaus, Attorney General, of the State of Minnesota. They are, by virtue of their offices, responsible for the implementation and enforcement of Minnesota's charitable solicitations Act. This Act, in effect since 1961, provides for a system of registration and disclosure respecting charitable organizations, and is designed to protect the contributing public and charitable beneficiaries against fraudulent practices in the solicitation of contributions for purportedly charitable purposes. A charitable organization subject to the Act must register with the Minnesota Department of Commerce before it may solicit contributions within the State. . . .

From 1961 until 1978, all "religious organizations" were exempted from the requirements of the Act. But effective March 29, 1978, the Minnesota Legislature amended the Act so as to include a "fifty per cent rule" in the exemption provision covering religious organizations. This fifty per cent rule provided that only those religious organizations that received more than half of their total contributions from members or affiliated organizations would remain exempt from the registration and reporting requirements of the Act.

Shortly after the enactment of § 309.515–1(b), the Department notified appellee Holy Spirit Association for the Unification of World Christianity (Unification Church) that it was required to register under the Act because of the newly enacted provision. Appellees Valente, Barber, Haft, and Korman, claiming to be followers of the tenets of the Unification Church, responded by bringing the present action [seeking] a declaration that the Act . . . constituted an abridgment of their First Amendment rights of expression and free exercise of religion, as well as a denial of their right to equal protection of the laws, guaranteed by the Fourteenth Amendment. . . .

The clearest command of the Establishment Clause is that one religious denomination cannot be officially preferred over another. Before the Revolution, religious establishments of differing denominations were common throughout the Colonies. But the Revolutionary generation emphatically disclaimed that European legacy, and "applied the logic of secular liberty to the condition of religion and the churches:" If Parliament had lacked the authority to tax unrepresented colonists, then by the same token the newly independent States should be powerless to tax their citizens for the support of a denomination to which they did not belong. The force of this reasoning led to the abolition of most denominational establishments at the state level by the 1780s, and led ultimately to the inclusion of the Establishment Clause in the First Amendment in 1791.

This constitutional prohibition of denominational preferences is inextricably connected with the continuing vitality of the Free Exercise Clause. Madison once noted that "Security for civil rights must be the same as that for religious rights; it consists in the one case in a multiplicity of interests and in the other in a multiplicity of sects." Madison's vision—freedom for all religion being guaranteed by free competition between religions—naturally assumed that every denomination would be equally at liberty to exercise and propagate its beliefs. But such equality would be impossible in an atmosphere of official denominational preference. Free exercise thus can be guaranteed only when legislators—and voters—are required to accord to their own religions the very same treatment given to small, new, or unpopular denominations. . . .

Since *Everson* v. *Board of Education* this Court has adhered to the principle, clearly manifested in the history and logic of the Establishment Clause, that no State can "pass laws which aid one religion" or that "prefer one religion over another." This principle of denominational neutrality has been restated on many occasions. . . . In short, when we are presented with a state law granting a denominational preference, our precedents demand that we treat the law as suspect and that we apply strict scrutiny in adjudging its constitutionality.

The fifty per cent rule of § 309.515–1(b) clearly grants denominational preferences of the sort consistently and firmly deprecated in our precedents. Consequently, that rule must be invalidated unless it is justified by a compelling governmental interest . . . and unless it is closely fitted to further that interest. . . .

[After discussion, the Court concluded] that the fifty per cent rule in § 309.515–1(b) [was not] "closely fitted" to further a "compelling governmental interest."

In *Lemon* v. *Kurtzman,* we announced three "tests" that a statute must pass in order to avoid the prohibition of the Establishment Clause.

> First, the statute must have a secular legislative purpose; second, its principal or primary effect must be one that neither advances nor inhibits religion. . . ; finally, the statute must not foster "an excessive governmental entanglement with religion."

[T]he *Lemon* v. *Kurtzman* "tests" are intended to apply to laws affording a uniform benefit to *all* religions, and not to provisions, like § 309.515–1(b)'s fifty per cent rule, that discriminate *among* religions. Although application of the *Lemon* tests is not necessary to the disposition of the case before us, those tests do reflect the same concerns that warranted the application of strict scrutiny to § 309.515–1(b)'s fifty per cent rule. . . . We view the third of those tests as most directly implicated in the present case. Justice Harlan well described the problems of entanglement in his separate opinion in *Walz,* where he observed that governmental involvement in programs concerning religion

> may be so direct or in such degree as to engender a risk of politicizing religion. . . . [R]eligious groups inevitably represent certain points of view and not infrequently assert them in the political arena, as evidenced by the continuing debate respecting birth control and abortion laws. Yet history cautions that political fragmentation on sectarian lines must be guarded against. . . . [G]overnment participation in certain programs, whose very nature is apt to entangle the state in details of administration and planning, may escalate to the point of inviting undue fragmentation.

The Minnesota statute challenged here is illustrative of this danger. By their "very nature," the distinctions drawn by § 309.515–1(b) and its fifty per cent rule "engender a risk of politicizing religion"—a risk, indeed, that has already been substantially realized.

It is plain that the principal effect of the fifty per cent rule in § 309.515–1(b) is to impose the registration and reporting requirements of the Act on some religious organizations but not on others. . . . We do not suggest that the burdens of compliance with the Act would be intrinsically impermissible if they were imposed evenhandedly. But this statute does not operate evenhandedly, nor was it designed to do so: The fifty per cent rule of § 309.515–1(b) effects the *selective* legislative imposition of burdens and advantages upon particular denominations. The "risk of politicizing religion" that inheres in such legislation is obvious, and indeed is confirmed by the provision's legislative history. For the history of § 309.515–1(b)'s fifty per cent rule demonstrates that the provision was drafted with the explicit intention of including particular religious denominations and excluding others. For example, the second sentence of an early draft of § 309.515–1(b) read, "A religious society or organization which solicits from its religious affiliates who are qualified under this subdivision and who are represented in a body or convention *that elects and controls the governing board of the religious society or organization* is exempt from the requirements of . . . Sections 309.52 and 309.53." The legislative history discloses that the legislators perceived that the italicized language would bring a Roman Catholic archdiocese within the Act, that the legislators did not want the amendment to have that effect, and that an amendment deleting the italicized clause was passed in committee for the sole purpose of exempting the archdiocese from the provisions of the Act. . . . On the other hand, there were certain religious organizations that the legislators did not want to exempt from the Act. One state senator explained that the fifty per cent rule was "an attempt to deal with the religious organizations which are soliciting on the street and soliciting by direct mail, but who are not substantial religious institutions in . . . our state." Another senator said, "what you're trying to get at here is the people that are running around airports and running around streets and soliciting people and you're trying to remove them from the exemption that normally applies to religious organizations." Still another senator, who apparently had mixed feelings about the proposed provision, stated, "I'm not sure why we're so hot to regulate the Moonies anyway."

In short, the fifty per cent rule's capacity—indeed, its express design—to burden or favor selected religious denominations led the Minnesota legislature to discuss the characteristics of various sects with a view towards "religious gerrymandering." As THE CHIEF JUSTICE stated in *Lemon,* "This kind of state inspection and evaluation of the religious content of a religious organization is fraught with the sort of entanglement that the Constitution forbids. It is a relationship pregnant with dangers of excessive government direction . . . of churches.". . .

United States v. Lee (1982)[23]

Congress has exempted from the filings and taxation required by the Social Security system individuals who are members of "a recognized religious sect" that has "established tenets or teachings" which are opposed to participation in retirement benefits, insurance, and other components of Social Security. This exemption only applies to the self-employed and, in this case, a member of the Old Order Amish claimed a constitutional right not to pay social security taxes for his employees. The Supreme Court found no such right, and it may be interesting to compare the reasoning here with the opinion in *Wisconsin* v. *Yoder*, where the Court sustained a challenge to compulsory education requirements by allowing Amish children to leave school at an early age.

Chief Justice Burger delivered the opinion of the Court. . . .

* * *

Appellee, a member of the Old Order Amish, is a farmer and carpenter. From 1970 to 1977, appellee employed several other Amish to work on his farm and in his carpentry shop. He failed to file the quarterly social security tax returns required of employers, withhold social security tax from his employees, or pay the employer's share of social security taxes.

In 1978, the Internal Revenue Service assessed appellee in excess of $27,000 for unpaid employment taxes; he paid $91—the amount owed for the first quarter of 1973—and then sued . . . for a refund, claiming that imposition of the social security taxes violated his First Amendment free exercise rights and those of his Amish employees. . . .

The preliminary inquiry in determining the existence of a constitutionally required exemption is whether the payment of social security taxes and the receipt of benefits interferes with the free exercise rights of the Amish. The Amish believe that there is a religiously based obligation to provide for their fellow members the kind of assistance contemplated by the social security system. Although the Government does not challenge the sincerity of this belief, the Government does contend that payment of social security taxes will not threaten the integrity of the Amish religious belief or observance. It is not within "the judicial function and judicial competence," however, to determine whether appellee or the Government has the proper interpretation of the Amish faith. . . . We therefore accept appellee's contention that both payment and receipt of social security benefits is forbidden by the Amish faith. Because the payment of the taxes or receipt of benefits violates Amish religious beliefs, compulsory participation in the social security system interferes with their free exercise rights.

The conclusion that there is a conflict between the Amish faith and the obligations imposed by the social security system is only the beginning, however, and not the end of the inquiry. Not all burdens on religion are unconstitutional. . . . The state may justify a limitation on religious liberty by showing that it is essential to accomplish an overriding governmental interest. . . .

Because the social security system is nationwide, the governmental interest is apparent. The social security system in the United States serves the public interest by providing a comprehensive insurance system with a variety of benefits available to all participants, with costs shared by employers and employees. The social security system is by far the largest domestic governmental program in the United States today, distributing approximately $11 billion monthly to 36 million Americans. The design of the system requires support by mandatory contributions from covered employers and employees. This mandatory participation is indispensable to the fiscal vitality of the social security system. . . . Moreover, a comprehensive national social security system providing for voluntary participation would be almost a contradiction in terms and difficult, if not impossible, to administer. Thus, the Government's interest in assuring mandatory and continuous participation in and contribution to the social security system is very high.

The remaining inquiry is whether accommodating the Amish belief will unduly interfere with fulfillment of the governmental interest. . . . The Court has long recognized that balance must be struck between the values of the comprehensive social security system, which rests on a complex of actuarial factors, and the consequences of allowing religiously based exemptions. To maintain an organized society that guarantees religious freedom to a great variety of faiths requires that some religious practices yield to the common good. . . .

Unlike the situation presented in Wisconsin v Yoder, . . . it would be difficult to accommodate the comprehensive social security system with myriad exceptions flowing from a wide variety of religious beliefs. The obligation to pay the social security tax initially is not fundamentally different from the obligation to pay income taxes; the difference—in theory at least—is that the social security tax revenues are segregated for use only in furtherance of the statutory program. There is no principled way, however, for purposes of this case, to distinguish between general taxes and those imposed under the Social Security Act. If, for example, a religious adherent believes war is a sin, and if a certain percentage of the federal budget can be identified as devoted to war-related activities, such individuals would have a similarly valid claim to be exempt from paying that percentage of the income tax. The tax system could not function if denominations were allowed to challenge the tax system because tax payments were spent in a manner that violates their religious belief. . . . Because the broad public interest in maintaining a sound tax system is of such a high order, religious belief in conflict with the payment of taxes affords no basis for resisting the tax. . . .

Congress and the courts have been sensitive to the needs flowing from the Free Exercise Clause, but every person cannot be shielded from all the burdens incident to exercising every aspect of the right to practice religious beliefs. When followers of a particular sect enter into commercial activity as a matter of choice, the limits they accept on their own conduct as a matter of conscience and faith are not to be superimposed on the statutory schemes which are binding on others in that activity. Granting an exemption from social security taxes to an employer operates to impose the employer's religious faith on the employees. . . . The tax imposed on employers to support the social security system must be uniformly applicable to all, except as Congress provides explicitly otherwise. . . .

Bob Jones University v. United States (1983)[24]

Taxation not only produces revenue for the government, it also provides a method for the state to enforce its policies. In the *Bob Jones University* case, the controversy arose from a challenge to the tax-exempt status of a religious school that had racially discriminatory admissions standards.

Chief Justice Burger delivered the opinion of the Court. . . .

We granted certiorari to decide whether petitioners, nonprofit private schools that prescribe and enforce racially discriminatory admissions standards on the basis of religious doctrine, qualify as tax-exempt organizations under § 501(c)(3) of the Internal Revenue Code of 1954.

No. 81–3, Bob Jones University v. United States

Bob Jones University is a nonprofit corporation located in Greenville, South Carolina. Its purpose is "to conduct an institution of learning . . . , giving special emphasis to the Christian religion and the ethics revealed in the Holy Scriptures." The corporation operates a school with an enrollment of approximately 5,000 students, from kindergarten through college and graduate school. Bob Jones University is not affiliated with any religious denomination, but is dedicated to the teaching and propagation of its fundamentalist Christian religious beliefs. It is both a religious and educational institution. Its teachers are required to be devout Christians, and all courses at the University are taught according to the Bible. Entering students are screened as to their religious beliefs, and their public and private conduct is strictly regulated by standards promulgated by University authorities.

The sponsors of the University genuinely believe that the Bible forbids interracial dating and marriage. To effectuate these views, Negroes were completely excluded until 1971. From 1971 to May 1975, the University accepted no applications from unmarried Negroes, but did accept applications from Negroes married within their race.

Following [a federal court] decision prohibiting racial exclusion from private schools, the University revised its policy. Since May 29, 1975, the University has permitted unmarried Negroes to enroll; but a disciplinary rule prohibits interracial dating and marriage. . . .

No. 81–1, Goldsboro Christian Schools, Inc. v. United States

Goldsboro Christian Schools is a nonprofit corporation located in Goldsboro, North Carolina. Like Bob Jones University, it was established "to conduct an institution of learning . . . , giving special emphasis to the Christian religion and the ethics revealed in the Holy scriptures." The school offers classes from kindergarten through high school, and since at least 1969 has satisfied the State of North Carolina's requirements for secular education in private schools. The school requires its high school students to take Bible-related courses, and begins each class with prayer.

Since its incorporation in 1963, Goldsboro Christian Schools has maintained a racially discriminatory admissions policy based upon its interpretation of the Bible. Goldsboro has for the most part accepted only Caucasians. On occasion, however, the school has accepted children from racially mixed marriages in which one of the parents is Caucasian.

Goldsboro never received a determination by the IRS that it was an organization entitled to tax exemption under § 501(c)(3). Upon audit of Goldsboro's records for the years 1969 through 1972, the IRS determined that Goldsboro was not an organization described in § 501(c)(3), and therefore was required to pay taxes under the Federal Insurance Contribution Act and the Federal Unemployment Tax Act. . . .

[T]he IRS [has] formalized the policy first announced in 1970, that . . . to qualify for a tax exemption pursuant to § 501(c)(3), an institution must show, first, that it falls within one of the eight categories expressly set forth in that section, and second, that its activity is not contrary to settled public policy.

Section 501(c)(3) provides that "[c]orporations . . . organized and operated exclusively for religious, charitable . . . or educational purposes" are entitled to tax exemption. Petitioners argue that the plain language of the statute guarantees them tax-exempt status. They emphasize the absence of any language in the statute expressly requiring all exempt organizations to be "charitable" in the common law sense, and they contend that the disjunctive "or" separating the categories in § 501(c)(3) precludes such a reading. Instead, they argue that if an institution falls within one or more of the specified categories it is automatically entitled to exemption, without regard to whether it also qualifies as "charitable.". . .

It is a well-established canon of statutory construction that a court should go beyond the literal language of a statute if reliance on that language would defeat the plain purpose of the statute. . . .

Section 501(c)(3) therefore must be analyzed and construed within the framework of the Internal Revenue Code and against the background of the Congressional purposes. Such an examination reveals unmistakable evidence that, underlying all relevant parts of the Code, is the intent that entitlement to tax exemption depends on meeting certain common law standards of charity—namely, that an institution seeking tax-exempt status must serve a public purpose and not be contrary to established public policy. . . .

We are bound to approach these questions with full awareness that determinations of public benefit and public policy are sensitive matters with serious implications for the institutions affected; a declaration that a given institution is not "charitable" should be made only where there can be no doubt that the activity involved is contrary to a fundamental public policy. But there can no longer be any doubt that racial discrimination in education violates deeply and widely accepted views of elementary justice. . . .

An unbroken line of cases following *Brown* v. *Board of Education* establishes beyond doubt this Court's view that racial discrimination in education violates a most fundamental national public policy, as well as rights of individuals. . . .

Few social or political issues in our history have been more vigorously debated and more extensively ventilated than the issue of racial discrimination, particularly in education. Given the stress and anguish of the history of efforts to escape from the shackles of the "separate but equal" doctrine, it cannot be said that educational institutions that, for whatever reasons, practice racial discrimination, are institutions exercising "beneficial and stabilizing influences in community life," or should be encouraged by having all taxpayers share in their support by way of special tax status. . . . Whatever may be the rationale for such private schools' policies, and however sincere the rationale may be, racial discrimination in education is contrary to public policy.

Racially discriminatory educational institutions cannot be viewed as conferring a public benefit within the "charitable" concept discussed earlier, or within the Congressional intent underlying § 170 and § 501(c)(3). . . .

Petitioners contend that, even if the Commissioner's policy is valid as to nonreligious private schools, that policy cannot constitutionally be applied to schools that engage in racial discrimination on the basis of sincerely held religious beliefs. As to such schools it is argued that the IRS construction of § 170 and § 501(c)(3) violates their free exercise rights under the Religion Clauses of the First Amendment. This contention presents claims not heretofore considered by this Court in precisely this context.

This Court has long held the Free Exercise Clause of the First Amendment an absolute prohibition against governmental regulation of religious beliefs. . . . As interpreted by this Court, moreover, the Free Exercise Clause provides substantial protection for lawful conduct grounded in religious belief. . . . However, "[n]ot all burdens on religion are unconstitutional. . . . The state may justify a limitation on religious liberty by showing that it is essential to accomplish an overriding governmental interest."

On occasion this Court has found certain governmental interests so compelling as to allow even regulations prohibiting religiously based conduct. In *Prince* v. *Massachusetts,* for example, the Court held that neutrally cast child labor laws prohibiting sale of printed materials on public streets could be applied to prohibit children from dispensing religious literature. The Court found no constitutional infirmity in "excluding [Jehovah's Witness children] from doing there what no other children may do.". . . Denial of tax benefits will inevitably have a substantial impact on the operation of private religious schools, but will not prevent those schools from observing their religious tenets.

The governmental interest at stake here is compelling. As discussed [above] the Government has a fundamental, overriding interest in eradicating racial discrimination in education—discrimination that prevailed, with official approval, for the first 165 years of this Nation's history. That governmental interest substantially outweighs whatever burden denial of tax benefits places on petitioners' exercise of their religious beliefs. The interests asserted by petitioners cannot be accommodated with that compelling governmental interest . . . and no "less restrictive means" . . . are available to achieve the governmental interest.

Goldman v. Weinberger (1986)[25]

The *Wisconsin v. Yoder* case suggested that bona fide religious beliefs might provide the grounds for a free-exercise right to be exempted from generally applicable laws, in that case, laws requiring the schooling of children. Here, a member of the armed forces sought an exemption from military regulations that would prevent him from wearing a yarmulke.

Justice Rehnquist delivered the opinion of the Court.

Petitioner S. Simcha Goldman contends that the Free Exercise Clause of the First Amendment to the United States Constitution permits him to wear a yarmulke while in uniform, notwithstanding an Air Force regulation mandating uniform dress for Air Force personnel. . . .

Petitioner Goldman is an Orthodox Jew and ordained rabbi. In 1973, he was accepted into the Armed Forces Health Professions Scholarship Program and placed on inactive reserve status in the Air Force while he studied clinical psychology at Loyola University of Chicago. During his three years in the scholarship program, he received a monthly stipend and an allowance for tuition, books, and fees. After completing his Ph.D. in psychology, petitioner entered active service in the United States Air Force as a commissioned officer, in accordance with a requirement that participants in the scholarship program serve one year of active duty for each year of subsidized education. Petitioner was stationed at March Air Force Base in Riverside, California, and served as a clinical psychologist at the mental health clinic on the base.

Until 1981, petitioner was not prevented from wearing his yarmulke on the base. He avoided controversy by remaining close to his duty station in the health clinic and by wearing his service cap over the yarmulke when out of doors. But in April 1981, after he testified as a defense witness at a court-martial wearing his yarmulke but not his service cap, opposing counsel lodged a complaint with Colonel Joseph Gregory, the Hospital Commander, arguing that petitioner's practice of wearing his yarmulke was a violation of Air Force Regulation (AFR) 35–10. This regulation states in pertinent part that "[h]eadgear will not be worn . . . [w]hile indoors except by armed security police in the performance of their duties." AFR 35–10. ¶ 1–6.h(2)(f) (1980).

Colonel Gregory informed petitioner that wearing a yarmulke while on duty does indeed violate AFR 35–10, and ordered him not to violate this regulation outside the hospital. Although virtually all of petitioner's time on the base was spent in the hospital, he refused. Later, after petitioner's attorney protested to the Air Force General Counsel, Colonel Gregory revised his order to prohibit petitioner from wearing the yarmulke even in the hospital. Petitioner's request to report for duty in civilian clothing pending legal resolution of the issue was denied. The next day he received a formal letter of reprimand, and was warned that failure to obey AFR 35–10 could subject him to a court-martial. Colonel Gregory also withdrew a recommendation that petitioner's application to extend the term of his active service be approved, and substituted a negative recommendation.

Petitioner then sued respondent Secretary of Defense and others, claiming that the application of AFR 35–10 to prevent him from wearing his yarmulke infringed upon his First Amendment freedom to exercise his religious beliefs. . . .

Petitioner argues that AFR 35–10, as applied to him, prohibits religiously motivated conduct and should therefore be analyzed under the standard enunciated in Sherbert v Verner. . . . But we have repeatedly held that "the military is, by necessity, a specialized society separate from civilian society." . . .

Our review of military regulations challenged on First Amendment grounds is far more deferential than constitutional review of similar laws or regulations designed for civilian society. The military need not encourage debate or tolerate protest to the extent that such tolerance is required of the civilian state by the First Amendment; to accomplish its mission the military must foster instinctive obedience, unity, commitment, and esprit de corps. . . .

These aspects of military life do not, of course, render entirely nugatory in the military context the guarantees of the First Amendment. . . . But "within the military community there is simply not the same [individual] autonomy as there is in the larger civilian community.". . . In the context of the present case, when evaluating whether military needs justify a particular restriction on religiously motivated conduct, courts must give great deference to the professional judgment of military authorities concerning the relative importance of a particular military interest. . . .

The considered professional judgment of the Air Force is that the traditional outfitting of personnel in standardized uniforms encourages the subordination of personal preferences and identities in favor of the overall group mission. Uniforms encourage a sense of hierarchical unity by tending to eliminate outward individual distinctions except for those of rank. The Air Force considers them as vital during peacetime as during war because its personnel must be ready to provide an effective defense on a moment's notice; the necessary habits of discipline and unity must be developed in advance of trouble. We have acknowledged that "[t]he inescapable demands of military discipline and obedience to orders cannot be taught on battle-fields; the habit of immediate compliance with military procedures and orders must be virtually reflex with no time for debate or reflection.". . .

To this end, the Air Force promulgated AFR 35–10, a 190-page document, which states that "Air Force members will wear the Air Force uniform while performing their military duties, except when authorized to wear civilian clothes on duty." The rest of the document describes in minute detail all of the various items of apparel that must be worn as part of the Air Force uniform. It authorizes a few individualized options with respect to certain pieces of jewelry and hair style, but even these are subject to severe limitations. . . . In general, authorized headgear may be worn only out of doors. . . . Indoors, "[h]eadgear [may] not be worn . . . except by armed security police in the performance of their duties.". . . A narrow exception to this rule exists for headgear worn during indoor religious ceremonies. . . . In addition, military commanders may in their discretion permit visible religious headgear and other such apparel in designated living quarters and nonvisible items generally. . . .

Petitioner Goldman contends that the Free Exercise Clause of the First Amendment requires the Air Force to make an exception to its uniform dress requirements for religious apparel unless the accouterments create a "clear danger" of undermining discipline and esprit de corps. He asserts that in general, visible but "unobtrusive" apparel will not create such a danger and must therefore be accommodated. He argues that the Air Force failed to prove that a specific exception for his practice of wearing an unobtrusive yarmulke would threaten discipline. He contends that the Air Force's assertion to the contrary is mere ipse dixit, with no support from actual experience or a scientific study in the record, and is contradicted by expert testimony that religious exceptions to AFR 35–10 are in fact desirable and will increase morale by making the Air Force a more humane place.

But whether or not expert witnesses may feel that religious exceptions to AFR 35–10 are desirable is quite beside the point. The desirability of dress regulations in the military is decided by the appropriate military officials, and they are under no constitutional mandate to abandon their considered professional judgment. Quite obviously, to the extent the regulations do not permit the wearing of religious apparel such as a yarmulke, a practice described by petitioner as silent devotion akin to prayer, military life may be more objectionable for petitioner and probably others. But the First Amendment does not require the military to accommodate such practices in the face of its view that they would detract from the uniformity sought by the dress regulations. The Air Force has drawn the line essentially between religious apparel that is visible and that which is not, and we hold that those portions of the regulations challenged here reasonably and evenhandedly regulate dress in the interest of the military's perceived need for uniformity. The First Amendment therefore does not prohibit them from being applied to petitioner even though their effect is to restrict the wearing of the headgear required by his religious beliefs. . . .

* * *

Justice Brennan, with whom Justice Marshall joins, dissenting.

Simcha Goldman invokes this Court's protection of his First Amendment right to fulfill one of the traditional religious obligations of a male Orthodox Jew—to cover his head before an omnipresent God. The Court's response to Goldman's request is to abdicate its role as principal expositor of the Constitution and protector of individual liberties in favor of credulous deference to unsupported assertions of military necessity. I dissent.

* * *

In ruling that the paramount interests of the Air Force override Dr. Goldman's free exercise claim, the Court overlooks the sincere and serious nature of his constitutional claim. It suggests that the desirability of certain dress regulations, rather than a First Amendment right, is at issue. The Court declares that in selecting dress regulations, "military officials . . . are under no constitutional mandate to abandon their considered professional judgment.". . . If Dr. Goldman wanted to wear a hat to keep his head warm or to cover a bald spot I would join the majority. Mere personal preferences in dress are not constitutionally protected. The First Amendment, however, restrains the Government's ability to prevent an Orthodox Jewish serviceman from, or punish him for, wearing a yarmulke.

The Court also attempts, unsuccessfully, to minimize the burden that was placed on Dr. Goldman's rights. The fact that "the regulations do not permit the wearing of . . . a yarmulke," does not simply render military life for observant Orthodox Jews "objectionable.". . . It sets up an almost absolute bar to the fulfillment of a religious duty. Dr. Goldman spent most of his time in uniform indoors, where the dress code forbade him even to cover his head with his service cap. Consequently, he was asked to violate the tenets of his faith virtually every minute of every workday.

* * *

Dr. Goldman has asserted a substantial First Amendment claim, which is entitled to meaningful review by this Court. The Court, however, evades its responsibility by eliminating, in all but name only, judicial review of military regulations that interfere with the fundamental constitutional rights of service personnel.

Our cases have acknowledged that in order to protect our treasured liberties, the military must be able to command service members to sacrifice a great many of the individual freedoms they enjoyed in the civilian community and to endure certain limitations on the freedoms they retain. . . . Notwithstanding this acknowledgment, we have steadfastly maintained that "'our citizens in uniform may not be stripped of basic rights simply because they have doffed their civilian clothes.'" . . . And, while we have hesitated, due to our lack of expertise concerning military affairs and our respect for the delegated authority of a coordinate branch, to strike down restrictions on individual liberties which could reasonably be justified as necessary to the military's vital function, . . . we have never abdicated our obligation of judicial review. . . .

Today the Court eschews its constitutionally mandated role. It adopts for review of military decisions affecting First Amendment rights a subrational-basis standard—absolute, uncritical "deference to the professional judgment of military authorities.". . . If a branch of the military declares one of its rules sufficiently important to outweigh a service person's constitutional rights, it seems that the Court will accept that conclusion, no matter how absurd or unsupported it may be.

A deferential standard of review, however, need not, and should not, mean that the Court must credit arguments that defy common sense. When a military service burdens the free exercise rights of its members in the name of necessity, it must provide, as an initial matter and at a minimum, a *credible* explanation of how the contested practice is likely to interfere with the proffered military interest. Unabashed ipse dixit cannot outweigh a constitutional right.

In the present case, the Air Force asserts that its interests in discipline and uniformity would be undermined by an exception to the dress code permitting observant male Orthodox Jews to wear yarmulkes. The Court simply restates these assertions without offering any explanation how the exception Dr. Goldman requests reasonably could interfere with the Air Force's interests. Had the Court given actual consideration to Goldman's claim, it would have been compelled to decide in his favor.

* * *

The Government maintains in its brief that discipline is jeopardized whenever exceptions to military regulations are granted. Service personnel must be trained to obey even the most arbitrary command reflexively. Non-Jewish personnel will perceive the wearing of a yarmulke by an Orthodox Jew as an unauthorized departure from the rules and will begin to question the principle of unswerving obedience. Thus shall our fighting forces slip down the treacherous slope toward unkempt appearance, anarchy, and, ultimately, defeat at the hands of our enemies.

The contention that the discipline of the Armed Forces will be subverted if Orthodox Jews are allowed to wear yarmulkes with their uniforms surpasses belief. It lacks support in the record of this case, and the Air Force offers no basis for it as a general proposition. While the perilous slope permits the services arbitrarily to refuse exceptions requested to satisfy mere personal preferences, before the Air Force may burden free exercise rights it must advance, at the *very least,* a rational reason for doing so. . . .

* * *

The Government also argues that the services have an important interest in uniform dress, because such dress establishes the pre-eminence of group identity, thus fostering esprit de corps and loyalty to the service that transcends individual bonds. In its brief, the Government characterizes the yarmulke as an assertion of individuality and as a badge of religious and ethnic identity, strongly suggesting that, as such, it could drive a wedge of divisiveness between members of the services.

First, the purported interests of the Air Force in complete uniformity of dress and in elimination of individuality or visible identification with any group other than itself are belied by the service's own regulations. The dress code expressly abjures the need for total uniformity . . .

> "Neither the Air Force nor the public expects absolute uniformity of appearance. Each member has the right, within limits, to express individuality through his or her appearance. However, the image of a disciplined service member who can be relied on to do his or her job excludes the extreme, the unusual, and the fad."

It cannot be seriously contended that a serviceman in a yarmulke presents so extreme, so unusual, or so faddish an image that public confidence in his ability to perform his duties will be destroyed. Under the Air Force's own standards, then, Dr. Goldman should have and could have been granted an exception to wear his yarmulke.

The dress code also allows men to wear up to three rings and one identification bracelet of "neat and conservative," but nonuniform, design. . . . This jewelry is apparently permitted even if, as is often the case with rings, it associates the wearer with a denominational school or a religious or secular fraternal organization. If these emblems of religious, social, and ethnic identity are not deemed to be unacceptably divisive, the Air Force cannot rationally justify its bar against yarmulkes on that basis.

Moreover, the services allow, and rightly so, other manifestations of religious diversity. It is clear to all service personnel that some members attend Jewish services, some Christian, some Islamic, and some yet other religious services. Barracks mates see Mormons wearing temple garments, Orthodox Jews wearing tzitzit, and Catholics wearing crosses and scapulars. That they come from different faiths and ethnic backgrounds is not a secret that can or should be kept from them.

I find totally implausible the suggestion that the overarching group identity of the Air Force would be threatened if Orthodox Jews were allowed to wear yarmulkes with their uniforms. To the contrary, a yarmulke worn with a United States military uniform is an eloquent reminder that the shared and proud identity of United States serviceman embraces and unites religious and ethnic pluralism.

Finally, the Air Force argues that while Dr. Goldman describes his yarmulke as an "unobtrusive" addition to his uniform, obtrusiveness is a purely relative, standardless judgment. The Government notes that while a yarmulke might not seem obtrusive to a Jew, neither does a turban to a Sikh, a saffron robe to a Satchidananda Ashram-Integral Yogi, nor do dreadlocks to a Rastafarian. If the Court were to require the Air

Force to permit yarmulkes, the service must also allow all of these other forms of dress and grooming.

The Government dangles before the Court a classic parade of horribles, the specter of a brightly-colored, "rag-tag band of soldiers.". . . Although turbans, saffron robes, and dread-locks are not before us in this case and must each be evaluated against the reasons a service branch offers for prohibiting personnel from wearing them while in uniform, a reviewing court could legitimately give deference to dress and grooming rules that have a *reasoned* basis in, for example, functional utility, health and safety considerations, and the goal of a polished, professional appearance. . . . (identifying neatness, cleanliness, safety, and military image as the four elements of the dress code's "high standard of dress and personal appearance"). It is the lack of any reasoned basis for prohibiting yarmulkes that is so striking here.

Furthermore, contrary to its intimations, the Air Force has available to it a familiar standard for determining whether a particular style of yarmulke is consistent with a polished, professional military appearance—the "neat and conservative" standard by which the service judges jewelry. . . . No rational reason exists why yarmulkes cannot be judged by the same criterion. Indeed, at argument Dr. Goldman declared himself willing to wear whatever style and color yarmulke the Air Force believes best comports with its uniform. . . .

* * *

Through our Bill of Rights, we pledged ourselves to attain a level of human freedom and dignity that had no parallel in history. Our constitutional commitment to religious freedom and to acceptance of religious pluralism is one of our greatest achievements in that noble endeavor. Almost 200 years after the First Amendment was drafted, tolerance and respect for all religions still set us apart from most other countries and draws to our shores refugees from religious persecution from around the world.

Guardianship of this precious liberty is not the exclusive domain of federal courts. It is the responsibility as well of the States and of the other branches of the Federal Government. Our military services have a distinguished record of providing for many of the religious needs of their personnel. But that they have satisfied much of their constitutional obligation does not remove their actions from judicial scrutiny. Our Nation has preserved freedom of religion, not through trusting to the good faith of individual agencies of government alone, but through the constitutionally mandated vigilant oversight and checking authority of the judiciary.

It is not the province of the federal courts to second-guess the professional judgments of the military services, but we are bound by the Constitution to assure ourselves that there exists a rational foundation for assertions of military necessity when they interfere with the free exercise of religion. "The concept of military necessity is seductively broad," and military decisionmakers themselves are as likely to succumb to its allure as are the courts and the general public. Definitions of necessity are influenced by decision-makers' experiences and values. As a consequence, in pluralistic societies such as ours, institutions dominated by a majority are inevitably, if inadvertently, insensitive to the needs and values of minorities when these needs and values differ from those of the majority. The military, with its strong ethic of conformity and unquestioning obedience, may be particularly impervious to minority needs and values. A critical function of the Religion Clauses of the First Amendment is to protect the rights of members of minority religions against quiet erosion by majoritarian social institutions that dismiss minority beliefs and practices as unimportant, because unfamiliar. It is the constitutional role of this Court to ensure that this purpose of the First Amendment be realized.

The Court and the military services have presented patriotic Orthodox Jews with a painful dilemma—the choice between fulfilling a religious obligation and serving their country. Should the draft be reinstated, compulsion will replace choice. Although the pain the services inflict on Orthodox Jewish servicemen is clearly the result of insensitivity rather than design, it is unworthy of our military because it is unnecessary. The Court and the military have refused these servicemen their constitutional rights; we must hope that Congress will correct this wrong.

Bowen v. Roy (1986)[26]

This case involves another religiously based request for an exemption to a generally applicable law or regulation: to receive food stamps and other federal benefits, every recipient is required by law to have a social security number. The appellants in this case sought an exception from this requirement for their two-year-old daughter, Little Bird of the Snow, on the grounds that under their Native American religious beliefs the social security number would "rob the spirit" of the little girl.

Chief Justice Burger announced the judgment of the Court and delivered the opinion of the Court with respect to Parts I and II, and an opinion with respect to Part III, in which Justice Powell and Justice Rehnquist join.

The question presented is whether the Free Exercise Clause of the First Amendment compels the Government to accommodate a religiously based objection to the statutory requirements that a Social Security number be provided by an applicant seeking to receive certain welfare benefits and that the States use these numbers in administering the benefit programs.

I

Appellees Stephen J. Roy and Karen Miller applied for and received benefits under the Aid to Families with Dependent Children program and the Food Stamp program. They refused to comply, however, with the requirement . . . that participants in these programs furnish their state welfare agencies with the Social Security numbers of the members of their household as a condition of receiving benefits. Appellees contended that obtaining a Social Security number for their 2-year-old daughter, Little Bird of the Snow, would violate their Native American religious beliefs. The Pennsylvania Department of Public Welfare thereafter terminated AFDC and medical benefits payable to appellees on the child's behalf and instituted proceedings to reduce the level of food stamps that appellees' household was receiving. Appellees then filed this action . . . arguing that the Free Exercise Clause entitled them to an exemption from the Social Security number requirement. . . .

At trial, Roy testified that he had recently developed a religious objection to obtaining a Social Security number for Little Bird of the Snow. Roy is a Native American descended from the Abenaki Tribe, and he asserts a religious belief that control over one's life is essential to spiritual purity and indispensable to "becoming a holy person." Based on recent conversations with an Abenaki chief, Roy believes that technology is "robbing the spirit of man." In order to prepare his daughter for greater spiritual power, therefore, Roy testified to his belief that he must keep her person and spirit unique and that the uniqueness of the Social Security number as an identifier, coupled with the other uses of the number over which she has no control, will serve to "rob the spirit" of his daughter and prevent her from attaining greater spiritual power. . . .

II

Our cases have long recognized a distinction between the freedom of individual belief, which is absolute, and the freedom of individual conduct, which is not absolute. This case implicates only the latter concern. Roy objects to the statutory requirement that state agencies "shall utilize" Social Security numbers not because it places any restriction on what he may believe or what he may do, but because he believes the use of the number may harm his daughter's spirit.

Never to our knowledge has the Court interpreted the First Amendment to require the Government *itself* to behave in ways that the individual believes will further his or her spiritual development or that of his or her family. The Free Exercise Clause simply cannot be understood to require the Government to conduct its own internal affairs in ways that comport with the religious beliefs of particular citizens. Just as the Government may not insist that appellees engage in any set form of religious observance, so appellees may not demand that the Government join in their chosen religious practices by refraining from using a number to identify their daughter. . . .

As a result, Roy may no more prevail on his religious objection to the Government's use of a Social Security number for his daughter than he could on a sincere religious objection to the size or color of the Government's filing cabinets. The Free Exercise Clause affords an individual protection from certain forms of governmental compulsion; it does not afford an individual a right to dictate the conduct of the Government's internal procedures.

As Roy points out, eight years ago Congress passed a Joint Resolution concerning American Indian religious freedom that provides guidance with respect to this case. As currently codified, the Resolution provides:

> "On and after August 11, 1978, it shall be the policy of the United States to protect and preserve for American Indians their inherent right of freedom to believe, express, and exercise the traditional religions of the American Indian, Eskimo, Aleut, and Native Hawaiians, including but not limited to access to sites, use and possession of sacred objects, and the freedom to worship through ceremonials and traditional rites.". . .

That Resolution—with its emphasis on protecting the freedom to believe, express, and exercise a religion—accurately identifies the mission of the Free Exercise Clause itself. The Federal Government's use of a Social Security number for Little Bird of the Snow does not itself in any degree impair Roy's "freedom to believe, express, and exercise" his religion.

Consequently, appellees' objection to the statutory requirement that each state agency "shall utilize" a Social Security number in the administration of its plan is without merit. . . .

III

The First Amendment's guarantee that "Congress shall make no law . . . prohibiting the free exercise" of religion holds an important place in our scheme of ordered liberty, but the Court has steadfastly maintained that claims of religious conviction do not automatically entitle a person to fix unilaterally the conditions and terms of dealings with the government. Not all burdens on religion are unconstitutional. . . .

The statutory requirement that applicants provide a Social Security number is wholly neutral in religious terms and uniformly applicable. There is no claim that there is any attempt by Congress to discriminate invidiously or any covert suppression of particular religious beliefs. The administrative requirement does not create any danger of censorship or place a direct condition or burden on the dissemination of religious views. It does not intrude on the organization of a religious institution or school. It may indeed confront some applicants for benefits with choices, but in no sense does it affirmatively compel appellees, by threat of sanctions, to refrain from religiously motivated conduct or to engage in conduct that they find objectionable for religious reasons. Rather, it is appellees who seek benefits from the Government and who assert that, because of certain religious beliefs, they should be excused from compliance with a condition that is binding on all other persons who seek the same benefits from the Government.

This is far removed from the historical instances of religious persecution and intolerance that gave concern to those who drafted the Free Exercise Clause of the First Amendment. . . . We are not unmindful of the importance of many government benefits today or of the value of sincerely held religious beliefs.

However, while we do not believe that no government compulsion is involved, we cannot ignore the reality that denial of such benefits by a uniformly applicable statute neutral on its face is of a wholly different, less intrusive nature than affirmative compulsion or prohibition, by threat of penal sanctions, for conduct that has religious implications. . . .

We conclude then that government regulation that indirectly and incidentally calls for a choice between securing a governmental benefit and adherence to religious beliefs is wholly different from governmental action or legislation that criminalizes religiously inspired activity or inescapably compels conduct that some find objectionable for religious reasons. Although the denial of government benefits over religious objection can raise serious Free Exercise problems, these two very different forms of government action are not governed by the same constitutional standard. A governmental burden on religious liberty is not insulated from review simply because it is indirect, . . . but the nature of the burden is relevant to the standard the government must meet to justify the burden.

The general governmental interests involved here buttress this conclusion. Governments today grant a broad range of benefits; inescapably at the same time the administration of complex programs requires certain conditions and restrictions. Although in some situations a mechanism for individual consideration will be created, a policy decision by a government that it wishes to treat all applicants alike and that it does not wish to become involved in case-by-case inquiries into the genuineness of each religious objection to such condition or restrictions is entitled to substantial deference. Moreover, legitimate interests are implicated in the need to avoid any appearance of favoring religious over nonreligious applicants. . . .

As the Court has recognized before, given the diversity of beliefs in our pluralistic society and the necessity of providing governments with sufficient operating latitude, some incidental neutral restraints on the free exercise of religion are inescapable. As a matter of legislative policy, a legislature might decide to make religious accommodations to a general and neutral system of awarding benefits, "[b]ut our concern is not with the wisdom of legislation but with its constitutional limitation.". . . We conclude that the Congress' refusal to grant appellees a special exemption does not violate the Free Exercise Clause. . . .

Lyng v. Northwest Indian Cemetery Protective Association (1988)[27]

Many of the Supreme Court's cases involving the religion clauses of the First Amendment have originated in questions concerning education, taxation, and employment. This case is one of few involving another area of government activity—the country's roads and highways. Here the Supreme Court weighs the free-exercise claims of Native Americans against the government's desire to build a road through land long held sacred.

Justice O'Connor delivered the opinion of the Court.

This case requires us to consider whether the First Amendment's Free Exercise Clause prohibits the Government from permitting timber harvesting in, or constructing a road through, a portion of a National Forest that has traditionally been used for religious purposes by members of three American Indian tribes in northwestern California. We conclude that it does not.

* * *

As part of a project to create a paved 75-mile road linking two California towns, Gasquet and Orleans, the United States Forest Service has upgraded 49 miles of previously unpaved roads on federal land. In order to complete this project (the G-O road), the Forest Service must build a 6-mile paved segment through the Chimney Rock section of the Six Rivers National Forest. That section of the forest is situated between two other portions of the road that are already complete.

In 1977, the Forest Service issued a draft environmental impact statement that discussed proposals for upgrading an existing unpaved road that runs through the Chimney Rock area. In response to comments on the draft statement, the Forest Service commissioned a study of American Indian cultural and religious sites in the area. The Hoopa Valley Indian Reservation adjoins the Six Rivers National Forest, and the Chimney Rock area has historically been used for religious purposes by Yurok, Karok, and Tolowa Indians. The commissioned study, which was completed in 1979, found that the entire area "is significant as an integral and indispensible part of Indian religious conceptualization and practice.". . . Specific sites are used for certain rituals, and "successful use of the [area] is dependent upon and facilitated by certain qualities of the physical environment, the most important of which are privacy, silence, and an undisturbed natural setting.". . . The study concluded that constructing a road along any of the available routes "would cause serious and irreparable damage to the sacred areas which are an integral and necessary part of the belief systems and lifeway of Northwest California Indian peoples.". . . Accordingly, the report recommended that the G-O road not be completed.

In 1982, the Forest Service decided not to adopt this recommendation, and it prepared a final environmental impact statement for construction of the road. The Regional Forester selected a route that avoided archeological sites and was removed as far as possible from the sites used by contemporary Indians for specific spiritual activities. Alternative routes that would have avoided the Chimney Rock area altogether were rejected because they would have required the acquisition of private land, had serious soil stability problems, and would in any event have traversed areas having ritualistic value to American Indians. . . . At about the same time, the Forest Service adopted a management plan allowing for the harvesting of significant amounts of timber in this area of the forest. The management plan provided for one-half mile protective zones around all the religious sites identified in the report that had been commissioned in connection with the G-O road.

* * *

The Free Exercise Clause of the First Amendment provides that "Congress shall make no law . . . prohibiting the free exercise [of religion]." It is undisputed that the Indian respondents' beliefs are sincere and that the Government's proposed actions will have severe adverse effects on the practice of their religion. Those respondents contend that the burden on their religious practices is heavy enough to violate the Free Exercise Clause unless the Government can demonstrate a compelling need to complete the G-O road or to engage in timber harvesting in the Chimney Rock area. We disagree.

. . . In this case, it is said that disruption of the natural environment caused by the G-O road will diminish the sacredness of the area in question and create distractions that will interfere with "training and ongoing religious experience of individuals using [sites within] the area for personal medicine and growth . . . and as integrated parts of a system of religious belief and practice which correlates ascending degrees of personal power with a geographic hierarchy of power.". . . ("Scarred hills and mountains, and disturbed rocks destroy the purity of the sacred areas, and [Indian] consultants repeatedly stressed the need of a training doctor to be undistracted by such disturbance").

* * *

The building of a road or the harvesting of timber on publicly owned land cannot meaningfully be distinguished from the use of a Social Security number in Roy. In both cases, the challenged Government action would interfere significantly with private persons' ability to pursue spiritual fulfillment according to their own religious beliefs. In neither case, however, would the affected individuals be coerced by the Government's action into violating their religious beliefs; nor would either governmental action penalize religious activity by denying any person an equal share of the rights, benefits, and privileges enjoyed by other citizens.

* * *

Whatever may be the exact line between unconstitutional prohibitions on the free exercise of religion and the legitimate conduct by government of its own affairs, the location of the line cannot depend on measuring the effects of a governmental action on a religious objector's spiritual development. The Government does not dispute, and we have no reason to doubt, that the logging and road-building projects at issue in this case could have devastating effects on traditional Indian religious practices. Those practices are intimately and inextricably bound up with the unique features of the Chimney Rock area, which is known to the Indians as the "high country." Individual practitioners use this area for personal spiritual development; some of their activities are believed to be critically important in advancing the welfare of the tribe, and indeed, of mankind itself. The Indians use this area, as they have used it for a very long time, to conduct a wide variety of specific rituals that aim to accomplish their religious goals. According to their beliefs, the rituals would not be efficacious if conducted at other sites than the ones traditionally used, and too much disturbance of the area's natural state would clearly render any meaningful continuation of traditional practices impossible. To be sure, the Indians themselves were far from unanimous in opposing the G-O road, . . . and it seems less than certain that construction of the road will be so disruptive that it will doom their religion. Nevertheless, we can assume that the threat to the efficacy of at least some religious practices is extremely grave.

Even if we assume that we should accept the [lower court's] prediction, according to which the G-O road will "virtually destroy the . . . Indians' ability to practice their religion," . . . the Constitution simply does not provide a principle that could justify upholding respondents' legal claims. However much we might wish that it were otherwise, government simply could not operate if it were required to satisfy every citizen's religious needs and desires. A broad range of government activities—from social welfare programs to foreign aid to conservation projects—will always be considered essential to the spiritual well-being of some citizens, often on the basis of sincerely held religious beliefs. Others will find the very same activities deeply offensive, and perhaps incompatible with their own search for spiritual fulfillment and with the tenets of their religion. The First Amendment must apply to all citizens alike, and it can give to none of them a veto over public programs that do not prohibit the free exercise of religion. The Constitution does not, and courts cannot, offer to reconcile the various competing demands on government, many of them rooted in sincere religious belief, that inevitably arise in so diverse a society as ours. That task, to the extent that it is feasible, is for the legislatures and other institutions. . . .

* * *

Justice Brennan, with whom Justice Marshall and Justice Blackmun join, dissenting.

"'[The Free Exercise Clause,'" the Court explains today, "'is written in terms of what the government cannot do to the individual, not in terms of what the individual can exact from the government. . . .'" Pledging fidelity to this unremarkable constitutional principle, the Court nevertheless concludes that even where the Government uses federal land in a manner that threatens the very existence of a Native American religion, the Government is simply not *"doing"* anything to the practitioners of that faith. Instead, the Court believes that Native Americans who request that the Government refrain from destroying their religion effectively seek to exact from the Government de facto beneficial ownership of federal property. These two astonishing conclusions follow naturally from the Court's determination that federal land-use decisions that render the practice of a given religion impossible do not burden that religion in a manner cognizable under the Free Exercise Clause, because such decisions neither coerce conduct inconsistent with religious belief nor penalize religious activity. The constitutional guarantee we interpret today, however, draws no such fine distinctions between types of restraints on religious exercise, but rather is directed against any form of governmental action that frustrates or inhibits religious practice. Because the Court today refuses even to acknowledge the constitutional injury respondents will suffer, and because this refusal essentially leaves Native Americans with absolutely no constitutional protection against perhaps the gravest threat to their religious practices, I dissent.

* * *

For at least 200 years and probably much longer, the Yurok, Karok, and Tolowa Indians have held sacred an approximately 25 square-mile area of land situated in what is today the Blue Creek Unit of Six Rivers National Forest in northwestern California. As the Government readily concedes, regular visits to this area, known to respondent Indians as the "high country," have played and continue to play a "critical" role in the religious practices and rituals of these tribes. . . . Those beliefs, only briefly described in the Court's opinion, are crucial to a proper understanding of respondents' claims.

As the Forest Service's commissioned study, the Theodoratus Report, explains, for Native Americans religion is not a discrete sphere of activity separate from all others, and any attempt to isolate the religious aspects of Indian life "is in reality an exercise which forces Indian concepts into non-Indian categories.". . . Thus, for most Native Americans, "[t]he area of worship cannot be delineated from social, political, cultur[al], and other areas o[f] Indian lifestyle.". . . A pervasive feature of this lifestyle is the individual's relationship with the natural world; this relationship, which can accurately though somewhat incompletely be characterized as one of stewardship, forms the core of what might be called, for want of a better nomenclature, the Indian religious experience. While traditional western religions view creation as the work of a deity "who institutes natural laws which then govern the operation of physical nature," tribal religions regard creation as an ongoing process in which they are morally and religiously obligated to participate. . . . Native Americans fulfill this duty through ceremonies and rituals designed to preserve and stabilize the earth and to protect humankind from disease and other catastrophes. Failure to conduct these ceremonies in the manner and place specified, adherents believe, will result in great harm to the earth and to the people whose welfare depends upon it. . . .

In marked contrast to traditional western religions, the belief systems of Native Americans do not rely on doctrines, creeds, or dogmas. Established or universal truths—the mainstay of western religions—play no part in Indian faith. Ceremonies are communal efforts undertaken for specific purposes in accordance with instructions handed down from generation to generation. Commentaries on or interpretations of the rituals themselves are deemed absolute violations of the ceremonies, whose value lies not in their ability to explain the natural world or to enlighten individual believers but in their efficacy as protectors and enhancers of tribal existence. . . . Where dogma lies at the heart of western religions, Native American faith is inextricably bound to the use of land. The site-specific nature of Indian religious practice derives from the Native American perception that land is itself a sacred, living being. . . . Rituals are performed in prescribed locations not merely as a matter of traditional orthodoxy, but because land, like all other living things, is unique, and specific sites possess different spiritual properties and significance. Within this belief system, therefore, land is not fungible; indeed, at the time of the Spanish colonization of the American southwest, "all . . . Indians held in some form a belief in a sacred and indissoluble bond between themselves and the land in which their settlements were located.". . .

For respondent Indians, the most sacred of lands is the high country where, they believe, prehuman spirits moved with the coming of humans to the earth. Because these spirits are seen as the source of religious power, or "medicine," many of the tribes' rituals and practices require frequent journeys to the area. Thus, for example, religious leaders preparing for the complex of ceremonies that underlie the tribes' World Renewal efforts must travel to specific sites in the high country in order to attain the medicine necessary for successful renewal. Similarly, individual tribe members may seek curative powers for the healing of the sick, or personal medicine for particular purposes such as good luck in singing, hunting, or love. A period of preparation generally precedes such visits, and individuals must select trails in the sacred area according to the medicine they seek and their abilities, gradually moving to increasingly more powerful sites, which are typically located at higher altitudes. Among the most powerful of sites are Chimney Rock, Doctor Rock, and Peak 8, all of which are elevated rock outcroppings.

According to the Theodoratus Report, the qualities "of silence, the aesthetic perspective, and the physical attributes, are an extension of the sacredness of [each] particular site.". . . The act of medicine making is akin to meditation: the individual must integrate physical, mental, and vocal actions in order to communicate with the prehuman spirits. As a result, "successful use of the high country is dependent upon and facilitated by certain qualities of the physical environment, the most important of which are privacy, silence, and an undisturbed natural setting."... Although few tribe members actually make medicine at the most powerful sites, the entire tribe's welfare hinges on the success of the individual practitioners.

* * *

The Court does not for a moment suggest that the interests served by the G-O road are in any way compelling, or that they outweigh the destructive effect construction of the road will have on respondents' religious practices. Instead, the Court embraces the Government's contention that its prerogative as landowner should always take precedence over a claim that a particular use of federal property infringes religious practices. Attempting to justify this rule, the Court argues that the First Amendment bars only outright prohibitions, indirect coercion, and penalties on the free exercise of religion. All other "incidental effects of government programs," it concludes, even those "which may make it more difficult to practice certain religions but which have no tendency to coerce individuals into acting contrary to their religious beliefs," simply do not give rise to constitutional concerns. . . . Since our recognition nearly half a century ago that restraints on religious conduct implicate the concerns of the Free Exercise Clause, . . . we have never suggested that the protections of the guarantee are limited to so narrow a range of governmental burdens. The land-use decision challenged here will restrain respondents from practicing their religion as surely and as completely as any of the governmental actions we have struck down in the past, and the Court's efforts simply to define away respondents' injury as nonconstitutional are both unjustified and ultimately unpersuasive. . . .

I . . . cannot accept the Court's premise that the form of the Government's restraint on religious practice, rather than its effect, controls our constitutional analysis. Respondents here have demonstrated that construction of the G-O road will completely frustrate the practice of their religion, for as the lower courts found, the proposed logging and construction activities will virtually destroy respondents' religion, and will therefore necessarily force them into abandoning those practices altogether. . . .

Ultimately, the Court's coercion test turns on a distinction between governmental actions that compel affirmative conduct inconsistent with religious belief, and those governmental actions that prevent conduct consistent with religious belief. In my view, such a distinction is without constitutional significance. The crucial word in the constitutional text, as the Court itself acknowledges, is "prohibit," . . . a comprehensive term that in no way suggests that the intended protection is aimed only at governmental actions that coerce affirmative conduct. Nor does the Court's distinction comport with the principles animating the constitutional guarantee: religious freedom is threatened no less by governmental action that makes the practice of one's chosen faith impossible than by governmental programs that pressure one to engage in conduct inconsistent with religious beliefs. The Court attempts to explain the line it draws by arguing that the protections of the Free Exercise Clause "cannot depend on measuring the effects of a governmental action on a religious objector's spiritual development," . . . for in a society as diverse as ours, the Government cannot help but offend the "religious needs and desires" of some citizens. . . . While I agree that governmental action that simply offends religious sensibilities may not be challenged under the Clause, we have recognized that laws that affect spiritual development by impeding the integration of children into the religious community or by increasing the expense of adherence to religious principles—in short, laws that frustrate or inhibit religious *practice*—trigger the protections of the constitutional guarantee. Both common sense and our prior cases teach us, therefore, that governmental action that makes the practice of a given faith more difficult necessarily penalizes that practice and thereby tends to prevent adherence to religious belief. The harm to the practitioners is the same regardless of the manner in which the Government restrains their religious expression, and the Court's fear that an "effects" test will permit religious adherents to challenge governmental actions they merely find "offensive" in no way justifies its refusal to recognize the constitutional injury citizens suffer when governmental action not only offends but actually restrains their religious practices. Here, respondents have demonstrated that the Government's proposed activities will completely prevent them from practicing their religion, and such a showing . . . entitles them to the protections of the Free Exercise Clause.

* * *

In the final analysis, the Court's refusal to recognize the constitutional dimension of respondents' injuries stems from its concern that acceptance of respondents' claim could potentially strip the Government of its ability to manage and use vast tracts of federal property. . . . In addition, the nature of respondents' site-specific religious practices raises the specter of future suits in which Native Americans seek to exclude all human activity from such areas. . . . These concededly legitimate concerns lie at the very heart of this case, which represents yet another stress point in the longstanding conflict between two disparate cultures—the dominant western culture, which views land in terms of ownership and use, and that of Native Americans, in which concepts of private property are not only alien, but contrary to a belief system that holds land sacred. Rather than address this conflict in any meaningful fashion, however, the Court disclaims all responsibility for balancing these competing and potentially irreconcilable interests, choosing instead to turn this difficult task over to the Federal Legislature. Such an abdication is more than merely indefensible as an institutional matter: by defining respondents' injury as "non-constitutional," the Court has effectively bestowed on one party to this conflict the unilateral authority to resolve all future disputes in its favor, subject only to the Court's toothless exhortation to be "sensitive" to affected religions. In my view, however, Native Americans deserve—and the Constitution demands—more than this. . . .

Church of Lukumi v. Hialeah (1993)[28]

Animal sacrifices played an important role in many religions for millennia, although the practice has been relatively uncommon in modern America. Nevertheless, the Santeria religion, a syncretistic blend of aspects of traditional African religion with elements of Roman Catholicism, employs annual sacrifice as an important devotional practice. A Santeria group announced plans to locate in

Hialeah, Florida, prompting the city to enact several ordinances designed to prohibit animal sacrifices. The Santeria church then sued to have the ordinances declared unconstitutional as a violation of the free-exercise clause.

Justice Kennedy delivered the opinion of the Court. . . .

The principle that government may not enact laws that suppress religious belief or practice is so well understood that few violations are recorded in our opinions. . . . Concerned that this fundamental nonpersecution principle of the First Amendment was implicated here, however, we granted certiorari. . . .

Our review confirms that the laws in question were enacted by officials who did not understand, failed to perceive, or chose to ignore the fact that their official actions violated the Nation's essential commitment to religious freedom. The challenged laws had an impermissible object; and in all events the principle of general applicability was violated because the secular ends asserted in defense of the laws were pursued only with respect to conduct motivated by religious beliefs. We invalidate the challenged enactments. . . .

I

A

This case involves practices of the Santeria religion, which originated in the nineteenth century. When hundreds of thousands of members of the Yoruba people were brought as slaves from eastern Africa to Cuba, their traditional African religion absorbed significant elements of Roman Catholicism. The resulting syncretion, or fusion, is Santeria, "the way of the saints." The Cuban Yoruba express their devotion to spirits, called orishas, through the iconography of Catholic saints, Catholic symbols are often present at Santeria rites, and Santeria devotees attend the Catholic sacraments. . . .

The Santeria faith teaches that every individual has a destiny from God, a destiny fulfilled with the aid and energy of the orishas. The basis of the Santeria religion is the nurture of a personal relation with the orishas, and one of the principal forms of devotion is an animal sacrifice. . . . The sacrifice of animals as part of religious rituals has ancient roots. . . . Animal sacrifice is mentioned throughout the Old Testament, . . . and it played an important role in the practice of Judaism before destruction of the second Temple in Jerusalem. . . . In modern Islam, there is an annual sacrifice commemorating Abraham's sacrifice of a ram in the stead of his son. . . .

According to Santeria teaching, the orishas are powerful but not immortal. They depend for survival on the sacrifice. Sacrifices are performed at birth, marriage, and death rites, for the cure of the sick, for the initiation of new members and priests, and during an annual celebration. Animals sacrificed in Santeria rituals include chickens, pigeons, doves, ducks, guinea pigs, goats, sheep, and turtles. The animals are killed by the cutting of the carotid arteries in the neck. The sacrificed animal is cooked and eaten, except after healing and death rituals. . . .

Santeria adherents faced widespread persecution in Cuba, so the religion and its rituals were practiced in secret. The open practice of Santeria and its rites remains infrequent. . . . The religion was brought to this Nation most often by exiles from the

Cuban revolution. The District Court estimated that there are at least 50,000 practitioners in South Florida today. . . .

B

Petitioner Church of the Lukumi Babalu Aye, Inc. (Church), is a not-for-profit corporation organized under Florida law in 1973. The Church and its congregants practice the Santeria religion. The president of the Church is petitioner, Ernesto Pichardo, who is also the Church's priest and holds the religious title of Italero, the second highest in the Santeria faith. In April 1987, the Church leased land in the city of Hialeah, Florida, and announced plans to establish a house of worship as well as a school, cultural center, and museum. Pichardo indicated that the Church's goal was to bring the practice of the Santeria faith, including its ritual of animal sacrifice, into the open. The Church began the process of obtaining utility service and receiving the necessary licensing, inspection, and zoning approvals. Although the Church's efforts at obtaining the necessary licenses and permits were far from smooth, . . . it appears that it received all needed approvals by early August 1987.

The prospect of a Santeria church in their midst was distressing to many members of the Hialeah community, and the announcement of the plans to open a Santeria church in Hialeah prompted the city council to hold an emergency public session. . . .

In September 1987, the city council adopted three substantive ordinances addressing the issue of religious animal sacrifice. Ordinance 87–52 defined "sacrifice" as "to unnecessarily kill, torment, torture, or mutilate an animal in a public or private ritual or ceremony not for the primary purpose of food consumption," and prohibited owning or possessing an animal "intending to use such animal for food purposes." It restricted application of this prohibition, however, to any individual or group that "kills, slaughters or sacrifices animals for any type of ritual, regardless of whether or not the flesh or blood of the animal is to be consumed." The ordinance contained an exemption for slaughtering by "licensed establishment[s]" of animals "specifically raised for food purposes." Declaring, moreover, that the city council "has determined that the sacrificing of animals within the city limits is contrary to the public health, safety, welfare and morals of the community," the city council adopted Ordinance 87–71. That ordinance defined sacrifice as had Ordinance 87–52, and then provided that "[i]t shall be unlawful for any person, persons, corporations or associations to sacrifice any animal within the corporate limits of the City of Hialeah, Florida." The final Ordinance, 87–72, defined "slaughter" as "the killing of animals for food" and prohibited slaughter outside of areas zoned for slaughterhouse use. The ordinance provided an exemption, however, for the slaughter or processing for sale of "small numbers of hogs and/or cattle per week in accordance with an exemption provided by state law." All ordinances and resolutions passed the city council by unanimous vote. Violations of each of the four ordinances were punishable by fines not exceeding $500 or imprisonment not exceeding 60 days, or both. . . .

II

The Free Exercise Clause of the First Amendment, which has been applied to the States through the Fourteenth Amendment, . . . provides that "Congress shall make no law respecting an establishment of religion, or *prohibiting the free exercise thereof. . . .*" The city does not argue that Santeria is not a "religion" within the meaning of the First Amendment. Nor could it. Although the practice of animal sacrifice may seem abhorrent to some, "religious beliefs need not be acceptable, logical, consistent, or comprehensible to others in order to merit First Amendment protection.". . . Given the historical association between animal sacrifice and religious worship, . . . petitioners' assertion that animal sacrifice is an integral part of their religion "cannot be deemed bizarre or incredible.". . . Neither the city nor the courts below, moreover, have questioned the sincerity of petitioners' professed desire to conduct animal sacrifices for religious reasons. We must consider petitioners' First Amendment claim.

In addressing the constitutional protection for free exercise of religion, our cases establish the general proposition that a law that is neutral and of general applicability need not be justified by a compelling governmental interest even if the law has the incidental effect of burdening a particular religious practice. . . . Neutrality and general applicability are interrelated, and, as becomes apparent in this case, failure to satisfy one requirement is a likely indication that the other has not been satisfied. A law failing to satisfy these requirements must be justified by a compelling governmental interest and must be narrowly tailored to advance that interest. These ordinances fail to satisfy these requirements. . . .

A

In our Establishment Clause cases we have often stated the principle that the First Amendment forbids an official purpose to disapprove of a particular religion or of religion in general. . . . These cases, however, for the most part have addressed governmental efforts to benefit religion or particular religions, and so have dealt with a question different, at least in its formulation and emphasis, from the issue here. Petitioners allege an attempt to disfavor their religion because of the religious ceremonies it commands, and the Free Exercise Clause is dispositive in our analysis.

At a minimum, the protections of the Free Exercise Clause pertain if the law at issue discriminates against some or all religious beliefs or regulates or prohibits conduct because it is undertaken for religious reasons. . . . Indeed, it was "historical instances of religious persecution and intolerance that gave concern to those who drafted the Free Exercise Clause.". . .

* * *

Although a law targeting religious beliefs as such is never permissible, . . . if the object of a law is to infringe upon or restrict practices because of their religious motivation, the law is not neutral, . . . and it is invalid unless it is justified by a compelling interest and is narrowly tailored to advance that interest. There are, of course, many ways of demonstrating that the object or purpose of a law is the suppression of religion or religious conduct. To determine the object of a law, we must begin with its text, for the minimum requirement of neutrality is that a law not discriminate on its face. A law lacks facial neutrality if it refers to a religious practice without a secular meaning discernable from the language or context. Petitioners contend that three of the ordinances fail this test of facial neutrality because they use the words "sacrifice" and "ritual," words with strong religious connotations. . . . We agree that these words are consistent with the claim of facial discrimination, but the argument is not conclusive. The words "sacrifice" and "ritual" have a religious origin, but current use admits also of secular meanings. . . .

We reject the contention advanced by the city, . . . that our inquiry must end with the text of the laws at issue. Facial neutrality is not determinative. The Free Exercise Clause, like the Establishment Clause, extends beyond facial discrimination. . . . Official action that targets religious conduct for distinctive treatment cannot be shielded by mere compliance with the requirement of facial neutrality. The Free Exercise Clause protects against governmental hostility which is masked, as well as overt. . . .

The record in this case compels the conclusion that suppression of the central element of the Santeria worship service was the object of the ordinances. First, though use of the words "sacrifice" and "ritual" does not compel a finding of improper targeting of the Santeria religion, the choice of these words is support for our conclusion. There are further respects in which the text of the city council's enactments discloses the improper attempt to target Santeria. . . . recited that "residents and citizens of the City of Hialeah have expressed their concern that certain religions may propose to engage in practices which are inconsistent with public morals, peace or safety," and "reiterate[d]" the city's commitment to prohibit "any and all [such] acts of any and all religious groups." No one suggests, and on this record it cannot be maintained, that city officials had in mind a religion other than Santeria.

It becomes evident that these ordinances target Santeria sacrifice when the ordinances' operation is considered. Apart from the text, the effect of a law in its real operation is strong evidence of its object. To be sure, adverse impact will not always lead to a finding of impermissible targeting. For example, a social harm may have been a legitimate concern of government for reasons quite apart from discrimination. . . . The subject at hand does implicate, of course, multiple concerns unrelated to religious animosity, for example, the suffering or mistreatment visited upon the sacrificed animals, and health hazards from improper disposal. But the ordinances when considered together disclose an object remote from these legitimate concerns. The design of these laws [is] an impermissible attempt to target petitioners and their religious practices.

It is a necessary conclusion that almost the only conduct subject to [the] Ordinances is the religious exercise of Santeria church members. The texts show that they were drafted in tandem to achieve this result. We begin with Ordinance 87–71. It prohibits the sacrifice of animals but defines sacrifice as "to unnecessarily kill . . . an animal in a public or private ritual or ceremony not for the primary purpose of food consumption." The definition excludes almost all killings of animals except for religious sacrifice, and the primary purpose requirement narrows the proscribed category even further, in particular by exempting Kosher slaughter. . . . We need not discuss whether this differential treatment of two religions is itself an independent constitutional violation. . . . It suffices to recite this feature of the law as support for our conclusion that Santeria alone was the exclusive legislative concern. The net result . . . is that few if any killings of animals are prohibited other than Santeria sacrifice, which is proscribed because it occurs during a ritual or ceremony and its primary purpose is to make an offering to the orishas, not food consumption. Indeed, careful drafting ensured that, although Santeria sacrifice is prohibited, killings that are no more necessary or humane in almost all other circumstances are unpunished.

Operating in similar fashion is Ordinance 87–52, which prohibits the "possess[ion], sacrifice, or slaughter" of an animal with the "inten[t] to use such animal for food purposes." This prohibition, extending to the keeping of an animal as well as the killing itself, applies if the animal is killed in "any type of ritual" and there is an intent to use the animal for food, whether or not it is in fact consumed for food. The ordinance exempts, however, "any licensed [food] establishment" with regard to "any animals which are specifically raised for food purposes," if the activity is permitted by zoning and other laws. This exception, too, seems intended to cover Kosher slaughter. Again, the burden of the ordinance, in practical terms, falls on Santeria adherents but almost no others: If the killing is—unlike most Santeria sacrifices—unaccompanied by the intent to use the animal for food, then it is not prohibited by Ordinance 87–52; if the killing is specifically for food but does not occur during the course of "any type of ritual," it again falls outside the prohibition; and if the killing is for food and occurs during the course of a ritual, it is still exempted if it occurs in a properly zoned and licensed establishment and involves animals "specifically raised for food purposes." A pattern of exemptions parallels the pattern of narrow prohibitions. . . .

Ordinance 87–40 incorporates the Florida animal cruelty statute, Fla Stat § 828.12 (1987). Its prohibition is broad on its face, punishing "[w]hoever . . . unnecessarily . . . kills any animal." The city claims that this ordinance is the epitome of a neutral prohibition. . . . The problem, however, is the interpretation given to the ordinance by respondent and the Florida attorney general. Killings for religious reasons are deemed unnecessary, whereas most other killings fall outside the prohibition. The city, on what seems to be a per se basis, deems hunting, slaughter of animals for food, eradication of insects and pests, and euthanasia as necessary. . . .

The legitimate governmental interests in protecting the public health and preventing cruelty to animals could be addressed by restrictions stopping far short of a flat prohibition of all Santeria sacrificial practice. If improper disposal, not the sacrifice itself, is the harm to be prevented, the city could have imposed a general regulation on the disposal of organic garbage. It did not do so. Indeed, counsel for the city conceded at oral argument that, under the ordinances, Santeria sacrifices would be illegal even if they occurred in licensed, inspected, and zoned slaughterhouses. . . . Thus, these broad ordinances prohibit Santeria sacrifice even when it does not threaten the city's interest in the public health. . . .

Under similar analysis, narrower regulation would achieve the city's interest in preventing cruelty to animals. With regard to the city's interest in ensuring the adequate care of animals, regulation of conditions and treatment, regardless of why an animal is kept, is the logical response to the city's concern, not a prohibition on possession for the purpose of sacrifice. The same is true for the city's interest in prohibiting cruel methods of killing. Under federal and Florida law . . . killing an animal by the "simultaneous and instantaneous severance of the carotid arteries with a sharp instrument"—the method used in Kosher slaughter—is approved as humane. . . . If the city has a real concern that other methods are less humane, however, the subject of the regulation should be the method of slaughter itself, not a religious classification that is said to bear some general relation to it. . . .

In sum, the neutrality inquiry leads to one conclusion: The ordinances had as their object the suppression of religion. The pattern we have recited discloses animosity to Santeria adherents and their religious practices; the ordinances by their own terms target this religious exercise; the texts of the ordinances were gerrymandered with care to proscribe religious killings of animals but to exclude almost all secular killings; and the ordinances suppress much more religious conduct than is necessary in order to achieve the legitimate ends asserted in their defense. . . .

B

We turn next to a second requirement of the Free Exercise Clause, the rule that laws burdening religious practice must be of general applicability. . . . All laws are selective to some extent, but categories of selection are of paramount concern when a law has the incidental effect of burdening religious practice. . . .

The principle that government, in pursuit of legitimate interests, cannot in a selective manner impose burdens only on conduct motivated by religious belief is essential to the protection of the rights guaranteed by the Free Exercise Clause. . . . In this case we need not define with precision the standard used to evaluate whether a prohibition is of general application, for these ordinances fall well below the minimum standard necessary to protect First Amendment rights.

Respondent claims that [the] Ordinances advance two interests: protecting the public health and preventing cruelty to animals. The ordinances are underinclusive for those ends. They fail to prohibit nonreligious conduct that endangers these interests in a similar or greater degree than Santeria sacrifice does. The underinclusion is substantial, not inconsequential. Despite the city's proffered interest in preventing cruelty to animals, the ordinances are drafted with care to forbid few killings but those occasioned by religious sacrifice. Many types of animal deaths or kills for nonreligious reasons are either not prohibited or approved by express provision. For example, fishing—which occurs in Hialeah, . . . is legal. Extermination of mice and rats within a home is also permitted. Florida law . . . sanctions euthanasia of "stray, neglected, abandoned, or unwanted animals," . . . destruction of animals judicially removed from their owners "for humanitarian reasons" or when the animal "is of no commercial value," the infliction of pain or suffering "in the interest of medical science," the placing of poison in one's yard or enclosure, and the use of a live animal "to pursue or take wildlife or to participate in any hunting," and "to hunt wild hogs.". . .

The ordinances are also underinclusive with regard to the city's interest in public health, which is threatened by the disposal of animal carcasses in open public places and the consumption of uninspected meat. . . . Neither interest is pursued by respondent with regard to conduct that is not motivated by religious conviction. The health risks posed by the improper disposal of animal carcasses are the same whether Santeria sacrifice or some nonreligious killing preceded it. The city does not, however, prohibit hunters from bringing their kill to their houses, nor does it regulate disposal after their activity. . . .

We conclude, in sum, that each of Hialeah's ordinances pursues the city's governmental interests only against conduct motivated by religious belief. The ordinances "ha[ve] every appearance of a prohibition that society is prepared to impose upon [Santeria worshippers] but not upon itself." . . . This precise evil is what the requirement of general applicability is designed to prevent.

III

A law burdening religious practice that is not neutral or not of general application must undergo the most rigorous of scrutiny. . . . A law that targets religious conduct for distinctive treatment or advances legitimate governmental interests only against conduct with a religious motivation will survive strict scrutiny only in rare cases. It follows from what we have already said that these ordinances cannot withstand this scrutiny.

First, even were the governmental interests compelling, the ordinances are not drawn in narrow terms to accomplish those interests. . . . The proffered objectives are not pursued with respect to analogous non-religious conduct, and those interests could be achieved by narrower ordinances that burdened religion to a far lesser degree. The absence of narrow tailoring suffices to establish the invalidity of the ordinances. . . .

Respondent has not demonstrated, moreover, that, in the context of these ordinances, its governmental interests are compelling. Where government restricts only conduct protected by the First Amendment and fails to enact feasible measures to restrict other conduct producing substantial harm or alleged harm of the same sort, the interest given in justification of the restriction is not compelling. . . .

IV

The Free Exercise Clause commits government itself to religious tolerance, and upon even slight suspicion that proposals for state intervention stem from animosity to religion or distrust of its practices, all officials must pause to remember their own high duty to the Constitution and to the rights it secures. Those in office must be resolute in resisting importunate demands and must ensure that the sole reasons for imposing the burdens of law and regulation are secular. Legislators may not devise mechanisms, overt or disguised, designed to persecute or oppress a religion or its practices. The laws here in question were enacted contrary to these constitutional principles, and they are void. . . .

Aid to Religious Schools

JOHN COURTNEY MURRAY, S.J.

Remarks on Aid to Parochial Schools[29]

Father Murray was professor of theology at Woodstock College and a member of the Society of Jesus. His influential writings on the church-state question from the perspective of American Catholics include the following brief defense of government support for religious schools.

[This is] the argument that has been made by Catholics in this country for more than a century with regard to the distribution of tax funds for the support of the school system. The structure of the argument is not complex. Its principle is that the canons of distributive justice ought to control the action of government in allocating funds that it coercively collects from all the people in pursuance of its legitimate interest in universal compulsory schooling. The fact is that these canons are presently not being observed. The "solution" to the School Question reached in the nineteenth century reveals injustice, and the legal statutes that establish the injustice are an abuse of power. So, in drastic brevity, runs the argument. For my part, I have never heard a satisfactory answer to it.

This is a fairly serious situation. When a large section of the community asserts that injustice is being done, and makes a reasonable argument to substantiate the assertion, either the argument ought to be convincingly refuted and the claim of injustice thus disposed of, or the validity of the argument ought to be admitted and the injustice remedied. As a matter of fact, however, the argument customarily meets a blank stare, or else it is "answered" by varieties of the fallacy known as *ignoratio elenchi.* At the extreme, from the side of the more careerist type of anti-Catholic, the rejoinder takes this form, roughly speaking (sometimes the rejoinder is roughly spoken): "We might be willing to listen to this argument about the rights of Catholic schools if we believed that Catholic schools had any rights at all. But we do not grant that they have any rights, except to tolerance. Their existence is not for the advantage of the public; they offend against the integrity of the democratic community, whose warrant is fidelity to Protestant principle (or secularist principle, as the case may be)." This "answer" takes various forms, more or less uncomplimentary to the Catholic Church, according to the temper of the speaker. But this is the gist of it. . . .

EDD DOERR

The People Speak: Parochiaid and the Voters

Edd Doerr's attack on government funding for parochial schools represented a position of Americans United for the Separation of Church and State, an organization that is devoted to maintaining a strict separation between church and state, especially in education. Americans United (originally Protestants and Other Americans United) has often participated as a party or friend of the court in major cases involving the establishment clause.

Parochiaid—any form of direct or indirect tax aid for sectarian private schools from any level of government—has been a controversial political issue in the United States since the early nineteenth century. Generally speaking, however, the policy followed throughout the country until the present has been one of confining public support to public schools, usually on the ground that parochiaid would violate the constitutional principle of separation of church and state and would damage public education.

Since World War II controversies have raged over parochiaid in Congress and most state legislatures, in the courts, and in the arena of public opinion. Most parochiaid plans were defeated in the legislative process, while those which were enacted were challenged in the courts by Americans United and other organizations. All but the most minor and peripheral forms of parochiaid have been struck down as unconstitutional by the courts, particularly in a remarkable series of U.S. Supreme Court rulings beginning in 1971.

Advocates of parochiaid have tried to win over public opinion but their efforts proved to be ineffective. Between 1966 and 1978 twelve statewide referenda dealt with parochiaid in one form or another. In every case the parochiaiders lost. These referendum elections, then, shed a great deal of light on how the American people view proposals to provide public aid to denominational schools. . . .

As these . . . referenda . . . make clear, the American people are solidly opposed to any form of public aid for parochial and private schools. By inference they support the Supreme Court and lower court rulings which have ruled unconstitutional all but minor and peripheral forms of parochiaid.

The referenda were won by church-state separationists, incidentally, despite the fact that they were outspent in every political campaign by the advocates of parochiaid. In a number of the referenda, such as the one in Michigan in 1970, political and business leaders flocked to the parochiaid banner, though to no avail. In most of the referendum states, separationists formed formal or informal coalitions representing religious, teachers, parents, civil rights, and a variety of other groups. Americans United for Separation of Church and State was active in all of the referenda, often playing a key advisory role in view of its many years of experience in dealing with the parochiaid issue.

Americans oppose parochiaid for a variety of reasons. The most salient are probably these: It is unconstitutional. It means forcing all citizens to contribute involuntarily to the support of religious institutions. It would harm the public education system that enrolls 90% of American children. It would use public funds to divide children by creed, class, race, and in other ways. It would endanger the freedom and independence of religious private schools.

The lesson for politicians is obvious. Most Americans support the constitutional principle of separation of church and state as essential to the preservation of religious liberty and other democratic values. There is rarely any real gain for politicians in moving against this main stream.

A. E. DICK HOWARD

Up Against the Wall: The Uneasy Separation of Church and State[30]

A. E. Dick Howard is professor of law at the University of Virginia and was executive director of the commission that wrote Virginia's most recent constitution. In the following excerpts from his essay titled "Up Against the Wall," Professor Howard discusses the numerous complicated Supreme Court cases dealing with aid to religious schools. Note the difference in treatment between higher education on the one hand and primary and secondary education on the other.

Aid to Church-Related Education

In his first term on the Court, the new Chief Justice [Burger] wrote *Walz* v. *Tax Commission,* a near-unanimous decision (only Douglas dissenting) upholding property tax exemptions for religious property. Noting that all fifty states provide for tax exemptions for places of worship, Burger saw the First Amendment as permitting "benevolent neutrality" by government toward religion. Burger found "deeply embedded in the fabric of our national life" the principle that government could fashion policies grounded in benevolent neutrality towards religion "so long as none was favored over others and none suffered interference." Tax exemptions, he reasoned, did not constitute sponsorship as the government does not transfer revenue to churches "but simply abstains from demanding that the church support the state."

The Court's 1968 *Allen* opinion, permitting New York to lend textbooks to parochial schoolchildren, had fired the hopes of proponents of more general aid to church-related schools. Burger's *Walz* opinion, two years later, stirred those hopes even further. Concerned about the flagging finances of parochial schools, Catholic educators and parents saw in the language of "benevolent neutrality" the opportunity to carry *Everson*'s general welfare legislation notion quite beyond such narrow aids as bus transportation or textbooks. Indeed, even before *Walz,* in the late sixties state legislatures had begun to enact significant programs of aid to private education—among them supplements to teachers' salaries, money to pay for text-books and instructional materials, appropriations for maintenance and repair of schools, tuition grants to parents, and income tax credits. Opponents of such aid promptly went to court, and the stage was set in the early seventies for a major round of Supreme Court decisions on aid to church-related schools.

In 1971, in *Lemon* v. *Kurtzman,* the Court passed on aid programs from Rhode Island and Pennsylvania. Rhode Island's statute provided for a 15% salary supplement to be paid to teachers in nonpublic schools. Pennsylvania's act authorized the "purchase" of "secular" educational services from private schools, reimbursing those schools for teachers' salaries, textbooks, and instructional materials. Both states, conscious of the sensitive First Amendment questions raised by such aid, had laced the programs about with safeguards and restrictions. For example, Pennsylvania required that reimbursement be limited to courses in specified secular subjects, that textbooks and materials must be approved by the state, and that payment was not to be made for any course having religious content.

The safeguards proved the programs' undoing. To the purpose and effect test of establishment used in the 1963 prayer cases, Burger in *Walz* had added a third test—that a program not result in an "excessive governmental entanglement with religion." The property tax exemptions in *Walz* had passed that test, but the Pennsylvania and Rhode Island school aid programs in *Lemon* failed it. The very fact that the state had "carefully conditioned its aid with pervasive restrictions" meant that "comprehensive, discriminating, and continuing state surveillance" would be necessary to ensure that the schools honored the restrictions; the result would be "excessive and enduring entanglement between state and church.

The Chief Justice had yet another ground for striking down the Pennsylvania and Rhode Island programs—their "divisive political potential." Burger saw political division along religious lines one of the principal evils against which the First Amendment was directed. State programs channeling money to a relatively few religious groups—Roman Catholics were the overwhelming beneficiaries of the challenged programs—would, Burger thought, intensify political demands along religious lines.

Undaunted, the proponents of parochaid kept trying. The result was another round of major Supreme Court decisions, in June 1973. In the principal case, *Committee for Public Education & Religious Liberty* v. *Nyquist,* a divided Court struck down three New York programs—direct grants to private schools for "maintenance and repair" of facilities and equipment, a tuition reimbursement plan for low-income parents of children in private schools, and tax deductions for parents who did not qualify for tuition reimbursement. In the 1971 decisions, it had been "entanglement" that proved fatal for the Pennsylvania and Rhode Island programs. In 1973 it was the "effect" test that was fatal; the three programs were found to have the effect of advancing religion. Justice Powell, who wrote the majority opinion in *Nyquist,* found it unnecessary to consider whether the New York program would result in entanglement of state and religion. He did, however, bolster his opinion by invoking the political entanglement argument—that the programs carried a "potentially divisive political effect."

Nyquist brought a new lineup on the Court. The justices had been nearly unanimous in *Lemon;* only Justice White would have permitted the kinds of aid there struck down. In *Nyquist* the Court was more divided, three justices dissenting in whole or part. The case split the four Nixon appointees; Blackmun joined Powell's majority opinion, while Burger—hitherto the spokesman for the Court in every religion case—and Rehnquist dissented in part (they would have upheld the tuition grant and tax credit statutes). Burger thought "simple equity" supported aid to parents who sent their children to private schools; moreover, to give such aid would promote a "wholesome diversity" in education.

Since 1973, the Court has decided yet other parochaid cases, but the course has been largely charted by *Lemon* and *Nyquist.* In *Meek* v. *Pittenger* (1975), the Court reviewed three Pennsylvania programs—the loan of textbooks to students in private schools, the loan to the schools themselves of instructional equipment and materials, and provision of "auxiliary" services, such as counseling, testing, speech and hearing therapy, and similar services. Only the textbook program passed muster—and even that dispensation largely on the strength of the precedent set by *Allen.* Effect, entanglement, political divisiveness—all figured in the Court's opinion. The loan of instructional material was found to have the effect of advancing religion, while provision of auxiliary services raised the spectre of excessive entanglement in order to police the program, as well as the opportunity for divisive conflict along religious lines. As in 1973, Burger, White, and Rehnquist would have allowed more aid to church-related schools than permitted by the majority.

The Court relaxed the barriers somewhat, but only slightly, in *Wolman* v. *Walter* (1977). Reviewing several Ohio programs, the Court refused to permit the state to lend instructional materials and equipment for use in sectarian schools or to pay for field trips. The Court did, however, permit the state to provide specialized diagnostic, guidance, and other services to students in nonpublic schools, as the services were not performed on school premises.

The majority's continuing suspicion of any form of aid to sectarian schools at the primary and secondary level stands in sharp contrast to the Court's more deferential posture on aid to church-related colleges. The same day that the Court ruled against parochaid in *Lemon* v. *Kurtzman,* the justices upheld federal construction grants to four church-related colleges in Connecticut. The federal statute placed limits on the purposes for which grants could be used, among them the exclusion of facilities to be used for sectarian instruction or religious worship. Writing for a five-man majority, Chief Justice Burger in *Tilton* v. *Richardson* concluded that the grant program satisfied all the Court's establishment tests—purpose, effect, entanglement, and political divisiveness. Key to the decision were the differences Burger noted between higher education and primary and secondary schools. College students, he thought, are less impressionable and less susceptible to religious indoctrination than younger students. Moreover, other forces, such as traditions of academic freedom, operate to create a more open climate at the college level.

All four of the Connecticut colleges were controlled by religious orders, and the faculty and student body at each were predominantly Catholic. Nevertheless, Burger noted that non-Catholics were admitted as students and were given faculty appointments. None of the colleges required students to attend religious services. Although all four schools required students to take theology courses, it was stipulated that the courses covered a range of religious experience and were not limited to Catholicism. In fact, some of the required courses at two of the colleges were taught by rabbis. In short, Burger was able to conclude that, although the colleges had "admittedly religious functions," their predominant educational mission was to provide their students with a secular education.

The Court has continued to maintain a sharp distinction between aid to sectarian primary and secondary schools and aid at the level of higher education. The justices' consistent rebuffs to parochaid in all its forms have been matched on the other side by a relaxed posture on aid to church-related colleges and their students. In 1973, in *Hunt* v. *McNair,* the Court rejected First Amendment challenges to the issuance by a South Carolina state authority of revenue bonds to help a Baptist college borrow money for capital improvements. No state money was involved, but having the authority's backing enabled the college to borrow money at more favorable interest rates. Justice Powell, who wrote the majority opinion, noted that the college's board of trustees was elected by the South Carolina Baptist Convention, that its charter could be amended only by the Convention, and that the Convention's approval was required for certain financial transactions. But Powell concluded that the college was not "pervasively sectarian" and that South Carolina had laid down sufficient safeguards to ensure that aid did not flow to religious activities.

Yet another case, decided in 1976, reflects the majority's ability to be more permissive toward aid to church-related colleges than to primary and secondary education. In that decision, *Roemer* v. *Board of Public Works,* the Court upheld Maryland's appropriation, on an annual basis, of noncategorical grants to private colleges, some of them with religious affiliations. For each fulltime student (not including seminary and theology students), a college received an amount equal to 15% of the state's appropriation for fulltime students in the state college system. At issue were appropriations to four Roman Catholic colleges. The district court had concluded that the four colleges were not "pervasively sectarian," and Justice Blackmun, reviewing findings as to curriculum, faculty, and other factors, held that the lower court's conclusion was not "clearly erroneous." Moreover, Maryland's system operated to ensure that aid would go only to "the secular side" of the colleges' activities. Nor, finally, was there "excessive entanglement" between government and religion.

Lemon v. Kurtzman (1971)[31]

Lemon v. *Kurtzman* is not only an important discussion of the constitutional limits on aid to religious schools, but it also formally introduced the concept that "political divisiveness" may be part of the "entanglement" test.

Mr. Chief Justice Burger delivered the opinion of the Court.

* * *

Pennsylvania has adopted a statutory program that provides financial support to nonpublic elementary and secondary schools by way of reimbursement for the cost of teachers' salaries, textbooks, and instructional materials in specified secular subjects. Rhode Island has adopted a statute under which the State pays directly to teachers in nonpublic elementary schools a supplement of 15% of their annual salary. Under each statute state aid has been given to church-related educational institutions. We hold that both statutes are unconstitutional. . . .

In *Everson* v. *Board of Education,* this Court upheld a state statute that reimbursed the parents of parochial school children for bus transportation expenses. There MR. JUSTICE BLACK, writing for the majority, suggested that the decision carried to "the verge" of forbidden territory under the Religion Clauses. Candor compels acknowledgment, moreover, that we can only dimly perceive the lines of demarcation in this extraordinarily sensitive area of constitutional law.

The language of the Religion Clauses of the First Amendment is at best opaque, particularly when compared with other portions of the Amendment. Its authors did not simply prohibit the establishment of a state church or a state religion, an area history shows they regarded as very important and fraught with great dangers. Instead they commanded that there should be "no law *respecting* an establishment of religion." A law may be one "respecting" the forbidden objective while falling short of its total realization. A law "respecting" the proscribed result, that is, the establishment of religion, is not always easily identifiable as one violative of the Clause. A given law might not *establish* a state religion but nevertheless be one "respecting" that end in the sense of being a step that could lead to such establishment and hence offend the First Amendment.

In the absence of precisely stated constitutional prohibitions, we must draw lines with reference to the three main evils against which the Establishment Clause was intended to afford protection: "sponsorship, financial support, and active involvement of the sovereign in religious activity." . . .

Every analysis in this area must begin with consideration of the cumulative criteria developed by the Court over many years. Three such tests may be gleaned from our cases. First, the statute must have a secular legislative purpose; second, its principal or primary effect must be one that neither advances nor inhibits religion . . . ; finally, the statute must not foster "an excessive government entanglement with religion."

Inquiry into the legislative purposes of the Pennsylvania and Rhode Island statutes affords no basis for a conclusion that the legislative intent was to advance religion. On the contrary, the statutes themselves clearly state that they are intended to enhance the quality of the secular education in all schools covered by the compulsory attendance laws. There is no reason to believe the legislatures meant anything else. A State always has a legitimate concern for maintaining minimum standards in all schools it allows to operate. . . . The legislatures of Rhode Island and Pennsylvania have concluded that secular and religious education are identifiable and separable. In the abstract we have no quarrel with this conclusion.

The two legislatures, however, have also recognized that church-related elementary and secondary schools have a significant religious mission and that a substantial portion of their activities is religiously oriented. They have therefore sought to create statutory restrictions designed to guarantee the separation between secular and religious educational functions and to ensure that State financial aid supports only the former. All these provisions are precautions taken in candid recognition that these programs approached, even if they did not intrude upon, the forbidden areas under the Religion Clauses. We need not decide whether these legislative precautions restrict the principal or primary effect of the programs to the point where they do not offend the Religion Clauses, for we conclude that the cumulative impact of the entire relationship arising under the statutes in each State involves excessive entanglement between government and religion.

* * *

In *Walz* v. *Tax Commission* . . . the Court upheld state tax exemptions for real property owned by religious organizations and used for religious worship. That holding, however, tended to confine rather than enlarge the area of permissible state involvement with religious institutions by calling for close scrutiny of the degree of entanglement involved in the relationship. The objective is to prevent, as far as possible, the intrusion of either into the precincts of the other.

Our prior holdings do not call for total separation between church and state; total separation is not possible in an absolute sense. Some relationship between government and religious organizations is inevitable. . . . Fire inspections, building and zoning regulations, and state requirements under compulsory school-attendance laws are examples of necessary and permissible contacts. Indeed, under the statutory exemption before us in *Walz,* the State had a continuing burden to ascertain that the exempt property was in fact being used for religious worship. Judicial caveats against entanglement must recognize that the line of separation, far from being a "wall," is a blurred, indistinct, and variable barrier depending on all the circumstances of a particular relationship.

This is not to suggest, however, that we are to engage in a legalistic minuet in which precise rules and forms must govern. A true minuet is a matter of pure form and style, the observance of which is itself the substantive end. Here we examine the form of the relationship for the light that it casts on the substance.

In order to determine whether the government entanglement with religion is excessive, we must examine the character and purposes of the institutions that are benefited, the nature of the aid that the State provides, and the resulting relationship between the government and the religious authority. . . .

Rhode Island Program

The church schools involved in the program are located close to parish churches. This understandably permits convenient access for religious exercises since instruction in faith and morals is part of the total educational process. The school buildings contain identifying religious symbols such as crosses on the exterior and crucifixes, and religious paintings and statues either in the classrooms or hallways. Although only approximately 30 minutes a day are devoted to direct religious instruction, there are religiously oriented extracurricular activities. Approximately two-thirds of the teachers in these schools are nuns of various religious orders. Their dedicated efforts provide an atmosphere in which religious instruction and religious vocations are natural and proper parts of life in such schools. Indeed the role of teaching nuns in enhancing the religious atmosphere has led the parochial school authorities to attempt to maintain a one-to-one ratio between nuns and lay teachers in all schools rather than to permit some to be staffed almost entirely by lay teachers. . . .

The substantial religious character of these church-related schools gives rise to entangling church-state relationships of the kind the Religion Clauses sought to avoid. Although the District Court found that concern for religious values did not inevitably or necessarily intrude into the content of secular subjects, the considerable religious activities of these schools led the legislature to provide for careful governmental controls and surveillance by state authorities in order to ensure that state aid supports only secular education.

The dangers and corresponding entanglements are enhanced by the particular form of aid that the Rhode Island Act provides. Our decisions have permitted the States to provide church-related schools with secular, neutral, or nonideological services, facilities, or materials. Bus transportation, school lunches, public health services, and secular textbooks supplied in common to all students were not thought to offend the Establishment Clause. . . .

We cannot . . . refuse here to recognize that teachers have a substantially different ideological character from books. In terms of potential for involving some aspect of faith or morals in secular subjects, a textbook's content is ascertainable, but a teacher's handling of a subject is not. We cannot ignore the danger that a teacher under religious control and discipline poses to the separation of the religious from the purely secular aspects of pre-college education. The conflict of functions inheres in the situation.

In our view the record shows these dangers are present to a substantial degree. The Rhode Island Roman Catholic elementary schools are under the general supervision of the Bishop of Providence and his appointed representative, the Diocesan Superintendent of Schools. In most cases, each individual parish, however, assumes the ultimate financial responsibility for the school, with the parish priest authorizing the allocation of parish funds. With only two exceptions, school principals are nuns appointed either by the Superintendent or the Mother Provincial of the order whose members staff the school. By 1969 lay teachers constituted more than a third of all teachers in the parochial elementary schools, and their number is growing. They are first interviewed by the superintendent's office and then by the school principal. The contracts are signed by the parish priest, and he retains some discretion in negotiating salary levels. Religious authority necessarily pervades the school system.

The schools are governed by the standards set forth in a "Handbook of School Regulations," which has the force of synodal law in the diocese. It emphasizes the role and importance of the teacher in parochial schools: "The prime factor for the success or the failure of the school is the spirit and personality, as well as the professional competency, of the teacher. . . ." The Handbook also states that: "Religious formation is not confined to formal courses; nor is it restricted to a single subject area." Finally, the Handbook advises teachers to stimulate interest in religious vocations and missionary work. Given the mission of the church school, these instructions are consistent and logical. . . .

We need not and do not assume that teachers in parochial schools will be guilty of bad faith or any conscious design to evade the limitations imposed by the statute and the First Amendment. We simply recognize that a dedicated religious person, teaching in a school affiliated with his or her faith and operated to inculcate its tenets, will inevitably experience great difficulty in remaining religiously neutral. Doctrines and faith are not inculcated or advanced by neutrals. With the best of intentions such a teacher would find it hard to make a total separation between secular teaching and religious doctrine. What would appear to some to be essential to good citizenship might well for others border on or constitute instruction in religion. Further difficulties are inherent in the combination of religious discipline and the possibility of disagreement between teacher and religious authorities over the meaning of the statutory restrictions.

We do not assume, however, that parochial school teachers will be unsuccessful in their attempts to segregate their religious beliefs from their secular educational responsibilities. But the potential for impermissible fostering of religion is present. The Rhode Island Legislature has not, and could not, provide state aid on the basis of a mere assumption that secular teachers under religious discipline can avoid conflicts. The State must be certain, given the Religion Clauses, that subsidized teachers do not inculcate religion—indeed the State here has undertaken to do so. To ensure that no trespass occurs, the State has therefore carefully conditioned its aid with pervasive restrictions. An eligible recipient must teach only those courses that are offered in the public schools and use only those texts and materials that are found in the public schools. In addition the teacher must not engage in teaching any course in religion.

A comprehensive, discriminating, and continuing state surveillance will inevitably be required to ensure that these restrictions are obeyed and the First Amendment otherwise respected. Unlike a book, a teacher cannot be inspected once so as to determine the extent and intent of his or her personal beliefs and subjective acceptance of the limitations imposed by the First Amendment. These prophylactic contacts will involve excessive and enduring entanglement between state and church.

There is another area of entanglement in the Rhode Island program that gives concern. The statute excludes teachers employed by nonpublic schools whose average per-pupil expenditures on secular education equal or exceed the comparable figures for public schools. In the event that the total expenditures of an otherwise eligible school exceed this norm, the program requires the government to examine the school's records in order to determine how much of the total expenditures is attributable to secular education and how much to religious activity. This kind of state inspection and evaluation of the religious content of a religious organization is fraught with the sort of entanglement that the Constitution forbids. It is a relationship pregnant with dangers of excessive government direction of church schools and hence of churches. . . .

[The Court then conducted a similar analysis of the Pennsylvania program.]

* * *

A broader base of entanglement of yet a different character is presented by the divisive political potential of these state programs. In a community where such a large number of pupils are served by church-related schools, it can be assumed that state assistance will entail considerable political activity. Partisans of parochial schools, understandably concerned with rising costs and sincerely dedicated to both the religious and secular educational missions of their schools, will inevitably champion this cause and promote political action to achieve their goals. Those who oppose state aid, whether for constitutional, religious, or fiscal reasons, will inevitably respond and employ all of the usual political campaign techniques to prevail. Candidates will be forced to declare and voters to choose. It would be unrealistic to ignore the fact that many people confronted with issues of this kind will find their votes aligned with their faith.

Ordinarily political debate and division, however vigorous or even partisan, are normal and healthy manifestations of our democratic system of government, but political division along religious lines was one of the principal evils against which the First Amendment was intended to protect. . . . The potential divisiveness of such conflict is a threat to the normal political process. . . . To have States or communities divide on the issues presented by state aid to parochial schools would tend to confuse and obscure other issues of great urgency. We have an expanding array of vexing issues, local and national, domestic and international, to debate and divide on. It conflicts with our whole history and tradition to permit questions of the Religion Clauses to assume such importance in our legislatures and in our elections that they could divert attention from the myriad issues and problems that confront every level of government. The highways of church and state relationships are not likely to be one-way streets, and the Constitution's authors sought to protect religious worship from the pervasive power of government. The history of many countries attests to the hazards of religion's intruding into the political arena or of political power intruding into the legitimate and free exercise of religious belief.

Of course, as the Court noted in *Walz*, "[a]dherents of particular faiths and individual churches frequently take strong positions on public issues." We could not expect otherwise, for religious values pervade the fabric of our national life. But in *Walz* we dealt with a status under state tax laws for the benefit of all religious groups. Here we are confronted with successive and very likely permanent annual appropriations that benefit relatively few religious groups. Political fragmentation and divisiveness on religious lines are thus likely to be intensified.

The potential for political divisiveness related to religious belief and practice is aggravated in these two statutory programs by the need for continuing annual appropriations and the likelihood of larger and larger demands as costs and populations grow. . . .

* * *

In *Walz* it was argued that a tax exemption for places of religious worship would prove to be the first step in an inevitable progression leading to the establishment of state churches and state religion. That claim could not stand up against more than 200 years of virtually universal practice imbedded in our colonial experience and continuing into the present.

The progression argument, however, is more persuasive here. We have no long history of state aid to church-related educational institutions comparable to 200 years of tax exemption for churches. Indeed, the state programs before us today represent something of an innovation. We have already noted that modern governmental programs have self-perpetuating and self-expanding propensities. These internal pressures are only enhanced when the schemes involve institutions whose legitimate needs are growing and whose interests have substantial political support. Nor can we fail to see that in constitutional adjudication some steps, which when taken were thought to approach "the verge," have become the platform for yet further steps. A certain momentum develops in constitutional theory and it can be a "downhill thrust" easily set in motion but difficult to retard or stop. Development by momentum is not invariably bad; indeed, it is the way the common law has grown, but it is a force to be recognized and reckoned with. The dangers are increased by the difficulty of perceiving in advance exactly where the "verge" of the precipice lies. As well as constituting an independent evil against which the Religion Clauses were intended to protect, involvement or entanglement between government and religion serves as a warning signal.

Finally, nothing we have said can be construed to disparage the role of church-related elementary and secondary schools in our national life. Their contribution has been and is enormous. Nor do we ignore their economic plight in a period of rising costs and expanding need. Taxpayers generally have been spared vast sums by the maintenance of these educational institutions by religious organizations, largely by the gifts of faithful adherents.

The merit and benefits of these schools, however, are not the issue before us in these cases. The sole question is whether state aid to these schools can be squared with the dictates of the Religion Clauses. Under our system the choice has been made that government is to be entirely excluded from the area of religious instruction and churches excluded from the affairs of government. The Constitution decrees that religion must be a private matter for the individual, the family, and the institutions of private choice, and that while some involvement and entanglement are inevitable, lines must be drawn. . . .

Mueller v. Allen (1983)[32]

Mueller v. *Allen* has been attacked and lauded, depending on the speaker's perspective, as permitting unprecedented support for parochial schools.

Justice Rehnquist delivered the opinion of the Court.

* * *

Minnesota, like every other state, provides its citizens with free elementary and secondary schooling. It seems to be agreed that about 820,000 students attended this school system in the most recent school year. During the same year, approximately 91,000 elementary and secondary students attended some 500 privately supported schools located in Minnesota, and about 95% of these students attended schools considering themselves to be sectarian.

Minnesota . . . permits state taxpayers to claim a deduction from gross income for certain expenses incurred in educating their children. The deduction is limited to actual expenses incurred for the "tuition, textbooks and transportation" of dependents attending elementary or secondary schools. A deduction may not exceed $500 per dependent in grades K through six and $700 per dependent in grades seven through twelve. . . .

Petitioners . . . sued . . . claiming that [this deduction] violated the Establishment Clause by providing financial assistance to sectarian institutions. . . .

One fixed principle in this field is our consistent rejection of the argument that "any program which in some manner aids an institution with a religious affiliation" violates the Establishment Clause. . . . For example, it is now well-established that a state may reimburse parents for expenses incurred in transporting their children to school and that it may loan secular textbooks to all school-children within the state. . . . [O]ur decisions also have struck down arrangements resembling, in many respects, [programs we have upheld.] In this case we are asked to decide whether Minnesota's tax deduction bears greater resemblance to those types of assistance to parochial schools we have approved, or to those we have struck down. . . .

The general nature of our inquiry in this area has been guided, since the decision in *Lemon* v. *Kurtzman,* by the "three-part" test laid down in that case:

> First, the statute must have a secular legislative purpose; second, its principle or primary effect must be one that neither advances nor inhibits religion . . . ; finally the statute must not foster "an excessive government entanglement with religion."

While this principle is well settled, our cases have also emphasized that it provides "no more than [a] helpful signpost" in dealing with Establishment Clause challenges. . . .

Little time need be spent on the question of whether the Minnesota tax deduction has a secular purpose. Under our prior decisions, governmental assistance programs have consistently survived this inquiry even when they have run afoul of other aspects of the *Lemon* framework. This reflects, at least in part, our reluctance to attribute unconstitutional motives to the states particularly when a plausible secular purpose for the state's program may be discerned from the face of the statute.

A state's decision to defray the cost of educational expenses incurred by parents—regardless of the type of schools their children attend—evidences a purpose that is both secular and understandable. An educated populace is essential in the political and economic health of any community, and a state's efforts to assist parents in meeting the rising cost of educational expenses plainly serves this secular purpose of ensuring that the state's citizenry is well-educated. Similarly, Minnesota, like other states, could conclude that there is a strong public interest in assuring the continued financial health of private schools, both sectarian and non-sectarian. By educating a substantial number of students such schools relieve public schools of a correspondingly great burden—to the benefit of all taxpayers. In addition, private schools may serve as a benchmark for public schools. . . .

> Parochial schools, quite apart from their sectarian purpose, have provided an educational alternative for millions of young Americans; they often afford wholesome competition with our public schools; and in some States they relieve substantially the tax burden incident to the operation of public schools. The State has, moreover, a legitimate interest in facilitating education of the highest quality for all children within its boundaries, whatever school their parents have chosen for them. . . .

[E]ach [of these justifications] is sufficient to satisfy the secular purpose inquiry of *Lemon.*

We turn therefore to the more difficult but related question whether the Minnesota statute has "the primary effect of advancing the sectarian aims of the nonpublic schools.". . . In concluding that it does not, we find several features of the Minnesota tax deduction particularly significant. First, an essential feature of Minnesota's arrangement is the fact that [it] is only one among many deductions—such as those for medical expenses and charitable contributions,—available under the Minnesota tax laws. Our decisions consistently have recognized that traditionally "[l]egislatures have especially broad latitude in creating classifications and distinctions in tax statutes," in part because the "familiarity with local conditions" enjoyed by legislators especially enables them to "achieve an equitable distribution of the tax burden." Under our prior decisions, the Minnesota legislature's judgment that a deduction for educational expenses fairly equalizes the tax burden of its citizens and encourages desirable expenditures for educational purposes is entitled to substantial deference.

Other characteristics . . . argue equally strongly for the provision's constitutionality. Most importantly, the deduction is available for educational expenses incurred by *all* parents, including those whose children attend public schools and those whose children attend non-sectarian private schools or sectarian private schools. . . .

In this respect, as well as others, this case is vitally different from the scheme struck down in *Nyquist.* There, public assistance amounting to tuition grants, was provided only to parents of children in *nonpublic* schools. . . . Moreover, we intimated that "public assistance (*e.g.,* scholarships) made available generally without regard to the sectarian-nonsectarian or public-non-public nature of the institution benefited" might not offend the Establishment Clause. . . .

[B]y channeling whatever assistance it may provide to parochial schools through individual parents, Minnesota has reduced the Establishment Clause objections to which its action is subject. It is true, of course, that financial assistance provided to parents ultimately has an economic effect comparable to that of aid given directly to the schools attended by their children. It is also true, however, that under Minnesota's arrangement public funds become available only as a result of numerous, private choices of individual parents of school-age children. . . . It is noteworthy that all but one of our recent cases invalidating state aid to parochial schools have involved the direct transmission of assistance from the state to the schools themselves. . . . Where, as here, aid to parochial schools is available only as a result of decisions of individual parents [that] no "imprimatur of State approval," can be deemed to have been conferred on any particular religion, or on religion generally. . . .

> At this point in the 20th century we are quite far removed from the dangers that prompted the Framers to include the Establishment Clause in the Bill of Rights. The risk of significant religious or denominational control over our democratic processes—or even of deep political division along religious lines—is remote, and when viewed against the positive contributions of sectarian schools, and such risk seems entirely tolerable in light of the continuing oversight of this Court.

The Establishment Clause of course extends beyond prohibition of a state church or payment of state funds to one or more churches. We do not think, however, that its prohibition extends to the type of tax deduction established by Minnesota. The historic purposes of the clause simply do not encompass the sort of attenuated financial benefit, ultimately controlled by the private choices of individual parents, that eventually flows to parochial schools from the neutrally available tax benefit at issue in this case. . . .

Thus, we hold that the Minnesota tax deduction for educational expenses satisfies the primary effect inquiry of our Establishment Clause cases.

Turning to the third part of the *Lemon* inquiry, we have no difficulty in concluding that the Minnesota statute does not "excessively entangle" the state in religion. The only plausible source of the "comprehensive, discriminating, and continuing state surveillance" necessary to run afoul of this standard would be in the fact that state officials must determine whether particular textbooks qualify for a deduction. In making this decision, state officials must disallow deductions taken from "instructional books and materials used in the teaching of religious tenets, doctrines or worship, the purpose of which is to inculcate such tenets, doctrines or worship." Making decisions such as this does not differ substantially from making the types of decisions approved in earlier opinions of this Court. . . .

Aguilar v. Felton [33] (1985)

This case, and its companion, *Grand Rapids* v. *Ball,* highlight a potential catch–22 within establishment clause jurisprudence. Both involved programs in which public school teachers were assigned to teach certain subjects in nonpublic schools, many of which were religious schools; these subjects ranged from home economics to remedial reading. In *Grand Rapids* v. *Ball,* the Court concluded that the programs in Michigan had the unconstitutional effect of promoting religion because (1) the publicly funded teachers in the religious schools, "influenced by the pervasively sectarian nature of the . . . schools," may subtly or overtly indoctrinate the students in particular religious tenets at public expense, (2) the "symbolic union of church and state" inherent in the program "threatens to convey a message of state support for religion," and (3) the programs "subsidize the religious functions of the parochial schools by taking over a substantial portion of their responsibility for teaching secular subjects. . . ."

The comparable program in New York City, which was considered in *Aguilar* v. *Felton,* attempted to address these issues by having publicly funded "field supervisors" who would make unannounced visits to the private schools to ensure that the program would, in fact, not have the effect of promoting religion.

Justice Brennan delivered the opinion of the Court.

* * *

The program at issue in this case, [Title I,] . . . authorizes the Secretary of Education to distribute financial assistance to local educational institutions to meet the needs of educationally deprived children from low-income families. . . . Since 1966, the City of New York has provided instructional services funded by Title I to parochial school students on the premises of parochial schools. Of those students eligible to receive funds in 1981–1982, 13.2% were enrolled in private schools. Of that group, 84% were enrolled in schools affiliated with the Roman Catholic Archdiocese of New York and the Diocese of Brooklyn and 8% were enrolled in Hebrew day schools. With respect to the religious atmosphere of these schools, the Court of Appeals concluded that "the picture that emerges is of a system in which religious considerations play a key role in the selection of students and teachers, and which has as its substantial purpose the inculcation of religious values."

The programs conducted at these schools include remedial reading, reading skills, remedial mathematics, English as a second language, and guidance services. These programs are carried out by regular employees of the public schools (teachers, guidance counselors, psychologists, psychiatrists, and social workers) who have volunteered to teach in the parochial schools. The amount of time that each professional spends in the parochial school is determined by the number of students in the particular program and the needs of these students.

The City's Bureau of Nonpublic School Reimbursement makes teacher assignments, and the instructors are supervised by field personnel, who attempt to pay at least one unannounced visit per month. The field supervisors, in turn, report to program coordinators, who also pay occasional unannounced supervisory visits to monitor Title I classes in the parochial schools. The professionals involved in the program are directed to avoid involvement with religious activities that are conducted within the private schools and to bar religious materials in their classrooms. All material and equipment used in the programs funded under Title I are supplied by the Government and are used only in those programs. The professional personnel are solely responsible for the selection of the students. Additionally, the professionals are informed that contact with private school personnel should be kept to a minimum. Finally, the administrators of the parochial schools are required to clear the classrooms used by the public school personnel of all religious symbols. . . .

At best, the supervision in this case would assist in preventing the Title I program from being used, intentionally or unwittingly, to inculcate the religious beliefs of the surrounding parochial school. But . . . the supervisory system established by the City of New York inevitably results in the excessive entanglement of church and state, an Establishment Clause concern distinct from that addressed by the effects doctrine. Even where state aid to parochial institutions does not have the primary effect of advancing religion, the provision of such aid may nonetheless violate the Establishment Clause owing to the nature of the interaction of church and state in the administration of that aid.

The principle that the state should not become too closely entangled with the church in the administration of assistance is rooted in two concerns. When the state becomes enmeshed with a given denomination in matters of religious significance, the freedom of religious belief of those who are not adherents of that denomination suffers, even when the governmental purpose underlying the involvement is largely secular. In addition, the freedom of even the adherents of the denomination is limited by the governmental intrusion into sacred matters. "[T]he First Amendment rests upon the premise that both religion and government can best work to achieve their lofty aims if each is left free from the other within its respective sphere.". . .

The critical elements of the entanglement . . . are . . . present in this case. First, . . . the aid is provided in a pervasively sectarian environment. Second, because assistance is provided in the form of teachers, ongoing inspection is required to ensure the absence of a religious message. . . . In short, the scope and duration of New York City's Title I program would require a permanent and pervasive state presence in the sectarian schools receiving aid.

This pervasive monitoring by public authorities in the sectarian schools infringes precisely those Establishment Clause values at the root of the prohibition of excessive entanglement. Agents of the city must visit and inspect the religious school regularly, alert for the subtle or overt presence of religious matter in Title I classes. . . . In addition, the religious school must obey these same agents when they make determinations as to what is and what is not a "religious symbol" and thus off limits in a Title I classroom. In short, the religious school, which has as a primary purpose the advancement and preservation of a particular religion must endure the ongoing presence of state personnel whose primary purpose is to monitor teachers and students in an attempt to guard against the infiltration of religious thought.

The administrative cooperation that is required to maintain the educational program at issue here entangles church and state in still another way that infringes interests at the heart of the Establishment Clause. Administrative personnel of the public and parochial school systems must work together in resolving matters related to schedules, classroom assignments, problems that arise in the implementation of the program, requests for additional services, and the dissemination of information regarding the program. Furthermore, the program necessitates "frequent contacts between the regular and the remedial teachers (or other professionals), in which each side reports on individual student needs, problems encountered, and results achieved."

The numerous judgments that must be made by agents of the city concern matters that may be subtle and controversial, yet may be of deep religious significance to the controlling denominations. As government agents must make these judgments, the dangers of political divisiveness along religious lines increase. At the same time, "[t]he picture of state inspectors prowling the halls of parochial schools and auditing classroom instruction surely raises more than an imagined specter of governmental 'secularization of a creed.'"

Despite the well-intentioned efforts taken by the City of New York, the program remains constitutionally flawed owing to the nature of the aid, to the institution receiving the aid, and to the constitutional principles that they implicate – that neither the State nor Federal Government shall promote or hinder a particular faith or faith generally through the advancement of benefits or through the excessive entanglement of church and state in the administration of those benefits.

Witters v. Washington Department of Services for the Blind (1986)[34]

The Supreme Court has reviewed numerous cases that it considered "ingenious plans for channeling state aid to sectarian schools." The question here is whether the use of funds from a state vocational-assistance program for attendance at a Christian college was such an unconstitutional scheme or just a neutral government program pursuant to which people can make legitimate private choices to study religious subjects.

Justice Marshall delivered the opinion of the Court. . . .

I

Petitioner Larry Witters applied in 1979 to the Washington Commission for the Blind for vocational rehabilitation services pursuant to Wash Rev Code § 74.16.181. That statute authorized the Commission, inter alia, to "[p]rovide for special education and/or training in the professions, business or trades" so as to "assist visually handicapped persons to overcome vocational handicaps and to obtain the maximum degree of self-support and self-care." Petitioner, suffering from a progressive eye condition, was eligible for vocational rehabilitation assistance under the terms of the statute. He was at the time attending Inland Empire School of the Bible, a private Christian college in

Spokane, Washington, and studying bible, ethics, speech, and church administration in order to equip himself for a career as a pastor, missionary, or youth director.

The Commission denied petitioner aid. It relied on an earlier determination embodied in a Commission policy statement that "[t]he Washington State constitution forbids the use of public funds to assist an individual in the pursuit of a career or degree in theology or related areas . . ." That ruling was affirmed by a state hearings examiner, who held that the Commission was precluded from funding petitioner's training "in light of the State Constitution's prohibition against the state directly or indirectly supporting a religion.". . . The hearings examiner cited Wash Const, Art I, § 11, providing in part that "no public money or property shall be appropriated for or applied to any religious worship, exercise or instruction, or the support of any religious establishment," and Wash Const, Art IX, § 4, providing that "[a]ll schools maintained or supported wholly or in part by the public funds shall be forever free from sectarian control or influence.". . .

II

The Establishment Clause of the First Amendment has consistently presented this Court with difficult questions of interpretation and application. . . .

We are guided . . . by the three-part test set out by this Court in Lemon. . . . Our analysis relating to the first prong of that test is simple: all parties concede the unmistakably secular purpose of the Washington program. That program was designed to promote the well-being of the visually handicapped through the provision of vocational rehabilitation services, and no more than a minuscule amount of the aid awarded under the program is likely to flow to religious education. . . .

The answer to the question posed by the second prong of the Lemon test is more difficult. We conclude, however, that extension of aid to petitioner is not barred on that ground either. It is well-settled that the Establishment Clause is not violated every time money previously in the possession of a State is conveyed to a religious institution. For example, a State may issue a paycheck to one of its employees, who may then donate all or part of that paycheck to a religious institution, all without constitutional barrier; and the State may do so even knowing that the employee so intends to dispose of his salary. It is equally well settled, on the other hand, that the State may not grant aid to a religious school, whether cash or in-kind, where the effect of the aid is "that of a direct subsidy to the religious school" from the State. . . . The question presented is whether . . . extension of aid to petitioner and the use of that aid by petitioner to support his religious education is a permissible transfer similar to the hypothetical salary donation described above, or is an impermissible "direct subsidy."

Certain aspects of Washington's program are central to our inquiry. As far as the record shows, vocational assistance provided under the Washington program is paid directly to the student, who transmits it to the educational institution of his or her choice. Any aid provided under Washington's program that ultimately flows to religious institutions does so only as a result of the genuinely independent and private choices of aid recipients. Washington's program is "made available generally without regard to the sectarian-nonsectarian, or public-non-public nature of the institution benefited," . . . and is in no way skewed towards religion. . . . It creates no financial incentive for students to undertake sectarian education. . . . It does not tend to provide greater or broader benefits for recipients who apply their aid to religious education, nor are the full benefits of the program limited, in large part or in whole, to students at sectarian institutions. On the contrary, aid recipients have full opportunity to expend vocational rehabilitation aid on wholly secular education, and as a practical matter have rather greater prospects to do so. Aid recipients' choices are made among a huge variety of possible careers, of which only a small handful are sectarian. In this case, the fact that aid goes to individuals means that the decision to support religious education is made by the individual, not by the State.

Further, and importantly, nothing in the record indicates that, if petitioner succeeds, any significant portion of the aid expended under the Washington program as a whole will end up flowing to religious education. . . . The program, providing vocational assistance to the visually handicapped, does not seem well suited to serve as the vehicle for such a subsidy. No evidence has been presented indicating that any other person has ever sought to finance religious education or activity pursuant to the State's program. The combination of these factors, we think, makes the link between the State and the school petitioner wishes to attend a highly attenuated one.

On the facts we have set out, it does not seem appropriate to view any aid ultimately flowing to the Inland Empire School of the Bible as resulting from a *state* action sponsoring or subsidizing religion. Nor does the mere circumstance that petitioner has chosen to use neutrally available state aid to help pay for his religious education confer any message of state endorsement of religion. . . . On the facts present here, we think the Washington program works no state support of religion prohibited by the Establishment Clause. . . .

Zobrest v. Catalina Foothills School District (1993)[35]

This case also involves an establishment-clause challenge to a government program that may indirectly aid religious education. Under the federal Individuals with Disabilities Education Act, public school districts must provide sign language interpreters for deaf students in both public and private schools. Can they constitutionally provide such a service to a student in a religious school where the interpreter might be one involved in prayers, worship services, and other devotional activities?

Chief Justice Rehnquist delivered the opinion of the Court.

Petitioner James Zobrest, who has been deaf since birth, asked respondent school district to provide a sign-language interpreter to accompany him to classes at a Roman Catholic high school in Tucson, Arizona, pursuant to the Individuals with Disabilities Education Act [IDEA].. . . We hold that the Establishment Clause does not bar the school district from providing the requested interpreter.

James Zobrest attended grades one through five in a school for the deaf, and grades six through eight in a public school operated by respondent. While he attended public school, respondent furnished him with a sign-language interpreter. For religious reasons, James' parents (also petitioners here) enrolled him for the ninth grade in Salpointe Catholic High School, a sectarian institution. When petitioners requested that respondent supply James with an interpreter at Salpointe, respondent referred the matter to the County Attorney, who concluded that providing an interpreter on the school's premises would violate the United States Constitution. . . .

We have never said that "religious institutions are disabled by the First Amendment from participating in publicly sponsored social welfare programs.". . . For if the Establishment Clause did bar religious groups from receiving general government benefits, then "a church could not be protected by the police and fire departments, or have its public sidewalk kept in repair.". . . Given that a contrary rule would lead to such absurd results, we have consistently held that government programs that neutrally provide benefits to a broad class of citizens defined without reference to religion are not readily subject to an Establishment Clause challenge just because sectarian institutions may also receive an attenuated financial benefit. . . .

In Mueller, we rejected an Establishment Clause challenge to a Minnesota law allowing taxpayers to deduct certain educational expenses in computing their state income tax, even though the vast majority of those deductions (perhaps over 90%) went to parents whose children attended sectarian schools. . . . Two factors, aside from States' traditionally broad taxing authority, informed our decision. . . . We noted that the law "permits *all* parents—whether their children attend public school or private—to deduct their children's educational expenses.". . . We also pointed out that under Minnesota's scheme, public funds become available to sectarian schools "only as a result of numerous private choices of individual parents of school-age children," thus distinguishing Mueller from our other cases involving "the direct transmission of assistance from the State to the schools themselves.". . .

Witters was premised on virtually identical reasoning. In that case, we upheld against an Establishment Clause challenge the State of Washington's extension of vocational assistance, as part of a general state program, to a blind person studying at a private Christian college to become a pastor, missionary, or youth director. . . .

That same reasoning applies with equal force here. The service at issue in this case is part of a general government program that distributes benefits neutrally to any child qualifying as "handicapped" under the IDEA, without regard to the "sectarian-nonsectarian, or public-nonpublic nature" of the school the child attends. By according parents freedom to select a school of their choice, the statute ensures that a government-paid interpreter will be present in a sectarian school only as a result of the private decision of individual parents. In other words, because the IDEA creates no financial incentive for parents to choose a sectarian school, an interpreter's presence there cannot be attributed to state decisionmaking. . . . When the government offers a neutral service on the premises of a sectarian school as part of a general program that "is in no way skewed towards religion," . . . it follows under our prior decisions that provision of that service does not offend the Establishment Clause. . . . Indeed, this is an even easier case than Mueller and Witters in the sense that, under the IDEA, no funds traceable to the government ever find their way into sectarian schools' coffers. The only indirect economic benefit a sectarian school might receive by dint of the IDEA is the handicapped child's tuition—and that is, of course, assuming that the school makes a profit on each student; that, without an IDEA interpreter, the child would have gone to school elsewhere; and that the school, then, would have been unable to fill that child's spot. . . .

The IDEA creates a neutral government program dispensing aid not to schools but to individual handicapped children. If a handicapped child chooses to enroll in a sectarian school, we hold that the Establishment Clause does not prevent the school district from furnishing him with a sign-language interpreter there in order to facilitate his education. . . .

Kiryas Joel Village School District v. Grumet (1994)[36]

A New York law allowed virtually any group of residents to form a new village. Members of the Satmar Hasidic branch of Judaism formed such a village composed exclusively of its adherents. The state legislature constituted the village as an independent public school district, and the district formed a school with special education programs for handicapped children who had previously been sent out of the community and suffered considerable fear and trauma. Justice Souter's opinion spoke only for a plurality of the Court; altogether, there were five concurring opinions and one dissenting. Although this case technically involves a public school program, the justices' analyses of the issues tend to link it more closely to the other cases in this section concerning aid to religious schools.

Justice Souter delivered the opinion of the Court.

The Village of Kiryas Joel in Orange County, New York, is a religious enclave of Satmar Hasidim, practitioners of a strict form of Judaism. The village fell within the Monroe-Woodbury Central School District until a special state statute passed in 1989 carved out a separate district, following village lines, to serve this distinctive population. . . . Because this unusual act is tantamount to an allocation of political power on a religious criterion and neither presupposes nor requires governmental impartiality toward religion, we hold that it violates the prohibition against establishment.

* * *

The Satmar Hasidic sect takes its name from the town near the Hungarian and Romanian border where, in the early years of this century, Grand Rebbe Joel Teitelbaum molded the group into a distinct community. After World War II and the destruction of much of European Jewry, the Grand Rebbe and most of his surviving followers moved to the Williamsburg section of Brooklyn, New York. Then, 20 years ago, the Satmars purchased an approved but undeveloped subdivision in the town of Monroe and began assembling the community that has since become the Village of Kiryas Joel. When a zoning dispute arose in the course of settlement, the Satmars presented the Town Board of Monroe with a petition to form a new village within the town. . . . Neighbors who did not wish to secede with the Satmars objected strenuously, and after arduous negotiations the proposed boundaries of the Village of Kiryas Joel were drawn to include just the 320 acres owned and inhabited entirely by Satmars. The village, incorporated in 1977, has a population of about

8,500 today. Rabbi Aaron Teitelbaum, eldest son of the current Grand Rebbe, serves as the village rov (chief rabbi) and rosh yeshivah (chief authority in the parochial schools).

The residents of Kiryas Joel are vigorously religious people who make few concessions to the modern world and go to great lengths to avoid assimilation into it. They interpret the Torah strictly; segregate the sexes outside the home; speak Yiddish as their primary language; eschew television, radio, and English-language publications; and dress in distinctive ways that include head-coverings and special garments for boys and modest dresses for girls. Children are educated in private religious schools, most boys at the United Talmudic Academy where they receive a thorough grounding in the Torah and limited exposure to secular subjects, and most girls at Bais Rochel, an affiliated school with a curriculum designed to prepare girls for their roles as wives and mothers. . . .

These schools do not, however, offer any distinctive services to handicapped children, who are entitled under state and federal law to special education services even when enrolled in private schools. . . . Starting in 1984 the Monroe-Woodbury Central School District provided such services for the children of Kiryas Joel at an annex to Bais Rochel, but a year later ended that arrangement in response to our decisions in *Aguilar* v *Felton,* . . . and *School Dist. of Grand Rapids* v *Ball..* . . Children from Kiryas Joel who needed special education (including the deaf, the mentally retarded, and others suffering from a range of physical, mental, or emotional disorders) were then forced to attend public schools outside the village, which their families found highly unsatisfactory. Parents of most of these children withdrew them from the Monroe-Woodbury secular schools, citing "the panic, fear and trauma [the children] suffered in leaving their own community and being with people whose ways were so different," and some sought administrative review of the public-school placements. . . .

By 1989, only one child from Kiryas Joel was attending Monroe-Woodbury's public schools; the village's other handicapped children received privately funded special services or went without. It was then that the New York Legislature passed the statute at issue in this litigation, which provided that the Village of Kiryas Joel "is constituted a separate school district, . . . and shall have and enjoy all the powers and duties of a union free school district. . . ." . . .

[T]he Kiryas Joel Village School District currently runs only a special education program for handicapped children. The other village children have stayed in their parochial schools, relying on the new school district only for transportation, remedial education, and health and welfare services. If any child without handicap in Kiryas Joel were to seek a public-school education, the district would pay tuition to send the child into Monroe-Woodbury or another school district nearby. Under like arrangements, several of the neighboring districts send their handicapped Hasidic children into Kiryas Joel, so that two thirds of the full-time students in the village's public school come from outside. In all, the new district serves just over 40 full-time students, and two or three times that many parochial school students on a part-time basis.

* * *

"A proper respect for both the Free Exercise and the Establishment Clauses compels the State to pursue a course of 'neutrality' toward religion," . . . favoring neither one religion over others nor religious adherents collectively over nonadherents. . . . [T]he statute creating the Kiryas Joel Village School District, departs from this constitutional command by delegating the State's discretionary authority over public schools to a group defined by its character as a religious community, in a legal and historical context that gives no assurance that governmental power has been or will be exercised neutrally. . . .

Authority over public schools belongs to the State, . . . and cannot be delegated to a local school district defined by the State in order to grant political control to a religious group.

It is, first, not dispositive that the recipients of state power in this case are a group of religious individuals united by common doctrine, not the group's leaders or officers. Although some school district franchise is common to all voters, the State's manipulation of the franchise for this district limited it to Satmars, giving the sect exclusive control of the political subdivision. In the circumstances of this case, the difference between thus vesting state power in the members of a religious group as such instead of the officers of its sectarian organization is one of form, not substance. It is true that religious people (or groups of religious people) cannot be denied the opportunity to exercise the rights of citizens simply because of their religious affiliations or commitments, for such a disability would violate the right to religious free exercise, . . . which the First Amendment guarantees as certainly as it bars any establishment. . . . That individuals who happen to be religious may hold public office does not mean that a state may deliberately delegate discretionary power to an individual, institution, or community on the ground of religious identity. Where "fusion" is an issue, the difference lies in the distinction between a government's purposeful delegation on the basis of religion and a delegation on principles neutral to religion, to individuals whose religious identities are incidental to their receipt of civic authority.

[This statute] effectively identifies these recipients of governmental authority by reference to doctrinal adherence, even though it does not do so expressly. We find this to be the better view of the facts because of the way the boundary lines of the school district divide residents according to religious affiliation, under the terms of an unusual and special legislative act.

It is undisputed that those who negotiated the village boundaries when applying the general village incorporation statute drew them so as to exclude all but Satmars, and that the New York Legislature was well aware that the village remained exclusively Satmar. . . . The significance of this fact to the state legislature is indicated by the further fact that carving out the village school district ran counter to customary districting practices in the State. Indeed, the trend in New York is not toward dividing school districts but toward consolidating them. The thousands of small common school districts laid out in the early 19th century have been combined and recombined, first into union free school districts and then into larger central school districts, until only a tenth as many remain today. . . .

The origin of the district in a special act of the legislature, rather than the State's general laws governing school district reorganization, is likewise anomalous. Although the legislature has established some 20 existing school districts by special act, all but one of these are districts in name only, having been designed to be run by private organizations serving institutionalized children. They have neither tax bases nor student populations of their own but serve children placed by other school districts or public agencies. . . . Thus the Kiryas Joel Village School District is exceptional to the point of singularity, as the only district coming to our notice that the legislature carved from a single existing district to serve local residents. . . .

Because the district's creation ran uniquely counter to state practice, following the lines of a religious community where the customary and neutral principles would not have dictated the same result, we have good reasons to treat this district as the reflection of a religious criterion for identifying the recipients of civil authority. Not even the special needs of the children in this community can explain the legislature's unusual Act, for the State could have responded to the concerns of the Satmar parents without implicating the Establishment Clause, as we explain in some detail further on. We therefore find the legislature's Act to be substantially equivalent to defining a political subdivision and hence the qualification for its franchise by a religious test, resulting in a purposeful and forbidden "fusion of governmental and religious functions." . . .

The fundamental source of constitutional concern here is that the legislature itself may fail to exercise governmental authority in a religiously neutral way. The anomalously case-specific nature of the legislature's exercise of state authority in creating this district for a religious community leaves the Court without any direct way to review such state action for the purpose of safeguarding a principle at the heart of the Establishment Clause, that government should not prefer one religion to another, or religion to irreligion. . . .

In finding that [the statute] violates the requirement of governmental neutrality by extending the benefit of a special franchise, we do not deny that the Constitution allows the state to accommodate religious needs by alleviating special burdens. Our cases leave no doubt that in commanding neutrality the Religion Clauses do not require the government to be oblivious to impositions that legitimate exercises of state power may place on religious belief and practice. But accommodation is not a principle without limits, and what petitioners seek is an adjustment to the Satmars' religiously grounded preferences that our cases do not countenance. . . .

In this case we are clearly constrained to conclude that the statute before us fails the test of neutrality. It delegates a power this Court has said "ranks at the very apex of the function of a State" . . . to an electorate defined by common religious belief and practice, in a manner that fails to foreclose religious favoritism. It therefore crosses the line from permissible accommodation to impermissible establishment.

Agostini v. Felton (1997)[37]

In the 1985 case of *Aguilar* v. *Felton,* the Supreme Court held unconstitutional a New York City program that provided publicly funded remedial-education teachers to parochial schools. New York then spent over $100 million to be able to continue to provide these services via mobile instruction units parked on the streets in front of the parochial schools, computer-aided instruction, and other techniques to avoid the establishment-clause concerns expressed in *Aguilar.* After subsequent cases suggested that the Supreme Court's views on the establishment clause had changed, New York City requested relief from the decision in *Aguilar.* In this case, Justice O'Connor's majority opinion takes the relatively rare step of acknowledging that *Aguilar* is "no longer good law."

Justice O'Connor delivered the opinion of the Court.

In *Aguilar* v. *Felton,* this Court held that the Establishment Clause of the First Amendment barred the city of New York from sending public school teachers into parochial schools to provide remedial education to disadvantaged children pursuant to a congressionally mandated program. Petitioners maintain that *Aguilar* cannot be squared with our intervening Establishment Clause jurisprudence and ask that we explicitly recognize what our more recent cases already dictate: *Aguilar* is no longer good law. We agree with petitioners that *Aguilar* is not consistent with our subsequent Establishment Clause decisions. . . .

Our more recent cases have undermined the assumptions upon which *Ball* and *Aguilar* relied. To be sure, the general principles we use to evaluate whether government aid violates the Establishment Clause have not changed since *Aguilar* was decided. For example, we continue to ask whether the government acted with the purpose of advancing or inhibiting religion, and the nature of that inquiry has remained largely unchanged. . . . Likewise, we continue to explore whether the aid has the "effect" of advancing or inhibiting religion. What has changed since we decided . . . *Aguilar* [and its companion case, *School District of Grand Rapids v. Ball]* is our understanding of the criteria used to assess whether aid to religion has an impermissible effect.

As we have repeatedly recognized, government inculcation of religious beliefs has the impermissible effect of advancing religion. Our cases subsequent to *Aguilar* have, however, modified in two significant respects the approach we use to assess indoctrination. First, we have abandoned the presumption . . . that the placement of public employees on parochial school grounds inevitably results in the impermissible effect of state sponsored indoctrination or constitutes a symbolic union between government and religion. In *Zobrest* . . . [, b]ecause the only *government* aid . . . was the interpreter, who was herself not inculcating any religious messages, no *government* indoctrination took place and we were able to conclude that "the provision of such assistance [was] not barred by the Establishment Clause.". . . *Zobrest* also implicitly repudiated another assumption on which *Ball* and *Aguilar* turned: that the presence of a public employee on private school property creates an impermissible "symbolic link" between government and religion. . . .

Second, we have departed from the rule relied on in *Ball* that all government aid that directly aids the educational function of religious schools is invalid. In *Witters* . . . we held that the Establishment Clause did not bar a State from issuing a vocational tuition grant to a blind person who wished to use the grant to attend a Christian college and become a pastor, missionary, or youth director. Even though the grant recipient clearly would use the money to obtain religious education, we observed that the tuition grants were "'made available generally without regard to the sectarian nonsectarian, or public nonpublic nature of the institution benefited.'" . . .

Zobrest and *Witters* make clear that, under current law, the Shared Time program in *Ball* and New York City's Title I program in *Aguilar* will not, as a matter of law, be deemed to have the effect of advancing religion through indoctrination. Indeed, each of the premises upon which we relied in *Ball* to reach a contrary conclusion is no longer valid. First, there is no reason to presume that, simply because she enters a parochial school classroom, a full time public employee . . . will depart from her assigned duties and instructions and embark on religious indoctrination, any more than there was a reason in *Zobrest* to think an interpreter would inculcate religion by altering her translation of classroom lectures. . . .

We turn now to *Aguilar*'s conclusion that New York City's . . . program resulted in an excessive entanglement between church and state. Whether a government aid program results in such an entanglement has consistently been an aspect of our Establishment Clause analysis. We have considered entanglement both in the course of assessing whether an aid program has an impermissible effect of advancing religion, . . . and as a factor separate and apart from "effect," . . . Regardless of how we have characterized the issue, however, the factors we use to assess whether an entanglement is "excessive" are similar to the factors we use to examine "effect.". . . Thus, it is simplest to recognize why entanglement is significant and treat it . . . as an aspect of the inquiry into a statute's effect.

Not all entanglements, of course, have the effect of advancing or inhibiting religion. Interaction between church and state is inevitable, . . . and we have always tolerated some level of involvement between the two. Entanglement must be "excessive" before it runs afoul of the Establishment Clause. . . .

In *Aguilar*, the Court presumed that full time public employees on parochial school grounds would be tempted to inculcate religion, despite the ethical standards they were required to uphold. Because of this risk *pervasive* monitoring would be required. But after *Zobrest* we no longer presume that public employees will inculcate religion simply because they happen to be in a sectarian environment. Since we have abandoned the assumption that properly instructed public employees will fail to discharge their duties faithfully, we must also discard the assumption that *pervasive* monitoring . . . is required. There is no suggestion in the record before us that unannounced monthly visits of public supervisors are insufficient to prevent or to detect inculcation of religion by public employees. . . .

To summarize, New York City's . . . program does not run afoul of any of three primary criteria we currently use to evaluate whether government aid has the effect of advancing religion: it does not result in governmental indoctrination; define its recipients by reference to religion; or create an excessive entanglement. We therefore hold that a federally funded program providing supplemental, remedial instruction to disadvantaged children on a neutral basis is not invalid under the Establishment Clause when such instruction is given on the premises of sectarian schools by government employees pursuant to a program containing safeguards such as those present here. The same considerations that justify this holding require us to conclude that this carefully constrained program also cannot reasonably be viewed as an endorsement of religion. . . .

Mitchell v. Helms (2000)[38]

The desire of state governments to provide funding for religious schools has led to vexing constitutional cases for over fifty years. In the latter part of the twentieth century, some of the justices began to look more favorably on such programs, while others decried this jurisprudential shift away from a strict separation of state and church schools. Although the Court upheld the program in this case, no opinion commanded a majority of the justices.

Justice Thomas announced the judgment of the Court and delivered an opinion, in which The Chief Justice, Justice Scalia, and Justice Kennedy join.

As part of a longstanding school aid program known as Chapter 2, the Federal Government distributes funds to state and local governmental agencies, which in turn lend educational materials and equipment to public and private schools, with the enrollment of each participating school determining the amount of aid that it receives. The question is whether Chapter 2, as applied in Jefferson Parish, Louisiana, is a law respecting an establishment of religion, because many of the private schools receiving Chapter 2 aid in that parish are religiously affiliated. We hold that Chapter 2 is not such a law. . . .

The Establishment Clause of the First Amendment dictates that "Congress shall make no law respecting an establishment of religion." In the over 50 years since *Everson,* we have consistently struggled to apply these simple words in the context of governmental aid to religious schools. . . .

In *Agostini,* however, we brought some clarity to our case law, by overruling two anomalous precedents (one in whole, the other in part) and by consolidating some of our previously disparate considerations under a revised test. Whereas in *Lemon* we had considered whether a statute (1) has a secular purpose, (2) has a primary effect of advancing or inhibiting religion, or (3) creates an excessive entanglement between government and religion, . . . in *Agostini* we modified *Lemon* for purposes of evaluating aid to schools and examined only the first and second factors . . . , acknowledged that our cases discussing excessive entanglement had applied many of the same considerations as had our cases discussing primary effect, and we therefore recast *Lemon*'s entanglement inquiry as simply one criterion relevant to determining a statute's effect. . . . We also acknowledged that our cases had pared somewhat the factors that could justify a finding of excessive entanglement. . . . We then set out revised criteria for determining the effect of a statute:

"To summarize, New York City's Title I program does not run afoul of any of three primary criteria we currently use to evaluate whether government aid has the effect of advancing religion: It does not result in governmental indoctrination; define its recipients by reference to religion; or create an excessive entanglement." *[Agostini]*

In this case, our inquiry under *Agostini*'s purpose and effect test is a narrow one. Because respondents do not challenge the District Court's holding that Chapter 2 has a secular purpose, . . . we will consider only Chapter 2's effect. . . . Considering Chapter 2 in light of our more recent case law, we conclude that it neither results in religious indoctrination by the government nor defines its recipients by reference to religion. We therefore hold that Chapter 2 is not a "law respecting an establishment of religion." . . .

[T]he question whether governmental aid to religious schools results in governmental indoctrination is ultimately a question whether any religious indoctrination that occurs in those schools could reasonably be attributed to governmental action. . . . We have also indicated that the answer to the question of indoctrination will resolve the question whether a program of educational aid "subsidizes" religion, as our religion cases use that term. . . .

In distinguishing between indoctrination that is attributable to the State and indoctrination that is not, we have consistently turned to the principle of neutrality, upholding aid that is offered to a broad range of groups or persons without regard to their religion. If the religious, irreligious, and areligious are all alike eligible for governmental aid, no one would conclude that any indoctrination that any particular recipient conducts has been done at the behest of the government. For attribution of indoctrination is a relative question. If the government is offering assistance to recipients who provide, so to speak, a broad range of indoctrination, the government itself is not thought responsible for any particular indoctrination. To put the point differently, if the government, seeking to further some legitimate secular purpose, offers aid on the same terms, without regard to religion, to all who adequately further that purpose, . . . then it is fair to say that any aid going to a religious recipient only has the effect of furthering that secular purpose. The government, in crafting such an aid program, has had to conclude that a given level of aid is necessary to further that purpose among secular recipients and has provided no more than that same level to religious recipients.

As a way of assuring neutrality, we have repeatedly considered whether any governmental aid that goes to a religious institution does so "only as a result of the genuinely independent and private choices of individuals." . . . We have viewed as significant whether the "private choices of individual parents," as opposed to the "unmediated" will of government, . . . determine what schools ultimately benefit from the governmental aid, and how much. For if numerous private choices, rather than the single choice of a government, determine the distribution of aid pursuant to neutral eligibility criteria, then a government cannot, or at least cannot easily, grant special favors that might lead to a religious establishment. Private choice also helps guarantee neutrality by mitigating the preference for pre-existing recipients that is arguably inherent in any governmental aid program, . . . and that could lead to a program inadvertently favoring one religion or favoring religious private schools in general over nonreligious ones. . . .

[The] second primary criterion for determining the effect of governmental aid is closely related to the first. The second criterion requires a court to consider whether an aid program "define[s] its recipients by reference to religion." . . . This second criterion looks to the same set of facts as does our focus, under the first criterion, on neutrality, but the second criterion uses those facts to answer a somewhat different question—whether the criteria for allocating the aid "creat[e] a financial incentive to undertake religious indoctrination." In *Agostini* we set out the following rule for answering this question:

"This incentive is not present, however, where the aid is allocated on the basis of neutral, secular criteria that neither favor nor disfavor religion, and is made available to both religious and secular beneficiaries on a nondiscriminatory basis. Under such circumstances, the aid is less likely to have the effect of advancing religion."...

Applying the two relevant ... criteria, we see no basis for concluding that Jefferson Parish's Chapter 2 program "has the effect of advancing religion."... Chapter 2 does not result in governmental indoctrination, because it determines eligibility for aid neutrally, allocates that aid based on the private choices of the parents of schoolchildren, and does not provide aid that has an impermissible content. Nor does Chapter 2 define its recipients by reference to religion....

Justice Souter, with whom Justice Stevens and Justice Ginsburg join, dissenting....

The establishment prohibition of government religious funding serves more than one end. It is meant to guarantee the right of individual conscience against compulsion, to protect the integrity of religion against the corrosion of secular support, and to preserve the unity of political society against the implied exclusion of the less favored and the antagonism of controversy over public support for religious causes.

These objectives are always in some jeopardy since the substantive principle of no aid to religion is not the only limitation on government action toward religion. Because the First Amendment also bars any prohibition of individual free exercise of religion, and because religious organizations cannot be isolated from the basic government functions that create the civil environment, it is as much necessary as it is difficult to draw lines between forbidden aid and lawful benefit. For more than 50 years, this Court has been attempting to draw these lines. Owing to the variety of factual circumstances in which the lines must be drawn, not all of the points creating the boundary have enjoyed self-evidence.

So far as the line drawn has addressed government aid to education, a few fundamental generalizations are nonetheless possible. There may be no aid supporting a sectarian school's religious exercise or the discharge of its religious mission, while aid of a secular character with no discernible benefit to such a sectarian objective is allowable. Because the religious and secular spheres largely overlap in the life of many such schools, the Court has tried to identify some facts likely to reveal the relative religious or secular intent or effect of the government benefits in particular circumstances. We have asked whether the government is acting neutrally in distributing its money, and about the form of the aid itself, its path from government to religious institution, its divertibility to religious nurture, its potential for reducing traditional expenditures of religious institutions, and its relative importance to the recipient, among other things.

In all the years of its effort, the Court has isolated no single test of constitutional sufficiency, and the question in every case addresses the substantive principle of no aid: what reasons are there to characterize this benefit as aid to the sectarian school in discharging its religious mission? Particular factual circumstances control, and the answer is a matter of judgment....

[T]his case comes at a time when our judgment requires perspective on how the Establishment Clause has come to be understood and applied. It is not just that a majority today mistakes the significance of facts that have led to conclusions of unconstitutionality in earlier cases, though I believe the Court commits error in failing to recognize the divertibility of funds to the service of religious objectives. What is more important is the view revealed in the plurality opinion, which espouses a new conception of neutrality as a practically sufficient test of constitutionality that would, if adopted by the Court, eliminate enquiry into a law's effects. The plurality position breaks fundamentally with Establishment Clause principle, and with the methodology painstakingly worked out in support of it. . . . From that new view of the law, and from a majority's mistaken application of the old, I respectfully dissent.

Zelman v. Simmons-Harris (2002)[39]

A Cleveland, Ohio, program provided parents with vouchers that could be used to pay some of the costs of private schools, including religious schools. This program was inaugurated at a time when a state auditor had determined that the public schools in Cleveland were suffering from a "crisis that is perhaps unprecedented in the history of American education." Challenged on Establishment Clause grounds, this approach to the use of vouchers engendered vigorous debate among the members of the Supreme Court.

Chief Justice Rehnquist delivered the opinion of the Court.

The State of Ohio has established a pilot program designed to provide educational choices to families with children who reside in the Cleveland City School District. The question presented is whether this program offends the Establishment Clause of the United States Constitution. We hold that it does not.

There are more than 75,000 children enrolled in the Cleveland City School District. The majority of these children are from low-income and minority families. Few of these families enjoy the means to send their children to any school other than an inner-city public school. For more than a generation, however, Cleveland's public schools have been among the worst performing public schools in the nation. . . .

It is against this backdrop that Ohio enacted, among other initiatives, its Pilot Project Scholarship Program.

The program provides two basic kinds of assistance to parents of children in a covered district. First, the program provides tuition aid for students in kindergarten through third grade, expanding each year through eighth grade, to attend a participating public or private school of their parent's choosing. . . . Second, the program provides tutorial aid for students who choose to remain enrolled in public school. . . .

The tuition aid portion of the program is designed to provide educational choices to parents who reside in a covered district. Any private school, whether religious or nonreligious, may participate in the program and accept program students so long as the school is located within the boundaries of a covered district and meets statewide educational standards. . . . Participating private schools must agree not to discriminate on the basis of race, religion, or ethnic background, or to "advocate or foster unlawful behavior or teach hatred of any person or group on the basis of race, ethnicity, national origin, or religion." . . . Any public school located in a school district adjacent to the covered district may also participate in the program. . . . Adjacent public schools are eligible to receive a $2,250 tuition grant for each program student accepted in addition to the full amount of per-pupil state funding attributable to each additional student. . . .

Tuition aid is distributed to parents according to financial need. . . . For [the] lowest-income families, participating private schools may not charge a parental co-payment greater than $250. . . . Where tuition aid is spent depends solely upon where parents who receive tuition aid choose to enroll their child. If parents choose a private school, checks are made payable to the parents who then endorse the checks over to the chosen school. . . .

The tutorial aid portion of the program provides tutorial assistance through grants to any student in a covered district who chooses to remain in public school. Parents arrange for registered tutors to provide assistance to their children and then submit bills for those services to the State for payment. . . .

The program has been in operation within the Cleveland City School District since the 1996–1997 school year. In the 1999–2000 school year, 56 private schools participated in the program, 46 (or 82%) of which had a religious affiliation. None of the public schools in districts adjacent to Cleveland have elected to participate. More than 3,700 students participated in the scholarship program, most of whom (96%) enrolled in religiously affiliated schools. Sixty percent of these students were from families at or below the poverty line. In the 1998–1999 school year, approximately 1,400 Cleveland public school students received tutorial aid. This number was expected to double during the 1999–2000 school year.

The program is part of a broader undertaking by the State to enhance the educational options of Cleveland's schoolchildren. . . . That undertaking includes programs governing community and magnet schools. . . .

The Establishment Clause of the First Amendment, applied to the States through the Fourteenth Amendment, prevents a State from enacting laws that have the "purpose" or "effect" of advancing or inhibiting religion. . . . There is no dispute that the program challenged here was enacted for the valid secular purpose of providing educational assistance to poor children in a demonstrably failing public school system. Thus, the question presented is whether the Ohio program nonetheless has the forbidden "effect" of advancing or inhibiting religion.

To answer that question, our decisions have drawn a consistent distinction between government programs that provide aid directly to religious schools . . . and programs of true private choice, in which government aid reaches religious schools only as a result of the genuine and independent choices of private individuals. . . . While our jurisprudence with respect to the constitutionality of direct aid programs has "changed significantly" over the past two decades, . . . our jurisprudence with private choice programs has remained consistent and unbroken. Three times we have confronted Establishment Clause challenges to neutral government programs that provide aid directly to a broad class of individuals, who, in turn, direct the aid to religious schools or institutions of their own choosing. Three times we have rejected such challenges. [These were the *Mueller, Witters* and *Zobrest* cases.] . . .

Mueller, Witters, and *Zobrest* thus make clear that where a government aid program is neutral with respect to religion, and provides assistance directly to a broad class of citizens who, in turn, direct government aid to religious schools wholly as a result of their own genuine and independent private choice, the program is not readily subject to challenge under the Establishment Clause. A program that shares these features permits government aid to reach religious institutions only by way of the deliberate choices of numerous individual recipients. The incidental advancement of a religious mission, or the perceived endorsement of a religious message, is reasonably attributable to the individual recipient, not to the government, whose role ends with the disbursement of benefits. . . .

We believe that the program challenged here is a program of true private choice, consistent with *Mueller, Witters,* and *Zobrest,* and thus constitutional. As was true in those cases, the Ohio program is neutral in all respects toward religion. It is part of a general and multifaceted undertaking by the State of Ohio to provide educational opportunities to the children of a failed school district. It confers educational assistance directly to a broad class of individuals defined without reference to religion, *i.e.,* any parent of a school-age child who resides in the Cleveland City School District. The program permits the participation of *all* schools within the district, religious or nonreligious. Adjacent public schools also may participate and have a financial incentive to do so. Program benefits are available to participating families on neutral terms, with no reference to religion. The only preference stated anywhere in the program is a preference for low-income families, who receive greater assistance and are given priority for admission at participating schools.

There are no "financial incentive[s]" that "ske[w]" the program toward religious schools. . . . Such incentives "[are] not present . . . where the aid is allocated on the basis of neutral, secular criteria that neither favor nor disfavor religion, and is made available to both religious and secular beneficiaries on a nondiscriminatory basis.". . . The program here in fact creates financial disincentives for religious schools, with private schools receiving only half the government assistance given to community schools and one-third the assistance given to magnet schools. Adjacent public schools, should any choose to accept program students, are also eligible to receive two to three times the state funding of a private religious school. Families too have a financial disincentive to choose a private religious school over other schools. Parents that choose to participate in the scholarship program and then to enroll their children in a private school (religious or nonreligious) must copay a portion of the school's tuition. Families that choose a community school, magnet school, or traditional public school pay nothing. Although such features of the program are not necessary to its constitutionality, they clearly dispel the claim that the program "creates . . . financial incentive[s] for parents to choose a sectarian school.". . .

Respondents suggest that even without a financial incentive for parents to choose a religious school, the program creates a "public perception that the State is endorsing religious practices and beliefs.". . . But we have repeatedly recognized that no reasonable observer would think a neutral program of private choice, where state aid reaches religious schools solely as a result of the numerous independent decisions of private individuals, carries with it the *imprimatur* of government endorsement. . . . Any objective observer familiar with the full history and context of the Ohio program would reasonably view it as one aspect of a broader undertaking to assist poor children in failed schools, not as an endorsement of religious schooling in general.

There also is no evidence that the program fails to provide genuine opportunities for Cleveland parents to select secular educational options for their school-age children. Cleveland schoolchildren enjoy a range of educational choices: They may remain in public school as before, remain in public school with publicly funded tutoring aid, obtain a scholarship and choose a religious school, obtain a scholarship and choose a nonreligious private school, enroll in a community school, or enroll in a magnet school. That 46 of the 56 private schools now participating in the program are religious schools does not condemn it as a violation of the Establishment Clause. The Establishment Clause question is whether Ohio is coercing parents into sending their children to religious schools, and that question must be answered by evaluating *all* options Ohio provides Cleveland schoolchildren, only one of which is to obtain a program scholarship and then choose a religious school.

JUSTICE SOUTER speculates that because more private religious schools currently participate in the program, the program itself must somehow discourage the participation of private nonreligious schools. . . . But Cleveland's preponderance of religiously affiliated private schools certainly did not arise as a result of the program; it is a phenomenon common to many American cities. . . . Indeed, by all accounts the program has captured a remarkable cross-section of private schools, religious and nonreligious. It is true that 82% of Cleveland's participating private schools are religious schools, but it is also true that 81% of private schools in Ohio are religious schools. . . . To attribute constitutional significance to this figure, moreover, would lead to the absurd result that a neutral school-choice program might be permissible in some parts of Ohio, such as Columbus, where a lower percentage of private schools are religious schools, . . . but not in inner-city Cleveland, where Ohio has deemed such programs most sorely needed, but where the preponderance of religious schools happens to be greater. . . . Likewise, an identical private choice program might be constitutional in some States, such as Maine or Utah, where less than 45% of private schools are religious schools, but not in other States, such as Nebraska or Kansas, where over 90% of private schools are religious schools. . . .

Respondents and JUSTICE SOUTER claim that even if we do not focus on the number of participating schools that are religious schools, we should attach constitutional significance to the fact that 96% of scholarship recipients have enrolled in religious schools. They claim that this alone proves parents lack genuine choice, even if no parent has ever said so. We need not consider this argument in detail, since it was flatly rejected in *Mueller*, where we found it irrelevant that 96% of parents taking deductions for tuition expenses paid tuition at religious schools. . . . The constitutionality of a neutral educational aid program simply does not turn on whether and why, in a particular area, at a particular time, most private schools are run by religious organizations, or most recipients choose to use the aid at a religious school. . . .

In sum, the Ohio program is entirely neutral with respect to religion. It provides benefits directly to a wide spectrum of individuals, defined only by financial need and residence in a particular school district. It permits such individuals to exercise genuine choice among options public and private, secular and religious. The program is therefore a program of true private choice. In keeping with an unbroken line of decisions rejecting challenges to similar programs, we hold that the program does not offend the Establishment Clause. . . .

It is so ordered.

Justice Thomas, concurring.

Frederick Douglass once said that "[e]ducation . . . means emancipation. It means light and liberty. It means the uplifting of the soul of man into the glorious light of truth, the light by which men can only be made free." Today many of our inner-city public schools deny emancipation to urban minority students. Despite this Court's observation nearly 50 years ago in *Brown v. Board of Education*, that "it is doubtful that any child may reasonably be expected to succeed in life if he is denied the opportunity of an education," . . . urban children have been forced into a system that continually fails them. These cases present an example of such failures. Besieged by escalating financial problems and declining academic achievement, the Cleveland City School District was in the midst of an academic emergency when Ohio enacted its scholarship program. . . .

To determine whether a federal program survives scrutiny under the Establishment Clause, we have considered whether it has a secular purpose and whether it has the primary effect of advancing or inhibiting religion. . . . I agree with the Court that Ohio's program easily passes muster under our stringent test, but, as a matter of first principles, I question whether this test should be applied to the States.

The Establishment Clause of the First Amendment states that "Congress shall make no law respecting an establishment of religion." On its face, this provision places no limit on the States with regard to religion. The Establishment Clause originally protected States, and by extension their citizens, from the imposition of an established religion by the Federal Government. Whether and how this Clause should constrain state action under the Fourteenth Amendment is a more difficult question.

The Fourteenth Amendment fundamentally restructured the relationship between individuals and the States and ensured that States would not deprive citizens of liberty without due process of law. It guarantees citizenship to all individuals born or naturalized in the United States and provides that "[no] State shall make or enforce any law which shall abridge the privileges or immunities of citizens of the United States; nor shall any State deprive any person of life, liberty, or property, without due process of law; nor deny to any person within its jurisdiction the equal protection of the laws." As Justice Harlan noted, the Fourteenth Amendment "added greatly to the dignity and glory of American citizenship, and to the security of personal liberty.". . . When rights are incorporated against the States through the Fourteenth Amendment they should advance, not constrain, individual liberty.

Consequently, in the context of the Establishment Clause, it may well be that state action should be evaluated on different terms than similar action by the Federal Government. . . . Thus, while the Federal Government may "make no law respecting an establishment of religion," the States may pass laws that include or touch on religious matters so long as these laws do not impede free exercise rights or any other individual religious liberty interest. By considering the particular religious liberty right alleged to be invaded by a State, federal courts can strike a proper balance between the demands of the Fourteenth Amendment on the one hand and the federalism prerogatives of States on the other.

Whatever the textual and historical merits of incorporating the Establishment Clause, I can accept that the Fourteenth Amendment protects religious liberty rights. But I cannot accept its use to oppose neutral programs of school choice through the incorporation of the Establishment Clause. There would be a tragic irony in converting the Fourteenth Amendment's guarantee of individual liberty into a prohibition on the exercise of educational choice.

The wisdom of allowing States greater latitude in dealing with matters of religion and education can be easily appreciated in this context. Respondents advocate using the Fourteenth Amendment to handcuff the State's ability to experiment with education. But without education one can hardly exercise the civic, political, and personal freedoms conferred by the Fourteenth Amendment. Faced with a severe educational crisis, the State of Ohio enacted wide-ranging educational reform that allows voluntary participation of private and religious schools in educating poor urban children otherwise condemned to failing public schools. The program does not force any individual to submit to religious indoctrination or education. It simply gives parents a greater choice as to where and in what manner to educate their children. This is a choice that those with greater means have routinely exercised. . . .

Although one of the purposes of public schools was to promote democracy and a more egalitarian culture, failing urban public schools disproportionately affect minority children most in need of educational opportunity. At the time of Reconstruction, blacks considered public education "a matter of personal liberation and a necessary function of a free society.". . . Today, however, the promise of public school education has failed poor inner-city blacks. While in theory providing education to everyone, the quality of public schools varies significantly across districts. Just as blacks supported public education during Reconstruction, many blacks and other minorities now support school choice programs because they provide the greatest educational opportunities for their children in struggling communities. Opponents of the program raise formalistic concerns about the Establishment Clause but ignore the core purposes of the Fourteenth Amendment.

While the romanticized ideal of universal public education resonates with the cognoscenti who oppose vouchers, poor urban families just want the best education for their children, who will certainly need it to function in our high-tech and advanced society. . . . An individual's life prospects increase dramatically with each successfully completed phase of education. For instance, a black high school dropout earns just over $13,500, but with a high school degree the average income is almost $21,000. Blacks with a bachelor's degree have an average annual income of about $37,500, and $75,500 with a professional degree. . . . Staying in school and earning a degree generates real and tangible financial benefits, whereas failure to obtain even a high school degree essentially relegates students to a life of poverty and, all too often, of crime. The failure to provide education to poor urban children perpetuates a vicious cycle of poverty, dependence, criminality, and alienation that continues for the remainder of their lives. If society cannot end racial discrimination, at least it can arm minorities with the education to defend themselves from some of discrimination's effects.

* * *

Ten States have enacted some form of publicly funded private school choice as one means of raising the quality of education provided to underprivileged urban children. These programs address the root of the problem with failing urban public schools that disproportionately affect minority students. Society's other solution to these educational failures is often to provide racial preferences in higher education. Such preferences, however, run afoul of the Fourteenth Amendment's prohibition against distinctions based on race. . . . By contrast, school choice programs that involve religious schools appear unconstitutional only to those who would twist the Fourteenth Amendment against itself by expansively incorporating the Establishment Clause. Converting the Fourteenth Amendment from a guarantee of opportunity to an obstacle against education reform distorts our constitutional values and disserves those in the greatest need.

As Frederick Douglass poignantly noted "no greater benefit can be bestowed upon a long benighted people, than giving to them, as we are here earnestly this day endeavoring to do, the means of an education."

Justice Souter, with whom Justice Stevens, Justice Ginsburg, and Justice Breyer join, dissenting.

. . . If there were an excuse for giving short shrift to the Establishment Clause, it would probably apply here. But there is no excuse. Constitutional limitations are placed on government to preserve constitutional values in hard cases, like these. . . .

The applicability of the Establishment Clause to public funding of benefits to religious schools was settled in *Everson v. Board of Ed. of Ewing*, . . . which inaugurated the modern era of establishment doctrine. The Court stated the principle in words from which there was no dissent:

"No tax in any amount, large or small, can be levied to support any religious activities or institutions, whatever they may be called, or whatever form they may adopt to teach or practice religion.". . .

The Court has never in so many words repudiated this statement, let alone, in so many words, overruled *Everson*.. . .

In the city of Cleveland the overwhelming proportion of large appropriations for voucher money must be spent on religious schools if it is to be spent at all, and will be spent in amounts that cover almost all of tuition. The money will thus pay for eligible students' instruction not only in secular subjects but in religion as well, in schools that can fairly be characterized as founded to teach religious doctrine and to imbue teaching in all subjects with a religious dimension. Public tax money will pay at a systemic level for teaching the covenant with Israel and Mosaic law in Jewish schools, the primacy of the Apostle Peter and the Papacy in Catholic schools, the truth of reformed Christianity in Protestant schools, and the revelation to the Prophet in Muslim schools, to speak only of major religious groupings in the Republic.

How can a Court consistently leave *Everson* on the books and approve the Ohio vouchers? The answer is that it cannot. It is only by ignoring *Everson* that the majority can claim to rest on traditional law in its invocation of neutral aid provisions and private choice to sanction the Ohio law. It is, moreover, only by ignoring the meaning of neutrality and private choice themselves that the majority can even pretend to rest today's decision on those criteria.

The majority's statements of Establishment Clause doctrine cannot be appreciated without some historical perspective on the Court's announced limitations on government aid to religious education, and its repeated repudiation of limits previously set. . . . My object here is not to give any nuanced exposition of the cases . . . but to set out the broad doctrinal stages covered in the modern era, and to show that doctrinal bankruptcy has been reached today.

Viewed with the necessary generality, the cases can be categorized in three groups. In the period from 1947 to 1968, the basic principle of no aid to religion through school benefits was unquestioned. Thereafter for some 15 years, the Court termed its efforts as attempts to draw a line against aid that would be divertible to support the religious, as distinct from the secular, activity of an institutional beneficiary. Then, starting in 1988, concern with divertibility was gradually lost in favor of approving aid in amounts unlikely to afford substantial benefits to religious schools, when offered evenhandedly without regard to a recipient's religious character, and when channeled to a religious institution only by the genuinely free choice of some private individual. Now, the three stages are succeeded by a fourth, in which the substantial character of government aid is held to have no constitutional significance, and the espoused criteria of neutrality in offering aid, and private choice in directing it, are shown to be nothing but examples of verbal formalism. . . .

[Justice Souter then discusses the prior cases in detail and argues that the voucher program violates the principles established in those cases and even the new approach offered in the majority opinion.]

[E]very objective underlying the prohibition of religious establishment is betrayed by this scheme. . . , the first being respect for freedom of conscience. Jefferson described it as the idea that no one "shall be compelled to . . . support any religious worship, place, or ministry whatsoever," . . . even a "teacher of his own religious persuasion.". . .

As for the second objective, to save religion from its own corruption, Madison wrote of the "'experience . . . that ecclesiastical establishments, instead of maintaining the purity and efficacy of Religion, have had a contrary operation.'" . . .

The risk is already being realized. In Ohio, for example, a condition of receiving government money under the program is that participating religious schools may not "discriminate on the basis of . . . religion," . . . which means the school may not give admission preferences to children who are members of the patron faith; children of a parish are generally consigned to the same admission lotteries as non-believers. . . . Nor is the State's religious antidiscrimination restriction limited to student admission policies: by its terms, a participating religious school may well be forbidden to choose a member of its own clergy to serve as teacher or principal over a layperson of a different religion claiming equal qualification for the job. . . . Indeed, a separate condition that "[t]he school . . . not . . . teach hatred of any person or group on the basis of . . . religion," . . . could be understood (or subsequently broadened) to prohibit religions from teaching traditionally legitimate articles of faith as to the error, sinfulness, or ignorance of others, if they want government money for their schools. . . .

Increased voucher spending is not, however, the sole portent of growing regulation of religious practice in the school, for state mandates to moderate religious teaching may well be the most obvious response to the third concern behind the ban on establishment, its inextricable link with social conflict. . . . As appropriations for religious subsidy rise, competition for the money will tap sectarian religion's capacity for discord. . . .

[The] intensity of the expectable friction can be gauged by realizing that the scramble for money will energize not only contending sectarians, but taxpayers who take their liberty of conscience seriously. Religious teaching at taxpayer expense simply cannot be cordoned from taxpayer politics, and every major religion currently espouses social positions that provoke intense opposition. Not all taxpaying Protestant citizens, for example, will be content to underwrite the teaching of the Roman Catholic Church condemning the death penalty. Nor will all of America's Muslims acquiesce in paying for the endorsement of the religious Zionism taught in many religious Jewish schools, which combines "a nationalistic sentiment" in support of Israel with a "deeply religious" element. Nor will every secular taxpayer be content to support Muslim views on differential treatment of the sexes, or, for that matter, to fund the espousal of a wife's obligation of obedience to her husband, presumably taught in any schools adopting the articles of faith of the Southern Baptist Convention. Views like these, and innumerable others, have been safe in the sectarian pulpits and classrooms of this Nation not only because the Free Exercise Clause protects them directly, but because the ban on supporting religious establishment has protected free exercise, by keeping it relatively private. With the arrival of vouchers in religious schools, that privacy will go, and along with it will go confidence that religious disagreement will stay moderate.

* * *

If the divisiveness permitted by today's majority is to be avoided in the short term, it will be avoided only by action of the political branches at the state and national levels. Legislatures not driven to desperation by the problems of public education may be able to see the threat in vouchers negotiable in sectarian schools. Perhaps even cities with problems like Cleveland's will perceive the danger, now that they know a federal court will not save them from it.

My own course as a judge on the Court cannot, however, simply be to hope that the political branches will save us from the consequences of the majority's decision. *Everson*'s statement is still the touchstone of sound law, even though the reality is that in the matter of educational aid the Establishment Clause has largely been read away. True, the majority has not approved vouchers for religious schools alone, or aid earmarked for religious instruction. But no scheme so clumsy will ever get before us, and in the cases that we may see, like these, the Establishment Clause is largely silenced. I do not have the option to leave it silent, and I hope that a future Court will reconsider today's dramatic departure from basic Establishment Clause principle.

The Scope of Religious Liberty

Torcaso v. Watkins (1961)[40]

Loyalty oaths were quite common in Europe during the colonial period, and many religious dissenters left European countries to come to America, at least in part to avoid such oaths. One of these immigrants was the first Lord Baltimore, George Calvert, a Roman Catholic who fled both England and the Colony of Virginia to settle in Maryland. It is thus ironic that this case involves a challenge to a Maryland loyalty oath requiring public officeholders to declare a belief in the existence of God.

Mr. Justice Black delivered the opinion of the Court.

Article 37 of the Declaration of Rights of the Maryland Constitution provides:

"[N]o religious test ought ever to be required as a qualification for any office of profit or trust in this State other than a declaration of belief in the existence of God. . . ."

The appellant Torcaso was appointed to the office of Notary Public by the Governor of Maryland but was refused a commission to serve because he would not declare his belief in God. He then brought this action . . . to compel issuance of his commission. . . .

There is, and can be, no dispute about the purpose or effect of the Maryland Declaration of Rights requirement before us—it sets up a religious test which was designed to and, if valid, does bar every person who refuses to declare a belief in God from holding a public "office of profit or trust" in Maryland. The power and authority of the State of Maryland thus is put on the side of one particular sort of believers—those who are willing to say they believe in "the existence of God." It is true that there is much historical precedent for such laws. Indeed, it was largely to escape religious test oaths and declarations that a great many of the early colonists left Europe and came here hoping to worship in their own way. It soon developed, however, that many of those who had fled to escape religious test oaths turned out to be perfectly willing, when they had the power to do so, to force dissenters from their faith to take test oaths in conformity with that faith. This brought on a host of laws in the new Colonies imposing burdens and disabilities of various kinds upon varied beliefs depending largely upon what group happened to be politically strong enough to legislate in favor of its own beliefs. The effect of all this was the formal or practical "establishment" of particular religious faiths in most of the Colonies, with consequent burdens imposed on the free exercise of the faiths of nonfavored believers.

There were, however, wise and far-seeing men in the Colonies—too many to mention—who spoke out against test oaths and all the philosophy of intolerance behind them. One of these, it so happens, was George Calvert (the first Lord Baltimore), who took a most important part in the original establishment of the Colony of Maryland. He was a Catholic and had, for this reason, felt compelled by his conscience to refuse to take the Oath of Supremacy in England at the cost of resigning from high governmental office. He again refused to take that oath when it was demanded by the Council of the Colony of Virginia, and as a result he was denied settlement in that Colony. A recent historian of the early period of Maryland's life has said that it was Calvert's hope and purpose to establish in Maryland a colonial government free from the religious persecutions he had known—one "securely beyond the reach of oaths. . . ."

When our Constitution was adopted, the desire to put the people "securely beyond the reach" of religious test oaths brought about the inclusion in Article 6 of that document of a provision that "no religious Test shall ever be required as a Qualification to any Office or public Trust under the United States.". . . Not satisfied, however, with Article 6 and other guarantees in the original Constitution, the First Congress proposed and the States very shortly thereafter adopted our Bill of Rights, including the First Amendment. That Amendment broke new constitutional ground in the protection it sought to afford to freedom of religion, speech, press, petition and assembly. Since prior cases in this [Court] have thoroughly explored and documented the history behind the First Amendment, the reasons for it, and the scope of the religious freedom it protects, we need not cover that ground again. What was said in our prior cases we think controls our decision here. . . .

We repeat and again reaffirm that neither a State nor the Federal Government can constitutionally force a person "to profess a belief or disbelief in any religion." Neither can constitutionally pass laws or impose requirements which aid all religions as against non-believers, and neither can aid those religions based on a belief in the existence of God as against those religions founded on different beliefs.

In upholding the State's religious test for public office the highest court of Maryland said:

"The petitioner is not compelled to believe or disbelieve, under threat of punishment or other compulsion. True, unless he makes the declaration of belief he cannot hold public office in Maryland, but he is not compelled to hold office."

The fact, however, that a person is not compelled to hold public office cannot possibly be an excuse for barring him from office by state-imposed criteria forbidden by the Constitution. This was settled by our holding in Wieman v Updegraff, 344 US 183. . . . We there pointed out that whether or not "an abstract right to public employment exists," Congress could not pass a law providing "'. . . that no federal employee shall attend Mass or take any active part in missionary work.'"

This Maryland religious test for public office unconstitutionally invades the appellant's freedom of belief and religion and therefore cannot be enforced against him.

Sherbert v. Verner (1963)[41]

The records of the debates in the First Congress in Chapter III show that it is difficult to identify a clear set of rights the founding fathers sought to protect by the First Amendment. Whatever the founders may have had in mind in the late eighteenth century, it is hard to imagine that they were thinking about unemployment compensation programs; yet this topic has repeatedly engaged the modern Supreme Court's attention, especially in response to claims under the free-exercise clause. In this case, the Court grapples with the issues raised by a denial by the state of South Carolina of state unemployment benefits to a Seventh-day Adventist who lost her job because she refused to work on Saturday, her Sabbath day.

Mr. Justice Brennan delivered the opinion of the Court. . . .

The door of the Free Exercise Clause stands tightly closed against any governmental regulation of religious *beliefs* as such. . . . Government may neither compel affirmation of a repugnant belief, . . . nor penalize or discriminate against individuals or groups because they hold religious views abhorrent to the authorities, . . . nor employ the taxing power to inhibit the dissemination of particular religious views. . . . On the other hand, the Court has rejected challenges under the Free Exercise Clause to governmental regulation of certain overt acts prompted by religious beliefs or principles, for "even when the action is in accord with one's religious convictions, [it] is not totally free from legislative restrictions. . . ." The conduct or actions so regulated have invariably posed some substantial threat to public safety, peace or order. . . .

Plainly enough, appellant's conscientious objection to Saturday work constitutes no conduct prompted by religious principles of a kind within the reach of state legislation. If, therefore, the decision of the South Carolina Supreme Court is to withstand appellant's constitutional challenge, it must be either because her disqualification as a beneficiary represents no infringement by the State of her constitutional rights of free exercise, or because any incidental burden on the free exercise of appellant's religion may be justified by a "compelling state interest in the regulation of a subject within the State's constitutional power to regulate. . . ."

We turn first to the question whether the disqualification for benefits imposes any burden on the free exercise of appellant's religion. We think it is clear that it does. In a sense the consequences of such a disqualification to religious principles and practices may be only an indirect result of welfare legislation within the State's general competence to enact; it is true that no criminal sanctions directly compel appellant to work a six-day week. But this is only the beginning, not the end, of our inquiry. For "[i]f the purpose or effect of a law is to impede the observance of one or all religions or is to discriminate invidiously between religions, that law is constitutionally invalid even though the burden may be characterized as being only indirect. . . ." Here not only is it apparent that appellant's declared ineligibility for benefits derives solely from the practice of her religion, but the pressure upon her to forgo that practice is unmistakable. The ruling forces her to choose between following the precepts of her religion and forfeiting benefits, on the one hand, and abandoning one of the precepts of her religion in order to accept work, on the other hand. Governmental imposition of such a choice puts the same kind of burden upon the free exercise of religion as would a fine imposed against appellant for her Saturday worship.

Nor may the South Carolina court's construction of the statute be saved from constitutional infirmity on the ground that unemployment compensation benefits are not appellant's "right" but merely a "privilege." It is too late in the day to doubt that the liberties of religion and expression may be infringed by the denial of or placing of conditions upon a benefit or privilege. . . . [T]o condition the availability of benefits upon this appellant's willingness to violate a cardinal principle of her religious faith effectively penalizes the free exercise of her constitutional liberties.

Significantly South Carolina expressly saves the Sunday worshipper from having to make the kind of choice which we here hold infringes the Sabbatarian's religious liberty. When in times of "national emergency" the textile plants are authorized by the State Commissioner of Labor to operate on Sunday, "no employee shall be required to work on Sunday . . . who is conscientiously opposed to Sunday work; and if any employee should refuse to work on Sunday on account of conscientious . . . objections he or she shall not jeopardize his or her seniority by such refusal or be discriminated against in any other manner.". . . No question of the disqualification of a Sunday worshipper for benefits is likely to arise, since we cannot suppose that an employer will discharge him in violation of this statute. The unconstitutionality of the disqualification of the Sabbatarian is thus compounded by the religious discrimination which South Carolina's general statutory scheme necessarily effects.

We must next consider whether some compelling state interest enforced in the eligibility provisions of the South Carolina statute justifies the substantial infringement of appellant's First Amendment right. It is basic that no showing merely of a rational relationship to some colorable state interest would suffice; in this highly sensitive constitutional area, "[o]nly the gravest abuses, endangering paramount interests, give occasion for permissible limitation. . . ." No such abuse or danger has been advanced in the present case. The state suggests no more than a possibility that the filing of fraudulent claims by unscrupulous claimants feigning religious objections to Saturday work might not only dilute the unemployment compensation fund but also hinder the scheduling by employers of necessary Saturday work. But . . . there is no proof whatever to warrant such fears of malingering or deceit. . . . Even if consideration of such evidence is not foreclosed by the prohibition against judicial inquiry into the truth or falsity of religious beliefs, . . . it is highly doubtful whether such evidence would be sufficient to warrant a substantial infringement of religious liberties. For even if the possibility of spurious claims did threaten to dilute the fund and disrupt the scheduling of work, it would plainly be incumbent upon the appellees to demonstrate that no alternative forms of regulation would combat such abuses without infringing First Amendment rights. . . .

In holding as we do, plainly we are not fostering the "establishment" of the Seventh-day Adventist religion in South Carolina, for the extension of unemployment benefits to Sabbatarians in common with Sunday worshippers reflects nothing more than the governmental obligation of neutrality in the face of religious differences, and does not represent that involvement of religious with secular institutions which it is the object of the Establishment Clause to forestall. . . . Nor does the recognition of the appellant's right to unemployment benefits under the state statute serve to abridge any other person's religious liberties. Nor do we, by our decision today, declare the existence of a constitutional right to unemployment benefits on the part of all persons whose religious convictions are the cause of their unemployment. This is not a case in which an employee's religious convictions serve to make him a non-productive member of society. . . . Finally, nothing we say today constrains the States to adopt any particular form or scheme of unemployment compensation. Our holding today is only that South Carolina may not constitutionally apply the eligibility provisions so as to constrain a worker to abandon his religious convictions respecting the day of rest. This holding but reaffirms a principle that we announced a decade and a half ago, namely that no State may "exclude individual Catholics, Lutherans, Mohammedans, Baptists, Jews, Methodists, Non-believers, Presbyterians, or the members of any other faith, *be-*

cause of their faith, or lack of it, from receiving the benefits of public welfare legislation." . . .

In my opinion, Congress did not authorize the prosecution of a civilian who accepted a military base Commander's invitation to attend an open house on the base simply because the civilian had been "removed therefrom" and "ordered not to reenter" some nine years earlier.

I respectfully dissent.

McDaniel v. Paty (1978)[42]

The *Torcaso* v. *Watkins* case established in 1961 that a century-old religious test for public office violated the provisions of the First Amendment. Almost two decades later, the Supreme Court was asked to come to terms with another colonial practice: a ban on "Ministers of the Gospel" serving as members of the Tennessee legislature found in that state's constitution. Does such a provision legitimately protect the state from the risk of ecclesiastical encroachments or does it offend the free-exercise clause? Among others, Chief Justice Burger consulted the opinion of John Witherspoon, president of Princeton University in the eighteenth century, and the only clergyman to sign the Declaration of Independence. Commenting on a similar clergy disqualification proposal, Witherspoon proposed the following amendment: "No clergyman . . . shall be capable of being elected a member of the Senate or House of Representatives . . . Provided . . . that if at anytime he shall be completely deprived of the clerical character [for] swearing, drunkenness or uncleanness, he shall then be fully restored to all the privileges of a free citizen. . . ."

Mr. Chief Justice Burger announced the judgment of the Court and delivered an opinion in which [three justices] joined. . . .

In its first Constitution, in 1796, Tennessee disqualified ministers from serving as legislators.* That disqualifying provision has continued unchanged since its adoption; it is now Art 9, § 1 of the State Constitution. The state legislature applied this provision to candidates for delegate to the State's 1977 limited constitutional convention when it enacted ch 848, § 4, of 1976 Tenn Publ Acts: "Any citizen of the state who can qualify for membership in the House of Representatives of the General Assembly may become a candidate for delegate to the convention. . . ."

McDaniel, an ordained minister of a Baptist Church in Chattanooga, Tenn., filed as a candidate for delegate to the constitutional convention. An opposing candidate, appellee Selma Cash Paty, sued in the Chancery Court for a declaratory judgment that McDaniel was disqualified to serve as a delegate and for a judgment striking his name from the ballot. . . .

---

*Whereas Ministers of the Gospel are by their profession, dedicated to God and the care of Souls, and ought not to be diverted from the great duties of their functions; therefore, no Ministers of the Gospel, or priests of any denomination whatever, shall be eligible to a seat in either House of the Legislature." Tenn Const, Art VIII, § 1 (1796).

The disqualification of ministers from legislative office was a practice carried from England by seven of the original States; later six new States similarly excluded clergymen from some political offices. . . . In England the practice of excluding clergy from the House of Commons was justified on a variety of grounds: to prevent dual office-holding, that is, membership by a minister in both Parliament and Convocation; to insure that the priest or deacon devoted himself to his "sacred calling" rather than to "such mundane activities as were appropriate to a member of the House of Commons"; and to prevent ministers, who after 1533 were subject to the Crown's powers over the benefices of the clergy, from using membership in Commons to diminish its independence by increasing the influence of the King and the nobility. . . .

The purpose of the several States in providing for disqualification was primarily to assure the success of a new political experiment, the separation of church and state.

Prior to 1776, most of the 13 Colonies had some form of an established, or government-sponsored, church. Even after ratification of the First Amendment, which prohibited the Federal Government from following such a course, some States continued proestablishment provisions. . . .

In light of this history and a wide-spread awareness during that period of undue and often dominant clerical influence in public and political affairs here, in England, and on the Continent, it is not surprising that strong views were held by some that one way to assure dis-establishment was to keep clergymen out of public office. Indeed, some of the foremost political philosophers and statesmen of that period held such views regarding the clergy. Earlier, John Locke argued for confining the authority of the English clergy "within the bounds of the church, nor can it in any manner be extended to civil affairs; because the church itself is a thing absolutely separate and distinct from the commonwealth.". . . Thomas Jefferson initially advocated such a position in his 1783 draft of a constitution for Virginia. James Madison, however, disagreed and vigorously urged the position which in our view accurately reflects the spirit and purpose of the Religion Clauses of the First Amendment. Madison's response to Jefferson's position was:

> "Does not The exclusion of Ministers of the Gospel as such violate a fundamental principle of liberty by punishing a religious profession with the privation of a civil right? does it [not] violate another article of the plan itself which exempts religion from the cognizance of Civil power? does it not violate justice by at once taking away a right and prohibiting a compensation for it? does it not in fine violate impartiality by shutting the door [against] the Ministers of one Religion and leaving it open for those of every other."

As the value of the dis-establishment experiment was perceived, 11 of the 13 States disqualifying the clergy from some types of public office gradually abandoned that limitation. . . . Only Maryland and Tennessee continued their clergy-disqualification provisions into this century and . . . Tennessee remains the only State excluding ministers from certain public offices.

The essence of this aspect of our national history is that in all but a few States the selection or rejection of clergymen for public office soon came to be viewed as something safely left to the good sense and desires of the people.

This brief review of the history of clergy-disqualification provisions also amply demonstrates, however, that, at least during the early segment of our national life, those provisions enjoyed the support of responsible American statesmen and were accepted as having a rational basis. Against this background we do not lightly invalidate a statute enacted pursuant to a provision of a state constitution which has been sustained by its highest court. The challenged provision came to the Tennessee Supreme Court clothed with the presumption of validity to which that court was bound to give deference.

However, the right to the free exercise of religion unquestionably encompasses the right to preach, proselyte, and perform other similar religious functions, or, in other words, to be a minister of the type McDaniel was found to be. . . . Tennessee also acknowledges the right of its adult citizens generally to seek and hold office as legislators or delegates to the state constitutional convention. . . . Yet under the clergy-disqualification provision, McDaniel cannot exercise both rights simultaneously because the State has conditioned the exercise of one on the surrender of the other. Or, in James Madison's words, the State is "punishing a religious profession with the privation of a civil right.". . . In so doing, Tennessee has encroached upon McDaniel's right to the free exercise of religion. . . .

If the Tennessee disqualification provision were viewed as depriving the clergy of a civil right solely because of their religious beliefs, our inquiry would be at an end. The Free Exercise Clause categorically forbids government from regulating, prohibiting, or rewarding religious beliefs as such. . . . In Torcaso v Watkins, . . . the Court reviewed the Maryland constitutional requirement that all holders of "any office of profit or trust in this State" declare their belief in the existence of God. In striking down the Maryland requirement, the Court did not evaluate the interests assertedly justifying it but rather held that it violated freedom of religious belief.

In our view, however, Torcaso does not govern. By its terms, the Tennessee disqualification operates against McDaniel because of his *status* as a "minister" or "priest." The meaning of those words is, of course, a question of state law. And although the question has not been examined extensively in state-law sources, such authority as is available indicates that ministerial status is defined in terms of conduct and activity rather than in terms of belief. Because the Tennessee disqualification is directed primarily at status, acts, and conduct it is unlike the requirement in Torcaso, which focused on *belief*. Hence, the Free Exercise Clause's absolute prohibition of infringements on the "freedom to believe" is inapposite here.

This does not mean, of course, that the disqualification escapes judicial scrutiny or that McDaniel's activity does not enjoy significant First Amendment protection.

Tennessee asserts that its interest in preventing the establishment of a state religion is consistent with the Establishment Clause and thus of the highest order. The constitutional history of the several States reveals that generally the interest in preventing establishment prompted the adoption of clergy disqualification provisions, . . . Tennessee does not appear to be an exception to this pattern. . . . There is no occasion to inquire whether promoting such an interest is a permissible legislative goal, however, . . . for Tennessee has failed to demonstrate that its views of the dangers of clergy participation in the political process have not lost whatever validity they may once have enjoyed. The essence of the rationale underlying the Tennessee restriction on ministers is that if elected to public office they will necessarily exercise their powers and influence to promote the interests of one sect or thwart the interests of another, thus pitting one against the others, contrary to the anti-establishment principle with its command of neutrality. . . . However widely that view may have been held in the 18th century by many, including enlightened statesmen of that day, the American experience provides no persuasive support for the fear that clergymen in public office will be less careful of anti-establishment interests or less faithful to their oaths of civil office than their unordained counterparts.

We hold that § 4 of ch 848 violates McDaniel's First Amendment right to the free exercise of his religion made applicable to the States by the Fourteenth Amendment. . . .

Thomas v. Review Board (1981)[43]

Two decades after *Sherbert* v. *Verner* the Supreme Court was again asked to decide whether the free-exercise clause creates a right to unemployment compensation. In this case, the claimant, a worker in a sheet steel factory, was transferred to a plant that made parts for military equipment. He found this work inconsistent with his Jehovah's Witness commitment to pacifism, and he quit when he could not be given other work. Using *Sherbert* as precedent, he claimed a right to state unemployment benefits.

Chief Justice Burger delivered the opinion of the Court. . . .

Thomas, a Jehovah's Witness, was hired initially to work in the roll foundry at Blaw-Knox. The function of that department was to fabricate sheet steel for a variety of industrial uses. On his application form, he listed his membership in the Jehovah's Witnesses, and noted that his hobbies were Bible study and Bible reading. However, he placed no conditions on his employment; and he did not describe his religious tenets in any detail on the form.

Approximately a year later, the roll foundry closed, and Blaw-Knox transferred Thomas to a department that fabricated turrets for military tanks. On his first day at this new job, Thomas realized that the work he was doing was weapons related. He checked the bulletin board where in-plant openings were listed, and discovered that all of the remaining departments at Blaw-Knox were engaged directly in the production of weapons. Since no transfer to another department would resolve his problem, he asked for a layoff. When that request was denied, he quit, asserting that he could not work on weapons without violating the principles of his religion. The record does not show that he was offered any nonweapons work by his employer, or that any such work was available.

Upon leaving Blaw-Knox, Thomas applied for unemployment compensation benefits under the Indiana Employment Security Act. At an administrative hearing where he was not represented by counsel, he testified that he believed that contributing to the production of arms violated his religion. He said that when he realized that his work on the tank turret line involved producing weapons for war, he consulted another Blaw-Knox employee—a friend and fellow Jehovah's Witness. The friend advised him that working on weapons parts at Blaw-Knox was not "unscriptural." Thomas was not able to "rest with" this view, however. He concluded that his friend's view was based upon a less strict reading of Witnesses' principles than his own.

When asked at the hearing to explain what kind of work his religious convictions would permit, Thomas said that he would have no difficulty doing the type of work that he had done at the roll foundry. He testified that he could, in good conscience, engage indirectly in the production of materials that might be used ultimately to fabricate arms—for example, as an employee of a raw material supplier or of a roll foundry. . . .

Only beliefs rooted in religion are protected by the Free Exercise Clause, which, by its terms, gives special protection to the exercise of religion. . . . The determination of what is a "religious" belief or practice is more often than not a difficult and delicate task. . . . However, the resolution of that question is not to turn upon a judicial perception of the particular belief or practice in question; religious beliefs need not be acceptable, logical, consistent, or comprehensible to others in order to merit First Amendment protection. . . .

Where the state conditions receipt of an important benefit upon conduct proscribed by a religious faith, or where it denies such a benefit because of conduct mandated by religious belief, thereby putting substantial pressure on an adherent to modify his behavior and to violate his beliefs, a burden upon religion exists. While the compulsion may be indirect, the infringement upon free exercise is nonetheless substantial. . . .

The mere fact that the petitioner's religious practice is burdened by a governmental program does not mean that an exemption accommodating his practice must be granted. The state may justify an inroad on religious liberty by showing that it is the least restrictive means of achieving some compelling state interest. However, it is still true that "[t]he essence of all that has been said and written on the subject is that only those interests of the highest order . . . can overbalance legitimate claims to the free exercise of religion." . . .

The purposes urged to sustain the disqualifying provision of the Indiana unemployment compensation scheme are twofold: (1) to avoid the widespread unemployment and the consequent burden on the fund resulting if people were permitted to leave jobs for "personal" reasons; and (2) to avoid a detailed probing by employers into job applicants' religious beliefs. These are by no means unimportant considerations. When the focus of the inquiry is properly narrowed, however, we must conclude that the interests advanced by the State do not justify the burden placed on free exercise of religion.

There is no evidence in the record to indicate that the number of people who find themselves in the predicament of choosing between benefits and religious beliefs is large enough to create "widespread unemployment," or even to seriously affect unemployment. Similarly, although detailed inquiry by employers into applicants' religious beliefs is undesirable, there is no evidence in the record to indicate that such inquiries will occur in Indiana, or that they have occurred in any of the states that extend benefits to people in the petitioner's position. Nor is there any reason to believe that the number of people terminating employment for religious reasons will be so great as to motivate employers to make such inquiries.

Neither of the interests advanced is sufficiently compelling to justify the burden upon Thomas' religious liberty. . . .

Frazee v. Illinois Department of Employment Security (1989)[44]

Sherbert, Thomas and other cases established that membership in religious groups such as the Jehovah's Witnesses or the Seventh-day Adventists can lay a foundation for the assertion of free-exercise rights by church members seeking unemployment benefits. This case arose because Mr. Frazee refused employment that would conflict with his religious belief that he should not work on the "Lord's day," although he was not a member of any particular church or religious group.

Justice White delivered the opinion of the Court. . . .

In April 1984, William Frazee refused a temporary retail position offered him by Kelly Services because the job would have required him to work on Sunday. Frazee told Kelly that, as a Christian, he could not work on "the Lord's day." Frazee then applied to the Illinois Department of Employment Security for unemployment benefits claiming that there was good cause for his refusal to work on Sunday. His application was denied. Frazee appealed the denial of benefits to the Department of Employment Security's Board of Review, which also denied his claim. The Board of Review stated: "When a refusal of work is based on religious convictions, the refusal must be based upon some tenets or dogma accepted by the individual of some church, sect, or denomination, and such a refusal based solely on an individual's personal belief is personal and noncompelling and does not render the work unsuitable."

The Board of Review concluded that Frazee had refused an offer of suitable work without good cause. . . .

We have had more than one occasion before today to consider denials of unemployment compensation benefits to those who have refused work on the basis of their religious beliefs. . . . It is true . . . that each of the claimants in those cases was a member of a particular religious sect, but none of those decisions turned on that consideration or on any tenet of the sect involved that forbade the work the claimant refused to perform. Our judgments in those cases rested on the fact that each of the claimants had a sincere belief that religion required him or her to refrain from the work in question. Never did we suggest that unless a claimant belongs to a sect that forbids what his job requires, his belief, however sincere, must be deemed a purely personal preference rather than a religious belief. . . .

There is no doubt that "[o]nly beliefs rooted in religion are protected by the Free Exercise Clause," . . . Purely secular views do not suffice. . . . Nor do we underestimate the difficulty of distinguishing between religious and secular convictions and in determining whether a professed belief is sincerely held. States are clearly entitled to assure themselves that there is an ample predicate for invoking the Free Exercise Clause. We do not face problems about sincerity or about the religious nature of

Frazee's convictions, however. The courts below did not question his sincerity, and the State concedes it. . . .

Frazee asserted that he was a Christian, but did not claim to be a member of a particular Christian sect. It is also true that there are assorted Christian denominations that do not profess to be compelled by their religion to refuse Sunday work, but this does not diminish Frazee's protection flowing from the Free Exercise Clause. . . . Undoubtedly, membership in an organized religious denomination, especially one with a specific tenet forbidding members to work on Sunday, would simplify the problem of identifying sincerely held religious beliefs, but we reject the notion that to claim the protection of the Free Exercise Clause, one must be responding to the commands of a particular religious organization. Here, Frazee's refusal was based on a sincerely held religious belief. Under our cases, he was entitled to invoke First Amendment protection. . . .

The State offers no justification for the burden that the denial of benefits places on Frazee's right to exercise his religion. The Illinois Appellate Court ascribed great significance to America's weekend way of life. The Illinois court asked: "What would Sunday be today if professional football, baseball, basketball, and tennis were barred. Today Sunday is not only a day for religion, but for recreation and labor. Today the supermarkets are open, service stations dispense fuel, utilities continue to serve the people and factories continue to belch smoke and tangible products," concluding that "[i]f all Americans were to abstain from working on Sunday, chaos would result.". . . We are unpersuaded, however, that there will be a mass movement away from Sunday employ if William Frazee succeeds in his claim. . . .

[T]here is nothing before us in this case to suggest that Sunday shopping, or Sunday sporting, for that matter, will grind to a halt as a result of our decision today. And, as we have said in the past, there may exist state interests sufficiently compelling to override a legitimate claim to the free exercise of religion. No such interest has been presented here. . . .

Employment Division v. Smith (1990)[45]

In one of the 1990's most controversial cases concerning the free-exercise clause, the Supreme Court denied the constitutional claims asserted by two Native American drug rehabilitation counselors who were fired for ingesting peyote during a religious ceremony. The workers were denied unemployment compensation benefits because they had been discharged for misconduct.

Justice Scalia delivered the opinion of the Court.

This case requires us to decide whether the Free Exercise Clause of the First Amendment permits the State of Oregon to include religiously inspired peyote use within the reach of its general criminal prohibition on use of that drug, and thus permits the State to deny unemployment benefits to persons dismissed from their jobs because of such religiously inspired use.

Oregon law prohibits the knowing or intentional possession of a "controlled substance" unless the substance has been prescribed by a medical practitioner. . . . As compiled by the State Board of Pharmacy under its statutory authority, [the definition of "controlled substance" includes] the drug peyote, a hallucinogen derived from the plant Lophophora williamsii Lemaire. . . .

Respondents Alfred Smith and Galen Black (hereinafter respondents) were fired from their jobs with a private drug rehabilitation organization because they ingested peyote for sacramental purposes at a ceremony of the Native American Church, of which both are members. When respondents applied to petitioner Employment Division (hereinafter petitioner) for unemployment compensation, they were determined to be ineligible for benefits because they had been discharged for work-related "misconduct.". . .

The free exercise of religion means, first and foremost, the right to believe and profess whatever religious doctrine one desires. Thus, the First Amendment obviously excludes all "governmental regulation of religious *beliefs* as such.". . . The government may not compel affirmation of religious belief, . . . punish the expression of religious doctrines it believes to be false, . . . impose special disabilities on the basis of religious views or religious status, . . . or lend its power to one or the other side in controversies over religious authority or dogma. . . .

But the "exercise of religion" often involves not only belief and profession but the performance of (or abstention from) physical acts: assembling with others for a worship service, participating in sacramental use of bread and wine, proselytizing, abstaining from certain foods or certain modes of transportation. It would be true, we think (though no case of ours has involved the point), that a State would be "prohibiting the free exercise [of religion]" if it sought to ban such acts or abstentions only when they are engaged in for religious reasons, or only because of the religious belief that they display. It would doubtless be unconstitutional, for example, to ban the casting of "statues that are to be used for worship purposes," or to prohibit bowing down before a golden calf.

Respondents in the present case, however, seek to carry the meaning of "prohibiting the free exercise [of religion]" one large step further. They contend that their religious motivation for using peyote places them beyond the reach of a criminal law that is not specifically directed at their religious practice, and that is concededly constitutional as applied to those who use the drug for other reasons. They assert, in other words, that "prohibiting the free exercise [of religion]" includes requiring any individual to observe a generally applicable law that requires (or forbids) the performance of an act that his religious belief forbids (or requires). As a textual matter, we do not think the words must be given that meaning. It is no more necessary to regard the collection of a general tax, for example, as "prohibiting the free exercise [of religion]" by those citizens who believe support of organized government to be sinful, than it is to regard the same tax as "abridging the freedom . . . of the press" of those publishing companies that must pay the tax as a condition of staying in business. It is a permissible reading of the text, in the one case as in the other, to say that if prohibiting the exercise of religion (or burdening the activity of printing) is not the object of the tax but merely the incidental effect of a generally applicable and otherwise valid provision, the First Amendment has not been offended. . . .

Our decisions reveal that the latter reading is the correct one. We have never held that an individual's religious beliefs excuse him from compliance with an otherwise valid law prohibiting conduct that the State is free to regulate. On the contrary, the record of more than a century of our free exercise jurisprudence contradicts that proposition. As described succinctly by Justice Frankfurter in Minersville School Dist. Bd. of Ed. v Gobitis,. . . : "Conscientious scruples have not, in the course of the long struggle for religious toleration, relieved the individual from obedience to a general law not aimed at the promotion or restriction of religious beliefs. The mere possession of religious convictions which contradict the relevant concerns of a political society does not relieve the citizen from the discharge of political responsibilities (footnote omitted)." We first had occasion to assert that principle in Reynolds v United States, . . . where we rejected the claim that criminal laws against polygamy could not be constitutionally applied to those whose religion commanded the practice. . . .

Subsequent decisions have consistently held that the right of free exercise does not relieve an individual of the obligation to comply with a "valid and neutral law of general applicability on the ground that the law proscribes (or prescribes) conduct that his religion prescribes (or proscribes).". . .

The only decisions in which we have held that the First Amendment bars application of a neutral, generally applicable law to religiously motivated action have involved not the Free Exercise Clause alone, but the Free Exercise Clause in conjunction with other constitutional protections, such as freedom of speech and of the press, see [for example] Cantwell v Connecticut,. . . (invalidating a licensing system for religious and charitable solicitations under which the administrator had discretion to deny a license to any cause he deemed nonreligious):. . . [and] Wisconsin v Yoder,. . . (invalidating compulsory school-attendance laws as applied to Amish parents who refused on religious grounds to send their children to school).. . .

The present case does not present such a hybrid situation, but a free exercise claim unconnected with any communicative activity or parental right. Respondents urge us to hold, quite simply, that when otherwise prohibitable conduct is accompanied by religious convictions, not only the convictions but the conduct itself must be free from governmental regulation. We have never held that, and decline to do so now. There being no contention that Oregon's drug law represents an attempt to regulate religious beliefs, the communication of religious beliefs, or the raising of one's children in those beliefs, the rule to which we have adhered ever since Reynolds plainly controls. . . .

Values that are protected against government interference through enshrinement in the Bill of Rights are not thereby banished from the political process. Just as a society that believes in the negative protection accorded to the press by the First Amendment is likely to enact laws that affirmatively foster the dissemination of the printed word, so also a society that believes in the negative protection accorded to religious belief can be expected to be solicitous of that value in its legislation as well. It is therefore not surprising that a number of States have made an exception to their drug laws for sacramental peyote use. . . . But to say that a nondiscriminatory religious-practice exemption is permitted, or even that it is desirable, is not to say that it is constitutionally required, and that the appropriate occasions for its creation can be discerned by the courts. It may fairly be said that leaving accommodation to the political process will place at a relative disadvantage those religious practices that are not widely engaged in; but that unavoidable consequence of democratic government must be preferred to a system in which each conscience is a law unto itself or in which judges weigh the social importance of all laws against the centrality of all religious beliefs.

* * *

Because respondents' ingestion of peyote was prohibited under Oregon law, and because that prohibition is constitutional, Oregon may, consistent with the Free Exercise Clause, deny respondents unemployment compensation when their dismissal results from use of the drug. . . .

Religious Freedom Restoration Act (1993)

Following an outpouring of public opposition to the decision in the *Employment Division v. Smith* case, Congress enacted the "Religious Freedom Restoration Act." It was signed into law by President Clinton on November 16, 1993.

SEC. 2. CONGRESSIONAL FINDINGS AND DECLARATION OF PURPOSES.

(a) FINDINGS.—The Congress finds that—

(1) the framers of the Constitution, recognizing free exercise of religion as an unalienable right, secured its protection in the First Amendment to the Constitution;

(2) laws "neutral" toward religion may burden religious exercise as surely as laws intended to interfere with religious exercise;

(3) governments should not substantially burden religious exercise without compelling justification;

(4) in Employment Division v. Smith, . . . the Supreme Court virtually eliminated the requirement that the government justify burdens on religious exercise imposed by laws neutral toward religion; and

(5) the compelling interest test as set forth in prior Federal court rulings is a workable test for striking sensible balances between religious liberty and competing prior governmental interests.

(b) PURPOSES.—The purposes of this Act are—

(1) to restore the compelling interest test as set forth in Sherbert v. Verner . . . and Wisconsin v. Yoder . . . and to guarantee its application in all cases where free exercise of religion is substantially burdened; and

(2) to provide a claim or defense to persons whose religious exercise is substantially burdened by government.

SEC. 3. FREE EXERCISE OF RELIGION PROTECTED.

(a) IN GENERAL.—Government shall not substantially burden a person's exercise of religion even if the burden results from a rule of general applicability, except as provided in subsection (b).

(b) EXCEPTION.—Government may substantially burden a person's exercise of religion only if it demonstrates that application of the burden to the person—

(1) is in furtherance of a compelling governmental interest; and

(2) is the least restrictive means of furthering that compelling governmental interest.

(c) JUDICIAL RELIEF.—A person whose religious exercise has been burdened in violation of this section may assert that violation as a claim or defense in a judicial proceeding and obtain appropriate relief against a government. . . .

SEC. 5. DEFINITIONS.

As used in this Act—

(1) the term "government" includes a branch, department, agency instrumentality, and official (or other person acting under color of law, of the United States, a State, or a subdivision of a State;

(2) the term "State" includes the District of Columbia, the Commonwealth of Puerto Rico, and each territory and possession of the United States;

(3) the term "demonstrates" means meets the burdens of going forward with the evidence and of persuasion; and

(4) the term "exercise of religion" means the exercise of religion under the First Amendment to the Constitution.

SEC. 6. APPLICABILITY.

(a) IN GENERAL.—This Act applies to all Federal and State law and the implementation of that law, whether statutory or otherwise, and whether adopted before or after the enactment of this Act. . . .

(c) RELIGIOUS BELIEF UNAFFECTED.—Nothing in this Act shall be construed to authorize any government to burden any religious belief.

Boerne v. Flores (1997)[46]

Following the Court's decision in *Employment Division* v. *Smith,* the Congress passed the Religious Freedom Restoration Act (RFRA) to attempt to return to an approach to the free exercise clause that resembled the Court's opinion in *Sherbert* v. *Verner.* In this case, the Supreme Court declares RFRA to be an unconstitutional attempt by Congress to affect substantive constitutional provisions.

Justice Kennedy delivered the opinion of the Court.

A decision by local zoning authorities to deny a church a building permit was challenged under the Religious Freedom Restoration Act of 1993 (RFRA) . . . The case calls into question the authority of Congress to enact RFRA. We conclude the statute exceeds Congress' power. . . .

II

Congress enacted RFRA in direct response to the Court's decision in *Employment Div v. Smith.* . . . There we considered a Free Exercise Clause claim brought by members of the Native American Church who were denied unemployment benefits when they lost their jobs because they had used peyote. Their practice was to ingest peyote for sacramental purposes, and they challenged an Oregon statute of general applicability which made use of the drug criminal. In evaluating the claim, we declined to apply the balancing test set forth in *Sherbert* v. *Verner,* under which we would have asked whether Oregon's prohibition substantially burdened a religious practice and, if it did, whether the burden was justified by a compelling government interest. . . .

The application of the *Sherbert* test, the *Smith* decision explained, would have produced an anomaly in the law, a constitutional right to ignore neutral laws of general applicability. The anomaly would have been accentuated, the Court reasoned, by the difficulty of determining whether a particular practice was central to an individual's religion. We explained, moreover, that it "is not within the judicial ken to question the centrality of particular beliefs or practices to a faith, or the validity of particular litigants' interpretations of those creeds.". . .

The only instances where a neutral, generally applicable law had failed to pass constitutional muster, the *Smith* Court noted, were cases in which other constitutional protections were at stake. In *Wisconsin* v. *Yoder,* for example, we invalidated Wisconsin's mandatory school-attendance law as applied to Amish parents who refused on religious grounds to send their children to school. That case implicated not only the right to the free exercise of religion but also the right of parents to control their children's education.

The *Smith* decision acknowledged the Court had employed the *Sherbert* test in considering free exercise challenges to state unemployment compensation rules on three occasions where the balance had tipped in favor of the individual. . . . Those cases, the Court explained, stand for "the proposition that where the State has in place a system of individual exemptions, it may not refuse to extend that system to cases of religious hardship without compelling reason.". . . By contrast, where a general prohibition, such as Oregon's, is at issue, "the sounder approach, and the approach in accord with the vast majority of our precedents, is to hold the test inapplicable to [free exercise] challenges." *Smith* held that neutral, generally applicable laws may be applied to religious practices even when not supported by a compelling governmental interest.

Four Members of the Court disagreed. They argued the law placed a substantial burden on the Native American Church members so that it could be upheld only if the law served a compelling state interest and was narrowly tailored to achieve that end. . . .

These points of constitutional interpretation were debated by Members of Congress in hearings and floor debates. Many criticized the Court's reasoning, and this disagreement resulted in the passage of RFRA. . . .

RFRA prohibits "[g]overnment" from "substantially burden[ing]" a person's exercise of religion even if the burden results from a rule of general applicability unless the government can demonstrate the burden "(1) is in furtherance of a compelling governmental interest; and (2) is the least restrictive means of furthering that compelling governmental interest." The Act's mandate applies to any "branch, department, agency, instrumentality, and official (or other person acting under color of law) of the United States," as well as to any "State, or . . . subdivision of a State.". . . RFRA "applies to all Federal and State law, and the implementation of that law, whether statutory or otherwise, and whether adopted before or after [RFRA's enactment].". . .

Under our Constitution, the Federal Government is one of enumerated powers. . . . The judicial authority to determine the constitutionality of laws, in cases and controversies, is based on the premise that the "powers of the legislature are defined and limited; and that those limits may not be mistaken, or forgotten, the constitution is written."...

Respondent contends that RFRA is a proper exercise of Congress' remedial or preventive power. The Act, it is said, is a reasonable means of protecting the free exercise of religion as defined by *Smith.* It prevents and remedies laws which are enacted with the unconstitutional object of targeting religious beliefs and practices. . . . To avoid the difficulty of proving such violations, it is said, Congress can simply invalidate any law which imposes a substantial burden on a religious practice unless it is justified by a compelling interest and is the least restrictive means of accomplishing that interest. If Congress can prohibit laws with discriminatory effects in order to prevent racial discrimination in violation of the Equal Protection Clause, . . . then it can do the same, respondent argues, to promote religious liberty.

While preventive rules are sometimes appropriate remedial measures, there must be a congruence between the means used and the ends to be achieved. The appropriateness of remedial measures must be considered in light of the evil presented. . . . Strong measures appropriate to address one harm may be an unwarranted response to another, lesser one.

A comparison between RFRA and the Voting Rights Act is instructive. In contrast to the record which confronted Congress and the judiciary in the voting rights cases, RFRA's legislative record lacks examples of modern instances of generally applicable laws passed because of religious bigotry. The history of persecution in this country detailed in the hearings mentions no episodes occurring in the past 40 years. . . .

This lack of support in the legislative record, however, is not RFRA's most serious shortcoming. Judicial deference, in most cases, is based not on the state of the legislative record Congress compiles but "on due regard for the decision of the body constitutionally appointed to decide."...

Regardless of the state of the legislative record, RFRA cannot be considered remedial, preventive legislation, if those terms are to have any meaning. RFRA is so out of proportion to a supposed remedial or preventive object that it cannot be understood as responsive to, or designed to prevent, unconstitutional behavior. It appears, instead, to attempt a substantive change in constitutional protections. Preventive measures prohibiting certain types of laws may be appropriate when there is reason to believe that many of the laws affected by the congressional enactment have a significant likelihood of being unconstitutional. . . .

RFRA is not so confined. Sweeping coverage ensures its intrusion at every level of government, displacing laws and prohibiting official actions of almost every description and regardless of subject matter. RFRA's restrictions apply to every agency and official of the Federal, State, and local Governments. RFRA applies to all federal and state law, statutory or otherwise, whether adopted before or after its enactment. RFRA has not termination date or termination mechanism. Any law is subject to challenge at any time by any individual who alleges a substantial burden on his or her free exercise of religion. . . .

The stringent test RFRA demands of state laws reflects a lack of proportionality or congruence between the means adopted and the legitimate end to be achieved. If an objector can show a substantial burden on his free exercise, the State must demonstrate a compelling governmental interest and show that the law is the least restrictive means of furthering its interest. Claims that a law substantially burdens someone's exercise of religion will often be difficult to contest. . . . Laws valid under *Smith* would fall under RFRA without regard to whether they had the object of stifling or punishing free exercise. We make these observations not to reargue the position of the majority in *Smith* but to illustrate the substantive alteration of its holding attempted by RFRA. Even assuming RFRA would be interpreted in effect to mandate some lesser test, say one equivalent to intermediate scrutiny, the statute nevertheless would require searching judicial scrutiny of state law with the attendant likelihood of invalidation. This is a considerable congressional intrusion into the States' traditional prerogatives and general authority to regulate for the health and welfare of their citizens.

The substantial costs RFRA exacts, both in practical terms of imposing a heavy litigation burden on the States and in terms of curtailing their traditional general regulatory power, far exceed any pattern or practice of unconstitutional conduct under the Free Exercise Clause as interpreted in *Smith*. Simply put, RFRA is not designed to identify and counteract state laws likely to be unconstitutional because of their treatment of religion. In most cases, the state laws to which RFRA applies are not ones which will have been motivated by religious bigotry. If a state law disproportionately burdened a particular class of religious observers, this circumstance might be evidence of an impermissible legislative motive. . . . RFRA's substantial burden test, however, is not even a discriminatory effects or disparate impact test. It is a reality of the modern regulatory state that numerous state laws, such as the zoning regulations at issue here, impose a substantial burden on a large class of individuals. When the exercise of religion has been burdened in an incidental way by a law of general application, it does not follow that the persons affected have been burdened any more than other citizens, let alone burdened because of their religious beliefs. In addition, the Act imposes in every case a least restrictive means requirement—a requirement that was not used in the pre-*Smith* jurisprudence RFRA purported to codify—which also indicates that the legislation is broader than is appropriate if the goal is to prevent and remedy constitutional violations.

When Congress acts within its sphere of power and responsibilities, it has not just the right but the duty to make its own informed judgment on the meaning and force of the Constitution. This has been clear from the early days of the Republic. In 1789, when a Member of the House of Representatives objected to a debate on the constitutionality of legislation based on the theory that "it would be officious" to consider the constitutionality of a measure that did not affect the House, James Madison explained that "it is incontrovertibly of as much importance to this branch of the Government as to any other, that the constitution should be preserved entire. It is our duty.". . . Were it otherwise, we would not afford Congress the presumption of validity its enactments now enjoy.

Our national experience teaches that the Constitution is preserved best when each part of the government respects both the Constitution and the proper actions and determinations of the other branches. When the Court has interpreted the Constitution, it has acted within the province of the Judicial Branch, which embraces the duty to say what the law is. . . . When the political branches of the Government act against the background of a judicial interpretation of the Constitution already issued, it must be understood that in later cases and controversies the Court will treat its precedents with the respect due them under settled principles, . . . and contrary expectations must be disappointed. RFRA was designed to control cases and controversies, such as the one before us; but as the provisions of the federal statute here invoked are beyond congressional authority, it is this Court's precedent, not RFRA, which must control. . . .

God and Country: Cultural Issues

ROBERT N. BELLAH

Civil Religion in America[47]

Robert N. Bellah is professor of sociology and comparative studies at the University of California–Berkeley. When his essay titled "Civil Religion" first appeared in 1967, it touched off decades of scholarly discussion and debate. The question addressed by Professor Bellah is, Does there exist "alongside of and rather clearly differentiated from the churches an elaborate and well-institutionalized civil religion in America"?

While some have argued that Christianity is the national faith, and others that church and synagogue celebrate only the generalized religion of "the American Way of Life," few have realized that there actually exists alongside of and rather clearly differentiated from the churches an elaborate and well-institutionalized civil religion in America. This article argues not only that there is such a thing, but also that this religion—or perhaps better, this religious dimension—has its own seriousness and integrity and requires the same care in understanding that any other religion does. . . .

The Idea of a Civil Religion

The phrase "civil religion" is, of course, Rousseau's. In . . . *The Social Contract,* he outlines the simple dogmas of the civil religion: the existence of God, the life to come, the reward of virtue and the punishment of vice, and the exclusion of religious intolerance. All other religious opinions are outside the cognizance of the state and may be freely held by citizens. While the phrase *civil religion* was not used, to the best of my knowledge, by the founding fathers, and I am certainly not arguing for the particular influence of Rousseau, it is clear that similar ideas, as part of the cultural climate of the late-eighteenth century, were to be found among the Americans. For example, Franklin writes in his autobiography,

> I never was without some religious principles. I never doubted, for instance, the existence of the Deity; that he made the world and govern'd it by his Providence; that the most acceptable service of God was the doing of good to men; that our souls are immortal; and that all crime will be punished, and virtue rewarded either here or hereafter. These I esteemed the essentials of every religion; and, being to be found in all the religions we had

> in our country, I respected them all, tho' with different degrees of respect, as I found them more or less mix'd with other articles, which, without any tendency to inspire, promote or confirm morality, serv'd principally to divide us, and make us unfriendly to one another.

It is easy to dispose of this sort of position as essentially utilitarian in relation to religion. . . . But there is every reason to believe that religion, particularly the idea of God, played a constitutive role in the thought of the early American statesmen. . . .

There are four references to God [in the Declaration of Independence.] The first speaks of the "Laws of Nature and of Nature's God" which entitle any people to be independent. The second is the famous statement that all men "are endowed by their Creator with certain inalienable Rights." Here Jefferson is locating the fundamental legitimacy of the new nation in a conception of "higher law" that is itself based on both classical natural law and Biblical religion. The third is an appeal to "the Supreme Judge of the world for the rectitude of our intentions," and the last indicates "a firm reliance on the protection of divine Providence." In these last two references, a Biblical God of history who stands in judgment over the world is indicated.

The intimate relation of these religious notions with the self-conception of the new Republic is indicated by the frequency of their appearance in early official documents. For example, we find in Washington's first inaugural address of 30 April 1789:

> It would be peculiarly improper to omit in this first official act my fervent supplications to that Almighty Being who rules over the universe, who presides in the councils of nations, and whose providential aids can supply every defect, that His benediction may consecrate to the liberties and happiness of the people of the United States a Government instituted by themselves for these essential purposes, and may enable every instrument employed in its administration to execute with success the functions allotted to his charge.
>
> No people can be bound to acknowledge and adore the Invisible Hand which conducts the affairs of man more than those of the United States. Every step by which we have advanced to the character of an independent nation seems to have been distinguished by some token of providential agency. . . .
>
> The propitious smiles of Heaven can never be expected on a nation that disregards the eternal rules of order and right which Heaven itself has ordained. . . . The preservation of the sacred fire of liberty and the destiny of the republican model of government are justly considered, perhaps, as *deeply,* as *finally,* staked on the experiment intrusted to the hands of the American people.

Nor did these religious sentiments remain merely the personal expression of the president. At the request of both Houses of Congress, Washington proclaimed on October 3 of that same first year as president that November 26 should be "a day of public thanksgiving and prayer," the first Thanksgiving Day under the Constitution.

The words and acts of the founding fathers, especially the first few presidents, shaped the form and tone of the civil religion as it has been maintained ever since. Though much is selectively derived from Christianity, this religion is clearly not itself Christianity. For one thing, neither Washington nor Adams nor Jefferson mentions Christ in his inaugural address; nor do any of the subsequent presidents, although not one of them fails to mention God. The God of the civil religion is not only rather "unitarian," he is also on the austere side, much more related to order, law, and right than to salvation and love. Even though he is somewhat deist in cast, he is by no means simply a watchmaker God. He is actively interested and involved in history, with a special concern for America. Here the analogy has much less to do with natural law than with ancient Israel; the equation of America with Israel in the idea of the "American Israel" is not infrequent. What was implicit in the words of Washington already quoted becomes explicit in Jefferson's second inaugural when he said: "I shall need, too, the favor of that Being in whose hands we are, who led our fathers, as Israel of old, from their native land and planted them in a country flowing with all the necessaries and comforts of life." Europe is Egypt; America, the promised land. God has led his people to establish a new sort of social order that shall be a light unto all the nations.

This theme, too, has been a continuous one in the civil religion. . . . We find it again in President Johnson's inaugural address:

> They came here—the exile and the stranger, brave but frightened—to find a place where a man could be his own man. They made a covenant with this land. Conceived in justice, written in liberty, bound in union, it was meant one day to inspire the hopes of all mankind; and it binds us still. If we keep its terms, we shall flourish.

What we have, then, from the earliest years of the republic is a collection of beliefs, symbols, and rituals with respect to sacred things and institutionalized in a collectivity. This religion—there seems no other word for it—while not antithetical to, and indeed sharing much in common with, Christianity, was neither sectarian nor in any specific sense Christian. At a time when the society was overwhelmingly Christian, it seems unlikely that this lack of Christian reference was meant to spare the feelings of the tiny non-Christian minority. Rather, the civil religion expressed what those who set the precedents felt was appropriate under the circumstances. It reflected their private as well as public views. Nor was the civil religion simply "religion in general." While generality was undoubtedly seen as a virtue by some, as in the quotation from Franklin above, the civil religion was specific enough when it came to the topic of America. Precisely because of this specificity, the civil religion was saved from empty formalism and served as a genuine vehicle of national religious self-understanding.

But the civil religion was not, in the minds of Franklin, Washington, Jefferson, or other leaders, with the exception of a few radicals like Tom Paine, ever felt to be a substitute for Christianity. There was an implicit but quite clear division of function between the civil religion and Christianity. Under the doctrine of religious liberty, an exceptionally wide sphere of personal piety and voluntary social action was left to the churches. But the churches were neither to control the state nor to be controlled by it. The national magistrate, whatever his private religious views, operates under the rubrics of the civil religion as long as he is in his official capacity. . . . This accommodation was undoubtedly the product of a particular historical moment and of a cultural background dominated by Protestantism of several varieties and by the Enlightenment, but it has survived despite subsequent changes in the cultural and religious climate.

Civil War and Civil Religion

Until the Civil War, the American civil religion focused above all on the event of the Revolution, which was seen as the final act of the Exodus from the old lands across the waters. The Declaration of Independence and the Constitution were the sacred scriptures and Washington the divinely appointed Moses who led his people out of the hands of tyranny. The Civil War, which Sidney Mead calls "the center of American history," was the second great event that involved the national self-understanding so deeply as to require expression in the civil religion. . . . Not only did the Civil War have the tragic intensity of fratricidal strife, but it was one of the bloodiest wars of the nineteenth century; the loss of life was far greater than any previously suffered by Americans.

The Civil War raised the deepest questions of national meaning. The man who not only formulated but in his own person embodied its meaning for Americans was Abraham Lincoln. For him the issue was not in the first instance slavery but "whether that nation, or any nation so conceived, and so dedicated, can long endure.". . . The phrases of Jefferson constantly echo in Lincoln's speeches. His task was, first of all, to save the Union—not for America alone but for the meaning of America to the whole world so unforgettably etched in the last phrase of the Gettysburg Address. . . .

With the Civil War, a new theme of death, sacrifice, and rebirth enters the civil religion. It is symbolized in the life and death of Lincoln. . . . With the Christian archetype in the background, Lincoln, "our martyred president," was linked to the war dead, those who "gave the last full measure of devotion." The theme of sacrifice was indelibly written into the civil religion.

The new symbolism soon found both physical and ritualistic expression. The great number of the war dead required the establishment of a number of national cemeteries [including Gettysburg and Arlington, in particular]. Memorial Day, which grew out of the Civil War, gave ritual expression to the themes we have been discussing. . . . [T]he Memorial Day observance, especially in the towns and smaller cities of America, is a major event for the whole community involving a rededication to the martyred dead, to the spirit of sacrifice, and to the American vision. Just as Thanksgiving Day . . . serves to integrate the family into the civil religion, so Memorial Day has acted to integrate the local community into the national cult. Together with the less overtly religious Fourth of July and the more minor celebrations of Veterans Day and the birthdays of Washington and Lincoln, these two holidays provide an annual ritual calendar for the civil religion. The public-school system serves as a particularly important context for the cultic celebration of the civil rituals.

The Civil Religion Today

. . . [T]he civil religion at its best is a genuine apprehension of universal and transcendent religious reality as seen in or, one could almost say, as revealed through the experience of the American people. Like all religions, it has suffered various deformations and demonic distortions. At its best, it has neither been so general that it has lacked incisive relevance to the American scene nor so particular that it has placed American society above universal human values.

The American civil religion was never anticlerical or militantly secular. On the contrary, it borrowed selectively from the religious tradition in such a way that the average American saw no conflict between the two. In this way, the civil religion was able to build up without any bitter struggle with the church powerful symbols of national solidarity and to mobilize deep levels of personal motivation for the attainment of national goals.

Such an achievement is by no means to be taken for granted. It would seem that the problem of a civil religion is quite general in modern societies and that the way it is solved or not solved will have repercussions in many spheres. One needs only to think of France to see how differently things can go. The French Revolution was anticlerical to the core and attempted to set up an anti-Christian civil religion. . . .

American civil religion is still very much alive. Just three years ago we participated in a vivid re-enactment of the sacrifice theme in connection with the funeral of our assassinated president. The American Israel theme is clearly behind both Kennedy's New Frontier and Johnson's Great Society. Let me give just one recent illustration of how the civil religion serves to mobilize support for the attainment of national goals. On 15 March 1965 President Johnson went before Congress to ask for a strong voting-rights bill. Early in the speech he said:

> Rarely are we met with the challenge, not to our growth or abundance, or our welfare or our security—but rather to the values and the purposes and the meaning of our beloved nation.
>
> The issue of equal rights for American Negroes is such an issue. And should we defeat every enemy, and should we double our wealth and conquer the stars and still be unequal to this issue, then we will have failed as a people and as a nation.
>
> For with a country as with a person, "What is a man profited, if he shall gain the whole world, and lose his own soul?"

And in conclusion he said:

> Above the pyramid on the great seal of the United States it says in Latin, "God has favored our undertaking."
>
> God will not favor everything that we do. It is rather our duty to divine his will. I cannot help but believe that He truly understands and that He really favors the undertaking that we begin here tonight.

The civil religion has not always been invoked in favor of worthy causes. On the domestic scene, an American-Legion type of ideology that fuses God, country, and flag has been used to attack non-conformist and liberal ideas and groups of all kinds. Still, it has been difficult to use the words of Jefferson and Lincoln to support special interests and undermine personal freedom. The defenders of slavery before the Civil War came to reject the thinking of the Declaration of Independence. Some of the most consistent of them turned against not only Jeffersonian democracy but Reformation religion; they dreamed of a South dominated by medieval chivalry and divine-right monarchy. For all the overt religiosity of the radical right today, their relation to the civil religious consensus is tenuous, as when the John Birch Society attacks the central American symbol of Democracy itself.

With respect of America's role in the world, the dangers of distortion are greater and the built-in safeguards of the tradition weaker. The theme of the American Israel was used, almost from the beginning, as a justification for the shameful treatment of the Indians so characteristic of our history. It can be overtly or implicitly linked to the idea of manifest destiny which has been used to legitimate several adventures in imperialism since the early-nineteenth century. Never has the danger been greater than today [in light of the Viet-Nam war]. . . .

The civil religion is obviously involved in the most pressing moral and political issues of the day. But it is also caught in another kind of crisis, theoretical and theological, of which it is at the moment largely unaware. "God" has clearly been a central symbol in the civil religion from the beginning and remains so today. This symbol is just as central to the civil religion as it is to . . . Judaism or Christianity. In the late-eighteenth century this posed no problem; even Tom Paine, contrary to his detractors, was not an atheist. From left to right and regardless of church or sect, all could accept the idea of God. But today, as even *Time* has recognized, the meaning of the word *God* is by no means so clear or so obvious. There is no formal creed in the civil religion. We have had a Catholic president; it is conceivable that we could have a Jewish one. But could we have an agnostic president? Could a man with conscientious scruples about using the word *God* . . . be elected chief magistrate of our country? If the whole God symbolism requires reformulation, there will be obvious consequences for the civil religion, consequences perhaps of liberal alienation and of fundamentalist ossification that have not so far been prominent in this realm. The civil religion has been a point of articulation between the profoundest commitments of the Western religious and philosophical tradition and the common beliefs of ordinary Americans. It is not too soon to consider how the deepening theological crisis may affect the future of this articulation.

The Third Time of Trial

In conclusion it may be worthwhile to relate the civil religion to the most serious situation that we as Americans now face, what I call the third time of trial. The first time of trial had to do with the question of independence, whether we should or could run our own affairs in our own way. The second time of trial was over the issue of slavery, which in turn was only the most salient aspect of the more general problem of the full institutionalization of democracy within our country. The second problem we are still far from solving though we have some notable successes to our credit. But we have been overtaken by a third great problem which has led to a third great crisis, in the midst of which we stand. This is the problem of responsible action in a revolutionary world, a world seeking to attain many of the things, material and spiritual, that we have already attained. Americans have, from the beginning, been aware of the responsibility and the significance our republican experiment has for the whole world. . . .

Without an awareness that our nation stands under higher judgment, the tradition of the civil religion would be dangerous indeed. Fortunately, the prophetic voices have never been lacking. . . . The spirit of civil disobedience that is alive today in the civil rights movement and the opposition to the Viet-Nam war was already clearly outlined by Henry David Thoreau when he wrote, "If the law is of such a nature that it requires you to be an agent of injustice to another, then I say, break the law."...

Out of the first and second times of trial have come, as we have seen, the major symbols of the American civil religion. There seems little doubt that a successful negotiation of this third time of trial—the attainment of some kind of viable and coherent world order—would precipitate a major new set of symbolic forms. . . . It would necessitate the incorporation of vital international symbolism into our civil religion, or, perhaps a better way of putting it, it would result in American civil religion becoming simply one part of a new civil religion of the world. It is useless to speculate on the form such a civil religion might take, though it obviously would draw on religious traditions beyond the sphere of Biblical religion alone. Fortunately, since the American civil religion is not the worship of the American nation but an understanding of the American experience in the light of ultimate and universal reality, the reorganization entailed by such a new situation need not disrupt the American civil religion's continuity. A world civil religion could be accepted as a fulfillment and not a denial of American civil religion. Indeed, such an outcome has been the eschatological hope of American civil religion from the beginning. To deny such an outcome would be to deny the meaning of America itself. . . .

JOHN F. WILSON

The Civil Religion Proposal as a Revitalization Movement in American Culture[48]

John F. Wilson is professor of religion at Princeton University and an editor of this volume. The following are excerpts from the last chapter of his book *Public Religion in American Culture,* in which he reviews the evidence for and against a well-institutionalized and differentiated civil religion in America. In the following discussion, Professor Wilson sees the proposals about civil religion as themselves an attempt to revitalize American society.

[Recently,] discussion of public religion has entered a new stage in the proposal that it be understood as a differentiated and institutionalized positive religious tradition, as in "Civil Religion in America." That thesis [can be] reviewed as a construction put upon the data, but brief consideration of it from another point of view is [also] appropriate. This is to ask several questions in the framework of religious analysis: How may we interpret the development of the proposal that there is a civil religion in America? What significance should we assign to the emergence of a religious movement based upon such a proposal?

Elaboration of religiously grounded claims frequently entails an explicit historical trajectory set out in terms of origin and destiny. Under Robert Bellah's construct, the American civil religion is believed to point toward a world order; its destiny is to become transformed into a global civil religion. The religion of the republic, the construction proposed by Sidney Mead, is thought to carry the burden of a cultural revolution originating with the Enlightenment. This event, possibly the most momentous cultural event in history, is believed to reach fullest expression in the ideal of the American republic. Thus, each of these particular constructs includes a historical interpretation placed upon public religion cast in terms of universalistic claims. When viewed with some detachment, however, both of these proposals appear to be highly ethnocentric. In the framework of a critical approach to religious movements, the logically necessary question is how such worldviews function as social constructions. How might we understand the appeal of civil religion, or the religion of the republic, as the basis for a social movement?

One of the conditions under which religious movements appear to develop is that of rapid social change, especially when an older and possibly waning culture is threatened by a newer and dynamic one. . . . Anthony F. C. Wallace has suggested an analytical model of the revitalization movement as a means of conceptualizing how a beleaguered society reaches for religious self-understanding out of the past, in terms which are familiar from the tradition at hand. This is a means of coping with an uncertain present and a threatening future. In this most general framework, revitalization movements are interpreted as attempts to recover, heighten, and strenuously advocate adherence to the religious legacy believed to be the center of the particular endangered culture. The anticipated outcome is preservation of that culture, possibly including the achievement of a more perfect embodiment of its central commitments. Of course, in a critical perspective, the recovered or revitalized culture is actually different from the older one. It has undergone a selective adaptation. In that process, elements have been dampened or heightened and the whole reorganized, usually in response to particular interest groups in the society.

If we seek an interpretation of the recent proposals about public religion in America in terms available from critical studies of religious movements, we can probably do no better than to view them as potential revitalization movements occasioned by widespread loss of internal confidence in American society and changed external cultural relationships. It is obvious that subcultures, such as those of black Americans or Spanish-speaking Americans (and a host of others), have become ethnically self-conscious enough to call into question the viability of traditional American society. This is in part because a broadly Protestant hegemony is experienced as alien and oppressive. Those sensitive to this situation have responded in different ways. One kind of response to this perceived condition has been resonance to the call for recovery of a civil religion or religion of the republic. While the manifest symbols of these proposals may be universal and global, the latent basis for interest in and support of them has more likely been a concern that the old familiar ways are directly challenged and severely threatened.

Interestingly enough, from this perspective, the ideological contents of revitalization movements turn out to be culturally specific versions of American Protestant Christianity, more classical than modern, which have been given a content of broadly political symbols and events. These constructs, in line with accepted critical interpretations of such movements, probably have more currency as reconceptualizations of past ideologies than as direct continuations of them.

Why should an idealized past be so prominent in these proposals? Partly because particular versions of Protestantism have repeatedly proved to be divisive, especially in the American setting. But at least as important, the latent strategy of a revitalization movement is to counter a threat to the whole social fabric and, generally, to enlist Americans under more inclusive symbols and commitments than the narrower inherited construction would permit. In some respects, then, it may be helpful to interpret the civil religion phenomenon more properly as a latent political revitalization movement than as a manifestly religious one. At one level, this is because politics is the realm in which consensus is achieved in modern societies in spite of other divergent opinions. But at another level, the perceived threat may be that politics as a means of governing communities is proving to be anachronistic; societies seem less readily subject to control through classical political means. If this is the felt threat, the culture threatened is one in which the political process is taken seriously as a means of significantly affecting society. . . .

If by suggesting that the American civil religion proposal may be identified as the ideological core of a revitalization movement, we have seemed to diminish its significance (by associating it with the Ghost Dance movement, as an example), that is unfortunate. Better parallels to it might be found in such religio-social movements as pietism in the German Lands (and others) in the eighteenth century, or Stuart Puritanism in seventeenth-century England. Versions of millenarianism in nineteenth-century America may provide a yet closer parallel, even antecedent. The point is that in each case an older culture was deeply challenged by new social conditions, and its existence seemed to be threatened. As a cultural strategy, it moved to consolidate and reexpress what it took to be its essential commitments. Usually through a prophet or a cadre of leaders, the movement worked to conserve the old in the face of social change. So the civil religion proposal, or the advocacy of a religion of the republic, might be seen, finally, as the attempt, through a variety of particular forms, to distill the old political culture of the United States which was supported by a broadly Protestant establishment. The purpose is to conserve that culture even as it, and the associated establishment, is threatened from within and without. . . .

Robert Bellah suggested that "Civil Religion in America" had gone undetected precisely because a western concept of religion as differentiated had prevented observers from recognizing something so obvious. Americans resist acknowledging in their own culture, he thought, something as obvious as Shinto in a foreign culture. But the further irony may be that emphasis upon civil religion itself betrays the other side of that same impulse—namely, to conceive of religion as developed and institutionalized. The materials [of public religion] . . . seem not to require that interpretation, but are better understood as aspects of an incredibly rich and internally complex culture.

Notes

1. 370 U.S. 421 (1962).
2. 374 U.S. 203 (1963).
3. 393 U.S. 97 (1968).
4. 449 U.S. 39 (1980).
5. 454 U.S. 263 (1981).
6. 472 U.S. 38 (1985).

7. 482 U.S. 578 (1987).
8. 505 U.S. 577 (1992).
9. 515 U.S. 819 (1995).
10. 530 U.S. 290 (2000).
11. Excerpts from statement of Bishop James W. Mallone, President, United States Catholic Conference on Relevance of Moral Values to Public Issues, October 14, 1984. Used with permission.
12. 366 U.S. 420 (1961).
13. From *The Church's Public Role,* ed. Dieter T. Hessel (Grand Rapids, Mich.: Eerdmans, 1993), pp. 263–284. Copyright 1993 by Wm. B. Eerdmans Publishing Co.
14. Reprinted with permission from *Political Science Quarterly*, 115 (Fall 2000): 377–394.
15. 366 U.S. 420 (1961).
16. 463 U.S. 783 (1983).
17. 465 U.S. 668 (1984).
18. 492 U.S. 573 (1989).
19. 515 U.S. 753 (1995).
20. 397 U.S. 664 (1970).
21. 406 U.S. 205 (1972).
22. 456 U.S. 228 (1982).
23. 455 U.S. 252 (1982).
24. 461 U.S. 574 (1983).
25. 475 U.S. 503 (1986).
26. 476 U.S. 693 (1986).
27. 485 U.S. 439 (1988).
28. 508 U.S. 520 (1993).
29. From *Religion in America* by John Cogley, copyright © 1958, 1986 by Fund for the Republic, Inc. Used by permission of Dutton Signet, a division of Penguin Putnam Inc.
30. Copyright 1981 by The Roscoe Pound-American Trial Lawyers Foundation, *Church, State and Politics* 1981 Chief Justice Earl Warren Conference on Advocacy. Used by permission.
31. 403 U.S. 602 (1971).
32. 463 U.S. 388 (1983).
33. 473 U.S. 402 (1985).
34. 474 U.S. 481 (1986).
35. 509 U.S. 1 (1993).
36. 512 U.S. 687 (1994).
37. 521 U.S. 203 (1997).
38. 530 U.S. 793 (2000).
39. 536 U.S. ___ (2002).
40. 367 U.S. 488 (1961).
41. 374 U.S. 398 (1963).
42. 435 U.S. 618 (1978).
43. 450 U.S. 707 (1981).
44. 489 U.S. 829 (1989).
45. 494 U.S. 872 (1990).
46. 521 U.S. 507 (1997).
47. Reprinted, with permission, from "Religion in America," *Daedalus* (Journal of the American Academy of Arts and Sciences, Boston, Massachusetts), Winter 1967.
48. Copyright 1979 by Temple University. Used by permission.

Chronology

This book is primarily concerned with the kinds of relationship between religious institutions and civil governments that have developed through American history. Little emphasis falls on institutions, events, or documents except as they illustrate or represent broader patterns. Accordingly this chronological table provides a list of relevant events to supplement the primary emphasis.

1607 Jamestown, Virginia, settled with a Church of England chaplain.
1631 Franchise restricted to church members in Massachusetts Bay.
1649 An Act Concerning Religion in Maryland provides a measure of toleration.
1654 Maryland Act repealed, Catholics suppressed by Puritans.
1662 Half-Way Covenant adopted in Massachusetts Bay; in effect gives franchise to those formally baptized though without necessarily having become full members of the established Congregational churches.
1663 Rhode Island and Providence Plantations receive royal charter through efforts of John Clarke; allows for "lively experiment" of complete religious toleration.
1665 Duke's Laws in New Amsterdam allow the Dutch toleration.
1669 First draft of the Fundamental Constitutions of Carolina proposes multiple establishment.
1691 New Massachusetts Bay Charter replaces the one revoked in 1684; provides liberty of conscience to all Christians except Roman Catholics.
1708 Connecticut allows non-Congregational Protestant worship but requires payment of taxes to support the standing order.
1722–1727 A party, led by Timothy Cutler, rector of Yale, defects from Connecticut Congregationalism to the Church of England. Anglicans subsequently released from supporting the establishment.
1739 First American tour by Whitefield; subsequently the Great Awakening rends the established church patterns.
1767–1768 Extensive public controversy regarding the introduction of Church of England Bishops into America.
1777 Religious freedom in New York State.
1785 Jefferson's Bill for Establishing Religious Freedom passed in the Virginia Assembly.

1789 Congress adopts Bill of Rights, including the two religion clauses in what becomes the First Amendment.

1791 Bill of Rights ratified and put into effect.

1802 Jefferson's occasional letter to the Danbury Baptists mentions "wall of separation between Church and State."

1811 Massachusetts Religious Freedom Act exempts members of non-Congregational churches from taxation for support of establishment.

1818 Disestablishment in Connecticut.

1819 Toleration Act in New Hampshire.

1833 Congregational Church disestablished in Massachusetts.

1868 Fourteenth Amendment ratified—would be used by Supreme Court to apply religious provisions of First Amendment to states in twentieth century.

1879 *Reynolds v. U.S.:* first Mormon case in Supreme Court.

1890 *The Late Corporation of the Church of Jesus Christ of Latter-Day Saints v. U.S.* reviews Congressional act of 1887, which annulled Mormon charter.

1908 Roman Catholic Church given fully independent status within international Catholicism (removed from control of the Congregation of Propaganda).

1919 National Catholic Welfare Conference proposed following War Council experience with central agency.

1925 *Pierce v. Society of Sisters* strikes down Oregon law requiring attendance at public school; this is considered the "charter" of parochial schools.

1928 Governor Alfred E. Smith becomes Democratic candidate for president; issue of his faith present in campaign.

1940 *Cantwell v. Connecticut:* Jehovah's Witness case, which explicitly applied religion clauses of the First Amendment to the States through the Fourteenth Amendment.

1947 *Everson v. Board of Education:* reimbursement to parents of parochial- as well as public-school children for bus fares upheld in a five to four decision that explicitly considered the question of establishment.

1960 John F. Kennedy elected first Roman Catholic president of the United States in a very close election; religious issue prominent.

1962 *Engel v. Vitale:* Regents' Prayer Case outlaws the recitation of school prayer in New York State.

1963 *Abington School District v. Schempp* outlaws reading of the Bible in public-school opening exercises.

1963–1965 The Second Vatican Council is held in Rome.

1968 *Flast v. Cohen* gives taxpayers standing in federal court. This allowed challenge of public expenditures on First Amendment grounds.

1973 *Roe v. Wade* recognizes women's constitutional right to an abortion in certain circumstances.

1979 The Moral Majority is organized by the Rev. Jerry Falwell to encourage people to vote for school prayer and a variety of conservative social issues.

1984 The United States and the Vatican establish full diplomatic relations for the first time in 117 years.

1988 Buddhist Churches of America obtain permission to supply chaplains to the military—first time a religion outside Judaism and Christianity given this privilege.

1992 Supreme Court declines opportunity to overturn the controversial *Roe v. Wade* decision in *Planned Parenthood v. Casey.*

1993 Religious Freedom Restoration Act becomes law in a legislative effort to reverse the effects of the Supreme Court's decision in *Employment Division v. Smith.*

1997 Supreme Court decision in *Boerne v. Flores* declares Religious Freedom Restoration Act unconstitutional.

2001 President George W. Bush signs an executive order establishing a White House Office of Faith-Based and Community Initiatives.

Suggestions for Further Reading

For readers who seek further understanding of the time period discussed in each chapter, we have included a short list of pertinent books. We then list additional works dealing more broadly with church and state in American history. The reader should note that these works often are (explicitly or implicitly) designed to foster a particular perspective on the church-state question. Accordingly, no one work (whether or not cited here) should be taken as the final word on any aspect of politics, history, or religion. Thus many "suggestions for further reading" have been selected not because they are necessarily the "best" works on a subject but because they are useful texts or are representative of one or more schools of thought present in the literature.

Chapter 1

Breen, Timothy H. *The Character of the Good Ruler: A Study of Puritan Political Ideas in New England (1970).*

Davidson, Elizabeth H. *The Establishment of the English Church in Continental American Colonies* (1936).

Frost, J. William. *A Perfect Freedom: Religious Liberty in Pennsylvania* (1993).

Haskins, G. L. *Law and Authority in Early Massachusetts* (1960).

______. *Roger Williams: His Contribution to the American Tradition* (1953).

Morgan, Edmund S. *Puritan Political Ideas, 1588–1794* (1964).

______. *Roger Williams: The Church and the State* (1967).

Chapter 2

Bonomi, Patricia. *Under the Cope of Heaven: Religion, Society, and Politics in Colonial America* (1980).

Bridenbaugh, Carl. *Mitre and Sceptre: Transatlantic Faiths, Ideas, Personalities, and Politics, 1689–1775* (1962).

Bushman, Richard. From Puritan to Yankee: Character and the Social Order in Connecticut 1680-1765 (1971).

Cobb, Sanford H. *The Rise of Religious Liberty in America* (1902).

Curran, Francis X. *Catholics in Colonial Law* (1963).

Greene, M. Louise. *The Development of Religious Liberty in Connecticut* (1905).
McLoughlin, William G. *New England Dissent, 1630–1833: The Baptists and the Separation of Church and State* (1971).
McLoughlin, William G., ed. *Isaac Backus on Church, State, and Calvinism: Pamphlets, 1754–1789* (1968).

Chapter 3

Adams, Willi Paul. *The First American Constitutions* (1980).
Alley, Robert, ed. *James Madison: A Free Conscience in a Secular Republic* (1985).
Antieu, Chester James, A. T. Downey, and E. C. Roberts. *Freedom from Federal Establishment: Formation and History of the First Amendment Religion Clauses* (1964).
Antieu, Chester James, P. M. Carroll, and T. C. Burke. *Religion under the State Constitutions* (1965).
Buckley, Thomas. *Church and State in Revolutionary Virginia 1776-1787* (1977).
Cord, Robert L. *Separation of Church and State: Historical Fact and Current Fiction* (1982).
Dreisbach, Daniel L. *Thomas Jefferson and the Wall of Separation between Church and State* (2002).
Eckenrode, H. J. *Separation of Church and State in Virginia* (1910).
Hatch, Nathan O. *The Sacred Cause of Liberty: Republican Thought and the Millennium in Revolutionary New England* (1977).
Howe, Mark DeWolfe. *The Garden and the Wilderness: Religion and Government in American Constitutional History* (1965).
Isaac, Rhys. *The Transformation of Virginia 1776-1787* (1982).
Kinney, Charles B., Jr. *Church and State: The Struggle for Separation in New Hampshire* (1955).
Levy, Leonard. *The Establishment Clause: Religion and the First Amendment* (1986).
Malbin, Michael J. *Religion and Politics: The Intentions of the Authors of the First Amendment* (1978).
Meyer, Jacob C. *Church and State in Massachusetts, 1750–1833* (1930).
Moehlman, Conrad H. *The American Constitutions and Religion* (1938).
Peterson, Merrill D., and Robert C. Vaughan, eds. *The Virginia Statute for Religious Freedom: Its Evolution and Consequences in American History* (1988).
Shaw, Peter. *American Patriots and the Rituals of Revolution* (1981).
Sheldon, Garrett W. and Daniel L. Dreisbach (eds.), *Religion and Political Culture in Jefferson's Virginia* (2000).
Wood, Gordon. *The Creation of the American Republic, 1776–1787* (1972).

Chapter 4

Billington, Ray Allen. *The Protestant Crusade, 1800–1860* (1938).

Bodo, John R. *The Protestant Clergy and Public Issues: 1812–1848* (1954).
Culver, Raymond B. *Horace Mann and Religion in the Massachusetts Public Schools* (1929).
Handy, Robert. *A Christian America: Protestant Hopes and Historical Realities* (1971).
Hudson, Winthrop, ed. *Nationalism and Religion in America: Concepts of American Identity and Mission* (1970).
Marty, Martin E. *Righteous Empire: The Protestant Experience in America* (1970).
Niebuhr, H. Richard. *The Social Sources of Denominationalism* (1954).
Story, Joseph. *Commentaries on the Constitution* (1833).

Chapter 5

Gordon, Sarah B. *The Mormon Question: Polygamy and Constitutional Conflict in Nineteenth Century America* (2002).
Michaelson, Robert. *Piety in the Public School: Trends and Issues in Relationship between Religion and the Public Schools in the United States* (1970).
Moorhead, James H. *American Apocalypse: Yankee Protestants and the Civil War, 1860–1969* (1978).
Schaff, Philip. *Church and State in the United States* (1888).
Smith, Timothy L. *Revivalism and Social Reform: American Protestantism on the Eve of the Civil War* (1957).

Chapter 6

Bennett, John C. *Christians and the State* (1958).
Blanshard, Paul. *American Freedom and Catholic Power* (1949).
Giannella, Donald A., ed. *Religion and the Public Order,* no. 5 (1969).
Herberg, Will. *Protestant—Catholic—Jew: An Essay in American Religious Sociology* (1955).
Kauper, Paul. *Civil Liberties and the Constitution* (1962).
Kurland, Philip. *Religion and the Law: Of Church and State and the Supreme Court* (1962).
Lenski, Gerhard. *The Religious Factor* (1960).
Murray, John Courtney. *We Hold These Truths: Catholic Reflections on the American Proposition* (1964).
Regan, R. J. *American Pluralism and the Catholic Conscience* (1963).
Ryan, J. A., and M. F. X. Millar, eds. *The State and the Church* (1922).

Chapter 7

Bellah, Robert N. *The Broken Covenant: American Civil Religion in Time of Trial* (1975).
Boles, D. E. *The Bible, Religion, and the Public Schools* (1964).

Dolbeare, Kenneth M., and Philip E. Hammond. *The School Prayer Decisions: From Court Policy to Local Practice* (1971).
Douglas, Mary, and Stephen M. Tipton, eds. *Religion and America: Spiritual Life in a Secular Age* (1983).
Frankel, Marvin E. *Faith and Freedom: Religious Liberty in America* (1994).
Miller, Robert T., and Ronald B. Flowers. *Toward Benevolent Neutrality: Church, State, and the Supreme Court* (1977).
Moehlman, Conrad H. *The Wall of Separation between Church and State: An Historical Study of Recent Criticism of the Religious Clauses of the First Amendment* (1951).
Morgan, Richard E. *The Supreme Court and Religion* (1972).
Muir, William K., Jr. *Prayer in the Public Schools: Law and Attitude Change* (1967).
Neuhaus, Richard John. *The Naked Public Square: Religion and Democracy in America* (1984).
O'Neill, James M. *Religion and Education under the Constitution* (1949).
Oaks, Dallin, ed. *The Wall between Church and State* (1963).
Richey, Russell E., and Donald G. Jones, eds. *American Civil Religion* (1974).
Roof, Wade Clark, and William McKinney. *American Mainline Religion: Its Changing Shape and Future* (1987).
Wilson, John F. *Public Religion in American Culture* (1979).
Wuthnow, Robert. *The Restructuring of American Religion: Society and Faith Since World War II* (1988).

General

Ahlstrom, Sydney, E. *A Religious History of the American People* (1972).
Bercovitch, Sacvan. *The Puritan Origins of the American Self* (1975).
Berman, Harold J. *Faith and Order: The Reconciliation of Law and Religion* (1993).
Beth, Loren P. *The American Theory of Church and State* (1958).
Carter, Stephen L. *The Culture of Disbelief: How American Law and Politics Trivialize Religious Devotion* (1993).
Clebsch, William A. *From Sacred to Profane America: The Role of Religion in American History* (1968).
Cookson, Catherine. *Regulating Religion: The Courts and Free Excersise* (2001).
Cuninggim, Merrimon. *Freedom's Holy Light* (1955).
Curry, Thomas John. *The First Freedoms: Church and State in America to the Passage of the First Amendment* (1986).
Dawson, Joseph M. *America's Way in Church, State, and Society* (1953).
Drinan, Robert F. *Religion, the Courts, and Public Policy* (1963).
Greenawalt, Kent. *Religious Conviction and Political Choice* (1988).
Hamburger, Philip. *Separation of Church and State (2002).*
Johnson, Alvin N., and F. H. Yost. *Separation of Church and State in the United States* (1948).
Kerwin, Jerome G. *The Catholic Viewpoint on Church and State* (1960).

Littell, Franklin H. *From State Church to Pluralism: A Protestant Interpretation of Religion in American History* (1971).
McBrien, Richard P. *Caesar's Coin: Religion and Politics in America* (1987).
McLoughlin, William. *Revivals, Awakenings, and Reform: An Essay on Religion and Social Change in America, 1607–1977* (1979).
Mead, Sidney. *The Lively Experiment: The Shaping of Christianity in America* (1963).
Miller, William E., and Ronald B. Flowers. *Toward Benevolent Neutrality: Church, State and the Supreme Court.* 5th ed. (1996).
Miller, William Lee. *The First Liberty: Religion and the American Republic* (1986).
Morgan, Richard E. *The Politics of Religious Conflict: Church and State in America* (1968).
Niebuhr, H. Richard. *The Kingdom of God in America* (1937).
Noll, Mark A., ed. *Religion and American Politics: From the Colonial Period to the 1980s* (1990).
Noonan, John T. *The Lustre of Our Country: The American Experience of Religious Freedom* (1997).
Pfeffer, Leo. *Church, State, and Freedom* (1967).
Sanders, Thomas G. *Protestant Concepts of Church and State* (1964).
Sorauf, Frank J. *The Wall of Separation: The Constitutional Politics of Church and State* (1976).
Stokes, Anson Phelps. *Church and State in the United States* (1950).
Strout, Cushing. *The New Heavens and New Earth: Political Religion in America* (1974).
Sullivan, Winnifred F. *Paying the Words Extra: Religious Discourse in the Supreme Court of the United States* (1994).
Thomas, John L. *Religion and the American People* (1963).
Wills, Garry. *Under God: Religion and American Politics* (1994).
Wilson, John F., ed. *Church and State in America: A Bibliographical Guide.* 2 vols. (1986, 87).

Index